FROM HERE BEGAN THE JOURNEY TO FAR OFF LANDS

HATS OFF TO ESTONIAN WAR PARENTS

MAI MADDISSON

COMPILER AND NARRATOR

Copyright notice

First Published in 2015

Copyright © in this compilation, Mai Maddisson 2015

Copyright in the individual pieces and photographs remain with the authors

All rights reserved. No part of this publication may be reproduced in any form, by any mechanical or electronic means including information storage or retrieval systems, without the prior permission in writing from the publisher.

Brolga Publishing
GPO Box 12544 A'Beckett St Melbourne 8006

ISBN: 9781922175861

Enquires should be addressed to the publisher via email at
 mai@maddissoon.com

Design, cover and typesetting by Mai Maddisson

The front cover image: It is derived from a photo I took on my fist visit to Estonia: It was all too much and I didn't clearly note its location but in the photo series it is set among a group between Paldiski and Saaremaa. I wish I had had the presence of mind to record its location. It just 'grabbed me' and I stood mesmerized and then we moved on!

Photo of Pastor Karl Raudsepp on refugee ship:

Enn his son writes that this photo has made a deep impression on him. It is a photo of his father sitting on the deck of the German ship that brought them out of Estonia on September 28, 1944. He is hunched over hands clasped (in prayer perhaps), mouth pursed and cheeks puffed out in worry. He must have been very anxious and sad, since no one on board knew whether they would ever be able to get back to see their parents, friends and homes. (My parents never did get back but they died knowing that Estonia was becoming free once more).

There were nearly 3000 passengers on the ship (which we only know as R 22, a military category, I think rather than an actual name). Most of the Estonian passengers stood on deck singing the Estonian national anthem, with tears rolling down their cheeks, when the ship began to pull away from the shore. I often wonder how I would have coped in such a situation at that time, since I also had three small children at his age. But I am glad I never had to find out. We really do owe our parents a lot.

Photo by courtesy of Enn Raudsepp.

WHERE IT ALL HAPPENED

Map of terrain traversed during our parents' flight

TABLE OF CONTENTS

What is an autobiography: MM
MAI MADDISSON (MM): PRELUDE — 13
Siberia where the raging rivers run: MM
MAI MADDISSON: PROLOGUE — 15
MAI MADDISSON: IS A GOOD BOOK SYNONYMOUS WITH A MEANINGFUL BOOK?
MAI MADDISSON: NOBODY'S, CHILDREN, NOBODY'S ADULTS — 27
MAI MADDISSON: HOW ACCURATE IS THE CHILDHOOD NARRATIVE OF ORAL HISTORY? A REFLECTION — 30
ARDO TARVO (AGT): I WAS A DP — 36
TÕNU LOORPÄRG (TL): HISTORY OF OUR PAST: NARRATIVE — 37
ARVED PLAKS: SINIMÄED — 40
KALEV EHIN (KE): SNIPPETS ABOUT REMINISCING — 41
ANNE TONDI/ ELLIOT: A HUMAN TRAGEDY — 47
BORIS LEES: SINKING OF THE MOERO- A CATASTROPHE IN 1944* — 49
GUNNAR NEEME (GN): AN AWESOME MAN — 54
Photos collage: Ravages of War: TL
TOOMAS STEINBERG: VOYAGE OF THE RO 22 — 59
KALEV EHIN : SNIPPETS ABOUT THE FLIGHT — 61
KYRA PALANGO/ARONSON: DISPLACED — 65
ILO SOOVERE (IS): FOR THOSE WHO DID NOT PASS THAT WAY: A PHOTO STORY — 68
GEISLINGEN GROUP 'MANYLOGUE'(GGM): THE MYSTERIES OF THE ESCAPE ON THE GERMAN TROOPSHIPS — 70
KALEV EHIN: OUR ULM R.A.F. BOMBING EXPERIENCE — 81
ANDRES KURRIK: WHEN THE NOISE BEGAN- A CHILDHOOD STORY FROM WW II — 85
PAUL ÖPIK (PÖ): STAYING IN TOUCH WHILE THE WAR CONTINUES TO RAGE — 88
HANNES JÜRMANN (HJ): STORMOVIKS — 90
ANTS TAMM (AT): AN ANT TRAVELLING IN EUROPE — 91
HELLE PUUPILL/ GIREY: MY MEMORIES OF THE END OF THE WAR — 95
AINO PAAL/ MARSHALL: FROM THE BEGINNING — 101
LINDA VOOSAAR/ DOLAN: CHILDHOOD MEMORIES FROM ESTONIA TO THE CAMPS — 109
The graveyards of man's politics: AT
KALEV EHIN: SNIPPETS OF WHEN THE WAR CEASED RUMBLING — 117
TÕNU LOORPÄRG: FREEDOM IS ANOTHER WORD FOR EVERYTHING TO GAIN — 123
Birds and bees and wriggly things: GGM
TOOMAS PILL: CHILDHOOD MEMORIES — 137
War ends and peace descends: reminiscing with Bruno Leepin
KALEV EHIN: FATHER'S ENIGMATIC IMAGE — 143
JÜRI TULTS: FLEEING FROM ESTONIA — 145
BRUNO LEEPIN: BOMB-BURST : OUR WORLD IS SHATTERED — 148
JAAN TABUR: FROM TALLINN TO GEISLINGEN — 149
EHA TREUFELD/ CARR: WHEN THE NOISE BEGAN — 153
AIMI KIBENA/ ZECHANOWITSCH: A LONG ROAD TO GEISLINGEN — 161
AIRE KOLBRE/ SALMRE: AND SO IT HAPPENED* — 169
ENE MAIDRE/ MIKLI: FROM THE SUMMER OF 1944* — 179

MAIE KAARSOO/ HERRICK & ALFRED KAARSOO: ESCAPE 181
Rare fish or fishing: Hilde Kaarsoo
Memmingen another early camp
MALL JUSKE/ KARP: MY MEMOIRS* 199
Idle hands were not permitted: the USA army work corps
ARDO TAREM: A MAN WITH FORESIGHT TO TELL A LOST TALE 209
It was from the disabled that we learned the ultimate lessons: AGT
HANNES JÜRMANN: FROM TARTU TO GENOA 213
Reminiscing with Bruno Leepin
HELGA MERITS: IN THE PARENTS' SHOES-A DIALOGUE WITH ILVI JOE 221
GUNNAR NEEME: LIFE AS A DP 222
MAARE KASK/ TAMM: MY ROAD 225
BRUNO LEEPIN: UNKNOWN DANGERS 235
Less "glam" images relating to the same epoch: IS
LIA NOORMETS/NICHOLSON: LEAVING OUR HOMELAND 237
Estonian DP camps in Germany
ARNE ELLERMETS: A FREE ESTONIA, THEN AN OCCUPIED ESTONIA FOLLOWED BY CAMP LIFE 245
SANNU MÕLDER: VENUS 258
ARNE ELLERMETS: DIALOGUES WITH HIS BROTHER AND COUSINS 260
SANNU MÕLDER: DIALOGUE WITH HIS COUSINS 263
Frequent mobility was the norm for the first twelve months: AT
INDRIK LINASK: ALONE- WITH FOUR CHILDREN 266
SIR ARVI PARBO: MY AUTOBIOGRAPHY- PART 1: MY YOUTH IN EUROPE* 275
JAAN PAARSONS: DONNA, HIS WIDOW REMINISCES 278
PAUL ÖPIK: A FATHER BEFORE HIS TIME (including photo collages)* 279
JÜRI RAID (JR): WAR ORPHANS 289
SNIPPETS FROM OTHER WAR ORPHANS (including photo collages) 300
HARRY SAKJAS (HS): YOU CAN'T GO HOME 303
Kalju Suitsev: a courageous young lad became a war hero in his new land
AIN TOHVER AKA ANDY DEUBLE 305
JÜRI RAID: MY FAMILY 307
BORIS LEES: VERY MUCH ON THE RUN-TO SOMEWHERE* 309
MART KASK: 14 JUNE 1941- AS I REMEMBER IT 323
Families had to begin all over again: ATG
BRUNO LAAN: WAR TIME TRAVELS WW II 328
Photography while in transit: E-mail snippets from conversations with the authors
Mythology, soul, spirit, serendipity or intuition: GGM
ILO SOOVERE: SERENITY -WELL MOST OF THE TIME 346
EPP LÕOKE/BAUERN: GEISLINGEN- A PHOTO STORY 348
MARJE LIMION/ MEDRI: GEISLINGEN-A PHOTO STORY 350
INGE PRUKS/IZZO: A LULLABY LOST-A PHOTO STORY 360
Let us not forget them: MM
Harrowed children: they too became captains of their lives: MM
Grimmer tales
ILLE LISCINSKI/USCINSKI: CHILDREN WITHOUT TOYS 375

Fork tongued lizards :MM
The tale of the salamander: MM
Relics of the world we left behind
Well for some their shoes still contained prickly burs

MAI MADDISON: ON THE OUTSIDE LOOKING IN — **383**

These are some of the children: What happened to the rest? AGT, MM

ENDEL TULVING: WE, THE YOUNG — **389**

Geislingen Gümnaasium (high school) collage

ARVED PLAKS: TEACHERS I HAVE ADMIRED AND SOME OTHERS NOT SO MUCH — **393**

EVE SILLAOTS/NOWACKI: GEISLINGEN DP CHILDREN REMEMBER — **397**

Recycled ugliness becomes a limbo for some
Artwork from Geislingen Gumnaasium (high school) annual
Addressing angst, uncertainty and frustration: MLM
As DPs our folks marked time-handicrafts: MM

ALAN ADAMS: PORTABLE ASSETS FROM ESTONIA (PHOTO COLLAGE) — **404**

Music and performing arts: GGM
Maybe Santa Claus had hierarchies: AGT,MM
Author group manylogue: Preparing for the new lands

HANNES JÜRMANN: FATHER WAS A MILITARY DOCTOR — **413**

ENN RAUDSEPP: FATHER WAS A COMMUNITY LEADER AS WELL AS A PASTOR — **415**

Author group manylogue: Name tags: They had many types of symbolism
How does a youngster's memory select its 'menu'?: TGA, MM
Donna Parson shares some relics of her late husband's trans-Atlantic transit
The best Christmas presents ever: TL

MAI MADDISON: " MITTE VIIMSE HETKE RAVI" — **427**

Harry Sakjas folks braved the bureaucracy to visit him in USA
A second generation's disbelief: JR. MM
Our dreams met became different to dreams to those of yore

TÕNU LOORPÄRG: REUNION WITH HIS FATHER — **435**

AGO LOORPÄRG: PARTING THE IRON CURTAIN- A VISIT FROM TÕNU AND HIS FAMILY — **441**

Purple twilight: MM
Despite our chagrin closure is an integral part of moving on

MAI MADDISON: REFLECTION- PEACE AMONG THE RUINS — **448**

MAI MADDISON: EPILOGUE: THE MEETING OF THE MINDS AND SOULS — **452**

"HOP" through the retrospectoscope: MM

MEET THE AUTHORS — **455**

The longer pieces will by annotated by the author's name: Initials in brackets will appear after the first such piece: They will be used to indicate memory clips and shorter reflections by the same author.

At times other stories will have previously appeared/are intended to appear in other publications: They have been published with the permission of the relevant bodies and annotated as such. And of course any author may chose at some date in the future publish their story elsewhere: That will always remain their prerogative.

> Among the pages you will find relics of old documents. Some of them will bear my/my family names. They in no way form part of my story. They are merely generic documents which obviated wasted time searching for equivalents: Which because they bear my name remove the time consumption in clearing copyrights etc. allowing me to move on with the task of the compilation of further data. MM

WHAT IS AN AUTOBIOGRAPHY?

An autobiography is essentially the first voice narrative of how a person views their past life: The only constants usually the diorama on which such a life was set, and the places and dates of the events which occurred. They are immutable.

It is essentially an interpretation, according to that person's memory, of their life. It is subjective and may change in subsequent editions of their recording of their life's events. Information may come to hand which will alter their perception of the various windows of time: This is more likely to occur for those windows when the author was very young or when they were under heightened stress, at times fighting for survival. And it is not impossible that the author may return to their original perception after yet more information coming to hand and rendering intervening edits void.

Such accounts are commonly written for the author's descendants or for secondary authors to base writings on. At times such writings are specifically written for secondary authors and may indeed be shared with many such authors at differing times: At times in close proximity.

What quandaries such similarity or dissimilarity can cause for the readers. Statistically the closer the writings of two secondary authors the less likely a revised edition of the autobiography.

The reader can become quite perplexed by what they are reading in the various publications which may differ or vacillate variably in details.

I am very grateful to my writing colleague Vasilios Vasilis, who shares my passion for exploring the autobiographical narrative of people who travelled through historical epochs. He shared quite significant time as we explored the complexities of books containing material from the same epoch of time, pertaining to the same authors, and as they pertained to their readership. How many such complexities occur! MM

* after a story indicates that some part/all of a story will have appeared in Vasilios Vasilis book "Across lands and oceans to freedom"

FOREWORD

This book is a collection of memories written by former Estonian World War II refugee children who are now in their 60s,70s and 80s .They look back on the period of their lives when they were uprooted from their ancient homeland of Estonia on the Northern Baltic Sea by the invading occupying powers of Soviet Russia and Nazi Germany. The memories, depending on age, are of events occurring in the immediate pre war and war time Estonia that lead to their parents fleeing for their lives from Soviet terror, taking their families with them. The stories describe the children's memory of escape journeys, survival in the midst of World War II, becoming one of the millions of Displaced Persons in Europe after the War and finally of being despatched globally to any country willing to take them. For their parents, a return to Estonia was not a viable option. Only despatch to slave labour camps of Siberia awaited those who did return.

Throughout the book Mai Maddisson acts as both compiler and narrator weaving her observations of the exodus to "far off lands" together with the memories of our cohorts.

The books genesis, as part of the title "Hats off to our Estonian Parents!" implies, is really a salute to our care givers of those years. A belated salute for parent/s or others who somehow, despite overwhelming odds, maneuvered their way through an earthly hell to reach sanctuary, often at the "Ends of the Earth", in places like New Zealand and Australia. Encumbered by offspring, mothers and grandmothers (where fathers were missing or dead) often had to start new lives for their families in foreign lands with minimal knowledge of the language.

Unsurprisingly many found it all too hard and so did some of the children. Sadly their memories are unavailable to be included in this volume. For those of our cohorts that have survived to old age the book is a timely recording and sharing of events long gone which collectively helps fill gaps in our individual memories. The cohort and Estonian Diaspora world wide can be energized once more for the benefit of our descendents so that they too may share in the knowledge of how their ancestors found strength for the Estonian Exodus which established them in distant lands. The book can also be seen as a timely reminder of the consequences of war on civilian populations and its long lasting impact. Today we have in Europe all too familiar echoes of the 1930's with conflict in Ukraine and the Middle East not to mention other continents where civilian casualties and refugees are being created in the millions.

Far too often the impact on innocent children is being overlooked when they are forced into Concentration Camp type incarceration to their lifelong detriment. Sadly even some Western Liberal Democracies have adopted such policies. It is hoped that the stories in this book can contribute to the burgeoning academic interest in "war children refugees" and provide additional understandings from a by-gone era which will help shape Government and NGO policies today for the better treatment and understanding of their plight. This applies equally to professionals working in health and education sectors.

Last but not least the book has a message for the current citizens of Estonia, Germany and Russia (albeit written in English). It is a record of memories from some of the Estonian children removed from their native land in 1944 by the aggressive actions of Totalitarian Powers which were of detriment to us all. May we all learn from it and prevent a repetition of such actions in the future.

Contributors to this book span an age group born between approximately 1925-1955. Those of the cohort born between say 1925 -1935 have clear memories of "Free Estonia" a period where the young Estonian Republic was being established as a democratic state. Memories of the period are often idyllic and speak of life on the land and in the towns surrounded by family and friends. As the War clouds approach these recollections start to darken particularly after the signing of the Ribbentrop /Molotov Pact between Germany and Soviet Union with its secret protocols dividing Eastern Europe between them. This resulted in demands by the Soviets for large Military Bases on Estonian soil and in other Baltic States. Those born between 1936 -1945 have some awareness of the lead up to the War and events during the War, particularly the older members of this cohort but not those younger children with pre –verbal memory only. Significantly some of the older children's memories can recall the forced occupation and subsequent take over and terror created by the new Soviet State between 1940 and 1941 and the consequent effect on their families, particularly after the mass deportations to Siberia began. Memories of fathers and uncles going into hiding and avoiding sleeping at home to avoid the "midnight knock" or forced mobilisation into the Red Army. Many others went into the forest to join Estonia's Forest Brothers a guerrilla resistance group.

When Hitler broke the Pact with the Soviet Union and invaded the Soviet Union he also occupied the Baltic States of Estonia Latvia and Lithuania where the Germans were initially seen as "liberators" from Communism and proceeded to rule the areas largely through existing Estonian Authorities. A number of the memories describe these German

Occupation years of the War 1941-1943 as the "quiet period" in Estonia when conditions became relatively peaceful for the families, given there was also a war on. By 1943 as the tide turned for Germany in the War and they were being pushed back to Estonia's borders, so did Estonian attitudes toward participation in the War.

Nobody wanted a return of the Red Terror from a second Soviet Occupation. The Estonian Local Administration called for volunteers to create a fighting force, The Estonian Legion to help hold back the Red Army on Estonian borders. This was with the approval and cooperation with the Germans and was to be under their command. Some volunteers who did not wish to be under German command went to Finland (The Finnish Boys)and fought the Soviets there .They only came back after the Soviet/ Finnish Armistice to help reinforce Estonian borders as the German Forces withdrew from Estonia. These events are described in the memories and they relate to fathers, uncles and other relatives who were mobilized. Many disappeared forever, being killed in action on the front or subsequently being incarcerated in Stalin's Siberian Gulags.

A few of the lucky ones survived and even made it back to their loved ones in Refugee Camps. Most did not. These battles on the border, especially those around Sinimäe (Blue Hills) in August 1944 near Narva, held back the Red Army sufficiently in September 1944 to allow almost 10% (80-100,000) of the population to flee. Some boarded small boats to Finland and Sweden while others managed to scramble on German Hospital Ships and Merchant vessels departing for the Southern Baltic Ports. The cohorts memories of those who were attacked on the journey and sunk by torpedoes or fighter aircraft provide horrific descriptions of survival and loss.

For those who made it to the ports in Poland, their struggles as foreign refugees were only just beginning as the Red Army swept in from the East and the Allies from the West. In January/February 1945 the bombing and the attacks became intense as the Communist Forces bore down on Berlin. Members of our cohort remember being spread far and wide in Germany in a desperate move West, directions anywhere but the East from where the Soviets approached. Unlucky ones write of being caught up in the fall of Berlin and desperate escapes, others remember travelling through the horrors of the Dresden bombing which killed tens of thousands.

Eventually at war's end on the 8 May 1945, most were located in the relative safety of the American, British and French Zones under Military Administrative control. Numerous Displaced Persons (DP) Camps were set up by the newly created United Nations Relief and Rehabilitation Administration (UNRRA) around the Allied Zones in Germany, Austria and Italy where Estonian Refugees were sent along with millions of others. The largest of the Estonian Camps was Geislingen, memories of which are in this book and also another (Mai Maddisson & Priit Vesilind)publication, "When the Noise Has Ended". Here we were to remain for 4-6 years as the adults started organising to rebuild our lives at the same time avoiding constant attempts by the Soviets to remove us back to Estonia. Everyone knew that the real destination would be Siberia, a fate which we were desperate to avoid, some even by suicide. Eventually the Western Allies realized that most of the Eastern Europe refugees that the Soviets claimed as being "their" citizens were in fact from illegally occupied territories of the Soviet Union and refused to recognise the legality of those occupations.

Memories of the DP camps between the years 1945-1951 are extensive. Where there were large numbers of Estonians most of the children were soon able to attend Estonian schools. They ranged from Kindergartens to High schools and were organized by a highly educated group of Estonian professionals who had fled the country after being targeted by the Soviets for deportation during their first occupation. Others attended local German schools and they write about the difficulties of coping with a foreign language. There was even a Baltic DP University organized in Hamburg for a brief period where multinational DP's could study, however most of the older children who qualified attended German Tertiary Colleges once things stabilized.

The memories bring back a rich tapestry of camp life involving active participation at schools, scouts and guides for older children, cultural activities involving traditional song and dance and much else. It shows that even in a refugee community it is possible for adults to organise and sustain a protective and meaningful life, for their children at least, as they themselves waited desperately for some country to accept their families as prospective immigrants.

When that call eventually came for most, it resulted in the sadness of separation from each other as an established Community, a community once again torn apart and sent to the far corners of the earth where they re-established themselves as "Estonian Clubs" (Eesti Selts) to a greater or lesser extent depending on the numbers. Playmates were kept in touch across the oceans through their elders who managed to sustain a letter writing exchange over many years.

This post war Estonian Diaspora became active in holding cultural gatherings around the world and maintained political pressure in their new homelands for their Governments to support the reestablishment of political freedom for their homeland. This was finally successful in 1991 with the demise of the Soviet Union. Once the Republic of Estonia was re-established it became easier for the War Children to visit their homeland although a few had managed to brave a return much earlier after Kruschev's reforms. Memories of these emotional returns have been included as have the equally emotive reactions to reunions with those relatives who remained behind. The story of the journey to these new lands and the children's "first five years" there is the subject of a book of further memories to be published by Mai Maddisson in the near future.

This book deals with the contributions in a variety of ways. I think it would be fair to call it a "compendium" of memories and commentary illustrated by photos and artwork some of which has laid buried in family albums for decades. There are short flashbacks of memory, almost transcripts of live recordings which have been added to by what Mai Maddisson has called "Manylogues" or e-mail exchanges between some members of the cohort. Other contributions are extracted from more extensive work and/or books written by some of the War Children. The photos, though often well worn, give an additional edge to some of the written pieces whereas some of the art work helps illustrate the subjective mind of a child caught up in war as seen from the vantage point of old age. Selected songs/poems from the period and from a later exile help to illustrate the pathos that can involve a separated family/lovers caught up in Total War.

Throughout the book Mai as a clinician and as the book's narrator helps to weave the pieces and thoughts together by commenting on and clarifying psycho /social elements of memory. She especially relates this to children and the intricacies involved when looking back on childhood decades later. She explains that she has in some instances published the contributions largely unedited because to do otherwise risked losing the exact meaning "in translation". She points out that some contributors are of an age where further "recycling" could result in no contribution at all. Finally she comments on the limited sample of contributors from our cohort in the book and of the difficulty presented by obtaining memories of those who have passed on or are incapacitated for one reason or another. It seems there have been many of these.

Who then should read this book?

First and foremost the parents /caregivers who were instrumental in navigating us through that "earthly hell" of World War II and brought us out the other side. Sadly most are no longer around any longer to read it..

I would recommend this book to others in our cohort of War Children also, especially those who did not participate on this occasion. I am certain that there will be information in it which will fill in blank spots in one's memory. It certainly has for me. The opportunity is there also to reconnect with childhood friends who shared the same journey. Should you so wish of course. Regardless of whether one wishes to reconnect with old friends or not, I am certain that the memories in this book will provide valuable details for our children /grandchildren when they seek to find out about their ancestors hazardous journey to the new lands.

There will be many others from different nations who also travelled the DP journey to far off lands. For example the story of other Baltic peoples from Latvia and Lithuania is very similar to ours and should be shared with them.

The World today is again awash with millions of war refugees, with Refugee Workers and Researchers trying desperately to respond to their urgent demands. This book reveals a rather successful approach by which refugee communities can, with help, manage a great deal themselves. Perhaps the past can come to aid the present Refugee Organisations, Clinicians and Educators especially with regard to the War Children?

Finally I would like to recommend the book to Western Military Historians who have, in my reading with some notable exceptions, shown a paucity of understanding as to the impact of war on civilian populations in WWII. In particular the consequences resulting for civilians from Great Power machinations (such as the Ribbentrop/Molotov Pact between Soviet Union and Germany, Yalta Conference), and their lasting detrimental impact on those nations of Europe sandwiched between "East" and "West".

The title of this book is "Hats off to Estonian War Parents", without the guiding initiative of Mai Maddisson and her great perseverance over some five years the book would not have been published. She deserves our thanks and heartfelt gratitude .

For this I say: **"Hats off to Mai!"**

Tõnu (Tony)Loorpärg
Waikanae Beach,Wellington, New Zealand
21 August 2014

From: THE MIST OF TIME

Then there was a war,
Men lost their senses,
time was stained
with hatred, fear and violence.

Yet life had to be lived
and every moment
had to be embraced

Moments embraced
even as borrowed time
was sinking fast beneath the
horizon of death and destruction.

Gunnar Neeme

PRELUDE

Estonia, yes it is a place: One which has always been there. Estonia is where many war children first met the light of day. It is where they were allowed permission to feel sadness for that which was lost, pride for that which was retained, and a knowledge that those around too felt those pangs of uncertainty. It was home.

It was a place where they did not feel the need to feign excitement and happiness when their minds were occupied by the grimness which was all around and which they could not leave behind as the years passed by: grimness which had been for up to five years had been their normality. It was a place for many déjà vus as the older ones relate their experiences of those times: As they latterly wander around Tallinn's streets and its surrounding countryside.

Many of their visual memories are sketchy, but they are real: They can relate to each other's imagery of those times and know just what they are alluding to. The feelings that accompany them are even more real: Indeed for me it took until the first early morning of my first return to Tallinn in August 2002 to place that realness in situ again. The afternoon of my first return felt surreal but not truly tangible. I was in a place that was 'mine' but it felt wrong. The eeriness of the long early morning shadows rectified the confusion. Wartime had been a place where eeriness stalked us all night and day.

There were just so many questions to answer: Questions which other babies born at those times might also need answered. I hope that my book answers many of those questions for them . MM

SIBERIA, WHERE THE RAGING RIVERS RUN

and the hell where many of Estonia's folks perished as deportees of the invading regime

The flight from Australia to Estonia takes me over Siberia: It is only from the height of 10,000-13,000 metres altitude that one can truly appreciate what a desolate God-forsaken place Siberia is. I was fortunate on one flight to have reasonable clarity of vision, sans cloud or weather spattered windows and enough day-light to grab a series of photos.

There are proverbially thousands of kilometers of nothingness though which wide serpentine rivers wend their way to the coast and at times converge to produce vast lake like structures. The towns look like little toy towns connected by roads which look like little more than wispy, sparse threads of murky white. Occasionally one would spot a city situated on a major waterway.

The narrative of the survivors of those deportations tells of them crossing and travelling on the rivers Ob and Vasyugan which at times were more like inland seas. Many perished during that journey in decrepit boats. Others perished on the railroad 'cattle trucks' of that transit. Many, many more after arrival in the perishing cold, inadequate shelter and rampant starvation. At times entire families exited our world.

Peep Varju, the recent president of Memento (an organisation that is updating the fate of such children) was to be the only survivor from a family of seven: To talk with Peep and hear of his commitment to make each day have a meaning is to hear of his way of paying tribute to his mother's courage. There were endless such families.

One can only admire the Estonians' young brethren for their tenacity, and their mothers for their unimaginable sacrifices to spare their children: That is the subject of another book. MM

MAI MADDISSON
PROLOGUE: ECHOES OF A WAR CHILD'S PARENTS

Parenting has never been an easy task. In Estonia, like in many places most families lived meaningful lives with variable difficulties: Some did it easy, others struggled to survive. The free Estonians' pride in their identity kept morale at a high ebb.

By decree I am not an Estonian child, but I am still a child of the war born in Estonia. To a small child for whom the emotions only contained 'goodies and baddies' the memories are not too different.

When war struck the lives of children and their parents changed: Fear and insecurity walked into our parents' lives. Whatever was their everyday routine ceased to be. They became afraid of premature death and injury. They feared for the safety of their children. They no longer knew with reasonable certainty what lay ahead tomorrow. Life became a lottery. Priorities changed. Gone was the reassurance that basic necessities remained available. Also gone were the carefree times with friends and family.

Fear became a permanent immutable shadow which accompanied all families for an interminable time. Daylight or dark could not modify it. It had no face. It had no place. It was just everywhere. It walked, it rode, it sailed and it flew and somehow it always tried to wreak its vengeance on one and all. No longer did parents say 'I'll see you later' to their families as they went about their lives. 'Goodbye' became a permanent way of life.

Fear had many meanings to all parents. Death and injury could result from friendly or unfriendly foe. The large and small weaponry of war intruded the cities and country sides. It had no mercy on those in its path. Wolves in sheep's clothing mingled among people. No spoken word was safe. Each word became a potential invitation to the Gulags, internment camps, war prisons and even death.

During war the veneer between human loyalty and self preservation became very thin. Parents could not afford to trust those whom they would normally trust. The spoken word became minimalistic, the written word avoided. Parents began to fear betrayal by those around them. They feared betrayal by their children. This at times made spontaneous communication with their children difficult. They could never be sure that their children would not accidentally, by bribery or coercion betray them

Yet those same children were their parents' talismans. They were also their Achilles' heels. Albeit with time those heels became less prominent as naivety diminished and insight into danger thrived. Children have always been spontaneous creatures who had yet to learn how to hide their emotions. Initially their loud voices of fear and confusion, later their body language only, continued to imperil their parents in a world where no one was safe.

I cannot visually remember those times. My mind contains no specific shapes. I was under three when World War II ended. The feelings I cannot forget. The instinctive urgency to listen carefully to hushed voices, to internally clarify ambiguous statements, and to ensure that I keep abreast of people's body language has not deserted me. The legends of my elders fall on familiar ears. I remember with them. I recognize their body language. Mine mirrors theirs.

Nor have the visual images of what might befall if I am remiss there abandoned me. Fear of accidental betrayal of a friend by ill chosen words is a fear which still haunts me. In my mind is etched a fear of documents being found on my person. That is how I believe many documents at times travelled with us until the war's end.

Perhaps it requires a revisit to the same terrain to more fully connect with the emotions of one's elders. On the other hand one should never forget that childhood was a time which for many children did not exist.

No matter how mature the child, their parents' shoes cannot become totally accessible to them until similar circumstances prevailed. Reminders of good byes where people never returned remain a haunting memory of our pasts: Pasts where parents said goodbye to their children: Their children said good bye to them.

Family narrative has left an unclear imprint on us: I like most of the war time children and youth of Estonia continue to wish that there had been opportunity to share more of their families' experiences through their eyes at a time when our minds were receptive to the information: Times which the struggle for post war survival attenuated for all of us.

Narrative of the times spoke of torpedoed and sinking ships in the Baltic Sea, of serendipitous diversions from a planned journey where people were spared from the vengeance of bombs.

How I wish that I had had the courage to stay and listen. Perhaps many of my war child cohort now share this wish. But then perhaps intuition was an ally rather than an enemy. Maybe it bade us to walk away from that which our souls were not ready to touch. As peace-time objectivity set in my acuity of body language perception has allowed me to recognize patients' anguish with greater ease. And yet I do have visual memories of that time. They live on as déjà vu's as I continue on my journey through life. While street wisdom and instinctive guardedness was the norm of the day it could not be heeded at all times. Parents still needed to go to work. Their world could not totally stop. They had to abandon such safety as existed to find earnings, food and other amenities.

Shelter was never safe. It was vulnerable to bombs and other missiles of war. The house doors could become the entry portals of the enemy Air-raid shelters could hardly serve as permanent shelter. They were but a means to an end.

Parents were left to ensure that their children did not unwittingly attract the enemy by opening curtains or wandering into forbidden terrain. They were left to unobtrusively manoeuvre their children to safety. As they went out in search of basic needs they were left wondering what they might return to or if anything would remain to return to.

Food became increasingly scarce. Much of it was diverted to the war front. Those who lived on farms initially had more access to produce. City parents travelled long distances in dangerous terrain and traded valued possessions for that extra food which might sustain their children.

Stories of parental sacrifices abound among folk who have endured war. The gratitude of their children remains incomprehensible to the children of today.

Bleak winters were the norm where people endured World War II. Clothing became increasingly scarce. Mothers became very adept at repeatedly remaking clothing into smaller and smaller clothes for their children. Unworn parts of material were meticulously recycled. Woolens were repeatedly unpicked and re-knitted from salvaged yarn. Parents now tell of the threadbare rags which they themselves wore

In war time soldiers had priority with medical care. My predominating memory of hospitals seemed to have been one of places where compassionate adults toiled against the odds of injury and rampant disease. Older children have more lucid memories: They talk of compassion and the dedication of the hospital staff.

I still wonder how these adults managed to stay focused in the presence of such grotesquely damaged and dying children. I marvel at their fortitude to return to their families when off duty and keep their hopes alive. Others of the older youth relate what it felt like to be among so many wounded children: there is a resignation to 'what was there to do?'

The physical health of parents suffered mercilessly. Malnutrition and TB ravaged many lives. Injuries ravaged others. Many were left with permanently impaired health. It amazes me that so many of them survived to their eighth or ninth decade. What strong stuff they were made of.

I find the tenacity of war children's forefathers quite incredible. In the depths of despair they managed to bring hope to their children. Somehow they balanced the despair of their own losses with the hope that their children would one day live on beyond that boiling cauldron of war.

As they now share their childhood experiences it is becoming common-place to hear of brutal punishment of children: Most of them manage to temper their parents' outburst of violence with compassion. Life among chronic human destruction must have inevitably numbed those who saw this. Their frustration at re-exposure to human disrespect, perhaps at times by lack of insight was to threaten their new sense of well being and create anxiety about their future

Their children's insight into their lives has been determined by the children's own temporal relationship to the war which affected their lives. Those who were born before the war could share their parents' sense of loss and years of fear. Children born into the war have no memory of having had anything to lose but they can relate to their parents fears of the past. Post war children have no losses to grieve for and do not understand their parents' fears. At times unfortunate parents have been left to grapple with children from three different Diasporas who see the world through three differing pairs of eyes.

Many of these parents continue to live with the ignoble psychiatric labels imposed upon them at a time when they could not be understood by those around them. Some have accepted them. Others mourn them. I resent them.

Some of their children accept these labels for their parents. They see their parents as 'misfits' in the world in which they were cast to live. They too bear the scars. They are now being known to be suffering from the second generation effect.

Their parents are left to wonder if things might have been different had fate not struck its deadly blow.

Some of these parents have found peace in resignation to the status quo. Others have sought out numbing agents such as alcohol. Yet others have lost their identities from chronic exposure to psychotropic medication and I am sure that a few have fallen victim to their cancerous pall.

Perhaps too many found it all too hard many, many years ago

THE ANGST OF FATHERS AT WAR

This book tends to focus on the sacrifices of mothers with their small children, as they traipsed thru Europe's war's wilderness in the hope of finding a safe limbo, of one day returning to a safe Estonia and of again meeting with their husbands, older sons and brothers. Somehow the males seem to have been done an injustice: Nothing can be more horrifying than endlessly fearing and facing gunpoint. MM

TÕNU LOORPÄRG'S FATHER WROTE
in "Freedom is Another Word for Everything To Gain , Loorpärg Family History, Volume I"

"The month of June brought us a troubling surprise. In Narva they were saying that there were things out of place in Tallinn. They spoke of threatening demands to support a Russian coup d'état and of the danger that Estonia would be occupied. Nothing definite was heard about, who was to be appointed. On 15 June the officers and NCOs received a command that had already been prepared, that was a command not to leave the battery. There was a threatening sign of danger ahead, initially we heard nothing else.

Early on the morning of 17 June 1940 there was a battery alert. Political action was not yet in hand, and then came an instruction which we received with annoyance. Suspicious persons around the barracks were to be treated sternly. Along the Tallinn highway roadside were to be placed sentries and security guards, who were to prevent people going on the road. We were warned about the Red Army coming across the Estonian border. Incidents with Red Army soldiers were to be avoided. A little later we were informed that this avoidance order was pronounced under an ultimatum not to show resistance and that we were to capitulate.

Now there moved in Red Army Tanks, motor convoys of Infantry and without any hindrance towards Tallinn. We felt a mixture of anger and shame, which for some men drew tears to their eyes. The Estonian Defence Force was ready to resist the occupiers, but to alter the situation was not within our authority . I had to change the security guard every hour by the road side and the men watched from the barracks lines how the unkempt endless main body stretched towards Tallinn, one's own pitiful equipment being repaired in the ditch, this was our first impression of the enemy.

Some few days afterwards we noticed change. A new city government, which was now named as the executive committee, previously it had been and under the direction of communists earlier. They gave Captain Maanemaa a command for the battery to be completely stood down and together, march in formation, through the city towards Raekoja town square to a rally. On the Raekoja steps stood red slogan and red armband bearing communists. At the Plaza Square there were some people who had been ordered to attend, they were in the main Kreenholme factory workers who had been brought their. Our battery was lined up on the edge of the Plaza. The speech was made by a well-known Narva Communist whose name from memory was Pauk. He had chaired and heaped praise on the communists as Estonian People's saviours, on Lenin and Stalin and then announced that there was now located in Toompea a Workers Administration. President Pats was to have stood down and his assembly had voted in a new president. Also the Parliament had also voted for a new assembly and now comprised of "workers".

Our battery men stood with gloomy faces. Cheers and "hurrahs" were not united. The Speaker informed us that the army was united with the workers and Stalin's sun would now warm us all. When the meeting finished and the army marched in line back to Olgino through the town, the people were along the streets. They shouted "three cheers for Estonian soldiers"; they were waving to us and throwing flowers.

At the end of June 1 Battery entire group went to Kurtan Summer Camp. In the beginning the changes were not obvious. Only the soldiers became more nervous, as a lack of information existed about their future. There were ethnic Russians serving in the battery and it was felt that some of these were semi-affected. During the day and during training, relationships with Estonians were fairly good. But in the barracks during the evenings they gave rise to arguments, which often resulted in fights. I had to, as battery orderly officer separate fighters a couple of times. Essentially the soldiers did not hide their thoughts about the tanks and the Red Army creating a turning point for the state. Neither did I hide my thoughts. Nobody could imagine what this was shortly to mean for us.

In mid-June, the first Red Army officers appeared in camp. They were Political commanders or in other words political commissars. The battery commander received an order that they were to be accepted into the unit as officially appointed liaison officers. Soon we noticed that the commissars were much friendlier with the Russian speaking soldiers. The men of the platoon looked to me. However, the Russians had warned the commissars to be watchful of me. At the same time, they were encouraging the Estonian Army to be incorporated into the Red Army. That was important because for the Estonian Republic to be incorporated we could no longer have an Estonian Defence Force in existence. When I didn't want to be a Red Army commander, I had to quickly resign and go into the territorial volunteer Force . At the time there were rumours that officers of a similar mind-set to mine were being arrested.

I telephoned the Narva Artillery Group chief of staff Major Rubach and asked him what he thought about it . Rubach told me that he still had command authority to transfer me to the reserve and not to worry. He promised to have the necessary documents signed at the earliest day in the month. In one week I was to be in Narva . Capt. Maanemann was also aware of my intentions and he felt I was doing the right thing.

One week later I rode to Jõhvi railway station and journeyed to Narva. The horse was returned to camp by a soldier who had seen me off. Major Rabuch had prepared my release documents into the reserve at the earlier date and told me that I was the last one of like mind he was able to assist. Thus on 1 August 1940 I was discharged at my own request from the permanent staff of the Estonian republic's Defence Force and placed on the reserve. On the reserve document I was assigned as number 65, eighth of August 1940. The officers who moved to the reserve were to be promoted. This applied to all the "Sam Brown (sword belt) graduates" who had finished their leadership practical in the meantime and were now no longer on active service."

A WOUNDED SOLDIER: GN

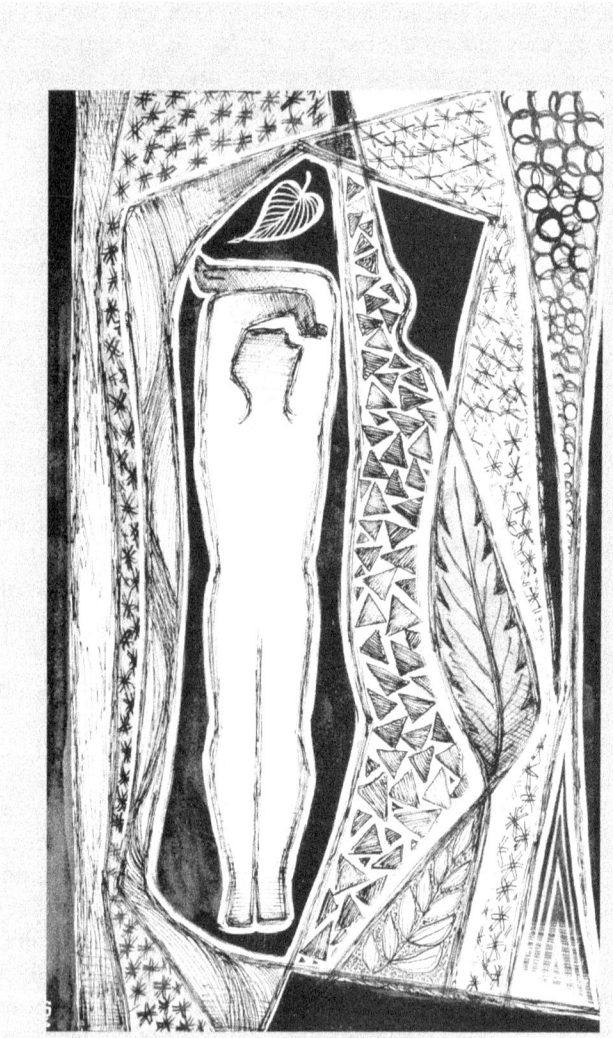

....another life was wasted and forgotten in timelessness

In the bloodied battlefield,
a wounded soldier cried,

"I don't need time any more.
Please take me, don't let me suffer,
O, the pain , the pain..."

His voice
became a soundless whisper
as he closed his eyes forever.

Another life
wasted and forgotten
in timelessness.

Yet, some miles away,
another soldier set down his weapons
and shared his bread with the captured enemy.

There are times
when it does not matter
what you are or who you are.

From the 'Mist of time'

Gunnar's two older children Aarne and Ants were born in the DP camps, their sister Ebe in Australia.
All three children are justly proud of their identity and of their father's creative skills in reconciling the past.

PERHAPS SOME THINGS CANNOT BE SAID SUCCINCTLY BY PROSE OR PHOTOGRAPHY

Over a decade ago I attended a mental health seminar on refugeeism. It included many photos: At times I squirmed at them. Some were clearly contrived: I recall one of refugees transiting on the back of a lorry. In my memory are indelibly imprinted a number of such occasions but without a definite time or place attached to them: I was aged between two and three years when time and location have no place. The ethos of the folk in that lorry was just wrong, wrong, wrong.

But then how does one derive authentic photos of critical fleeting moments of our lives? The photographers themselves are preoccupied with survival and should they perish so might their camera, and of course the camera is vulnerable to confiscation at times to become the key to their owner's demise.

And one does need to question the motives of some of such photography. Is the wish one of a ghoul, or is it one to truly convey to future viewers something of critical content. Many of the photos on that war time trek were taken while marking time ,like the ones Erik Soovere took during the Jena train ride: Yes it was a ghastly ride. Thankfully he had the courage to record it.

Mike McQuary wrote of Erik's courage

"CLIFTON- Sometime in the early 1940's, Eric Soovere traded Lithuanian lighter flints on the black market. He risked his life to take historic pictures of his family's journey through Northern Europe at the end of World War II.

'If the local Nazi population suspected you of being a spy... .it was under great risk. The pictures were taken under threat of death' said his son, Ilo Soovere......"

I am grateful to Ilo for sharing some of those photos for this book.

Erik's photos have been displayed in exhibitions relating to our trek.

War photographers have an unenviable task and among one of the magnificent representations of such times occurs in Donald Koppel's book titled "I saved them for you". It is written in both Estonian and English. His photography can only be described as soulful, as is his narrative. I thank Prof. Peeter Linnap for his wisdom on the intricacies of the pictorial representation of such material.

That which could not be photographed at times can be represented in paint and other visual art media. Perhaps visual art like poetry allows selective clipping of 'fleeting moments': Moments which one could write volumes about but volumes which in today's hurry and scurry of life not many would have the time to read. Such clips send the reader/viewer away to ponder, perhaps reinforced by such moments as they cross the reader's/viewer's path:
There is nothing like reality street to engage another.

Art work becomes particularly poignant in small children's accounts which are fragmented and tend to allude to that salient to them: Traumatic or unreconcileable given their naivety.

I am grateful to Gunnar Neeme's children two of whom were born in DP camps in Germany: They have shared some of their father's art work for this book. Albeit Gunnar was a young adult.

Moving film adds an additional dimension to any account. Such opportunities were rare given the times and street wisdom precluded much of their use where such rare resources existed. In such films one could see the what even photos can conceal: Emotions can only be concealed for short windows of time when the prevailing events preoccupy those being filmed.

They are certainly not a reality when one is really being shot at or avoiding this: This year I had the good fortune to be contacted by Mati Sööt who was born in Geislingen and has been editing moving films sans voices, of life in Geislingen in the latter 1940s. Ardo Tarem had made these films and his grandson, Erik Laidroo, the guardian of that edited film was kind enough to allow me to use "Screen grabs" to create little picture stories of the time. The available chronology definitely adds an added dimension to those stories.

Poetry also adds a depth to any tome on the journey of a people. Ex-pat Estonians have many wonderful poets. Among them is Gunnar Neeme: Both his poetry and his artwork leave one's mind to ponder. Gunnar lived in Melbourne after leaving the camps. Poetry allows the unspeakable to say cryptically, the unbearable to be said minimalistically and the ugly to be said impersonally. It is a much undervalued source of information for academics stating give us FACTS, FACTS, FACTS. I say to those academics- I challenge you try to do that in the shoes of the people who wrote that poetry.

A MOSAIC OF MEMORIES

Some mosaics can be completed and others can't. Some will contain indecipherable voids, others need to be cropped in such a way as to make the book look real and sometimes it is kinder to subtly change the name of the mosaic to minimise distressing another. Often there is a wish by coauthors to have the darkest shadows removed. Those whose authors are caught with the unenviable task of braving sharing their story and knowing that it has a high chance of being excluded on some technicality. Perhaps too their own dignity precludes them from risking another painful blow on their already battered souls.

As a clinician to me every story is important: Pain is a relative phenomenon as some endure it better than others, some are more practised at enduring it than others. Whichever be the case their voices are vital in completing the authenticity of that mosaic.

I have also had decades of experience of working among refugee and other traumatised cohorts to devise ways that they can disclose their pain with minimal discomfort or pain. That is why I have placed no constraints on the words per story.

The stories of the very young often only have short windows of time to traverse and at times their language development has not evolved to the level of words to convey any information: At other times they do have information but need more words to convey it in the only way they have: Clumsily. At times their information is a series of quandaries.

Among such stories are some which are extremely ugly, clearly not the product of the child's own actions. At times it is actions of their loved ones whom they are divided between protecting and questioning and yet at the same time trying to find a way to belong to the mainstream.

There are stories where detail is not sharable because of the nature of their parents' baggage: some were sworn to silence in groups like underground movements or intelligence: The children knew something but not something they could share directly: others to parents' actions which went beyond the call of their duties in an ignoble way. Such authors needed a way to depersonalize that material. Others could cope with using progressive disclosure.

Progressive disclosure is a word consuming exercise where at times chronology needs to be lost.
Such material is at times related with the most benign first, and at times fragmented to remove the impression that the author is incoherent. And at times they need opportunities to interleave lighter interludes among the ugliness. I was prepared to allow whatever number of words it took and allow anonymity if needed. Perhaps some vignettes will help clarify my reasoning.

Let us pretend that among the potential authors is the once child of an Estonian freedom fighter: Their father was court-martialed. It is well known that data on such events never become fully public: Conjecture certainly does. It may have because he betrayed his country, it may have been some indiscretion unrelated to loyalty or it may indeed have been the legacy of another's envy or dysfunctional behaviour. No matter, that child becomes one of the court-martialed and is inextricably tarred with the same murky brush. Such children inevitably have murky lives as do their mothers in the wake of the same event.

That child's story is not one to tell in a simple chronology. Much verbiage needs to be consumed painting a hazy diorama and in aliquots separated by other's voices begin to clarify the most benign parts first. They may chose to paint pen pictures of their parents as they knew them and gradually introduce what they know of what might have broken then. They might gradually begin to brave the locales of places they have visited in their youth: A preamble that their journey is not what or where mankind would have wished of them. At times disclosure may emerge, commonly in cryptic. They too have their dignity: They will wish to share how they have reconciled their place in life.

Perhaps on an equally ugly note, in the context of this book is the ex-nuptial child of an Estonian mother and a Russian soldier involved in the invasion: It may have been the legacy of infatuation between two young, it may have been the need for intimacy on the part of a young man who had been on a remote war front for years, and at times it could have been rape. The child had no part in their conception but all had plenty to do with their reception in society. They too might use the above strategy to share their story (well in a different book because they are not truly Estonian).

This book contains no such stories: My clinical experience would be that such children would rarely have survived long enough to tell their tale: Nobody's children find solace in self neglect, alcohol and suicide. They tend to die very prematurely. On that journey the girls tend to chose between detachment from society and promiscuity (yes, the trollops folk like to frequently malign): The guys seem to tend towards being comedians (then self soothing alone with alcohol, food or whatever), detachment and from my interest in forensic behavioural medicine I know that many tend to act out anti-socially. Fortunately not too many resort to extremes but one has to ask what might have been the extremes they might have resorted to had time granted them the opportunity: That they had not died in the wake of their own lack of will to live. Many conjecture that homicide and suicide are the flip-sides of the same coin: The coin that nobody's children were left to pocket.

During my years as a clinician I have learned more about a patient by the paintings that hung on the walls of my consulting room than I have ever learned from a formal genogram. At times they commented a dislike and could immediately feel comfortable in disclosing their distress: At others they would focus on a super -cheerful one: They liked it because it made them feel happy. It was often months later that they found the courage to tell me that their access to happiness during their lives had been at near starvation point and that that painting reminded them of one of the scarce happy interludes.

Thus in permitting optimal leniency with wordage and medium of conveyance of the stories I hope that I have allowed each of the authors to truly share their souls.

Perhaps a limitation of elective text is its respect for cultural mores: Some things are just not sharable by voice or writing. Yet ingrained in such silences are at times what may become the salvation of mankind: That which street wisdom mandates one to conceal: To allow the casualty of fate to live another day in the environment which they are not in a position to change at that epoch of time.

And perhaps another avoidant theme, as I have already alluded to, is where one's parents were involved with what then or subsequent times is not considered 'kosher' by the prevailing environment (regardless of its actual appropriateness at the times they were enacted). One can hardly ask any of their descendants to openly narrate such information. Yet narrated it should be, for it is amongst those streets of despair that the lives of those descendants were perhaps mutated to what was not their preference. Their despair does need to be understood. One cannot deny such constricting impacts on lives.

But narrated it cannot be: Those whose lives were enmeshed in such ugliness too have a right to make the best of what remains of their lives: Some continue as chameleons to not inflict discomfort on those around, some find solitude as a friend, yet others seek out the company of alcohol and other addictive substances and sadly many find their homes with tombstones as their roofs. Yes, as I repeat myself, that is the way of the world.

It would be wonderful to produce a tome which represented our youth proportionately and inclusively: Sadly this is a vain aim as Estonia's expat. flock are spread far and wide and not all can be reached be it by location, infirmity, a persisting desire to detach from the past or worse still death. My challenge became to arrange what was available into a meaningful mosaic: A mosaic which may lead you to further tiles to clarify the existing ones.

World War II finished in May 1945, nearly seventy years ago: The youngest of us born into the war would now be sixty-nine, those to reach adulthood by the end of that war eighty-five or so, to almost ninety if the time in camps is included in the demographics. We all saw the event through age appropriate eyes and saw our parents endure the unendurable: Even the littlest of us knew that something was not right .A number of children were born on the cusp, into refugee camps to also become Displaced People. Some of these children were to struggle with their identities in the years to come: Somehow ascribing nationality in times of peace, transit and war to have differing symbolisms.

This is not a history book. Nor can it be: The world looks different to children of different ages: They prioritize differently. Even children of the same age may be developing at a different rate and thus absorb different features of their world. Thus the book will seem to hold many incongruities when adults read them: Perhaps the truth consists of the composite of the stories. And maybe the differences are accounted by similar events occurring in many differing places.

 Children were not always privy to all that surrounded them and intrinsically had little sense of time and place. The youngest of the cohort knew nought of their parents' trek only the despair that followed. They would now be in their early sixties.

We are all at an age when time has taken its toll and many are no longer with us, no matter our demographics. The percentage I cannot estimate but the number increases rapidly with the years. How many of those deaths were premature I too cannot estimate. But then this is not a book about statistics or demography. Only those who remain able and free to tell the tale can be represented in the narrative. There will thus be many inevitable artifacts; be they by absence of the author or selective recollection of what transpired, or their sense of lack of inclusivity within the demographic.

In the book "When the Noise had Ended" rabbits popped up on many pages but their context varied. I personally have no recollection of such rabbits despite knowing from the addresses they would have been on my beaten track and the authors of a similar age: Clearly they had a low priority on my agenda.

Unfortunately I lack a possible other tool: As a clinician for nearly five decades I have seen many owners of the 'missing stories' pass through my consulting room. It is unethical to tell such stories without their permission: the latter perhaps obtainable to tell anonymously. Sadly many of these patients had an early demise. Some of the salient aspects of such stories where they can be de-identified I will attempt to tell in omniscient voice.

Most importantly, I stress that this is not a psychology book despite my interest in human behaviour. It would be quite inappropriate to place my interpretation of another's narrative into such a book: Perhaps rendered even more inappropriate as many of the authors have become my pals. Nor have I chosen to even ruminate on the matter.

To ensure this I have left all writings where possible in the first voice as the authors wrote them, albeit translating a few (and indicating this). To ensure accuracy through the authors eyes, their chapters (including any translations) have been returned to them for review: The final products as they still presented them. Any behavioral comments would be the inclusions of the authors which are their prerogative.

I have also left unaltered some stories where English is the author's third or subsequent language (unless requested to correct the English). Their standard would compare very well with many for whom English is their third/fourth etc language. It illustrates the remarkable plasticity of the young mind to adapt and learn many languages simultaneously or in rapid succession when necessity bids. The narrative would identify the stories which have been written in a third or subsequent language.

Let us not lose sight of the purpose of this book: Recall of events which occurred at a time when many of us were very small. Yes, it is a book about childhood and adolescent memory. A book where the children of Estonian DPs remember those precious people in their lives: Their parents and the events which were to mould their identities.

Somehow we all imagine that memory suddenly happens, that at some point in time we begin remembering: What is that magical age? Most of the narrative begins at about 6-8 years and of course becomes increasingly more detailed as the child approaches adolescence. Most of the stories begin around this age and the ones of older authors, the adolescents of the time, have quite a different flavour.

My own memories which are best described like a moth eaten curtain with some holes in it: At times a number of holes close are enough to offer some coherency. Some of these have been derived from very brief abrupt flashbacks which have remained as a hazy image, others as dreams to do the same. But it would be dishonest of me to include those into a book which does not pertain to my demographics.

Photoscapes have added to expand that: Some of us could remember some of the photo incidents at least partially and e-mail conversations containing snippets of information perhaps fill in the voids further. Yes, we the littlies were there, as were our minds albeit in different capacities..

A number of the authors have been fortunate to have their parents keep diaries or have been able to reconstruct those early years while their parents were still alive. I have included some such chapters and used Italics to separate what the author remembers and what has been derived from secondary sources. Among the manuscripts is the translation of the father of a toddler in transit: I have included this. Aino Marshall has marked in her recollections among that text. Tõnu Loorpärg and Maie Kaarsoo have combined their resources with those of their parents. They are a valuable addition to illustrate the insidious evolution of memory, its expression as verbal communication appeared and that feelings among us did exist.

It is poignant to remember that much of adolescence was fractured by either fleeing or survival needs to help parents. Yet others found themselves in military tasks. They returned to complete their adolescent tasks as adults. Such stories have also been included. And yet others sacrificed their remaining youth to become adults in their adolescence and cared for children who had become separated from their parents.

Excerpts (both as short stories and snippets and with permission from Lakeshore Press) from Kalev Ehin's book "Coming Home" take us through many reminiscences and these are at varying ages. I am grateful to have them to add some cohesion to the younger stories. Fortunately Kalev visited those places some years ago and had his family members to validate his memories: An experience which brought sadness, gladness and sometimes closure.

Another conspicuous glitch occurs for accounts which are ugly or disturbing: People tend to feel a taboo for sharing such material in their narrative. As this book evolved there were many intercurrent e-mail communications: I feel privileged that a few of the authors have agreed to snippets of such conversations being shared. How many such communications remain unshared one can only guess at. Given my clinical experience working in areas where many refugees lived I would say that we are only privy to the tip of the iceberg.

It is easy to return somewhere and state I remember that: Was it a memory jog or wishful thinking?
Before my first trip to Europe I thought that I would explore that theory and produced a small series of ink and wash paintings to illustrate what I thought that I remembered. The matches were scanty but there were times when I knew that something wasn't it and years later some 'matches' were to appear.

Perhaps more dramatic were the déjà vus and flashbacks: After their appearance their details never changed and they were never to abate unlike those of other nightmares. I have no idea where some of those occurred. I can only guess from our scanty documents, but I believe that their gist is true.

As I perused through the various manuscripts at times I felt that I was part of the journey and at others there was a clear feeling that we must have been elsewhere at that time. Given I was under three at that time something must have been imprinted.

Many of us will have photos which have passed though the generations and are now in our possession. Sometimes we are fortunate to find an inscription behind them and at others we are left in limbo to guess or wonder, as I have been. My last connection with any available information was lost when Mother died in 1964. The material gleaned prior to that fragmented given our complex lives in survival mode and Mother's shattered nerves rendering her less accessible to share information. At times there was more to be learned from where she 'lost the plot' and shared nought.

Very few of us have had the opportunity to retrace our steps as Kalev Ehin has and found validation of their quandaries. Even returning to what has been documented as a relevant place may leave one with quandaries as happened to me on my first return to Estonia. The house which was supposed to have been the right house didn't feel right. I left Estonia in 2002 questioning if we had really lived there, until back in Melbourne I stumbled over that photo without an inscription on the back. How fortunate it was that I took detailed photos of every face of the building. I have since confirmed that the people in the photo were our landlords.

Writing things retrospectively introduces a glitch: Our language changes as do our identities. A fellow. Geislingen 'young' sent me a copy of the Geislingen Gümnaasium (High school) journal written just post war. It contains writings which were those of the times:Howfortunate I was to find this gem to bridge the present with the past.

Some of the stories will also share memories of camp life in Germany: They will introduce an additional dimension to the book. Four years in limbo is a long time out of a youngster's life. A more extensive account of such camp life can be found in "When the Noise had Ended: Geislingen's DP Children Remember" (Vesilind and Maddisson). However many of your cohort were not fortunate enough to spend most of their DP sojourn in such an Estonian village in another land: For them the trek became one which lasted until they found niches in the countries they emigrated to.

No book is complete without a synopsis of the diorama on which it was set: Tõnu Loorpärg has written a family memoir "Freedom is another word for everything to gain" which he has generously shared. From this I have extracted his account of Estonia's history into which he has beautifully embroidered the story of his family: It could be the story of many Estonian families at those times. Also included in the book are Tõnu's memories of the times and relevant photos.

Each diorama has some silent characters: Among them are the doctors who looked after the troops and gave our mothers peace that our fathers while in danger where in caring hands should they become maimed. It is one aspect of the trek where we took anothers' lives for granted: War was a time when we, as people are won't to do: To reach out for reassurance to the Almighty. Hannes Jürmann's father was one of the doctors who tended our troops. Enn Raudsepp's father one of Estonia's many pastors. He continued to care for his flock when he migrated to Canada.

And definitely no book is complete without the tools that gave people the courage to keep morale alive. There is an old Estonian saying that Estonians sing and dance their way to heaven. I don't know that any of them had such ambitious aspirations in those bleak times but I can say for sure that they sang and danced their way away from Hell.

The photos accompanying the various writings were supplied by their authors: Any exceptions will be specified by appropriate acknowledgements.

Sadly some of the photos are not optimal in clarity: They are at times third/fourth degree reproductions. They convey what needs to be conveyed. I make no apology for not diverting time to photo shopping them: Such time is better diverted to further exploring the journey of our youth: Our increasing age a poignant reminder that one needs to prioritize one's time.

Perhaps there is a seeming artefact in the book: That the material from Geislingen camp is over-represented. I wish that there had been a way to make the representation accurately proportional. This of course was a vain wish as many of the camps were smaller and the subsequent opportunities to network were reduced. Given Geislingen was by far the largest of the camps and many Estonians at least transiently passed through it or participated in its activities the statistical chances of recorded material were higher as were the opportunities to generate such activities.

The smaller camps were attenuated variants of Geislingen: There is no doubt that they too optimized their opportunities and at no stage did their morale of tenacity flounder: The soul of Estonia thrived where ever its people were to spend those years in limbo.

In some chapters the authors have used Estonian names for parents and geographical features; The most commonly used are

Isa: Father	**Mägi:** Hill
Ema: Mother	**Strasse:** Street
Härra: Mr	**Weihe:** Way
Proua: Mrs	**Herr:** Mr
Preili: Miss	**Frau:** Mrs
Tänav: Street	**Fraulein:** MIss
Maantee: Highway	**WNE:** "When the Noise had Ended": Vesilind and Maddisson
Ema: Mother	**Gumnaasium:** Estonian word for high school

MAI MADDISSON
IS A GOOD BOOK SYNONYMOUS WITH A MEANINGFUL BOOK?

I like to begin with definitions to ensure that everyone is on the same page. Let us define the word book!

Each dictionary has its variations but essentially the ingredient is a written work that is published, either as printed pages inside a cover or electronically. It is as simple as that: Nowhere is it indicated that a specific format is required be it in layout or language.

Nor is a book necessarily intended to have a meaning: and the same material can be subjectively interpreted as being meaningful or not so by different people. It depends what the readership is seeking. If that which they are seeking is contained then they may classify the book as good and meaningful, or they may challenge its value in terms of the literary skills of the writings contained. For those that way inclined I remind them that this book is not intended to effect a Ph. D. in the English language for any of us.

Books are written for many reasons but the only one relevant in this instance is the compilation of the narrative of Estonia's cohort of war children: Implied that it is completed in a time frame that it remains relevant to the readership. That creates endless complexities, perhaps the greatest one that none of us has a crystal ball to ensure that each of the authors and the narrator will remain alive and physically and mentally accessible until its completion. Time is of the essence.

I am among the youngest of the cohort of children who were removed from Estonia in 1944: Many of the older ones are now approaching ninety. When working with multiple authors there needs to be significant to and fro feedback. In the fourth and fifth decade of life that is a realistic task while it may be intrusive to the authors occupationally. By the seventh and eighth decade occupational intrusion becomes uncommon but ill health becomes increasingly intrusive and one cannot just set a timetable of reviewing variable lengths of narrative. One has to accept that each author has a lifetime of valuable experiences to share and has shared it their way. Their way may not be my way and it may not be the local linguistics department's way but is that so critical: Perhaps the reverse holds too, given how many local departments there are spread over our various adoptive lands. Could they even agree among themselves!

The English spoken in USA, Canada, UK, Australia and indeed nearby New Zealand differs: There are idiomatic variants which are unrealistic to find a common expression for: To do that is to lose the flavour of the author's writing. Perhaps a poignant vignette is the expression "Sent to Coventry". Anyone who has lived in a country of British origin would feel the pungent emotions associated with such an exile of a small child. I cannot think of a synonym for it and the reader does not need to in these days of computers: They rapidly offer a coherent explanation to those unfamiliar with such idiom.

I am certain that USA, Canada, and New Zealand all have their own idiom for all manner of situations. To begin to edit all those stories would be a formidable task and the chances of my altering the meaning significantly very high: While the edited narrative may be grammatically correct it would deny the author their right to share their emotions on a theme: Not to mention the frustration it would create for those involved: And let us not forget that time will not wait for any of us, myself included! The task of recording takes priority over how it is recorded.

I have spent my life as a family physician, mostly working among those who live among adversity. Their mode of expression varies to that of those who live in prosperity: And we have not even moved out of Melbourne yet!

Something becomes lost in those linguistic conversions: Patients at times feel that they need to speak in 'doctor language'. I quickly ask them to talk as if they were talking to their neighbour. How much more spontaneous the communication becomes. It has feeling: It has the ability to express both the pain and mirth of their lives. The Linguistics departments of our various universities may challenge their presentation: They don't need to reach the patient nor the patient's friends and neighbours.

This book is about many memories when feelings ran high: Good and bad were inextricably entwined. Estonia's DPs derived from various demographics each with their own idiom and nuances, or what they call "Murraks". They have grown up spread far and wide across this globe: some of them had access to elite education, others didn't. There are probably as many linguistic variants as there are authors in this book. This book is about all of them. As Frank Sinatra once crooned "I did it my way", so did the authors of this book: They did it their way. Who am I to challenge that their way is not the right way for them.

I hope that the readership can engage in the spirit of the narrative and not waste precious time pondering on the linguistics of the stories: For each of the authors time is measured: They have a story to pass on: Imbibe it and continue to pass it on. Each story is worthy of such privilege.

I have perused the commentaries on the backs of books of similar ilk (albeit the ilk being mostly that of the 'oldies') and some stand out to me as ones that 'hit the spot' to use Oz lingo.

On the back of "Hitler versus Stalin" by Professor John and Ljubica Erickson among the words written are "..it is not a book of proposed propaganda images......a moving, authoritative and unforgettable account..."

Vaclav Havel writes on the back cover of (as part of the foreword): "We are children just the same" selected and edited by Marie Rut Krizkova, Kurt Jiri Kotouc and Zdeneck Ornest : "Art springs from truthful...experience...;..how many poets left a record of their true birth in the shadow of death?". The book is about artwork from those incarcerated in Terezin.

On the back cover of "Changi" by John Doyle are the words ". This *Changi* dwells on the lucky ones. Six men, who on the surface have enjoyed happy and fulfilling lives, reveal that over fifty years later, reconciling the past is still a day-to-day proposition".

The back cover of "This war never ends" written by Michael McKernan alludes to yet another dimension of retrospective writings on war. Perhaps there is some mimicry to the book "Changi" as the cover words unfold "Homefront and prisoners constructed an idealized world that would be there when the war is over and they fantasized about home life, jobs and harmony.

This book is about a world that military history has preferred to ignore: The impact of war on wives, mothers, sons, daughters, relatives, friends - and on the soldiers themselves, once they were left to their own resources."

Both of the latter books confirm my own impressions that the heaviest of human baggage will only be shared with those who too speak their language of life, and it is perhaps only in the twilight of their lives, sadly at times under the effect of narcotic analgesia that the ugly truths emerge.

But a kid I am no more, nor was I when I began the project of compilation of narrative of Estonia's war time youth. There was a clearly planned strategy to collect as much information as I could access given the authors' demographics: To format the book in such a way that should time take its toll be it at 100, 200 or even 2000 pages, that it would with minor external editing be a complete book for another to build a successive book on. It had to allow for insertions, rearrangements and fragmentation into more than one book without leaving the material fragmented at any stage.

In such situations one does not dwell on niceties such as grammar, and even minor typos: They, time permitting become the icing on the cake. At this stage there is another layer of cake in the oven and a third partly mixed in the bowl.

If I have even partly met the above cover comments which I admire, I will feel that the last five years have been meaningfully spent.

In the same vein I hope that while I have tried to be very careful, that the odd typo is excused: The time spent on repeated screening is better spent on compiling further narrative for which the resources are facing attrition.

And yes I could have perhaps done more in learning to photo-shop: It captures my imagination as a technical challenge but somehow it dampens my enthusiasm in regard to this book. The time spent is again better spent on compiling further material: Perhaps more importantly to my eye destroying the authenticity of a time travelled image is to destroy its very soul.

This book is what it is: I hope that in putting it away after hopefully many hours spent perusing it, the reader will have learned much about what that war time trek meant to Estonian children and adolescents. That is the sole meaning of this book. The time to produce another one will never return, to revise it time squandered to leave further material unshared.

From: **THE WAVE**
The human right is to love and be loved.
Gunnar Neeme

MANYLOGUES

For about 8-9 years I have been researching the journey of our ex-pat cohort of young who fled with their parents in the 1944 exodus.

One of the most stimulating methods has evolved to be a system of e-mail dialogues where someone would raise a quandary, and others would respond bringing forth new perceptions. At times something tangential would be included and engage the group in a secondary, tertiary dialogue.

One can hardly call a many way communication a dialogue: 'Manylogue' seems far more apt, while not in the current dictionary perhaps to the linguistic purists' chagrin. But then that is something I have been doing since my intern days: At those times just to conserve time recording information. I was commonly in strife with my seniors, but the words seem to have become infectious and are now to be found in orthodox literature.

Perhaps from our youth we have confirmed that necessity is the mother of invention.

And how much useful information has derived from our manyloguing!

At times those manylogues tend to hop in erratic fashion: The material has been recorded in the chronology with which it arrived: Not to relate a specific story: The emergence of the latter of course the major fringe benefit.

One needs to remember that when we first began exploring the epoch many of us had lost contact with people from the past and there was an array of 'tiles' of thought which we gradually arranged in some form of chronological order: And the order may have varied among us!

This book contains a number of these, both long and short.

Perhaps a salient observation is how little any of us knew of our early journeys, which of course were prioritized by the need for survival. We each had fragments: At times very different ones!

 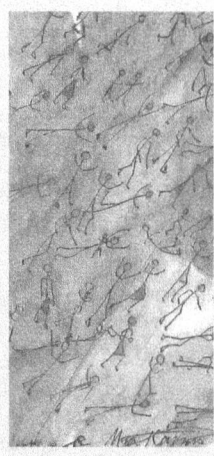   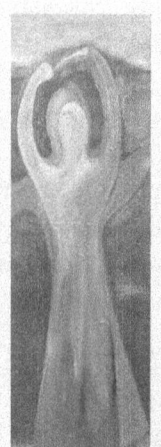 

MAI MADDISSON
NOBODY'S CHILDREN, NOBODY'S ADULTS

HOP as the book has become hieroglyphed among those concerned in it production, perhaps has an incomplete title, long as it is. Implied in the subtitle is another dimension: Perhaps the subtitle should read "Hats off to our Estonian war parents for all their sacrifices in helping us reach a place where we could become some society's people and later its adults". Theirs was a noble cause as the stories in this book tell.

Also implied in the title is that it about Estonian parents (in plural). I have accordingly modified the title as no human can cut themselves in half, or worse still disown one half of themselves.

Perhaps a limitation of the book is the paucity of memory fragments of those acquired before the age of six to eight years. Most of these reside in children's preverbal memories but some can be eventually translated into words in some language.

Some children also become verbal very early: Perhaps a genetic trait: One which I would not have believed until I found my younger son with a vocabulary of about fifty clumsily pronounced words by his first birthday and using simple garbled phrases three months later. That facility available he was able to describe the death of our dog from a convulsion and exactly where it had occurred. The dog died when he was about seven months old.* He narrated that story for some years until he had enough insight to understand why a sick dog had been placed outside: Until then he was too young to comprehend that a very mobile baby with a limited sense of danger and a dog in post-epileptic furore after a very brief unwitnessed fit was a dangerous combination. He was then at peace with the predicament, and now has forgotten the event to which he would and could have been the only witness.

*it is possible to be accurate about the dates due to inter-current events at the time.

The only significant available memory clips of those first few years are ones which would have been in my account of those years. Perhaps part of the same genetic variant as my younger son carries together with of course many less desirable shared traits! Given I was already also speaking Baltic German by the time I reached Geislingen (a tangible age) it suggests that I too had a good grasp of words by the age of three: And perhaps need being the mother of action I had good reason to be bilingual.

However given the title in its strung out version, it is dishonest to be a participant if one's account is irrelevant to the theme. This book had taken five years to mature and a lot of water has passed under the bridge in that interval. Some of it has been HOP related, some other writing related, some inter-current Estoniana related and much totally unrelated to the latter. The culmination of all the observations that I do not have the qualifications to be part of this book, except as a narrator: I thank all concerned for that privilege. I have learned a lot and made some wonderful friendships on the journey. And even if I qualified to do so, the story is so complex and disturbing that it would require to be presented by progressive and at times cryptic disclosure: Such a technique would involve my consuming more than my fair share of the book's verbiage.

On a battlefield camaraderie is the mainstay of the troops' morale: They understand when to support each other and when one of them needs to stand back to allow the others to move on with maximal safety.

We the littlies and young too were part of that battlefield and now wear variable 'tattoos' embossed in those times. Perhaps even as littlies many of us had already needed to learn the soldiers' axiom of camaraderie: I would suggest that were one of our parents in visible danger we would have made whatever sacrifices our little minds could contrive to keep them alive: Many of us had learned that silence is the language of war and we did not indulge in idle chatter which we did not understand:

We all, be it by our elders mythology or personal experience knew that loved ones vanished with that knock on the door and perhaps there was some kind of symbolism in the choice of that door. For many years that memory was dissociated for me: I was for decades perplexed why I could tolerate war films (which my ex had a penchant for), even when soldiers invaded a civilian house, no matter where the house or what their uniform: There was one exception, when the soldiers wore German uniforms. My Estonian family weren't Jewish. The explanation for all that was to evolve only about a decade ago, the explanation for my clumsiness a little before.

Yes, I as a little tyke less than two years old had got in the way and concluding from the remaining scarring (and other variables) was stood on to sustain a crushed chest, and a near fatal pneumonia. Mother too was caught in the scrimmage and perhaps that was the last straw for her shattering nerves. Had there been a video-tape recording of the time it might not have been exactly like that. But somehow I knew without knowing, and that had permanently imprinted on me that one aims for the optimal outcome for all even if it means personal sacrifice for one or another: The explanation of that too complex for this book.

As Estonian war children you all admire your parents for their tenacity to bring you to a meaningful belonging to a society. I admire my parents too, but the reasons largely differ and don't belong to this book.

I've modelled my life on the camaraderie of those battle fields: That one should always minimise the carnage be it physical or emotional.
Perhaps I got too close to the battle fields as bunkers, garrisons, and such like loom in my mind in addition to the bombing raids and imagery which many of you relate. I am acutely aware of my wish to be near them rather than wishing them further. I am also aware of sights which are not included in the narratives in this book: Of rendezvous where I was too scared to cry, of seeing in the distance structures which could have been camps and possibly could include Terezin, of long absences from mother to the point where separations had long ceased to bother me, even as a little tyke.

The scanty documents (perhaps deliberately so) suggest that I yo-yoed between the Estonian trek trail and somewhere in East Prussia and that one day which I have only recently dared to remember it all came to an end: A very ugly end. In my narrative the same references keep cropping up in varying guises, perhaps as relics of recurrent events.

My world was a different world to yours while albeit both were treacherous. But life is about horses for courses. Your parents picked the best of what they deemed in your family's interests. Maybe mine did too: there are too many glitches to be certain .

Very early in my life I recognized that my demographics, as seen through the eyes of a child could be a blight to my family, as seen through the eyes of the culture of the relevant times. Even before understanding 'the birds and bees' I committed myself to never blight the lives of my father's family and chose not seek him out: It was a decision based on compassion not to be vindictive.

Yes, I was a blight to my remaining and future family: They did their best but mother's shattered nerves were not a reliable compass in life. I cannot be sure how much input my father had into my destiny after his escape from Siberia: There is some anecdotal evidence that my parents did meet and certainly being half German I had a right to remain there.

Perhaps the immigration authorities of our youth were less naive than those of today. As a small child I can recall mother's recurring bemoaning that no one wanted us: Perhaps the truth was that the weight of the crooked cross would be too heavy for a small child and even a young adult to bear: That Sweden would have been a less weighty place to for me to live out my life.

When one tampers with the rules bad things happen: We were accepted in Australia finally. While learning how to use the Oz immigration archives for the WNE project I felt that the most honest place to practice was on our own documents. I learned how I came by the 'stolen ticket' to Australia. Father's first name was Fritz, a name which even the naivest of officials would have considered needing further scrutiny: That did not occur: Father's name was not there to scrutinise: Nor did anyone scrutinise the reason for its absence.

Nor were the medical records too carefully scrutinised: Albeit with my now clinical knowledge the crucial questions were not present. A recently paralysed arm surely needed accounting for four years post war: Why was that not done? It has now recovered but in those days it was in the lap of the Gods: The Gods who for whatever reason did not complete that examination fully. Of course maimed children have the right to move on in life, but maybe the road needs to be different.

There are more voids in my memory of life in Geislingen than for the pre-verbal years: Detailed as is the former. I have far more emotional memories of what would be considered attributable to a preverbal child. To this day I cannot remember the basic details of our room in Geislingen or what occurred within it in the three years we lived there. Nor do I wish to remember much of the decades which followed, while I have included the first five years in Oz (In the story of Estonia's children's fractured generation) to illustrate how bad things occur with 'stolen tickets': **to validate my conviction that children's documents and predicaments should be carefully scrutinised to ensure that child's safety at the mercy of an unfamiliar land's disconnecteds: That they do not become the prey of the latter:** For those are the only relationships aliens can hope for. It can never be assumed that the parent's best outcome equates to that of the child's.

My early memories of Australia include the loss of my little friend from Geislingen to another state a couple of weeks after our arrival and loss of contact, the newspaper accounts a few years later of the grizzly death of my little playmate on the ship to Australia and perhaps most painfully the loss of my little Australian born sister to a foundling home when aged four weeks: Of visiting her there and leaving her behind week after week, month after month for eighteen months until she finally came home. I still wonder what became of all those other little mites: Given my job as a clinician I know.

And of course the shadow of the crooked cross continued to live on over the decades and impact on all who touched my life: Life as a chameleon is complex. One is expected to get close to people and relate to them: How does one do so when one's life narrative is that of an alien. Being a fugitive is complex for one and one's loved ones. Everyone pays its price.

How much simpler would life had been for all concerned had mother been able to have a clean start without me as a marker of her past.

There were so many opportunities when a change of fate was possible. Someone, I suspect not mother, took me to the doctor: Once there, he was obliged to do as he had promised to Hippocrates: Emotional pain had never been considered a valid parameter in medicine: Nor did the doctor have a crystal ball to know the dynamics of how that pneumonia evolved. Surely there was some adult who could recognise that there are worse fates than death and who would have allowed me the dignity to be buried in Estonian soil: The notion of doing so on German soil perhaps yet too opaque in that crystal ball.

Was there not someone who could see that, what would have been a hypoxically brain damaged child would not travel well in flight: That they would be a hazard to all concerned. That their mother was hardly in a state to address such complex decisions. Perhaps a far more humane outcome for all, especially for my future extended family, would have been to at the eleventh hour leave me unidentified in an orphanage. Mother given the German connection would definitely not have been safe to stay.

There I may or may not have survived, but at least I would have lived out my days in a world where those around me too were nobody's children to become nobody's adults: We could have shared the camaraderie of each other. The pain it would have generated for mother would have more than been outweighed by the pain it would have spared her in the years to come: She could have left behind all stigmata of the crooked cross, she would have spared my Australian born sister of different genetics spending the first eighteen months of her life in a foundling home: The list is endless. I still shed a tear should I need to drive past where that foundling home stood.

I dearly wish that I could have been granted the rights of an honest soldier on a battlefield: The right to step back with dignity to allow others I treasured to move on.

Given the above I cannot be an honest part of the story which you are all are wishing to share: Yours is a story to commemorate, mine one I would prefer to forget and only share where it would improve the outcome of another. And were I to share it, it is one which cannot be shared by traditional narrative means. There is too much detail, too many quandaries and too much disillusionment to cram into this book.

But as I have walked beside you, I have watched many of you Estonian children reach fulfilment in your new worlds (and of course seen the tragedies too):

For this book I can only be your narrator.

MAI MADDISSON
HOW ACCURATE IS THE CHILDHOOD NARRATIVE OF ORAL HISTORY? A REFLECTION

This article was published in "Children in War" Vol VI, No 11, ISSN 1745-7211

I have based my reflection on my experiences with four books relating to the exodus of my people's young from the Communist occupation of Estonia during World War II. Entwined in this is the narrative of decades of verbal memory clips of patients who derived from the local refugee hostels in Melbourne post World War II. In the course of their management it has been necessary to return to the genesis of their current perceptions and tread the paths of their youth. There has been a seeming concurrency given there was a commonality among the two groups of aggressors. The differences in their narrative have generally been readily ascribed to local cultural and geographic factors. The human emotional response has been surprisingly constant.

The books I allude to are
- When the Noise had Ended (WNE)
- Its Estonian translation which was launched in Estonia in 2013 (EWNE)
- The ongoing compilation of the story of the trek of my cohort of youth through war time Estonia to the DP camps:"From here began the journey to far off lands: Hats off to our parents" (HOP). The book you are now reading , but with its subtitle amended to read "Hats off to Estonian War parents"!
- The ongoing compilation of the story of our young during their first five years in their new lands: Those who were taken as DPs to faraway places, those who were deported to Siberia, and those who remained on the same soil now with a different flag: "Estonian war children: A fractured generation" (#G). This compilation is about half complete currently.

Oral history is essentially the personal recollections of people who participated in historical events. One tends to think of such narrative in terms of the military or the historians. The ordinary civilians have written accounts of personal circumstances, especially if their experiences have been significantly different or more traumatic than those of their cohort: Cohortal narrative is perhaps uncommon and maybe hard to access if the cohort is very large: The Estonian cohort because of its smaller size rendering this a tangible task.

The narrative of children again has been sporadic: Children have largely been considered to be passengers in their parents' journeys: The notion of differing perceptions of the same milieu a fairly recent notion: The cohortal recording of such again a tenuous process except for a compact group such as the Estonian children.

Such narrative can be recorded on a diversity of media: Written, electronic and indeed song and artwork.
Such events can consist of brisk interludes: Usually relating to a major impact of an event on the author, or of epochs of time: The latter perhaps a reinforcement of the recurring turmoil of war and its aftermath's erosive effect on optimal survival for that author and those who form part of their lives.

Despite the presence of more than one witness, no two are at exactly at the same place be it by foot space or mind space. Each person will be preoccupied by their own survival of the event but each person will be translating their mode of survival in context of the life skills they have learned to date: Their preceding demographics and life experiences will colour their current perceptions. In critical events the exact proximity to the danger will have a major impact on its translation into the survival story: A small increment of space can provide more ready access to an escape route and hence very different narrative to other only metres away.

Such narrative can occur in first or second voice. The first voice would be by the person whom the narrative is about: The second by someone communicating with them.

Where there is more than one person present inevitably each will give a variably different first voice account: The number of second voice accounts as numerous as the number of interviewers multiplied by the number of interviewees. That variation may be subtle or significant. Some interviewers will be basing their questions on a mythical reality, others on sensory reality.

Mythical reality may range from never met the predicament at all to having met it via the newspapers or electronic media. Some of those preceding accounts may be from the index person being interviewed: Others from their interviewer. And let us not forget that for the mythical exposure this can always be terminated when it becomes "all too much". The TV can be turned off or the page of the paper changed, and indeed the interviewer can make a "Knight's Move" to remove themselves from something which is beyond their resources to continue. Whichever the case they present a punctate image: Only the size of the window of narrative will vary as will its impact

Sensory reality is the reality of someone who has been there and done it: Their narrative will have a continuum about it. It can only be aborted by escape from the event.

Interviewers, no matter how experienced in their research will always have imbibed and polarized their background information through their own eyes.

Perhaps a vignette will be helpful here: My last twenty years of clinical work were largely spent at a clinic which evolved in an area where one of our large Victorian DP camps was situated. That camp's characteristics were not too different to the ones I lived in across the other side of Melbourne: The conditions of life after we left the hostels too, to remain similar. Each person sought out with their meagre resources places where basic survival was possible.

When I began working there one could hardly see an illusion to the genesis of these peoples emotional ails: Much of the formulation had been derived without that piece of insight. The older doctors were aware of the presence of that now defunct hostel and the journeys of its inhabitants to a limited extent. The younger doctors were totally unaware of the history of the region all those decades ago and that it was vastly different to many less cosmopolitan regions of Melbourne.

The patients, of course believing that doctor knows all, didn't consider it necessary to introduce the doctors to the history of their past or even of the region.

The appearance of a twin soul changed the patients' and clinicians' perceptions of their ailments. When I was on after hours' duty, one of my ways of engaging anothers' patient was to look at their name and date of birth and play a guessing game of where they might have spent their youth. Given my name, to the unfamiliar, does not look foreign many patients would play down their past traumas. The stiff upper lip culture had become firmly entrenched decades earlier.

Their narrative changed fast when I indicated that my memories of those times were different: they shed their chameleon's cloak. They felt free to tell how it had really been because the imagery would no longer be unfamiliar to the other present and that other present gave them permission to share that which had been left unshared.

Children present an additional interface: They are rarely interviewed by other children of the same ilk, or even of a different one
: A retrospective interview by an adult perhaps to imply adult transposition of those events rather than retaining the imagery as it presented at the time.

Perhaps the most poignant confounding determinants of the flavour of the narrative are the characteristics of

- *The interviewee.*

The words refugee, displaced person and asylum seeker can have endless connotations. No two stories are alike and different people may describe their status differently.

- *The interviewer:*

The same words can have many connotations for the interviewer and each interviewer may in turn place their own inflections on each of these.

It can depend on how that person and their contacts have previously related to such groups and what they know about them generically.

- *An interface is created.*

It is a thing called chemistry. It can depend on whether the interviewee views themselves as a victim, a survivor or just one who has walked a different road.

It depends on how the interviewer sees those roles and how they see their role: Is it to rescue, sympathise, and empathise or to just improve their insight on such a journey.

Differences in orientation can alter the polarity of the narrative

Perhaps a poignant example of political polarity arose because I am a German-Estonian cross breed. This created a diversity of conundrums and for me some initial uneasiness with spontaneity, learned over ensuing years while clarifying what was acceptable communication: At times by quite traumatic methods. On one occasion when too young to understand the historical diorama of my youth, I was flung into a burning primus when questioning another's ire at my status: My escape from serious burns more luck than my agility. Many years later a badly traumatised colleague, during a long operation read from my omissions why I was silent and lost the plot: Fortunately the patient's management was not compromised but I had learned a valuable lesson: That omission and commission can say the same thing. But silence doesn't tell any kind of story to those who were neither the afflicted or the 'perpetrators' of the predicament. To the unwary the story would have been told out of context with those events missing.

Perhaps in the Estonian context the Russian Orthodoxy which might have appeared sporadically hasn't appeared in any of my compilations. Is this due to absence of Orthodox folk or is there another explanation? I find it hard to believe that there were no half cast Russian children amongst us.

Estonians, like all cultures had the different echelons of society each with their own system of self esteem and the problems of the exodus contained differing mores. The random dispersion and mixing post war would have created clusters of mixed echelons where those whom society tended to devalue perhaps feeling bound to conceal their identities and even to falsify their reality. Children are quick to learn and conceal their place in their world.

Let us look at the factors which may determine the flavour of the narrative;

•*Small children seem to remember less.* Their world was definitely more constricted.

But perhaps they remembered it all in a different way given some were at a preverbal stage.

And of course they remained in proximity of their oldies narrative more frequently, albeit perhaps with also a more limited comprehension of life. How much of the narrative was inadvertently plagiarized? Could they separate the two narratives and perhaps more importantly were they confounded by the discrepancies to dissociate theirs to avoid confusion while in survival mode.

•*Some children are just more observant.* Perhaps one could add, given the environment of the time they may have been preoccupied by other issues to their elders.

Perhaps the ones who were more securely cocooned needed to imbibe less from their environment for their own and their loved ones safety.

The stories in WNE certainly tend to illustrate this quite clearly. Rabbits it seems just about burrowed and ran under my feet when I lived in Geislingen. With my clumsiness I should have endlessly tripped over them or their burrows and yet I have no recollection of them, unlike many other kids of my age, who lived nearby and who have warm fuzzy memories of them some to be blighted by finding Mr. Bunny on their meagre plate at a time to follow.

Nor can I remember the cat in some of my photos apart from consternation over it. Mother quite naturally felt that it would be cute to have a photo of me with a cat sitting on my shoulder: She could not conceive that I wanted nothing on my shoulders: Given my memories of a past strangling a cat, a scarf, or a polo neck were all too close for my comfort. Translated into my language of life the absence of a polo neck or a scarf did not mean that it was too warm to wear one. One would only begin to question such absence if there are other children in the same photo more warmly clad. Yes, isolated narrative and photos do need to be placed into context of the times.

And that cat had no place despite its physical proximity to me.

•*Precarious narrative may vary with safety of environment.* In narrative involving an exodus to safety each parent had their own reasons, fears and secrets. They had their own strategies for coping with them and their children were left to adapt their priorities in such contexts.

It took me little time to learn that German was a dirty word in many places and I fast learned not to be where such a word was to complicate my life.

The corollary: what occurred at those places I was not privy to! Sans the knowledge of my parentage one might concede that I had my facts wrong: The reality that had no narrative of that place because I was elsewhere.

Within our Estoniana culture alone the fathers were variably involved in military responsibilities. While it appears that Ruskis was an even dirtier word than Germans, there would have been those who were at least ambivalent on such an issue.

I still ask if there were kids among us who remained silent despite the passage of years to ensure their parents' comfort.

•*Some children are naturally able to be more graphic and colourful in their language*. It may partly be the legacy of the language they are exposed to in their environment.

In the DP cohort there may also be variation related to the degree to which the children were cocooned or exposed to their rumbling world.

Perhaps those that saw it face to face could describe it and associated emotions more graphically.

Perhaps those whose parents were more vocal adopted those parents idiom.

There is much to be learned about the language development of children in a fast moving environment.

That fast moving environment if visible to the child could have introduced them to increasing street wisdom. The absence of an event in their narrative was not necessarily an indication of an absence of it in their memory.

•*Distortion may have been employed as an adjunctive language tool for survival.* Omissions, additions and misrepresentations could become a form of masking one's identity: At times it was necessary to present as stupid to save one's skin.

All children learn fast to protect their own skin and that of their loved ones. Even small children learn to fudge narrative or render it ambiguous.

I can remember from the time I was a little tyke to state that my father had been lost in the war: That he had become a POW.

A few years later I learned not to discuss family at all because there was always a sticky beak that needed to know more about how this had happened and where he had served. Eventually I learned that solitude could at times be my best friend.

Imagine the problems of an Estonian- Russian half cast travelling in our midst! Did they ask to be born!

•*Memories can be suppressed or dissociated to facilitate survival.* Many of our cohort's early lives were not pretty and far too hard to deal with for years, even decades. Their memories of those times at times vanished into the recesses of unconscious memory never to peek out again.

•*The language of the narrative can influence the written records*. How easy it is to present a graphic image in English with its vast vocabulary.

Try it in Estonian and one becomes more reliant on inflections of voice and idiom (if one still has it and it remains current).

Currency of language too can influence writings. Translating WNE into Estonian has provided some interesting challenges.

Standardizing it to American English introduced some occult distortion but readily coped with because of our familiarity with American films.

The translation into Estonian for the stories written by Australian authors became an effective second translation and was not quite so lenient.

Perhaps in retrospect we mused at the complications the word 'schleif' caused. A 'schleif' was a large ostentatious bow which was considered a sign of being someone at the time when I was young. There is no equivalent in the current Estonian dictionary because these days no one wears such 'daggy' hairpieces and the available translation is even more 'daggy'.

•**The culture it is being shared with is always poignant**: One would be a twit to cross the Narva Bridge with some of the Estonian publications under one's arm. If one lived across that bridge one would censor one's narrative far more carefully.

What is manna to one's ear is poison to another's: The narrator has to consider their audience and at times the distortion may occur subconsciously out of a habitual need to do this.

•**The length of the time warp between the writings and the events alluded to,** inevitably creates an artefct: language changes and narrators become lost by location death and infirmity. The sample may no longer be representative.

Why write anything at all?

Does it have any purpose apart from creating inevitable dissent among the readership? People seem to have a penchant for accuracy: Well accuracy as it looks through their own eyes. They also seem unable to separate the words history and memory.

•**For the historian** maybe there is little to be gained as there as endless more coherent accounts available. But maybe the children's accounts because of their relative naivety can challenge the known and with luck begin a search for greater objectivity. Children seem able to be ubiquitous and hear new things with an unbiased pair of ears. At times their memories lack context but at others in fact they do remove preconceived biases when the narrative is reviewed to clarify it.

Perhaps it does remind the historians that children too are passengers in the affairs of the world and thus not irrelevant to them. The movement of families has always been dictated by an attempted optimizing safety for children. However again errors of judgement may effect the opposite outcome: Cross bred children of the enemy had a less predictable destiny than children of parents of the same ilk and their narrative could be reflected on to assess the impact of parental biases.

•**To the sociologist** such narrative will finally convey that the needs of adults and children are not necessarily the same or even compatible:

That when they plan rescue strategies they may need to reflect on what harm may occur to a child when their parent makes a decision based on their own insight only.

They need to have read other accounts of such transits and their impacts on children: Each such transit can broaden the scope of their data base.

The relocation of DP children needs to be done with such contexts in mind. I often wonder what future children will feel about their destinations: who were they eventually to help. With military cross breeds, the mother may have loved the father but would the mother's chosen destination love that child: What other factors and supports need to be engaged in such a transition!

•**For the psychologist** that a person's journey and coping skills are determined by the road that they have walked: that therapy cannot be based on a model built on a diorama seen through adults' eyes: That mythical reality.

I squirm at many clinical meetings where this has been disregarded. I too squirmed when folk have suggested that I formulate more specific questions for my books: Questions which the patient/author may not be in a position to answer.

Whatever a child believes to be the truth, unless they have opportunities to review it and reflect on it, will remain the truth upon which they collectively with their cohort build the next adult generation. It is quite inappropriate to impose an adult's perception on the child's reconciliation of their events. That would only add to the child's lack of trust in themselves and their world. Any such revisions must be done safely and perhaps only to allow the child to place their perceptions into the context of the world they now find themselves in.

And maybe the time has come to review Dr. Asperger's work.

Those writings derive from about 350 km from where I spent much of my early childhood. With troop and refugee movement news travelled fast: The children's folks were commonly embroiled in it and communication of realties created peril for all concerned: What sensible child would not learn to stay silent when they and their loved ones were in danger. I would suggest that there are dangers in exhuming material which has been sequestrated from its historical context and basing further research on this.

Can we truly be sure that mini-wars are not waging in the modern children's homes? Perhaps children will always ensure that their carers are not separated from them no matter how desperate their environmental plight. Perhaps the ultimate in mental health research for children will derive when we can place Methuselah like flies on all children's shoulders and ensure that those who interpret this do not introduce their own biases: That the latter have conquered their own demons prior to beginning to address those of others.

•*For the children of historical epochs,* those words will build a shared and collective experience which they can bounce off each other to clarify the glitches in their memories of the times when they met their greatest challenges in life.

They will have access to the facts in the language of life of young children where adult bias has not left such an intense imprint on the narrative.

False memory is a conjectured notion
•*Retrieval has been a controversial topic in our society*: perhaps it has become so because there is that inevitable axe to grind. There are risks in encouraging a person to prematurely retrieve but there are also gains in spontaneous retrieval when they read of others' experiences and fill in glitches in their own. Curiously what they recall is not mimicry of what they hear and may be diametrically opposite: It is the regeneration of the diorama where it occurred that becomes the pivotal event.

They for the first time can make sense of what seemed to be an irrational behaviour and it is for this reason that I challenge the notion of CBT. (Cognitive behavioural therapy) The latter is based on the notion that Pandora's Box does not exist for anyone. It is again a concept derived from a mythical reality perspective.

To save face a person can be tempted to exhume a reality prematurely or feel guilt if they cannot make sense to the therapist without that risky step. They assume that the therapist knows all and do the unrealistic to move on. What may be the consequences if the therapist lacks experience in that domain to retrieve the situation?

•*Denial is perhaps the true form of false memory.*
A child to move on shuts out a reality which is beyond their resources to cope with.
Perhaps one of the enigmas of therapy will always remain whether to exhume what lies in denial. What can be exhumed in one's latter years with greater life skills may prove dangerous in a person's earlier years where they are exposed to a more unpredictable and heterogeneous world.

For the many reasons above I made an immutable decision that any narrative I would indulge in would always be in first voice.
It would be what that young person remembered as it looked through their eyes.
•This will minimise the risk of dangerous retrieval of material.
•It will not ask questions which risk bias in another's answer.
•It won't risk omitting disclosure of something which that person wishes to share and I have no awareness of.

WHAT HASN'T HAPPENED CANNOT BE MEASURED

And part of us will have always live in another place far from where we have lived our lives. We were to forever wonder about the fate of loved ones and friends whom our folks left behind. We were to always wonder about their safety and their ongoing exposure to what we left behind. We knew that in some way they lived on in the world we left behind, and continued to retain the fears which we gradually learned to suppress.

They perhaps too, were to wonder what became of their family members and to wonder why our folks acted as they did abandoning them in their darkest hour. Love is said to be unconditional but our folks imposed conditions under which they would wish their children to live on and at times families became divided: How does one reconcile such circumstances. How does a father or mother reconcile to maybe not seeing their children again. How does their child reconcile not seeing a parent again. For some emotions there can be no answers.

Some of us have had the opportunity to retrace our steps and try to close that time warp. How could that ever be. We have all moved on. Those whom we left behind were to become imprinted with a way of life which those of us in the west, no matter how compromising our lives, could ever again imagine. **Those who were left behind, who knows how they truly see us: We hope that they can reconcile our leaving and not returning. We have to respect their feelings if they can't. The reality remains that no matter what our parents' reasons, we just were not there to endure that journey.** MM

THE NOMENCLATURE OF GERMAN TROOPSHIPS

During dialogues and manylogues among the author group and the wider e-mail data base, at times there was confusion and /or dissent over the names of ships.

Some of this could be attributable to memory lapses, misinterpretation of information heard when we were very small: Indeed there could be any number of variants of these and more.

Something which had not even occurred to me was that the ships could have been renamed: Maybe that is the legacy of a bit of local superstition which has lodged into my interpretation. I have always had this notion that it was bad luck to rename a ship.

But then did war ships ever have luck- albeit better luck than maybe a ship near by: At least until a subsequent trip.

While seeking out a photo of the Hilfskreuzer "Hansa" I found this material. It is an extract from a longer article from **www.lexicon-der-wehrmacht.de** on the internet

".......Originally the Glen Line freighter Glengarry, Schiff 5 was still being built by Burmeister and Wain for the British Alfred Holt Company in Copenhagen, when the Germans seized her.

Re-named Meersburg for the Hamburg-Amerika line, she served first as a target ship for the 27th U-boat Flotilla in the Baltic, but was then ordered to Rotterdam, and later to Blohm & Voss Hamburg, to be converted into a raider.

As the work was repeatedly delayed by labour and material shortages, and by the air raids that had set the schedule back two years, particularly the raid of July 25 1943, the SKL finally gave up, and the ship served as a gunnery training and target ship again.

Gerlach relinquished his command to serve as naval commander at Leningrad, and Kapitän zur See Hans Henigst took over command of the ship from April to August 1943.

Schiff 5, the intended raider Hansa, was the last vessel to be converted into an auxiliary cruiser and was to be by far the most heavily armed, with eight 150 mm guns, eight 37 mm anti-aircraft guns, thirty-six 20 mm anti-aircraft guns, four 53.3cm torpedo tubes, an aircraft catapult and radar.

Under the command of Kapitän zur See Fritz Schwoerer, appointed in February 1944, she participated in the evacuation of refugees from Reval in August 1944, and from the Hela peninsula, continuing in this desperate service until the end of the war, sustaining damage when hitting a mine on May 4 1945....."

But the "Hansa" certainly brought some fortune to at least one of our authors and her family: They survived the journey from Estonia to Gotenhafen, which in those times was located in East Prussia.

And one wonders how the parents survived: The older children were complex enough to cope with, but......

.....how many such little bundles, born into the chaos where our parents had to move across torrid terrain: How many such bundles they had to grieve over at times: And how many sacrifices they had to make to ensure that those bundles reached adulthood unscathed while they worked for perhaps a decade after the DP days in survival mode. MM

The signpost truly indicated the ethos of the times: No one knew what lay ahead. The future looked very grim: That essentially is the translation on the signpost.

This is the title-page of Ardo Tarem's contemporaneous silent film of life in Geislingen.

 Throughout the book will be pages and spreads of collages of 'screen grabs'. These pages/spreads will be designated by the insignia to the left: No part of those collages, nor parts of the parent film may be reproduced without the written permission of the guardian of the film.

TÕNU LOORPÄRG
HISTORY OF OUR PAST

An extract from "Freedom is another word for everything to gain": Volume II

My story really begins with what I have been told by my father and what I have read about the History of Estonia once I had access to history books on Estonia and the Soviet Union/Russia. Unfortunately after my arrival in New Zealand my education in matters Estonian ceased by the age of 10, particularly after the circumstance surrounding my home life changed; including my mother's re-marriage. This took me away from contact with the small Estonian Community in Auckland.

Very little was available on Estonian history or my past as my mother, who did not have the opportunity of a tertiary education, had preferred to close off that part of her life almost entirely. She would, however, answer my specific questions from time to time. By the time I was 14, I was away in boarding school and later in the army so this type of education became haphazard at best, deriving mainly from the books sent to me from USA by my grandmother and my aunt.

As my Estonian education had finished at kindergarten level, I preferred to read those books written in English relating to Estonia and these were very scarce. From the 1960s I began to have greater access to history books which related to Russian Czarist history and to the more recent Soviet period. With these I began to piece together the frequent anti-Communist utterances I heard from my elders with my more detailed understanding gained from the books. This enabled me to develop my own world view on past events.

It was not until I was able to visit my father and his family in Estonia 1974 that I started to gather family history in any coherent way. As the years went by and the frequency of my visits to Estonia increased, so did my knowledge. This verbal learning from my father was considerably enhanced when he responded to my frequent requests to write about the family and his personal life history. This record is documented in Volume 1. For now I will only briefly outline the period prior to my birth.

According to my father our original surname "Loorberg" originated around the early 18th century, probably after the Swedish - Russian wars which Sweden lost. After Russian hegemony was established in 1710 it is said a Swedish soldier who remained behind in Estonia married *an Estonian woman in or around the Helme district of Southern Estonia or Northern Livonia as it was then known.

At this time surnames were not common among the Estonian peasantry who were under the control of the Baltic German nobility who had arrived many centuries before with the Teutonic Knights of the Sword and who had succeeded in colonizing Estonia. They were followed by a series of other rulers who coveted this strategic part of the Baltic coast: They included Danes, Germans, Poles/Lithuanians, Swedes and Russians. After the departure of the Teutonic Knights the Baltic German nobility had been able to continue to run their estates by swearing allegiance to the ruling class and now in the 18th and 19th Century they submitted to the authority of the Russian Czar. Around this time some of the more prosperous Estonian farmers were able to free themselves from the Feudal system and were adopting family names.

Many took the name of the estate they had been part of as their family name. So it is possible, though unconfirmed that the name "Loorberg" could be derived from an estate name or from the Baltic German nobility who ran the estate. This name in turn could have come from a geographic region in Germany/Holland from whence the original family had come from. Indeed there is a location in southern Holland called Loorberg which today hosts popular hill climbs circuit for cyclists. The earliest record we have on my father's side is that of Ado Loorberg recorded in the Helme Parish records as being born there in 1781. From Ado, can be traced the family history through to the start of the 20th century in Southern Estonia.

After that some members of the family emigrated within the Czarist Empire to Saint Petersburg and others to Kiev located in today's Ukraine: any place where they could find employment. My grandfather Alexander was one of those, as was the family Leesman of my paternal grandmother who went to Saint Petersburg around the 1900's.

On my paternal grandmother's side of the family we are able to trace family records back through my great grandmother Mari Leesman (nee Olesk),tracing back to Olesk (1690-1757)and wife Liisu Olesk 1699-1782.

*The name was changed to "Loorpärg" by my grandfather during the "Estonianization" period in the 1930's when many families adopted "Estonian names".
On my mother's side, the Koppel family history has to rely on anecdotes passed down by my Aunt Alide (Aili), my mother Helene's elder sister before she died. The name "Koppel" is one of the ten most common names in Estonia so researching it becomes quite hard. This has been made more complicated by the destruction of records in Narva during World War II.

Narva is where my mother and Uncle Alexis were born. From what my aunt related, it appears the family Koppel had in the early 1900's also emigrated from Narva to the district now called Kingisepp (formerly Weimar) which was East of Narva

My maternal grandparents Juhan and Juuli Koppel's wedding day

Narva Bridge

Mamma feeding chickens in Narva

in the lands of the Ingrians, an ethnic group related to Estonians and Finns. In the town and the estates around Kingisepp there lived a large Estonian Community including the extended Koppel family and also the Reinoks, my maternal grandmother Juuli Maria Koppel's family. Her mother's maiden name was Kala (my great-grandmother) .I am told that grandfather Juhan Koppel and grandmother were both working on a Russian General's estate near Weimar (now Kingisepp). The General was of Polish/Scottish heritage. Grandfather Juhan was his book keeper and my grandmother (Mamma) worked as a chef.

Soon after his return, the Bolshevik Revolution occurred and fighting broke out between the Bolshevik (communist)Reds and the Czarist (anti-communist) Whites. after demobilization The strife was soon moving further afield from its origins in St. Petersburg and swept over the area where they lived.

Aunt Aili remembers being frightened as an eight year old when she heard that the fighting was going on close by and that the "Reds were shooting the Whites". She went and hid her white pet lamb to save her from the slaughter! When the Reds did arrive in trucks shooting into the air to scare the locals they also started to steal farm animals. My great-uncle Koppel who was a community leader went to the Reds complaining about the theft of a cow and was summarily shot and killed by the Bolsheviks.

This event caused the families to take fright and for safety they moved back to Estonia just before Estonia declared Independence after winning the war in Estonia against the Reds in 1918.

Their youngest children Alexander and Helene were both born in Narva. After the family established themselves in Narva, grandfather was able to find work as a cobbler and Mamma worked as a chef at a children's health camp at Narva Jõesuu (river mouth). They had living with them grandmother Reinok. She was a very religious person and no doubt had a big influence on my grandmother's religious persuasion throughout her life.

My mother tells the story of when Great-grandmother Reinok was coming towards the end of her life and how she believed she saw her "guardian angel" looking after her as she lay on her sick bed. Great-grandmother died in 1940.

In those days Narva was a beautiful Hanseatic city built originally during Swedish rule in Estonia. The family lived in various locations initially and towards the end of the 1920's they had moved into rooms at Endla Kalda's parents house. Endla's father was a tailor and her mother was a businesswoman running a shop. I was to meet Endla some 70 years later on one of my visits to Estonia.

As the finances were limited, the children's education to a tertiary level was not possible. Aunty Aili completed a commercial course and left school, she was working outside of Narva up until 1930 when she returned to assist Mamma after my grandfather Juhan died.

Grandfather had been suffering from TB ever since he first contracted it at the POW camp in Hungary during the war. In these tight economic circumstances, my mother and uncle finished their schooling at high school technical colleges. My mother was learning home science and my uncle completed an apprenticeship. Both of them had belonged to the Estonian equivalent of Boy Scouts and Girl guides.

Mamma on grandfather's death continued to work as a chef at the Narva Jõesuu Health Camp and at one stage was employed by the Estonian President Pats at his summerhouse near Narva. Uncle Lexis, who was of short stature, possibly due to food shortages during the revolution when he was born, was also unusually strong as a teenager. He was also growing a beard while still a child and was of some medical research interest to researchers from Tartu University

My parents met in Narva when my father was posted on graduation from the Estonian Military Academy, as a young officer, to the Estonian Army Artillery Battery located outside Narva.

After the occupation of Estonia by the Soviet Army in 1940 my father decided to resign and be posted to the Reserve. He was one of the last able to do so prior to the transfer of Estonian soldiers into the Soviet Army and their subsequent removal to labour battalions in Russia.

On his return to Tallinn my father was able to find work and on the weekends continued to visit my mother in Narva or else my mother would come to stay in Tallinn.

On one of these occasions my grandmother Alide became very ill with pneumonia and died on Christmas Eve 1940. This prompted my parents to review their wedding plans, especially in view of the international situation and the possibility of the war reaching Estonia.

They were married in Narva on 30th April 1941 and made their home initially at my grandfather's house in Nõmme. They were living here at the time when Germany attacked the Soviet Union in July 1941 and occupied the Baltic States including Estonia.

The German occupation pushed out the Soviet Army and was initially welcomed by most Estonians who were hoping for the restoration of the Estonian Republic.

During the Soviet occupation the NKVD (Secret Police) had murdered large numbers of Estonians and transported whole families to Siberia where they languished in very harsh conditions never to return. The country had become very anti-communist as a result.

My father relates the mood of the times in his memoirs. Soon after this new occupation my father and his brother started a radio repair business and around the time of my birth moved the family to an apartment above the workshop where they conducted their business in central Tallinn.

The story of our people through the eyes of a historian can be learned from Ferdinand Kool's "DP Kroonica". This book is but the voice of individual travellers, those too young to have a voice when it was all happening. MM

EXODUS 20

Most children of Estonian descent, no matter their religious denomination, have been brought up on the tenets of the Old Testament Ten commandments.

The poignant ones of course for this book being:
- Honour thy father and mother.
- Thou shalt not kill.
- Thou shalt not steal.
- Thou shalt not covet---anything that is your neighbours.

They do not directly clarify what one is to do when another forcibly tramples on one's turf. Perhaps implied is that one is not expected to turn the other cheek: That one is permitted to use necessary force to retain that which one has honestly begotten.

To Estonian born children the Battle of Sinimäed is perhaps the ultimate symbol of the latter: One which no child of our birthright can ignore, and indeed given we have all lost loved ones to it, we can never forget.

We have a right to be justly proud of the courage of our fathers, siblings and extended family members.

Yes, the Battle of Sinimäed was the ultimate bastion of our parents, and countrymens' courage to retain that which was theirs and ours. Something in me jolted me to remember that there are many voids in this book, but particularly one which must be filled. Arved Plaks whose age at the time of Estonia's freedom failing was almost on the cusp of joining into its fight for freedom has powerful feelings for that epoch: MM

ARVED PLAKS: SINIMÄED

Arved wrote

Mai, ...I gave the painting to the museum in Viimsi, since I commissioned it .....
It is based on interviews that I conducted with Meedi Hiielo who visited after the battle when corpses (bones) and war materiel (disabled tanks, guns etc.) still littered the whole battlefield. However paths had been cleared of mines so she could gather mushrooms. She is now quite old but still lives and teaches Estonian folk art to related clubs.

The article of interviews appeared in Eesti Elu under the title "Kas ida rinne peab veel?" Or something like that. The sketch that I made with her guidance looks like the thing to the left

I intentionally did not want a painting of someone throwing a grenade so as not to focus just on one item, but to capture the whole horror of the battle that was. For this painting I got a young artist to do it by the name of Klemmer. Two earlier painting that I commissioned did not really do what I wanted and so I had to keep going.
Arved

KALEV EHIN
SNIPPETS ABOUT REMINISCING

REVISITING THE PAST IN ESTONIA

...Maimu's (My sister) compassionate smile and general demeanor reminded me so much of my mother as I remembered her when I last saw her less than three months before my ninth birthday. The three of us had been very close. Laine on the other hand, noticeably exhibited many of my father's characteristics which were generally less even tempered and caring.

Maimu asked me what I wanted to do. Without a second thought, I replied that I wanted to visit mother's grave. ....

Maimu pointed to a large parking lot adjacent to the hotel .. "That's where you were born Kalev. It's where the old Children's Hospital stood......Mother became a nurse after the war and worked there until shortly before her untimely death...It was a place that was very dear to her since it reminded her so much of you, her beloved son who vanished without a trace....What a heart rending first encounter with my lost past.

Mother and Maimu had desperately searched for us after the war, not knowing that we had actually made it out of the country...They knew that on the evening of September 19, 1944, my father and I had left for the harbour, with whatever we could comfortably carry with us. However from that point there was no documentation to verify that we had actually boarded a ship or whether we were on one of the boats sunk by the Russians......

The first indication that Maimu and Laine had that my father and I had actually survived the war is when the first letter arrived from the United States in 1957.

Maimu ..reappeared with extra drinking glasses and then with a flourish pulled a bottle of Russian champagne from her oversized handbag...for the next seven days, she and Laine would keep pulling loaves of bread, other bottles, smoked fish, and all sorts of goodies. We were just told to just accept what they had gathered and not to worry where the things came from or how scarce they were... We drank several toasts to this monumental occasion.

At times when we did take a cab Maimu had forewarned us the watch what we were saying because many of the drivers were KGB agents or informers.

...we were able to fill in much of the missing details of what happened to our families in the years since my hasty departure with my father almost forty years earlier. I discovered that mother had been in Tallinn when we fled. Maimu as at our maternal grandparents farm about sixty miles directly south of the city. After discovering we had departed the country, mother could probably have caught another German ship and followed us, but she had no intentions of leaving without Maimu, who was fifteen years old at the time.

EMOTIONS RUN HIGH

In Tallinn I learned to laugh and cry, and to love and hate. Here I felt the tenderness and security of my mother's embrace while at the same time experiencing life under two of the most brutal dictatorial regimes in times past. And before I was nine, my boyhood dreams and family ties were abruptly shattered in this historic place.

Old Tallinn is my shrine for joy and laughter as well as for suffering and tears. It was hard for me to fully comprehend that I was back again in Estonia to decipher more of the mysteries of my life and next of kin that had eluded me for more than forty years.

Time stood still as awe hugged and kissed each other. We exchanged no words. There was no need for such trivialities. We simply sensed each other's thoughts and feelings. ...morning was rather cool and rainy. Maimu had arranged ...to drop us off at the back entrance of the Rahumae (Peaceful mountain) Cemetery, my mother's resting place......I felt fitting that it was raining. As Betty (wife) would confide in me later, her mother used to say that the heavens cry on sad and sombre occasions, such as was the case at the moment....Maimu turned left, took a few more steps and stopped. With her hands clasped and her head bowed as if in prayer, she stood before a well groomed plot.....I joined her....she pulled me closer to her. Mother had been so close to both of us.

As I began to read the inscription on the white marble gravestone, Maimu whispered to me, **"Here rests our mother. She waited such a long, long time for you, with a broken heart. She missed you so much."** The dedication reads Nurse Salme Ehin, 23 March 1906 to 2 April 1952- in remembrance, the Tallinn Children's Hospital". For a long time we stood in silence, tears streaming down our faces. This was the culmination of years of searching; wondering and worrying.

She had finally told me what mother whispered to her minutes before she passed away **"Kalev will return!"** I was finally in my mother's presence. It devastated me not having been able to tell her how much I loved her before she came to her final resting place on Peaceful Mountain. Now all I could do was to whisper under my breath

"Mother, I'm so sorry for not being able to return earlier. I love you: Now rest in peace."

Finally I had to part with Maimu... we hugged each other as long as we could. Words weren't necessary – feelings said it all. It was gut wrenching to leave her behind again.

Words that I had heard repeated over and over again during our visit echoed in my ears. "We will survive!"

Part of this ancient, beautiful land was leaving with me. Besides the memories, I also had a small bag of sand from Ulemiste Järv (Lake Ulemiste) situated above Tallinn, given to me by my relatives.

After the initial euphoria faded, too many pieces of the puzzle of my past were still missing. I knew that I had only barely parted the curtains to much of my life's mysteries...Come hell or high water, I would return again as often as possible.

VISITING OLD HAUNTS

In addition to talking about past events, we visited the old houses where our family had lived over the years.

I longed to have a chance to visit......the fortifications behind the frontline in south eastern Estonia that my father and I had helped to build shortly before we fled.

I saw that all street names were printed both in Russian and Estonian....large hammer and sickle symbols were permanently posted on most buildings.. I could invariably hear Russian together with Estonian being spoken

...we entered the Tallinn suburb of Nõmme where our family had lived at the beginning of the war, my mood began to change. Here...most houses still had tree covered yards and gardens stimulating one's senses with a feeling of tranquillity.

I felt so much at home. Our family had moved here from another part of the city when I was less than five years old and not surprisingly my capacity to recall past events of my life also dates back to that period.

Maimu.... knew that I wanted to explore our old home more closely if possible.

Suddenly it seemed as though as if I had arrived home after a life long journey. We stood facing a tiny house that was situated in the middle of a huge fenced yard. Sixty foot pine trees pointed skyward in one corner of the yard and other types of shrubbery and flowers dotted the rest of the landscape.

Nothing much seemed to have changed since my sister and I lived and played there. Only the pines had grown taller and the small neighborhood grocery store that was once situated across the street was now a private home. ...a tiny grey haired lady in her sixties appeared from behind the dwelling. "Tervist" (to your health) said Maimu caringly to the approaching woman. "My brother and I lived here at the beginning of the Second World War....could we come in and look around for a few moments. My brother now lives in America."...

We wandered around the yard and later toured the inside of the house, more and more early childhood memories began to surface. After all, this was the very first home I could clearly remember living in...... I was amazed what this old landmark had done to revitalise my childhood memories. The emotional highs had been simply overwhelming....My trek through the tranquil streets of Nõmme deliberately took me again past our old house of former Kreutzwald Street. There I paused for a moment and took another close look at the lurking shadows of my early life when our family had still been intact ...

Põlva and Aunt Olga's farm nearby will surely rekindle many, many pleasant childhood memories of a time long past. Regrettably, in Põlva the war also steadily crept back into our lives and eventually the fate of our entire family took a turn for the worst, I thought to myself in a serious vein.... Bewildered and disappointed because I didn't recognise any of the landmarks (Põlva) ...the place had grown tremendously... Old Põlva was only minutes away around the next bend.

.....Mesmerized, I stood looking around as if I had been beamed back in time. The arched gate of the cemetery and the high massive walls made from multicolored stones extending far in either direction seemed to have changed little over the years. Only the canopies of the ancient trees in the graveyard appeared to be reaching higher towards the midsummer sky. Across the street from the cemetery, the first house in a row of houses stood our house. It was exactly as I remembered it except that it appeared smaller and was in much worse condition than we had left it. However, the beautiful lush meadow and the river flanking it behind the house, where I had spent endless hours playing with my friends and horsing around in the cool stream on warm summer days was no longer there. In its place was a newly completed road running along a dyke behind which was a small reservoir.

The old narrow cobblestone bridge spanning the river now only appeared to serve pedestrians...On a hill across the river surrounded by ancient oak trees was the old familiar Lutheran Church with its towering white steeple. The main street and many of its buildings to the left of the church also appeared to have changed little.

I sighed with relief and exclaimed, "Now this is how I remembered Põlva!......."......we stood in from of our former house that faces a narrow street which runs parallel to the wall of the cemetery. It seemed strange standing in the middle of a deserted street that used to be the main thoroughfare leading from the center of town to the train station and middle of a deserted street that used to be the main thoroughfare leading from the center of town to the train station and other points north. ..from a slightly elevated vantage point... Maimu and I looked down at the back side of our former home. Again it appeared that little had changed over the past four decades. The now dilapidated six foot cedar fence still enclosed the back yard... the shed where we used to keep about a dozen chickens had managed to stay upright and intact. How could I forget my little barn, since feeding my feathered friends and collecting their eggs had been one of my daily household chores?

As we slowly walked back towards the cemetery gate while continuing to take in all the sights around us I mentioned to Maimu **"Põlva sure is nice and peaceful today."**

"It certainly is. However, as August approached back in 1944 the situation was quite different, wasn't it?" she replied. How well I remembered.

We first noticed the increased clandestine activities of partisans in our vicinity. As more and more of them were dropped behind the front lines by the Russian planes each night, travel after dark became increasingly perilous. Everyday there were reports of people being ambushed on country roads and of entire farm families being executed in their homes.

Next, we had to house German soldiers in our home as did other families in town. These were combat troops happy to be away from the war for a few precious days before being sent back. The three or four men who bedded down in our living room all had families at home and were friendly towards kids. They had been away from their own children for a long time and knew that they might not survive to see them again.

One night we were shaken out of our beds by large explosions. We had experienced our first air raid. Luckily the Russians missed their mark and dropped the entire bomb load into a swamp less than half a mile from our home. The only damage that we sustained was a cracked window.

Several days later another Soviet bomber flew over the town. This time it had made the mistake of flying its mission during the daylight hours. It was promptly shot down by a German fighter and went down in flames in a field not far outside of town. Although the crew bailed out, none survived because all their parachutes caught on fire as they exited the aircraft. I got to the scene of the crash with several of my friends just as the bodies were being loaded into a military truck.

It was in Põlva where I started my schooling in first grade. In those days in Estonia, kids didn't attend kindergarten but were expected to already have acquired basic reading and maths skills through home instruction before registering for their initial classes. I had been well prepared by my mother with additional assistance from my sister.

Sadly, my formal education was abruptly cut short and delayed for several years. In the spring of 1944, prior to the end of the regular school year, Põlva Elementary was closed and converted into a military hospital. The war was getting closer and closer. For a while, however, I looked at the situation on the bright side. I now had more time to do other things like fishing and playing soccer in the meadow and swimming in the river behind our home.

Even at the relatively young age of eight, not all of my memorable experiences of life in Põlva were pleasant... I had finally become mature enough to grasp that Father suffered from delusions..apparently his mind had been permanently affected by an accident.. he was electrocuted.....our meagre wartime rations were generously supplemented with food from the pantries of four friends as a reward for our help.

Over the bridge was the old Lutheran Church....the massive door to the church was unfortunately locked. ...how I wished that I could have peeked inside just for a few seconds to refresh my memories of the many Sunday services and other ceremonies that I had attended in that ancient church.

I wondered if the old wooden schoolhouse where I started first grade is still standing......a few minutes later we turned right onto an unpaved street...I couldn't believe my eyes. There stood the old two –storey structure where I had started my formal education albeit not for very long: For some strong reason I had thought until now that it had burned down as the Red Army over ran the town.

.....gave us a quick tour of the ancient Tallinn town hall and then accompanied us in a casual stroll to the Viru Hotel. **It was an eerie yet exhilarating walk through the silent, narrow cobbles-stone covered street of mediaeval Tallinn. It seemed as though we had been transported back in time.**

REMINISCENCES

One of the first things that came to mind was the time I put my father's boots on, which almost came up to my hips, and caught a nearby train all by myself in the hopes of visiting my cousin on the other side of Tallinn.

I wasn't running away from home. I simply wanted to see my cousin who was about ten at the time and who had a far greater and more sophisticated selection of toys than I did. I distinctly remember being especially fond of one of his large model airplanes....I succeeded in getting downtown before being gently handed over to a police officer as I tried to board a trolley for the final leg of my journey. According to Maimu, father wasn't overly cheerful, to say the least, after receiving a call to pick me up at the central police station.

I also recalled playing with Maimu's precious paper dolls while she was at school. Those cut out dolls came with all sorts of exchangeable wardrobes and were as popular then as today's Barbies. I chuckled at when envisaging how irate she had been on several occasions after uncovering my clandestine activities involving her toys...we laughed uncontrollably when Maimu showed me the window that she had pushed me out of during one of her rages after I reminded her of the doll encounters.

Even mother wasn't immune to my pranks. One day when she was out, either shopping or visiting a neighbor, Maimu was responsible for keeping an eye on me. Regrettably she decided to play in the yard with a girlfriend while I remained in the house. So in order to entertain myself I used up mother's brand new lipstick to paint my entire face red. (one must remember what a good lipstick was worth then) To my utter surprise I couldn't get rid of the red color with just plain soap and water no matter how hard I tried.

For the first and only time in my short life with mother, I recollect her completely losing her composure when she came home and saw me with my "war paint". Maimu vividly remembers how she took most of mother's wrath since she had neglected to keep an eye on me. What a beginning, I thought, for a guy who later earned his undergraduate degree at Colgate University playing football.

The innocence of youth is a precious commodity, I thought to myself as Maimu and I walked towards the corner of the yard where our garden once flourished. The spot immediately rekindled the memories of some of the initial phases of the war. True innocence makes youngsters gullible and prone to error, but it also acts as an invisible shield protecting children from the fears and horrors of the world around them. I'm convinced that it was this innate capacity and my mother's tender loving care that preserved my sanity through childhood amidst the turmoil of war.

On June 17, 1940 soviet troops occupied Estonia. I recall initially sensing that things had radically changed during the course of another train ride, this time in the company of my father. **As we took our seats I noticed two uniformed Russian soldiers sitting across from us. Their odd appearance instantly stirred my curiosity. "Who are those funny-looking men?" I asked my father moments later.** Evidently, I had asked the question loud enough so that most of the passengers in our compartment could hear it. Instantly everyone, except the soldiers, began to laugh or giggle.

For a moment my father seemed to panic. But he too began to smile when it became obvious that the men in uniform didn't understand Estonian. Later, father tried to explain to me that from now on I needed to be careful what I said in public, especially when there were strangers present. That was my first conspicuous encounter with the perilous changing world around me- a world that would become less and less forgiving.

Within days after the Red Army occupied Estonia their secret police, the notorious KGB (then known as the NKVD), began to make arrests all across the country.

Even though I was only five, I still recollect how my fears at those night time raids intensified.
It was also after that notorious night that my father began his nightly vigil in anticipation of a possible KGB raid as the rest of our family slept fully dressed for a quick getaway. After dark he would hide in a cluster of berry bushes in the corner of the yard. Standing at that spot Maimu and I could see that it was a superb vantage spot. One could see traffic approaching from all directions.

Father's plan was simple. Knowing that there was no normal vehicular traffic at night during this period, his intent was to waken us if he observed headlights coming in our direction. We would then disappear through the backyards of our neighbors. Fortunately, we never had to put that plan into action. Moreover, while my father kept watch in our yard, many of his friends retreated to the swamps and forests outside the city. There they formed the "Metsavennad' (Brothers of the Forest) armed units and started systematic surprise attacks against Soviet targets.

Soon after my father had begun his nightly vigil in the garden Nazi Germany attacked the Soviet Union. Instead of gloom there was now a growing sense of guarded optimism and controlled excitement in our neighborhood in anticipation of the possibility that Estonia would somehow have an opportunity to regain its independence in the ensuing conflict. Suddenly it appeared that it was only a question of time before the Red Army would be pushed out of Estonia.

Our parents and neighbors were also well aware that as the fighting drew closer to the city, fire fights would spring up everywhere between the retreating Russian and the advancing German units.

As the battle intensified many Estonians took steps to protect their most valuable belongings. Walking back to the house I remembered how exciting it had been for me to watch my father, with the help of a couple of neighbors, digging a large square pit six to eight feet deep in the back of the house. I stopped where I thought that excavation had been. Pointing to what I thought to be the approximate spot I asked Maimu. "Wasn't the secret pit about here?' with a bewildered look, she stared at me for several seconds. "You sure have a good memory. I had forgotten all about the hiding place until you just brought it up"...

Smiling, I mentioned to Miamu how I had tried to pitch in until the hole got so deep that I couldn't reach the top with my shovel. Further, I recalled how all sorts of things including some furniture were carefully wrapped and placed in the pit. Once full, the top of the trench was covered with dirt. When the job was completed the yard looked undisturbed.

The eight day battle for Tallinn was, to say the least, was quite exciting for a boy who was almost six. Shortly after the Wehrmacht began to press their attack the Soviets blew up their main ammunition storage depot situated about only a mile from us. **Although the fireworks were spectacular, the loud explosions and**

the immenseness of the spectacle worried me. In fact, Maimu remembered that I had anxiously asked Father whether the entire downtown area of Tallinn as being destroyed since the explosions came from the direction of the city. When he reassured me that the detonations were coming from an ammunition storage area not far from us, I calmed down and enjoyed the continuing pyrotechnic displays for several hours.

Actually, we were rather fortunate during the battle for Tallinn. Even though there was considerable action around us daily, no fire fights ever came close to our house and we were never in immediate danger. Although we never had to abandon our home, father was continuously out scouting the surrounding area for any signs of activity that might head our way.

......I continued to run without a destination in mind. My jog took me through some wooded areas and swamps as I began to follow sandy tree-covered foot-trails in several locations... As I ran by what obviously were the remnants of a World War II German fortified anti-aircraft battery, my memories of the battle for Tallinn began to dominate my thoughts. What further reinforced these reflections was the fact that I was also scurrying past sites where many bloody skirmishes had taken place in the summer of 1941.

I remembered going with my father to several of the battle fields, roughly where I was at the moment, soon after things had quietened down. Up to that point I had experienced war from a distance. **Standing in the midst of a field, swamp or wooded area where men had been fighting and dying only hours before was another story.** The only things missing were the noise, smell, and the actions of the men and their weapons. Now the places were quiet, with hastily dug shallow graves and bloody bandages all around us.

Beside the makeshift graves, abandoned and destroyed weapons were everywhere, some smeared with blood. There were anti-tank guns, light artillery pieces and mortars. Some were twisted hulks; others looked like they were still poised for further action. Scattered among the larger military hardware were countless spent shells, boxes of ammunition and grenades. Even an occasional bolt-action rifle could be seen here and there but all the automatic weapons had been carried away.

Shortly after the Germans occupied the country in 1941 our family moved from Tallinn to Antsla, a small town roughly forty miles south of Tartu near the Latvian border...I recalled how we lived there in a downstairs flat of a two storey wooden house as father worked across the street in the post office.

Life for us in Antsla was relatively uneventful. Maimu completed elementary school and tended cattle in the summers for a farmer right outside of town...we both had memories of helping mother in the fall chopping up cabbages and washing cucumbers. Both commodities eventually ended up in two separate large wooden barrels that supplied our family with ample quantities of sauerkraut and pickles during the winter months when vegetables were in short supply.

I remembered two other events in Antsla that my sister had forgotten....For the Christmas of 1942; I received my first pair of cross country skis. Boy, was I elated! Never had I received such an expensive and practical gift before. Unfortunately the next morning I also experienced the greatest tragedy of my life. Immediately after putting on the skis, in the middle of a roaring blizzard and heading down the street, I hit a good sized rock breaking off the tip of one of the skis. All attempts to fix the ski with the help of my father failed and so did my world's shortest cross-country skiing career.

The second incident was far more sombre and a reminder to all of us that the war still lay on our doorstep. Above us lived a young couple. Her husband was an amateur athlete and a tremendous trumpet player. He was a charming person and I always looked forward to listening to his almost daily practice sessions. Unfortunately he was also a member of the Home Guard, similar to our National Guard.

One day he was on patrol with his squad attempting to track down a Russian partisan who had parachuted into our area. During the search of a hay barn he was shot through the chest by the partisan hiding in the shed that was then killed in the ensuing fire-fight. **Our upstairs neighbor eventually recovered, but never again did I hear the welcome sound of his trumpet.....**

BOYS BEING BOYS

....we were jolted back into the present... I looked around for familiar landmarks. Soon I spotted the footpath that I had used frequently as a shortcut to the woods on the other side of the cemetery. There I had played all sorts of games with my cohorts....I had to stop myself from laughing as I recalled one of the last games I engaged in there. I suppose that it could be called a version of "chicken".

Several of us were rather proficient at making our own bows and arrows. The arrows were quite deadly, tipped with two inch nails with heads removed. One day, having gotten bored with target practice in the clearing behind the cemetery, a friend and I decided to do something more daring with our weapons. We agreed to play a game which required both skill and daring. The rules were simple. We would stand about fifty feet apart and take turns shooting arrows with high trajectories at each other. If the one being fired on was forced to move in order to avoid being struck, he would lose a point.

After several rounds the score was practically even and, therefore, I couldn't be too cautious for fear of losing the match. I watched the arrow whistling towards me and estimated that it would pass my motionless right arm by a couple of inches. In the next split second I heard a muffled thump and a sudden burning sensation in my right wrist. Looking down at my wrist I saw that the tip of the arrow had disappeared into it. As I pulled the projectile out of my wrist there was hardly any bleeding or pain. **I was too scared and embarrassed to mention the incident to my parents. We never played that game of chicken again.....**

...towards the center of the town I looked to the left down the narrow twisting river. For a moment I thought that I'd spotted an old familiar fishing hole some distance downstream...**I commented gleefully "Down there is where I first learned to fish with explosives"....**shortly before we had fled Põlva two Estonian soldiers who were friends of the family stopped by our house on their way through town.

During the course of their short visit they asked me to show them a good fishing spot along the river. I was more than willing to oblige, but I was surprised when they didn't want to take any of our fishing gear with them. I soon discovered why when they hurled two hand grenades into one of my favorite fishing holes. After the muffled explosions and two huge water spouts shot skyward, at least a dozen fish floated to the surface. **Needless to say, we had plenty of fish for dinner that evening..**

....our conversation momentarily centered on the old sauna...as a very young lad I'd traditionally gone to the sauna with women and other small children on this farm. One day, however, my mother had noticed me looking around the sauna much more attentively than before as the women were busy bathing. On our way back to the house mother pulled me gently to the side and whispered, **"Kalev, you appear to be getting a little too curious in there so I think it's time that you start going to the sauna with the men." It's funny how I've never forgotten that little incident with my mother**

German barracks in Rakvere   MM

ANTS TAMM REFLECTS ABOUT GERMAN TIMES

The years 1942 and 1943, as I understand it, were more like, for example, the occupation of Denmark, a good place for German soldiers. Many of them have told about the "good years", of service.

Were the Estonians and the Danes Nazis? Of course not, that's not the point. Denmark helped more or less "all" their Jews to flee to Sweden, and the Germans where quite aware of the situation and remember, the only country which allowed Jewish refugees into the country until the Soviet occupation, was Estonia.

In Sweden they were not allowed to come before the war. By the way, Swedish authorities asked the Germans to mark Jewish passports with a" Jewish star", so they could stop them at the border. Estonians never stopped Jews. The only country in the world which gave Jews full citizenship was Estonia. The Jewish World Congress gave Estonia its gold medal. It was for the first and the only time they made that for a country.

ANNE TONDI/ELLIOT
A HUMAN TRAGEDY

It was in September 1944, when I was only six, that my sister and I were wakened one night by our parents. Heavy coats were wrapped around our nightshirts, felt boots pulled on our bare feet, and in a few minutes we were speeding on a crowded truck. This was not the first night in which my slumber was often disturbed with strange happenings. Early, with the dawn, I woke to discover that we were on a train. The September morning was beautiful as the hours dragged and the train rolled on. There was tension in the air as the devastated countryside opened before us and as the train stopped while broken rails were repaired.

At noon the train finally stopped in a harbor beside a large warship which was already occupied by many refugees. While the rest were delivering our luggage on board, I was left sitting on some of our suitcases. I was far too exhausted to notice all the confusion around me. Stretcher after stretcher must have been carried from our hospital train aboard the ship, but it is very dim in my memory. Then suddenly enemy planes were over the city. They were aiming at the ships in the harbor, but the ground artillery skillfully kept the fire from us. I was numb to the loud explosions, red leaping flames, and black smoke. I had seen them so often now.

But then I had a strange feeling: a feeling I can still recall clearly, but which I have never experienced since. I began to cry quietly. These were not tears of fear: Fear was unknown to me now. I was crying because I realized that I was leaving this land and a home that was no longer a home. Even after the night in the cellar when we had slept on the shelves with the preserves, and our beautiful home had been torn to pieces by a bomb, my little mind had grasped the meaning of war. Then I knew that one scene in my life had ended. And now I was leaving and my loving and protective grandparents were not coming with us. In a way I had to look after my own life from now on. It was going to be different, how completely different. I could no longer live in ignorance of my surroundings.

In the late afternoon the machines began to work and the ship departed with more than three thousand refugees. More than half of them were wounded soldiers on stretchers. As the expanse of water widened, it grew dark. Then over the rumble of the black and treacherous waves even more terrible sounds arose. Fearful explosions sent ghastly flames high up into the night sky and soon the horizon was a long line of blood-red flames. And between the sea and the fires - a well known silhouette of an old and once famous city: long, piercing steeples and ancient grey towers. Already they appeared as black as ash.

A storm had blown up during the night, but now our agitated dozing was disturbed by brilliant sunlight. This soon eased our hearts slightly and when our sleeping blankets had again been bundled together on the crowded deck, a pleasant, even cheerful atmosphere came to existence. But eventually word went around that the ships were entering more treacherous waters, and an air raid or submarine attack would not be impossible, not to mention running into the mines that had been blown loose by the storm. Life belts (far too few) which had been distributed during the night were now fastened on and at eleven the dreaded alarm came. An air raid was on our ship. We sought safety below the deck and here I became fully aware of stretcher beside stretcher, all tightly packed together. These soldiers were completely in the hands of fate. How would they reward those who had fought so bravely for their homes and their country? The wounded were now unable to move a finger in their own defense.

The guns on deck were blaring ceaselessly. The planes were repelled time and time again, but still they returned. Hope and fear became greater as the minutes ticked on. But then a sudden rollicking of the boat quieted the guns and the planes. It was plain that the ship had been hit by a torpedo. The task of the planes was completed. Now it only remained to be questioned how serious the blow had been. But already the ship tumbled to one side. Now it was important to get on the deck, and as quickly as possible. On the stairs a nurse who was hurrying down, calmly informed us that nothing serious had happened. How could she descend so calmly to an impossible task? How could she comfort now the weeping, the praying, the hysterical wounded heroes? She could give them no more assistance for an immense explosion had already sent an immense cloud of black smoke to the heavens. At the same time the bow was swallowed into the depth of the waves. One thousand people perished in seconds. They had no chance.

But meanwhile, menacingly the helm was rising, inch by inch. Our position was already too high for jumping overboard. Besides, the water was swarming with desperate people who were trying to reach for planks or life buoys. To jump would mean to take somebody else's life.

There was only one way left – to go down with the ship. The helm rose, rose…. Final good-byes were said as my mother held my sister and my father me. Then he realized that his heavy coat would certainly drag him below. He threw off his coat, but before his hand could again reach mine, our feet had left the deck. What went down with us is unaccountable – suitcases, boxes, heavy metal, all at the same time when the guns and the masts all broke off the deck. Only a miracle could have saved our lives then.

Yet I found my head above the water, only a hundred feet or so from the towering ship. I had been so light that I had not descended very deep into the water. And then quietly the ship slid into the water and I was sucked swiftly downward. Gradually the force changed and I was dragged upward, upward …, it was a long way. I saw light! Then bubbles, but my conscious mind never reached the surface. Thus around thirty-five hundred persons went painlessly to their muddy graves in a few seconds.

It might have been an hour, maybe two, before I regained consciousness. I saw articles of every description floating around me in the oily and icy waters. Exhausted humans were still fighting against the waves but numerous heads were lifelessly below the water. How my head, wrapped in a large, wet wool shawl was still above the sizeable waves was a wonder. Some hours passed before the rest of the fleet arrived at the scene of the tragedy and before lifeboats started gathering the living. I was pulled into a lifeboat but I returned into unconsciousness. Four hours in the cold currents had taken all strength out of my limbs.

From time to time I began to take note of kind and hurrying faces peering down at me. I sensed that I was warm and lying between white sheets in a well lighted cabin. For a long time I dozed on and off, but gradually I began to think and wonder. Of how I tried to flee from those tormenting thoughts. I felt that I was the only one who had been saved. I shrank from the future that appeared so clearly in my mind. How could they tell me that I was going to be safe and that I would soon see my parents? To me it seemed hopeless, and indeed the following day showed no proof to the improbability of my fears. And they knew it too. Fortunately I had received no bodily harm, however my felt boots had shrunk so much that I had to be fitted with a pair of sailor's socks, three times too big for me. But I was in such a state of shock, physically and mentally fatigued that I cannot even remember when I was finally received into the eager arms of my parents.

My parents and my aunt had been saved by the lead convoy ship. The ship had been so crowded that there was no room to move a limb. And so for a day each one of them had lived in agony, exhausted, wondering the same I had wondered: "Am I the only one?"

Then for a week I lay in a crowded room with terrible small animals and my enormous socks. Often I would find some sweets thrust into my hand by a kindly sailor. I was like a miracle. I was a child who had been saved from the shipwreck. Less than five hundred people had reached land from that crowded ship, among them very few children.

Meanwhile my father, with a blanket wrapped around him (his clothes had been torn almost to shreds) hunted for a few provisions. For a week my mother haunted the harbour. Only after that time was she persuaded to leave Danzig and thereby pronounce her younger daughter 'drowned'. Thereby with empty hands, empty pockets, and a few water soaked rags on our back and older by ten years we left the seashore for more tragic and horror filled days.

This is an essay that I wrote in high school about a memorable event in my life. I have transcribed it word for word from my handwritten original, only correcting spelling errors. My English was not very good then.

This happened almost 70 years ago and my memories have faded, but when I wrote the essay, about ten years after the tragedy, they were still quite fresh. However, many of the images are still with me to-day.

I will always wonder why the nurse chose certain death over possible life.

For some of the factual information I probably used information from the article that I have enclosed. It and the pictures I scanned from magazine pages that I have saved but I no longer know the name of the magazine nor whether it was printed in Geislingen or in Canada, although I think it was Canada.

Notes: In the essay I never mentioned the name of the ship. It was the Red Cross ship 'Moero'.

My parents and aunt were saved by the lead ship in the convoy. The ship that saved me came along much later.

ANTS TAMM
REFLECTS ON ESTONIAN SOLDIERS CO-OPTED INTO GERMAN MILITARY

The Estonians joining the German forces be it willingly or not, are very well seen in Estonia. The Russians and old Estonian communists says otherwise, but nobody really cares about them. We have a cemetery and memorial in Vistla for Estonians in German uniforms, and it is very respected. The cemetery for Estonians in Russian uniforms, near Vistla, is more or less never visited, only by Russians from Russia and relatives to the soldiers still living.

During the "calm" years, in 1942 to 1944, many German soldiers married Estonian girls, even more so in Denmark, Norway, France and other countries.

BORIS LEES
THE SINKING OF THE MOERO, A CATASTROPHE IN 1944

It was Tuesday 19th September 1944. My mother and I had been carrying various items into the basement as well as packing a few things to take with us, should we succeed in leaving our own Rakvere. The sound of shell fire in the east of Estonia was becoming more frequent and also louder. We also placed various items of jewelry in a glass jar and buried this in the sand under the house. We opened a bottle of excellent quality homemade apple wine, bottled a number of years previously, as we felt we did not want to leave it to the Russian communist forces, although there were still several bottles left in the cellar.

It was twilight when my mother noticed that in the house across the road, where the Lukmann family and the chief surgeon of the Rakvere Hospital, Dr. Huik lived, people were carrying suitcases onto the street. Outside their house was an army truck with a couple of German soldiers. My mother spoke to the soldiers who said that they were taking the Lukmanns and their luggage to Tallinn and if we did not have too many things we could go with them.

It was already quite dark when the entire luggage was on the truck and we started our journey towards Tallinn. The back of the truck was partly covered and we sat on our suitcases without having any view to the front. The evening was cloudy, but it was not raining, and the truck moved relatively slowly along the road with a dim army light on the front mudguard faintly lighting the road.

We arrived in Tallinn in the early morning and as my godmother, with whom we intended to stay, lived near the center of the city, the truck dropped us off first, and the destination of the rest of the people remained unknown to us. My godmother was not particularly surprised that we arrived at her place and she helped us find out how we could flee further.

We found out that to get on a ship we needed a permit which could be obtained from the government offices on Toompea, and my mother decided to go there. There was a short queue at the door when my mother arrived, but it grew rapidly. Although my mother was close to the door, it opened only now and then to let in a few people at a time. My mother and another lady then told those behind them that as soon as the door opened to let some people out, they should push really hard so that the first couple of people would be pushed in through the door.

This worked and my mother succeeded in getting permits to get on a ship. My mother thought that we should leave the city for the night and in the late afternoon we went to the Central Railway Station to find out what possibilities there were, but we were not successful.

As we were leaving we noticed a high ranking German officer, probably a colonel or a major. My mother approached him and asked him if he could help us in some way to get our suitcases and ourselves to the port next day. He was a very friendly man and mentioned that he also had a family in Germany and was happy to help us.

He took a notebook from his pocket, tore out a page and wrote something on it. He then pointed to Tornide Väljak (Square of the Towers), where some army stores were located, and told us to show his note to the gatekeeper who would tell us where to go next. He assured us that they would organise the necessary transport.

We walked to the place concerned and showed the note to the gatekeeper, who sent us to a small office, where an army official looked at the note and grumbled that his boss is too soft hearted. He told us to turn up with our luggage on the morning of the next day, Thursday the 21st of September, and they would organize transportation to the port.

We slept at my grandmother's that night. In the morning we found a horse-drawn cab to take us and our suitcases to the army stores at Tornide Väljak. We found several other people waiting to go to the port as well, among them Mrs. Glaudan, who told us that her husband was of Polish extraction and had been the owner of a cigarette factory. Sometime mid morning an army truck arrived to take us all and our luggage to the port.

There was no problem getting through the checkpoint and we were taken to the wharf, where on the right was the hospital ship "Moero" and on the left were "Lappland" and "RO 22".

The two latter ones were larger than "Moero" and those people opting "RO 22" had their luggage lifted on board with a crane. Although we thought it was a good idea, Mrs. Glaudan thought it was better to chose "Moero" as she thought that a hospital ship was safer and she may have liked the white color of the "Moero" as well. We had to take our luggage up the gangway ourselves and when we arrived at the top we were told that the hatch which was meant for private individuals and was located at the stern was fully occupied and we would have to stay on deck, preferably towards the front of the ship.

We placed out luggage on the cover of the second hatch, but were soon told to take our suitcases down, as they were about to place some machinery on top of the hatch. We moved them to the starboard side of the hatch and placed them in a semicircle to protect ourselves from wind during travel. The side of the hatch was about a metre high, thus giving us protection as well. In the late afternoon when the wounded had been taken on board, the gangway was removed and we awaited departure.

I went for a walk on the deck and found that near the bridge next to the cabins were benches attached to the wall, the seats of which could be lifted and which contained life-vests. An Estonian man stood next to the bench and offered life-vests to anyone wishing to take one. I took two vests and went back to my mother. They were soft and flexible, filled with something akin to kapok or cotton wool, and we decided to put them on straight away as we thought that they would protect us later against the wind.

It was twilight when the ship left port and stopped a couple of kilometers off the coast where a convoy was being formed.
From the direction of Tallinn we heard and saw explosions and it seemed that the port which we had recently left was being blown up, as we saw a strip of fire lighting up the silhouette of the city. We were relieved that we had left the port in good time.

Meanwhile a small ship the size of a mine sweeper had moved in front of us and we also started moving towards the open sea. As our travelling speed increased, the wind, which had not been particularly strong while we were standing still, increased considerably and became quite penetrating, so we were happy that we had our life vests.

We arranged our suitcases around us as best we could and the side of the hatch and the upright suitcases reduced the force of the wind. The lights on the horizon dimmed gradually and we lay down between our suitcases. We were obviously very tired to be able to sleep under these conditions.

The morning of the 22nd September was clear and windy, and white crests were appearing on the waves. In front of us was the small minesweeper, a fair distance behind us was "Lappland" and finally quite far away another ship, thus forming a convoy. There was a short-lived air-raid warning but nothing happened. I brought us some coffee from the stern, and we had something to eat.

A little before 11 am there was another air-raid warning, and this time we heard the drone of an aircraft approaching. The antiaircraft guns opened fire and in between we heard machine gun fire from the aircraft. We disappeared rapidly into the hold of the ship, where hundreds of injured were lying on stretchers on the floor.

"Moero" had once been a freighter, but on conversion to a hospital ship four or five floors were built into the holds, thus holding a large number of wounded.

Suddenly there was a loud bang, the ship shook to the core, and dust and rubble rained from the coiling, the engine stopped and the lights went out. The nurses attending to the wounded told the people impatiently that nothing had happened and to go back up on deck and get out of the way. Actually there was no need to say anything at all as the couple of dozen people who had come down, rushed back up the stairs to the deck where all the shooting had shopped.

On deck we saw a depressing sight. From the stern rose a large thick column of black smoke, which was getting heavier, and we felt how the stern started sinking. Strangely there was no panic, only indecisiveness. It seemed somehow impossible that such a large ship, possibly 5-6000 tonnes, could disappear from under our feet. Some people started throwing life-rafts over board. These consisted of approximately 30 cm diameter metal pipes, which had been welded into square shaped rafts, with webbing in the center. We saw some soldiers bashing their arms or legs, which were in plaster casts against the railing to free them of the plaster and thus improve their chances of staying afloat.

From the bridge a member of the crew shouted "Einspringen" (jump in) and people started to one after the other to climb overboard, taking hold of ropes hanging down the side. Right next to us a man climbed over the railing, over which was hanging a 5 cm thick rope. "Pray and go overboard!" said my mother. I prayed quietly. "Dear God, please don't let me die!" then got hold of the rope and started climbing down the side of the ship. It is difficult to judge at this stage, but I think the distance between the deck and the water was at least 15 metres.

About 3 cm short of the surface of the water the rope came to an end and as I had no option I let go and splashed feet first into the water. I disappeared under water, but a few seconds later was back on the surface. It is probably worth mentioning here that, although I had spent time at the beach on a number of occasions I could not swim, and without the life vest I would not have survived. The same applied for my mother.

From among the waves I had a dramatic view of the ship. The stern sank faster and faster and the bow was rising out of the water.

Then all of a sudden, in the course of a few seconds, the bow rose into a vertical position, throwing everything on the deck on a wide arc into the water, and the ship sank vertically, stern first, bubbling ad hissing into the waves. The whole drama lasted only a few minutes, in the view of some survivors five minutes at the most, but one thing is certain, anyone who did not climb overboard had no chance at all.

In the meantime a life raft of the type described above had drifted into my vicinity. In the middle of the raft, sitting on the woven bottom, was a soldier, and around the raft were another four or five people. I also tried to hold onto the raft, but it had a fault: Normally these rafts had a rope attached to the outside, so that people could grab hold of it, but this one only had the metal pipe. I tried to lift may arm over the pipe, but my arm was too short. The arm of the German soldier next to me reached over the curve of the pipe and I hooked myself around his elbow in such a way that I would not pull his arm down or off the pipe. The waves were tall, the raft rose and fell, and at times I got water into my nose and mouth.

Time passed and I felt cold and tired. Slowly a small ship was approaching and when it got closer I recognized the minesweeper which had joined us near Tallinn. The deck of the ship was so low in the middle, maybe a meter to a metre and a half from the water that the sailors were pulling people out of the water with their outstretched arms. Our little raft was already quite close, only 10-20 metres from the ship, when due to hypothermia or for some other reason, I lost consciousness.

My mother had immediately followed me into the water, but did not see me anywhere. A wooden beam appeared close to her with a couple of survivors holding onto it, and shouted that she should take hold of it. Apparently there was a lot of drifting material in the vicinity as my mother was bumped by a number of objects.

Suddenly someone grabbed her by the hair, pulling her under water. The culprit was a dog, which was chased away by one of the survivors.

They drifted for a long time until a ship was getting close. Now a new problem arose, as the ships waves were tossing people and objects against the sides of the ship, and some actually were hurt at this late stage. The beam with my mother also hit the ship a couple of times before a seaman's strong arms pulled her on board. She was taken with the others into a small room which was already full of dripping people. One mother was holding her dead child in her arms, and the other survivors could only console her by telling her of losing their own son or daughter, mother or father. My mother also said that she had lost her son.

On awakening I became aware of a light shining into my eyes, and on regaining complete consciousness it turned out to be a ceiling lamp above me, as I was lying on the dining table in the seamen's mess. At first I could not understand what had happened to me or where I was, everything was so strange. Next to me on the table were another couple of men asleep and on the bunks near the wall were several more men asleep, as it was already night time. The ship was rolling quite strongly, and when someone entered the room, one could hear the wind whistling outside.

Seeing me awake, a seaman came to me and asked if I had any relatives. I replied that I had a mother if she hadn't drowned. He promised to make some inquires and went upstairs.

After a long time he came back and told me that he may have found my mother and shortly thereafter she came down to the dining room where I was still lying on the table. Our joy at seeing each other was immeasurable. I had taken off most of my wet clothes, now I had to get dressed again, as we were approaching Gotenhafen.

It was a cool grey morning, when the ship berthed. On the quay there were some buses to take us from Gotenhafen (at present Gdynia) to the nearby transit camp of Grabau.

Here it was discovered that I had a high fever and I was taken to the camp hospital, where I was found to have pneumonia. I spent the week in a rather primitive hospital, where I was given Prontosil (an early sulphonamide antibiotic), and where men and women were in the same room. One of these was a woman approximately twenty years old, Miss Kutti, who had sustained a head wound from an object floating in the water. Miss Kutti's father was a solicitor in the town of Rakvere and both he and his wife were said to have gone down with the "Moero".

In 1994, while I was staying in Rakvere, I heard that Miss Kutti had fallen into Russian hands on the collapse of Germany and was sent to Siberia from where she returned to Rakvere many years later. My mother told me while I was in hospital that among the rescued was the aforementioned Mrs. Glaudan, who apparently was an excellent swimmer and managed to survive without a life vest. Another survivor was Mrs. Gerstock, who had been hanging onto the same beam as my mother, and was the lady who had chased away the dog from my mother's hair.

Accurate figures concerning lives lost are not known. No registration of people on board was ever carried out. Later estimates put the figure over 3000 persons. Of these only those who were on deck at the time of the catastrophe had a chance to survive. The fifth hold which had been assigned to civilian refugees was the one that receive the direct hit from the torpedo. According to available information the Soviet Union only manufactured torpedoes to be used by submarines. It seems therefore that the torpedo was released from a low flying aircraft, and which sank the "Moero" would have been supplied by the Allies, ie, Britain or the United States.

The number of those rescued, who were taken to the transit camp in Grabau, would have been around 120- plus a couple of dozen military personnel. The other ships in the convoy also rescued small numbers of people from the water, but for the larger ships this was also more difficult than for the low minesweeper. Later it was estimated that a total of less than 200 people were saved.

We heard later that the air attack on the "Moero" took place 80-100 km west of the Latvian port of Ventspils and before Soviet troops had reached the coast of the Baltic Sea.

The photos of the Moero sinking are from another publication of the time. I have been unable to trace the source: The clipping was contributed by Anne Elliot.

Paljudest kurbmängudest, mis lavastusid sügissuvel 1944 Läänemerel, omades osalt elavaid tunnistajaid, osalt mitte, on üks raskemaid laatsaret-laeva „Moero" hukkumine 22. septembri keskpäeval Liibavi lähedal. Selle kurbmängu tunnistajaid ei ole palju, sest vähe on neid, kes suudeti laevalolnuist päästa. Enamik 21. septembril Tallinnas „Moerole" asunuist vaikib igavesti oma märjas ja jäljetus hauas, keegi ega miski ei rebi enam puruks musta ja sünget saladuslinikut nende viimastelt tundidelt ja minutitelt. Aga need, kellele saatus jättis elu, jutustavad, nagu jutustab teisel küljel üks pääsnuist. Need jutustused ja siia toodud pildid on süüdistuseks nende vastu, kes ei suuda elada rahus.

Argem unustagem neid kurb-raskeid mälestusridu lugedes — nad on üsna väikeseks, aga meie südameis kasvanud kauneimatest ja närtsimatuist elavlilledest pärjaks paljude meie hulgast kistute mälestusele. .

This clipping has been derived from a publication of the time: Given the vast time void I have been unable to trace their source.
Anne Elliot forwarded this to me: she too is uncertain of its genesis.

GUNNAR NEEME: AN AWESOME MAN

Gunnar was a twin soul: He too had a creative bent which roamed across visual arts, poetry, narrative and philosophy.
I was fortunate the become better acquainted with him during the last decade of his life. A time when he was becoming frail and enthusiastic to share his pondering with the next generation. I worked nearby at the time and relished the opportunity for such mental stimulation. The job moved but the stimulation remained irresistible.

Gunnar was born in Tartu at the close of World war I: In 1918. His creative talents began to emerge quickly at school and he proceeded to study art among Estonia's best.

Upon fleeing from Estonia in 1944 he found himself in the American Zone of Germany: He quickly found work as a teacher and a judge of handwork (at which Estonians excelled even with rudimentary tools. He was a dynamo who organized painting and handicraft exhibitions for the refugees and was commissioned to produce a mural for an American Church.

Gunnar's house walls were covered by his paintings but eventually there was more to learn about them. He would always take me to his studio and discuss the techniques he used and the rationale of these. His paintings always had substance as did his drawings: They always said something.

Then we would proceed to talk about that something: at times it was existential issues to which he so adeptly alludes to in his books: At times in verse , at other times in prose. Of course such existential issues were commonly vignetted by our shared trek from Estonia.

His pride of the time was his illustration for a new edition of Kalevipoeg; Traditional Estonian mythology.

After all those years the material I had vamoosed from as grandfather narrated our trek became touchable. He talked about life in Tartu and Otepaa nearby, with the beautiful "Pühajärv": Holy Lake not too far further away. I have since visited that spot many a times with my Estonian hosts: It truly is an artist's paradise.

He talked about the fateful journeys of those German troop ships and shared with me that while people were queued up for permits a policeman rode back and forth on his motor bike to avoid people jumping the queue.

It was Gunnar who finally clarified the story of the three ships which came to grief en route to Gotenhafen. One got a major hit and sunk but did not split into two- that was my perception: Another was also hit and many Estonians perished. It of course limped onto Gotenhafen and the third one amidst the missiles managed to escape being hit.

That as I recall is the story of the Moero which sunk, the RO 22 which limped home and the Nordstern which was to take its fateful sail on a subsequent voyage.

Gunnar had a way of sharing what needed to be shared, faced and yet allowing one to move on.

ARTIST, POET, AUTHOR, PHILOSOPHER & MORE

Gunnar was one of my painting colleagues, We had many an interesting reminiscing of his life in Estonia, the flight from Estonia and his family's life in the camps.

PAINTINGS ABOUT THE FLIGHT

His younger son Ants writes: I've managed to put together a handful of drawings made by my father which chronicle his and my mothers flight from Tartu to Nõmme in Tallinn, and finally their flight from Eesti via , Hiiumaa and finally Kuressaare.

My wife and I are heading for Eesti ....or the song festival after which we will be retracing Ema and Isa's flight through Haapsalu, Hiiumaa and Kuressaare, a journey which I am very much looking forward to.

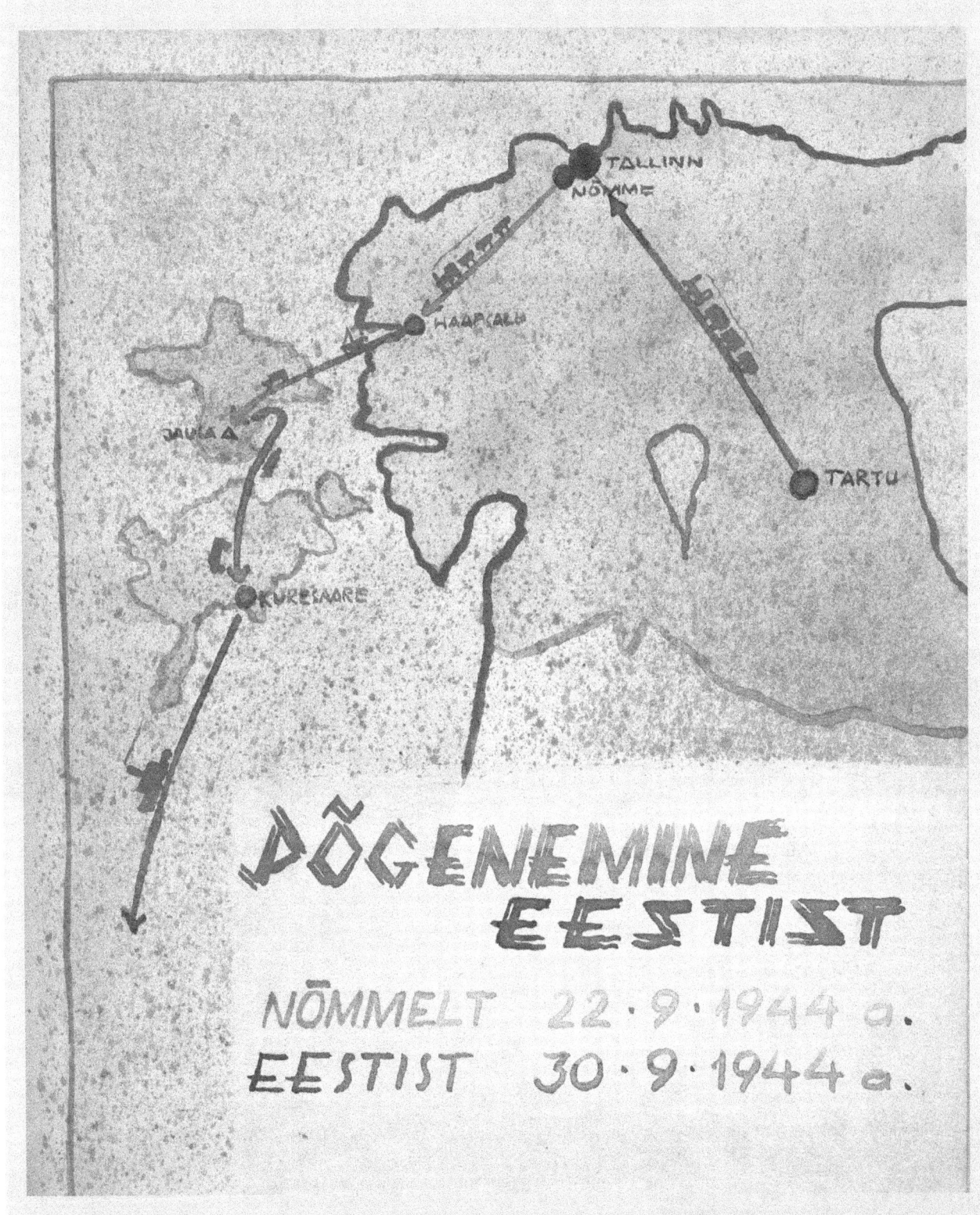

THE RAVAGES OF WAR
PHOTOS FROM TÕNU LOORPÄRG

Turbulence at the Estonian Russian border: Parade over the bridge at Narva River.

Mobilization parade Tallinn 1943

No longer President Päts's residence

Tallinn bombing the day after from a ship at sea: 20th March 1944- source of photo unknown

TOOMAS STEINBERG
VOYAGE ON THE RO 22

My mother and I left our home in Pirita on the morning of 21st September 1944. I was seven years old. My mother had a suitcase and a rucksack and so did I except they were smaller to fit my size.

I want to relate something of what happened before we boarded the armed merchant vessel RO 22 because these events perhaps saved our lives.

During the German occupation of Estonia my mother worked as sound monitor in the Soldatenkino in Tallinn. In those days the sound volume of films could vary considerably and there was a master volume control in the cinema. My mother used to sit by this control and regulate the volume. Maybe she had other duties as well. If my memory is correct the cinema used to be called Bi-Ba-Bo (and was destroyed when Russians entered Tallinn).

Because of my mother's work she was able to procure papers, tickets if you like, for us to leave Estonia on one of the ships taking refugees from Estonia. The designated ship was the Moero. I remember of it being talked about as large and comfortable ship.

On the morning of the 21st, again because of my mother's work, a small pickup with two German soldiers turned up in our yard. They were helpful and friendly and soon we and our baggage were settled in the back tray, which was open. It did not matter as the sun was shining and I could look around. It was not often that I had been able to ride in motor vehicle. Horse and cart were our normal mode of transport.

Just as we entered the port area the air raid warning sounded. The soldiers said that they had to hide their car and that we should hide in the ruins that were nearby and that they would be back when the air raid was over. This was about mid morning. Mother and I sat in the ruins wondering if we would ever see our luggage again.

It was nearly evening when the two soldiers returned. Our luggage seemed to be intact. They drove us the few hundred meters to where the ships were moored at the quay side. There may have been other ships tied up but I remember only the Moero and what turned out to be RO 22.

Because we were so late the Moero was no longer accepting passengers. I am not exactly sure what mother did but we were allowed to board the RO 22. Because we were really late and the ship was really full we were allocated space in a cage made from wooden slats that normally contained life jackets. This cage was one level down from the deck and was reached by a reasonably wide set of stairs. The cage was practically opposite the foot of the stairs.

As dusk was falling I remember being at the railing as the Moero slowly pulled away from the wharf and passed close on its way to the bay and open sea. The railings of both ships were crowded and on both ships the people were singing the same song. I can no longer remember the song but I have a vague feeling it was one of sad farewell.

Came night. Mother and I were bedded down in our cage. The ship must have been anchored in the bay. During the night there was an air raid. The ship's anti-aircraft guns were thumping away. One seemed to be mounted just over our heads. I could hear empty shell cases falling on the deck. Yet I cannot remember seeing a gun where I thought it was.

When I emerged on deck in the morning we were under way. The coastline of Estonia was still visible off to port. And then the air raid warning sounded. I went below where my mother was. I cannot remember how long it was until we heard a loud bang. The ship started to list. Through loudspeakers, I think, people were ordered to go to the high side. Mother and I were on deck by this time and did that. Now although the sun was shining the wind was cold and the sea was bit choppy. I think that was the only time I felt some fear. I could not swim and the last summer I had seen two kids about my own age drown in the water at Pirita beach. Practically under my nose. I was wondering how I was going to deal with the waves. I noticed a fairly large raft in the water, full of German sailors. I thought to myself, by gum they were quick off the mark. Maybe they were there to save anybody who fell in the water.

After a while the crew seemed to think that the ship would not sink. Slowly the ship assumed a more normal position and we returned to our cage. Because the ship was still tilted and there must have been some pushing on the stairs my mother fell down and landed on her knees. This would cause trouble later.

What caused the damage? I remember people talking of a torpedo yet other accounts say that it was bomb. Yet the ship had a huge hole in its side. It was below water level that could not be seen from the outside. The damage was to the aft hold. The hold cover had disappeared together with the shiny black car and another vehicle that had been parked on the hold cover. Looking into the hold from the deck I saw the hold filled with water and dead bodies floating in the water. I also remember a couple of brightly colored quilt blankets.

Women and children had been placed in the aft hold. The story was that this was the only hold that could be heated. People spoke of 600 people dying. Another estimate had 300 people dying. This is what I remember people saying. Later accounts seem to indicate 130 to 200 people who died. I cannot remember when I heard that the Moero had been sunk.

The voyage to Gotenhafen (Gdynia) should not have taken more than two days. We were at sea much longer than that. I became very seasick. One day I ventured outside. I noticed the ship's crane boom was swung out and there was a stretcher attached to the end of the cable.

Looking over the side I saw a tug-like ship close alongside. It seemed wounded were being transferred to this ship. Some stretchers were already on the smaller vessel. The sea was fairly rough. I had to sit down again. I could see the tip of the mast of the other ship disappear only to rise until most of the wheelhouse was visible. Even as a small boy I could understand that what was being done required great skill. I presume the heavily wounded were being taken off so that they could be transported to hospital sooner. I cannot remember hearing of accidents.

As usual, where many people are crowded together, the toilets block up. And so it was on the RO 22. Even before we set sail. I was lucky. On the first day, on one deck up on the superstructure, I found my very own toilet. Accessible through a door from the outside. It was clean and warm. Talk of heaven on earth.

On the whole the voyage passed in a kind of fog. I am not very observant when seasick. I was glad when we entered the harbour at Gotenhafen. The 'ground' under my feet felt steady again.

It was a grey overcast day. I was standing at the railing in the stern when two, to my mind, very small submarines passed the stern of the ship. Also painted grey.

Waiting on the quay was a column of lorries. They were loaded with coffins. I do not remember what happened after that. We must have boarded a train to Chemnitz because that was our first camp in Germany.

The German troop carrier Kalev Ehin and his father boarded:
Photo derived from Kalev's book "Coming home".

KALEV EHIN
SNIPPETS ABOUT THE FLIGHT

OUR FLIGHT BEGINS
Before we left the city limits....we parked in front of the station and walked around the building to the main platform...we were well aware that we stood at the very spot that marked the beginning of the end for our family ties.....

I was thinking back to Sunday, August 13, 1944. I still remembered that it had been an unusually warm day. Father was noticeably worried. There was no question that the situation was getting worse by the minute. We could hear the steady rumbling of artillery getting closer and closer.

……**As our family waited for the train I wandered into the station's sauna: There I saw the most grisly sight which I haven't seen duplicated to this day.** On the bench in the sauna was a half- naked corpse of a Russian soldier. The man looked like a giant to me. His hair was standing straight up matted with dried blood, his hands still held his head, and there was an outsized hole through the sides of his neck. Horrified, I ran to my parents and reported to them, in detail what I had seen, but they had already been informed about the dead prisoner in the sauna. Apparently the man had got into an argument with several other prisoners. His adversaries had eventually ganged up on him and proceeded to beat their comrade unconscious with their belt buckles. Finally as the coup de grace, they had stuck a knife through his neck and twisted it around. **It was my first graphic example of the limitless human capacity for cruelty.**

After it got dark, tracers filled the night sky as we anxiously gazed down the tracks towards the south-east, the direction from where we and several other families standing on the platform hoped a train would soon come into view. Shortly before two, as the sounds of battle inched ever close, a train laden with severely wounded combatants slowly pulled into the station.

It was a chilling sight. The wounded were on stretchers stacked in three tiers in open freight cars. As the wagons rolled by us before the train came to a halt, I could clearly see blood dripping, in some cases more like pouring, from the bottoms of countless stretchers. Oddly, I can't recall hearing a single scream, only an occasional subdued moan.

I was personally witnessing the results of the human sacrifices being made on our behalf. They were loyal everyday people, not a bunch of fanatics who had stepped forward to defend their ancient homeland from the re-approaching Communist terror and oppression. That night I had an unforgettable lesson why war is the ultimate nightmare and what a precious commodity freedom is.

The moment of truth was finally at hand. Was there enough room on the train from hell to take us and several other families to temporary safety? Somehow everyone who had been waiting managed to get on board. As the train inched out of Põlva Railway Station at two o'clock on the morning of August 14, the night behind us suddenly lit up. Within minutes we found out that the Kiisu railroad bridge less than three miles behind us had been blown up by retreating troops. There was now no doubt that we had escaped on the last train.

As Maimu and I peered down the track in the direction from where the last train had pulled into the station forty years ago, tears streamed down our cheeks. What kind of lives would the two of us led had it not been for World War II and its continuing aftermath?

LEAVING ESTONIA
....pointed to an old yellow, brown trimmed two-storey stucco house building, **"This is the house from where you and father headed for the harbour when you fled....**..a short distance from the waterfront. It seemed off that I remembered more where the place was located in relation to the docks rather than what the house looked like. Our family had stayed there for a little while after we fled from Põlva. But, that was not all.

...It was from this house that father and I walked several blocks downhill to the harbour. There we were able to board a German freighter overcrowded with troops and fleeing civilians. The ship, part of a convoy of three other vessels, let go of its mooring precisely at five in the morning on September 19, 1944.

It turned out to be the darkest Tuesday of my life since I never saw my mother again.... only within the last few days had I learned the circumstances under which we had departed....Maimu has actually been happy that father was planning to take off by himself. She couldn't think of a better way to get rid of him permanently.... she was overcome by a tremendous sense of guilt when she discovered that father had taken me with him.

By the time we arrived in Tallinn, it was common knowledge that the Soviets were massing vast numbers of troops and armor on the front for the final assault against the Baltic Republics.... all able bodies men and women in Tallinn... were taken by train to various locations behind the front lines to construct infantry trenches and bunkers..lightheartedly referred to as the earthworks. These defence networks were intended to be used as a last ditch effort to help stop the enemy ....

Father decided to take me with him when he reported for the 'Earth works'. He told me that he didn't want to leave me alone in the city in case the Russians bombed Tallinn... he promised it would be adventurous being in the middle of such exciting activity .... much more than either of us could have anticipated... his reasons for taking me with him was far from the truth...at forty six....could have been detained by the military and ordered to report for combat duty immediately. There was little time for training....What better way to avoid being placed on the front line than having to take care of an eight year old

He also knew that the final Soviet offensive could begin any moment. Having a youngster with him would make it easier for him to find transportation back to Tallinn...Father was well aware that Mother was still in Tallinn... He would not have found me .... That meant that he would not only have lost his son but his "cover". Self-preservation is a very powerful human drive.

Father and I departed for the earthworks on September 5.... the destination less than 20 miles south of Tartu. The mood of the men and women riding on the flatbeds and open freights was almost festive.....Estonians are known to sing for any reason....we were housed in the main building of an old German manor... did very little digging. I mostly watched father and the others...I more or less kept me entertained...

Most of those twelve days ... were uneventful. Occasionally we could hear muffled artillery from the direction of Tartu. Once we were even strafed by a lone Soviet fighter... by the time Father had pulled me into one of the dugouts the aircraft had already disappeared.

Before long however the peace and quiet of the countryside was shattered by the thunder of war...... At precisely six on the morning of September 17, we were awakened by the sudden shaking of the concrete floor. The Russians had launched their anticipated massive attack. For two hours the ground shook beneath our feet and from the south we heard the continuous rumbling of heavy weapons. Eventually the defenders were overwhelmed by the sea of Soviet troops, tanks, artillery and planes.......

Since it was Sunday, the trucks that normally ferried us back and forth were not available....that they would be available on Monday morning...they could take us farther northwards away from danger....Father's survival instincts were as sharp as ever.... I'll take my son and start walking towards the nearest train station immediately.

Father then asked a friend for directions...Father's friend gave me his jack knife which I had admired for days.

We walked for what for me, seemed like forever and we were without any food or water. At one point ...we even came close to being run over by a column of Germans Panzers.. by nightfall we arrived at the station. We were momentarily scared.... when we were informed that no more trains were expected to arrive from... Tartu since the city had been overrun by Communists....

A German troop train ....already at the station ready to depart for Tallinn at any moment....I remember nervously going into the caboose with my father...German officers began to smile and pat me on the head. They also offered me some food and drink. We stayed in the caboose until we reached Tallinn.

On September 18, 1944 father and I finally got back to Tallinn.... We saw thousands of people pouring into the city fleeing... Some of them were trying desperately to find space on the few remaining German transport ships in the harbour. Others continued westward hoping to get on board fishing vessels, sail boats or anything else that would float in order to get across the Baltic Sea to Sweden. Many were simply trying to decide whether to flee or to wait and see what fate would bring.

In late afternoon Father began to pack the bare necessities for both of us into a large duffle bag. After dinner he cooked some pancakes, smothered them in butter and put them into a covered milk pail. We were ready to leave before midnight and that's when he told me that we couldn't wait any longer for mother and Maimu. He was certain that Tallinn would fall within a day or two. ...Soviet tanks entered the city on September 22.

Aunt Ella... somehow she'd gotten wind that father was leaving and taking me with him...she desperately tried to hide me behind her back....to no avail. Father had finally pushed her aside and taken me by the hand..... On our way down to the harbour Father assured me that mother and Maimu would follow us on another ship as soon as they got back from Viljandi. We would be reunited again somewhere in Germany....

As we approached the pier on that fateful night, I suddenly saw a large grey ship looming in the darkness to our left..I was awestruck. Father ...seemed to know exactly where he was going..headed straight for the gray ship, a German troop carrier whose decks were already packed with soldiers and refugees.

At the ship's gangway we were stopped by an armed German soldier and asked for boarding passes. Casually, father reached in his breast pocket and pulled out an important looking document that he handed to the sentry. I never did find out what that paper was. Most likely it was some sort of an official document that was given to him when he worked for the counter intelligence people in Põlva. The guard did not accept these documents and told father that we needed papers from both the evacuating German and the new Estonian harbour commander before he could let us on board.

Father was noticeably trembling from nervousness when he asked the guard when the ship was scheduled to depart. "At four o'clock," was the response. Father now had only three hours to find the right offices and to obtain proper passes for us. Under the existing chaotic conditions this was an impossible feat. His fears were heightened by the fact that the newly established Estonian government was placing all able bodied man under arms for the last ditch defence of Tallinn. After a long pause, Father asked if the sentry could keep an eye on our belongings while we tried to get the passes. He nodded and we raced off into the night.

My presence again saved the day for father. ..the new Estonian authorities were only allowing old men, and men with wives and young children to leave the country. Each time Father was asked why he hadn't responded to the general mobilization order he replied, "What will I do with my eight year old son? How can I leave him alone without someone to care for him?" Years later it dawned on me that I'd been his ticket out of the country.

Although we had to visit a considerable number of offices, we managed to acquire all the necessary documentation fairly quickly and headed back to the ship with only minutes to spare. ...by now there was a new guard on duty at the gangway. Our duffle bag was still there but our pail with the pancakes had vanished. We would have hardly anything to eat for the next two days.

Before dawn, at precisely five in the morning on December 19, we steamed out of the harbour. Darkness hid the skyline of the city where I had been born on a snowy December morning almost nine years earlier. I prayed for my mother and sister that somehow they would follow soon.

THE BALTIC CROSSING
For two days my father and I sailed southwards on the Baltic on board the German troop carrier after we left the Tallinn harbour. On the crowded decks there was continuous talk about possible Russian submarine attacks. In fact before we landed in Poland, we heard through the ship's rumor mill that the two ships travelling some distance in front of us had been torpedoed. Apparently, both ships had sunk quickly and left few survivors. I've never been able to confirm the actual fate of those two ships although father firmly believes that they were sunk.

On the first day our ship was fired on by a single Soviet fighter aeroplane. I saw the plane flying fairly high above us, but I don't recall anybody, or anything being hit by its guns. I guess the pilot was in no mood to test the skill of the transport's anti-aircraft crews since he disappeared out of sight rather quickly.

Had he taken a couple more runs at us we would just have stood there anyway and watched the action as there was no place to take cover on the overcrowded decks. Where do you go when there is standing room only? In any case that was the only excitement we had for the duration of the voyage. By the end of the day, father and I sure could have used that pail full of pancakes that vanished as we were busy getting boarding passes from the harbor master.

There were no provisions for the thousands of refugees and military personnel crammed into every nook and cranny of the ship I don't remember if there was even any drinking water accessible to passengers. Fortunately, a gentleman standing near us noticed our predicament and kindly gave us a small can of sardines.
That wouldn't be the last time we would experience hunger during our flight from Estonia. It was just a prelude to what was in store for us in the very near future.

On the night of September 21 we docked in Danzig, Poland. Red Cross women, in crisp spotless black and white outfits, greeted us with warm milk and sandwiches as we came ashore. It was a welcome relief after having existed on half a can of sardines for two days. All the refugees were then herded to a documentation processing area where we stood in line for the rest of the night.

Early the next morning we were given tickets for a train destined to Vienna. I felt that we were moving too quickly from one location to another and I became extremely worried that Mother and Maimu would not find us if they left Tallinn on a later ship. Father, however assured me that they wouldn't have much difficulty locating us since he had left word with the Danzig Harbour authorities as to where we were headed.

Besides, my thoughts were soon distracted by the Austrian mountains as out train got closer and closer to Vienna. Considering that Suur Munamagi (Big Egg Mountain) in south-eastern Estonia, with an elevation of 318 metres above sea level is the highest peak in Estonia, one can grasp why I became so preoccupied with the majestic beauty of Austria's landscape passing by our window. I have ever seen mountains like that before in my life.

We only stayed in Vienna for two weeks in a tiny hotel filled to capacity with refugees like us.
We had to move on because the Russian forces were closing in on us again.

KEEPING MY SPIRITS UP
In Götzig..it was again pleasant to converse with others in our native tongue. Also by this time it had become standard practice for Father to ask every Estonian we met if, by chance, they had heard anything of Mother and Maimu. For the

next thirteen years we'd get the negative answers in return. Of course, unbeknownst to me,...father always knew what the response would be

AT BIRKENFELD

Father worked long hours, from dawn to dusk, and although he had grown up on a farm he wasn't accustomed to hard physical labour, having worked behind a desk most of his adult life.   He confided in me that the job was almost killing him.

At Birkenfeld I also attended my first non-Estonian school. All I can recall is that I was more of an item of curiosity for the local children than a student. I was simply a blond kid from an unknown country somewhere near Russia who wore the same clothes daily, had no 'lederhosen' like the local youngsters, spoke almost no German, but played quite good soccer for his age.

Even in this seemingly quiet rural community there were constant reminders that we lived in a state of war. At least weekly someone was shot by the German border guards as they got to close to the Swiss border, trying to escape to Switzerland, a neutral country. Since the village was less than a mile from the Rhine River, designated as the boundary between the Third Reich and Switzerland, it was very easy to wander into no man's land where one received no warning before being instantly killed by a single bullet from a concealed sharp shooter. Occasionally, I would accompany my father to a potato field near the river. While there, father never failed to warn me not to go too close to the killing zone while playing with the other kids, who knew the area much better than I did.

A STEEP LEARNING CURVE

In Götzig I learned two important lessons through first hand experiences. One was that making a pair of skis is much more complicated than it appears. Also, when you're learning a brand new language, don't say things in public if you don't know the meaning behind the innocent sounding words you are uttering.

To me it seemed that every man, woman and child in this quaint little alpine village had both a pair of skis and ice skates. I became increasingly resentful that I didn't at least have a pair of skis of my own so that I would better fit in with the kids who I occasionally played with. One day I stumbled across two equal sized boards as I was moseying around the lodge and they seemed to be perfect for making skis.

Using my pocket knife, the one given to me by Father's friends as we fled the earth works near Tartu, I went to work on the planks to shape them into something resembling skis. Once that was completed I made some bindings from rope and attached them to the middle of the boards. I then stuck the tips of the boards into hot water and bent them upwards and let them cure overnight.

Early the next morning, and out of sight of anyone on the lodge, I strapped on my new skis and attempted to go down a small hill near the hostel. Without poles and a lot of drag, I promptly found myself tumbling through the snow. To my dismay, I also discovered that the tips of my skis, which didn't have much curvature to begin with, had completely straightened out as soon as they came in contact with the cold snow. Thoroughly frustrated and embarrassed, I quickly discarded the skis before any of the hostel residents had a chance to humiliate me.

The second lesson involved several of my so-called village friends. They seemed intent on having me learn a short slogan that they would occasionally utter themselves. It turned out to be an anti-Nazi cataphrase. My compatriots were quite amused how quickly I learned to flawlessly say "Heil Hitler, unter mit Die Partei" (Hail Hitler, down with the party) and how freely I began to use it, since it was obvious that I wasn't aware of what I was saying. Later, when I tried the slogan on my father and several other Estonians present, they weren't amused at all. Rather, **they sternly advised me that repeating that phrase in public would be one of the fastest ways to get Father and me arrested if the wrong people hear it.**

KYRA PALANGO/ARONSON
DISPLACED

As I stood on the upper deck of the German transport ship named RO 22, clutching my mother's hand, it occurred to me that this was probably the last time I would ever see my beloved Tallinn.

The city was bombarded by Soviet planes and I saw houses being swallowed by raging orange flames. In the distance, the majestic Gothic church spires .continued to stand erect as if in defiance. The sky above the city glowed with a crimson hue. We were fleeing our homeland and all the things dear and familiar to us as the dreaded Soviet forces were approaching the city. While my parents did not know what awaited us in Germany, they were willing to risk facing the unknown in order to escape the well-known Communist terror.

Even though I was only ten years old, it broke my heart to see Tallinn destroyed. My little tow haired brother Hillar was crying. He was only six and was frightened by the sight of the burning city. Since I was older, I felt that I should act like an adult in this disaster and be poised as my mother. She stood there clasping our hands, her back straight as a ramrod and her head held high. The funny striped rooster feathers sprouting from her hat twirled in the wind.

Earlier in the evening, the harbor had been swarming with frenzied people carrying suitcases, hurrying pell-mell to the German ships anchored at the pier. After sounding their booming horns, one ship after another began to pull away from the pier and head out to sea. We had been told that all ships were to rendezvous a distance away to form a convoy before heading for Germany. However, the RO 22 was not leaving, for reasons unknown to us.

As darkness descended on the city, the airplanes began to concentrate their attacks on the harbor. We heard bombs falling in the water around the ship. Several brilliant Magnesium flares in the sky lit up the harbor and made it seem as if daylight had arrived.

Finally, to everyone's relief, the ship pulled out of the harbor. We went below decks to find our cabin located in the middle portion of the ship, assigned for women and children. There was not much light and there were no beds or seats. Women and children had to sit on the floor or on top of their luggage. My mother made lumpy beds for my brother and me on our suitcases. She herself lay down on her folded coat. We had all been given life preservers and commanded to wear them all the time. There was no ventilation in the cabin and the heat was oppressive, but I was so exhausted that I fell asleep.

Early next morning we heard talk among other women that our ship had been abandoned by the convoy and we were navigating alone in the midst of the Baltic Sea. Suddenly, there was a piercing shriek of an alarm. "It's just a warning, don't worry," my mother said. At the next moment, an ear-shattering explosion rocked us with a blinding flash of fire and black smoke.

I remember that much, then blackness, nothing. When I regained consciousness, I was alone. I called for my mother but she was nowhere in sight. There was only total darkness and smoke, with cries and moans surrounding me, along with the ominous roar of sea water rushing into the cabin through a gigantic hole in the ship's side. Too terrified to move, I cried for my mother.

Suddenly I heard my mother calling me. Then I saw her splashing through the water, carrying my brother. She had found him pinned under a huge steel pole and somehow had the strength to pull him out. We moved slowly through the rising water toward a source of light shining from the upper deck. My mother carried Hillar, who was sobbing feebly, while I gripped her soaked skirt. We ploughed among people who cried out for help, but there was no one to help them since the crew was frantically working to keep the ship afloat.

Someone had thrown a rope ladder down and we were crawling up, my mother pushing Hillar's bottom and me dragging behind. My mind felt numb and blank from shock, so that I did not see or remember anything beyond the rope ladder. My mother told me later that she had seen a woman's disembodied leg clad in a high-heeled shoe float by. When we reached the upper deck, I do remember seeing a multitude of people in the water but I don't know if they were saved or drowned.

After what seemed like an endless period of time, the ship righted itself and sat upright in the water. News was passed around that we were not going to sink after all.

Shortly after that, the wounded were taken to the ship's medical staff to be examined. They found that I had only a few minor cuts on my face and back. Hillar, on the other hand, could not walk because the heavy metal pole had injured his back. My mother's left eye was embedded with small glass fragments, which the doctor feared might cause her to lose her eyesight. She had to wait until we reached our destination so she could be treated in the hospital.

We learned later that a torpedo had hit the cabin allocated for women and children, the very same one where we had spent the night. The explosion had made a huge hole in the side of the ship, through which sea water poured in and filled the cabin. However, since the walls were structurally watertight, they contained the water and did not allow it to penetrate other sections of the ship. So the ship was able to limp along toward Germany.

Upon arrival, we were placed in a hospital in Gotenhafen and were cared for by their excellent staff. After two weeks, my mother's eye and my scars had healed, but Hillar continued to have trouble walking.

My father, who had come on a different ship, was waiting for us. All our suitcases were lost in the Baltic Sea, including our winter clothes, my mother's fine jewelry and documents. We felt naked like newborn infants, stripped of everything but our lives. But I did not care. I was just glad to be alive and to have my mother, to whom I clung with all my might.

After being released from the hospital, we were transported from one refugee camp to another. At the end of October we found ourselves in a camp in Neumünster, near the Danish border.

Neumünster had been spared from the daily onslaught of bombing raids and it sheltered a multitude of German women and children who had fled there for safety. We were sheltered in drafty but clean clapboard barracks. The big problem was still the scarcity of food. The limited rations we were given had trickled down to a bare minimum. As a result, Hillar and I developed a death-like pallor and became weak and sickly. The camp's doctor took a look at us and decided to place us in the hospital, another barrack on the other side of the camp. After a couple of days our strength began to return.

One morning we heard an air raid siren. We thought nothing of it at first, but then we began to hear an ominous rumble above us. At the next moment bombs began to fall on our camp. Suddenly an ear-splitting explosion rocked our barrack and Hillar and I were thrown on the floor and showered by debris. The other end of the barrack had sustained a direct hit. Still in our white hospital gowns, Hillar and I crawled out of the rubble and jumped into a crater created by a bomb explosion.

Bombs continued to fall every few minutes. Whenever we heard the whistle of a falling bomb, we prayed with our palms grasped together, mumbling feverishly: "Meie Isa kes Sa oled taevas*. . ." and so forth. When we heard a bomb explode somewhere, we held our breath and stopped mumbling. When we heard another whining sound, we started again: "Meie Isa kes Sa oled taevas ...."

* The Estonian translation of the Lord's Prayer: "Our Father who art in Heaven.....

Finally the bombs stopped falling and we saw our mother running toward us, out of breath. She pulled us out of the crater and led us back to safety. We found out later that one third of the city had been destroyed. Evidently there was an airplane factory near our camp, the real target of the Allied Air Force. They had made a mistake in bombing the refugee camp.

After a while we were transported again to another camp, in Sudetenland, a region in Czechoslovakia. We were housed in a medieval castle called Schloss Enzovan, with musty, tomb-like corridors and vaulted ceilings. Although the rooms were an improvement from the previous clapboard barracks, a huge problem remained. Hunger.

Toward the end of the war, all the stores were empty. At first my mother was able to buy winter apples, pears and kohlrabi from local farmers, but after a while the farmers said they had nothing to sell. Some of the enterprising women made surreptitious nightly visits to the fields and pulled the frozen kohlrabi from the soil. The smell of boiled kohlrabi permeated the entire castle, which we found nauseating, but hunger prevailed and we kept eating this prosaic vegetable.

The other problem was the approaching Russian front. We could hear the sounds of cannon get closer to us and we knew we had to leave Sudetenland as soon as possible: The only fear greater than the fear of bombs was falling into Soviet hands. My mother wrote several letters to my father, who had been placed in another camp in north-western Germany, asking for his help. My father was unable to do anything. We saw huge convoys of trucks and horse-drawn carriages loaded with German civilians fleeing toward the West. I felt my mother's fear and terror and was affected by it in turn.

Then, almost at the eleventh hour, an angel came to save us. My mother had written a desperate letter to her good friend, Mrs. Kibena, begging for help. Mrs. Kibena and her daughter Aimi were living in a small town called Murnau near the Bavarian Alps. She sent a telegram to my mother saying that she had an apartment and a job for my mother, a white lie.

This allowed my mother to obtain permission to leave our camp and head for Bavaria. My mother lost no time. She packed our few belongings and purchased tickets for a train leaving the next morning. The train was packed, with people piled up on all the seats, some of them sitting on the floor or the roof of the train. The train crawled westward at a snail's pace, making numerous stops. At each station more people tried to board. At one point the train stopped and we were told that the rails ahead of us had been destroyed by bombs. We were frantic. Then all the passengers were to continue their trip on buses. After a few hours, the buses also came to a stop and we were to continue our journey on horse-drawn wagons.

Finally, we reached another railroad station and were able to board a train heading for Munich. In Munich we had to wait the whole night for a train for Murnau, sitting on a platform cracked up by a recent bombing. As the sun began to rise we travelled southward, away from the ruins of war. I sat by the window and stared at the beautiful landscape, the rolling hills and fields beginning to show a green hue.

After scrambling off the train at Murnau, my mother asked a sleepy clerk for direction to the address Mrs. Kibena had given her. It turned out that they lived quite a distance from the station. As we walked through the town with our bundles, I stared with an open mouth at the quaint Bavarian houses with their slanting roofs and balconies. I was looking for the Alps but they were hidden by clouds. When we approached the house in which Mrs. Kibena lived, Aimi burst out of the house and hugged me. She said that I had arrived a day after her birthday. I was overwhelmed with joy, seeing my good friend and finally feeling safe after the ordeals we had been through.

At that moment, the clouds departed from the Alps and I could see their majesty. That was a miraculous day.

Kyra and her brother Hillar in 1944 in Sudentenland

FLEEING:

Maarja Kiesel Paris: My Bother Tõnu was born in Tallinn in 1940 and was in that group who had to take baggage in hand to get out of Estonia. I was born in Geislingen in 47.

........my mother as a member of the women's choir (she had a beautiful voice). She was very thin and looked depressed after having lost a little son of 2 years on the way from Estonia.

My parents Dr. Ilmar Kiesel and Hilja Kiesel and brother Tõnu lived at #16. I was born in 1947 and lived there too until we came to the USA to North Dakota where my father was the doctor for a small community. I have some very clear memories of the place even though I was not quite 4 when we left.

Photos were hardly a priority as our folks fled in their angst from Estonia.

Few carried cameras and of those carried some were interred in the Baltic Sea and others were perhaps traded for necessities such as food.

The absence of such photos perhaps to void the perception that tragedy and deprivation had been our long standing companions.

How many small children looked just as forlorn and distressed as Kyra and Hillar for years to come: The more lighthearted and better clad images at the camps perhaps deceptive of those times.   MM

FOR THOSE WHO HAVE NOT PASSED THAT WAY OR WERE TOO YOUNG TO REMEMBER THE TREK

On the open road fleeing towards Helterma harbor. Leili Soovere has just said goodbye to her mother, and Ilo Soovere is not yet a year old. August 1944, Tallinn will fall to the Red Army in weeks.

The Jena Refugee train on the way to Augsburg DP camp. The flags of the 3 Baltic countries are seen with the Estonian tricolor in the front. June 1945

Jena Refugee train with all seeming exhausted and fatigued. Lying on his side is Ardo Tarem, a well known youth leader in Estonia, and who had no future in now occupied Estonia

*Ardo's silent film screen grabs feature in this book

IMAGERY IS A WONDERFUL MEDIUM TO SET THE DIORAMA
THANK YOU ILO SOOVERE FOR SHARING YOUR FATHER'S PHOTOS

Displaced orphan kids, they have made it to Estonia from Russia, and are hanging around Tartu Railroad Station . 1943.

An attic kindergarten in Augsburg 1945: The teacher is pr. Viilu

Karl Koljo Augsburg Gümnaasium head is presiding over graduating class. Mihkel Viise is standing with the colors; he would become an Army chaplain and serve in Estonia after independence to organize their chaplain program.

GEISLINGEN GROUP 'MANYLOGUE'
THE MYSTERIES OF ESCAPE ON THE GERMAN TROOP SHIPS

While the book "When the Noise Had ended" (WNE) was being compiled we had many an interesting "Manylogue" where folk on the data base enthusiastically chimed in with many a quandary and thought. The tradition has continued with new 'once young' from our Estonian ex-pat cohort joining in. This is one of the later communications.

There are many notions and myths but given our ages at that time combined with our parents' angst, harried recurring movement and then the long drawn out days in survival mode in camps and later in our new adoptive lands, there are endless glitches in our perceptions: Perhaps helpful in survival mode and now less helpful in reminiscing mode: Perhaps that is the fate for future generations of refugee children!

Liivi Joe began one of these

"Indeed there are some salient points we must consider - first of all, I am reminded that Jüri Linask pestered me ad infinitum to get the name of the ship we left Tallinn on into my story - I told him that my older brother Tiit b. 1930 was old enough to remember such things but I was not - he once told me the name of the ship was Molken Feldt and it got bombed and sunk on its next trip - I wrote that down somewhere but couldn't remember where when exchanging these e-mails with Jüri - now I have it in front of me - on my brother's card in my Rolodex - where else?

The matter of the ship named Lappland has come up - we know that some of our WNE (When the Noise had Ended) authors were on it and it was part of the convoy that departed Tallinn harbor on September 21, 1944 - back in the 1990s when I was recording memoirs in Connecticut on my video camera I recall the Vester family and the Siismets family reported they were both on that ship - but as late as the late 1990s they didn't know that as it was a subject that hadn't gotten discussed 'in the new land'

I felt I was the link that could organize a Lappland reunion - of sorts - by now we seem to have uncovered so many people who were on the Lappland that it seems to be taking on a myth like the Mayflower - in my more skeptical moments I hope that it isn't the case that people who knew they were on the 'last boat out of Tallinn' who have heard that there was a ship named Lappland that it must have been that one ... sometimes memory works that way ... certainly accounts for the Mayflower phenomenon - for our own purposes **we must remember that the Lappland was not the only 'last ship out of Tallinn' but that there was a whole convoy...**

In any case, if I am to trust my brother's memory that our ship was the Molken Feldt I expect that someone doing historical research of original documents can verify the date ...

Donna Parson writes:

As Liivi knows my husband Jaan Paarson left Pärnu on a Lithuanian ship named Johan Arens. I wonder if there are others among this group who were on this ship.

Liivi again writes:.

......some details had to be clarified - **foremost the impression that those who were financially better-off left (and the poor people stayed behind). I could not go along with this misperception as our own family was certainly not well off** (and the Kutsar family we were traveling with who were definitely better-off stayed behind) - I don't recall that my mother ever talked about having to pay for passage on the ship to Germany. **My contention was that it wasn't those who were wealthier who left, but those who were quicker** - i.e., some people felt they had to take care of some matters before leaving and therefore missed the last boats out though they had full intention of leaving - the logic of my argument I think is substantiated - the more property you own or business affairs you have to tend to the more time it takes - at the same time I know the easiest way to console yourself is to say you didn't have the money to do one thing or another anyway ... These are my thoughts on the matter ....

Now that I have lived in Estonia for nine years some other issues have become evident ....it is the issue of how those who stayed behind consoled themselves - by telling themselves we would never be returning - **official soviet propaganda even flat-out stated that we 'emigrated' rather than 'refugeed'** - realistically, given the Iron Curtain made conversations on this topic impossible, **the subject of intent to return has not really been in the collective conscious here** and again I see that only those older than me can address the various ways attachment to the homeland and intent to return got played out in the DP camp. We know that both the attachment to homeland and intent to return were the groundwork for later political activity in the new lands emigrated to 1948 That political activity has been well-documented but **as far as I can tell there is still that gap in the documentation of the 1944 departures.**

Ilvi Joe has added

I could add to the reasons why some people fled - or succeeded in fleeing - and why some didn't. In the book "Carrying Linda's Stones", historian Ea Jansen tells in her story that she could not imagine living abroad and her family certainly was not poor. Many people felt the same way. **Perhaps the myth of the better-off having fled** (supposedly they had the money to do that) **is based on the fact that for the most part these people had the most to fear when the Communists returned to power,** i.e., they had been either politically active or had assets coveted by the Communists, as we now have learned more and more. In our family's case, we were to be deported in June 14, 1941, and feared that after the return of the Red Army, the deportation would be carried out. .

Kalju Kubits added his thoughts

Why some fled and some didn't (and the residue of misunderstanding) has been on my mind lately. I spoke on this some at the recent Minneapolis symposium. Three things:

1) **Some of us had no choice.** We had info that we were on the 1941 lists for Vorkuta, and my father was a career military man (Estonian Air Force fighter pilot.)

2) Looking around our DP community in Minneapolis, it wasn't that they had money, **it was that they had some position of leadership in their community in any field and were therefore targets** in the drive to turn society upside down, like turning over a garden in the spring.

3) **We did not plan to flee to the West.** We were in Tallinn on March 9, 1944, and we left to get away from the bombing - went to Saaremaa to my father's family. We could not afford to fall into the hands of the communists. We left Saaremaa (Roomasaare) on a burned and abandoned freighter after the Germans had left on Oct 1, 1944. We kept fleeing the bombings and the Red Army and waited for the fighting to stop so we could go home. **When the war did stop it was with a result that left us without a country - so we sought asylum.**

Ülo Kuhi added

I was born June 3.1944 in Tartu. My mother and I left Eesti September 22,1944. My mother had no money and lived with her Aunt in Tartu. My question to everyone is "How did anyone, other than my mother, know my father was a German?". **Mai refers to Nepotism getting on a ship But how would anyone know I had a German father.** My mother could have said my father was Juhan Kuhi, who would know? I never had a birth certificate. Where there some papers for passage revealing my lineage? My mother did mention once something re to Geislingen that we had to go to Ulm because of my German father. I was the child of a German therefore there were some issues living in Geislingen. My mother got some help in the Fall of 1945 we did move to Hospitalweiher Strasse in Geislingen.

Mai Maddisson replied

You certainly clarify some issues, including my perception that some boats did leave after September 21.

Maybe there is a paranoia on my part but **I do sense an overall defensiveness on this issue about what was needed to board those German military ships.** My initial quandary arose from the (inaccurate) knowledge that mother and I were in no more danger than the average Joe, and had less money than the average Joe and yet managed to get on board one of those ships (I assume because I don't know all the details of our transit for many reasons). I always had a notion of nepotism given that I was the kid of a German soldier: Of course **nepotism can have many variants.** There are certain givens and have always been.

• That money buys access to all manner of commodities, be they access to medical management (as is the case in USA but less so in Oz), better housing, better education etc. And of course our much publicized and I 'm told derided by the world, current refugee situation indicates that these folk pay vast sums for their passages to our north-western coast.

• That money is a commodity that is more accessible to those with a better education or sociological position, or better business skills and sadly the odd rogue.

• That there was a hierarchy of danger levels to our people during 1944: Some were on deportation lists, others by way of occupation posed a threat to the invading regime and then there were all the others who were at some lower risk so that the Russians could make up their deportation quotas.

• That some people whose lives already fell under the negative tail of life's adversity Bell curve may have done their arithmetic and reasoned that they would neither emotionally nor financially survive fleeing into the unknown where their support systems would be zilch. This is something I have had to deal with in a lesser context all my working life: patients who need to remove themselves from a precarious environment still need to decide whether the transit for them would be even more precarious. At times people resign to the lesser evil.

• That among our poorer folk were those with limited life opportunities but high level reasoning and coping skills and they would quickly have deduced the status quo and acted accordingly.

But then there is another variable: The people who were issuing the permits to get on the ships; what were their criteria?

• Were the decisions made by the Estonians or the Germans?

• If they were made by which ever did they prioritize risk to the individual or was it first in best dressed? In my compilation of the book on the trek from Estonia I get the impression that it was largely a matter of first in best dressed but whether that was the official policy we might never know. But then those in the know would have had more available contacts: Someone working in a factory for long hours with little opportunity to socialize might not hear of what was transpiring until too late.

Possibly such groups were more accommodating of the left wing politics: On my first return to Estonia in 2002 as I roamed around the district where I had lived, it was not unusual for the folks to bemoan the change of regime: that they had felt more secure in what had been lost to them. And of course world politics is declaring that in many modalities: The turmoil among our politics is quite scary: Once those who don't like getting their hands dirty get the balance of power it becomes hard to reverse. "Entitlement" must be the hardest word to define!

• And is humanity infallible: Did nepotism exist? That is a question I did pose many years ago in a confidential setting: The answer was a very definite yes. And it has been further affirmed if further such settings. But that does not make anyone guilty of wishing to flee because it is human nature to look after one's own self and one's flesh and blood.

So maybe we can just speak more freely remembering that no one is presenting the accusative.

My feeling (one which I can never prove) is that mother and I did access some nepotism but that also in fact we were at very high risk: Father was involved in the Leningrad siege i.e. actually in the invasion of Russia unlike our 'metsavennad' who were protecting our own turf. **I doubt that there is any ideology where invasion would be more acceptable than protecting one's own turf!** We would certainly have been dead meat. (My beginnings in Oz for some decades were ample proof of that: That the invader in never welcome and usually remains in fugitive mode*). Had I been born of an Estonian father, with our demographics I would feel that we would have fitted on the lower end of the risk scale.

*Of course one has to make allowance for people's vulnerabilities but also one needs to question how much say a child under 3 years old had in the dynamics of war time Europe: That none of us whatever our parents' reasoning or position in society were responsible for their decisions.

Now for some other bits of wisdom,

Hannes Jürmann shared his impressions: These will be annotated in the 'microscope' further in the book. Hannes is a little older than the WNE authorship and hence his comments correlate better there.

Mai responding
Liivi has made some interesting comments. Each needs to be viewed in two contexts.
•What was the reality- **of course only the older of us had any concrete information there** . The younger of us had our parents' info which mostly was reliable but a long time ago and some aspects may have become enmeshed in similarities.
•What remained with us as the 'memory' of our journey. Compiling more of our narrative it occurs to me that similar events occurred in more than one place, foreign names were confusing for the littlies but some form of 'mythology' remains with each of us. **Some of us will wonder why we remember what we did and others will want to know how it really was.**
Let's keep our minds open to both tangents.

Mai responding to Ulo Kuhi
Ulo, there are shades of knowing! There are differing personalities within oldies of the time. One can only conceal that which no one knew- I have 12 letters father sent to our Paldiski Maantee address- even the damned postie knew and everyone who would have had occasion to be involved in the transit of those letters! In the book HOP there are allusions of flashes of memory- not very pretty.

Aino (Murk) Naeris wrote:
 Not everyone left Eesti by boat.....I know my mother went thru Riga (she lived by the Latvian border) but after that ??? Lithuania? Poland ? she never mentioned a boat and I never thought to ask her. I wasn't born until she reached Germany. My birth certificate actually has a swastika on it .

Aino (Murk) Naeris comments
I am heartened by the response to my query - the basic question of which was ´How can we know more detail on this time period that determined the rest of our lives ......
Below (Now above due to e-mail formatting) is Ülo Kuhi´s outright statement about how financially not-well-heeled his mother was when she fled as well as additional questions (hence my own query has two parts:
1. How did a person with no money get from Tartu to Geislingen? and
2. How can those who stayed behind perpetuate the myth that only those with the financial means left?). Those of you who do not know Ülo, he is a retired history teacher, grew up in the Seabrook-Lakewood Estonian community -

Mai continues

Synapses are whizzing around and trying to format and answer from the material I have in the book (HOP) which narrates a number of varied stories and from it I surmise that the answer is a hybrid of much that I wrote the other day. I have also done a little asking around many years ago because as I indicated my trek has many glitches and voids which I needed to reconcile.

There is a saying : One swallow doesn't make a summer. That applies equally to Ulo and myself. As far as the kids of German soldiers are concerned they generally are not too forth coming whatever their nationality re their trek and we have done well to get Ulo and I to speak up at all so we won't find many swallows. Human nature being what it is there are bound to be a few Russian- Estonian cross breeds- their trek would perhaps be a really interesting one to learn about but I suspect that their accessible numbers would be even less than the two swallows we have with Ulo and me.

Aino quite rightly stated that a number of people travelled by land: I have skimmed HOP and formatted a summary of the trek route from the stories I have. Riga, Tilsit, -Lemsalus, Tukum Ost, Libau, Memel, Königsberg, Danzig. It seems that the trains were cut off very early in the transit and it seems that only a small percentage of the stories relate the land route.

Perhaps another variable that is not factored in for the older of us is that many became part of the military system in its variants and arrived in Germany in that context- at times by land.

Epp Lõoke wrote

I've always assumed my parents left by boat too but with Aino mentioning Riga I had another look through my father's papers and discovered a document stating we arrived in Danzig from Riga on 22nd Sept 1944.

I was born in Ronneburg in Nov 1944 and we passed through several camps including Wildflecken arriving in Geislingen Oct 1945.

Kalju makes some further observations

Re: **The last ship from Tallinn on Sept. 21st - West of Tallinn there were still other possibilities.** We left from Roomasaare on Oct. 1st, but the Germans were already gone and the Russians were coming. No permissions. Got to Gotenhafen and were put in a refugee camp. Re: How did we get to the west with little or no money - we walked from the East Prussian border, across Poland and part of Germany (the winter of '44-'45) till we came to an area controlled by American troops (twice.) Many people did the same.

I say twice because we thought we had made it when we go to an American occupied zone. There was a rumor that the zone was being turned over to the Russians. My mother, who spoke some (British) English, got into an extended argument with an American Captain, who swore up and down that NO- that was NOT going to happen.

In the middle of the night, with the ground shaking and rumbling, there were tanks on all the roads and in the distance, men's voices singing (something...voina). My father said "American troops don't sing..." grabbed for his clothes under his arm, and ran for the woods. My mother, myself and my younger brother his in the attic of a farmhouse.

Next day we were found by two Russian soldiers and as they were poking through our packs they found a first aid kit my mother had put together. In it was a large bottle of isopropyl alcohol (for disinfecting wounds). They started drinking it and my mother grabbed one child on each arm and started walking away, and was not stopped.

There were now many people trapped behind the Russian lines. The military aged men were hiding in the woods. On a new moon night my father swam the river border of east and west with a cable, and they used a boat and the cable to ferry many of us across. Spring, fast water, it was dangerous. I was pressed against the bottom of the boat and not allowed to look over the edge.

Once across, the American soldiers arrested my father (no papers) and took him to a POW camp, from which he escaped. My father had papers, but they were hidden.

Having papers could be a life or death issue.

Priit Vesilind adds

These are all good observations. There is another factor that hasn't been mentioned: **Those who could flee had few ties to the land itself. They were city people.** Farmers were responsible not only for the family, but also for the welfare of their help as well as their livestock. I have heard people say that they simply could not bring themselves to abandon their horses and cattle and sheep, with the realization that they would either suffer and die, or end up on a dinner table. When you're a steward of the land, there is a powerful drive not to desert it.

Liivi shares some more thoughts

Priit et al - good observation - certainly those who fled because the common knowledge was that during the Russian Occupation of 1940-41 the Communists had taken measures to rid society of the bourgeoisie in order to establish a society of proletariats - bourgeoisie tend to be urban - shopkeepers, policemen, bureaucrats, lawyers, professors, etc., - they certainly had reason to flee in 1944. **The farmers would get their turn in March 1949 when deportation to Siberia was used to intimidate them to join the collective farms.**

Certainly my own grandmother, as I have written in my story, stayed behind as we left, saying no Russians are going to drive her off her farm. There are always exceptions - last summer when I visited Ruhnu Saar I found out that the entire population fled to Sweden in 1944 and the authorities brought in women from Kihnu and Sõrve Saar to tend to the animals they left behind.

Now that Kalju Kubits has done a ´reply to all´ can I ask about the ´asylum´ - are you using that in a generic term or did your family actually formally apply for asylum somewhere. My family got **the famous Jaakson pass which identified us as stateless** and moving on to the US we were formally immigrants - green card status -

Ilvi clarifies Epps' quandary
Epp, it still could mean that the fleeing was by sea (ship), because both Riga and Danzig are harbor towns. The person filling the document may have marked Riga, because it was the point from which the ship had arrived in Danzig. The ship on which we fled stopped in Latvia also to pick up people who wanted to flee. **There was no more room below and I remember vividly these families sitting on top of their bundles on the open deck**.

Kalju clarifies a word usage
--generic. I should have said "shelter," instead of "asylum," as we melded into the refugee camp system. I know of no formal application. **We did not go directly to Geislingen, but were shifted through a number of camps.** We arrived later at Geislingen.

Merike Tamm joins in
(Merike is one of the children born of Estonian parents in Geislingen, as she indicates below. She has been actively involved in our dialogues largely because her interest in her past has involved has involved significant exploring of her family mythology : The inclusion of her commentary while not directly related to the troop ship quandary does illustrate how the younger of us go about piecing together information which has been dislocated from other information they have. The older of us have always ensured that we filled in any voids for such queries if we could. Killingi-Nõmme was one of the mysteries of her folks' transit. MM)
I was born in Geislingen, in 1946, so I did not experience leaving Estonia myself, but my parents did. In his old age, at my urging, my father wrote his memoirs, "Elulookirjeldus". I am summarizing (and translating) a small part of his story below.

My father was a career Estonian army officer. From 1941 to 1944, he was in Omakaitse in Elva. He left Estonia on 26 August 1944, driving a small truck, which the Germans weren't interested in, since its maximum speed was 35 kph. He took about 12 people with him. They drove toward Germany for 14 days, to Danzig, crossing the Estonian border on 26 September 1944. In Danzig he encountered Col. Saarsen, who recommended to my father that he go to the American zone. (My father wrote in his memoir that Saarsen was a double agent, for Germany and Great Britain.) Saarsen gave him documents that got him on a train to Ulm. At this point 7 remained from their original group of 12.

At another time in his old age (not in his memoirs) my father told me his specific driving route from Estonia, which I recorded. He wanted that information included in the obituary he wanted me to write for Vaba Eesti Sõna. I can't locate that obituary now, but I do remember that the town of Killingi-Nõmme was en route. That was such an unusual name, which I hadn't heard before.

Kalju ponders
One thing about this discussion and money keeps bothering me. If I was the other guy taking payment whose currency would I actually accept? I wouldn't want Eesti kroon or Deutschmarks. Western currencies were probably not very available there at that time. How is this money thing actually done?
One traditional way of transporting some of your net worth in smaller chunks across borders and through war zones was to convert it into stuff, e.g., camera(s), watch(es), use your imagination. What was done?

Liivi responds to Merike
Merike....my mother was from Mõisaküla and Killingi-Nõmme was somewhere near there. My mother and step-father talked about it often...I got the feeling it was more of a town than a village in the area.
and to Kalju -

Good going - getting specific - do you have any particular, specific memories about the various camps you spent time in before arriving in Geislingen?

I ask because for example the Kaar family got directed to a work camp where they made cheese - we ourselves, for all that my mother had the address of a relative to go to wound up in what in effect was a work camp (although housed in a palace) for Dutch people brought in from Occupied Holland to work there - and my 14 year old brother got assigned the duty of ironing German soldiers uniforms -

Actually Kilingi-Nõmme is the last town you pass through before Mõisaküla if you were pushing westward - Mõisaküla, an important railroad center near the Latvian border, was burning when the Kaar family from Vana Antsla passed through it with their horse and carriage. Rein Männik who I think you both know from Lakewood once told me his father was Vallavanem (Manor elder) of Kilingi-Nõmme just before the war ..... naturally I can´t force Rein Männik to write down what he himself knows - it seems all our long years of exile we chatted about everything else except where our families were from in Estonia - at least looking back it seems that way. **What has helped me a great deal in reconstructing our own family history has been actually living on the farm my great-grandfather built** - about a half-hour east of Kilingi-Nõmme -

Mai reengages

All this history stuff was starting to sound more concrete until the concrete mixer went into reverse gear.

Until starting resourcing WNE I only had a sketchy notion of Estoniana and the trek to the camps: Perhaps like a haze which one day might clear. It just didn't seem relevant over those early decades.

To resource WNE I did visit the Australian Immigration archives to start finding where people were. I figured that a good way to get the hang of it was to begin sifting out the stuff for my own folks. I thought that it would be there all nicely presented just for me to transcribe. Nope! Part of the stuff was in Melbourne and the rest of it was in Canberra. Accessing the Melbourne stuff was easy- all I had to do was to come back another day when they had fished the stuff out. Canberra of course is not that far from Melbourne (but awkward to access) and one still had to go there and that meant waiting until one can combine it with other agendas.

My overall impression was that there as a mismatch between what grandfather had written and what mother had written: the dates of their arrival in Germany did not coincide by a day or two: grandfather definitely had all his marbles. Maybe mother under duress got the dates wrong. And did I really want to know right then? Putting on my clinicians hat I told myself that while it wasn't preoccupying my mind maybe that was how it was best left: And compiling WNE had priority.

While compiling the material about the trek from Estonia I have learned a lot more about that trek: And one of the realities is that there were endless variants: **When one is on the run one is not documenting history and endless hardships create a mental blur.** But there has been a recurring phenomenon of my thinking to myself "that is not how I remember it" while not actually initially remembering anything else instead. As I have indicated that upon perusing the Fremden pass I found out that there was much else to remember: Whatever the German's shortcomings, they tended to be meticulous in what they wrote down- **that Fremden pass was correct: and who wouldn't be meticulous with the possibility of a firearm at one's temple if one goofed.**

Yesterday I got back to the Melbourne Archives again and found something even more perplexing: Grandfather's naturalization request papers stated that he had lived in Estonia from 1883- > 19-8-44. And that he had lived in Germany 19-8-44-> 19-10 50. I had filled in the form and as a teenager with other preoccupations I probably just wrote down whatever I was told to write.

Wow, supersonic ships and /trains. How could Germany possibly have lost the war with such technology!

And what's more during WW I Samara (south of Moscow) must have been on another planet, like Czechoslovakia was in 1944-5. One begins to wonder how reliable our planet really is.

I have always been aware that I spent time with my German grandmother somewhere down that journey: I couldn't quite visualize how but made some reasonable guesses from fragmented info. All those were based on the notion that father actually came from the city of Konigsberg. I have since accessed father's military documents (albeit a little fragmented) and found out his birthplace. It is a smallish hamlet in Poland near the Konigsberg border-it has only over the last 12 months appeared on the net.

I now wonder if grandfather took me down to my paternal grandmother earlier for whatever reason by whatever means. In which case, given the above dates, I would not have been an asylum seeker/refugee/or a DP until my grandmother's demise. I have asked for the Canberra documents which as I recall had a lot of detail for grandfather and almost zilch for mother. They should arrive on my computer within the next month: A facility not available when I last went down that track- interesting!!

I suspect that many of us will have similar enigmas to resolve if we go cruising through the transit archives documents. But I would be interested to hear from anyone who has braved such documents.

Anyway, I'll hop off the see-saw for now; kerplonk!!

Liivi suggests

I have one idea off the top of my head - as **we know Germans kept meticulous records** - now that you know the name of the town that your paternal grandmother lived in you might be able to find out if she actually registered you there as a resident? We know that refugees didn't´have free passage any more than during the German occupation in Estonia 1941-1944 written permission was necessary to move about - just a thought here - (now that I´ve written that **I am wondering how they could keep track of tens of millions of people trekking about on foot, by train, by bicycle** - according to my mother there was NSVAU at every train station keeping track of the welfare of refugees - seemingly an area that needs corroboration with official records - the work camps very definitely kept good records.)

Other than that I find myself going back to previous discussions **where when we have no concrete information fiction can somehow come closer to the truth of what the human experience really was** (see Sofie Oksanen´s work) - but that takes a different skill and orientation - I am clearly, as you can tell, doing my darnedest to reconstruct what details those of us - the last of the generation with any memory at all - fleeting as it is - who experienced this particular chapter - record anything and everything they remember. This is to say that I hope anyone who feels offended that I ask specific questions understands I am not trying to pin you against a wall - just trying to help jog that old memory cell -

Good going Hannes - please keep going if anything else comes to mind - this is precisely the level of detail that children remember - intertwined with remembering details of what the grown ups discussed - throughout the evolution of both the English and Estonian versions of our WNE book I was frustrated by authors who felt they had to write an ´acceptable´ history book when personal memories of the sort that only children remember is what we were after - we know that the actual historical events were but just a backdrop for what each individual family had to live through - **what makes memoirs so valuable is that they explain a lot of history.** By the way, Kensico Cemetery is in NY - north of the city in Westchester County in the township of Valhalla - the Estonian section there is quite large.

Again, please keep writing if you can - for now I´m sending this on to only Mai and Priit and my sister Ilvi who is helping arrange publicity for EWNE in Tallinn this summer when Mai is in town.

Ilvi responding to Hannes
So glad you wrote these recollections! Fascinating!

I happened to see the Kornel family once after the war when the Estonians who had fled to Sweden organized for about 50 orphaned kids from the Geislingen camp to spend a summer (1949) in Sweden. My sister Linda and I were among those kids. All of us were housed in Gläborg (it was sort of run as a camp for us), north of Göteborg. Toward the end of that period in Gläborg, I visited the Kornels in Göteborg (I think I was there couple days). I recall that their housekeeper from Tartu was with the family and she prepared for breakfast cream wheat that had the tastiest strawberry jam in the center. I also recall that their apartment was small, but sunny.

I got a kick out of your reference to the Wilhemshöhe Kindergarten. I used to go to Wilhemshöhe every week where our relative Erika Laos lived with family; she gave me piano lessons.

Marje Limion-Medri added
Remembered you were interested in how people arrived in Germany.

Mom told me that she and Heikki got on the ship in Tallinn during the day and the ships all sailed at night. They were aboard the middle ship of a three-ship convoy. The ship in front and the ship behind were bombed and sank. She told me she was strangely calm throughout the whole thing thinking that if they were hit and sank, well that's just the way it would be.

Of course, she was unspeakably sad at having to leave Estonia but her parents told her she had to get to safety with Heikki. They took her to the port in Tallinn. Dad was away somewhere fighting in the war. Like everyone else, she always believed they would go back after the war. How tremendously, achingly, wrenchingly sad it must have been for her when that did not happen.

What a generation our parents were in every single way.

I have been unable to contact the author of this segment of thoughts by publication time to access permission to quote their words: They are thoughts which are not specific to them apart from family details.
I have rendered the comment generic to de identify the author.
It goes thus:
Quite a number of our cohort were to grow up in Germany. They participated in Estonian summer camps, but some were too young to attend the song and dance fests which were called "ESTO's. This was particularly so in the early years, for others it continued longer.

Some Estonian parents arrived in Germany in 1941 and became German citizens soon after. They were to become documented as Aryans. They were refugees but had some advantages over 'stateless' refugees it seems. Those families too had different complexities which affected them.

There was nobody in Europe who escaped being affected by that war: Each had their own history both before and after that epoch.

How many such long 'manylogues' we have had over the years! This one has but touched the tip of the iceberg of all the quandaries which have arisen. Oh, if I hadn't always done the disappearing act when the oldies of the time reminisced.

And of course Mr. Hippocrates' Oath puts constraints on what one shares: I can state generically that I have heard of allusions to nepotism existing.

MICROSCOPE ON DEPARTURES FROM ESTONIA: SNIPPETS FROM E-MAIL COMMUNICATIONS: MM

The escape from Estonia was but a fleeting few days set among a decade of war and turmoil both in the Europe's war zones and later the camps. Those fleeting days and moments perhaps pivotal in our lives and memories.

Life moved fast and our parents made many quick decisions which it did not occur to us to reflect on until decades later: Our parents and older relatives have since died. Others have moved away to places remote from ready communication, which while possible through cyber- connection age wise are past the resources of our increasingly mentally less agile extended family and friends. The answers of course to have been lost forever. Perhaps some of the older of us heard the flickering thoughts and retained those cascading images.

Those images too however were set into a context relevant to that age cohort and not imbibing its subtle nuances.

CLIPS FROM HANNES JÜRMANN'S COMMUNICATIONS

....First cousin, Kristi Rammo had some younger brothers and sisters, told me **her mother having a baby in arms when they were picked up from a raft off the coast of Estonia.....**

.....in various books on the war in Estonia I have read that the Germans were making much effort in trying to get a many soldiers (including Estonian) and their dependents onto the last ships leaving Tallinn. Mum's record states that we left on the freighter "Donau" on the 18th or 19th Sept, together with mum's parents, but I always remembered getting an early birthday present because we were probably going to be on a ship on the 22nd.

I gather that we were accepted on the grounds that father had been conscripted into the German Wehrmacht. I believe he instructed mum to go on one of his last leaves to grandfather Rehe's farm at Järva-Jaani where we had gone from our farm SW of Tartu, at Nõo (14 km) in August. I still remember the truck and narrow-gauge train trip to Tamsalu, where mum's parents came to meet us. We stayed some days in Tallinn at the flat of a friend of mum's, called Mitsi. We also went to Nõmme to visit my father's mother and sister.

They had **a rather harrowing escape by raft to a passing German ship from the west coast an had to climb a rope ladder while aunt Helga was pregnan**t. Kristi (Rammo – father a painter), my cousin of about the same age as I. They were in Geislingen before us and Kristi was in the same class as I for a short time. They emigrated to the US about 1950. Kristi told me about the raft when I rang her in Toronto from Alberta. She always seemed a bit childish. When she died in about 2007 due to a fall down the steps at home. ......Very sad.

Meanwhile, back on the "Donau", we were on the first level below the deck at the front. All the people were spread over the floor on their blankets and baggage. **A guard with sub-machine gun stood at the top of the stairs during an air-raid to discourage people from crowding onto the deck.** However, later when we did emerge, he gave me and Peeter some of his chocolate. We stopped at Libau (?) and we all had to crowd to the sides of our floor for them to open the floor access to lower levels in order to winch some artillery pieces onto shore.

At Tallinn docks and later, Peeter had the job of carrying my teddy-bear, that mum had made, and I was in charge of mum's expensive Italian violin, for the whole journey to Hagenow.

There was some fuss at Tallinn, because some distraught woman had thrown herself from the ship onto the wharf and committed suicide. Mum had also taken the precaution of removing the valves from our valued Phillips radio. It was stolen on the ship but mum traded the valves for a win-up portable gramophone (Odeon) and records in Germany. We still had them in Stockwell, SA. My son Brett has the teddy bear in Dapto, near Wollongong.......

I remember mum telling us in Australia **that we were lucky, as not everyone found it as easy to get out.** I am sure that it was Ants Kitsing, a class mate in Geislingen who told of an escape on his father's tractor with trailer loaded up.

I wish I had been more persistent in trying to get written accounts of his retreat across Estonia. I do remember one account of where they had a close call when father went back into their temporary 'clinic' to grab some essential medical supplies wit his medic and found that the Soviets were already approaching and they had to use their sub- machineguns to fight their way out. He had a tendency to lose track of time and also to make long-winded speeches (according to mum).

Another tale was of having to drain a cupful of pus from a septic skull wound, but the man surviving. But that is about all of my childhood tales from him in Geislingen. ....

CLIPS FROM ARNE ELLERMETS COMMUNICATIONS

With **Gusten Lutter** his cousin,

Your story is different than ours, but equally interesting and probably riskier! I'll add a bit here about our departure.

After returning from your home at Kuusiku we spent some time, probably around a week, with our grand parents, dad's parents, in Nõmme, a suburb of Tallinn. Heiki and I never returned to our own apartment in Pelgulinn where we had lived before moving about sixty miles to a far safer place in your home in the country.

We left Nõmme on the morning of August 19, 1944 and Isa drove us in the same EMLO delivery van to the Tallinn harbor. ....Heiki, Ema and I were about a month ahead of the real refugee mass that left Estonia in September. The ship that brought us out of Tallinn, Estonia was empty.

The reasoning behind our early departure, if you want to call four weeks early! was related to the confiscation of a boat that Dad had reserved with some fishermen to take us to Sweden. Gusten, you mentioned that in your message how the German military was confiscating boats and arresting the fishermen who made money by quick trips to Sweden. "Our" boat was one of those that was confiscated.

Apparently Dad had no other contacts for an immediate escape to Sweden. He and Mom looked at the options available to us that led to our departure.

Dad had many contacts in Germany because of his foreign travels for EMLO, the liquor factory that he managed. He decided to send Mom, Heiki and me to Germany with the hope that we would be welcomed by his friends in Auerbach im Vogtland. He stayed in Tallinn and planned that If the Russian assault would continue he would leave Tallinn at the last moment and join us. On the other hand, if the Russian assault would be stopped and Estonia remain under German control then we were to return home.

Staying in Estonia under Russian control wasn't an option since he had been arrested by the Russians in 1941. He had been on a ship "Eesti Rand" destined to carry him as well as my uncle Endel to a Siberian prison camp, when it was sunk and they were both saved.

...........the total freedom that Heiki and I had, running about the empty ship. The cooks in the galley became our friends and we were well fed!

When we arrived in Gotenhafen a band was there to play some snappy music and greet us to German controlled Poland. Busses took us to a refugee camp that was surrounded by barbed wire fences.

We spent one night killing lice in our straw tick beds and Mom bought our way out of there the next day with a bottle of liquor! The commander even arranged for a vehicle to take us to the train station!

The reception in Auerbach was very nice. I don't remember whether the family who hosted us spoke Estonian or only German. In any case they helped us find a tiny attic apartment at Sorgaer Straße 45.

Dad left Tallinn on one of the last ships to leave the harbor before it fell into Russian hands on September 22nd. Gusten I notice that you left Saaremaa on September 28th - six days after our Dad left Tallinn. The time difference would account for the time that the Russian forces would have taken to get from the area of Tallinn to Saaremaa.

Dad's ship was attacked on the Baltic Sea by a Russian dive bomber that put a torpedo through the smoke stack of the ship without exploding.

The tiny apartment we rented was the one I described earlier when I told about opening the flipping widow in the slanted roof, climbing on the roof and watching the allied bombers fly in good formation to bomb either Dresden or Leipzig. Mom came home with Heiki and dragged me off the roof and we went to the air raid shelter! The rest of our escape has been described previously... It is interesting to see how our stories trigger memories in each other's minds!

I have no idea what special permission may have been required for Estonian refugees to board German cargo ships at Tallinn for the escape to - in our case - Gotenhafen (Gdynia).

Since Ema bought our way out of the internment camp after arriving in Gotenhafen with a bottle of liquor, the same kind of liquid may have been offered to the German Captain of the ship in Tallinn, but I haven't heard even any rumors about that part of our escape!

The ship that carried us from Tallinn to Gotenhafen was completely empty. We shared a large cabin with another family from Dad's office by the name of Proua Huuk and her daughter who was about the same age as I was

CLIPS FROM GUSTEN LUTTER'S COMMUNICATIONS
Arne wrote:
Here is something about our experience leaving Estonia, vis-a-vis permissions/clearance for passage on a German transport.

For a month before leaving Eesti on September 28, 1944, our family was laying low and moving around in Saaremaa, searching for a way to Sweden. The shore was "closed". German border guards confiscated boats that would emerge from hiding places and arrested people involved in escape attempts.

Rumors had the Red Army about to invade Muhu island. Approaching the end of September, the weather turned stormy, and we had totally, in the maximum sense possible, given up any hope of escape. Then we heard of troop ships taking refugees to Germany. For many reasons, we had not viewed Germany as a way out for us, but in desperation we went to Kuressaare, anyway. We found a disorderly, milling mass of refugees gathered along the harbor road. Wagons were abandoned, horses were turned loose in the fields.

Two big ships were anchored outside the harbor, and couple of barges ferried people to the ships. An orderly, but slow access to the harbor area itself was maintained and controlled by soldiers. Then one of the ships caught fire, spewing billows of black smoke.

My parents concluded that with this many people ahead of us, and with one ship burning, we would have no chance to get on a ship. In the "every man for himself" situation, my dad decided on a, sadly dishonorable, "HÄDA VALE" (Emergency lie!) deception. He elbowed us through the crowd to the cordon of soldiers and claimed that "our aged and feeble grandparents were ahead of us already on the ship, needed our help, and we simply had to join them".

No questions were asked, no ID papers were checked. We were escorted to what turned out to be one of the last barges leaving the harbor. The name of the ship was Peter Wessel. It started moving at dusk, along with the burning ship and a small naval escort vessel. The long strip of Sõrve peninsula fading into the night was my last view of our homeland. When I think of it, I can picture it still. And people crowding on deck, some groups singing patriotic and soldier songs of the day.

After dark there was an attack. Escort vessel fired some guns. Everyone was ordered off the deck, but we hid under a leaning life raft to remain away from any closed spaces. The other ship continued to burn and smoke all the way to Gotenhafen, where it was boarded by the harbor fire brigade.

In Gotenhafen, efficiently and without any fuss or probing questions, everyone was registered by uniformed officials at dock side tables, issued a "Durchlass Schein" (sp?) authorizing entry to Gross Deutschland, fed soup from an army field kitchen, with milk for children, loaded on passenger train cars with plenty of seats, issued a personal food ration (bread, piece of sausage, cube of "Markenbutter") for overnight train ride through Berlin, ending in Brandenburg. We were quartered in military garrison buildings and were free to visit the city. Another basic registration took place the next day.

CLIPS FROM KALEV EHIN'S COMMUNICATIONS
Father and I feverishly walked to several offices (the harbor master and members of the recognized Estonian Government now recruiting able bodied men to hold back the Russians--the Germans by this time were pretty much out of the picture other than organizing the departing ship traffic) in the harbor in order to get our boarding passes.

I still vaguely remember the discussions between father and the officials. The primary focus of the discussions was why father was not part of the now hastily being formed Estonian unites that were being positioned to hold back the approaching Russian forces. His response was simple, I was under his care and that there was no one else that I could be left with to be properly cared for.

Although it took us several hours to get the proper clearances and the boarding passes, I don't recall anyone really challenging him or generally giving him a hard time why he was fleeing. Essentially, what would happen to his son if he was suddenly drafted into one of the unites being formed?

AND AT TIMES THERE MAY HAVE BEEN OTHER MOTIVES FOR LEAVING
That type of material is not conducive to family harmony and has only been shared in confidence: Not isolated communications, to be further validated by patient comments of that ilk.

Small children of course did not understand adult complexities in life: They considered the predicaments as they seemed through their own limited experiences in life and perhaps extrapolated from mythology, gossip or whatever one might call it from those around. This of course needs to be interpreted with an open mind for there are those wishing to create havoc and malice among all nationalities and walks of life: Who knows where the truth lies for some.

But one does need to acknowledge that not all Estonians lived in circumstances which they considered optimal, regardless of the war and wishful thinking that the grass might be greener in other paddocks is not an unrealistic hope.

In such families the children may have felt greater regret at leaving their homeland. And one has to consider whether among such families were dysfunctional systems where the children's fate would be equally daunting where ever they trod: The holy dollar is not the only parameter of a positive outcome: Nor is a string of academic glorias. MM

AND OF COURSE WE DIDN'T REMAIN AT GDANSK OR GOTENHAFEN
Aimi Zechanowitsch writes

Mai, **you wonder why so many went to Czechoslovakia: There were special camps set up for women and children.** In September 1944, it seems, no one thought of what was in store by spring.

'SURVIVAL KITS' IN ESTONIA DURING GERMAN TIMES

KALEV EHIN
OUR ULM RAF BOMBING EXPERIENCE

(An excerpt from his book "Coming Home")

We'd been on the farm barely a month when Father was suddenly reassigned to another job. Apparently there was a shortage of qualified workers in an electronics factory in Ulm, Germany. Thus, when the employment office in Bregenz searched its files, they discovered that Father was a "funkman" by profession which seemed to instantly qualify him for work at the electronics plant. He was, therefore, ordered to travel to Ulm as quickly as possible.

Ulm straddles the Danube River roughly eighty-five miles straight north from Bregenz. In this medieval city we were housed in an old inn on the outskirts of town. I remember that there were several other Estonians, some with their families, staying at the same lodge. Most of them had been living there for some time and working at the electronics factory. It was fun to be able to share old and new experiences with people who you could identify with and who spoke the same language.

Almost nightly the air-raid sirens would sound. Hardly anyone, however, paid any attention to them. Some nights we could hear allied bombers flying over the city at high altitudes after the sirens had gone off. Even on those occasions few people showed any concern. The hostel inhabitants had simply become complacent, since Ulm had suffered only one relatively light attack about a year and a half before our arrival.

It was about nine-thirty on the evening of December 17th when the sirens began to play their nightly serenade. Father and I were sitting on our beds in an open bay on the second floor of the inn getting ready for bed. The room was heated by a large tile-covered stove positioned in the middle of the floor so that the fifteen or so residents would all have an equal amount of heat distributed to them. Some people were still busy talking in small groups while others were reading on their beds.

Suddenly, I had a strange feeling that something unusual was about to happen. I expressed my uneasiness to Father, but he only smiled and said that there was nothing to worry about. I then begged him to go outside with me for a few minutes before we turned in for the night. He finally agreed to take a short walk.

As soon as we were outside behind the lodge, we could hear the roar of aircraft engines coming toward us from the west. A few minutes later we saw the first set of "Christmas Trees" (nickname for parachute flares) lighting up the crisp clear December sky as they slowly descended towards the ground. My intuition had been correct. This time the target was Ulm.

Father, for some reason, thought it best to get away from the building since we had no idea where the inn's air-raid shelter was. Given that the hostel was built on the side of a steep hill it seemed most logical to move down to the bowl-shaped orchard below the house rather than waste more time and effort running up the hill.

We had only gotten halfway down to the bowl when I saw the bright flashes and columns of dirt flying skyward as the first three bombs, in rapid succession, exploded on the ridge in front and above us. The ground shook beneath our feet and the roar of the detonations was deafening. At the same time, shrapnel from the bombs whizzed by hitting many of the fruit trees round us.

Clearly, that was not the direction to go. As we turned around and started to run back up towards the lodge several more bombs hit fairly close behind us. Father shouted at me, on top of his lungs, to hit the ground, and I did instantly. Unknowingly, I had left my rear end up in the air. Father slapped my butt down and sarcastically asked me if I wanted to have it blown away.

Unexpectedly, out of nowhere one of our compatriots from the second floor landed next to us. Father immediately asked the man whether he knew where the nearest shelter was. He nodded his head and told us to follow him as he jumped up and headed for the inn. As luck would have it, we'd walked right by the shelter's entrance when we were in back of the hostel. That is, the cellar of the lodge was our air-raid shelter, and it was only accessible through a trap door behind the building. How could we have known that since before the start of the attack hardly anybody thought that we would ever need to use it.

As the man in front of us pulled up the trap door to the shelter, a huge bomb detonated on the other side of the building and all three of us were hurled down a steep set of stairs by the force of the explosion. As we picked ourselves off the concrete floor and our eyes got accustomed to the darkness, we noticed that all the other occupants of the inn had beaten us to the sanctuary. Fortunately, the whole group had only suffered a single casualty. A man about my father's age had been hit by a bomb fragment which had sliced through both sides of his buttocks. He lost a lot of blood but survived.

For the next twenty minutes the building shook relentlessly, and debris fell from the ceiling as bombs exploded around the inn. We could also see the brilliant flashes accompanied by the explosions as the trap door was continuously lifted up and then slammed down by the shock waves of the detonating ordinance.

Finally, as suddenly as it all had begun, the bombing stopped. After waiting for a few minutes we began, in single file, to cautiously ascend the stairs that led out of the cellar to the outside world.

As we emerged from the darkness of the shelter we were confronted by the glare of fires burning all around us. One of the first things that caught my eye were several raging fires lighting up the sky on top of the steep hill directly behind the hostel. Minutes later a number of German soldiers, clad only in trousers, undershirts and boots, came stumbling down the embankment.

It immediately became apparent that the burning buildings on top of the hill were the quarters of a sizable military unit. The complex had been a well kept secret. None of the residents of the inn had known anything about it until now. Clearly, the garrison above us had been one of the major targets, if not the principle objective, of the allied raid. It appeared that the British, who normally conducted their attacks at night while the Americans carried out daylight raids, had done their homework well. Unbeknownst to us we'd been within the bull's-eye of the attack and were lucky to have walked away from it alive.

As we wandered to the front of the inn we saw the entire old part of the city of Ulm burning below us. It was an eerie sight. Only hours before the medieval metropolis with its ancient churches and other historic structures had been glistening in the sunlight. Now from the distance it appeared as if every building on this side of the Danube River was ablaze and an otherworldly glow hung over the city.

Fearing that a follow-up attack was imminent, Father asked one of the residents about a bomb-proof bunker that he'd heard about earlier. Minutes later we and several other members of our group were on our way to a larger shelter dug into the side of the hill directly below the orchard from where father and I had barely escaped less than thirty minutes earlier. Although, as we discovered, the concrete reinforced bunker was only about a half mile away as the crow flies, we had to take the narrow winding road from the hostel down to one of the main streets and follow it to the entrance of the shelter. This route would take us across part of the bombed-out town smoldering below us.

As we descended to the city street closest to us, I couldn't see a solitary structure that had been left intact by the raid. In fact, in order to get through the rubble we had to carefully walk down the middle of the road.

Soon, however, I witnessed an even more grisly sight. Apparently, most of the residents of the houses in this section of the city had either suffocated or burned to death in their crushed basements. As we slowly passed by we could see police and firefighters pulling the dead from ruins and placing them on the sidewalks. From there the bodies were stacked onto flat-bed trucks and taken away. In the glow of the houses burning around us, it was a sight I would never forget, particularly the different discolorations — some red, some blue and some black — of the victims as they lay on the pavement.

We spent the rest of the night in the overcrowded community shelter that appeared to be more like a railroad tunnel with heavy steel doors than anything else. There were no more raids that night and in the morning we walked back up to the inn. Once there we stood and looked around in absolute amazement at the amounts and different types of ordinance that had rained down around our "country manor." The ferocity of the attack was astounding.

It was hard to believe that the inn hadn't been hit directly and obliterated.

In the orchard below the lodge where Father and I had run at the beginning of the raid were six large bomb craters. There was no doubt in our minds that had we stayed there for several more minutes or seconds we wouldn't have survived the attack. Further, only a few steps from one corner of the inn was a huge thirty-foot crater whose depth reached at least fifteen feet. The only thing that had saved the building and us from being literally blown away was its ancient three-foot thick stone and concrete walls.

Finally, on two sides of the building were at least a dozen hexagonal firebomb canisters stuck in the ground right next to the foundation. It appeared as if someone had walked around the dwelling and systematically embedded the cylinders as close to the base of the structure as possible. Miraculously, none of them had ignited on impact. Had they burst into flames there would have been no way to put them out since the major ingredient in the fire-bombs was phosphorous.

As expected, the second floor of the hostel where all of our worldly belongings were was an absolute mess. Glass and debris was everywhere and in everything. For example, many of our possessions, including food, were in small cardboard boxes stored under our beds. Every one of those cartons had been riddled with debris (mostly glass) blown in from the windows by the bomb blasts so most of the food had to be thrown away and much of our scant "fashionable attire" appeared to have been made from cheese cloth.

Yet, what remains foremost in my mind is the shape of the solid cast-iron plate that covered the top of the tile stove in the middle of the floor after the raid. This solid piece of metal, roughly two by three feet and a half inch thick, was used by the floor residents to cook food on. During the course of the attack it had been bent into a "U" shape by the air pressure or shock waves of the exploding bombs, but miraculously still remained on top of the stove. For me, and many others, it was a vivid lesson in physics.

As we carefully gathered everything that was salvageable, Father decided that we should leave the city as quickly as possible and head back to Bregenz.

Looking around the inn for something to transport our goods in we found an "abandoned" wheelbarrow. After placing our belongings into our newly acquired vehicle we again descended into the razed city below. Once there, we followed the nearest set of railroad tracks out of town in hopes of eventually finding a station that was still intact and in operation.

After walking for several hours we arrived at the Ruhetal Railway Station, a southern suburb of Ulm. Seeing that we were two of the victims from the previous night's allied raid, the station master or the local constable (I can't recall specifically who it was although I still have the document) issued us an "Ausweis für Fliegergeschädigte" (An identification paper authenticating that a person/s had been victims of a bombing attack) and an advance of one hundred marks. With the new identification paper in hand we boarded the next available train south to Bregenz.

In Bregenz we immediately went to our favorite "Hangout," the employment office. This time, though, we were treated with obvious contempt. The administrator with whom Father dealt with considered him to be a deserter having fled a city that needed all the help it could muster in order to restore its vital functions. Eventually, we were given train tickets for Salzburg, Austria, and "resolutely" directed to report to a camp on the outskirts of the city.

A day later we disembarked at a railway station on the fringes of Salzburg. The camp, where we had been told to report, was only a short walking distance from the station. As we arrived at the main gate we saw hundreds of people who appeared to be refugees like us, slowly coming from the direction of the station with their belongings, making their way into the facility. To put it mildly, the place looked quite ominous and suspicious, particularly to my father. By word of mouth he had heard of concentration camps but never mentioned a word about them to me. That well-kept secret would shortly end up saving our lives.

In any case, the camp was quite large and made up of multiple extended rows of wooden barracks. It was surrounded by about a fifteen foot high barbed wire fence curved inward at the top, obviously meant to keep people from "leaving." In addition, two armed soldiers were posted at the gate. After being liberated by the French, father told me that the place had probably been a temporary holding area for "undesirables" who later would most likely end up in a concentration camp.

Father and I were among a large group of people as we entered the camp. We had barely gone through the gate when father stopped suddenly. He intuitively sensed danger and wasn't about to be interned voluntarily.

Without looking directly at me, he whispered to me that we would slowly turn around and walk back out of the gate. He also asked me to be as casual as possible in order not to attract any undue attention from the guards. I remember that it all came about so quickly that Father didn't even set down either the suitcase or duffle bag he was carrying. We lucked out simply

In Bregenz, Austria, in 1944

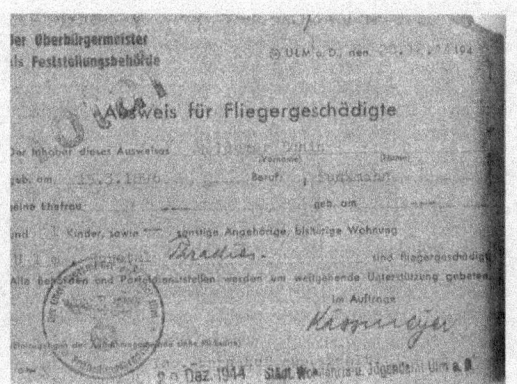

Document certifying that we had been bombed out in Ulm

Document permitting father to work in the shoe factory

Lancaster bomber

Photos from Kalev Ehin's "Coming home"

Ulm after the air raid

because a lot of people were still entering the camp and the sentries weren't paying much attention to what was going on around them.

We walked quickly back to the railway station and boarded the next train headed back to Bregenz. I suppose that father's newly acquired identification paper from Ulm was still working since I don't recall anyone at the station questioning us as to where we were going. As fate would have it, we met an Estonian refugee on the train who was on his way to a small village called Götzig, not far south from Bregenz near the Liechtenstein border. He was going to work in a shoe factory there and suggested to Father that he might also want to seek employment at the same plant when we got to Bregenz.

Father did exactly that when we arrived in Bregenz andfortune continued to smile on us as we once again reported to the employment bureau.The man who out of spite had sent us to Salzburg wasn't there that day andwithout much ado, Father was assigned to work at the shoe factory in theAustrian Alps.

It's amazing how serendipitously and unexpectedly life's major events seem to play themselves out at times.

AND FOR SOME IT WAS ALL TOO MUCH:

Hannes Jürmann: Just remembered another piece of trivia from those days. At one of our temporary accommodations in Schlosshalde we found an artificial aluminium leg with elastic sprung knee in the attic.

We were told that it had belonged to a disabled Estonian ex-soldier who had hung himself. Possibly when the ex-army men were hunted out of DP camps with the help of fellow Estonian administrators.

ANDRES KURRIK
WHEN THE NOISE BEGAN: A CHILDHOOD STORY FROM WW II

The first memories of my childhood go back to the year 1940 when my family lived in Tartu. I clearly remember riding with my parents in a red city bus, the white swans on the pond at Raadi where we visited my aunt who worked at the Estonian Folk Museum there, and repeatedly throwing an orange out of my pram thinking it was a ball to be played with.

That beautiful summer we took the train to Kärkna to spend the summer on my grandparents farm in Sootaga. My first recollection of fear was when we had to walk on a log to cross a ditch on the way to the farm. Once there, my terror was forgotten as I immersed myself in discovering and exploring this exciting new world full of all kinds of animals and machines. Life was beautiful and the world I knew was fascinating and peaceful. Or so it seemed to this 3 year old.

In the realm of a larger world, the Noise had already begun in Europe the year before and my free homeland was on the verge of being annexed by the Soviet Union. My father saw great danger looming for himself and for his family, as he would have been branded by the new masters a triple traitor to the Soviet motherland. First, as an officer in the Tsarist army he had fought against the reds during the Russian revolution. Then he joined the army of the nascent Estonian Republic to fight again against the reds, this time for Estonian freedom. And to top it off, he was an Estonian reserve officer ready to be called to active duty had mobilization been proclaimed. All this was more than enough for a sure ticket to Siberia for himself and his family.

Thanks to his position as secretary and archivist of a church in Tartu, my father was able to do some creative research into our ancestral history and to convince the new Soviet masters that we had some German roots. Thus we were allowed to leave Estonia in the winter of 1941 to resettle in Germany. I still remember that very cold February morning when we were standing on the platform at the Tartu train station waiting to board the train that would take us to Germany. We three children were practically hidden in new sheepskin coats and hats that were many sizes too large to give us "room to grow into", but barely allowed us to move as the coats reached to the ground. Our relatives from the farm had brought us large smoked hams to keep us from starving on the trip and to tidy us over in an unknown future in a new and strange land.

It was only four months later that we - but for the foresight of my father - most likely would have been forced to join the thousands of other Estonians who were herded at gunpoint on trains that took them in the opposite direction, this time without new sheepskin coats and without smoked hams.

In 1944, after a number of temporary stays in various relocation centers in Germany, we were finally settled in Freiburg in an apartment of our own. By now, the adventures of travel and exploration had become a part of my life that I very much enjoyed. Freiburg brought a new aspect to this as I for the first time started going to school. This did not prevent me from using all my free time to explore this colorful historic city. I found a way to do this and at the same time indulge my curiosity for technical matters by befriending the streetcar drivers of Freiburg. Apparently they appreciated my curiosity and reciprocated by allowing me to ride for free, standing next to them and watch all of their actions. I did this for days on end and I was certain that when I grew up I was going to be a streetcar driver myself.

Up to this time, war had been to me a remote abstraction with no apparent adverse impact on my life. Our much relocation I had seen as exciting adventures that everybody should have a chance to enjoy. Occasionally I heard radio news broadcasts of battles in strange places far away from Freiburg and of air raids on cities that had no special meaning for me. My parents did not explain or discuss the war with us children and to me it all seemed as another exciting but normal part of everyday life.

This rose-colored childhood perception was shaken very abruptly on the night of November 27, 1944. I remember this date very well because it was the fifth birthday of my brother Juhan.

During the war foodstuffs were rationed in Germany and by this time had become meager even with ration cards. Father had become friendly with some farmers in Glottertal, a village near Freiburg where we had stayed before moving to the city. Now he used to make forays there to supplement our table. On that November day he had again gone to Glottertal in the early morning.

I myself was again riding the streetcars, this time to the end of the lines in the outer suburbs of Freiburg. I had lost track of time and failed to return home in the usual afternoon hour. I knew that punishment would await me and I strained to find a way to avoid this. Eureka! Father was expected to return home on the late afternoon train. What better way to save my skin than to meet him at the train station and to return home with him! Certainly such a show of affection would impress him and save me from punishment.

I went to the train station and placed myself on the platform where the train from Glottertal would soon arrive. But father did not emerge from the train. Father must have missed this train and would be on the next train later that evening. Or so I hoped. But now it was getting really late and I was in real trouble. Besides, it was getting dusk and I was afraid we would not see each other in the oncoming darkness and the blackout that was rigorously enforced during the war. To make myself visible to father, I decided to sneak home, get a candle, return to the train station, and hold the candle to my face when the train arrived.

When I got home and tried to sneak into our apartment, I was immediately caught by my aunts Helmi and Elly who were living with us. They told me that father had accomplished his foraging early and instead of waiting for the train, had returned to Freiburg by an earlier bus.

Father and mother had planned to go to the movies that evening for the premiere of a long-awaited movie for which they had been able to get rare tickets. When I had not returned home by late afternoon, they became worried and had decided to sacrifice the movie and instead go into town to try to find me. My aunts were left to baby-sit the three other young boys.

It was not long after I had returned home that we heard the pre-alert air raid sirens. Such precautionary pre-alerts were fairly common and indicated that enemy bombers had been detected flying in the general direction of the alerted areas. Once the actual targets were established, those locations were given the full alert, requiring mandatory evacuation into air-raid shelters. A full alert was never given for Freiburg that night.

When we heard the pre-alert, we turned off the lights to peek out from behind the heavy curtains. What we saw was spectacular and ominous: colored "Christmas Trees" drifting slowly down over the city. These were parachute flares dropped by scout planes to mark targets for following bombers. My aunts decided not to wait for the full alert and rushed us all into the communal air raid bomb shelter in the basement of our apartment building. We soon heard explosions that seemed to come from some distance and were muffled by the concrete walls of the air raid shelter.

The "Noise" had finally caught up with me in a real way.

When the pre-alert was sounded, my parents had been walking in the blacked-out old town trying to find me. They wanted to continue to do so, but were persuaded by the sight of the "Christmas Trees" and by a friendly air-raid warden to go into a nearby public air raid shelter. After the raid was over, they emerged to find burning buildings and the streets piled with rubble from the destroyed old town.

In the movie theater my parents had planned to attend, a message was flashed on the screen advising the attendees that a pre-alert had been issued for Freiburg, that evacuation to the air raid shelter was voluntary, and that the movie would be continued until a full alert was given. As it turned out, only about 3 people left the auditorium for the air raid shelter. That theater took a direct hit during the raid, killing all those in attendance in the sold-out house. But for my adventurism, my parents could well have been among them.

That evening was also a close call for myself, as the train station to which I had planned to return, was totally destroyed during the raid

During this phase of the war, the "Noise" was building up to a crescendo, and the inhabitants of larger and more exposed cities were encouraged to relocate at least their families to presumably safer rural area. Numbers published after the war show that after the air raid on Freiburg on November 27, which claimed about 2,800 killed and 9,600 injured, this city experienced a reduction of its population by almost a half, from previously more than 101,000 to around 58,000.

My parents decided to become part of this exodus and to move further away from the Allied air bases to the west and from the front that was moving closer to the French-German border near Freiburg. We were able to put our belongings and ourselves on a train that headed for Ulm, at the Württemberg-Bavarian border, another historic city that had so far escaped bombing. In Ulm we were temporarily assigned to a transient hotel near the railway station. Eventually we were sent for more permanent lodgings to Herrlingen, a small village not far from Ulm.

We had not been in Herrlingen for more than a few days when the Noise continued with another big bang. It was on the evening of December 17 that we observed a flaming red sky and flashes of explosions coming from the direction of Ulm. **To me it was an exciting spectacle, the kind of which I had never seen before. Little did I realize the suffering and devastation that was being visited upon the victims of this spectacle.**

As we later found out, the transient hotel where we had stayed only a short while ago had taken a direct hit, with a loss of life of everybody who had stayed there. **After the Noise was over and I was able to safely roam the spectacular devastation of Ulm, I saw the large crater where our transient hotel had stood.**

A final and perhaps the most personal encounter with the Noise took place in Herrlingen in early 1945 just before the end of the war. I was just on the verge of turning 8 when, on a bright and sunny day, I was playing in a green meadow across the road from the house on the edge of Herrlingen where we had been lodged in the attic.

All of a sudden I saw a single-engined plane approaching low from the distance directly toward me. I was certain the plane was coming for me, an easy target with my bright yellow shirt standing out against the green grass. I flung myself to the ground, desperately trying to hide in the short grass. Sure enough, I heard the rat-tat-tat of gunfire as the plane flew over me. Only after the plane had disappeared and I got up did I realize that not I had been the target, but a truck that was just passing on the road behind me. The truck was carrying some passengers who were standing in the open back – a common mode of travel in those days. Apparently the only casualty of this attack was a German soldier who - I was later told – had his head blown off. I saw he woman who had been standing next to him when she came into our house to clean off the blood that had splattered over her black coat.

And then the Noise ended. But this stone that had not grown any moss kept on rolling. First into the UNRRA refugee camp for Estonians in Geislingen as a DP (Displaced Person): Then being "screened" out from the camp by UNRRA because we were not considered refugees (we had left Estonia "too early"): Then kindness of the Estonian camp managers who continued us on rations and allowed us three boys to stay in the Estonian school. Then readmittance "into the fold" as Dps by the apparently more liberal UNRRA team in Aschaffenburg. The closing of that camp a year later and transfer to the camp in Kempten: Closing of that camp after another year and transfer to another camp in the remnants of the former German air base in Memmingen. The end of an era when IRO (the former UNRRA) closed its doors and turned over the remaining remnants of its former DP wards to the German government. German high school for which I was not able to develop a liking:

After I had turned 16 I left home to work in the Labor Service of the US Army in Ettlingen, then Worms, then Mannheim. One had to be at least 18 to qualify. I had given my age as 17 and was told in effect: close enough for government work – you will be 18 next year! Apparently no close background checks in those days.

When I finally – and really – turned 18 two years later, I rolled on by myself to the USA, leaving my parents and my four siblings back in Memmingen.

But that is a story for another

BOMBINGS:

Ilvi Joe: Re Kalev Ehin's comments: Kalev's comments on the bombing of Ulm by the British Air Force makes me wonder whether I wasn't at the same barracks (kaserne) years later (early 1950) when the camp in Geislingen was closed and we were transferred to a former German military base on the outskirts of Ulm.

I do recall the destruction in the city (had to go there several times, because our mother was hospitalized in Ulm), but the cathedral (did it not have the tallest steeple in Germany - at least in the southern part?) stood unharmed.

The base had a swimming pool, neglected and filled with dirty water. I recall clearly when some of the camp residents on a warm spring day gathered around the pool and one man dove to the bottom, found the plug, and pulled it. The pool was drained, cleaned and filled with clean water. It became the center of community life in the summer and that's when and where I learned to swim, taught by a veteran who had lost one foot at the war.

Regarding the Allied bombing, I'm sure many of us met later in the US men who recalled their bombing raids over Germany and we've had to tell them that we were below, trying to stay alive.

Then, in another context, more than 10 years ago I joined my good friend from Indiana University graduate studies days (a professor emerita of music residing in Colorado) to walk in Bach's footsteps on the 250th anniversary of his death. We visited his childhood home in Eisenach, now a museum, and there were on display photos of the bombed house with an explanation of when it was hit by Allied bombing. My friend exclaimed: "I didn't know we bombed Bach's house!" I said to her that much of history we did not know about is gradually seeing the light of day now that the Cold War is over.

Postscript by Mai.
And such occurrences were not absent in Australia. Perhaps the perspective is a little different because Oz is a once British colony: Dunkirk a place where many Australians lost their lives when deployed to Britain's aid. Their families would have found the presence of Germanic names painful. Yes, the obstetrician who delivered my sons lost his father in that heavenly hell.

I recall at a clinical meeting, some years ago, sitting opposite a colleague with whom I had always related well. Somehow the conversation turned to the Allied bombing: Indeed he had been in one of those crews.

With a mischievous grin I remarked "So you were one of the guys who lit up our skies with those fireworks decades ago". He was taken aback and we chatted on: In cold hard reality he was far worse off than we were. We had permission to run to safety if any could be found: He could not desert his fearful post.

We still relate well.

STAYING IN TOUCH WHILE THE WAR CONTINUES TO RAGE

Our folk fled from Estonia with a instinctive determination to return to there as soon as it was safe: Eesti Sõna (Estonian Word) began its publication in late 1944. It related the ongoing terror in Estonia and of Moscow's agents trying to persuade our folk to return from Sweden to Estonia. Of course that time was never to come again until 1991 when Estonia again became free. We littlies, too understood what was amiss in simpler terms of goodies and baddies and empathized with our families.

But while we remained in limbo, life needed to continue and a Estonian News sheet was published in Danzig. In it were many contact points where our folks could obtain help from the local hierarchies, and other useful information. Indeed it is on opening this document last year that I for the first time in my life knew what the hieroglyphics of the remaining half of an old envelope, still among my memorabilia, pertained to.

WHERE THERE IS A WILL THERE IS A WAY: DETERMINATION COUNTS: PÖ

HANNES JÜRMANN
STORMOVIKS

This is Hannes' reply to some curious imagery I had alluded to in the e-mail dialogues: Of three winged airplanes, waship s being built out of what seemed to be Lego blocks and soldiers coming on shore an dtaking things off children. I was perplexed at the notion of three winged planes. MM

From reading war books I know the Stormovik was a heavily armored ground attack monoplane There was a Lagg biplane fighter and the Germans gave Estonian pilots a biplane bomber with which to perform night raids over the Estonian border against the Russians.

I think it was some kind of Fokker. Our family friend Hans Aschendorf (who I think was in charge of Tartu Rail transport where father was a doctor) gave me a wooden model of a biplane with German markings. He was 2 m tall and after release from Russian prison camp, joined the new Wehrmacht. Mum corresponded with him and his wife from Australia.

I can remember being on the freighter from Tallinn. We were on the first level below the deck camped on the floor with blankets and belongings. When going up the stairs onto the deck, the guard with sub-machine gun gave me and Peeter some chocolate. Apparently he was to stop anyone from venturing on deck when there was an air raid warning. We stopped at Libau (?) and had to clear the removable floor to the hold, from which artillery pieces were hoisted to shore. I had the task of carrying mum's expensive Italian violin and Peeter was in charge of my teddy bear, which my son Brett now has.

From Estonia, I found that the storage building at our Nõo (pertaining to nõgu or hollow) farm was exactly as I remembered, a red stone building. I asked the locals why it was that most of the Estonian place names were in the possessive case. Friend Eeva suggested it could be because in the old times the name was followed by the word town or village – sounds reasonable.

All signs of grandfather's retirement cottage he built at the edge of the farm land, had completely vanished. I remembered grandfather teaching me to play the harmonica there and have been able to do it ever since.

Father had leave from near Narva (at Jõhvi) and came to grandfather's cottage. He and grandfather practised shooting with a pistol he wanted to leave with grandfather (mother's father). I got into trouble for trying to cock one of the pistols by pushing the hammer on grandmother's table.

I had my first dose of tonsillitis there in the autumn of '44 while we were digging a bomb shelter trench with grandfather. Before departure, we visited aunt Helga (buried at Geislingen – breast cancer 1950) and father's mother at Nõmme, south of Tallinn.

When we visited the locality in 2001 it was just as I remembered it. Due to aircraft engine problems, I did not get any sleep for over 36 hours before arrival on that visit. Due to that and years of fear about escaping horrible conditions in Estonia, and our inevitable deportation to Siberia, that I felt most uneasy about being in Estonia. It wasn't helped by frequently hearing Russian spoken and the decaying buildings around Tallinn. I felt trapped. It took me some time to relax. Just shows how sleep deprivation can affect the mind.

Hans Aschendorf is long dead. Mum had been writing to his wife, and after her death I tried to correspond with his wife. However, it was mostly small-talk and a major task for my limited German, so it ceased after 12 months. Es war mir eine grosse Schwierigheit! My RAAF friend Dieter Ableitner and I play around with German terms and phrases when we call each other. He had forgotten a lot but has made a point of re-learning his German and is much better at it than I.

AND OTHER PLANES

(Arne Ellermets) I am very familiar with the Junkers aircraft. From the time I was 10 years old in 1941 until 1944 my brother Heiki and I spent much time on my grandfather's small farm abut 10 miles from Tallinn, Estonia. The farm was on the edge of a forest and directly under the flight path to the Tallinn Airport. The JU 52's made multiple daily approaches and flew low over the farm while German forces occupied our home country!

In 1943/4 the bombing of Tallinn became a routine trip for Russian bombers. We were once again under the flight path. One of those aircraft must have run into trouble since it dropped its bombs before reaching Tallinn. They fell on the small community of farms, one of which belonged to my grandpa. The bombs hit in a plowed field and became a "Sehenswürdigkeit", loosely translated as "something worth seeing". People from the neighborhood came to see the bomb craters. Actually there wasn't much to see since the craters were no larger than good size swimming pools!

ANTS TAMM
AN ANT TRAVELLING IN EUROPE

My father was a businessman, a sales manager at Oskar Kilgas Trikoo, pitsi ja sukuvabrikus.(Lace and hosiery factory)

He had been married once before he married my mother, to a Polish lady named Claudia. He divorced her because she could not give him a child. My father bought her a hat boutique in Helsingi, but she did not like the place, so she sold it and bought another shop in Stockholm.

My aunt told me about her after her death. My mother had forbidden her to tell me about Claudia. People are odd in many ways.

My aunt visited her many times and even when she was dying she held a diamond ring in her hand and cried out for my father Morits. Unbelievable!

My father met my mother in Pärnu. She had become Miss Pärnu. He saw her photo in some shop and went to my grandmother with roses and asked her if he could take her daughter out. Father was somewhat well known, and my grandmother was somewhat "worn out" with my mother, Ira, then 17 years old. Ira smoked and dated boys and so on, so my grandmother said "yes". I believe that my mother was not pleased at first, my aunt however was. Regardless, mother and father married and they lived in Tallinn.

They had to flee, in Estonia, during the first Soviet occupation. My father had been an honoured freedom fighter during the independence war. He was one of the famous Kuperjanov battalion soldiers. I know that my grandfather and grandmother were distressed when they understood the predicament. However he fought one year, got hurt and survived.

The Russians aimed to shoot him during the occupation. They looked for him. He was also a member of Kodukaitse. (Home guard).

They hid in Nõmme.

When the Russians fled in 1941 my family moved back to our house. Father had to renovate everything, the house was truly a mess. The Russians had used it as an office and living quarters for Russian authorities; people without European manners.

When the Russians occupied Estonia the real hell broke loose. Everything was forbidden. My parents hid in the countryside, many relatives were shot dead, jailed or sent to Gulags. It was a terrible and unbelievable time.

Then the Germans entered.

Our family got their houses back, our relatives got their farm back, our media friends started to work again. They were not Nazis, but of course very careful with what and how they wrote.

"As long as I did not write bad things about Nazis and Hitler, I could more or less write whatever I liked, even bad things about the Germans in Russia", said Peep Kärp, a journalist, now deceased.

My father had to renovate his houses and the Germans asked if they could rent the empty rooms for offices: the Russians, as one expected had stolen everything.

Life did not change to normal, but compared to the Communist time, it became more or less "normal".

Estonians were not pleased with the German occupation, they had their doubts about Hitler's further ideas, about national socialism, but like the Finns they said, "Everything is better than the big devil Stalin, even a 'light' devil."

I was born in Oct. 1942 in Pärnu during the "Calm period", but we lived in Tallinn.

My mother got very ill when she gave birth to me, and during my first six month I lived with my aunt. Her name was Tatiana/Tanja Klaassen, who owned the Pärnu bakery and a farm in Sindi.

You (MM) wrote to me that you lived in Pärnu your first years. I found your house on Google, it´s barred just now, but the odd and funny thing is that I lived just some hundreds of meters from that house in the "Valge Villa", owned by my mother's sister.

We spent summer 43 and 44 at my mother's childhood home, just some hundred meters from the sea, near the famous "Rannahotel". My mother's father was a director at the Russian gümnaasium. He was not Russian but he was orthodox. Before the so called "revolution" he was a school inspector in various parts of Estonia and even for some time in the environment of Moscow.

He is the only person I know who was chased by a wolf pack, when he was travelling through a wood near Moscow, with my grandmother and my aunt Tanja, in a sleigh, drawn by two horses. He killed a wolf with whip, the other wolves stopped and ate the dead wolf, and grandfather managed to save their lives.

My uncle was in the German army. Not willingly, but he was proud until his death that he had defended Estonia against the reds and of course his hope was to free Estonia. But we know now, that it was not Hitler's intention.

I left Tallinn 22 September 1944 with my parents, aboard the ship Nordstern and arrived two days later at Gotenhafen which is now situated in Poland.

The boat was shelled by Russian aeroplanes and the deck was full of dead people. Of course my mother was very scared; my father too of course, but my mother was more angry at an Estonian lady who had stolen my potty, and when she met the lady in New York many years later, she did not say hello.

From Gotenhafen we went by train towards Germany. Many refugees were on their way to Dresden, and so were we. We were in Dresden during the bombing in February 1945.

My mother's brother, George, had fled from the German army and was together with us. My father discovered that he had kept his military gun. My father threw it away immediately. George was just an eighteen years young boy, and he wanted to defend us against SS or Gestapo.

He went to the Estonian Gümnaasium in Geislingen and then to university. My father paid for him.

In Berlin my mother showed a lot of guts. We had German occupation money with us and my mother went to a railway station to by a cheap ticket and to pay with big occupation time note.

The clerk said, "no you cannot use that money here...and so on". My mother yelled: "BUT OUR FÜHRER, ADOLF HITLER PROMISES.. and so on". She got her ticket and the money was changed to "Reichmarks".

We stayed in Dresden for some months and the Estonians there started a little theatre and my mother, who was a leather artist, got some work with a publisher. What, my father did I don't know.

I don't know how long we stayed in Berlin, but father tried all the time to get in touch with the American or English forces; but the Germans wanted refugees nearby, so they could hide behind them and made it difficult for them to leave.

We ended up in Flensburg, Hitler was dead and Dönitz surrendered.

The war was over.
When Dönitz surrendered in Flensburg we where there, or we came soon after. Herr Kommendant phoned my father -it sounds very civilized- and asked him to come to Geislingen where he and an architect friend were staying: I believe his name was Liiband, and he had a firm building bridges and manufacturing concrete. My father went to the English authorities in Flensburg and asked for permission to go to Geislingen, but it was denied.

Kommendant wished to employ my father as a salesman for bridges in Germany. Most of the bridges there were of course destroyed, therefore it was, of course, a good plan. My father spoke German fluently. Kommendant had good relations with the Americans, so it seemed viable.

The Americans could not help my father so he devised an original idea.

He hired a railroad wagon for goods; he wrote Geislingen on the wagon, and I and my father, mother and my mother's brother, Ossi moved on. Ossi built a stove so we could cook, but it began to burn.

I liked the journey very much and got "mad" when it was over. So I am told anyhow.

At every stop my father asked the railroad workers where we were, they told him, and nobody called the military police. And one day they said "Geislingen".

In Geislingen we moved in with the Kommendant family and my father started his "bridgework". The house we lived in belonged to a former Nazi who was probably jailed.

My grandmother left Estonia on the Moero a medical troop ship, as did her sister Olja who worked as a nurse on it.

She had been a teacher of mathematics and Estonian language. She told us the story this treacherous journey when we were teenagers. We believed her, she was very religious and she never lied: Nor did her sister Olja.

Olja had been a hospital nurse and she had seen terrible things in a sanatorium in the south of Finland during the communist "revolution". She never told us, but she told grandmother who told us when we were grown up. She was very religious too. She really believed that one can talk to God!? When my father died, I was thirteen years old, she said; "No Ants, you cannot read comic stories now. Read the Bible or talk to God!" Sic!.

Well. While on the Moero she went to the WC. When she sat there the bombs began falling. She said to God, if you let me die here, I will never forgive you."

Bang, everything was blown up and she found herself swimming and she said: "Thank you God."

In Sweden she continued as Metropolite Alexanders assistant: That she was in Tallinn too.

Yes, now onto Geislingen. One day there came a delegation from Geislingen Estonian refugee camp and asked my father if he would be the camps "politsei chef"? Well he said "yes" Given my father was in Kuperjanovs battalion during the war of liberation in Geislingen he became one of the leaders of the refugee camp. His name was Morits Tamm.

After that he had nothing to do with Kommendants firm, but they where best friend until my father's death in New York 1955.

I lived in Geislingen 1945 to 1948, but I am not mentioned in the book WNE.

In one photo some children are "building" a little "house". I believe that I am the blond boy on the roof. The boy, half laying on the ground is Jüri Kommendant I believe. He was my best friend in Geislingen, he disappeared in Vietnam during the Vietnam war, (*correction -Ado was lost in the Vietnam Campaign-MM), and if the other person on the roof is a girl, it must be Merike Kommendant, whom I have been looking for several times without any luck. I know she became an architect.

My best friends there were Ado, Jüri and Merike Kommendant. Ado was a pilot in American Air Force and was lost on duty while in Vietnam. Ado had the appropriate military funeral in USA in 2013 when his fate was confirmed. We came to Geislingen in summer 1945, and I lived there to 1948.

We lived together with the Kommendant-family in a rather big house. After that we moved to a house near "tondiloss", (ghost castle): Father hired or bought a house "above the railroad", along the path of "tondi loss".

I have many photos and I have visited Geislingen once and looked at the houses we lived in. Our friends in Geislingen was the Kommendant and the Liband families, as I remember. My first love was Maimo, but unfortunately she was twice my age.

My parents divorced and I and my mother went to Sweden in 1948 and my father went to New York when the refugee camp closed some years later.

I believe that the best part of my childhood was in Geislingen. The rock climbing, the ice-cold mountain lakes, the Geislingen theatre, sailing at Bodensee in summertime, my playmates: everything was great as I remember it or they told me.

In 1948 I was told that we should visit my mother's parents and sister in Sweden some weeks. They had fled from Pärnu in a little boat.

I was not pleased to leave Geislingen but I had of course no say in that decision.

It was a good trip and we reached Helsingför, the city where Hamlet said "To be or not to be?".

I do not know why, but suddenly I felt very unhappy, and it soon became apparent, that we would not return to Geislingen. My father and mother had divorced, due to some kind of affair she had with somebody and therefore we stayed in Uppsala with my grandparents in a small flat and I rapidly understood that we where political refugees in a frequently hostile environment.

When I started school my first teacher said: "Now we have Nazi kids here." She did not know that I already spoke fluently "kidswedish".

When the teacher called me a "Nazi kid", my mother got angry and contacted a lawyer, who, curiously, had the same name as we did; Tamm.

The strange thing is that the name Tamm in Sweden is a noble one,

Our house which we shared with the Kommendants.

1945 or 46.
From left Ado Kommendant, Merike and Jüri and me.

My mother and me and Merike and Jüri with their mother. 1948

My father and me 1948.

so all the Swedes with that name are members of the "knight order", and are socializing for example with the royal family.

The lawyer found it amusing and contacted the school and I have no idea what followed, but the "Nazi kid" bit came to an end.

Uppsala was a workers and student city, and after the war it was very "left wing", not to say, a communist city. I have later understood that my uncle and many Estonian students fought with their fists against communists now and then and, as you know, many Baltic people left Sweden because of the Swedish socialists and communists.

I believe we stayed because we had so many relatives and friends in Sweden and I suppose we where not afraid of the actions of Swedish government.

My mother, uncle and aunt found good jobs more or less immediately. My grandpa and grandmother worked for some time too: my grandfather in an archive and my grandmother in a restaurant, called "FLUSTRET" , in the kitchen.

By the way, when I had grown up, more or less all my teacher colleges told me, that they have had some Estonian classmates, and they where often "best in the class". And I know just one who became a little bit criminal, stealing a car, but he calmed down. (One swallow doesn't make a summer- an Oz saying: Mai)

So Estonians living in Sweden today have a very good reputation among the Swedes. But many Swedes have fallen for the Soviet and Russian propaganda and they believe that many Estonians in Estonia are fascist, and the Swedish communist are saying that all the time. (As happens in many countries, such as in South America:)

I was not very fond of school. Football, swimming, movies, reading stories and playing were my interests. Unfortunately, so to say, my grandparents were teachers, so I was asked EVERY day about school.

Daytime I went to the ordinary Swedish school, three or four evenings to Estonian school and always homework, homework and homework. And when I was totally uninterested, came extra lessons.

My grandmother was very religious, so some Saturdays and Sundays I had to accompany her and grandpa to church. Grandpa joined us to the orthodox ceremony where he sang in the choir and some relative was the priest, but grandma said: "Your father was very religious, but he was Lutheran, so you have visit that church too". So she took me there too, so first an Orthodox ceremony and the day after a Lutheran ceremony. I am not religious at all today.

The years in school were what they were. I was not the brightest in my class but not the dumbest either.

The school holidays were my haven and strangely   enough even when I was a teacher, although I liked my job, the holidays were my lure, until I got my pension.

Me and Jüri Kommendant. I am at the right. Christmas 1946 or 47.

Such was the typical refugee/ DP accommodation of the times: Note the sparse furnishings etc. MM

HELLE PUUPILL/GIREY
MY MEMORIES FROM THE END OF THE WAR

On September 22, 1944, at an age of six, I became a refugee.

These are my memories, as seen through the eyes of a child. I am convinced that a child's mind is programmed to protect itself from the horrors around her - remembering some scenes, forgetting others, and interpreting events with the child's understanding of the moment.

I remember leaving Paide for Tallinn, in the dark, in a German army truck with my mother and one suitcase. My father was with the Estonian army fighting against the invading Russian army. The Russian front was so close that the trains had stopped running, and our only way to the port of Tallinn was with the retreating German army.

My parents had decided that if the worst was to happen, that each would try to leave Estonia independently. The only toy I was able to bring was a small wind up frog that I made jump on the bench in the truck. I don't remember what happened to the frog.

The next memory is the chaos of the harbor with thousands of potential refugees, all trying to find a spot on the last few ships leaving for Germany. The Russian army was only hours away, and I sensed the urgency to get away. I remember the bombing of Tallinn. My mother and I crouched under a railway car during the raid as hundreds of Russian planes darkened the sky and the sound of exploding bombs filled the air. My fear was not of being hit by a bomb, but of the train starting to move!

My mother had found a spot for us on RO2 (not RO22) next to MOERO, a German infirmary ship taking wounded German soldiers back home. My mother had learned that many Estonian military families were also on Moero, and she went to ask the captain if we could also board this nice looking white ship. The captain reassured my disappointed mother that the ships would leave in convoy, and for us to stay where we had a space. We did not leave in convoy, and MOERO was sunk where over 600 perished. My mother's favorite saying until her death at age 97 was "you never know what something is good for!"

I have few memories of the sailing - they had mattresses on the floor for the children, and I played with other children.

Gotenhafen, Germany, was another chaotic moment with hundreds of refugees arriving. My mother left me to guard our suitcase as she went to find out our next destination. My mother owned a coat with a mink collar. Next to our suitcase stood a couple with their belongings and a coat with a mink collar. When they were ready to leave, I took hold of her coat, insisting that it was my mother's, and would not let go of it. My mother returned to a very angry woman, who told my mother to teach me between our belongings and those of strangers.

The German Red Cross fed the children some kind of porridge, and we were moved to barracks where we had to undergo the humiliating process of delousing. They should have also sprayed the straw mattresses, as the cockroaches were having a field day!

We were moved to a camp outside Berlin, where we could get passes to visit the city between the air raids.

I have two distinct memories of Berlin – watching a young strapping man approach us and recognizing him to be my 21 year old cousin Harald Laupa. He knew that his father (my mother's brother) had also escaped but did not know his whereabouts.

The second memory was being told by the German police to stand against the wall, as the Führer was coming down the road. Hitler was on a flatbed truck, yelling into a loudspeaker. I did not understand what he said, but I do remember his high pitched voice, and the crowd cheering "Heil Hitler." With the typical Estonian stubbornness, I remember being taught to say "ei ütle" which sounds close enough to Heil Hitler, but means "I won't say".

From Berlin we were moved to Trautenau at the Czech border. Daily bombings by the Allied troops have resulted in my never watching war movies – why bring back horrible memories?

Russian army again advanced and we moved to southern Germany to the village of Waal. The train that we travelled on was bombed (strafed) by planes, and I remember running in the pine forest and lying down by a big tree. My mother covered my body with hers. No one was hurt, the locomotive was demolished, and the train car was filled with bullet holes, one had struck some-ones feather quilt, and our car was filled with feathers. Again something for us children to play with!

In Waal we had an unheated room at a farmhouse (it was winter). I started school in first grade, not really speaking

German. The school was very strict and if there was an infraction, the penalty was a whipping on the knuckles with a switch. I was hit once, since I turned to look at a child behind me. Never did that again!

One day in the spring there was some furious shooting, couple of larger ammunition explosions and the American Army was entering the village. My mother was somewhere standing in a food line, and I was playing with German children. We were handed little American flags and were told to wave the flags at the tanks entering the village.

The soldiers walked next to the tanks and handed candies to the children. The soldier that approached me was very black, and since I had never seen a Negro in my life, I ran screaming back to the farmhouse. This moment has haunted me to this day, as I would like to say to that man "Thank you."

The German army supply train was stopped in Waal, and the villagers were told to go and take anything they wanted. The train carried butter and blue cheese. My mother borrowed a wheel barrow and came back with a barrel of butter (blue cheese was not familiar to us and smelled unpleasant). I remember my cousin cutting our rationed bread with surgical precision into very thin slices and then adding a slab of butter to it. He was a growing young man, and he was always hungry.

At that time the refugee camps were set up by United Nations Relief and Rehabilitation Administration (UNRRA) and we were moved to Augsburg (Hoffeld camp) in Southern Germany. This was to be my home for the next four and half years. Although we were foreigners in a foreign land, we were surrounded by our own people, and we could develop the sense of self within that society.

The camp consisted of grey three story apartment buildings that had been used by the German railroad workers. Our apartment had a kitchen, bathroom, and three rooms. Three families lived there, each had their own room, and shared the kitchen.

The first job for the adults was to set up schools for the children. Many adults wanted to help, and we ended up with artists teaching drawing, professional musicians teaching singing, and university professors teaching math and history to elementary school children.

Our first year class was held in an unheated attic, we had no paper or books, but used slate boards for our first efforts at writing. Things did improve and we had a heated room and also paper and pencils, most likely provided by refugee aid groups in United States.

I remember more about playing than I do about school. Math was easy and fun for me and I was an avid reader. Since there were very few children's books in Estonian, I read any adult book that I could put my hands on. One of my favorite ones was the translated copy of "Gone with the Wind." I don't remember learning about history, but I do have an elementary book of history still on my bookshelf – therefore we must have had that subject. Foreign languages consisted of German and English. German I had learned playing with children before the end of war, English was new but did not seem very difficult

We had heard that father was alive, and also in Germany, but most likely in a prisoner of war camp. My mother was determined to find him, but since travel across different occupation zones was very difficult, she had to find a spot for me.

I had suffered through a bad bout with whooping cough, and the doctors found a "shadow" on my lung (not sure what that meant). I was placed into a TB sanatorium and my mother went searching for my father. I was in the same room with another Estonian girl, Inna-Leena, I remember that her head had to be lowered, and mine raised, so our beds were placed next to each other so that we could see each other.

 I do remember the walks that we had to take in the pine forest surrounding the sanatorium, in rain and in sunshine. We were given grey hooded capes of various sizes to wear – some came to our ankles, others just mid thigh. A Catholic priest visited the children and I remember him bringing a goldfish bowl. He also gave us small religious icons – I still have the one of St. George killing the dragon! Inna-Leena lives in San Francisco, and we keep in contact with each other.

Mother found father in a POW camp in the English zone, and somehow was able to get him out of there and back to Augsburg. I remember crying when I was told that I had to leave the hospital, we were having such a good time!

Children are so creative – I remember the toys that we were able to make, since we had no store bought toys, but we certainly did not suffer because of that. We made animals out of acorns and chestnuts – whole farms with fences and barns from wood scraps and stones. Someone had given us a bag of marbles, and they became our kings and queens and ladies in waiting. We built houses in boxes for our royalty, with furniture and curtains. I do remember getting into trouble when I found my mother's sanitary napkin box, and I used the outer cover to make curtains and the soft inner part for mattresses! Needless to say my mother was not amused.

When the spring rain brought out the first snails, they became our toys. I am constantly surprised at how patient and giving the adults around us were. Snails do crawl out of boxes and end up in someone else's room.

Some excitement was available from the abandoned German military equipment that was sent to an equipment graveyard not far from the camp. This was an area supposedly out of bounds for the children, since there was the danger of some unexploded ammunition. Do you know that an unlocked tank turret makes for a wonderful merry-go-round? All you need to do is to climb up on the tank gun and wrap your arms around it, and get someone else to push the whole turret around.

Some close calls did happen. Ain was my age, our families were old friends, and we lived in the same building. Ain found a grenade, and like boys everywhere, they were going to see if it still worked. The plan was to pull the pin and throw the grenade against a bombed out building near us. I tagged along, but at the last minute chickened out and ran for home. Just at the apartment door I heard the "boom," obviously it was a live grenade.

Another "boys will be boys" episode was when Ain discovered that the American army metal gasoline cans had a few drops of gasoline in them. These containers were scattered all around in the fields near by. He carefully collected a small amount of gasoline in the can, and then lit a straw by the opening. When he arrived at our door and was asking urgently for his mother, my mother did not understand why his face was so red, until she saw that he had no eyebrows and no hair over his forehead.

Food was rationed, but we all had enough to survive. Our family status improved when my father's aunt and uncle in New Jersey found our names on the refugee list and started to send us care packages.

We did not understand why they sent us boxes of cereal, as we did not have milk, and the crispy cereals were not familiar to us. No food was to be wasted and my mother lined them up dutifully on a shelf.

One day the box had been damaged and out poked something red – a package of cigarettes! Mailing cigarettes from US was not allowed. We opened our cereal boxes, and each one contained a package of cigarettes. We were suddenly very wealthy, as for cigarettes you could trade anything else – fresh fruit, milk, meat, or a pair of shoes. The most desirable items were cigarettes, coffee and soap - in that order.

The adults organized themselves into committees, dealing with cleaning the streets, handing out relief food and clothing, starting choirs (Estonians are a singing nation), setting up youth groups such as girl scouts and boy scouts, sport teams – volley ball and basket ball were popular, policing the camp area, and voicing the objection to the barbaric overtaking of Estonia by Soviet Union.

The feeling of the adults was that our condition as refugees was temporary, and that soon we would be able to return to our homeland. No one would have believed that it would take almost 50 years before the Estonian blue, black and white flag was again seen on top of the Pikk Herman tower in Tallinn.

The social life among the refugees continued, as it had been in Estonia. Parties were held in family rooms, alcohol was secretly distilled, some form of food was prepared (I think my mother learned how to cook with dry cereal!).

I have fond memories of lying in my bed that seated many of our guests at the other edge, listening to discussions and

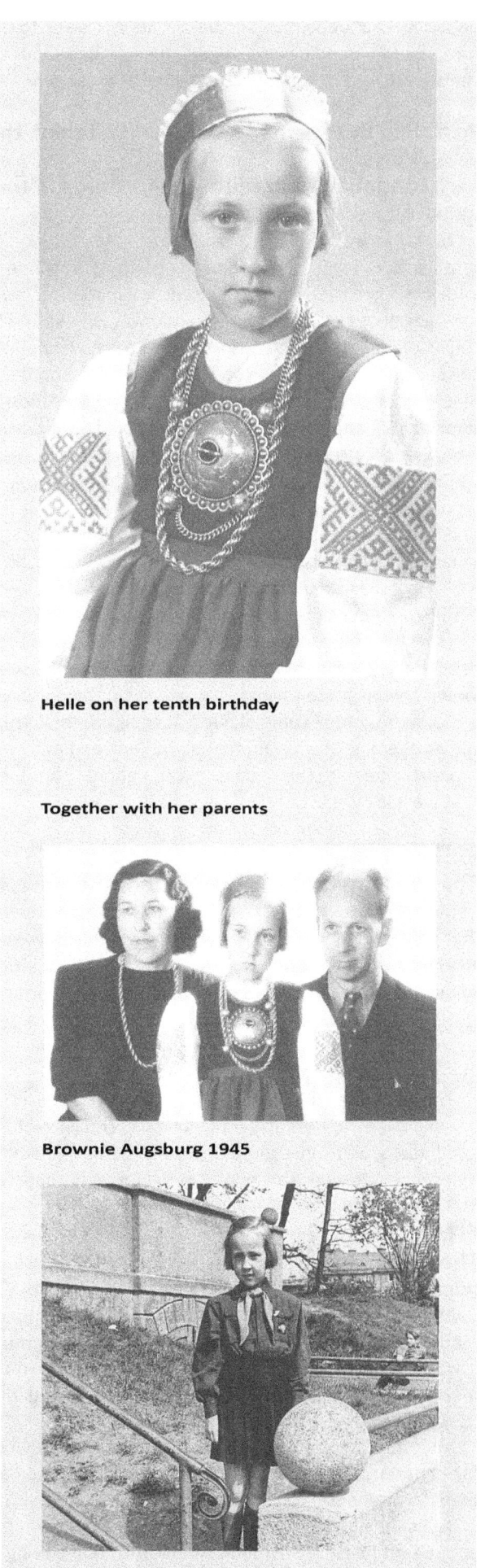

Helle on her tenth birthday

Together with her parents

Brownie Augsburg 1945

arguments about politics, and then drifting to sleep to the sounds of old Estonian songs. The parties seemed to have this format, always ending with singing, many songs about the longing for freedom or returning to our homeland. I am sure there were also many secret tears shed at those times.

To a child this seemed a normal life, I think they adjust very quickly to change.

I am continually amazed at the fortitude of the adults, as they carried the memories of what was left behind, including parents, siblings and friends.

My father's sister, mother and father were left in Viljandi. My mother's mother (father was deceased) stayed at the farm in Järva Jaani, of her surviving brothers, Johannes was with us in Augsburg, August and Rudolf stayed in Estonia with their families, Alfred was sent to Siberia (or shot before making it that far). No one has been able to find out anything about him. My cousin Harald was with us and his brother Hillar was killed at age 17 fighting the Soviets.

For the first couple of years we did not know about the fate of our families, but then slowly methods were devised to send information using coded words and descriptive phrases to let people know about our whereabouts.
Since father was in Estonian army and was listed for deportation by the Soviets, we did not dare to write directly to our family, as all letters were opened and it could have caused serious consequences to our relatives. The letters that arrived from Estonia often had carefully cut sentences removed and the paper resembled a lacy doily!

Grandmother's farm was taken over by the Soviet collective farm system. All the buildings were razed, except part of the farmhouse proper, and grandmother lived there until a few years before her death at age 89. How she managed, I do not understand, as she had to heat the house with wood (that needed to be chopped) and the water came from a well. At the same time she could grow some vegetables, potatoes, and possibly still had some berry bushes for jams. Her sons tried to bring her to Tallinn, but she declined steadfastly any move out of her beloved farmhouse. I am sure that my uncles were helping her with some of the work around the house, but they were two hours drive from the farm, did not own a car, and that meant a slow trip by train.

I saw the house location from a distance two years ago.- There is a slight rise where the farm used to be, and you can see parallel rows of old trees that used to align the road leading to the farm. As someone interested in archaeology, I would love to get to the property and see if there are any house foundations left.

My mother took some of our belongings to the farm, to protect them from possible bombing attacks in the city, and buried them, in the dream that all this will end and we will be living happily ever after! Therefore somewhere on the property there are the remains of her national costume, hand embroidered tablecloths, and all the best photo albums that we had.

GEISLINGEN

The camp in Augsburg was closed, and the refugees were moved to Geislingen. This was a small town in the hills of Southern Germany. To my eyes the hills were big mountains – it was in 1984 that I returned to Germany and drove through Geislingen, and realized the hills were really very modest is size.

The refugees were housed in sections of residential homes that had been commandeered by the American occupation forces. The Germans had to leave everything in their homes except their personal belongings.

Needless to say the refugees were despised by the Germans, but theirs was the fate of the losers in a war. On the way to school in the winter, German children threw snow balls at us, but they added rocks into the snowballs for effect. We learned to run fast, and dodge the snowballs.

The hills were our main playground – we made secret spaces under roots of trees and rock formations. We developed a secret code (no idea how that worked!), and left notes for each other in the code. Somehow we knew about cowboys and Indians, and some games involved chases and ambushes. Even at this difficult time, for children this was a time of innocence. We were able to play in the forest for hours at end, with no fear of abductions or killings.

ULM

The camp at Geislingen was closed, and we were moved to a temporary camp in Ulm. This was a former German military camp.

The space was limited to large rooms that a number of families shared. The use of blankets and sheets provided a modest amount of privacy. I have two memories of the stay in Ulm – there was a swimming pool (no shallow end – as it was meant for military training), where we learned to swim. We would hold on to the side of the pool, let go for a moment, paddle like crazy, and as we started to go under, grab hold of the side again. I presume we had adults present during these times, but I do not remember them.

My other memory of Ulm was a little black and white kitten that I had found somewhere. I fashioned a sand box for him/her and was responsible for getting new soil for it every day. The kitten's name was Miki. A kitten does not understand the division of space by blankets, and Miki moved freely from one family area to another.

Again the patience and understanding of other adults amazes me at this time. I don't remember anyone complaining about a cat being in the room, and I recall people bringing over food scraps to feed my pet. When we left Ulm, I had to leave Miki behind.

Our next move was to Sweden. My parents wanted to immigrate to United States where my father's aunt and uncle lived, but since father had fought against the Soviets (who were allies to United States) with the German army (who were enemies of the United States) we were refused entry visas to United States.

The next choice was Canada, but Canadians were not taking refugees from Germany. Sweden was accepting refuges from Germany, and Canada was taking refugees from Sweden. Therefore, we immigrated to Sweden, from there to Canada, and when the cold war between United States and the Soviets was in full bloom, our family was welcomed to United States.

What games our nations and their egos play!

ÖSTAFORS, SWEDEN
At the age of 11, I became an immigrant – no longer a refugee. I know this now, I don't think it made much of an impression on me at the time.

A number of men were recruited to work in Östafors, southern Sweden. We were housed in a large lodge like building in the rural area. Again every family had their own room – therefore not much of a change from Germany. All the children went to school. It was a two classroom school 1-3 grades in one room, 4-6 grades in another room. Swedish came quite easily to us, as we spoke some German and a bit of English.

In the winter we used out Finnish sleighs (Soome kelgud) to get to school, and I presume we just walked at other times of the year. The beauty of the country side was lost on us, but I do recall large boulders in the forest and the land was marshy with little streams running around the boulders. We spent a lot of time in the forest.

There was a fast running river behind the house, and the men placed hooks and lines for eels into the water in the morning.

My father was a city boy, and when he caught two eels, he placed them into a basin and poured salt on them. This was supposedly a way of killing them. Well the eels did not like the salt and vaulted directly out of the basin and under my bed. I was terrified and refused to eat eel for most of my life. Two years ago in Saaremaa, I discovered the absolute bliss of smoked eel and red wine!

MONTREAL, CANADA
Our side trip to Sweden was only to give us an opportunity to immigrate to Canada, with the hope that at some time we would be able to come to United States.

Crossing the Atlantic was stormy, with waves washing over the sides of the ship. Most were seasick, including me. My father bundled me warmly on the deck in a lounging chair, and I remember craving pickles, as I could not keep anything else down.

My parents had some friends in Montreal, and we had a room in their apartment for a few weeks until my parents had jobs. We finally moved into an apartment – first one since I was six years old. This meant I had my own room, and we had a living room! Barkley Avenue had many immigrants, including a number of Estonians.

My parents friends advised them to insist that I start school at 8th grade (first year of high school). My school documents showed that I had not completed 6th grade in Germany and that

Partying

My tenth birthday party

Ulm, Helle and Miki

I repeated 6th grade in Sweden, but did not complete the year there either. I started my school year at Montreal High School for Girls. Although there were other Estonians starting 8th grade, the administration made sure that we were not in the same classrooms.

During classroom breaks we gathered together and there was comfort in knowing that there were other Estonian speakers around. I remember studying very hard. Math and science was easy, the worst was history, where I memorized passages, and hoped that the questions on an exam would hit on one of my memorized parts. This did not always work and although most of the teachers were very supportive and encouraging, Miss Miller of history gave me a failing grade and stated that I did poorly. The other problem was French – the students in Quebec started learning French in 3rd grade, and there I was in 8th grade with not a word of French and struggling in English. Someone tutored me the first year and then things got a bit easier.

Estonians in Montreal were very active in church and social activities. It was like camp life all over again, except that we lived further apart. Our social gatherings had the same format – food, drinks, political discussions and singing. My father was very involved in Estonian military veterans organization, and endless petitions were sent demanding freedom for Estonia.

By the second year in school, I was integrated enough to start selecting friends other than Estonians. We found a foursome, but as adult it seems interesting that we consisted of one Hungarian, one Latvian, one White Russian and me.

The selection was not because we were outcasts, we selected each other because we felt that much closer to each other and to each others culture.

Teen years followed with crushes on boys, school, social activities in school and in Estonian community. Years passed with graduations, college, work, marriage and children. As we age, memories of our childhood remain clearly in our minds, reinforced by recalling our stories with other Estonians of our age. Most of us travel to Estonia every few years, and we feel great pride in seeing what a small nation has been able to accomplish in 22 years.

There is also a feeling of regret that we had to leave our homeland and to grow up in another country. Somehow it is fitting that we live in United States, as this is a country of immigrants, and only the Indians can call this land their own.

POSTSCRIPT:

I look at my Estonian friends – they are self assured, educated, cheerful individuals. Yet they all went through a similar experience during and after the war. Where are the psychological wounds that we in today's world would expect to have, and since we do seem normal, what is the reason for this?

The strong influence was the love of our parents and the community of refugees. Children were the future, and the time and effort was lavished in providing the best in education, youth organizations, and choir groups.

My personal conclusion is that we as children were encouraged to think of ourselves as special and capable by our parents, teachers, and other adults. How many times did we hear, that as Estonians, we can accomplish anything, as Estonians we were special?

I was fifteen in Canada when it dawned on me that no-one knew where Estonia was, and cared even less. By that time the deed had been done, my ego developed, my pride in my "Estonianess" firmly set, and I have carried that self assurance ever since.

BORN ON CUSPS

Most of our cohort was born in Estonia but there were children born in transit in the many places over which our folks needed to traverse to find safety.

Sometimes our folks left Estonia prematurely intuitively or otherwise to cross terrain which was to fall into enemy hands. Some among us were born into such now enemy countries. At times this proved to be an advantage, at others quite the opposite.

Others of us were fathered (and perhaps mothered) by someone who was not of Estonian origins: At times of friendly origins, at others not: And all this could change in a day or less.

Many of us have identity quandaries, not about our worth but about who we really are. Are we of the country we were born in, of our parentage: Do we discard the parent who was or became foe.

Perhaps the greatest number of us who were born on the cusp were born in Germany while in the camps. I have not heard it commonly expressed among our cohort that there is a wish to be considered German, or where ever else one was born, but I have certainly noticed this trait among my DP patient base, also the colleague base.

What concerns might belie in their identities when their wishes do not meet the expectations among whom they are cast to live. MM

AINO PAAL/MARSHALL
FROM THE BEGINNING

Preamble (from Aino's letter)

...I've included a couple of bits my brother came forward with. I've been trying to get bits and pieces from him but to no avail. He just keeps telling me he had a reasonably good time and the war did not hassle him in Germany- he means Geislingen. Of the rest of the trip he says I can get from my father's diaries so I get little insight or impressions from him.....

I arrived at a time in the history of my birth country when freedom did not exist but food rationing and formalities of protocol to be allowed to exist, did.

To register my birth was not enough. I had to be registered into the ledgers of various government departments so that I would be recognised as a citizen, have the right to live somewhere in the country and receive the necessary food quota vouchers - the procedure was:
1. Produce the landlord's list of residents as well as the 'building's records' of the place I intended to live in.
2. Produce an undertaking from the Residents Office allowing me to live at that address.
3. Enter as a resident at the given address at the Address Bureau.
4. Produce a declaration from the landlord for the food voucher supply centre
5. Register the declaration for food vouchers at the voucher office.
6. Obtain a declaration for the purchase book, from the food voucher office
7. Present the declaration to the relevant department to obtain the purchase book.
8. Register the food vouchers at the relevant stores to be able to receive the allowable quantities.

I was named after famous Estonian women, guess father had in mind that I would leave a mark somewhere in life. No doubt if we'd had a chance to stay in Estonia father would have made sure of this and things may have been different but that's just me making excuses.

I like anonymity and staying out of sight, I've always preferred working in the background. I often wonder if this is a by-product of my early years which were filled with the necessity to hide, staying low and being quiet while the war raged around me.

As my father explained to me when I was 3 weeks old, I was born when the country was at war. A war conducted by people, to kill and destroy for whatever reason one wanted to give, but the usual common denominators are greed and power.

I was born on 28th August 1942, in Tartu which had already been bombed and burnt. Destruction, death and fear had spread over the University town at the time of my arrival.

On my first birthday at 1 month old, I met my grandfather and my half brother Harald who travelled together to town from Lääne farm, near Nõo. My paternal grandparents, Peeter and Mari (nee: Peets) Paal, were then 79 years old and still worked the farm while my brother who was 12 often stayed with them.

My maternal grandparents, Peeter and Miina (nee: Kliimask) Luiga, had both passed away, my grandmother going to her rest just 28 days before I was born.

On 31st October 1942, I was christened. Father writes that they decide to have me christened 'in the Christian belief', I wonder if I might have had a choice of maybe some old Celtic, druid or pagan instead but realistically the probable alternative was Russian Orthodox.

At two months I had already decided sleep was irrelevant, especially during the day. Late nights were also my preference, going to sleep before 10pm was a waste of time. I still work by this creed.

I already knew that yelling got everyone's attention and I responded to my father's words. Took me 17 years to start responding to my own.

1942 comes to a close with stormy winds, cold and when looking out from the front window one saw Emajõgi starting to freeze over.

The war and its effect on everyone was at the forefront of everyday life and although the Bolsheviks Eastern Front assault had been halted, it was only a matter of time when it resumed.

Father reads in the newspaper of the people who have passed away during the year and muses that these are but a handful when considered against the war casualties. Even on New Year's Eve there are reports of fierce fighting in southern Russia from the Don through to the Caucasus. Comparing this period with the same in 1941 nothing much had changed or been achieved.

27th January 1943 the war came close to us in Tartu at 22.45.

The Bolshevik air force dropped four bombs in the middle of the town. One in the Botanical Gardens destroying the propagation building where Professor Lippmaa, his wife and 8 year old daughter were killed. Another was found in the cellar of the University pharmacy. The third damaged the building next to the telephone reception dish and the fourth hit a two storey building in Laia Street near Toome Hill, it had housed the art museum. This building was destroyed along with some important works of art. One could wonder why, and why 18 people died, 13 were hurt with 9 on the critical list. Sadly, they become statistics. We hid in the bathroom as father thought I was too young to be taken into the cold & damp cellar. And while my mother was frightened for us, I apparently stayed calm, but serious and wide eyed.

I developed a taste for books by 6 months of age. I spent a lot of time sitting at or under father's writing desk and devoured whatever reading matter I could hold onto. On one occasion mother spent considerable time trying to extract material from my mouth and apparently after this my access to printed works was restricted. No wonder I became a librarian - a hoarder of the printed word.

The planes kept coming, usually around midnight as the constant rumbling continued though it was difficult to tell who flew where as they passed over, 14th February 1942 saw major destruction in Tallinn around midnight.

24th February was the Estonia's anniversary of Independence Day but there were no celebrations for fear of bombings if a lot of people were gathered together in one place. Besides what a farce it would be to celebrate the day when Estonia obtained its independence from Russia while Russian forces are attacking. Instead, church services were held throughout the town and these were all well attended.

By 6 months I already have a weight problem. I'm 8kg which is 800 grams heavier than the accepted 'normal' weight. Actually I was stocking up for the tough times ahead - I'm forward planning already.

Spring has arrived with adverse weather conditions for crops and a poor harvest is expected. We have problems with staff at the farm with a young man who joins the Communist Party, another who thinks work now is a waste of effort and the older people who can't understand what is happening to the younger generation. Harald said that the two young men were Russian prisoners and they couldn't believe haw good Estonian conditions were.

Tallinn is being bombed continuously with explosive and incendiary bombs. The result is destruction and death - what else can one expect.

April sees me standing up against supports and I have also been confined to a large cardboard box where I seem to spend my time talking to myself and playing with smaller cardboard boxes (cardboard tastes awful so it was considered safe), bedtime for me is still closer to midnight rather than a reasonable earlier hour.

On Good Friday grandfather comes to town and with my mother we travel to the farm on horse and cart where I'm to meet my grandmother for the first time. She had been too frail to travel with grandfather when he visited so as yet we hadn't met. Father and Harald go by train to Nõo and then walk the last 9 kms

While the day is sunny, the evening brings a thunderstorm, rain and the cold. Mother and I stay at the farm but father and Harald need to return as Harald has school and father has a court sitting.

Farm life obviously suits me as I learn to wave good bye, say my version of 'thank you' and call out 'hui' when I want attention (how polite can a child be?). I still have my own language and carry on a good conversation with myself.

Getting back to town is a concern as to travel by train one needs a permit and mother doesn't have one. It is 25th April and at the end of the month all permits are to be cancelled as train travel will be restricted to war related only. No private cars are allowed either, only military and state vehicles.

After my first trip to the country I seem to have got the hang of travel as mother and I often travel to the farm as well as trips to Meerapalu where mother's relatives live. While away I finally cut my first tooth and learn to walk unaided (well sort of unaided)! The trips to Peipsi and Meerapalu are by boat across Lake Peipsi.

1943 saw Harald finish 6th grade and now enters Commerce School. During the break he spends time at grandparent's farm.

11th February 1944 my brother Ilmar is born, but on 12th July he is no longer with us. His funeral took place on 15th July 1944.

Meanwhile the war has been dancing around us as we have waited for some outcome. Now in August 1944 we are on the move. We have been advised to evacuate from areas in the south and move northward.

18th August saw us separate from father as he headed to join the Forces while the rest of the family went north towards Põltsamaa. Father joined the Home Defence Force Tartumaa 2nd Company, 5th Troop but the stay is short lived as the country's forces are no match for the Communists. He then does a lot of 'evacuation' work for the State and the Judiciary, work he continues after leaving the Defence Force.

My grandparents, aunties and their families along with mother and Harald left Lääne Farm together heading for Nõo, to Lutsivere and Põltsamaa as the Communist forces headed closer to Tartumaa.

On 21st August 1944 dad bids his final farewell to the farm and buries his two dogs in the apple orchard.

By 23rd we've managed to reach Punapea Farm owned by mum's relatives but by 10pm the same night we are moving again heading for Laeva. After another brief stop we head for Puurmani.

By 26th August we are staying in a barn about 2 km outside of Neanurme Village when father catches up to us.

I don't know what our trek was like but from what dad encountered along the way, it would not have been a pleasant one. We would have been like so many others who shared the road while the war raged around us.

The following day August Turp (father's brother-in-law) and father go looking for better 'accommodation' and the family is split between two nearby farms. Father, mother and I have a room at Vanari Farm while the rest of the family are at Pahla Farm.

Harald recalls that at one of the farms where we stayed there were two teenage girls, both older than him. They took him to a nearby creek to catch marron by putting their arms into the marron holes in the banks. They told Harald to try but he reckons there was no way he was sticking his arm in.

The older girl, about 17, went off with the army, she carried the machine gun.

By the 29th Bolshevik forces have captured a number of towns and left Tartu in ruins and although the Germans managed to halt some of the onward flow, it was only a temporary measure.

Father tries to convince mum to go on to Germany but she refuses so, eventually we all continue together along Tallinn Highway. As we are unable to now go direct to Viljandi we stop at Viruvere Village and dad organizes staying at Mrs. Alles' farm, sharing a couple of rooms and the barn.

Nearby in tents are a number of families father knows, Nõok from Luke Village, Petulai. Suut and Soot - who have lost their whole herd along the way. Soot and his daughter join up with dad, mum and Mrs. Alles to travel to Põltsamaa for news.

Then everything began to move too fast - on 21st September 1944 Mum, dad, Harald, me, Mrs. Alles and Henna, her 6 year old son travelled to Türi Station intending to get a train to Tallinn.

We had horses and a wagon from Mrs. Alles' place. My aunties and their families along with my grandparents took our horse and cart to go towards Rapla. They would make a decision as to what to do. My grandparents had made it clear they were too old to travel to Germany.

Harald also said that on the road to Põltsamaa heading for Türi Station, a plane came down in front of us and burst into flames. The men on the road ran to help but with the flames there little they could do. A horse also got killed.

While confusion, explosions and gun fire surrounded us, it was eventually found that the German Army had been ordered to withdraw leaving the Home Defence Force split and with near on no weapons.

In Türi we let the horses go and caught a train for Tallinn. As we left there was bombing of the railway from the direction of Võhma and we were told travel to Tallinn was impossible, instead we should head for Pärnu.

At Papiniidu Station, still trying to head to Tallinn via Pärnu, we were confronted with utter confusion. Dad had met a number of colleagues and the information on Tallinn was not good.

Now the difficult decision was made to travel by train to Riga and on to Germany. There is even confusion as to what train is going where and even if any are leaving, but finally we board a train supposedly going to Riga. Dad's colleagues help us on and say their good-byes since they are staying, hoping to get to Tallinn.

It was 21st September 1944, my brother is 14 and I am 2.

We travel through the night with many stops along the way, our last Estonian border towns are Heinaste and Ikla as we say goodbye to our homeland.

Sunrise sees us in Puikul Station in Latvia. The train is carrying Estonian evacuees as well as members of the German forces.

At Puikul we are told to leave the carriages and have to relocate onto open deck wagons. The train was about 100 metres up the track ready to go so it was a mad rush to make it. Dad was helping Mrs. Alles with her numerous luggage when the train suddenly moved backwards another 200 metres, dad and Harald were left on the platform while the rest of us were on the train. Dad was told not to worry as the train was just manoeuvring but after a while he got tired of waiting and walked up to the wagon to speak with mum. Harald stayed with Mrs. Alles's luggage. Then came a call that the train was leaving and began to move. Dad hurriedly reached for me while mum threw down our packages as she and Mrs. Alles and her son jumped off. The train left without us.

By evening we had managed to locate another train heading for Riga in Latvia, another open wagon and now continue.

I guess we all started off with as much luggage as we could humanly carry but the constant changing on off transport that eventually one was left with what could actually be carried. A lot of people left or lost many belonging along the way. Dad writes about some people who nearly got left off trains because of the amount of luggage, and how often it just got thrown onto trains or trucks regardless of who it belonged to, just to get people moving quickly.

At Lemsalus there was a long stop and then we were told to relocate to another wagon. Some German soldiers came to our aid and actually found a closed wagon for us. It was now going on 11pm.

We had barely got on board when an angry sergeant major bellowed that this was an ammunitions wagon and all luggage had to be removed. The wagons we were allowed to board were about 200 metres from the platform but they were all fully loaded, so we finally gave up searching.

The women, Henna and I curled up on the dirty floor in a corner of the small station house waiting room, sharing it with some soldiers while dad and Harald stayed with the luggage.

Here at Lemsalus dad also heard from Ruhja evacuees that the town was burning and they'd stop trying to evacuate many of the Latvian farmers. It was also reported that the Communists had reached Estonian border towns of Heinaste and Ikla

We had made it through just in time. Escape via Latvia was now cut off.

During the night, 23-24th September there is a glow from fires to the north and the east as massive destruction was wrought onto Latvia.

Monday 25th we arrived at Tukkum Ost Station having travelled on an open wagon squatting between shovels, pickaxes, motors and all sort of stuff destined for railroad and building work. Nights were very cold so we kept close to avoid the wind as best as we could, eventually arriving at Riga Station.

Here we were advised that a train will arrive around 5.30 pm which will go direct to Königsburg, so the time at the station was spent getting ourselves clean.

On time, at 5.30pm a long army supply train arrives and the Officer announces that civilians are not allowed on board. Somehow we manage to get on board the last wagon (open wagons) and position ourselves between the trailer wheels and under the gun barrels of the cannons. There are 5 Estonian families between the last two wagons. We left Riga at 6.30pm and for some reason I'm tired before my usual late night so father sings me a lullaby he wrote to help me sleep.

The trip is a slow stop - start affair as it picks its way along. We come to a stop in the morning and are told that we might continue in the evening. The countryside is desolate - ruins and empty farms. The Bolsheviks had been through this part of Latvia and razed it.

The "good news" is that we will probably continue along the seashore, a short way back to Tukkumist, the "bad news" is the Front will be just 3-4 kms away.

The weather had turned, it rained as we tried to shelter under the trailer and gun barrels and as we began to move, the wind picked up and the rain increased. Mum and I huddled together while Harald and dad sat back to back. It was an awful night as the rain and freezing wind found every opening to get inside you.

In the morning you could see the rocket fires and feel the thunder of the explosions. We were passing the Front.
When we stopped we were stiff and freezing cold, the only warmth was to stand against the train's engine hoping to thaw out, and when we continued it was much the same as before, freezing, wet with lots of stops, starts along the way. At Blieden there was obvious aftermath of recent bombing with burnt forest, some warehouses and barracks now smouldering piles of ash.

The rough weather, wind and rain continued all day: Whenever we stopped, dad and Harald found some bits of carpet, tin, even vegetable support netting (with dried peas still clinging ,on), this was fashioned around the cannon to give mum and me some shelter.

As we approached the Lithuanian border the Front was very near, some said it was in front of
us, and there were concerns we won't get through but with our usual stop, start edging along method we make it.

The soldiers left the train at Libaus but our "accommodation" did not change. The next night was worse than the previous and when we stopped at Memel station in the morning, everyone was freezing cold, wet, aching and stiff.

It is 21st September 1944, six days since we left Estonia.

At Memel dad and some friends try to find out where to register and after being given the run around, in the end are told "go to the railway station and buy a ticket to wherever you want to go!" So dad changed some money, purchased tickets to Danzig, got some food and we tried to get some sleep in a cold, windy railway waiting room.

Dad also bought a newspaper and already news about Estonia was missing.

This time we travel in a proper passenger carriage and **30th September sees us reach Danzig where we are told that there is a camp for Estonians and Latvians at Gotenhafen.** The camp is called Nüssdorf But after a day of being shunted around we finish up where the Poles and Russians are - camp named 'Durchgangslager für Ausländischer Arbeiter - Arbeiter Gotenhafen' (transit camp for foreign workers - work camp Gotenhafen).

In the evening we are given coffee and a loaf of bread between four people, a spoon, a bowl and a blanket each. It is a freezing night and I spend most of it coughing. In the morning there is coffee, for lunch it was something like thick soup or porridge. In the evening it was coffee. One may wonder where I developed an addiction to coffee!

There are no food vouchers and no opportunity to buy food.

Next day we move into the Estonian sector where the food is a bit better. Dad finds a list of 7 day supplies to be allocated to 'travellers': 2430g bread, 1450g rye bread, 250g meat, 150g butter, 70g margarine, 175g marmalade,

200g sugar, 60g coffee or substitute, 60g cheese, 24 Cigarettes each for men & women, 150g other foodstuffs, separate coupons for potatoes, vegetables and 1/4 litre skim milk each day., but we don't get any of these.

On 7th October we are on the move to a new camp at Frankfurt an der Oder. I'm still coughing and as
we eventually reach Bossen I'm running a temperature and vomiting.

At the camp the conditions are non existent, beds are just boards with no mattress, straw or any covering, no light, heating is supplied bit by bit, food is mainly bread, watery soup and coffee.

No one is allowed to leave the camp, there is a barb wire perimeter fence, a marksman at the gate and uniformed guards in the centre courtyard. Everyone is edgy, I now have diarrhoea. We wait. ,

The tension is even evident in the young as father writes that my brother is always out with the other boys 'just hanging around' and when spoken with we gets constant back answers and sulking.

Over the next 2 weeks father meets up with a number of friends and colleagues. Hendrik Visnapuu visits us and describes his escape. He was on the second ship which was not torpedoed while another of dad's friends, Dr. Kuisk, was on the first ship. He managed to save his wife but his mother drowned as he watched helpless.

Horror stories are filtering through everywhere and we consider ourselves lucky.
Dad and Mr. Kubol have arranged some work in Schweibus and we arrive there on 21st October 1944. Dad's work is in a rubber factory as camp security overseer. Our living quarters are a great improvement as we have two rooms, and for payment we have heating, power and food.

But the first day is not the best as nothing has been organized. We have no heating, no hot water, and the only food all day was 60g of sausage and a piece of bread each. By evening I'm letting everyone know I'm hungry and mum chops up a small piece of gammon she'd saved. Next day we manage some bread and soup but no food vouchers as yet. I'd say that by now I wouldn't have had a weight problem any more.

My brother recalls how he would save crusts from a meal so that he'd have something in the evening, and father writes that often my mother went without just so there'd be something for me to eat later.

Christmas day is spent together with an evening meal and a pray for family and friends in Estonia.
On 26th December we go to a cafe in town where, 'Aino behaved herself very well, she had a coffee and a piece of torte which she ate with a spoon'.

Winter has set in and 1945 New Year enters with a snow storm, but this doesn't seem to deter the war, as at 8pm the air raid sirens began.

Since the beginning of December Berlin had been bombed heavily and other cities followed.
New Year's Eve, before midnight, mother and I are already asleep while Harald was at a New Year dance organized. for the workers. Dad's updating his diary.

First week of January I go for a sled ride to town and finish up with a temperature for a few days but by 12th I'm back to my usual self, still up near midnight having long discussions with father.

The air raid sirens continue but it is difficult to say where or how close they are. The Bolsheviks have commenced a massive invasion from Karpaat to Memel to Danzig. The situation is depressing.

On 20th January mum went to Züllichau and saw an influx of refugees, by the next day (Sunday) the Front was just 105 km away. There was an endless row of refugees heading for Frankfurt on Oder and Züllichau. Crying children perched on top of loaded carts and wagons, weary parents, tired horses plodding along the ice-slippery roads. The official temperature was minus 10' but feels colder.

We had packed up but as yet no evacuation from the factory has been announced, instead a notice states, "under threat of punishment, no one is to leave".

We had no form of transport and the trains were all reserved for army personnel. Soldiers came and went through the camp as they are being reorganized.

A week later we were still waiting as a chance to go with some army personnel fell through when they were sent back to the Front.

While waiting Harald has built two sleds, to take our 3 suitcases and me but trying to push or pull them through the thick snow is useless so we discard everything that doesn't fit into backpacks. The January snow storms are fierce so we need to travel as light as possible.

On Sunday (28/01) dad makes one last attempt at the railway station but everything is locked up. A polite notice on the door reads "all enquires are pointless!'
4.45am the sirens start. All factory overseers had disappeared and the one left in any authority told everyone to fend for themselves. There were some very distraught people, especially women with children who had previously been promised assistance.

By 10am we started out, following a well trampled snow covered road, a freezing wind and minus 15-20 degree cold. We walked and had our and some other peoples bare essentials on the sleds Harald had built. With us were Mrs. Reuter, her year old daughter, Mihkel Ling and his 13 year old son Felix. Felix had been ill and had difficulty travelling, but there was no help. The snow storm just got thicker and walking got heavier.

We walked about 7km heading towards Wilkan Station when we heard there was a chance of a train which had set out from Schweibus Station. Dad went ahead and eventually we were scrambling to get on board a train apparently organized to take out refugee, we hadn't been notified when in Schweibus. It was a struggle to get on because those already on board, barricaded the doorways to stop others getting into the carriages and therefore over-crowding.

It was dark when we arrived in Frankfurt an der Oder Station.

For once I wasn't ill but Felix was worse, Mrs. Reuter's daughter was sick, and dad had caught a chill.

As usual there was confusion at the station but eventually we had a dry room at the high school for the night. It was 7pm when we arrived, registered and were given some soup, sandwiches and coffee ? first food for a couple of days, and it was past midnight by the time we'd found some straw to sleep on.

Next day 7.10am (31/01/45) we were standing in the morning cold as ordered, waiting to move out but no one knew where. Three hours later transport arrived to take us to the station where we then waited all day until 10pm to get under way. There was just soup and coffee available. Everyone was tired, freezing cold, hungry and on edge.

There was a young woman in our carriage who kept crying as her 10 month old baby had just died. She'd been on the move for 2 weeks.

We stopped in Templin in the dark but it was hard to say just where we were except that soon we were on the back of some dirty, wet, coal trucks, covered with soggy soot. After a cold, wet, windy ride we arrive near Flögel. We had a room to ourselves and although there was no electricity, it felt warm being out of the snow and wind.

Registration and food vouchers we got at the Town Hall.

Noon 03/02/45 - air raid sirens began with planes flying towards Berlin. We were situated on the flight path and had already been bombed with nearly 2000 people killed when the Town Hall and hospital were hit.

We had all been ill and although mum and I were still not well father wanted to move out as soon as possible. We left out at 4am on 9th February heading for Jena.

Mr. Ling and Felix were still with us, while Mrs. Reuter had stayed in Berlin with her daughter expecting to go on to Frankfurt am Main.

Train travel was getting worse as more and more people try to escape the advancing Bolshevik army. There is no polite way to go about it - just push and shove, grabbing what space you can to get on board.

We arrived at 2.30am and managed to get a room at a school that even had some straw mattresses. In the morning we were told to leave but father's bluff about working for the war effort was enough to give him time to find some Estonian friends and eventually secure us accommodation. We moved to Hotel der Tempelhof. Don't be fooled by the title of the building.

The day before we arrived (09/02/45), Jena had been bombed with the centre of town extensively damaged.

Now, about 50 Estonians got together and father meets up with a lot of his friends and learns about those lost. An Estonian church service was held.

With so many people on the move it is understandable that forms had to be filled in wherever one went. To get anything you had to register your existence. In some cases it took days to finalise forms and if your situation changed during the process, you started again.

On isth February we finally moved into a private house. The owner, a Mrs. Harz lived with her daughter at 6 Gartenstrasse, Jena. We have a small room on the 2nd floor. It is so cramped that Harald had to move in with another family on the 3rd floor. We had 2 beds, a small table and wardrobe. The kitchen is a shared affair downstairs, the bathroom a tub if you can fit it in somewhere for a quick wash.

The stay there is not at all pleasant as the landlady and her daughter prove to be a real problem. And make no secret that they hate foreigners. This is not just with us but all who share her house.

We stay as accommodation is very scarce and it is dangerous to venture too far. The bombing increased and this is a time when we spend some very long, unpleasant hours cramped in the cellar. I develop bad chest colds and ear aches. In March we still had snow falls.

The air raids sirens continue in town; news is that Erfurt was bombed overnight (19/02) as the Bolshevik army headed for Dresden. Later dad meets a friend who escaped the horror of Dresden.

The constant bombing continues, Harald and dad get caught up a couple of times when out getting coal or supplies. On another occasion we had been in the cellar for a long time when dad went out to check on the situation. The planes came in waves and groups of 9-12. Dad reckoned they were about 4km high and counted 5 waves. Then suddenly the bombs started, one dropped nearby and he only just made it to the cellar door when the explosion

ripped the street apart. There were about seven more waves before they stopped. Later dad explains what destruction had occurred and it is extensive. He and Harald go and help

But there is no help for over 3000 people who perished.
The things I recall from this period are walking through ruined streets with buildings on fire; knowing the different sounds of the alarm warnings and to stay quiet and flat on the ground whenever the raids started.

One of the Germans staying in the house talks to dad about the general feeling of the German people around him. The German army is now so depleted that 15 to 17 year olds were being ordered to enlist.

In March, Dr. Volmer's youngest son fell off a balcony but he was OK and Mr. Ling and Felix visited us, Felix is better now and they are trying to get to the coast to a fishing village.

The air raids continue through April and dad is making arrangements for us to move to the country where some friends have gone. On the 5th he checks out one area and when he returns, finds me very ill and the town closed off. There is no way out, Gotha had fallen and tanks were heading to Jena. There are ditches dug around the city to try and slow any invasion.

We manage to get 6kg of bread, some butter and potatoes which we hope will see us through for 3-4 weeks as getting supplies is now limited.

We spend most of 7th to 12th April in the cellar as air raids continue. Across the road from us, the Air Force Personnel Command Centre was damaged and a house directly across had its front blown up.

Escape by train was dangerous as the railway lines were also under attack.

Harald is ill and has nose bleeds, mother and I are both ill.

On 13th" April 1945 it is announced that Jena has fallen to the American Forces.

End of April sees Harald's health worse. He'd been bed ridden for a week and had a severe ear infection. Then I got an ear infection and on 15th May am rushed to hospital for an operation.

Early June moves are under way with assistance from the Americans to get people out before the Communist Army arrives which had been moving towards Jena. Refugees are continuously arriving from the east with the Communists at their backs.

We eventually make it out on 27th June 1945 and spend a night on bare concrete in a garage at Coburg. A stop at Bamberg where we see the bombed old town as well as get a coffee, but there is no room left for refugees. The same applies to Kotzau, Münchberg, Wirsberg and Kulmbach. Eventually (02/0745) we arrive in a disused concentration camp at Wildflecken. Other's.had been through before us and the place was dirty and messy. Here more than anywhere previously we needed the place disinfected.

As Harald told me, whenever we entered a camp we went through a process of being deloused. DDT dust was pumped into and onto our clothing so that we looked like walking flour sacks. Then again this was necessary as often we did not get to wash for days yet we were in constant close contact with others. We slept in what we were wearing, usually with our boots on.

By 26th July we are on the move again and finish up in Coburg. Our nights were spent in a horse stable hay loft as accommodation was very scarce. By 19th August we've left the stables and have accommodation at Blieden Camp near Ansbach. We share a garage building but at least it is dry and we are able to make it comfortable. I have bronchitis.

Dad reminiscences on the 12 months since leaving our home in Tartu on 1ih August 1944. We are still on the move with no idea where we will finish up.

While at Ansbach, there is a circus, Latvian ballet performance, Estonian musical performance and a sport's competition. So, life goes on despite the uncertainty.

We are told of a chance to move on with 405 people to Rotenburg or with 424 family people to Fürth. Luckily dad insists to know what is in store to avoid past problems, so a delegation is organized to check out the facilities. The end result was that no one at Rotenburg knew anything about refugees coming, and there wasn't anywhere to accommodate them.

At Fürth there was a camp for Poles and Russians and this was overflowing. No one knew of any camp established for Baltic people. After some reorganization several Estonian families are moved to Fürth and we are amongst them.

We relocate on 12th October 1945 and I call this "our new home" but remind dad that "our real home is far away".

A week later mum travelled with Harald to Geislingen where a large Estonian camp has been established and secured a room for us. Harald stayed behind, while mum and I join him a couple of days later. Dad followed on 4th November. Dad had also secured a teaching position taking the final year classes for commerce, economics, psychology and philosophy.

Mum described the trip by train to Geislingen as 'horrendous'. Trains were so packed that part of the trip one was hanging on standing on the steps or the outer porch. At one stop mum managed to get into a carriage but Harald didn't. He eventually climbed in through a window.

We live in Rappenacker Street in one house with just one room and then moved to another in the same street. We were on the 3rd floor in what was actually two attic rooms and Harald shared one with an ex soldier, Ludwig Annom.

Life takes on some form of normality but food is still rationed and scarce.

Dad works at teaching and as legal adviser for Baltic people, is involved in most Estonian organisations, the chess club and Scouts. He attends various courses, such as mechanics, English language, farming, photography. He also completes his PhD in Law.

Mum does dressmaking and her specialty in corsetry, this earns them some money, and I besides attending kindergarten, or being constantly ill with bronchitis, often go with mum to Augsburg to meet up with my godmother Sylvia Korju and mum's other friends. She manages to obtain food in Augsburg, items that were still scarce in Geislingen.

Harald continues his education and receives his final certificate in April 1949. He also passed his Scout's level 3 and is now an assistant leader.

I finish my final year of kindergarten in 1948. Along the way I've also had vitamin A deficiency, the measles, whooping cough - just for starters. I fell down the stairs and also saw my mother fall down two flights.

My sister Evi was born on 11th March 1948 - and apart from that life went on until we migrated to Australia.

We left Geislingen on 26th May 1949 and arrived in Italy, Bagnoli Camp. Processing was very quick, as if on a conveyor belt. Medical checks - eyes, any skin disorders; dusted with DDT powder, document checks, then allocation to buildings and rooms. We were in Block M, room 82.

17.06.49 we left the camp and headed for the goods train station in Napoli. There were about 610 people.

18.06.49 at 10am we board the ship 'Amarapoora' at Taranto port and by 13.30 have left the mainland behind.

Evi and I are excited, mum is crying, dad wonders if we will ever see Estonia again.

The Rhine-Ruhr Basin

Lubeck

THE LANDSCAPES OF OUR CHILDHOOD

Dresden

LINDA VOOSAAR/DOLAN
CHILDHOOD MEMORIES FROM ESTONIA TO THE CAMPS

Bombs whistling to earth viciously tearing apart neighborhoods, killing occupants. Townspeople trying to put out the spreading flames to near blocks of wooden framed and brick buildings. The heart of the Estonian city of Tartu was on fire from Russian bombing, spring 1944. Today that section is a park. The city chose never to build on this land.

That night, however, my godmother, Maie Seitam-Saar, telephoned my father at their apartment in the "soup kitchen" section of Tartu: So named because the streets were named after vegetables, like peas, beans, cabbage. My father, Osvald (Ozzie) Max Henri (Voikman) Voosaar told her the latest news of his helping putout the fires and of the birth of his second daughter. The families in the countryside had seen the glow of the red-yellow fire on the horizon towards the direction of Tartu about 10.37pm and were doubly anxious about the bombing and my mother.

That night, however, my godmother, Maie Seitam-Saar, telephoned my father at their apartment in the "soup kitchen" section of Tartu: So named because the streets were named after vegetables, like peas, beans, cabbage. My father, Osvald (Ozzie) Max Henri (Voikman) Voosaar told her the latest news of his helping putout the fires and of the birth of his second daughter. The families in the countryside had seen the glow of the red-yellow fire on the horizon towards the direction of Tartu about 10.37pm and were doubly anxious about the bombing and my mother.

This was the evening of March 22, 1944, as Ilme Linda Voosaar came into the world. Hello little girl. What a greeting.
The same evening as the bombing became more intensive, all the women at the clinic were moved to the basement level for safety. My mother Eleonora (Mardisoo) Voosaar sat on the cold cement floor throughout the night into the following morning holding me.

In 2002, I took my daughter Christina and son Brian Kalju, on a tour of Tartu conducted by cousin Eevi's husband Alfred Bender. I pointed out the women's clinic where I was born. Second floor, third window was what my mother described for her bed position: Certainly a terrible way to spend a night with a newborn in arms listening for the nearby scream of bombs and explosion.

It seems my little event of being born long ago compared with current events humankind is again tearing itself apart: Parents holding their dead children in their arms and weeping is nothing new. The recent (2011 2013) events of Aleppo, Syria, replay my life as a Displaced Person (DP). The pain of loss, the misery of living in camps, families walking through miles and miles of road to escape destruction: Evil seems to win out so many times.

Celebrating his daughter's birth was short lived for my father as he was commandeered with the Estonian Army to the Russian front by the German command. My mother and dad's mother lost all contact with him for months. As the German front was collapsing, chaos ruled the country. The silence and the stream of people evacuating with their feet or any cart, vehicle or train hustled past my great aunt and uncle's Kuresaar farm. My uncle and paternal grandmother came to the countryside weeks ago. There was more food available for my sister, Malle, and the new baby, me. The city food shelves were sparse by this time. Fear ruled the streets.

Almost six months later my father had broken ranks with a disintegrating German front. Estonian leadership was either dead or gone elsewhere. He told his fellow squad members he was going home to his family and they could chose whichever way they wished to travel. There was no one left to give orders.

My dad searched for us at our Tartu city apartment. An elderly neighbor told him that his family had gone to the great aunt and uncle's farm in the country and that the Russians were looking for him. Time to leave!

My mother had taken only what she could carry months earlier to the farm. Many mementos were left for others to enjoy. There were only so many dishes and blankets that could be hauled. When my father finally arrived at Kuresaar, death and terror was everywhere. As my mother's cousin Eevi, relates to me in 2002, the entire family of five at a neighboring farm was murdered by the Russians not more than one week after our family left my great aunt Louise's farm. This family had a baby not much older than me.

Before our family left, my father tried to convince Eevi's mother, Ella, to leave Estonia. She could not conceive abandoning her homeland. Going toward what and where she said? Year later in letters from Eevi to my father, she stated her regret at staying and the hard life under the Soviets they endured. Her husband Alfred was sent to the Gulag in the Arctic Circle for seven and one half years. His crime was (forced) playing in a band for the departing German army. Enemy of the people was is label for the rest of his life. When Alfred returned to Estonia, from the Russian labour camp he was not allowed a work permit. Ruling Russian committee chief said "Alfred should do us a favour and die."

WARTIME ESTONIA (1939-1944 AUGUST)
My father like many Estonian men was conscripted into the German army… through the Estonian army. He had no choice in the matter. It was World War II with its own rules. My father, like many other Estonian men were second class citizens.

He told me several stories of his life as an Estonian soldier like spending one of his birthdays (August 18) in a swampy area drinking water through his hanky because of thirst and hunger. He said the mosquitoes were big as horses and loud as an Orchestra. I have forgotten which country they were walking. Later in the day, his men "borrowed" a farmer's goose. The farmer had abandoned his house. Because it was too dangerous to have a fire, they 'low-steamed' it..but not enough it seems. All the men had the "revenge of the goose" that evening behind many, many trees.

Dad recalled several of the villages the Estonian squad passed though had people who only spoke Russian.

When he was a boy, his father was hired by the Russian Czar Nicholas II, to run a factory of many thousands of people outside of Irkutsk, Siberia. The Czar liked educated Estonians and trusted those more than his own people.... then again, who would choose to live in such an outpost? Dad's mother Alma, insisted he learn the Russian language, much to his disdain. Grandmother even bribed Ozzie with candy money. Instead of playing good guys and Robbers, he was into the joys of studying the spoken and written Russian language. This wise mother saved her son's life and many others' years later by her action.

The Estonian squad passed through one village looking for food. There a grandmother had hidden her fourteen year old grandson in the rafters of the house. Dad looked up at something floating down and said nothing. Grandmother noticed his eyes look up. He said she looked terrified at his discovery. Dad led the squad out. Told them he forgot something. He went to talk to the grandmother again. She begged in Russian, for her grandson's life. We are Estonians, not murderers of children. Before dad walked out, she offered him and the squad food, which they had hidden: Wonderful for weeks hungry men.

The second time the Russian language saved lives happened after the Estonian squad rejoined with the Germans. The night was pitch black. The low mist made it even harder to see even trees in front of them. They literally felt their way through the dense brush and heavily forested trees. The German orders were for the Estonians to proceed ahead of the Germans in advance toward the Russian lines. It was less than half an hour before my dad heard Russian whispers ahead of him. Dad warned his men what he had heard ahead. Death was behind and in front of them. In his head he knew that gunfire would give the Russian positions away to the German generals. Estonian would be collateral pawns in this slaughter house.

His quick plan was to save their squad's lives and free them from the Germans. Dad whispered that they were Estonians and for the Russians to feel the left arms for the identifying bands. Almost immediately Dad felt someone touching his left arm. Lowly Estonian soldiers were made to wear those armbands and now they saved their lives. In the ensuing conversation in Russian, a Russian Colonel told him they were not dumb enough to give away their position. The Colonel told the order up the line to feel for the Estonian armbands and that these people were merely buffers for the German army. The Russians, their troop walked past showed no interest in them.

Dad said "It was like walking through death untouched". His men said later that each was grasped as they passed. The look on my father's face left me with a lifelong impression. Within long minutes the silence of the forest awoke in a terrible volley thundering from rifles and heavy weapons behind the Estonians.

Death opened His frightful wings and consumed Men.

LEAVING ESTONIA: THE GREAT EXODUS (SEPTEMBER 1944)
The squad of men stood in a semi-circle not knowing what to do. The Russians were busy with the German Army. The plan was made to flee. My father went directly back to Tartu to search for his family. These other men did the same. Some fled with families to Finland and Sweden taking the sea route, others by land towards Germany and across Europe.

Now that my father was again at Kuresaar farm, my mother could stop wondering whether she was a widow. I was six months of age and much had changed in Estonia. The German Army was withdrawing from our country.

The Russian front was advancing towards the Baltic States and ready to conquer us again. The final decision was made by my parents to take my sister, my father's mother, my mother and me to leave our beloved Estonia forever.

My mother's aunt Louise's (Luise) husband packed all our family onto her back of a hay wagon and took us to the railroad station a little more than a mile away.

At the train station, my father decided to go back to Tartu, in order to convince other families to leave. Meanwhile his mother, Alma, decided that she had had enough escaping from place to place (Siberia, St. Petersburg) and wanted to go back to Tartu. Also grandmother had fallen on the train platform and broken her false teeth and injured her arm.

All this pain and confusion was too much for an elderly woman. My mother was in tears as what to say to Alma's son—her husband. Nana did not care. She was staying in Tartu. She was old and tired. We never knew what happened to grandmother. Lives are made of these deep heart breaks in evacuations...and worse. So many families lost family members and all knowledge of what happened to them.

Many decades later my parents found out that our family was three days short of being trapped into the colonialism of the "Workers' Paradise". It was also in the mid 1950's that my mother found out that her father, Karl Mardisoo had survived the Russian occupation. My mother had assumed for years that he was deceased possibly like her mother-in-law. Karl had been a warehouse watchman for several years. One night criminals broke into the warehouse, hit my grandfather over the head and killed him. Knowledge of what happened to various members of our families took decades to uncover and mourn their death or celebrate their survival.

When I took my daughter and son to Estonia in 2003, as an adult, other stories from family and friends of family made me ponder at the tragedy of our little Baltic country stuck between two powerhouses of Russia and Germany. My mother's cousin Eevi's mother Ella (Rooma), took in a young student who eventually became one of the foremost pediatric surgeons in present day Estonia. Her story to me was of her sixteen year old brother (?) who looked much older because of his height and the invading Russians took him to the edge of their farm woods, made him kneel down, and she heard the crack of the Russian bullet take his life without any justice or court of law. The look in her eyes, her face...

With war there is little justice: Just empty pain.

As an eight year old in Deerfield County New Jersey (USA) grade school, I remember watching World War II black and white newsreel movies. At one point the American children were laughing at the stream of women with baby carriages, others with bundles of what they could carry, and the sad looks of the stream of people escaping. What was there that caused the sight to be funny, I thought?

It took decades of pondering that that idea in my head to discover why: Simply sheer ignorance in understanding the suffering at the situation: That I too, with my mother, father and sister was among this miserable lot one time. I was ashamed to share that fact. It also, in my child's way made me angry.

THE ROAD FROM ESTONIA TO BERLIN
There are nothing but black and white photos now to keep me earliest memories and stories from my parents and other adults to keep the "Exodus" history alive from me.

The Great Abandonment from Estonia I understand actually began as early as August of 1944. Mostly women and children arrived in Danzig as the first displaced persons (DPs). Arrangements were hasty and what was left of the German government was trying their best to protect those escaping the Russians. Those first Estonian women at Danzig complained nightly over infestations of bedbugs, accommodations... but not having any Russians present was a good thing. Since my parents left later, there was time for the government and many valiant Estonians to arrange for camps.

At age three and four with the help of photographs I remember the travel and camps.

The memory of train rides have always remained with me. There was excitement and mystery. There was always a label, DP, pinned to my coat or dress. There I was standing with a group

Kucknitza Camp 1, Red Cross 1945

Ilme Linda Voosaar 1945 aged 2

Hindrich's birthday party

111

of other children and adults likewise labelled. Of course the train ride had to end at some point. The huge trucks the Estonian families were deposited onto were enormous to me. Army khaki colored, rough inside and very noisy as it drove along tour destination...a camp. I also remember doing a lot of walking and being very tired. My father carried me at times and at another time a carriage was used until we could no longer take it with us.

My father managed to get us to the British lines and under its protectorate. From there the first camp, which my father labelled on the back of the photograph as Camp 1: Kucknitz, had an American flag flying over it. The Red Cross was in charge of the food and medical efforts at this camp.

When I was three years old in June 1945, my parents were able to have me christened. I had two godmothers and two godfathers. The godfathers were older men and had limited contact with me. My godmother, Maie Seitam-Saar, was a lifelong guide in my emotional and religious life. My child's imagination pictured her always as an angel with very blonde hair and a soft manner.

In this camp, our family was assigned to an enormous room with rows and rows of three level bunk beds. The rows and sections of beds were laid so close that even I could touch two separate rows with my playful outstretched hands. I still possess the first British khaki blanket that was over my mother's and my bed. It has travelled well.

To this day, some possessions are worth keeping. One could even say hoarding. Though, on the other hand, my parents taught me generosity at every turn. Always share even if we had very little. Others had less than we did.

PEOPLE: YOUNG, AND OLDER: THE PARNA FAMILY

As a five year old, memory brings me to several children my own age. Nothing remarkable: Kids being kids. Families came and went from camps. My closer friends were children whose parents had ties with my parents.

In the tragedy of war and displacement comes disease. My older sister Malle was hit by three illnesses. She contracted scarlet fever initially. My parents took her to what hospital was still open. There was a patient in the bed next to Malle with open tuberculosis. She caught TB. My parents brought her back to the hospital again after which Malle contracted bacterial meningitis. It was too much for such a young child to withstand and the combination took her life.

Mother at the same time was pregnant with my baby sister, and she gave birth to a very weak baby girl: The baby managed to live less than two weeks. There were no antibiotics or oxygen tents for her. My mother explained to me years later, the German people were barely able to take care of themselves. Shortages of all kinds ruled. It was no one's fault.

Life is sometimes taken away and can be replaced again by something very special. My older playmate, Silvi (Parna) Trick happened to be my sister's age and became my lifelong friend. From DP Camp to college to godmother for her son Kevin: She became my surrogate sister through the years. Silvi introduced me to my husband John. I, in turn, became her son, Kevin Matthew's godmother and adored her daughter Ellen. Several other families who also came to the United States and emigrated to Seabrook Farms in New Jersey (USA) had sons and daughters who were lifelong friends. There are many stories connecting me to all these children and immigrants. They become extended brothers and sisters in life. I am so blessed. Unfortunately Silvi passed away in 2003 of breast cancer.

Silvi's mother, Juuli Parna, is to be remembered for being a courageous mother. Juuli was a survivor! The Parna family lived at another temporary DP camp before arriving in Kucknitz Camp. Her story was of her family of five with father (Aarno), older sister (Anita Parna Pallop), middle sister (Elvi) and Silvi. Berlin was still being bombed; however Juuli thought she remembered a farm field not far from the camp.

One dark night she spoke of her daughters and her with toddler, Silvi going to the potato field. In the dark of the night mother and two daughters dug for potatoes with their hands. Silvi sat playing with dirt clumps. Without warning the Russians started bombing again. Juuli saw it was a curse...they could be killed, and a blessing....the farmer would stay away. Starvation, Juuli, remembered, took away her fear...only determination to keep picking. Elvi said, she was afraid but agreed her stomach was in pain from hunger.

The next day Juuli at the camp asked the other women what produce they had. Let us put it into a pot for soup. It will last longer and feed more people. In went pitiful carrots, cabbage fairly wilted, and fresh dug potatoes.

The smell of the cooking wafted throughout the building and out the window. This brought several French DPs mainly and a few other ethnics to the camp kitchen. Could they please have some soup? Hand signals indicated that they had not eaten for many days. These people were starving. Juuli took pity on them. She hesitated, thinking of her family of five. However these people were in worse shape. Juuli gave them each a bowl of the watery soup warning them not to eat too fast as they would get sick. Too hungry people, words mean nothing nor hand signals. Several got 'starvation gut'.

BERLIN TO EUTIN, GERMANY

American, British, French sectors of Berlin during the bombing were still chaotic. The uncertainty of life, strange people coming and going, my parents were often quiet and spoke in quite voices between them. If they did not want me to understand the subject matter, they would shift languages either to German, Russian ...and possibly Finnish.

I started to understand German especially since my father found or traded for children's books to read for me at bedtime. Many times he would make up Russian or Estonian stories he remembered. Stories in books have and always will be magic for me. He would teach me how to be strong, never afraid, to listen and understand people, and to never prejudge what I viewed. Everything was a lesson.

Moving from place to place with my mother holding my hand was my point of security.

The feeling of impermanence, of not belonging stayed with me into adulthood.

Only in 1999, when I travelled back to Estonia for the first time since 1944, did I feel that I belonged somewhere, connected to a people, a place through a language so sweet to my ear. Indescribable joy!

Even from the time of these camps, the scary stories left an impression. I overheard during our time in Berlin, my father was almost shot to death by a drunken British soldier on leave and very lost. The soldier was looking to pay for feminine company and wandered into a family building of Estonian and other ethnic families. Lack of English language put my father at a disadvantage. My father happened to be in the hallway when the soldier grabbed a female friend of our family. She was shrieking in terror. Dad broke up the manhandling. Other people had called the British MPs, who arrived in time to see the soldier pull out his pistol, aim and fire at my father. Fortunately the gun misfired. All was straightened out later but put a scare into everyone.

Life in refugee camps was hard on everyone from those running them to those occupying them. As young as I was, I sensed the mood of the people, the faces, body postures, tenseness of individuals, and always on guard watching people. My parents did the best they could to normalize and all situations. We initially slept on the three tier cots, narrow railed bunks.

I remember my folks going for walks every evening to discuss their personal plans and events of the day. The walking and playing was simply fun for me. The parks and woodlands in Germany were especially beautiful in spring. My mother pointed out the Linden tree, which I could smell from so far away. For Easter, my father and I picked moss for the plate onto which a few colored eggs were placed. All of these had a story of some kind which lasts in my memory to be passed onto my grandchildren and others. Traditions are to be cherished.

THE SUBJECT WAS: FOOD IN A REFUGEE CAMP

The first items for any refugee to consider were a safe place to stay, clean water and food. So much of life was happening around me in my toddler/early childhood, which is rather hazy.

Food was always treated with serious respect as there was not much of it. I never had a good appetite and always wondered how my parents were ever able to keep me alive. I was always aware 'first food' was placed in front of me. As I grew older, I could sense my parents held back on what they ate and I in turn told them, "Mom.

I am full" to their astonishment. Years later my father forced me to eat and I immediately turned green and threw up.

The supplement to our family food allotment later in Eutin, Germany camp Kucknitz was from UNRRA in the form of CARE packages. These packages added to the sparse fat content in our basic diet.

Many years later living in Seabrook, New Jersey, USA, I remember American classmates making care package jokes. Why would they think CARE packages were funny, I thought? They had never faced hunger? This all went into my mental category of: Stupid: Never thought deeply about it again.

Decades later, after I married my Irish Catholic husband, John, the subject of CARE packages came up. He had just looked at a television broadcast and remembered his grade school years and declared "Oh, yes. My class and I donated to CARE." There it was. My husband was feeding me in Europe. Who knew?

When I was around four to five years old, the war was over. My father's coming and going on a secondhand bicycle brought supplemented food to our family. Our family was finally assigned a very small apartment with a toilet down the hallway. My play area was the cubical apartments of other children, stairway and stairwells, and grass mall in front of the huge building. This mall area contained more buildings than I can remember of the refugee camp. The buildings had black cherry tree lining the back part.

One late spring men with trucks came to pick the cherries. Any time some cherries escaped from the men, children and adults would descend on them. I was too little and too slow to snatch any to my disappointment. To this day, black cherries hold a distinct memory for me. Now I can eat myself silly with them.

The Estonian men were good at making documents which would allow travel around the cities and countryside of our refugee camp. My father was a bookbinder by trade. Had it not been for WW II, my father would have finished his master's level in the trade. I watched him repair books for people outside and in the camp. When he was able to make the shiny, gold edging for a Bible, I thought all kinds of magical abilities he had. Dad shot down that notion immediately. He showed me how from a hard-boiled egg yellow color, various powders chemicals actually worked 'their 'magic to transform the edging.

Father also made tools from pieces of woods he worked into making a book press. Other metal tools he would trade for when he started making cigarette holders from toothbrush handles: Again, to me, magic...and hard work. He showed me how to buff the end product and how I was adding an important part to bringing money to buy important things for our family.

My lessons of life came everyday with the mundane events of daily living. As I mentioned previously, making documents were important to any travel around post-war Germany. I cannot say how much of my father's hand or experience went into these activities but he had travel on train through Berlin.

On one of these travels to Berlin and then to the countryside to trade what father possessed, Red Cross cigarettes, a man was taken off the train never where he had sat by police and roughly escorted to the train station. He did not have 'proper papers' and from the look of pain on my father's face, the person would have a terrible end. Proper papers were extremely important to anyone moving around the country.

These Red Cross cigarettes, as my father was not a smoker, went to trade for all kinds of city goods, he surmised, that farmers might desire. Here came my father through our apartment door carrying, one time, a pound of butter, cheese, eggs for Easter, pencils, many other food items. The butter itself would have been a portion for a family for a year in a refugee camp.

Therefore, my mother shared the bounty with the other mothers in the building as supplement to their family's diets. Sometime in turn items would come back from these families for us.

The one other item my mother loved was German beer. This was a rare item during this time period and now I know she desired the item because she was pregnant with my young sister. Of course, I was clueless at the time.

The only time I was not personally happy with all the refugee camp sharing was when mother 'shared' my metal bathtub. With the world coming to a more peaceful and quiet state, people wanted to celebrate. Someone's great idea was to make beer! My mother happily lent the tub thinking it would be used either for a bathtub for little kids or making soup for a family. Wrong. It came back smelling like beer. I can distinctly remember the sour odor of fermented hops. Not pleasant at all. My mother was definitely upset and never lent the bathtub again. My father stated that he did not like his daughter smelling like sour beer.

The last two years in Germany at camp brings quieter memories. My father acquired a second hand bicycle. This bicycle saw many, many miles of German countryside. His best time was going to Potsdam to visit various historic sites. All these places, my father brought back in stories that he even brought up when I was a teenager. History was my father's favorite subject. When I left home and was married, he gave a two day seminar on WWII at the Latvian Centre for the Indianapolis Estonian Society.

Other memories of Germany and peacetime, were with several other families with whom we went on picnics at local parks and woods. Mrs. Linda Paar with her sons, Koivo and Kalju (later Americanised, Ron Paar) became long time family friends. Their step-father was Voldemar Salomon, a veteran who married their mother.

My father took me to a motor bike race taking place off road and another time a boxing match. My mother was not thrilled but I loved it. In this time I learned the names of trees, flowers, how things were made, how and why people behaved. We even managed to go to the circus one time. I thought the monkeys were funny. One put a chamber pot on his head and everyone shrieked in laughter. My mother had no love for monkeys and said why. I pondered her view from that time. As an adult, I understand her observation. They belong in the world. People should not interfere with them.

A Christmas trip to town of Eutin market brought my first toy, a second hand teddy that was being auctioned. At the same marketplace foods were prepared. The smell of smoked fish and its taste are wonderful to this day. They smoked the fish in what was a tarp covered tepee. Men were going in and out of it releasing the smoke and smell: So much color and texture in the plaza.

Not only foods were important but medicines and doctors were difficult to acquire. The one time I remember going to a doctor and not a camp nurse was around the age of four...or younger. The doctor and my mother were speaking in German. I was neither thriving nor strong. She came to the child specialist in desperation of losing her last child.

The German doctor took compassion on her and wrote a prescription for me of a grape tasting powder. It was given once every day and really worked. I tasted grape for the first time in my life and decided it was something that was good. The powder crystals exploded on my lips and tongue uniquely. I felt so much better. Mother told my father of the doctor's kindness and saying that, "There is little medicine to be had for the German people. It was helpful of this doctor to care for one refugee child. He could have dismissed my mother."

THE DISPERSAL JOURNEY

By 1949, the great dispersal journey had begun for many ethnic peoples. Politics after the war made it impossible for northern Europeans to stay in war torn Germany.

Opportunity was elsewhere across the globe. Rumors of emigration possibilities spread quickly. Australia was looking for young families willing to work. My mother had a distant uncle who had worked in the Australian 'outback' for decades. It sounded like an inviting place for our family to begin life again: Maybe a house of our own some day. Australian immigration had opened and my father went for application papers. It was several weeks before he heard that the papers had cleared and went to inquire about the length of the list.

The well being of the Estonians was in the hands of the Lutheran World Council. It was through them and the Red

Cross that our families received CARE packages from America. What a mysterious word it was for me just like Australia. When my father came back he was excited. My young ears pitched forward to hear every word. "Nora, they have opened America for refugees!" The Lutheran pastor my father knew had provided him with the information.

Before coming home, father had switched destinations and aimed our family for America. The pastor placed us on the American list. My parents were very excited and elated. My mother trusted my father's thinking and courage. His judgement was always correct.

The entire time I was in the refugee camp I was too young for kindergarten or any formal schooling. I learned from stories and either German or Estonian picture books. Letters and words in both languages were the basis for my education in later years.

Leaving the camp we did not have much to take. My father allowed me to play with the breakable Christmas ornaments until they all broke. He promised new ones in America. The buttons on my dress did not seem to hold the round ornaments well. I was sad to see them fall off and break. There is a lesson in what is important in material objects at a tender age: What to let go and their value.

My parents were allowed two suitcases: One for each adult. Large khaki-coloured army vehicles were parked outside the mall to take many families on board the ship at lodged at Port Bremerhaven. It was exciting to be leaving. I had little attachment to the apartment but just a mental check mark..I had lived there. The sound of the truck engine, the shifting noise of gears shifted, and the rumble of the road seemed familiar and normal.

My father pointed out the ship we were taking to America. The gray liner went on forever. I could not see where it started or ended. The ship was so high with many, many decks.

Holding hands we left our suitcases and walked on board. My father went to the men's section of the ship way down below. My mother and I went to...again bunks with many rows.

On the deck my father took photographs of us facing port side towards the ocean. The wind was cold that morning. Down one side of the ship through doors, down stairs and forever walking, we found the dining room. Food was strange but good. I filled up quickly.

The ship's horn indicated that we were on our way.

ARNE ELLERMETS DETAILS THEIR ACCOMMODATION IN HAUNSTETTEN CAMP
(A*rne has also shared his story)*

This is a communication Arne had with me in one our dialogues....MM

I'll add here that our fourth DP Camp was in Haunstetten, Germany. The house where we lived had five apartments. One under the roof and two each on the second and first floors. Our apartment consisted of two small bedrooms, a kitchen and a tiny WC without a sink.

We shared the apartment with a young husband and wife without any children. Our bedroom was shared by Mom and Dad and Heiki. I had a folding Army cot in the kitchen and a large wooden crate that stood upright with a built in shelf that Mom covered with a piece of cloth. Your comment about the earthen floor where the cooking and bathing was done reminded me of the huge kettle in our basement in Haunstetten.

That area with a rough basement floor was used for family baths as well as laundry. We had a list and all of the families in the house had their designated days for their use!

The water in the kettle was heated with birch logs that we bought from the German farmers who drove their horse drawn wagons through the area that housed the refugees.

I still have a clearly visible scar on my left hand that could have cost me a finger. I was the wood chopper for the family. I used the ax with great vigor and must have lost the presence of my mind and looked away on the down swing! The sharp ax cut a neat flap of skin from the first finger to the knuckle and caused what I considered a flood of blood. Mom cleaned the cut and tied it tightly with a strip pulled from a bed sheet, but didn't exclude me from the rotation of wood choppers!

THE GRAVEYARDS OF MAN'S POLITICS: ANTS TAMM REFLECTS

I travelled with my fellow teachers to Estonia between the years 1992 to 2001 once a year. I really taught them about Estonia, Soviet union, the Russian mentality and so on. I know orthodox mentality, half of my family was orthodox.

One of my colleagues was a Jewish woman. She is born in the city of STALIN. Believe it or not, the Rumanians had renamed some towns to the honour of Stalin. It induced some smiles at the Estonia border.

We came to a cemetery for German soldiers and she refused to follow us and look. In my opinion every person does what she wants, so the situation was okay to me. Afterwards, at the evening drinks, she asked me about the Estonians and the Germans. I tried to explain the big problem, that the worst that had happened in Estonia those days was the Russian occupation.

I said that "Hitler" for her was like "Stalin" for us. I told her that, believably or not, the Germans behaved as normal people, believe it or not.

Estonians were not pleased with the German occupation, they had their doubts about Hitler's further ideas, about national socialism, but like the Finns they said,

"everything is better than the big devil Stalin, even a ´light´ devil." And compared to Stalin he was a light devil for most Estonians, but of course not for the Jews. And by the way, what did people know about the truth 1941? We talked much that night and she was confused all the time.

Next morning she said: I have thought about everything during the night, now I follow you to your tourist places, even to German soldiers cemeteries.

Afterwards she had problems with her VERY Jewish children, they did not like her Estonian travel at all, but I have met them now and then and now they are very understanding. I also met one of her friends from Tel Aviv, and she said that she understand the Estonians fully.

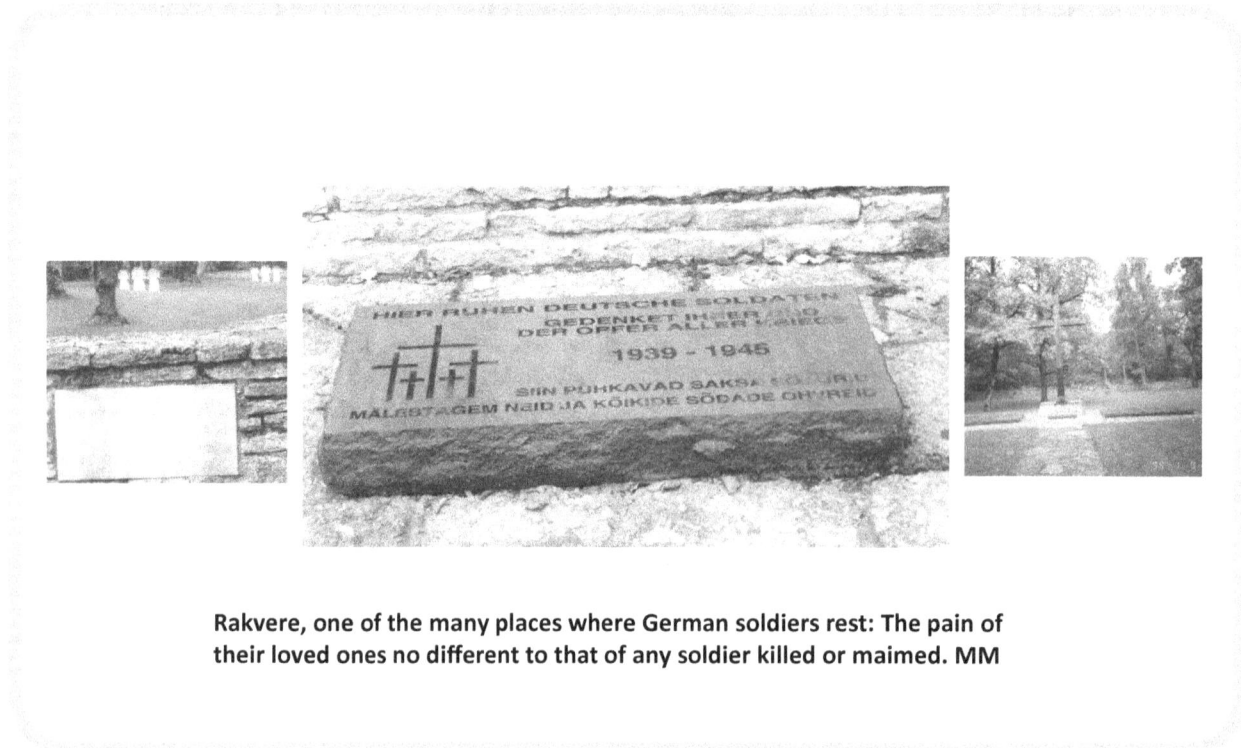

Rakvere, one of the many places where German soldiers rest: The pain of their loved ones no different to that of any soldier killed or maimed. MM

KALEV EHIN
SNIPPETS OF WHEN THE WAR CEASED ITS RUMBLING

HEADING FOR THE SWISS BORDER AGAIN
When it became obvious that the French would occupy the area in a matter of days, Father and I again headed for the Swiss border. This time however we went a few miles further south to Lustenau. It was now almost the end of April and the German authorities had essentially given up trying to stop anyone from crossing the border into Switzerland. Instead of the Germans, the Swiss were now controlling the influx of foreigners into their country.

For seven days father and I tried desperately to legally gain access to Switzerland from Lustenau. Everyday we would stand in line from morning to night in hopes of ultimately being interviewed and having our identification papers verified by the Swiss authorities. All of these activities took place on the German side of a large bridge that spanned the Rhine connecting the two countries. The Swiss, by some sort of an agreement, were using a large office complex on the German side situated not far from the bridge.

As we waited, more and more refugees gathered at the checkpoint heading across the river. Many of the new arrivals were high ranking Nazis who had discarded their uniforms and identities and were trying to flee from the allies. As the number of refugees swelled, our expectations of crossing the border diminished proportionately. The more people were trying to cross the more selective the Swiss could be.

For practical purposes the Swiss limited the access to their country to a small number of highly educated and physically fit individuals whose talents were in demand in Switzerland. Radio operators with young children, most likely were not on top of their priority list. By the time we had our credentials checked and had completed our physical examinations, the French arrived and the border was closed.

That full week at Lustenau was pure hell. During the day we would stand in countless queues, without food and hardly any water frantically trying to get all the required papers in order to be able to cross the Rhine.

Occasionally we would even have to repeat some process over again. At night our primary purpose was to hunt for a place where we would at least have a roof over our heads since there were no facilities to accommodate any of the people seeking refuge in Switzerland. Most of the nights we were lucky if we found a corner in some overcrowded building or abandoned house where we could sleep on the floor. Food was almost non-existent. I recall walking by a park or an open grassy area where people were cooking whatever they had found or brought with them on open fires. They were the fortunate few, but we weren't so lucky. On the first day in Lustenau, Father somehow got hold of a small bag of sugar. For the remainder of that week that is all we had to eat. I remember father parcelling out three or four tablespoonfuls of sugar during the course of each day to keep us going.

Several days before the French occupied the region our large duffle bag containing most of our clothes and mementos from home was stolen. As we had to hurry to another office or queue, we foolishly left the sack with a stranger who promised to take care of it until we came back. When we returned a short while later both the man and our bag were gone.

As the French units finally approached the town from the north, white flags (mostly bed sheets) began to be displayed on practically every building and the atmosphere on the streets became almost festive. The reason for the holiday like mood was quite understandable. Once the French moved in, World War II would be over for this part of Austria.

Within a day or two after the French had taken control, Lustenau, we, and other foreign refugees, were rounded up and placed into hospitals in the surrounding area for physical checkups and treatment for malnutrition. Father and I were first taken into a hospital in Bregenz where we were well fed and pampered. With the exception of the initial few days, we were free to come and go as we pleased; since we weren't being treated for any diseases. It was during this brief respite that we really had a chance to explore Bregenz: A place we'd travelled through so many times before but knew very little about. We ever took a cable car ride up to the top of Mt. Pfander on the eastern fringes of the city

DISPLACED PERSONS
The French occupation administration treated us well, and we felt and looked like fairly normal human beings again by the end of July, 1945. Father and I, however, were also aware of the living conditions beyond the boundaries of our little paradise. Germany was in ruins and unlikely to rise from the ashes any time soon. We neither wanted nor could remain in Birnau too much longer.

Father desperately searched for any means of gaining entry to any country that hadn't been ravaged by war as badly as Germany. More importantly, he was looking for ways to assure that we wouldn't be turned over to the Russians by the French or any other allies. That would have meant almost certain death for both of us in a slave labour camp in Siberia. We were keenly aware of several incidents where the allies had forcibly delivered several train loads of eastern European refugees to the Soviets. Many people on those trains had jumped to their deaths rather than end up in Russian hands.

Father finally managed to get his hands on a forged passport supposedly even validated by the French and the new

German authorities. I still have that document which was actually very cleverly designed piece of "art work" (including the use of hand carved stamps to make the artefact look as authentic as possible) by several young Estonian refugees. It stipulates that father was born in Norway but that his nationality since 1920 was "staatenlos" or "nationless". Essentially that he was allegedly a man without a country.

The intent of the passport was to make certain that father was not legally tied to any particular country, especially Communist Estonia. Further, at least theoretically, this was to permit us greater flexibility and accessibility in requesting travel to non-communist countries. It was all to no avail. We could remain in Germany for the next three years.

Having exhausted all our options in trying to get out of Germany, we now had to leave our Birnau sanctuary.

At least the French were kind enough to allow us to choose where in Germany we wanted to go. Father selected Hamburg since it was the closest city to Denmark with a refugee camp. Denmark came into the picture after father befriended a member of the Danish royal family during our stay in Birnau. Before the lady departed for Denmark she gave him her home address and asked that he write to her once we arrived in Hamburg.

In August we were on our way to Hamburg. **On our train trip north we had to pass through Ulm. During the course of a short layover at the main station, we had enough time to reminisce about our experiences in a once beautiful city. Ulm was still in ruins. Of course almost eighty percent of the old part of the city was destroyed by the raid we had endured.**

The city state of Hamburg, the once powerful member of the Hanseatic league (The League, organized in 1358 was a protective and commercial association of free cities in north-eastern Germany and the Baltic. Tallinn and Pärnu were members of the league). And the largest port city in Germany, looked pitifully humble as our train rattled towards the Hauptbahnhof (Central Station). Like Ulm and most other German cities it had been reduced to mostly rubble by allied air strikes.

As I would soon learn, this was not the first time Hamburg had been destroyed. Around 800 AD it had been a missionary outpost for the Christian Saxons and was constantly sacked by the Vikings and other non-Christian Germanic tribes north of the Elbe River. As late as 1066 it was burned down by the Wends. It was in Hamburg where I began to appreciate history

For several weeks after out arrival we stayed in a former military camp, almost in the heart of the city. All the refugees were housed in one-storey wooden barracks, and slept in open bays on bunk beds. Families had sectioned off portions of the open area with extra blankets in an effort to gain some privacy. Here we acquired our fair share of the required British (Hamburg was in the British zone) and local administrative documents.

Much of the rest of the time was spent exploring the city or trading some of father's cigarette rations for money, clothes, and other necessities on the black market.

Father also exchanged letters with his lady friend in Denmark. She apparently had been unable to pull the right strings, or she may have changed her mind about us altogether, in getting an official letter from the government inviting us to come to Denmark. That of course ended all our hopes of getting out of German in the near future.

It was in Hamburg that Father and I were officially given the new label- DP. To me being called a DP was humiliating. I hated this term from the very first day I heard it. I felt as if I was a lesser person than anyone else, with the exception of other refugees. Even the Germans, who had been defeated in war, had more self respect as far as I was concerned. They were still Germans and not some God-forsaken DPs.

In any case from downtown Hamburg Father and I were transferred to a larger ethnically diverse DP camp near the Hamburg suburb of Billbrook on the eastern outskirts of the city. The German name for the former military site was "Funkturm lager" or Transmitter Tower Camp which the British formally called Transmitter Camp. The name was quite appropriate since immediately to the east of the place stood a huge radio transmitter tower. Knowing that we would be there until we found a new homeland, Father and I settled in for a lengthy stay. We had no idea that we would remain residents of the camp for the next three years.

At the Transmitter Camp we also initially lived in one of the single-storeyed elongated wooden military barracks and slept in an open bay. I occupied the top bunk while Father slept on the bottom. The communal latrines and bathing areas were in separate buildings which were shared by the residents of several barracks. Half of each bath house was for the toilets which consisted of two rows of ten holes moulded into elevated cement benches built over a deep, elongated cesspool. The other half was the washroom. It contained several large, round wash basins about six feet in diameter with multiple faucets, and a separate common shower room. This was also the place where we did our laundry.

It was a typical German military camp, only the troops were no longer there and all the anti-aircraft weapons had been removed from their cement reinforced towers. That was also the reason the bath houses weren't designed to have hot water. The German military philosophy was based on Spartan ideals. Soldiers need to be accustomed to the harshest conditions possible. Thus, whether it was summer or winter hot water was not part of the deal.

Food was served in one centrally located mess hall. If you didn't want to stand in line for a long time, you had to queue up early or go late and hope that there as something left to eat. Everyone had to supply their own bowls or containers and utensils. Usually the meal consisted of some kind of stew or soup, bread and beverage. If you wanted fresh milk you had to buy it outside the camp.

It was hard to subsist on only what you could find in the mess hall so we visited the local German stores (there was one right outside the camp entrance) to buy milk, bread or potatoes since that was about all they had. Most everything else we had to buy on the black market. For instance, cigarettes or even half cigarettes, especially of American brands were like pieces of gold. Most of Father's cigarette rations, provided by the British camp administrators on a weekly basis, were used to purchase food and other items on the black market or from other refugees.

As far as my education was concerned, I first began to attend a small school in the Transmitter Camp organized by several Estonian families. Instruction was in the Estonian language. The school barely got off the ground when all the families, except us, decided to move to the Estonian DP camp in Geislingen in southern Germany. Father for some reason didn't want to follow them.

A short while later an attempt was made to start an integrated German language camp school. The venture lasted less than a year when it was also discontinued because the population of the camp was slowly dwindling as more and more people relocated in other camps or left the country.

Finally in 1947 I began to attend the local elementary school in Bilbrook, less than two miles from Transmitter camp. When I think back, this was one of the most rewarding experiences in my life. It was in the "Schule Billbrookdeich" where I first developed a fundamental appreciation for education and knowledge in general that's lasted to this day. It was almost a magical combination of two wonderful teachers and a close considerate friend.

My mentors were Heeren Boge and Saphir. Both men had been wounded on the eastern front and had been fortunate to have been released early from Russian prisoner of war camps (huge numbers of German prisoners of war died in Russian prison camps and most who survived weren't released until ten or more years after the war). They were strict disciplinarians but, at the same time, warm, loving and caring individuals. Although both teachers worked our tails off, they made learning fun and meaningful. History, as an example was not only taught in the classroom but also by frequent trips to the museums and sites where past memorable events had taken place. We also drew many maps and wrote a lot of papers.

My best friend Ronald, I'll never forget him although we haven't kept in touch since 1950. He and I supported each other no matter how rough a situation we may have been facing on school or otherwise. I spent as much time in his small house, built brick by brick collected from destroyed buildings, as he did in our place in the barracks. He saved my hide a few times from older and bigger German kids, and a few times I saved his from the camp bullies. I also enjoyed the fresh corn from his family garden.

No matter what circumstances surround them, young folks generally still seem to find all sorts of ways to have fun. We were no different. In the summers we swam in the deep water of the barge canal bordering the camp to the south. The water in the canal wasn't very clean, but then who cared. In the winter we skated on the same surface. I remember how tricky it was getting on and off the ice when the water level rose during the high tide. We were occasionally even crazy enough to use large chunks of ice, which had been broken away from the main surface, to float back and forth from shore to the middle of the canal. In early winter and spring when the ice was dangerously thin, except for us, it took considerable skill and daring to skate faster than the cracks were noisily forming between and behind our feet.

Weather permitting; soccer was played almost daily after school.

Estonians in Transmitter camp, 1945

Father working in the camp kitchen, 1946

Kalev's seaman's certificate

The SS Dabaibe on the St. Lawrence River in Canada, 1949

The goals consisted of two rocks, which caused frequent arguments as to whether a ball was kicked inside or outside of a rock. The kid with the ball was usually the captain of the team. I don't recall how, but somehow I'd managed to become the proud owner of a soccer ball. I suspect Father had something to do with it. In any case, most of the matches were between a team from our camp and one composed of the neighboring German kids. Predictably, these matches were always fierce and bloody.

I still remember my most frequent teammate and closest friend in camp, Paul. He was a tall, well coordinated lad from Lithuania and we seemed to complement each other no matter what we got involved in. In 1949, while Father and I were at sea, Paul and his family immigrated to the Unites States.

Two other kids I hung around with come to mind. They were twins Witek and Jurek from Russia. They weren't the brightest nor the most well coordinated youngsters in the world. For example, no matter how Paul and I tried we just couldn't convince them that being a millionaire was not a 'profession". Their goal was to immigrate to America and become professional millionaires. Usually, the twins would only play when we were short of players. Their family ended up in Australia. I still chuckle over those two characters.

While I was going to school and horsing around with my friends Father worked. At first he was employed in the camp kitchen. Naturally, we never ran short of food while he was there although we still had to supplement our diet with fresh fruit and dairy products from external sources. While Father worked in the mess hall he also managed to get us a private room at the end of one of the empty barracks.

I remember keeping my pet rabbit in the vacant bay of the building until someone stole it.

Later father got a job in the camp's Administration Office run by the British. I don't remember what his duties were but he got to wear a British uniform that was dyed black (in the British and American zones of occupation DPs who were employed in any official capacity- administration, security, transportation etc- by UNRRA or the allied military forces wore the full uniforms of the respective allies that were dyed black).

He really enjoyed that. In his new capacity he also found us new accommodations. We moved into a large comfortable room right in the headquarters.

KALEV BECOMES AN EAGLE TRAINER

I even became an eagle trainer. On one of my daily forays in the nearby woods, accompanied by a friend, I discovered a young eagle resting in a large pine tree. Out of curiosity we began to climb the tree although I was sure the bird would fly away as I got closer. To my surprise the eagle remained perched on a branch about half way up the tree until I was practically next to him. He didn't seem to be injured, but he did make a lot of noise.

As I attempted to pick him up he jumped off the branch and fluttering its wings it slowly fell to the ground. My friend had been watching all the action from below and now began to chase the bird on the ground. Within seconds I got down from the tree and helping him in the pursuit. Soon the young eagle became exhausted and I was able to pick him up without much difficulty. With a sly look on his face my friend asked, "Now what are we going to do with it?" More as a dare than anything else, I told him I was going to take him home with me..

"Home" of course was one of the many three-storey brick dormitories on the spacious grounds of the hospital complex. Father and I lived on the second floor of one of those buildings with a number of other single men, most of who also happened to be Estonians. We had a small room with two beds in the back of one of the bays where our compatriots were housed. In order to get to our room we had to walk through the open bay.

As I brought in my eagle, the men present could hardly believe what they were seeing.

Eventually several of the chaps complimented me for having accomplished such a superb feat. Many remained mesmerized by my feathery companion while others started to laugh uncontrollably. Once the curiosity had subsided, Father asked me the same question as had my friend in the woods, "What are you going to do with the eagle? "I had no immediate answer, except that I wanted to hold onto it for a while. I then told Father that I could keep the eagle in one of the large empty closets in our room at night.

I already knew what his reaction would be. He first said that keeping a big bird like that in the dormitory would obviously be against the hospital rules. Besides, how would I keep the room and chest clear? The answer was "No!"

At this point many of the men around us got involved in our discussion and they egged Father to allow me keep my newly found friend. After a relatively lengthy debate and considerable ribbing, Father gave in and consented to allow me to keep the eagle for a couple of days. For two to three days I was in the limelight. Even people from the other dormitories would stop by to see my eagle when I had it outside, secured by a long string tied to one of its legs. Occasionally the bird would hop (You could hardly call it flying) on a low branch nearby tree or the flat roof of our building's utility shed.

It was only a question of time before the hospital staff got wind of my eagle training. The reason I had gotten away with it for this long was because the dormitories weren't visited by nurses or other attendants on a daily basis. After all, none of the residents were ill but merely convalescing.

As expected, my eagle training days ended abruptly. One morning our floor was routinely inspected by several nurses. When they came into our room and saw the eagle perched on the wooden rod *in the shape* from the several nights of roosting. In no uncertain terms I was told to get rid of the eagle immediately and clean up the mess.

Unlike the nurses, our compatriots in an open bay were laughing hysterically as the nurses marched out. They had long anticipated what would eventually happen to the eagle's nest and now the hour of reckoning was at hand. I was not amused.

Instead, for me it was a very sad moment. I took my feathered friend to the tree where I had found him and untied the string around his leg. We stood there looking at each other for a while as if in mourning. Eventually, he flew up the tree and I hoped that he would make it on his own.

A YEAR AT SEA AND THEN OFF TO A NEW HOMELAND

Unexpectedly, Father was offered a job as a radio operator on a ship in July 1948. The ship was as old Estonia freighter that had evaded the Russians and was now docked in Kiel Harbour, Germany....

To make the offer feasible I was later included on the deal and asked to sign on as a deck boy, a post that included any odd menial jobs that needed to be done around the ship. Father's salary was to be thirty-one British pounds, mine ten pounds. At the time the exchange rate for the pound was about five dollars. Of course free food and board would be part of the arrangement.

Father still had his old Mariners' Service Certificate issues back in 1920 when he worked on salvage ships as a radio operator. Before I could join the crew, however I needed one of my own. Father sent my picture and other necessary documentation to the free Estonian Legation in Stockholm in Sweden. Within thirty days I received an Estonian Mariner's Certificate of my own.....We then packed all our belongings into three newly purchased aluminium suitcases and headed for Kiel:. There we reported to the SS Dabaibe on September 21...

With the all-Estonian crew we had no problem speaking with or swearing at our shipmates.....

As we approached Dabaibe gangplank it was hard to believe that we would take this vessel to sea in seven days...... the propeller blade, which was exposed above the water, had been half sheared off probably as a result of enemy fire.......

Luck was with me again. Since Father was a ship's officer he was assigned his own cabin on the lower bridge, which of course also contained all the radio gear. I was now almost thirteen and the youngest crew member.....

The captain was kind enough to allow me to bunk with Father instead of the other sailors. That certainly made things more comfortable for me because the regular crew's quarters in the fore and the aft sections of the ship were dark, dingy and cramped.

Within an hour of our arrival Father was bury repairing the vessel's electrical system and I was peeling my first pail of potatoes for the evening meal... I really grew to hate the potato peeling job... chipping rust and paint was pure pleasure compared to slaving over spuds. Unfortunately that would be an almost daily job for me for the next three hundred and fifty-seven days....

The North Sea wasn't as kind to me as the Baltic had been on my first voyage when in September 1944 when Father and I fled from Estonia.... since on part of the propeller blade was missing, the propeller was out of balance.... caused the entire ship to vibrate even at abnormally slow speed we were travelling at. I got seasick for the first and last time in my life.....

On September 30 we entered a dry dock part of the way up the Tyne River. Everybody on board was relieved that our ship had made it to England for its major overhaul without a serious sea incident....... I saw many wartime ship wrecks littering the Dover Strait especially on the French side...

What stunned me most was the number of very young teenage girls, some not older than me, who were offering sexual favours by means of very explicit hand gestures, in exchange for two packs of cigarettes..... when it became clear that no one from our ship would respond to their offers. The girls began to show their disappointment and anger with all sorts of shouts and motions....

Father and I ended getting a case of oranges for two packs of cigarettes. Having not seen an orange since before the war, we devoured the entire crate in less than two days. You can only imagine how our digestive systems responded to that marathon fruit eating event.....

On another occasion my impatience nearly cost me my eyesight. Shortly after sunrise as the Dabaibe was approaching the gateway to the Seine River on our trip to Rouen, France I was in the galley getting things ready for breakfast before the chef arrived. My first task was to get a fire started in the coal burning stove. I checked the embers in the stove from the night before with my bare hand and they appeared to be completely out. I then added more coal. Since I was a little behind schedule, I thought that I could save some time by lighting the coals with kerosene. I fetched a cup of kerosene from the paint locker nearby and threw it onto the coals. Before I could stoop all the way down again to light the coals, the stove exploded and hot ambers flew into my face.

Quickly dousing my head with cold water I was able to stop most of the pain. Fortunately I received no injuries to my eyes and the burns that covered my face didn't become infected. Luck was with me again....

It was in Canada that I was first introduced to chewing gum and I made sure I had plenty of Wrigley's Double Mint gum before we departed Newcastle. I also remember thinking that if Canada was anything like United States I definitely wanted to live there.

Apparently two of my ship mates felt the way as I did. They were nowhere to be found when the ship was ready and we left without them. One of the sailors was the second youngest crew member whom I would meet again three years later in New Jersey......

Father and I also seriously considered jumping ship but decided against it. We were afraid that if we were caught crossing the border to the United States we would never be allowed to immigrate to our most favorite country. We were going to pursue our goal legally. Thus after we left Canada, Father and I agreed to sign off Dabaibe the next time the ship was in England. From there we would go back to Germany where we would try to follow the footsteps of many other refugees to the United States.

In September 13 1949 we docked in Barry, England as we returned from the Mediterranean by way of France. It was time to bid farewell to thirty shipmates who I had grown close to during those last twelve months. That obviously was not easy. Although the year at sea had been reasonably good to us, it was now high time for a change of venue. I needed to continue my formal education and, more importantly, we had to find a permanent home. Only one legal avenue remained open to us in our quest for a new homeland, and that required us to return to Germany. ...

Two days later we were back at our old home, the Transmitter camp.

Much had changed at the Transmitter Camp since we had departed a year ago. All of my old refugee friends were gone. They had departed for their new homelands. It was a severe let down for me to realize that although I had travelled much of the world for a year, I would-be the last of my friends to locate a permanent home.

Fortunately Ronald and his family still lived near the camp and I saw a lot of other familiar faces as I joined my former class at Schule Billbrookdeih. They were now in the last half of the sixth grade, the final elementary grade in the German school system.

After we returned to Transmitter Camp father immediately applied for immigration to the United States. In the request he stipulated that he'd accept any job for which he could qualify. That was the easy part. Now we had to wait and hope that one of the war relief services in America would be able to match Father's qualifications, including a thirteen year old dependant, with the employment needs of one of the employment needs of one of the registered sponsors

The Estonian refugees in Germany had appropriately named this sponsor matching process as the "Orjaturg" (slave market). We waited nervously for several months and with every passing day our confidence in being able to find a market). We waited nervously for several months and with every passing day our confidence in being able to find a way to the United States diminished accordingly. IN the meantime I completed elementary school on Bilbrook and father worked as a radio technician a factory in Gilde, another suburb of Hamburg.

Finally, in April of 1950,after almost giving up all hope of ever seeing America we were notified that a farmer in Northern New York State had agreed to sponsor us.

Father and I jumped for joy.

HELL'S FURY WAS ALL AROUND: BUT THE MORALE OF THEIR PEOPLE COULD NOT BE PLUNDERED

The stories in this book repeatedly allude to precarious situations where the parents prayed for remission of their perceived destiny, as did their children.

At every little gain, prayers for thanks for a little reprieve were offered.

TÕNU LOORPÄRG

Extract from

"FREEDOM IS ANOTHER WORD FOR EVERYTHING TO GAIN"
Volume II

I was born innocently enough into a world that was not so innocent.

Totalitarianism was in vogue in Europe and elsewhere. Both small and large nations were being swallowed up by circling dictatorial sharks.

Like my grandfathers and grandmothers before me in World War I, my parents and I had to suffer the same fate during world War II. My two surviving grandparents had to also go through it again for a second time. I had to survive disease, being bombed in Estonia, hunted by submarines in the Baltic Sea, attacked by a fighter aircraft in Poland plus all the horrors of World War II Europe, before we eventually journeyed on a refugee ship "to the ends of the earth" in faraway New Zealand for our place of refuge.

WAR BABY

In 1942 the international political situation was a mess. The Second World War had been in progress for three years and millions of lives had been lost in the fighting around the globe. The Estonian State had been under occupation first by the Soviet Union since June 1940 and then, after the breakdown of the Molotov Ribbentrop Pact between the Soviet Union and Nazi Germany, by a German occupation from July 1941. The earlier Soviet occupation resulted in thousands of Estonians being killed or sent to slave Labour camps in Siberia and had created great animosity towards the Soviet State and its Communist system amongst the Estonian population.

Thus when Germany attacked the Soviet Russia and pushed them out of the Baltic States and Estonia the local inhabitants initially saw them as liberators from Stalin's oppressive system. At this time there was little awareness of the wider geopolitical impacts of the war and the focus in Estonia became one of "my (Soviet) enemies enemy (Germany) was my friend" -- at least until the Estonian State could be re-established.

It was felt amongst former Estonian Defence Force officers and politicians that a key aspect of re-establishing the Republic of Estonia at the end of the war would have to be the creation of a military force comprising of Estonians that could resist any future attempt by the Soviets to occupy the country. They had witnessed the example of Finland which had resisted the Soviet occupation by armed resistance and how it had been able to preserve its independence. Indeed Estonian Volunteer Units had been formed which went to Finland to support the Finns in their struggle, the so called "Finnish Boys" (Suomi Poisid). It was clear by this time that Germany was likely to lose the war and that the German occupation forces in Estonia were now more amenable towards the formation of such a force and for its use against the Soviets on the eastern front. The expectation was that it would be used to defend Estonian borders against the Soviets

At the time of my birth on 15 October 1942 Germany was facing defeat after military disasters on the eastern front at Stalingrad and in North Africa. By 1943 it was facing the prospect of having to withdraw from its assault of Leningrad (St. Petersburg). This presented a direct threat to Estonia being reoccupied by the Soviet Army, a prospect which the population assessed as the worse of two evils, insofar as the German occupation had been relatively benign in Estonia compared to what had earlier been experienced under Soviet rule.

Most of the population was prepared to support the call of mobilisation from its leaders. Earlier in 1940 Estonian Armed Forces had been incorporated into the Soviet Army and had been moved to Russia for employment as "Labour battalions". The Soviets did not trust the Estonian troops. Many, like my father had managed to resign before they were moved to Russia and those who remained were badly affected by morale problems. This became obvious when they were used close to the front by the Soviets when the German assaults began in the northern sector of the eastern front in July 1941.

Large numbers became prisoners of war and others deserted the Soviet Armed Forces. The Germans on their part released Estonian POWs, who were still in their Estonian Army uniforms, after a short time and sent them home to Estonia which was now occupied by the Germans. Some were formed into small units which served on the eastern front with the Germans. By 1943 the situation on the Estonian border was critical and Estonian political leaders supported a call to mobilise young Estonian men to form a large Estonian military force to be equipped by the Germans. They saw this as the only possibility left to stop another Soviet occupation of Estonia. The expectation was to fight on Estonian borders in defence of Estonian soil.

This was the situation my father faced at the time of my birth, he was an Estonian Army officer by training, committed to the defence of Estonia at the time of the infamous Stalin/Hitler pact (Molotov-Ribbentrop Treaty)signed in August 1939. The secret protocols divided Eastern Europe up between Germany and Russia resulting in the occupation of

Estonia in 1940 and other Baltic states including Poland. There had been no support from Western governments who were distracted by the Western Front and the "phoney war" in Western Europe. The situation for Estonia was desperate especially after the first Soviet occupation in 1940 when tens of thousands of Estonians and other Baltic peoples were deported to Siberia or killed.

After my birth my father was reluctant to leave his young family, preferring to continue with his brother operating their wireless repair business which was becoming quite successful in repairing radios and selling battery powered radios to farmers. For a brief period during the German occupation my parents family life as a young couple seemed as "normal" as could be, given the world was at war.

I was born at the Tallinn hospital in Islandi Väljak street. This location was to became highly significant for me in the years to come in more ways than one. My family home had become an apartment located on Paldiski Highway on a fourth floor and which was conveniently located above my father's business on the ground floor. I was Christened at Kaarli Church on December --- 1942 by Pastor Koppel. My god parents were Helmut Arakas and Captain Saidra. My godmother was my mother's girlfriend.

Helmut was soon to be arrested by the Soviets in 1944 and died in a Soviet slave labour camp in Siberia that year. I was to be reunited with his wife Ellen and his daughter Anu many years later when I took my family back to Tallinn in 1974 for the first time.

My other Godfather survived the war and escaped to Canada. I was to meet him and his wife once more in 1990 when we were both visiting Tallinn at the same time.

Our Tallinn apartment was relatively modern, it had one bedroom, a living room, a kitchen and a bathroom. We were quite fortunate with our food situation as through the business, we were able to procure items from farmers wanting battery radios and also other items like liquor which was only obtainable through the Germans who sought to have their radios repaired.

It was a relatively quiet period for Estonia after the Soviets retreat and the subsequent fighting which erupted again on Estonian soil between the Germans and the Soviets in 1944. It would seem that in our brief family life together, when I was a baby, our lives were quite comfortable.
My mother did not work and was at home. Later she was joined by Mamma, during 1943. From this time on until 1949 Mamma became my principal caregiver. My mother's relationship with my paternal grandfather, from what she tells me seems to have been slightly distant. She found him to be a rather proud and demanding personality and a stickler for correctness traits he had possibly developed during the ten year period he was employed by the Czar's Adjutant, Count Fersen. She does not remember him altogether favourably. At that time my Auntie Aili and Uncle Volli Kallaspalu were working at the oil shale town of Kohtla Järve and my mother's brother, Uncle Lexis remained behind in Narva.

I don't of course remember any of this period in Estonia up to the time we left in September, as I was not yet two years old.
The Estonian population at this time was around 1.2 million, 92% of the population were ethnic Estonians. The rest were mainly Russians, Swedes and Finns. The Jewish population centered mainly on Tallinn and the other cities and was very small.

My father's cousin Helga had married a Polish Jew Pedro Goldmann who was a manager in the textile factory at Greenholme in Narva. They together with their daughter Ariana were caught up in the Soviet roundup of those individuals and their families who were considered a threat to the Soviet occupation in 1940 and was sent to Siberia during the forced removals. This meant that during the period of the Soviet/Nazi pact when Poland and other East European states were carved up between Germany and Russia they had been removed from Estonia.

After the pact broke down and Hitler attacked the Soviet Union, Stalin joined the Atlantic alliance against the Axis powers. This required the Soviets to release all those Polish citizens who had been incarcerated by the Soviets during the period they were allied to the Nazis. It resulted in the release of thousands of Poles from Siberia including our relatives the Goldmann's.

They also included the orphans of the Polish officers who had been slaughtered by the Soviets in the Katyn Forest when Poland was attacked by the Soviets from the East and the Germans from the West during September 1939. Some of these orphans came to New Zealand via Persia. Our relatives did not get back to Estonia until 1945 and were then able to emigrate initially to Austria and then later to Chile.

The irony of their situation soon became apparent, had they remained in Estonia during the Nazi occupation they could well have suffered the fate of the small Estonian Jewish community which was largely eliminated by the Gestapo. In other words their Siberian incarceration had probably saved them. I found out about the families fortunes in 1969 when Ariana wrote me a letter and we were later to meet in Paris and New York.

It would seem that my crisis experiences also started early in life. My mother tells me the story of how, soon after I was born, she had been breast feeding me on the bed and had dropped off to sleep. When she woke up I had "disappeared" a frantic search soon located me under the blankets curled up at my mother's feet and sound asleep. This perhaps explains a tendency I have acquired in later years to hold my breath and then take a deep sigh.

My grandmother (Mamma) came down to assist my mother (Ema), from Narva in early 1943 and she was to remain my close caregiver until May 1949 when my Ema and I departed Augsburg, Germany on our journey to New Zealand. Mamma was to follow once we arrived but for reasons still unclear she never received the correct papers and ended up going to USA with my Aunt Aili and Uncle Volli.

My father (Isa), was called up for mobilisation in March 1943 and after passing his medical examination was mobilized on 1 April 1943 and immediately dispatched for training at Heidelaager in Poland.

After some three months the Estonian Regiment he was assigned to the Nevel Front where they saw their first combat action. He managed to take a short leave at home in Tallinn for Christmas 1943 and soon after their Formation was moved to Narva, Estonia from Nevel in a move to block a major Soviet offensive on that strategic location.

During March 1944 the bombing of Tallinn by the Soviet Air Force intensified. On the night of 19 March 1944 there was a major assault on the city in particular the central city suburbs including our district which was near railway lines. Bombs landed some 50 metres away across the road killing many friends and acquaintances.

Tallinn was on fire. My mother (Ema) happened to be out visiting friends that night while Mamma and I were at home. Ema had to run back through the bombed streets of central Tallinn stepping over dead and wounded lying in the streets, to our apartment. She found us safe in the cellar of the building and we departed the city during the fire storm for a safe haven in the countryside with friends that Isa had arranged for us to stay with.

We went to Captain Sepling's farm located at Padise. The farm was located next door to the ancient ruins of the Roman Catholic Nunnery there.

I have some recollection of this night, at least I seem to remember being taken outside with the whole sky glowing red. However this may also have come from adult's descriptions of the scene afterwards in later years.

It was subsequently rumored that the attack on this night was carried out by a squadron of Soviet women aviators, who had been imbibing of alcohol prior to the mission! Whether this was propaganda or truth it does conjure up an unusual picture of the assault which is different from most. This then was another close call in my young life which with luck, I managed to survive together with my grandmother and mother.

We stayed on at the Sepling farm for almost 6 months as the international events got worse for Estonia. Isa had been stationed with the 20th Estonian Division near Narva since January and had been fighting on the front in a series of defensive battles.

During a lull in the Soviet offensive he was sent on a short training course to Tallinn. This was to be the last time we were together as a family in Estonia. It was also the last time that Isa saw his brother, my Uncle Lembit, who was also on leave at the same time from the Tartu front. We later learned from his platoon

Isa Ema

Ema taking Tõnu for a walk
Inset: Tõnu aged 3 months

Tõnu's christening day

commander that Lembit was badly wounded when his Estonian border defence unit was over run during a Soviet attack on 17 September 1944 in the area of Ema River at Kavastu near Tartu. He had remained behind wounded on the battlefield and had been murdered by Soviet soldiers. His grave is unknown and lies somewhere on the banks of the Ema River.

During our stay on the Sepling farm I had to face another challenge when I caught diphtheria. With wartime conditions in force it was difficult to get medicine. After considerable worry for Ema and Mamma who were nursing me I managed to pull through the illness and survive. In those days diphtheria was often a deadly disease for children.

By September the situation on the border had reached a critical point. Telephone links between Tallinn and the Front had been cut and my father was unable to contact us. He had given my mother instructions on how to get us on board merchant ships as an escape route, should the Red Army reach Tallinn.

Captain Sepling also had contact with the captain of one of the merchant ships .This was to prove to be our saviour when the time came. Had we stayed behind, being the family of an Estonian Army officer who was serving in an Estonian Unit with the Germans, this would have resulted in our dispatch to the Siberian Gulag forced labour camps or worse. Many were killed later also. This had already happened to thousands of our fellow citizens in 1940 when the Soviets first invaded and was to be repeated again in 1945 and in 1949 by Stalin's henchmen the NKVD (later named KGB).

In mid-September we received advice that the last German convoys evacuating the wounded would be leaving Paldiski Harbour, which was some 10 km away, in the next few days. We had not heard any news from Isa and rumors were rife about the German Army withdrawing from the Baltic states. Word was also received that there had been a Soviet breakthrough on the southern Estonian front near Tartu and that the Soviet Army was fast advancing on Tallinn.

This was the signal for us to take the few possessions we could carry with us and go to Paldiski wharf. Somehow we managed to get a ride on a truck to the harbour on the night of the 16th September together with the Sepling family and scramble on to the merchant ship commanded by Captain Sepling's acquaintance.

We later learned that after the collapse of the Narva front, my father and the Sepling son who was a staff sergeant serving with Isa's unit arrived at the farm to discover we had departed two days earlier. My father on discovering this decided to head south where other members of his Formation were retreating towards, instead of joining the Sepling son in his escape bid by small boat to Sweden. This he hoped would enable him to reunite with us in Danzig where our ship was headed.

I did not know until many years later on one of my visits to Estonia in 2007 that others close by on that Paldiski peninsula were not as lucky as we were. On visiting the site of the Concentration Camp Memorial on the peninsula in 2007, I discovered that on the same day as we managed to board the merchant ship, some 1000 concentration camp inmates comprising mainly of Jews were being slaughtered by their Gestapo jailers. The Gestapo were desperately trying to remove evidence of their inhumanity. I must say that as I stood in front of the Memorial in the snow surrounded now by a quiet forest of pine trees, I felt an enormous sadness welling up in me.

Questions came to my mind such as "why did I survive and not those people who died here?", I also felt an enormous anger towards the type of totalitarian leadership which led to the slaughter on this spot and many, many others all over the globe. The combined tyrannies of Stalin and Hitler were unparalleled in human history, yet a decade later Mao Tse Tung and others like Saddam Hussein were allowed to continue with their crazy ideas in the name of their extreme ideology.

During the voyage south on the Baltic Sea, many ships in our convoy were attacked by Soviet submarines and aircraft. We were lucky once again to escape with our lives as the ship in front and the ship behind us in the convoy were both sunk. More recently I have been able to get documentary movies of this journey from the archives.

Some months after we managed to slip through to Danzig, in January 1945 a former cruise ship turned refugee carrier, the "Wilhelm Gustloff" was sunk by a Soviet submarine after it left the Latvian coast. Some 9000 people most of them women and children fleeing from the advancing Red Army went down in the Baltic Sea, making it the deadliest maritime disaster of all time. On our journey south there were other Estonian families also. Ema tells me I was the youngest on the merchant ship and because of this the captain gave us his cabin to sleep in on the three day journey to "safe" harbour.

REFUGEE
When we arrived in Danzig after the three-day journey on the Baltic Sea, we were initially taken care of by a local Lutheran pastor and his family. He was a Baltic German who had lived in Estonia until recently but had been repatriated (evacuated?) at the time of the Hitler - Stalin Pact in August 1939 (Ribbentrop Pact). This agreement resulted in the transfer of German speaking populations to German held territory especially from those areas which had been occupied by the Russians after their agreement.

This is where we stayed for some months until February 1945. My father in the meantime had been able to evacuate south with the remnants of the Estonian 20th Division and arrived in Danzig in December. He was able to locate us through the Red Cross. The Estonian Division was to be reformed and resupplied at a training location in Neuhaemer.

For a period the families of Division members who had managed to reach Danzig were housed in a German Army holiday camp. We spent the Christmas of 1944 and the New Year in this location and Ema relates that Isa and her made a short trip to Prague for sightseeing.

Sadly she says the atmosphere in Prague was not very welcoming to those wearing a German uniform, although many Czechs once they knew Isa was part of the Estonian Division changed their attitudes. There was an understanding about what had happened to Estonians and other Balts under the Soviet occupation and therefore a degree of sympathy though this did not extend to those with communist sympathies.

Ema recalls, Isa was anxious for the locals to hear them speaking in Estonian so that they could be distinguished from the Germans. Isa's leave ended in February and he reported back to the reconstituted Estonian 20th Division which had been re-equipped and trained for operations on the Opeln Front.

This leave was the last time that my mother saw my father, I was not going to see him again for another 30 years. As Soviet armies were fast closing from the East it, became essential for us to move west away from them. The emphasis was to move south west towards Bavaria near where the Americans were advancing. We were now a group consisting of some 30 women and children and a few men.

Included amongst our group were some distant relatives of ours, Helga Junkur and her son Indrek. Travel was very difficult and consisted mainly of movement by train and which was often disrupted by the bombing of rail lines and consequent backtracking to follow a different route. This gradual zigzagging to the south-west took a period of some six weeks. My mother recalls that where ever we stopped at railway stations, the local population there had been very helpful to us. They provided adequate food and drink sometimes in exchange for the few ration coupons which we had obtained and at other times it was given for free.

On one occasion we were travelling through this forest in a passenger train when suddenly a fighter aircraft swooped down initially firing at the engine and it managed to knock it out of action with its machine guns. The train was brought to a standstill with the engine full of holes and water spiraling out of the water cylinders now useless to the steam engine.

All of the passengers jumped out of the carriages and entered the forest in order to escape the fighter aircraft which came back for a second attack this time along the row of carriages.

My mother and grandmother hauled me clear of the carriages at some distance and my grandmother planted herself on top of me in the undergrowth. Unfortunately I was desperate to go to the toilet, so her weight made this call of nature even more desperate.

Once the aircraft had emptied its magazines into the train it departed and I was able to get relief.

This moment of crisis I can now recall as my clearest first memory from my childhood, not so much for being strafed but more from the feeling I might fill my pants if my grandmother didn't get off the top of me.

After some time we got the all clear and returned to the carriages to rescue our belongings. My grandmother took

Grandfather Alexander, Uncle Lembit, Tõnu and Ema, Mamma at Grandmother Alide's gravesite at Rahumäe, Tallinn.

Uncle Lembit, Mamma, Ema, Grandfather Alexander and Tõnu.

Above: My parents with my Anu Arakas and my Godparents Helmut and Elen Arakas

**Tõnu and his mother   Anu Arakas and Tõnu
January 1944**

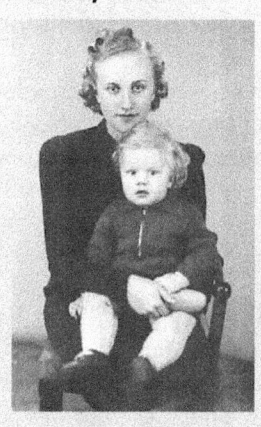

down the bag which had been hanging on a hook at about shoulder height as one was sitting by the window, looking in, she pulled out a dress which was now full of holes from machine gun bullets ripping through the bag during the attack. I often think that as Mamma was a very religious person she saw her "holy" dress as a sign of God's grace in keeping us from harm. After this train attack our group had to walk through the forest for some kilometers before we were able to continue our zigzag journey south. Eventually we managed to get to the Bavarian lake district close to the Swiss border.

At this stage, having been on the railway for weeks, normal hygiene precautions had become difficult. We were reduced to inspecting each other's hair for nits just like monkeys. Finally we found small Bavarian village of Erkheim where we were able to find accommodation with the local farmers in return for assisting them with the fieldwork and other chores. All this time the war fronts were coming closer as Germany was being squeezed from both East and West.

Now however we arrived at a point well away from the Soviet forces and which was close to the oncoming US combat units coming from the west. Prior to their arrival in our village by mother recalls another close encounter with an attack aircraft. She was in open fields with a few others gathering wood some distance from houses and forest cover, when they were suddenly attacked by an aircraft firing machine guns. Fortunately they made it to cover in the nearby forest.

The arrival of US troops in the village was a very tense time initially, for both groups, the villagers and the troops were both mutually suspicious of each other. After a few days the tension settled down and very soon military government bureaucrat's, closely following the front line troops, had us under scrutiny for our refugee status.

At the end of this scrutiny was another journey to the displaced persons (DP) camps at Augsburg. *I remember at the end of the war seeing the night sky lit up with flashes and hearing the boom of cannons in the distance. During the day we would sometimes look up into the sky and as far as the eye could see there were aircraft, mostly bombers moving across the sky hundreds of them. All were looking to drop their bombs on selected targets.*

The war ended on 8 May 1945. Sadly my mother tells me, there was not much in the way of celebrating for us Estonians at the war's end. Everyone was relieved that most of the killing and destruction had stopped however.

Estonian refugees had lost everything and we could not risk going home to another oppressive Soviet occupation. Now we did not know what destiny lay ahead .

Soon after the war ended my family and the other Estonians found ourselves concentrated with other DPs and being grouped into our national communities for housing at Hochfeld Camp, Augsburg.

Hochfeld turned out to be something of a lucky break for us. The housing there had been built for the workers at the nearby Messerschmitt factory where the Messerschmitt fighter aircraft were built for the German Air Force during the war.

By the time we arrived the factory had been bombed flat and bulldozers had pushed all of the rubble into long rows on the adjacent farm fields. The housing area we were in had been built by Hitler as a model of "National Socialist construction", specifically for Messerschmitt factory workers during the 1930s.

The doorways had above them various symbols depicting Hitler's National Socialist movement. Some of the buildings had suffered from bombs but they had been left relatively unscathed.

Very close to where we lived, the end of one apartment block had received a direct hit from a bomb and it became a place where we would often go to play our games of hide and seek. There were however a large number of broken windows which had to be boarded up.

With our arrival, all the workers had been tossed out and us refugees were crammed into their apartments. This of course was not taken kindly by the local population which had been evicted by the American Occupation Authorities.

Rumors about what could happen to refugees in some of the cities in Germany began to circulate, frightening stories about people being beaten to death with clubs were often heard. How true these were we had no way of knowing.

Soon after we arrived I remember in the evenings clustering around a radio with others listening to the crackling sound of a voice speaking in Estonian pleading for us refugees to return to the "homeland".

These propaganda messages were being broadcast by the Soviet authorities in an attempt to encourage the Baltic peoples to return. Sadly after the way they behaved in 1940, nobody was prepared to listen to them.

Around the housing area there was a great deal of debris lying around and on the embankment overlooking wheatfields below were the remains of German defensive positions.

From here the memories become largely Tõnu's own and hence will no longer be written in Italics.

As youngsters we would play along this bank and we would regularly find ammunition, helmets and other war debris. It was the first time I set eyes on Gillette razor blades which were lying about in great quantities with those distinctive paper covers with the bearded head on.

Fortunately, I didn't blow myself up like some of my playmates, who accidentally got injured by explosives and I remember in one case a friends bullet wound which had gone in one cheek and out the other, knocking out some teeth but enabling him to recover once it healed properly. By the time I got to know him the wound had healed in such a way that he was able to sort of "whistle" out of the exit point in hi scheek. Something he demonstrated frequently to us small boys with pride.

Many years later I discovered that when the Americans arrived on the outskirts of Augsburg, the American general in charge had come to an agreement with the mayor of Augsburg to surrender the city by calling it an "open city". This was done to save the beautiful medieval township from being obliterated by bombs and gunfire. It had not of course included the Messerschmitt factory at Hochfeld which had already been worked over thoroughly by the Americans and their bombing.

At the time I was living there I cannot remember being aware of any factory, only the debris around it. I remember going for long walks through the area with my grandmother and playing on piles of scrap containing anti- aircraft guns and other military equipment. There was certainly a lot of it. We would go to the nearby forest area in summer to swim in a stream and in winter I recall being taught how to ice skate on a small lake close by.

The US Army had a base nearby and every so often they would put on a sporting event. I recall going to watch a game of gridiron and another time we attended a rodeo. Those events caused me to take a great interest in them especially the oval ball used in gridiron (American football). When I arrived in New Zealand I mistakenly thought that rugby was the same game and took it up as my sport of choice. This was fortunate because it became a sport in which I was able to excel to my advantage as I integrated into the New Zealand Society.

During the winter months we were learning to ski on improvised wooden skis made from a pickle barrel and on other occasions we went tobogganing on sleds as the top activity. When the boys in the neighborhood got bored, they would be edged on by the older ones to form National "gangs" who would then go en-mass to the next apartment block where the Latvians or Lithuanians were housed. Here we would challenge their "gang" for a snowball fight.

I was one of the younger ones and made sure that I stayed on the fringes of these "fights". One of our favorite play areas was the children's sand pit in the middle of the apartment quadrangle. Here we would let our imaginations go wild, especially us younger ones .The bigger children did not usually bother us here. Sixty years later in 2005 I returned to this spot to once again find that childhood sandbox which had somehow been preserved and as I sat down in it a flood of memories returned to me of those long forgotten days. It brought tears to my eyes.

For those of us who had lost our fathers in the war or whose whereabouts were unknown, the first few years in the refugee camp was the hardest. This was because most of us found ourselves in this category and those at my age or younger could not remember what a father was.

Our daily lives tended to be filled by female guardians and the odd example of a male role model in the family could be found in perhaps one in ten of the families at Hochfeld.

Gradually over the period of some 24 months with the

Christmas 1943, Tallinn

Mamma, Ema and Tõnu at the Sepling farmhouse with Sepling mother (right) and Seppling daughter (left)

Tõnu's father being farewelled, with other Estonian Officers after mobilization, by my mother and grandfather April 1943 at Tallinn Railway Station

help of the Red Cross, fathers began to appear from POW camps and elsewhere. I remember being very jealous of a neighboring boy who was slightly older than me and whose father arrived back on the scene. In particular I was unhappy that I didn't have a father to show me how to ride a bike or teach me how to box.

I vaguely remember my mother showing me a letter she received from my father in a POW camp through the Red Cross around 1946. We knew then he was in the hands of the Soviets. After that we heard no more.

We shared our two roomed apartment with another family the Ülpers, there was Mr. and Mrs. Ülper and their daughters Reet and Tiina. Tiina was four years older than me. We lived as a sort of extended family sharing the kitchen and a cellar downstairs where Mr. Ülper had created a sauna or steam bath which all the extended family would use once a week.

On these occasions I was introduced to the proper routines of Estonian sauna bathing including the beating with birch leaves and dousing with buckets of cold water.

The cellar areas were used for much more also, some illicit, like making home brew and rearing of farm animals. Pigs in particular. This practice was forbidden by the UNRRA authorities and every so often the community police would carry out raids to identify the evildoers. When these occurred the word would go out and pigs would be quickly transported away from the cellar and hidden elsewhere. Often the location chosen was inside newly stacked wheat clumps on the wheat fields below our apartments. Us boys would sit on the embankment and watch the "politzei" move across the harvested wheat field with pitchforks, poking each clump to see if they could flush out a squealing piglet.

In the apartment we had a smaller bedroom where my grandmother, my mother and I slept and lived. It was also the area where I used to get bathed in a large bucket placed on a table. Mamma would do the scrubbing by stripping down to her waist and bare breasted give me a thorough wash and inspection to see that I was free of nits.

Indeed my earliest memories are mostly of my grandmother rather than my mother. Ema, was away working during the day in a canteen attached to the American Army base. She would bring home interesting new things like leftover Coca-Cola drink in a small tin bucket from which I was able to enjoy the taste though no longer the fizz from a bottle. Fruitcake was another treat I recall along with occasional sweets and doughnuts.

We had very little money so I did not have many toys to play with. I did receive birthday presents however and some which I received then I still have to this day and cherish, like "my own" cup and saucer for drinking coffee and tea and a little wooden figure with movable arms and legs on a stand.

In addition, once I started kindergarten in 1947 and was learning to read and write, I received my first books published in Estonian by the refugee authorities. Most of these I have managed to keep over the years and they now take pride of place on my bookshelf.

Mamma was with me all day long, sometimes we would go on long walks together. On occasions we would go into the Forest looking for mushrooms, an old favorite Estonian pastime, on other occasions we would wander around the area where the war debris had been piled up and I would climb up onto the anti-aircraft guns and other interesting relics.

One favorite pastime of my grandmother I remember particularly well, she enjoyed visiting the local cemetery. In Estonian culture this is not unusual as we quite frequently sit by the grave side of our ancestors and tidy up the grave sites. Now , here in Augsburg, there was no graves to tend so Mamma would take me to the local cemetery when there was a funeral and we would tack on the end of a group of mourners as they carried the coffin to the grave site.

She was a regular churchgoer and made sure that she taught me to have faith in God. This she did by teaching me a simple prayer in Estonian which I have had with me all my life. I did attend Bible classes at the camp but these did not leave a firm impression on me.

The only thing I remember of them were little scripture cards they gave out with a picture of a biblical event on one side and the story in English on the other side. I could not of course read English in those days and the best I could do was to try and mouth the letters and words. I recall this created a great deal of fun for us because Estonian is a phonetic language and English is not. In particular we used to be fascinated by the word "THE" which is very difficult to sound in Estonian.

At Christmas time we still managed to have a big celebration, proceedings began on Christmas Eve when Father Christmas arrived with his presents for all the " good " children. There were of course never any "bad" children, but just in case there was a symbolic "vits" (small bundle of branches) also.

A Christmas tree took pride of place with real candles and other home-made decorations on the tree. The smell of burning candles and scorched pine needles still lingers for me even after these many years. Outside there was usually a white carpet of snow. All the children had to learn a song or poem to recite as they received their Christmas gifts from Santa Claus.

Later, on New Year's Eve, we had a number of other events to welcome in the New Year. I particularly remember how we used to heat up lead and then drop the lead liquid into cold water to see what shapes they made. From the shapes we would try to see the future.

Another day I remember was in late October or early November, I think it was all Saints night when all the children would dress up in various ways and visit the next-door neighbors for treats. I remember it as a variation of what I later understood as Halloween as practised in USA. However I think this was an age-old Estonian tradition also.

Our closest friends at the camp I remember as Ali and Harald Kapp and the Allase family. Mr Allase when he got back from the war taught me a good lesson for not smoking after I persisted on one occasion asking him for a puff on his cigarette. He gave it to me and almost immediately I started to cough so badly that I didn't touch a cigarette again for a long time.

Anne Allase was my regular playmate both kindergarten and around the home. They have remained in contact with us through the years despite being continents apart. Kapps on the other hand were responsible for guiding us to New Zealand. My mother had started to work with Ali as a dressmaker in the camp and they became firm friends.

Harald and Ali met in Augsburg and were married there. Harald had an uncle in New Zealand who sponsored them to emigrate in 1948. After they arrived, they in turn would sponsor my mother and I to come to New Zealand and we then intended to bring my grandmother over.

Kindergarten was located in the next block of apartments and we would go there on a daily basis for organized play and a little learning. Here I made friends with my first playmates that I am able to remember. Names like Jumbo, Indrek Junkur, Toomas Rikken,Tõnu Sang and Anne Allase. There were also many others and these I recall from the birthday gift one received from classmates.

On a child's birthday caregivers would organise a folder containing a picture drawn by every member of the class. I still have two of these folders from my years at the kindergarten.

At Christmas time there would be a big party for all the children to enjoy. On occasions there would be organized at the community centre a film show, usually some rather nostalgic film about the lost homeland which in my memory always seemed to end with a shot of waving rye fields.

Other events would involve cultural recitals of poetry and song, sometimes from a visiting Estonian Concert Party from another DP Camp in Germany. The kindergarten children also got to perform, I got my first public speaking opportunity when I was chosen to recite a poem for the camp audience .

From those years together in Hochfeld we have been scattered far and wide around the world, mostly to USA and Canada. Nevertheless I have managed to maintain some contacts, especially those who were the children of my mother's friends and with whom she continued to correspond with over the years from New Zealand.

Anne Allase (Kiis), in particular maintained communication with me throughout the years, even when I became a little tardy with my letter writing, she would regularly correspond and keep me informed about those of our mutual friends with whom she still had contact with in North America.

Sadly Indrek Junkur and Tõnu Sang are no longer with us and Toomas Rikken's marriage to Mari-Ann ended in divorce. Mari-Ann remarried with Tunne Kelam, he was a prominent Estonian activist for Estonian Independence in the 80s and 90s and is now a Euro MP in Brussels. Mari Ann met Tunne in USA where she was active as a Estonian- American lobbyist in Washington

As the years passed in the DP Camp, by 1948 my mother had lost hope of my father ever returning and she feared the worst. We knew

Ema on her 25th Birthday (May 7 1947)

Our Estonian Refugee group resting in a forest Tõnu in centre front.

Reet Ülper   **Mamma 1947**

Tõnu and Anne Allase

he had been captured by the KGB and this meant that in all probability he was dead.

My knowledge of my father was limited to what Mamma and Ema said to me about him on occasions and also from a box of photographs which we had brought with us from Estonia. Even though I had been too young to remember him I was able to see him in the photographs, looking very smart in his Estonian Army Officers uniform and other photos where he was together with me and my mother. On my part I was oblivious of the politics and the dangers this brought and continued to have a strong faith that Isa would return. To this end the little prayer my grandmother taught me helped, as every night I would recite it and finish with the plea to God to bring my father back.

This prayer also had another useful purpose in later years when I was separated from other Estonian speakers at Boarding School and in the Army. It enabled me to hold on to my Estonian language to some extent as a sort of daily mantra to keep me in touch with the pronunciation of the language.

Eventually in 1958 my prayer was answered when word came through relatives in USA that Isa was alive and living in Tallinn.

I did get a little confused on one occasion when an Estonian POW arrived at our window and asked Mamma if this was where the Estonian Community was located. Mamma invited him in for a drink and from this kindness there developed a friendship which also included my mother. Initially I wasn't sure whether "Uncle Tarr" was my father or who he was.

I also recall being visited by my father's cousin Aksel Loorpere (Loorberg) who had managed to escape from Estonia and was living in a DP Camp at Geislingen near Frankfurt where my Aunt and Uncle were.

I would not see him again until 1984 when I visited Toronto on a business trip. Aksel had immigrated there and married another Estonian but they had no children. We would visit my aunt and uncle on occasions also in Geislingen.

There were other visits, also to Munich which was not far away. We would visit the rather dilapidated Zoo there and on one occasion go to a swimming pool where I had my first experience of panic as I floundered in water up to my chin at the shallow end.

By 1949 the situation for us Refugees was getting desperate. To go back to Estonia was not an option our only hope was the generosity of various Governments around the world opening their doors to us.

People were taking up the first opportunity that came up just to get out of their depressing circumstances in the DP camps. We were no exception. Our opportunity came when our friends the Kapps managed to get sponsored for entry into New Zealand by Harald's uncle who had been living there for some years. They departed Augsburg in 1948 and we arranged for them to sponsor our family once they arrived. In the meantime we made application to the New Zealand authorities and went through the relevant medical tests required.

Unfortunately while my mother and I were accepted, Mamma was turned down on the basis of her age and my aunt and uncle were not accepted because Aunty Aili had had TB when she was younger. We then were advised to wait until my mother and I arrived in New Zealand before making another request to sponsor my grandmother.

Arrangements for the journey were completed by February of 1949 and we awaited instructions to join the draft for our journey to New Zealand.

Had we stayed on at Hochfeld I was due to start primary school and I can recall being involved in the preparations for this event. I remember it as a very exciting few weeks during which we were introduced to a number of new activities which we would now embark upon. I remember music lessons were commencing along with being supplied with writing books. However this never eventuated for me until I got to New Zealand as we were to depart in May.

I do remember listening to the adults talking about the journey described by some as "a journey to the ends of the Earth". Also there was a vision of going to the South Pacific and arriving at islands where there were coconut palms, sandy beaches and balmy breezes.

Suddenly learning English became a priority for my mother and sorting out the few possessions we needed to take with us. Everything went into a big wooden chest which had written on it, "Mrs Helene Loorpärg, Wellington, Camp at Pahiatua New Zealand". Some things had to be excluded, the most significant being a small "ladies" pistol which my father had given to my mother in Danzig for protection if needed, on our escape route to the west.

Hopefully on our next journey we were now going to be beyond the reach of the KGB.

Anne and Tõnu

Tõnu, Ema Mamma prior to departure 1949

Aksel Loorpere (Loorberg)

Refugees escaping bombing. (Photo source unknown)

ON THE RUN TO THE DP CAMPS

On our way towards Bavaria. Tõnu being held at rear. Ema and Helga Junkur in front

Mrs. Rikken, Toomas Rikken, Mrs Ülper, Tiina Ülper, Mr Ülper (1949)

Temporary sanctuary in Bavarian Village of Erkheim: April 1945

Tõnu and Hochfeld playmates 1945

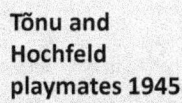

PHOTO COLLAGE FROM HOCHFELD: TL

Big children organizing us little ones for photo 1948, Tõnu middle in braces.

My (Tõnu at right) first swimming pool at Munich

......since the age of 10 I had managed to eliminate my foreign accent completely. If I had adopted Stan's surname, "Mckeon", I could have merged completely into this young and vigorous British outpost in the southern seas, which New Zealand still was in those days. But I had not done that. Something inside me told me to keep my Estonian identity alive. I think at base it was a feeling of injustice that I saw had been inflicted on the land of my birth by large totalitarian states, ... TL

First year at Estonian Kindergarten 1947. Tõnu on right of middle row

Estonian Kindergarten 1948, Tõnu on right in braces

THEY BECAME EXPERTS AT MARKING TIME

Hochfeld camp, Augsburg

Refugee housing at Hochfeld

Estonian adults party, Ema at end of table on left

Ema, Mamma, Alma Allase and Anne Allase

Estonian adults party in Augsburg, Ema in top right hand corner

Mr & Mrs Ülper, Helga Junkur and Ema outside apartment (note broken windows)

BIRDS AND BEES AND WRIGGLY THINGS: GGM

People in rapid transit in fear for their lives are hardly in a position to consider the niceties of life.
Many of the stories allude in variable detail to bed bugs among the bedding and to lice which infested many of our little and bigger bodies. The dusting powder used to delouse us also gets popular attention in our narrative while in Germany: But let us not wallow in our sense of being humiliated. The Germans did the same to their own folk in transit.
Small children were of course at greater risk and other things blighted them such as

WORMS:

Ilvi Joe: I don't remember how we hit on the topic of worms, but Liivi related the story when one of the group had mentioned that he had had worms in Geislingen and another person in the group had said "me too". Last evening, a third person remembered having worms in Geislingen, and I certainly also remember having worms. Then we discussed what could have been the possible cause and concluded that the worms were a result of the food and unhealthy conditions under which we had lived during the year before Geislingen camp was set up. It would be interesting to hear what others remember about this topic and what may have caused these worms.
I brought up the topic, because to us, discussing our childhood memories of Geislingen, this fact had been omitted. ....
(later in the communications) I appreciate Jüri Linask's scientific explanation for this condition and, indeed, I now remember the practice he described.
Jüri Linask: Kersti, Juri's widow has translated Juri's explanation:.
Yes, after all the traumas of war, worms were indeed eating at us. Pinworms are not that unusual.
It had to do with how the Germans grew vegetables. Germans used raw sewage that was pumped out of the privies in the houses as fertilizer and spread it on their vegetable beds in the gardens. By eating the vegetables, the eggs of the parasitic worms gained entrance to our intestines. Maybe some of us remember the stench that accompanied the spreading of the "fertilizer". A dirty song (lori laul) sang by the children comes to mind regarding the men "sibid" who emptied the privies. The song translated somewhat loosely:

> The moon shines, the stars twinkle
> Why are the "sibis" making all this noise?
> A barrel hit the gate (...)
> resulting in the lack of poise.

What is in parentheses are words that cannot be printed. I don't think that this entirely belongs in our accountings of Geislingen. But...Hopefully this helps to clear up the mystery around having pinworms that affected many.
Tiiu Kera wrote: Must have infected a lot of us. Ema & Isa said I had them too. Wonder what the lasting effects of the poison they gave us to kill the worms has been.
Ilvi Joe wrote: No doubt, my interest in facts - historical and otherwise - stems from the training given by good professors. I hope we don't get all bent up when facts are presented.
Someone alluded: "It's nice to have two scientists' - Mai and Jüri Linask - opinion on what may have caused the worms."
Mai replied: I can't claim any knowledge of such things: Biology never did grab me in medical school. I think I enjoyed the drawing bit better during prac classes.
Priit Vesilind : Although I've found that discussion of intestinal worms is always a good ice-breaker at parties, and is probably quite a chick magnet, I'm not sure I want to go much deeper into the subject except to say that I always thought it was from bad meat.
Mai: There are probably heaps of memories which we haven't included. Maybe some were omitted because we were too coy to share such material when we first 'met' per e-mail.
I can certainly remember the recurring song and dance about having worms and mother indicating them to me you know where: after a while I managed to self diagnose and recognise those beasties. I can't remember what mother did about them. I certainly can't remember any allusion to the notion that they were food or animal borne. But then how much access did most of us have to animals? And food being scarce I don't think that we were too preoccupied what came with it: And of course meat which appears to be the major vehicle was almost a novelty. So one has to wonder how long we were hosts to these beasties before they were evicted from our innards.

AND SMALL CHILDREN FOUND AMUSEMENT IN SIMPLE THINGS:

Ilvi Joe: Ulme also knew to say that UNRRA had distributed three condoms per month to men in the camp. Nobody mentioned that in the life story either!
As for the condoms, Mari-Liis asked me in an e-mail why would "mudilased" have known about such things. We didn't, except that at our Saturday evening conversation while dining and wining, Ulme also remembered (and I forgot to include that in my e-mail this morning) that we found discarded condoms on the ground and innocently thought them to be balloons and blew them up.
It's true - we knew nothing about the birds and bees, as Mai says.
Mai: As for condoms: I know modern kids learn about birds and bees before the go to kindergarten but I am sure that I was far too naive to even recognise one if saw one: for many years later! Thank goodness for medical school.

TOOMAS PILL
CHILDHOOD MEMORIES

I was born in Tartu on January 7, 1938. These are my memories as a 6 year old child of our flight from Estonia to Germany in the summer of 1944.

I spent the summer of 1944 with my maternal grandmother Bertha Kuiva in Põltsamaa, a sojourn of which I have the fondest memories. When I returned to this picturesque town in 1985, I had no trouble in finding her cottage, so vivid were my memories of the place, as if I had never left, allowing that I was only six years old at the time.

My parents, Johannes and Linda Pill and my aunt and her husband, Leino and Leida Tammemägi, unwilling to undergo the horrors of a second Soviet occupation, had decided to emigrate to Germany, with hopes of eventually reaching the west. On a balmy August evening in 1944 we set off on the back of a truck - in the company of numerous other people - to meet up with my parents in Tallinn.

We stayed there with the Tammemägi family and their little daughter Liina, in a massive 19th century granite building in Kadriorg, where Leino, as chief veterinary officer for Tallinn, had been given lodgings. The building still stands, but the narrow gauge railway, which terminated there and fascinated me, has long since gone. Tallinn, with its high, 6-7 storey buildings and trams, was quite a revelation for a young boy.

After a week or two we boarded the ship that was to take as to the formerly Polish port of Gdynia, which after being annexed by Hitler had been renamed Gotenhafen. I remember how my mother and aunt tried long and hard but in vain to convince grandmother to come with us. She could not, after all, leave her house and friends in Põltsamaa. Besides, it was then the hope that we would meet up again within a year or two, little did we think that the western democracies would allow Estonia to be swallowed up by Russia.

It was eighteen years when we saw her again. In 1962 with Khruschev's coming to power, there was a mini thaw in Soviet politics, in so far as parents of pension age were permitted to join their children abroad. Thus my grandmother was able to emigrate, as were the mothers of some of my parents' friends. These ladies constituted the first emigrants from Estonia since 1944, and meeting one another for the first time in Sydney became good friends.

I recall, that as the ship set sail from Tallinn harbour, passengers went on deck to catch a glimpse of the city's spires receding into the distance.

On disembarking at Gotenhafen the refugees were met on the quay by ladies of the German equivalent of the Red Cross, who welcomed us with tea and sandwiches. There was no visible war damage and food seemed more plentiful than in Estonia - the Germans certainly knew how to look after their own.

From there we boarded a train through Pomerania to Liegnitz in Silesia. Why Liegnitz? one might ask. A German officer, Hr. Tilgner, who had been billeted at my parents' place in Tartu, had suggested that we stay with his mother in Liegnitz. This turned out to be an unwise choice, as the lady was not at all agreeable to families with children staying there for any length of time. Fortunately a refugee camp was being established on the outskirts of the town for Germans fleeing Allied bombing raids in the west of the country. The camp consisted of timber two-room cottages, with stove and kitchen. Leino, who was working for the veterinary administration at Breslau, was able to obtain some pure alcohol, which helped our chances for obtaining accommodation with the camp administrator.

Alcohol had become an invaluable item of barter in Germany in the final months of the war. It came in handy a second time in Breslau, where he, having missed the last train out before the encirclement of the city by the Russians, was able to convince the driver of a solitary locomotive, which he spotted building up a head of steam, to take him on board in exchange for a litre of alcohol. They then proceeded through the night at snail's pace, so as not to draw the attention of the Russians. This was his second close encounter with Russians, previously he had left Tallinn on the last transport, a few hours before the arrival of the Russian tanks.

Liegnitz was a sleepy provincial town, with a mentality to match, which manifested itself in xenophobia and racism in so far as Poles and Jews were concerned. Its townsfolk, perhaps conscious of their own insignificance in the Reich, displayed excessive zeal in implementing Nazi doctrines by humiliating these so-called "untermensch".

My aunt saw an elderly Jewish man, emblazoned with a yellow star of David, walking in the kerb, though there was ample room on the footpath; my father saw a policeman order Polish passengers in a tram relinquish their seats to Germans; I myself saw a German boy, a few years my elder, mock a group of Polish men and women, engaged in forced labour in the presence of an armed guard, telling them to eat sand from his toy shovel. I was shocked at such conduct toward a grown person and was relieved to see one of the Polish women take the shovel from his hand and throw it into nearby bushes.

The poison of Nazism was being injected into the future generation virtually from infancy, and amazingly, the inhabitants of Liegnitz continued to fall for the propaganda of a regime whose days were clearly numbered.

In the evenings we could see the sky light up in the east as if by some false dawn - the battle for Breslau was raging, but no sounds could be heard, the distance was too great.

We caught the train for Dresden, which it was hoped would be spared on account of its treasures of baroque architecture and its insignificance industrially. The train was suddenly diverted to Leipzig, for reasons at the time unknown to us. Only later did we learn that Dresden had been obliterated. The train was stopped once in anticipation of an attack by enemy fighters. Some people ran out into the snow, but a German officer warned that we would be no safer outside. As for himself, he would prefer to die warm in the carriage than cold in the snow. Fortunately there had been a false alarm and we reached Leipzig without further incident.

Leipzig station, once Germany's biggest, had been reduced to a shell, but due to German ingenuity, the trains kept running. Contrast Sydney, where a suspected gas leak at Town Hall station immobilised the metropolitan network for most of the day. In Leipzig we stayed in a multi-storey housing block, next to which was a pub or bierstube. The city was bombed virtually nightly, and the wail of the sirens, the roar of the engines, the whistling sound of the falling bombs and explosions were for a long time afterwards etched on my mind.

We normally had enough warning to get to the air-raid shelter in time, except in one instance, when we would have most needed to do, we had barely time only to get to the cellar. The planes seemed, to judge from intensifying engine noise, heading straight towards our neighborhood. Then there was an almighty crash, the walls shook and lime dust poured from the ceiling. Elderly German women, dressed in black, were on their knees praying.

The next morning we saw a huge crater, where the bierstube had stood only the previous day - if the bomb had been released a second later, we would have perished.

There is surely something to be said in favour of prayer!

From Leipzig we proceeded by train to Hof, a medieval town, with a gate tower similar to that of Pikk Jalg in Tallinn. I remember passing through that gate twice in the middle of the night in a desperate search for accommodation - no easy task, when encumbered with all one's earthly possessions. We finally managed to rent a room from an old man, whom I remember distinctly for one thing: he would get himself dressed at 9 in the morning for a hairdresser's appointment at 12 noon. We called him "old man of Hof".

From Hof we proceeded to Furth, where due to excessive bombing, no accommodation was to be found. We eventually found a place. By that time food too was becoming scarce. I remember visiting an Estonian lady there, who showed us a plateful of cakes she had baked, but would not offer us any. At that time I fell ill with a 40 degree temperature, and father, emaciated as he was, insisted on carrying me to the cellar during bombing raids. As luck would have it, he managed to find lodgings for us in the nearby village of Stadeln with an asparagus farmer, Hr. Buchel. My father helped him with the harvest, and we ate asparagus 7 days a week. This was a huge boost in a time of famine.

The Buchels were a devoutly Catholic family - father, mother and daughter - and prayed at meal times for the return of their son, Hans, who was in the army. We all rejoiced greatly when Hans turned up, unscathed with not a scratch on him. The whole family joined in prayers of thanksgiving. As I remarked above, there is something to be said for prayer. Even when we were already settled in Australia, we exchanged Christmas cards with the Buchels.

One beautiful morning the Americans arrived in their jeeps and squashed in the middle Coca Cola bottles. They were a welcome sight for us, even if the Germans were initially somewhat apprehensive. It was also good news to the smoker: the Americans discarded their good quality cigarettes half way through, throwing them by the roadside. All one had to do was to put the discarded half into a cigarette holder and light up.

The Americans set up refugee camps in Augsburg. We, after a brief stay in Augsburg, ended up in Geislingen, living first in the district of Willemshöhe and subsequently in Schlosshalde. What caught my attention in Willemshöhe were the fossilized snakes, some of them enormous, all turned into a spiral, victims of some geological upheaval. The ridge behind Schlosshalde was crowned with a ruined castle, whose foundations date back to Roman times.

My interest in classical civilizations started when my father explained to me who the Romans were.

In Geislingen I attended the Estonian primary school. I recently discovered my final report card, best subject being art followed by Estonian and mathematics.

This was the extent of my education in the Estonian language. It came to end as we set out for Australia in April 1948.

Toomas, Liina in Estonia

WERE THEY SPECIAL OR IS REMINISCING WRONG?

During the compilation of this book and its predecessor there have been many interesting e-mail manylogues.

Somebody asked why we have so little sympathy among us towards the plight of today's refugees. Do we really feel that way or are we just exploring the way the saga is unfolding. It is in retracing one's steps that one at times finds ways to improve the road for those that follow. Let us not forget the words of the epilogue of "When the Noise had Ended" which states

It is a vain hope that the squabbles of mankind will ever stop. Three will always be refugee children But we hope that the children who share our misfortune can also find the rays of hope which sustained us in Geislingen, and use them to meet the challenges which lie ahead of them. We hope that they retain a trust and serenity in themselves to find meaningful futures and opportunities to support others, that they follow their conscience to generate warmth, not hostility, to others. In a world that often does not understand their journeys, they may need to find the courage to stand alone.

A question was also posed if we felt that we were somehow special: I would doubt that there is anything special about any one person on this earth. However when a topic is under discussion it is appropriate to discuss that subject and feel warmth for it: That does not preclude warmth for another topic. Simply put, if someone raises the subject of measles then measles is to be discussed not chicken pox!

And maybe all of us begin to look at a subject by considering how it looks to us personally. Much has been said about what is perceived to be Australia's intolerant immigration policy: Those words have tended to emerge from those who somehow feel that they were rejected by that policy many moons ago. Some spoke in response to my remarks that it is important for the hierarchy to take sufficient time to ensure that the children are correctly placed: A few years of misery beats potential decades of this.

My remarks of course speak of arriving in Oz with fudged documents: The children of German soldiers were personae non grata those days. It was no joy being in land of endless warmth when that warmth was not accessible by the ravages of history upon the host people. I still see myself being in Oz with a stolen ticket: One that belonged to another child that perhaps missed out on the quota.

Of course times have now changed! But **I still ponder where that child now lives and might they have become a greater asset to this country. Might they be embittered by their rejection because space had run out. MM**

National Socialist Crest for Messerscmidt Factory workers apartments in Hochfeld (photo taken 2004), where Estonian refugees were housed.
The doorways had above them various symbols depicting Hitler's National Socialist movement.

US Army Air Force Reconnaissance photo of bombing results on Messerscmidt Factory (top right) Hochfeld Camp buildings (top left) between field and railway workshops.

THE MESSERSCHMIDT FACTORY IN AUGSBURG: ONCE A GENESIS OF LETHAL FIREWORKS: TL

Remains of Messerschmidt Factory after bombing

WAR ENDS & PEACE DESCENDS: REMINISCING WITH BRUNO LEEPIN

Burned out trains in Schlosshalde. They were behind Bruno's house: Despite my nomadic streak they were a feature I had not noticed and no one else had commented about yet

The bridge over the train tracks- photo MM 2002

View if the train tracks from the Schlosshalde steps; MM 2002

The steps leading down to the track: MM with her mother circa 1948

The same view from a lookout nearby circa 1948

Bruno like most of us passed through many camps in Germany and what was then known as East Prussia and now is known as Poland, among those places he lists Augsburg which as I recall was late in that transit.

He was at one of those transit points when war finally ground to a halt. He can recall the American soldiers plunking themselves on their helmets and to see dancing and rejoining break out subsequently. It is there that he first saw a black American soldier.

Photos of the WMF factory, the one on the top L. taken from approximately same location as the lookout: MM 2002

He must have arrived in Geislingen early on when the WMF factory was still functioning war mode producing ammunitions. His mother worked there and he recalls his mother telling him about needing to wear special glasses when inspecting ammunition during some aspect of their production.

In those days they did not live in the houses on the hillsides, which were to become the camp. The factory had its own workers' quarters which consisted of dormitories of triple bunks. Bruno recalls sleeping on a table somewhere on his early trek.

The factory in those days was painted in camouflage colors.

On reflection, maybe mother early on worked there too: I can't remember much of her and it could account for my penchant for hanging around that factory.

Bruno and his family eventually moved to Schlosshalde and lived at the top end of the winding Schlosshalde Strasse. He would meander down the hill, down some steps to the railway bridge which led to the train station and the town.

The bridge was a fun place for small boys: From there they could watch the steam engines ferry their cargo of troops, military vehicles and hardware beneath them. The soldiers were of many nationalities and he call recall the red and while Polish flags being waved. Among those soldiers were POWs returning from their varying places of internment. Early on there were also old war stricken burned -out trains.

And of course, that bridge brought a 'magic' to those little boys: As the engines puffed their black smoke onto it: The children rushed into that smoke to make believe that they were now among the clouds: Clearly pollution was a peace time issue to be haggled over at a later date.

And troops and war hardware not confined to the railway transport. The trucks laden with the laden with such cargo passed through the town's main road: These of course were a magnet for small boys.

But perhaps the burned out trains were to become the beginnings of Bruno's journey in life. At the town end of Schlosshalde Strasse overlooking the valley was a more up-market house with big windows. It has a nice garden which Bruno had wandered through, and through one of those big windows Bruno saw an easel with a painting: Of those burned out trains. He continued to return there to become mesmerized by the paintings of that Estonian DP gentleman.

Life on that mountainside was fun for kids: That slope was also the plumbing facility for the differing modalities: Its legacy luxurious vegetation which the children enthusiastically gobbled up for their extra vitamin rations.

All good things come to an end: Kindergarten ended and school started. By that time, due to the DPs being relocated to their adoptive lands the camp began to shrink and Schlosshalde was closed down and its remaining folk relocated to Wilhelmshohe on the same mountain face: Steep steps led down to the school. They were fun, challenge and at times a site for disaster: Melting snow and slush made the passage more slippery. Bruno and Erika finished their first year of schooling there and had begun the second, when another trek began: To Australia.

Bruno and Erika didn't pass through transit camps and recall the long train haul to the Bagnoli camp in Italy. He doesn't recall the long dark tunnel stretch suddenly ending on what seemed a rickety bridge (I wondered what might happen if it collapsed- I suspect there were many such mangled bridges on our trek) which is imprinted in my memory but recalls that American MPs boarded the train and question its passengers, including his mother about an unwanted passenger on that train: Once they were found the train stopped at the next station and both police and their quarry alighted.

Perhaps boys and girls do absorb different aspects of whatever trek they travel.

REFUGEE 'SURVIVAL KIT' IN WW II GERMANY

Mother died fifty years ago while I was still a medical student and we had been very much in survival mode: Her narrative of the past perhaps a hybrid of windows of time and place names.

As I have perused the stories in this book there have been times when I have felt that the imagery felt familiar and at others despite being in the same terrain it felt 'wrong'.

That red book with its barely decipherable hieroglyphics was to be my reassurance that my instinct was mostly right: An entry on its pages suggesting I was elsewhere: Where and why may never become known.

Newer options are emerging to follow up such glitches.

In some ways this little book is the Bible of my preverbal days.

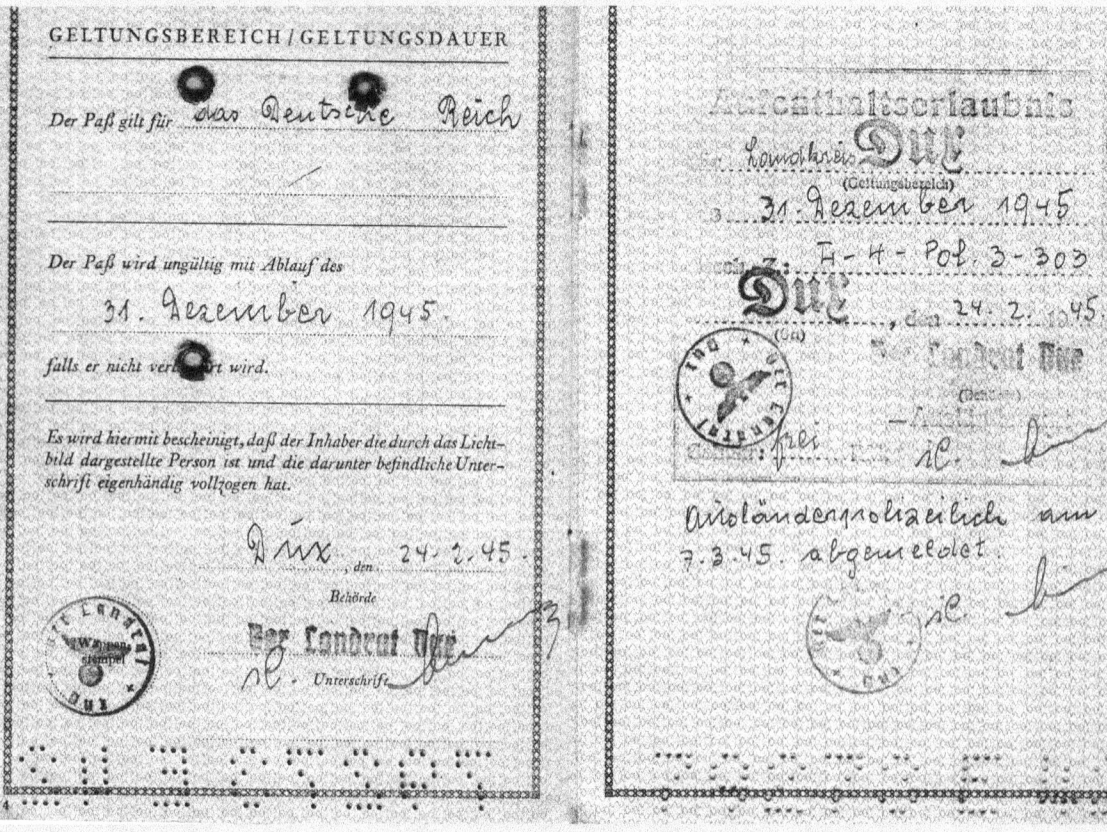

KALEV EHIN
FATHER'S ENIGMATIC IMAGE

Father also considered himself to be infallible. His judgement was always final.. I sensed that many more previously unknown facts would surface...

Mother and Maimu were never actually sure of what job father did during the war. ...he was occasionally referred to as 'Rahva Valgustaja" (People's enlightener). What that job entailed we never were really able to decipher. Mother suspected that it entailed collaborating with the German authorities

What she'd said now made a lot of sense to me. Three seemingly unrelated events from the past now fit perfectly into the puzzle. First, I remembered Father leading the local Song Festival parade during our last summer in Põlva. He'd been extremely proud to the point of arrogance in having been selected to lead the procession. He'd even acquired a solid white suit for the occasion. Unfortunately, none of us ever had the nerve to ask him where he had managed to get such a smashing outfit under wartime restrictions and how he'd been selected to lead the parade in the first place.

Part two of the collaboration puzzle involving my father fit into a few weeks after the Song Festival pageant. Father decided to take him with me to a funeral celebration at a farm some distance from town. Traditional Estonian funerals as well as weddings are merriments that last three solid days and wedding ceremonies and funerals are often difficult to tell apart. ... the church services and the burial had already taken place before we arrived at the farm...there were ample quantities of all sorts of food and freshly brewed beer.

My father and I sat at a table that included half a dozen Estonian soldiers in uniform. These were seasoned front-line troops, most of whom only hours before had been engaged in front line combat with the Red Army to the east. They were still armed with light automatic weapons and hand grenades which were not unusual since after the 1943 soviet winter offensive; Põlva was only about forty miles from the front lines.

Some of the soldiers had passes while others had received unofficial permission from their immediate superiors to go home to attend the funeral. Nearly all of them would be back in the trenches at the conclusion of the festivities helping their buddies fend off the Soviet invasion. These men were not fighting for the Third Reich. They were putting their lives on the line for Estonia and hoping that the Allied Fleet would soon steam up the Baltic Sea to the rescue as was the case at the end of World War I. Accordingly, if necessary they were also prepared to turn their weapons on the retreating Germans.

I remember listening with intense curiosity to these hardened veterans since much of their talk centred on hair-raising battles, many of which were raging as we sat there. In addition, these men brought fresh, uncensored and undistorted news straight from the trenches that were of significant interest to everyone present. After all, our lives were dependant on the valor and success of these troops.

Most of the soldiers and other guests around the table knew father and the tone of the conversations was initially very cordial. After several hours of heavy drinking, however, one of the men in uniform began to get increasingly hostile towards Father. Suddenly, without warning he grabbed Father by the front of his shirt and, almost nose-to-noose bellowed, "I suppose Volli (short for Voldemar), you are going to report everything you see and hear tonight to those bastards (German authorities). Do you know what we do with men like you? We shoot them! I think that I'll take you our right now to the barnyard and put a bullet in our head," he concluded and began to drag Father towards the open barn door.

Scared to death, I must have turned white as a sheet. At that moment there was absolutely no doubt in my mind that Father would be shot. Frozen in my seat, I didn't know whether to scream or cry. Fortunately, within seconds, which seemed like a lifetime to me, two grenadiers from our table jumped up and pulled the man away from Father and led him to another part of the barn.

Thinking that the horrifying confrontation was over: I relaxed and broke out in a cold sweat. However, minutes later, the drunken soldier was back, now armed with his sub-machine gun. "Come on, Volli; let's go outside so I can shoot you without injuring anybody else here.' he shouted as he tried to pull Father away from the table with his free hand. The same two soldiers rescued father again. This time they took their friend to the hayloft where they tucked him in for the night.

Immediately after daybreak Father and I headed home. On our way back he tried to explain to me that many Estonian really didn't know who their friends were. "By alienating the Germans, they are playing right into the Russian's hands." He repeated several times. **I wasn't sure what to believe any more.**

For years I wondered why Father had dragged ma along to the funeral in the first place. It finally dawned on me that Father had taken me with him for self-preservation. Who wouldn't feel sympathetic towards a man accompanied by an eight year old son? This episode it turns out was only the first of several episodes where Father used me for protection.

The third event which fits the collaboration issue occurred at our home in Põlva only days after the funeral celebration. Early one morning Father went to the outhouse next to the chicken shed. While sitting on the commode he heard a dull thud outside. Someone had lobbed a grenade over the back fence and he obviously had been the target. Miraculously, the grenade had failed to explode even though the pin had been pulled. That evening when Father returned home he brought with him a German Luger (a semi-automatic pistol). The weapon remained on the top of his bedroom closet until we abandoned our home.

MEETING THE CHAIN DOGS: KE

On one of our food safaris Father decided to hike to Birkenfeld and visit the farm where we'd lived in October, after the war he would confide in me that he primarily wanted to use the trip to the farm as cover. His real objective had been to get close to the border and see if there was an opportunity to make a break for Switzerland. He'd figured that at the time that risk to life had become minimal. He was aware that the French armies were getting closer by the day and that the German border guards were beginning to shirk their duties to the point where they would occasionally leave an entire section of the border unguarded.

In order to get to Birkenfeld we first had to cross a tributary or canal, which branches out from the Rhine River bordering Switzerland and flows north into Lake Bodensee. As we approached the familiar bridge leading over the waterway, we were stopped by two German Military Police Guards. I had seen such police before in Estonia and was well aware of their notorious reputation. They had the power to shoot you on the spot. In fact, the Estonian frontline soldiers had named the members of the German Military Police Units "Ketti Koerad" (Chain dogs) because of their unquestioned authority and since **they wore a breast plate around their necks by a chain designating them to be military police.**

The guards asked Father for a pass authorizing him to gain admittance to the more secure border area across the bridge. He showed them his papers from last October and told the men that we merely wanted to visit the farm where we'd worked in order to get some fruit and other foodstuffs which were not available at the camp.

Apparently these two guards were still fully devoted to their duties, since they didn't believe Father's story. Without any further discussion, one of the guards, who to me looked like a giant, simply told us to walk in front of him to a small building housing the military police detachment. As far back as I could remember I'd been terrified of the chain dogs but now I was scared to death.

As we entered the building Father was immediately separated from me and taken to a back room for interrogation. I was told to take a seat next to the front desk in an open bay where there were several other tables manned by military police officers. As I flopped down on the chair the guard sat down behind the desk and slowly took his Luger (pistol) out of its holster and placed it in front of him. He then **told me point blank that if I didn't tell him the truth they would shoot Father.**

Father had of course deliberately refrained from telling me his true intentions as we left the camp that morning. That foresight probably saved his life and possibly also mine. Hence, when repeatedly asked by my interrogator what our real purpose was in trying to cross the bridge I stuck to the same story. It was the only explanation I could provide, that we had no other intentions than to visit the farm where Father had worked last fall and ask them for any food they could spare. I don't know how long the grilling lasted but to me it seemed like hours. Finally Father, looking troubled and thoroughly drained emerged from the back room and we were both allowed to return to the refugee camp.

RELICS OF A RECENT PAST: KE

With the allies getting closer by the day things around the area were becoming fairly chaotic and thee employment office didn't even make an honest effort to find father a job on a nearby farm. Rather, we were placed hastily into a refugee camp southwest of the city, not far from the farm where we had stayed prior to being sent to Ulm. The camp had only recently been vacated by the Hitler Youth Organisation and when we arrived **I found a cat-of nine-tails and several black helmets in the barracks where Father and I were house**

Isn't each man's task to learn afresh, from what exists about him around the world? But who has walked through the world seeking nothing but simple truth? Why should each man be made a scapegoat for sins that were not his? Must we keep our pride, whatever the cost, knowing that once it is lost, all is lost? Don't we see that the waves are like us, destroying themselves against nothing?

from **Gunnar Neeme "The Waves"**

FLEEING FROM ESTONIA

As an introduction, it was early in 1944 when it had become clear that, barring a miracle, Germany under Adolf Hitler was rapidly losing the war on the eastern front where it was trying unsuccessfully to halt the rapidly advancing forces of the Soviet Union under the leadership of Stalin. For Estonians in their home country this meant soon again coming under the rule of the communist regime we had just experienced in the years 1940 and 1941.

During their 2-year period of occupation the communist rulers had made a great effort to eradicate the military of the former Republic of Estonia (independent from 1918 to 1940) and neutralize the influential segments of the society, e.g. Government officials, teachers, lawyers, and successful farmers.

One night in June of 1941 the persons on the first list of such "enemies of the working class" were rounded up with their families, locked into railway freight cars, and deported to Siberia to work there for the state under primitive and backbreaking conditions. The total number of people in this first wave of deportation was about 10,000. Among those were the following relatives of my mother, Lea Tults:
- Paternal uncle Anton Teetsov, his wife, 3 daughters, and 3 young grandchildren;
- Maternal aunt Gerda Toomsalu, her husband, and young daughter Hilja.

Additional lists of persons to be deported had been prepared by the communists, but the start of World War II and the arrival of German occupying forces in August of 1941 prevented the completion of the plan. As for our family, my parents Ernst and Lea Tults, 2-year old daughter Marje and 8-year son Jüri, on the very day our above-mentioned relatives were rounded up, we boarded a train to southern part of Estonia where one of my father's cousins owned a farm. The family stayed there in hiding for about 2 months until the German forces had pushed the Russian occupiers out of the country.

Based on what had happened under Russian occupation, it was natural that many Estonians, including my parents, were ready to leave their homeland rather than live again under the communist regime.

It so happened that my father's brother, my uncle Harald Tults, was at the time directing the construction of a dam on the Vistula River near the city of Bromberg (now Bydgoszcz) in what is now western part of Poland. He offered to prepare a requisition for a secretary and specified my mother as the person he wanted. She was allowed to take her children along, but my father had to stay in Estonia because at age 39 he was on call to be mobilized any day into the German army.

According to plan, on a sunny day in the first week of August 1944, my mother with her son and daughter, ages 11 and 5 respectively, boarded a train in Tallinn to start our journey to my uncle Harald's place of work

Our first destination was the Latvian capital Riga where we stayed overnight in a hotel to catch a train to Königsberg (now Kaliningrad) in what was formerly East-Prussia. Hopefully this was going to be just another train-ride, but armed forces of the Soviet Union had already advanced far into Latvia and were very close to breaching the railway line from Riga to points south.

The train departed from Riga late in the day and reached the dangerous area when it was already dark. It reduced its speed drastically and just crept along, most likely because of the possibility of shell-damaged or sabotaged rails. The rumbling of the moving train could not suppress the sound of artillery fire somewhere not very far away. We were fortunate being able to pass through the southern part of Latvia and also through neighboring Lithuania without any serious incidents.

It was still dark when the train stopped in Tilsit (now Sovetsk), a railroad center in East Prussia. From hearsay ours was the last train that made it from Riga to Germany.

The train had not stopped along the platform of the Tilsit railway station, but somewhere nearby where it was flanked by what looked like freight trains. Rumors started to circulate that the station had been heavily bombed the night before, and only one or two tracks had been repaired during daylight hours.

As we were sitting and waiting in the stationary train for something to happen, one of our many fears became true when the air-raid sirens started to blare, soon followed by ear-splitting sounds of exploding ammunition. Apparently another air attack was on the way. This commotion lasted for about an hour, but apparently without any serious damage to our train. A couple of Estonian soldiers wearing German army uniforms, returning from leave to rejoin their fighting units, explained that most of the loud noises we heard came from German antiaircraft guns.

At dawn everybody with their belongings was ordered out of our train. We were told it was not going anywhere, and we were to wait for another through-train presumably stopping on the adjacent track. Nobody knew when, if at all, this train would arrive. But it did, after we had waited for a few hours, except it was crammed with people.

My mother with her two children was helpless, but the Estonian soldiers I mentioned above came to our aid and lifted us all one by one into the train through an open window over the loud protests of passengers already tightly packed into the railroad car, including the small toilet. I don't know how many persons were able to get on that train, but we were among the lucky ones.

The train arrived in Königsberg without any major delays, and the railroad station there was intact and functioning. We now transferred to another train that took us to Bromberg where my uncle was presumably going to meet us at the railroad station. Of course, we did not arrive on the train we were originally scheduled to take in Königsberg. However, he knew that schedules in these times did not mean much and believed that we still might reach our destination before the end of the day.

As our train pulled into the station, imagine our delightful surprise to see our uncle standing alone on the platform, the only person meeting this train. We had made it and all was well, at least for the time being.

In our new temporary home my mother's help as a secretary was not really needed. I attended the local school, even though my knowledge of German language was limited to what I had learned in the 3rd and 4th grades of elementary school in Tallinn.

Soon my father rejoined his family having left Estonia in September on one of the German ships ferrying to Germany the many Estonians who could not bear the thought of living again under a communist regime, but would rather work in factories supporting the German war effort. Because the Russian army was already in Poland and advancing rapidly, we immediately had to start planning our second move to a location further west.

Our next destination in the fall of 1944 was the small town of Weissensulz in West Sudetengau, a district that Hitler annexed by taking it away from Czechoslovakia in the late 1930-s.

My uncle had married a Czech citizen while studying at the university in Brünn (now Brno), and she had relatives who lived in that area.

Trains were still running, although on unpredictable schedules. In two days we were very fortunate to reach our destination without any air attacks on the train and without long delays because of railroad tracks damaged by bombs from the numerous air-raids in the final year of the war.

In Weissensulz my father got a job at the local railroad station. I attended school again, this time with a somewhat improved knowledge of German.

We thought we had made the right move, because the area was occupied by US armed forces without meeting any resistance shortly before the war officially ended in May of 1945. However, at the conference in Potsdam during that summer, the victors (United States, England, France, and Soviet Union) agreed to make West Sudetengau part of Czechoslovakia again, and therefore the US occupation forces promptly vacated this region. We were now under scrutiny of the Czech police authority which basically consisted of communists. This presented the real danger that we would be forced to return to our homeland according to the wishes of Soviet Union.

There was no time to waste – we had to make another move westward into Bavaria which was governed by United States occupation forces. Fortunately the border was only about 10 miles from the town of Weissensulz. Moreover, the relatives of my uncle's wife had a farm even closer to the border and they were very familiar with the topography of the area.

One night, under the cover of darkness, our and my uncle's families set out on foot from the farm in the direction of the border. We followed a horse-drawn wagon track in a forest to sneak around a regular border crossing station on a gravel road passing through the woods.

Naturally all the grown ups were very tense, and even I at age 12 was scared. We could hear dogs barking now and then, and this made us think that the Czech border guards were on our trail. There was also the worry that my sister and my 2 cousins, all well below the age of 10, would be spooked in the dark woods and start crying loudly.

Our march through the woods seemed to take forever, but in a couple of hours we did reach a road in Bavaria that led to a small town where we found temporary shelter in a small guesthouse.

From this point on all of our problems were minor compared to what we had been through. Within a few days we secured passage on a large open-bed truck for a 2-day drive to Stuttgart where my father's sister had lived and practiced dentistry ever since she and her husband had left Estonia in 1940. Our family, as well as my father's cousin with her 2 sons, found temporary shelter in her 3 room apartment. I started attending a local German school, but tolerated the hostile attitude there towards me as a foreigner only for about a week. My parents believed me and let me stay home.

The housing and schooling problems were fortunately quickly solved when we moved to Geislingen where a large refugee camp for Estonians with its own schools had just been established in the fall of 1945.

AN ILL WIND WHICH BLEW GOOD ALSO:

Maarja Kiesel Paris' husband:

I read with great interest all the multiple exchanges of Estonians around the world who resided in Geislingen, as did my wonderful wife, as a child and her parents. I do agree with your last sentence. I came to the US forty years ago where I met Maarja my wife to be, not pushed or moved by horrible reasons such as yours or economic/religious reasons, just on my free will.

World War II , as all wars, are ultimate tragedy followed by a Diaspora of people far away but in this ultimate chaos positive elements occurred. It is because of this tragedy that my/our destinies joined, that I met my wife and we made a "new" life without forgetting, one second, our respective past and always respected it and passed onto our children the same approach and taught them Estonian History, Culture and Language.

It is with great delight and expectancy that we go now to Eesti, at least every 5 years, to meet our relatives for these "out of the world" first class and exceptional dance and song festivals, and each time we discover a new area of this beautiful country that is yours.

Unfortunately, it is because of the horrors of war, that people meet, tell others what they have witnessed with the great hope that it will not happen again!

My sister and I in Tallinn boarding a train to Riga (The girl to the left is a relative sending us off)

My family's belongings being transported to the railway station of Bromberg

Jüri Tults and Family in Geislingen, Germany in 1946

BRUNO LEEPIN
BOMB-BURST: OUR WORLD IS SHATTERED

Drawing by Bruno Leepin

This story needs no words. Bruno and his twin sister Erika were little tykes at time, as was I. In a split second their surrounds were reduced to shatters. There was rubble all around: It had no form: It had no predictability. It was to be reproduced repeatedly over those latter years of World War II as Bruno, Erika and their mother traipsed the road away from their homeland.

Bruno describes one occasion when they headed for safety in a crowded air raid shelter where water was gushing in: He has no idea where this took place. That is the story of many of us littlies. There were events but no pinpoint on the map for them.

JAAN TABUR
FROM TALLINN TO GEISLINGEN

LAST DAYS IN ESTONIA
When the bombing of Tallinn by Soviet bombers got severe as the war front approached, my father moved us out of town to Saku, where he had built a two room cottage just for such a reason. We still had our apartment in Tallinn, on Päikese street, and most of our belongings were there. We had just the bare minimum of things in Saku that we could get by with, because there was not much room in the cottage. We spent the spring and summer of 1944 there.

From Saku we could hear and see the bombing raids on Tallinn, and the searchlights shining at night. Saku is also where I thought that I would like to learn to fly an airplane, after I saw a German fighter airplane flying low enough that I could see the pilot.

When it became apparent that Germany was losing ground to the Russian forces, my parents decided that they had to leave Estonia to survive. My father had miraculously escaped deportation to Siberia during the previous Russian occupation, and he was sure he would not be so fortunate the next time. It turned out that he was right, because two of his brothers were later deported. Uncle Elmar finally got back to Estonia many years later, but in very ill health. My father would not have survived the hardships because of his heart problems.

So, they made arrangements to go to Germany on a troop ship that was returning to Germany. We gathered together what essential belongings we could carry, and got on a train to Tallinn. It was a pretty, sunny early September day, we rode sitting on a flatcar in the open air.

We boarded the large, gray ship and said good bye to Estonia and all our relatives who could not, or would not leave. We were facing a very unknown future in a foreign land, with my parents knowing only the little German they had learned in school. But it was certainly better than no future at all under Soviet Communist rule, and quite probable suffering and death in Siberia.

VOYAGE TO GERMANY
The ship had many Estonians on board. As it began to leave the port in the late afternoon, most of the people came on the main deck and spontaneously started to sing "Mu Isamaa Kaunis" (My Beautiful Fatherland). It was very moving experience, with no one knowing if they would ever see their homeland again. I don't think many people at that time thought that Russian occupation of Estonia would ever end. I finally did go back for a visit in August of 2003, 59 years after leaving.

The conditions below deck were quite crowded. There were many wooden bunks crammed very close together (what did I expect on a troop transport?) and there was not much room to walk around. Some acquaintances of my father were nearby, one of them was pastor Rebane and family. After Geislingen they wound up in St. Petersburg, Florida.

We were blessed to survive this voyage; several other similar ships with Estonian refugees were sunk by

Russian planes or submarines. One ship sunk was larger than ours, named "Moero", and went down with hundreds of Estonians. Many small boats trying to leave were also sunk, others sank due to storms. One such boat was the one my cousins Vello and Kalju Varangu and their families were attempting to sail to Sweden. A storm pushed them on the rocks on Finnish shore. They were helped to get to Sweden by some friendly Finns.

GRIEFENHAGEN, GERMANY
After disembarking in Germany, we were taken to a small town named Greifenhagen on the Oder river. When we arrived there, my uncles Jaan and Oskar with families were already there, as was our good friend Vello Rebane (no relation to pastor Rebane mentioned previously) with his wife. I don't recall them being on our ship, so they must have somehow gotten there earlier. They and some others had found fairly nice places to live in town. We were provided living quarters in a single-story resort building in a park just south of town, near the Oder river. We lived in a large room with some other families, separated from others with blankets hung from ropes.

We had some beautiful fall weather days there. The large chestnut trees in the park were losing their leaves **and the fallen leaves smelled good.** I liked to walk under the trees and along the river bank. During worse weather I read the large one-volume Estonian Encyclopedia we had brought with us.

We were close enough to the city of Stettin to see the bombing raids by American bombers. I saw the antiaircraft shells exploding in the sky. Once, I saw a bomber getting hit, there was a large fiery explosion in the air. At night we saw the searchlights scanning the sky.

A large troop of German Hitler Youth camped at the ball field of the park for several days. They had nice uniforms, long bugles, drums and flags. I was so impressed I told my father that I wanted to join the Hitler Youth, but he calmly told me that would not be a good idea. Besides, they did not take foreigners anyway.

In early part of the winter a portion of Vlasov's Army camped there for several days. Vlasov's Army was a Russian Army unit that joined the Germans in fighting against the Communists, as best as I recall. They were a ragtag group with tattered uniforms. After they moved on, the place was a mess! They had soiled the floors of the nice, large lavatory in the park as if they didn't know what the pots were made for. I know not all Russian soldiers were not like that, but many were from the less developed regions of Russia and didn't know proper behavior, or didn't care to.

It got cold enough later that winter to completely freeze over the river. By January the Russians had advanced sufficiently westward that we had to flee again. We packed our meager belongings on the best conveyances we could obtain and started walking westward. My father and uncle Jaan had gotten sleds to hold our belongings. Uncle Oskar, being a machinist, had assembled a cart with bicycle wheels. But by the time we had to leave, the snow was about a foot deep and the cart would not push with the load on it, and one of the wheels collapsed. He managed to obtain a sled also and we were on our way again. **The German soldiers in town told us that the bridge over the Oder would be closed soon and then blown up to slow the Russian's advance, so we hurried across.**

THE VOYAGE WESTWARD, part one

So we traveled westward any way we could. German farmers sometimes gave us rides on their horse-drawn sleighs and took us to the next town. The weather was cold with much snow on the ground, clear skies and sunshine. One day we saw many hundreds of bombers heading toward Berlin, which was just southeast of our route. I had never seen such a sight before, nor since. They were flying very high and left vapor trails, four behind each plane. The combined vapor trails covered about one third of the sky like a wide, white sheet being unfurled. The deep throbbing noise of all those engines was memorable.

A farmer's family, or someone in a town would let us sleep in their home at night. At one place they let me sleep in an upstairs bedroom in a nice mahogany bed, under a feather bed comforter. The people there believed that it was healthier to sleep with the windows open, even in the winter, so they warmed the bed with a hot water bottle and partly opened the window.

Somewhere along this journey we started traveling on trains. I recall towns along the way, with names like Halle (Saale), Erfurt, Weimar, Jena and Gera.

An air raid took place while our train had stopped in Weimar. Weimar was a beautiful university town. It was one of Hitler's favorite towns. It was the home of several of Germany's well known authors and composers, such as Goethe, Schiller, and Franz Liszt. The German National Assembly met there in 1919 and adopted a new constitution for the democratic republic, to be called The Weimar Republic. But the events led to Hitler being named the chancellor and then eventually taking over all power. Weimar had never before been bombed and the residents thought that the Allies had decided to spare their town because of its history and beauty, but the Allies apparently decided that the railroad station had to be destroyed, and bombed it while we were in town. I don't think most of the town was damaged very much, except the neighborhood of the station.

We got off the train when the sirens sounded and hurried away from the station as fast as we could. When we heard the bombers nearing, we started seeking shelter but the only thing we could find was under the concrete roof of a four-story apartment building's entrance. Just then a German soldier came running along, saw us standing there and told us we could not stay there because it was not safe.

Since the building's door was locked, he smashed a basement window with his rifle stock and told us to climb inside. While sitting on the floor next to a large pile of coal, I heard bombs exploding quite close to us. Some explosions were very loud and shook the ground.

I prayed for God to keep us safe and promised Him I would never become a drunkard. I don't know why I thought He would care, except that I had known of many men in Estonia who drank to excess and acted in a way that would not, in my opinion, please God,.

After the "all clear" sirens sounded, we emerged from the basement and looked around. Before we entered the basement, there was a car parked in front of the building. Now the car was in the side yard, upside down and crumpled. There were several deep bomb craters in the street, one directly in front of the doorway where we had been standing, before we climbed into the basement. The doorway and nearby walls were riddled with pockmarks from bomb shrapnel. So, I suppose God decided to preserve our lives again.

I think that the railroad station and the train we had been on were severely damaged during that raid, since I recall that we had to find other means of transportation to the next railroad station. This part of the journey to flee the Russians ended in a small town called Krölpa-Raanis.

KRÖLPA-RAANIS

We arrived in Krölpa-Raanis, which consisted of the neighboring villages of Krölpa and Raanis, in early spring of 1945. I don't know where my uncles lived during our stay there. Most of my memories there are of the summer and fall. After a few weeks in an empty schoolhouse, we got an upstairs apartment from a lady that my father called "Liebergott" because when something alarmed her she would throw up her chubby arms and say "Ach du liebergott" - meaning "oh my dear God".

Krölpa-Raanis had a small river running through it. The main street was on both sides of the river, the river ran in a concrete channel between the two traffic lanes. Several streets crossed the river over masonry bridges.

I befriended a blacksmith at the outskirts of the town and he gave me a bicycle wheel rim to play with. I was great fun to make that wheel go wherever I wanted to, using a wooden stick to hit it forward or to guide it. I watched the blacksmith weld using an arc welder, but afterward my eyes were sore from the bright ultraviolet light. No one had told me that the light from the arc would damage my eyes. I have been sensitive to bright lights ever since.

Our family went to the woods several times to gather firewood. It was permissible to pick up any branches that had fallen, but not to take any live trees or branches. One day when we were picking up firewood, some German soldiers on a nearby road started target practice with their pistols. We left just in case we might get in the way!

My stepmother Helmi used to send me to the store for what was available, like vegetables. Between what German I had been taught in the first two grades in Estonia ,and what I had picked up in Germany, I was able to get the job done. Whenever I went in a store, I had to use the greeting required by the Nazi regime: "Heil Hitler" and they would reply with same – sometimes unenthusiastically. I was under the impression that they were not allowed to sell to customers who did not use the proper greeting.

Germany was running out of men to fight the war, so they mobilized what they called the "Volksturm" or People's Storm to supplement the regular army. The Volksturm consisted of men too old or disabled to be in the regular army, and of teenaged boys.

When the war front got closer, some of them went through town toward the fighting, carrying "panzer faust" antitank weapons on their shoulders. It consisted of a large warhead propelled by an unguided rocket. I later learned that these weapons were not very accurate and were able to fly only a relatively short distance. I wonder how many of these people actually got to use these weapons, as it would have been quite dangerous to get that close to American tanks.

THE AMERICANS ARE COMING
We were still living in Krölpa-Raanis when the American army advanced through that part of Germany. My stepmother had taught us our first words of English: "I am an Estonian", because she thought it would be useful if questioned by the Americans.

One evening the artillery noise got quite loud and we all knew that the Americans were coming. My father had been assigned to work running a large air compressor where a large cavern was being bored into the side of a granite mountain for a munitions factory. Germany had many factories in such caverns to protect them from aerial bombing. We walked to this cavern to seek shelter from the approaching battle. I saw shells, some with red tracers, flying overhead as we walked. We stooped and walked in ditches whenever we could. We spent the night in the cavern, and by morning the German soldiers were gone and the front had passed our town.

There was a German government food warehouse not far from the cavern. When we exited the cavern, we heard that some people had broken into the warehouse and were helping themselves. Food, especially meat, had been scarce during the war. So, we joined others and took some food also. We got delicious canned meats, and canned soft chocolate and ginger cookies. Yes, I guess I was a "looter", but we were taking from Nazis, who had hoarded these goods for themselves and deprived even their own German people.

The next day I was in town, watching the American troops crossing the river on the main street. The retreating German army had destroyed

DP camp in Bremen

Jaan, Imbi and Andres Tabur

the bridges, but the Americans just filled the river channel with logs and drove across. Some vehicles were German army cars that they had captured. They consisted of a Volkswagen beetle chassis fitted with a military-style body.

Soon previously unavailable goods like Nabisco wafers, sunglasses, etc began to appear in store windows. I bought a pair of sunglasses with the little money I had, not that I needed them, but for the novelty of actually being able to buy something.

ROOSEVELT'S GIVEAWAY

It wasn't very long after the front passed that we began to hear rumors from the Germans that the "crazy Americans" had made a treaty with that murder Stalin, and had agreed to give over to his control part of Germany liberated by the U.S. Army, including the part where we lived! It would become part of the Soviet Zone of occupation, and later to become communist East Germany. Some ladies from town worked at the American army camp in the nearby town of Saalfeld, and had heard of this agreement. We walked to Saalfeld on a nice sunny day, and verified this with the American authorities. As a result, we had to make plans to go further westward to what would become the permanent American Zone of occupation.

THE VOYAGE WESTWARD, part two.

My father got a small hand wagon that the Germans called a "Wegele", and loaded all of our belongings on it. We started walking southwest from Krölpa-Raanis towards Bamberg. My parents probably had heard that there was a refugee camp there. The distance from Krölpa-Raanis to Bamberg by road is about 120 kilometers, or 75 miles. We walked through the towns of Coburg and Lichtenfels. The walk took at least three days, probably longer. We spent the nights in some kindly German's homes along the way. Father pulled the wagon, and the rest of us walked along except on some downhill parts of the road when he would let me or Helmi's daughter Imbi get a ride.

I recall some quite impressive mountains of pure black slate, the kind which was used to make slate tablets for writing. I don't recall any bad weather on this journey.

DP CAMP AT BAMBERG

We arrived at the city of Bamberg on the 28th of July, 1945. Much of Bamberg had been bombed or shelled to ruins. The Displaced Persons (D.P.) camp was a six-story schoolhouse that had a winding staircase with a smooth wooden banister that was ideal for sliding down from top to bottom. It's a wonder some children didn't get killed. The convent next door had a large grape arbor. We climbed over the masonry wall and sampled some delicious grapes.

We lived in a second-floor classroom with several other families, separated by blankets hung from cords. All of the families in our room were Estonians, although I think there were other nationalities in the building.

My father got a job working for UNRRA, the United Nations Refugee Relief Agency, at the Bamberg railroad station. He was able to obtain additional food for us from there, I especially remember the large hard salami he brought to us. That was a delicacy that we hadn't eaten for a long while. I also received candy and chocolate bars from American soldiers who were on the troop trains that stopped there, when I visited father at work. They called out to me as I walked on the station's platform alongside the train: "hey, boy c'mere" and handed me goodies. I also saw my first black people there.

There was an Estonian pastor at this camp in Bamberg who taught the children about God and the Bible. One evening he took a group of us out to the dark courtyard, to teach us that God's word is the light of life. He had a flashlight and shone it on the path as we children followed him. As we walked, he quoted and demonstrated Psalms 119:105 "Thy word is a lamp unto my feet, and a light unto my path". Of course, he said it in Estonian. This was the first Bible verse I learned, and it has stayed with me through my life.

My parents must have heard about an all-Estonian D.P. camp in Geislingen, and we soon moved there, most probably on a train. And that started the next stage of our refugee journey, which has already been documented in the book "When the Noise Had Ended".

People wagon transport between camps continued for some years post war. MM

EHA TREUFELD/CARR
WHEN THE NOISE BEGAN

Three chairs stood side by side next to my bed that late winter. I remember only too clearly that on one I could find warm underwear, the next a warm jumper and pants, and on the third were loaded my winter coat, hat, gloves and 'dilly' bag of favorite belongings. Dad and I used to have this 'game' of timing how quickly I could get changed out of my night clothes and race with him thru' our apartment on Kaupmehe Street in Tallinn. We then had to get down the back stairs, across the yard, squeezing past the fence planks onto the building lot next door, twixt Kaupmehe and Kentmann'i streets, to reach the bunker allotted to our address under a multi-storey edifice being erected. Every clear night we kind' of expected the sirens to warn of an air raid. Some game!

My Mom had joined friends at the ballet performance of 'Kratt' that night at the Estonia theatre just down the road. Dad was 'keeping me company'. It was to be the last night of my childhood in a way, as the horrors of the real world were about to explode: the noise was to become very real. The date was the 9th of March. The year was 1944. Like many others I was about to lose my home, my security – and very soon the land of my birth. The journey back to normality had a long way to begin. I was eight years old.

Dad had this premonition about what was to happen. The night was just perfect for a bombing raid. As often occurred, the ugly sound of the sirens began after the first bombs had already hit. The sight from our kitchen steps is with me to this day: the crisscrossing searchlights reaching into the sky, the ugly black shapes of the planes flying between them, the sound of first missiles falling, signs of fire and smoke, anti-aircraft guns adding to the terror. Virtually tumbling down the rickety steps into the bunker, I could but hide my head in Dad's lap, cover my ears and admit to being very scared.

Even that small safe feeling came to an end as all able bodied men were commanded topside to fight the fires started by the incendiaries. Sitting next to the First Aid room I was to witness an ever increasing lot of bloody, moaning, oft badly hurt casualties being helped into the bunker for the little help available. After some horrendously loud crashes almost atop us, the door opened again to have a tall, gangly guy being carried in – half his face had been blown away and his left eye was uselessly hanging by the stalk from its socket. I heard crying, loud crying, but until Dad rushed in to hold and comfort, I did not realize I was the one doing the screaming.

Much later there was a pause. Looking up I saw mother on the stairs, her silk frock in tatters, stockings torn, legs and arms bleeding and minus a shoe. The distance from Estonia was a matter of minutes, but when ne is falling into bomb craters to land on the dead or injured, surrounded by violent fire storms, alone and frightened . .

I don't remember much of the interim between the two waves of bombers. When the horror began again, I remember Dad quietly coming in: 'Frieda, could you come and help – the house is on fire, perhaps we can get some things out. I think the bombers have mostly gone'.

I must have gone to sleep on the wooden bench, because it was morning when my parents finally arrived to get me. Dad asked me not to be too upset – we had lost virtually everything. Our large library and salon were well and truly alight by the time my parents got to the house. They had managed to move much from the bedrooms, dining and kitchen, but the air was full of embers, and piles of what they had painstakingly rescued caught fire in the yard. Among other items we lost all our photos and other memorabilia. I could not believe the small, smoking pile, which had been home and safe haven for all of my nearly nine years, was all that was left.

Two days later Dad had relocated us to Nõmme, actually to the now famous Õie Street, where the lower floor once occupied by a Baltic German stood empty. There I was to spend the last six months in my birth country. No books, no theatre, no 'going out' and no children I could approach in the vicinity. Too peaceful by half! I seemed to be picking wildflowers and making daisy chains and, bloodthirsty and thoughtless, as only a child can be, getting a buzz when Russian and German planes had dogfights practically over the house. I remember actually clapping when one of them went into the final dive! Exciting aerial ballet to me!

There was the good and the bad. I realized Mom and Dad were having endless arguments. My paternal grandmother being Swedish, Dad would have quite legally been able to send us, and whatever we possessed, to Sweden. He could not and would not leave until the end, but promised to get out before the walls came tumbling down. Mom could not cope with the proposed separation. So we stayed and waited for the inevitable end.

And then there was the birthday. On the 10 June 1944 I became 9 years old and we had a party. An odd birthday party for a child – there was not one other child present, but I had the time of my life, with all of Mom's and Dad's friends, in our beautiful back garden. What did anything else matter because the love of my then life was there! His name was major Aksel Kristjan, he was a contemporary of Dad's and the closest thing Estonia then had to a '007'! Working undercover in Finland, he happened to be in the country – the beautiful story spun to me was that he had swum ashore that morning, under German patrol boat fire, with my birthday present of a finely crafted 'puss nuga' strapped to his chest. Decades later, people present that day remembered this not as a simple 'crush', but a young girl in the beginning throes of starting to grow up. Bold as brass I asked Uncle Aksel to marry me on that very day ten years hence – no doubt having a hard time to hold back a smile, he stated that, if I still felt the same ten years down the track, he would be honoured to share his name! What a wonderful lifelong memory!

Little did I realize that we were celebrating a wake: for Estonia, for a rather elite way of life in Tallinn, for the fear that we would never be together again. All three were to happen. In my much later travels with my first husband I had the opportunity to relive some of my childhood memories, my parents sadly never did.

During the German occupation Dad was Sisedirektor'i abi, ipso facto, second in charge of the practicalities of running the country under Oskar Angelus. As the latter moved to Germany ahead of the Front, Dad felt he could not flee.

This found us on the docks of Tallinn the day before the Russians marched in late September 1944 – and we arrived late! A child's memory: were the last two ships to leave the harbour called 'Wärteland' and 'Minden"? I know that Litzmann and Mae, together with most of the remaining government, were on the first. The dock land was a dangerous shambles by the time we got there. Totally panicking, people were screaming, pushing, shoving and threatening. Carrying their few portable belongings with them, they were pushing women and children aside to just get on anything that floated and seemed to be heading away from the Reds. Dad had a permit for 'Wärteland', but the ship was supposedly filled to the scuppers, and the young, frightened guards at the bottom of the gangplank actually threatened to shoot Dad and roughly pushed him aside. Somebody knowing him saw him from aboard the 'Minden' and managed to get us on board.

'Minden' must have been a cargo vessel, as, none too kindly, we were pushed down rickety steps into a hold. I was taken topside after we left harbour – there was smoke everywhere and frightening noises on all sides. I do not know how much later the plane came: a Russian spy affair, which made two or three low passes over both boats. Suddenly the two ships reversed positions and men on our ship swore. Indeed, not so much later we were very hurriedly pushed back into the hold. Covers were pushed atop the hole just in time for us to hear the first bombs/shooting. In fear we heard the loud prangs topside and soon felt the ship list. We were taking the bombs meant for Litzmann/Mae and the rest of the dignitaries. I am here to tell the story – the 'Minden' actually limped, with just a few casualties, into Gotenhafen (now Gdynia of Lech Walesa's fame) a day or two later.

A train was brought alongside the docks to take us to a transit camp, me thinks somewhere near Frankfurt/Oder. The shooting was not behind us. As the long train was crossing the Oder over a very high railway bridge, we were suddenly dive bombed by what must have been a Russian survey aircraft – surely there were no daylight flights by the Western Allies so far east? I don't remember the train itself suffering much damage, but the bridge infrastructure was seemingly weakened. It was oh so scary to be told not to move, not even to speak, whilst, carriage by carriage, it was emptied of its passengers. We had to walk between the rail tracks in single file, very slowly and very quietly, to the Western side. Only with everyone safely out, to the best of my recollection, did the train ever so slowly follow us and we were able to reboard.

Decades later I thought the camp, into which we were unceremoniously bundled, resembled a cross of what I had seen in The Great Escape and Auschwitz: row upon row of barracks with closely set bunks and little in the way of bedding. After some inedible soup and bread we collapsed into our allotted spaces. Not so much later lights were relit by an increasing number of complainers. Well, it seemed many of us had contracted measles or scarlet fever in very short order! With the coming of the night the bedbugs had come out to feast! And we were covered with them!

I cannot believe to this day that in the ten years of leisurely weekend walks Dad and I so enjoyed in Australia I never asked exactly what happened next. Although a child who obviously had nothing to do with the matters, I have somehow felt guilty all my life that then some were more 'equal' than others. Some 'escaped' – others were left to uncertainty. Perhaps I simply did not want to know that I had in some form been 'privileged'!

I remember Dad and a number of other guys being closeted with the Camp Commandant for all of the morning. The last two ships out of Tallinn harbour had many of the Occupation-time government officials on board. I guess some simply had documentation to the Germans to give all possible assistance? I guess Dad did?

In the afternoon he quietly moved Mom's/my suitcase out of our barracks and took us for a walk around the perimeter of the camp. Would we not get undressed that evening but pretend to go to the toilet at a certain time. Would we instead hurry to the camp gate where buses would be waiting.

The Camp Commandant had been able to secure just one railway carriage to take some of us to whichever destination in Germany suited us. Whose idea Freudenstadt in Schwarzwald or Black Forest, as we know it, was I have no idea. Perhaps his? Dad explained the benefits: we would be as far as possible from the Russian invaders; also Freudenstadt was a Lazarettstadt: its peacetime spa-hotels were housing convalescent soldiers and the International Red Cross had a promise from the Allies not to bomb the small town. And the latter was very close to both

Swiss and southern French borders – perhaps there would be a chance to cross over?

How the lists were drawn up I also have no idea – obviously and sadly this again depended not on what you knew but whom you did! There was talk of a hundred people getting out – but one rail carriage can't carry so many? So, I guess, there were about 70-80 to undertake the journey across Germany?

Even that number of people can't leave their barrack rooms before midnight without others noticing. By the time Mom and I almost reached the gate a very ugly scene was developing. Many, thinking all of us were leaving, had rushed to wake the Camp and grab their few possessions. When they did not find their names on the list pretty justifiable anger and violence arose. I personally remember the scene as worse than that on the Tallinn docks but a few days before. Mom and I barely got thru' the gate and into one of the two buses (?), when stones thrown in anger and frustration started breaking the bus windows.

It was incredible relief to reach the station to find the train and the carriage with Freudenstadt slotted into the destination slot. We were to be hooked as last carriage onto a number of trains getting ever closer to our destination. I'd say it took that night and the following – I could easily be wrong. One horribly frightening night lies in memory banks: we had reached a large city (perhaps Hannover or Hamburg?), where we had to wait till the next morning, shut in our carriage and shunted onto a huge rail siding. Well, 'smart bombs' were decades away in discovery and would have been aimed at rail facilities anyway! For two interminable bombing raids we were just holding one to the other, wondering why we had bothered to 'escape'?

Freudenstadt was small and pretty and, oh so very peaceful. We ended up at the local Gauleiter's (Military Area Commander) office being assigned our billets. Now why the poor locals were forced to accept refugees from the East, I again have no idea – a nine-year-old does what she is told! Our family was to have a room with an elderly lady living alone in a large top-floor apartment in Bahnhofstrasse – actually she was forced to hand over her own large bedroom and did not like it one little bit! I really thought she looked like a very wicked witch and behaved accordingly. I suppose she was only in her sixties, but with a tight bun of grey hair and floor length black garments, when she hissed, you ran. The first few days she tried to stop us going into the kitchen and attempted to trip me when I had to use the toilet.

There was nothing to do but to 'hang in there'. Oh, matters improved! Once the lady discovered we were willing to clean, bring up the split logs and even stand in the queue with her bread coupons also, she became increasingly mollified. Actually the last I heard of the bird was after we had been in Australia for a number of years and her grandson notified us of her demise in her 90's! There had always been a monthly letter! God bless her memory!

Meanwhile I had language problems! There were four kids roughly my age downstairs and more down the road. My home language had always been German – I hardly spoke a word of Estonian until 4-5, but these kids would spout at an incredible speed always finishing with 'gell?' I hardly understood a word and they must have thought me a good and proper idiot! How was I to know there was something called Schwabish? Swabian to the reader!

Matters resolved in a peculiar way. The Black Forest region was in the throes of diphtheria, which, in those days, could very much be a death sentence. When I developed a sore throat, I was bundled into the local hospital down the road before one could say Jack Robinson! Only a few hours later the hospital doctor pronounced all I had was a simple sore throat, but because I had been admitted into a quarantine ward I had to actually stay some 12-14 days! Well, it was a large ward of all ages and both sexes – mostly in a convalescent stage with nothing to do. Thus I had a multitude of 'teachers' to make sure I learnt the 'bl. . .y language' ere I left. When my relieved parents collected me at the gate they failed to understand I had the bragging rights to: 'I speak three languages; Estonian, German and Swabian'! No more problems with the Bahnhofstrasse kids either!

Whilst I was at language school a few of our Esto group had made a discovery. On the edge of town, in a most picturesque setting, they found a pretty inn doing absolutely nothing at this stage of the war. Having talked Madame (she actually turned out to be half-French) into selling some rather good cognac, and sampling the soup she had bubbling on the stove, they made a suggestion: if she allowed our Esto mob to come over for lunch most days but stay awhile to play cards, chess and just talk – we would make her place a kind' of local Esto club! This was to work with bells on!

Most of us, even if we got along with the people with whom we were billeted, felt uncomfortable in their kitchens – so a hot midday meal was more than welcome. With food supplies oft 'under the counter', even if you had coupons/money, sourcing fresh ingredients was also difficult. Madame's cooking I remember as heavenly: she had the innate French gift of making something wonderful out of nothing. A young gourmet, or should one correct this to gourmand, was in the making?

Early on in the piece she explained that if only we were willing to eat offal, she could get three times the amount printed on the coupons from the local abattoir and we could have a proper meal. Thus I came to know one of my all time favorite dishes 'Schwartemagen' – honeycomb tripe to you! Before you throw up your dinner or close the book – you cut it into fine strips, sauté it with heaps of onions in some form of shortening, add your favorite 'herbs and spices' (No, KFC, yours are not IT!), pour over a bottle of gentle red, cover the pot and put it overnight into the slowest of ovens. I remember us kids running into the inn and, after sniffing the air, screaming 'Oh,yea, Schwartemagen!'. By the bye, I also don't remember a single one of us refusing our greens – baked or fried with heaps of garlic and herbs, we just wolfed them down. OK, no one had thought of bribing us with dessert either. Parents of today, note!

And to give our parents a break, we were given baskets to fill with edible weeds from the nearby fields for the next day's soup. Our guys would sometimes go fishing and take the catch to the inn or take the horse/buggy from a neighbor down the road to fetch fresh vegetables/potatoes from the owner's friends' farms. I don't even know exactly how grateful we kids were when a soft-boiled egg from Madame's not so secret chickens ended on our plate or she beamed when pouring us a glass of still foaming warm milk straight from some cow mooing not so far away. Yuk! Never mind our pleased parents. The slightly alcoholic Apfelmöst was much more to our taste.

Then there were the mushrooms. Of course, in a hilly country area of endless needle-bearing trees and many, many misty days there were mushrooms! In Estonian we did use the term 'seenevihm' after all. The war was obviously drawing to a close and most of the local Germans were afraid to venture out of town, so the bolder Estos had the place largely to themselves. Or did we?

Well there were a few rabbits and the occasional pretty deer which had not made it into the pot.

On weekends there was the Hitlerjugend still pretending to be brave and bellowing the 'Horst Wessel Lied' – they could be quite dangerous, demanding to see our papers and the few Estonian guys stupid enough to laugh were roughed up and marched into the police station. And then there were the others . . . .

I'd just discovered this wonderfully promising patch of fungi, when, looking up, I simply froze. A pair of eyes was staring at me from the other side of the sparse bush. Just as well Dad had his eye on me and moved fast enough to clamp his hand over my mouth. I was ready to scream the proverbial blue murder. So clearly do I remember 'korras' to me and 'freund – friend' to the other party. Quietly I was told to climb down to the path about 10-15 metres downhill and just look both ways. If I saw ANY movement either side, I was to face that way and bend as if to tie a shoelace.. I was not to look back. I was my Daddy's daughter, but DID look back. Dad was in conversation of sorts with two worried-looking guys. Directions were obviously given and Dad gave something out of his wallet to each. They disappeared.

We found a sunny place on a rock that afternoon and sat quietly for quite awhile. I was then asked did I understand what had happened? Yes, I thought so. Had I been very frightened.? Only at the initial shock. Did I understand that Dad, being a soldier, had the obligation to help other soldiers? We had trod that path back in Estonia – oh, yes. I was born an army brat after all. So proud of it! My very favorite song was 'Ich hat einen Kameraden . . .' Then came the repeat question: 'Eha, what did you see this afternoon?' Somehow, just somehow, with the 'wisdom' of a child growing up in wartime, I knew only one answer would do: 'Nothing, Dad – oh, that pretty grey rabbit back in the bushes'. Nothing more was said. Not to anyone.

Many, with hindsight, would blame my father. For what it's worth, I never did and I never betrayed his trust .

Oh, yes, until the front moved much closer, we did pick mushrooms, for us and Madame. For some odd reason we also carried bits of bread, the occasional apple or hardboiled egg, the odd map of the surrounds and other incidentals. We never talked about it. Yes, we met others. Yes, I was a bit scared, but now prepared. And when an English airman risked his life to slip down the hill and kiss my forehead whispering: 'Ich - auch. - daughter – zehn Jahre alt – God bless you!', I prayed every night, for weeks on end, for him to get home to a little girl just like me.

Meanwhile matters were not smooth sailing back in town. The closeness of the Front could be seen by the number of daylight sorties undertaken by the Allies. Their bases in France must have been close enough for fighter aircraft to accompany them now. All people are individuals: the first time I was shocked out of my wits I was taking a shortcut across a field to a family friend to pick up a precious pair of eggs. Jolted out of my eternal flower picking I saw a fighter at tree height making straight for me. As the plane rushed past I saw the (expletive) pilot wiggling his wings and waving to me! Would you believe I waved back!! Clearly remember doing so!

The second time happened but days later and showed the other side of human nature. In the early afternoon I had just crossed our road to take my place in the queue at the baker's for that day's bread. Noise, a fusillade, screams and a fast moving metallic shadow dead ahead, racing up Bahnhofstrasse. Totally automatically, I threw myself against the cement wall of the school opposite. The path of the bullets was later discovered as but centimetres away. This time around the neighbours did the screaming and it took the docs at the local hospital most of the afternoon to pick out all the gravel thrown at me by the exploding roadway. Had to lie on my tummy for days. And these were the expected Allies - our friends? Two in the queue died, more were injured. The inhumanity of war. Some Allied fighter-pilot saying 'bu...r them!'? At least they did the promised thing in never properly bombing us – the odd bomb did land, but mostly jettisoned in the countryside.

The Front had reached us. We knew the French troops would enter town. Under a white flag an envoy was sent from their side to make a proposition – since there were many hundreds of wounded in the makeshift hospitals, if the Gauleiter simply allowed the French Army to march into town, there would be no shooting and no casualties. The proud Nazi refused and ordered everyone in town into two long tunnels dug, on Hitler's orders, into the hillsides some years before. The stupid, useless cannonade lasted for over a day with most of us close to asphyxiation n the airless surrounds. If I remember correctly, somebody simply put a gun to the fool's head and we were told to hurry home.

We did not have to wait long. A peculiar 'plopping' sound reached us indoors. Racing to the attic windows overlooking the park next door, a most unusual sight met our eyes. Column after column of donkeys, accompanied by bearded men in white nightshirts, were moving down the street to bed down in the park. I had never seen live Moroccans before – I did not know what the fact they had been allowed to precede regular French troops meant. The adults did. We had been handed to the wolves as revenge.

Peculiar things rapidly happened at our place. I did not understand a jot and thought the adults had gone just a little crazy! Mother got out of her normal gear and borrowed one of the old lady's floor length black garments. All makeup went and hair, covered with white powder, was covered by a head scarf. I was made to get into bed with my oldest nightie buttoned to the chin. Then the most hilarious bit began: Dad and Mom started to use Mom's makeup to put red and yellow spots both on her and myself – after a layer of white powder that is! I looked like ghost in fancy dress!

They came soon – in threes and fours mostly, for their safety. They stole and raped and murdered any who resisted. Father would meet each group and politely greet them in his impeccable French, thanking them for freeing us!! Some backed off, apologizing. Some laughed and stole. Watches and 'pretty' things like red and yellow and bright blue scarves. When they got to our bedroom door, Dad would sadly utter: 'Ma pauvre fille, elle est tres malade ' (My poor daughter, she is so ill!'. Well, typhus or typhoid or whatever I and Mother were supposed to have, did not appeal to them an iota. Some sort of a medico was found. He did not dare enter either but had a big sign to 'keep out' put on our front door. Eureka!.

But, there was a 'before'. I can still hear the screams! Every time I think of the day. Our downstairs neighbor had her 18-year-old niece by chance staying with her. She was a gloriously pretty and fun young lady. Scared by what was obviously happening, she tried to get into the attic to hide – just as a group of four Moroccans entered the front door. Her screams lasted for seemingly hours. Other groups were attracted by the noise and there seemed an endless number of soldiers tramping up the stairs. Much later, when she had obviously stopped being fun by passing out and bleeding just a little too much for their taste, they laughingly marched out. There was nothing Dad could do – he would just have been bayoneted to death

As is, he took his life in his hands. After it was over, he found her mangled body upstairs, carried her into the yard, found our wheelbarrow, and, right in front of the Moroccan campfires, trundled her half-alive body to the local hospital a few hundred metres down the road escaping back the long way around. Not one Moroccan bothered him, not a word was said, not a look was exchanged. Yes, there was an operation. All her female organs were removed. She survived physically. The day she returned to Auntie she hanged herself from the rafters in the same attic. She had been promised to a neighbor in her village. The shame was too great. That was just one story of the dozens that people talked about in whispers, hoping we children did not hear and did not understand. The carnage to women and children especially was unbelievable. It lasted for nearly two days. I was to see women raped against walls opposite our house – thank God I was too immature and ignorant to really know what was going on. Power play – revenge – war. How can such memories ever really go away?

We woke on the third morning to silence – a quick recce (slang for reconnaissance) to the attic window showed the park empty. What now? Soon trucks started arriving and regular French Forces descended upon town. The Military HQ was established in a school across our road. We held our collective breaths but were basically left alone. I do remember pairs of French MPs doing the rounds, asking who lived in the houses, searching for German soldiers or others dangerous to them. Soon the grapevine said that the new Commander was a Parisian lawyer and seemed a human being – 'ein Mensch', as the Germans call it. Fear began to leave us, tho' there were still stories of rapes and beatings.

Dad waited about a week or so. One late afternoon he donned suit and tie and marched across the street to see whether the Commandant would see him. He wondered whether our large group of refugees was known to him and what would happen to us now. Mom and I were pretty frightened in the aftermath of the barbarity shown until now. Watched as Dad spoke to the guards, was frisked and allowed in. I guess they did not expect to be approached in French and were careful about turning him away. We waited and waited and waited. Surely he had not been taken into custody. Well, it must have been around midnight when it took all three females in the house to put Dad to bed – I had never seen him three sheets to the wind before and thought it absolutely hilarious! I think I was the only one! Next morning, after cups and cups of the horrible 'coffee' we could brew, he grinned foolishly and said the Commandant kept really good cognac. Life and war had brought two military lawyers of the same age and similar background together. The Commandant had come on the scene after the Moroccan barbarism: his guilt and disgust had been palpable. Oh, more cognac was to be shared ere we left Freudenstadt – but neither guy wanted the headache of that morning after! Meanwhile Dad always had first-hand information as it happened.

We children had our own excitement: funny now, terribly puzzling then. Having been cooped up during the occupational moves, we were happy to be allowed out – as long as we played on the vacant allotment twixt our house and the next and stayed together It had been 'our place' before, as two brick walls faced one another and one could play ball against the walls and make noise without parents coming to complain.

Armed with balls and skipping ropes we raced around the corner to find an extra bonus to getting into the sunshine - there were heaps of white balloons on the ground! Well, they were a bit messy – it must have rained during the night? But who cared, we were going to blow them up and have a party. Just as well one of the boys from downstairs raced into his kitchen to ask his Mom for some twine to tie up our party accessories. All hell seemed to break loose! Suddenly extremely upset parents were dragging us into our respective bathrooms. I haven't a clue how many times my mouth was washed out with soap and how many times I had to clean my teeth. A horrible salt gargle followed – yet none of the parents would explain. Only when we stood in line in front of the local doc, and, accidentally, I saw him having a hard time from bursting out laughing, did I begin to think the world had not come to an unexpected end. What did we know of sex? Whispers said that part A fitted into a mysterious part B, but . . . .Army issue rubber condoms were definitely not part of our lexicon!

Dad's pleasant visits to the French Commander continued. Thus he was the first Estonian in town to know France and Russia had come to an understanding that refugees from Eastern Europe were to be forcibly returned to their home countries. A totally unexpected death sentence in the making! I doubt any of us would have got past the Russian border. The most desired document in the French Occupation Zone became a small slip of paper called the laissez passer: let the person pass/cross over – in this case into the US Zone. It appeared like a million dollar lotto win to all of us!

The Commandant was in a quandary. He so wanted Dad to be able to take us north, but it would have cost him his job, career, perhaps even led to a court martial. But, could Dad make up the name of an imaginary relative very ill/about to die up there? Somehow a reasonably legal pass for Dad for some 72 hrs duration appeared in his hands.

Quietly he slipped out of Freudenstadt, pretending to have a cold and be in bed. His lack of English was a problem at the checkpoint at Sindelfingen We had heard that the Yanks were forming camps for migrant folk of our ilk. Someone gave him directions and a lift to Goppingen – from there more fixed information about Geislingen appeared on the horizon and the proposed Camp was actually designed for Estonians! The person in charge seemed to be a Polish gentleman by the name of Czernecki, methinks.

Dad sat all day in the latter's busy ante-room before the gentleman had time to see him. Once that happened, it seemed a repeat of the Freudenstadt story: two gentlemen. with enough in common, got stuck into a bottle of cognac. No, he (C) could not see his way to get the Freudenstadt Estos en masse out of the French Zone. But – did Dad know anything about management? I wasn't there, but Dad's only answer could have been that he kind' of helped to 'manage' a whole unstable country under a foreign regime for some four years! Did he know anything about accountancy on a large scale? Affirmative! Could he manage to take care of large scale stores? Affirmative! Was he prepared to relocate from the French Sector within a week? You had to be joking! 'Give me three days'!

Dad appeared dead tired, but, oh so happy, in the middle of the third night. Mom and I had been so frightened. Before collapsing in bed, he waved a request by the US Occupational Forces for the French to release us into the US Zone, as 'no other person of equal and necessary qualifications' had been found to help build up the infrastructure in Geislingen! A place and a time . . . .

Next morning a delighted Commandant wrote out the famous laissez passer for our family and Dad raced to the station to get us tickets to the border on the evening train.
My parents had a large number of friends in the Freudenstadt artists' 'colony'. Some had old cars which ran on the smell of the proverbial oily rag. Everyone German became part of our 12-hour rush. Dad felt he could not tell any of the Estonian community. People were worried to their proverbial deaths – how did you say you had been able to manage to win the lottery?

It had to be me who did the deed! Since I was totally in the way of trying to fit three people's lives into two suitcases, I was ordered to cross the park to play with my Estonian girlfriend opposite. Huge mistake! I still remember the hopscotch on her pavement. Had I learnt my poem for the next day yet? Some national day celebrations were planned. My response was cheekily negative – No, but I did not have to: we had a laissez passer! Out of the mouths of babes! As soon as the little girl raced to her door: 'Dad, Eha does not have to learn her poem 'cause she's got a lessee-passee – I want one too!' I knew I was in trouble. Made it heaps worse by running straight back home. The moment Dad saw me it was a case of 'You could not give your mouth shut, could you? What if we all end up in Siberia now?'

Only an hour later we were visited by a number from the Esto community. Actually we were totally above board and legal, but . . . Dad had to spin a story of childish wishes and misunderstandings. There were threats of his face being rearranged if he was lying. Yet nothing illegal had occurred. Just - jealousies and fears were rife.

Our beloved old lady's grandson took us and our very few belongings to the station . I had been crying all afternoon, feeling a proper idiot and so afraid something would go wrong at the last moment. Dad knew the Station Master well and he waved us on board at the last moment. Suddenly, Dad ducked our heads below window level. The train to freedom had just started moving. Some of the guys who had visited us in the afternoon were there and trying to peek into all the carriages. The train gathered speed and they were left behind. I cried and shook all the way to the border post. Writing this, I do not know why? I just felt that Dad had wanted to do things his way and I had been a small, stupid kid and let him down! Ten had seemed so grown up until then!

At Sindelfingen we all had to line up single file on the French side to have our papers checked. It seemed to take forever. The same recurred on the US side, except friendly looking guys in uniform seemed to be passing lollies and what I later learnt was chewing gum to all the kids. As a new train gathered strength into the night, I started feeling better. 'Eha, it's alright – we all speak out of turn' came from Dad.

I guess it was the next morning we arrived in the town called Geislingen and some form of army transport took us up to Schlosshalde to the house and the room Dad had been able to pick out only a few days before. We were to live in the library of a four-room upper storey apartment on Weilerstrasse There was a big, round table with three chairs, a sofa to be my bed, a double bed which had arrived in the interim for Mom and Dad and a beautiful, large timber and glass bookcase, which we shoved by mutual strength against the glass doors to the room next door. We were home.

Whilst Mom and Dad went to check out the rest of the facilities I remember looking out towards the rail and town below. Children were playing on the next terrace. A couple of laughing ladies were heading towards town. A pussycat was hunting for dinner on the empty allotment next door. Little did I then know that I could never think of the words written decades later as pertaining to any other place than Geislingen:

For let it not be forgot
That once there was a spot
Where, for one bright, shining moment
There was a Camelot

The noise had ended.

KONIS AND TOBACCO PLANTS:

I can certainly remember grandfather smoking these. I can also remember him drying tobacco leaves in the attic of 144 Hospitalweihe in Geislingen and actually growing tobacco in our yard in Oz. I have no idea where he got the tobacco leaves or the plants from. I asked for others' observations. I personally was naive of the notion that proper cigarettes had a market value and that our folks would not squander them to calm their own nerves. MM

Olav Virro:
Regarding the question of tobacco plants, I do have some fairly vivid memories from Geislingen. My father, Artur Virro, who was a moderate if not heavy smoker (unfortunately), planted several rows of tobacco plants in the garden of the house in Rappenecker where we lived. The plants apparently thrived and grew quite tall, at least from the perspective of the small boy that I was. A reason I remember this is that one day my friend and I hid among these plants (I don't quite recall our objective in so doing) and we damaged some of the tobacco leaves. Some other men who also had an interest in these plants and my father got upset when they found out. As punishment I was to get a spanking. But guess what! My father spanked me alright but he took off his tie to do it with. It was probably the softest spanking I ever got. No wonder I remember it- and rather fondly at that.

Ilvi Joe:
I heard the word "koni" for the first time in 1945 when we were placed in a work-camp site (barracks) in Wasseralfingen after the war ended. From a near-by US military base, soldiers used to come on Saturday evenings to invite young women to their socials (transported in army trucks). A lot of them were smokers who left their extinguished cigarettes on the ground. On Sundays, I would see some of our men at the camp walking with their eyes to the ground, looking for konis. They would combine the tobacco found in several konis and fashion a cigarette for themselves.

Hannes Jürmann:
I remember one of the Estonians in the house next door at No. 86 in Wilhelmshöhe having tobacco growing in his garden plot behind the house. Back in Wentorf near Hamburg in '46, mum was disgusted that father had instructed us to keep an eye out for decent 'konis'. He said he took up smoking to cover the stink of formalin preserved corpses he had to dissect during anatomy prac. He actually dropped the habit in his mid 70s, but still survived to 88.

HOW GLIBLY WE USE THE WORD 'PRIVATION'

Many moons ago, well thirty years anyway, I returned home to find in my living room, a hoard of fast growing adolescent boys with holes in the bottoms of their feet, as they were wont to have.
I was greeted with "Mum, there's nothing to eat".
"What do you mean there's nothing to eat, I just did the shopping yesterday?"
I fast gravitated to the pantry and fridge to ensure that the omission was not mine. There were few voids in the capacious structures: Only the 'garbage food' had vamoosed.

Yes times had changed! MM

Gusten Lutter writes to Arne Ellermets, her cousin

There are books of suffering and hunger in Siberian prisons and labor camps. I have not read any of Solzhenitsyn's works. Unfortunately, of the several by Estonians deported in 1941 and 1949, only a few are available in English. The exception that comes to mind is the saga of Tiiu Lehtmets Hoyle's mother. (Cannot think of the name of her book right now).

A week ago I finished a great book that should be available in English, but, because of its length and depth, it would not be a commercial success. I found it in the Baltimore Estonian House book give-away, where people who are downsizing for retirement (NB: many to Florida !) bring their collections for anyone to take. Lorry and I are still kicking, so I keep picking up and collecting Estonian reading matter.

The notable book is by Rein Kasak, titled "50 Aastat Saatana Embuses" ("50 Years in Satan's Clutch"). Originally written in Russian, translated into Estonian by Margus Leemets, published 2011 in Tallinn by Kirjastus Varrak, hard cover 590 pages, weighing a hefty 1-1/4 kgs. HEAVY on all levels.
    It is the life story of (Merchant Marine Ocean Qualified) Kapten Rein Kasak, starting from about age 4 boyhood in 1939, remembering Russian soldiers occupying bases and quartered in Võru area, deported 1941 with mother and older brother (father separated, arrested, executed) to Siberian far north.
    Surviving cold and hunger with mother working in lumber camps, struggling through elementary and secondary schooling in Siberia, having to skip a year twice when he had no warm clothes to survive the winter walk to school, finally manipulating his way out of Siberia to merchant marine academy in Estonia.
    Assigned to Soviet Estonian Merchant Marine, he was restricted for years to work as second officer on coastal vessels and ferries -- being the son of an "enemy of the people", was denied international sailing and captain's positions until mid-1980's – and then only after being admitted to The Party and recruited by KGB as a "kopputaja" (snitch).

His description of years of hunger and freezing in Siberia brings me quickly "up to vertical", compared to what I remember experiencing and witnessing in the refugee life in Germany.

AIMI KIBENA/ZECHANOWITSCH
THE LONG ROAD TO GEISLINGEN

Sometimes during the night the ships, filled with refugees, left Tallinn. On the next morning, September 22. 1944, our LAPPLAND and other ships in the convoy were targeted with Soviet aerial torpedoes. Two torpedoes did not reach their intended victims, the third entered MOERO from the aft. The big hospital ship, with Red-Cross markings and the leader of the convoy, broke in half and sunk in a few short minutes. Thousands, the wounded, the refugees and others perished; a handful of souls were saved. LAPPLAND also stopped to save some of the very few, who had managed to jump into the chilly waters from where, if the fate thus decreed, were plucked into safety.

Mother and I were in a large cabin into which the seamen carried a survivor - a young woman, who did not know what had happened to her child and husband. My mother hurried to our own cabin and from the few dresses, that she had hastily managed to pack,, she chose one to take to the rescued one, so that the woman could change into something dry. It was a brick red dress, one of mother's better ones. Then mother turned to someone she knew and asked for a cigarette. A voice in the crowd murmured: "Some have lost everything, others cannot even do without a cigarette". The cigarette was already between my mother's fingers; she broke it in half and it took years before she smoked again.

Next I remember that we had arrived in Gotenhafen (present Gdynia), the port for Danzig (Gdansk) and were transferred onto trains, that were to take us to Berlin. I had a window seat and when at some point, during the journey, I once more became aware of my surroundings, it was night. There were no lights on the train, nor could any be seen in the world outside. But it was not totally dark I could observe that the landscape was incredibly flat and in the far horizon stood a line of trees, like sentinels, against the grey of the sky. The train shortly stopped at a station, I could read that it was called Posen (Poznan). Many, many years passed by before I was once more in that region - now Poland, of course, and couldn't help but notice that the landscape really is as flat as I remembered it from my night ride so long ago

At the end of the train ride we arrived at Potsdam Transit camp, a short distance from Berlin. At the Potsdam camp there were all kinds of refugees, who had started to pour in from the east - people, whose homes were in the German occupied areas, that were now being overrun by the Soviet troops: from Estonia, Latvia possibly Lithuania........

We were placed in some kind of barracks, that I can hardly remember. In order to move on, from the camp, one had to have a place in Germany, where one could go. An uncle of mine and his family, who had arrived in Germany, about a month earlier, had had time, while we were still in Tallinn, to send us their new address. They were in Werdau, not far from Leipzig; and had work and an apartment there. Thus mother was able to get a travel permit and we were allowed to leave.

Uncle's apartment turned out to be just one tiny room, hardly space for them, none for us. It was obvious that we quickly needed to find our own four walls. Next morning after our arrival, mother decided not to waste any time but to take our troubles straight to "the top". In this case to the " Oberbürgermeister " (the mayor) of Werdau. To make her case plainer, I was dragged along as the "suffering, homeless kiddie". No one from my uncle's family offered us escort, but we found the city hall and " the man in charge."

we must have looked pretty pathetic after all the traveling, that we had done, but the "Oberbürgermeister " kindly took us to his office. Mother's German was not good, but she managed to convey our plight and a few phone calls later we were told that there was a room for rent, but we had to wait until the landlady arrived to make things official. Before she arrived, the lunch hour was upon us and the " Oberbürgermeister " obviously decided that I needed sustenance more than he did and handed over, what must have been his own lunch: bread with butter, a tomato and an apple. To this day I remember the taste of that meal. Only much later I learnt to truly appreciate his kindness. Already at that time food was scarce in Germany - even for " Oberbürgermeisters ".

Then arrived our potential new landlady - "Fräulein" Enke; she looked as if she had stepped right out of a Dickens' novel. Thick hair was piled in huge curls and rolls on top of her head and she was nothing if not a dignified spinster. She took one look at us and assuming that mother's German was as good as nonexistent , she demanded to know, how she was supposed to trust into her proper establishment such as us? In her halting German mother made the point that though we were poor refugees, we were still totally honest.

The next day we moved into our new home: Bismarckstrasse, number one. It was a corner house and on the main floor, the corner room was a "Bierstube", a small pub, ruled by " Fräulein" Enke herself. At a large round table , in one corner of the room, she sat and " ministered" to her customers, the good "Bürgers" (citizens) of Werdau. There was either beer or dark beer, a sort of a mead. Nothing else was available. The rest of the house was divided into apartments. One of those, a small room, became ours.

As soon as we were settled, mother , like most women in Germany, during the winter of 1944, had to work. Officially she became a metal worker, whatever, that meant, at a workshop called MAFA-WERK just a few doors down from the building, where we lived. MAFA-WERK probably was, like many such work places connected with war production -making parts for one killing machine or another. I, at the age of nine, was supposed to go across the street to a"Kinderheim". It could have been partly an orphanage, but they also looked after children like me, who had no one at home to look after them. But I spoke no German, must have seemed very different to the other children and in those foreign surroundings I felt very uncomfortable. After a few days I refused to go there and was left to my own devices.

As sitting all day, alone, at home became boring, I soon learnt to wander around Werdau - a relatively small town. If there were any afternoon films for children I occasionally went to the cinema, but usually I just wandered about, keeping my eyes open for cardboard coverings for various size missiles. It was not an uncommon sight to see a truck roaring down the street, its load made up of such cardboard cargo. And as the trucks sometimes turned too quickly around a corner, some of these treasures were thrown out and I eagerly picked them up. Cardboard was precious - torn up, it was of great help to start a fire in our little stove, that we had both for cooking and heating.

We did not starve, but our food was very basic: mainly bread and potatoes. The latter with some gravy was the usual daily dinner. Coupons were needed to buy almost everything, that was eatable. And even coupons allowed one to get only minute quantities of meat, butter and such products. Only two items were available without coupons: a herring salad, basically of beats and potatoes with some herring for taste; and, a sort of meat jelly. The latter quickly disappeared from our menu, when we discovered that the "meat" was snails.. We had not become sophisticated enough to consider snails as food, even if they had been called " escargots ".

But above all else, that I remember from Werdau days, was the Christmas season of 1944. Already, a couple of weeks before the holidays, Christmas decorations began to appear on the shop-windows. Nothing elaborate. Perhaps a gingerbread house or some Christmas cookies, perhaps just couple of colored candles and a few fir tree branches.

Even though these were the last months of the war, every store still seemed to be eager to place something Christmassy on the windows. To me all these decorations were wonderful and I could admire them endlessly.

Then, almost daily, mother started to come home from work carrying a gift, that one or another of her co-workers had brought. Again these were simple gifts: a small bag of candies, a cushion, perhaps a coffee cup......... all given to bring some cheer to us, the refugees. Also the management of MAFA WERK was distributing Christmas gifts to all the children of its workers. Mother was asked what I would like. As all my toys were left in Tallinn, mother mentioned that a doll would be most appreciated. But the gifts contained only two dolls and both of those had been previously promised to some other workers. Yet, when the gifts were actually given out, one of the dolls was for me.

The day before Christmas Eve mother returned from work with several of her co-workers. I was told to go down to "Fräulein" Enke and stay until I was called. When the call finally came and I entered our room, I found myself in a "world of magic". The electric light was turned off, but several burning candles provided the light and on the table rested an exquisite doll's house, its four rooms perfectly furnished; there was even a minute Christmas tree in the "parlor". I was totally mesmerized and only after much prompting from my mother did I have the presence of mind to thank all the "fairy godmothers".

But the surprise didn't end there. Early in the afternoon of Christmas Eve, " Fräulein"Enke called us to her "Bierstube". After her initial negative reaction, she had quickly befriended us and both mother and I had often spent time, sitting at her personal round table, while like the rest of the folk in the room, we drank beer - the dark beer in my case. Now the round table was piled with gifts, all beautifully wrapped. Mother was embarrassed, she had not thought of giving any presents to our landlady and quickly returned to our room and made a little package containing soap - still from Estonia. Soap was especially hard to obtain at that time - " Fräulein" Enke seemed pleased.

Later that evening we had two guests, two Dutchmen. One middle aged, the other not much older than I. They had been brought to Werdau as "workers" and it was through my uncle that we had come across these men. As they were alone, their families back in Holland, mother had decided to offer them, at least a resemblance of a Christmas Eve.

The main meal was still potatoes and gravy, but there were sweets etc. to make the evening more festive. As the men were Catholic we all ended up going to the Midnight Mass- in a beautiful church, decorated with Christmas trees. It was the only Christmas Mass, that I have ever attended. After the church service the men walked us home...........I have often wondered what was their fate? Did they ever make it back home to Holland? I never saw them again.

About five weeks after the holidays our lives were once more uprooted - the four months stay in Werdau was coming to an end. These had been four hard months for mother. Many an evening, after work, she was quietly in tears. After all, we had no idea what had become of my father, who, when mother and I left Tallinn, had been somewhere on the front, participating in a futile effort to stop the Soviet advance into Estonia. Was he still alive? As for my own feelings, I can hardly describe them or now even understand them. It was as if I was suspended in time and space. Everything was different from what I had previously known, but I understood that the war was nearly over and that its end would once more bring all kinds of changes.

In between, finding the daily necessities and also making the frequent enough trips to the bomb shelter, were paramount in our lives. Werdau was not bombed while we were there, but many an evening and also during the night air- raid sirens made us hurry to the shelter, a couple of blocks away: always carrying a small suitcase, containing the most essentials for our existence.

Except for the Christmas period the most encouraging part in our lives was the Estonian newspaper, that was published in Berlin and which we began to receive shortly after our arrival in Werdau. The paper was full of names of people, who had managed to escape to Germany and were now looking for friends and family members with whom contact had been lost during the last panicky days while fleeing from the approaching Soviets. No one had any information about my father, but we once more got in contact with several of our friends and acquaintances. Being able to correspond, to share one's stories, worries and plans made one feel somehow less alone.

One day, in the last week of January, 1945, my aunt with my little cousin, with five other ladies and three other children arrived in Werdau. After fleeing Estonia they had lived for a while in Frankfurt an der Oder and now, as the Russian front was rapidly moving toward Germany, they were once more in flight . Together with my mother they wanted to keep on moving further South, where they hoped at the war's end to be in an Allied occupied area. Mother once more needed a travel permit, obtained it and we were ready to move on.

I do not remember exactly when or how we left Werdau. Of course, the beautiful doll's house had to be left behind, but in this new state of anxiety, of having to meet once more the unknown, it didn't seem to matter. Looking back, it seems to me that I was rapidly evolving out of my childhood.

Unknown station we had to change trains. Were some of the trains needed for troops: were some of the railway lines bombed out and we had to transfer to another route? Impossible to recall and most probably we weren't told anyway. Each change, however, meant a long wait on a cold platform and when a train arrived, in an enormous surge of people, to try to get on board.

In one of these unknown stations when we had somehow squeezed in, we saw to our horror that my aunt's large suitcase was still on the platform. Pushing kids and suitcases, one piece of luggage had obviously been overlooked. There was no chance to go and collect it - the train was far too full of humanity, besides the whistle let us know that at any moment the train would start. Somehow we managed to push our way to a window and to open it. It was nearly dark and the platform was almost empty. Near the suitcase was one soldier, who even to my eyes looked totally fatigued. We called out to get his attention and pointed to the suitcase. The train had slowly started to move. He ran to the case, grabbed it and then headed for our window; as he lifted it several hands pulled the case inside. That moment is still with me and I hope that in Valhalla, where he surely must be with all the other heros, he dwells in eternal good cheer and contentment.

Then it was daytime and we were still on a train. Some people were looking at a map of Germany. Geislingen, where we were headed, seemed surrounded by other towns - would there be air raids? Then mother noticed a place called Murnau where no large centers seemed close by. We must go to Murnau was my mother's decision. The rest of our group became terrified: our checked-in luggage was destined for Geislingen, our travel permits were for Geislingen, what would happen if an inspector would find us on a wrong train? Mother's decision prevailed and she promised to take care of everything.

At the next station, where we were to get on a train heading in the direction of Geislingen,we all got on a train heading for München (Munich) - ie. in the direction of Murnau. The inspector did come on the train and certainly wanted to know why we were not on a correct train to Geislingen? " We are still on the way", was my mother's reply. The rest of us had been ordered into silence. The inspector looked at our pathetic group and deciding that we had no idea what we were doing, he patiently explained that we were going in a wrong direction and once we arrived in München we had to change for the Geislingen line. We all nodded in earnest agreement and when we arrived in München clambered on a train to Murnau.

When we arrived at our destination it was very late and there were

Mother and I in Birling's farm, Weindorf

The autograph of the famous Maria Rokk on the back of a postcard

The Estonians in Camp Insul. I am the one in the national costume

no lights at all - even the railway station was in total darkness. So we all began to holler to see if anyone was around. Finally a sleepy and bad-tempered stationmaster appeared and demanded to know what all that noise was all about. Once he understood that we were refugees from the east and needed some sort of shelter, he immediately became helpful and went back to the station to make a phone call. When he re-emerged he told us that he had contacted the NSV (National-Sozialistische Volkswohlfahrt), a Nazi era social organization and we were to go to their shelter for the night. He offered to show us the way; thereupon he lifted my little cousin into one of his arms and with the other hand he carried the "almost lost" suitcase.

Between the station and the town was a large, snow covered area. I can still remember us drudging in that dark vastness, but once our eyes adjusted a bit, I wondered about the horizon - were there some strange clouds? It didn't look like any horizon, that I had ever seen before; but I couldn't exactly interpret what I was seeing.

And then we arrived at the NSV shelter. In a large room, where some other people were already asleep, the beds, bunk beds, were ready for us. We sunk into oblivion.

The next morning we were given some hot, herbal tea and the adults decided that we needed to find us something more permanent, where to stay. Mother had experienced kind treatment from the " Oberbürgmeister " of Werdau and decided that the "Obebürgmeister" of Murnau might be equally helpful.

My aunt and another young woman were in the best shape of the lot and they were designated to head for the city hall. They were gone but a minute when they returned, almost hysterical. "Mountains, mountains!"was all they could say. The rest of us dashed out with them to see what the excitement was all about. We saw that the street sloped down and at the end of it the Alps rose skyward. Snow covered, glittering in glorious sunshine they stood like pillars of hope and beauty. Actually, the mountains were quite a few kilometers away, but they seemed so very near on that crystal clear morning, as if declaring that the endless, dark train rides were finally over and something more promising was in store for us.

Eventually our two "emissaries" were sent off to the city hall and a while later they returned with the good news, that the mayor indeed had found places for all of us. Five separate farms in Weindorf, a small village just outside Murnau, had been ordered to provide rooms for us. By the evening we all had moved to Weindorf'.

 Mother and I were given the living room in Birling's farm. That evening the Birling family also invited me for supper in their kitchen. The supper was simple: in the middle of the table there was a bowl with boiled potatoes and a bowl of milk. Around the table sat several of the family members: the parents and their grown-up children. A long prayer,recited loudly and rapidly preceded the meal and then, as the rest were doing, I also sprinkled some salt on the potatoes and with a spoon helped myself to the milk. That was the meal - but even that was precious. The supper invitation was not repeated.

But the most important fact was that our harrowing journey from Werdau was over and we could once more settle into some kind of a daily routine. Also, in one week, our luggage, that had been sent to
Geislingen, caught up with us. In spite of the relentless destruction of the rail lines, not a single item was missing. And above all, we were finally far enough from the Russian front - we no longer needed to contemplate another flight. Now we were close enough to the advancing American army to hope that they would soon occupy the region.

It was also wonderful that Murnau and its surroundings were so picturesque. Besides the nearby Alps there were three lakes, rolling hills and meadows, small forest groves and almost everywhere one could come upon a quaint little chapel. Southern Bavaria was a very Catholic land.

We received a new set of food coupons, but on the whole, by March, food had become extremely scarce. Thus the main meal of the day was eaten at the "Barbara Restaurant" and almost always it was the " Stammgericht" - consisting of potatoes with some added kohlrabi (a turnip type of vegetable). It was excellent hog feed, it also filled our stomachs. Special were the days when mother used some coupons to order for me "Greissbrei". It was an oven-baked porridge, made of cream of wheat, with a touch of some fruit juice poured on top. But the "Greissbrei" days were few and far between. As the spring progressed going to the restaurant became more and more dangerous. The best route took us through some open fields, where the Allied "Tieffligers", low flying planes, were often circling above us and there was the danger of being fired at. We became experts in diving into the nearby ditches.

 Eventually even the " Stammgericht " days were over. In simple language the kind waitress explained to us: " Kein Transport; Kein Kartoffel; Kein Stammgericht " (No transport; No potatoes; No " Stammgericht "). From then on our diet became even plainer - only three food items were still available: bread, sugar and "ersatz" coffee; the latter being some substitute of the real thing.

However, before that state of affairs was reached, on March 20. was my birthday. The whole group with whom we had travelled from Werdau to Murnau must have given up the best part of their food coupons in order to arrive at our place with two birthday cakes. What joy ! At the end of the day, very satisfied with the state of affairs, I remarked that all would be perfect if only Kyra would also be with us.

Kyra's father and my father had been colleagues, our mothers were friends, Kyra and I had been playmates from our earliest age. Through the Estonian paper, that was published in Berlin, mother had made contact with Kyra's mother, who with her children was in a women's and children's refugee camp in Sudetenland, an area of Czechoslovakia. As the Russian front was also approaching in that direction, Kyra's mother wanted to leave but was not given a travel permit unless she could show that she had a place waiting for her. Thereupon my mother had sent her a letter with a fictitious offer of a place, where to come and stay. After that we had heard nothing more.

To my joyful surprise, on the next day after my birthday, as I looked out of the window I saw Kyra, her mother and young brother approaching the Birling farm. My mother's letter had done the trick. The kind " Oberbürgermeister "also found them accommodation, in a farm, about five kilometers from Murnau.

Mother had been right, Murnau did not suffer from Allied air raids (actually, neither did Geislingen). However one nice sunny day, possibly in April we were at the farm, where my aunt had obtained her room. The proprietress and her two children were also in that room and as usual the talk was about the approaching and much awaited end of the war. All of a sudden there were couple of bomb blasts; with ear-splitting noise they fell from the sky. In a moment mother and I were under the bed and cautiously peering out.

My aunt was protectively bending over my cousin while covering herself with the baby's bathtub and looking very much like a giant turtle. The German woman had managed to squeeze herself under the old "Singer" sewing machine while hugging her two youngsters close to her body. The sight of us, had there been anyone to witness the "tableau", must have been hilariously comical. Even then I wondered how strong must be one's self-preservation instinct?

No more bombs were dropped. We later learned that Hermann Göring, one of the leading Nazis, was expected that day at a near-by hunting lodge. Obviously the allied intelligence had learnt about it and had attempted to target him. However, that day fate decided to spare the man.

Then Kyra's mother let us know that she had obtained a small sack of flour and the farmer was willing to sell her daily some skim milk. I was invited to go and stay with them, to eat something a bit more nourishing, than was my usual diet of bread, sugar and coffee.

Mother stayed in Weindorf.

Off I went and for a week ate food, that tasted better than anything, that I have eaten since. In the morning we had flour gruel with a touch of milk. For lunch we had flour gruel with a touch of milk and the dinner "menu" was identical to the two earlier meals of the day. Yet, how tasty every meal was ! When we weren't eating, Kyra her brother and I endlessly played the same game. As Kyra was able to jump on the back of one of the farm horses, provided the animal came close enough to a fence, she was awarded with the plum role in our "imaginative world". She was the smart horse. Her brother became the big brother and I was the little sister. In our game we were eternally fleeing from an enemy and devising ways to avoid capture and ambushes. Obviously the "smart horse" usually got us out of our dilemmas.

When the flour in the sack was dangerously and rapidly decreasing Kyra's father, who some weeks earlier had located and joined his family, decided to walk to Murnau to see if any bakery was still selling bread. I decided that I wanted to get back to my mother and would walk along with him up to Weindorf. We noticed nothing special until we got closer to the highway, that led from Murnau to Bad Tölz.

The road was full of German soldiers all heading in the direction of Bad Tölz. Not only soldiers, but all kinds of equipment, that moves with an army. As Kyra's father still hurried on toward Murnau, I trotted along. Soon appeared the "Tieffliegers" The soldiers ran for the ditches. We made use of the barns, where hay was kept or simply tried to hide behind the trees. I remember clearly, as I was circling around a tree, hoping not to be seen, that one of the planes was so low, that I could see the pilot. The planes did not fire on anyone. And the Germans kept marching in one direction, we in the opposite one. Still on our way to Murnau.

Eventually all the soldiers had moved on, we had the road all to ourselves. Then a man appeared. As he came closer I could see that he was very thin and poorly dressed. When we met, he stopped and asked us if we knew in which direction was Hungary. He explained that before the army left, the gates of the large prisoners- of -war camp, just outside of Murnau, had been opened by the Germans and everyone could leave the camp. (I later learned that the camp was mainly for Polish officers, who received somewhat better treatment than the inmates of the majority of prisoners-of- war camps in Germany). However the man, that we met was an Hungarian and he told us that he had made a vow to God, that should he ever be set free, he would head straight for his country. And he was doing just that. Kyra's father pointed out the direction, that he believed would lead the man to Hungary. I have always wondered if he ever made it safely to his homeland?

Just before Murnau we parted ways. I took the road, that led directly to Weindorf,Kyra's father continued along the town's main street. Once at Weindorf, the first farm, that I passed was where my aunt was staying. There, to my horror, I found out that mother being aware of the imminent arrival of the Americans and not knowing if there would be German resistance, had headed, not by the highway, but through the fields and villages to the farm, that I had left to come to her. Fortunately my panic didn't last too long, for as soon as mother found out, what had happened, she hastened back to Weindorf. At that point I was still with my aunt. The next step was to rush back to Birling's place and there with the farm folk and a couple of other Estonians we all took shelter in the farm's cellar.

It seems to me that it was still full daylight when the news filtered to our hideaway, that the American army was already in Murnau and that there had been no fighting. Later we were told that the "Oberbürgermeister" and one of the high-ranking army officers, who had stayed behind, had driven a car, with a white flag, to meet the Americans and to declare, that there would be no resistance. Thus the American army just rolled in a couple of hours after the German army had left. The actual end of the Second World War came couple of days later.

While we were hiding in the cellar I learnt that during the previous night one of the village women had come to wake "Frau" Birling to tell her that government storages for food and clothing were opened for all.

Obviously some administrators had decided to make the contents of these warehouses available to the people before they would fall into the hands of the Americans. By the time my mother had spread the news to other Weindorf Estonians the pickings at the warehouses were pretty slim but she had managed to find some clothes for me (I remember a pretty blue dress) and she also carried home a huge block of dried cheese, "Trockenkäse". Mixing a little chunk from that huge block with a bit of water, provided us with tasty, spreadable cheese. In my memory we ate it for weeks.

The next morning, after the arrival of the Americans, an order came to all the farms in Weindorf, that everybody had to move out of the houses, which would be used by the army. If the farmers wanted to stay, to take care of the animals etc. they could stay in the barns or stables. In the farm, next to ours, another Estonian lady had found accommodation. She had long, beautiful legs and wore the shortest of shorts; she also spoke some English. By the evening she was given permission to stay on in her room. She invited mother and me to stay with her. That night for the first time in my life I ate US army rations' chicken noodle soup.

A few days later all of us were allowed to return to our "homes" - the army moved on and left behind a mighty "mountain" of various discarded items. Among these discarded items were large, unopened cans - seemingly containing some food stuff. "Frau" Birling and mother decided to open one of these cans; it contained some unknown, soft and milk-coffee colored substance. We knew that the Americans were using some "instant" food products; just add water and......... Was the mysterious mixture in the cans for making some soup or gravy?
Trials were made, sometimes more sometimes less water was added, the results were the same: whatever it was, it tasted awful. Sadly the cans were thrown back into the rubbish heap. Only a couple of weeks later we had learnt to eat that obscure product: it was good peanut butter. I don't know why the Americans had thrown those cans away? The peanut butter would have made a nice change to the "Trockenkäse".

Not too much later all the Estonians of the area were gathered together to form a refugee camp in Murnau One by one we left Weindorf. A story went around that when the "long-legged soup and room provider" left, a special service was held in the village church to thank God for removing the "evil one". The priest supposedly also sprinkled each farm house with the holy water to purify the whole village. Anyway, Hotel Post on the main street became the camp's centre ,while many, like mother and I found an apartment nearby.

The war was over, no more fears of air raids or approaching soviet troops. Many were jubilant, not mother - we have lost our homeland, she declared; and, of course, we still had had no word of my father's fate. Yet, once the constant black cloud of war was lifted, life did become more cheerful, especially for us children.

A sort of a "field kitchen" was set up at Hotel Post, where all of us refugees could eat. Some American army rations like chocolate bars, canned fruit cake and other long-forgotten "goodies" filtered down to us; sweets once more were a part of our existence.

And as the weather warmed there was swimming in the lakes and we, children, to our hearts' content, could wander around the flower- clad meadows, picking wildflowers and playing our games.

Then, toward the end of the summer, a school was set up at the camp. Most of the children had lost much more school than they had had a chance to attend, so classes and teachers were greeted with glee.

Unfortunately, there were not enough Estonians at the Murnau camp to make it more permanent, so later in the fall the people were transported to other more settled DP camps. (DP: a displaced person) The school ended, we even got report-cards for what we had accomplished during that short period. But to my sadness it was all over.

Mother preferred to stay on in Murnau and Kyra's family had also moved from the farm to the town.
Without any structured time Kyra, her brother and I once more began our wanderings.

We no longer played that we were eternally fleeing, simply walked around in the streets and surrounding areas of the town. One day we came across, what we considered, was a pretty special " loot" - some magnificent ceremonial swords. We found them in bushes along a small creek. Obviously they had been ditched by some high-ranking German officers before the army's hurried retreat from Murnau.

They were things of beauty; I can still remember one spectacular handle, decorated with gold and mother of pearl. There must have been three or four of these swords. After carting them around for a while, we tired of our new possessions and decided to hide them in a new place - where, when we desired, we could easily find them. We chose a barn full of hay and then never bothered to go back. Perhaps to this day a farmer in Murnau region is the proud owner of some beautiful war memorabilia.

On another occasion we came close to some barracks, where US army soldiers were stationed. In the nearby bushes we found a "treasure trove" of white balloons. We only wondered why the men , who were sitting in front of the buildings were laughing so hard?

Life changed once again when in February, 1946, mother and I went to visit my aunt, who by then was living in camp "Insula". The camp buildings, as we were told, were originally intended for German soldiers, who would defend Hitler, in case the German's "last stand" would take place in that region. Berchtesgaden, with Hitler's " villa ", was only a walking distance away. The scenery was magnificent. Camp "Insula" was surrounded by Alps and tree-covered hills and mountains. In the army barracks were now housed refugees from various Eastern European countries, among them some fifty plus Estonians, including my aunt. I discovered that there was an Estonian school at "Insula" - two students and three teachers. I refused to return to Murnau and staying with my aunt, I became the third pupil.

Besides the joy of being able to go to school, one other recollection, connected with camp "Insula", has been carved into my memory - it was the visit of Marika Rökk and her troupe, including many famous German revue artists of the time. Marika Rökk, of course ,had had a brilliant career in German musicals but after the arrival of the Allies many of the stars of German stage and film were considered Nazi collaborators and were left to fend for themselves. Hunger was the greatest enemy.

We, refugees, were now fed by various allied relief organizations, in case of "Insula" we got our daily meals in a large canteen. For many Germans the food situation in the early months of 1946 was rather desperate. Thus this troupe, consisting of the " creme de la creme" of entertainers had decided to form a traveling group, that performed at various refugee camps etc. Food was their big reward.

On the evening of the performance I squeezed myself into the large hall. Entrance fee was ten marks and two cigarettes. One cardboard box held the money, the other the cigarettes. I had neither and simply went in, choosing a seat in the middle of a row, not to get evicted too easily. The show was for adults only. Soon one of the ushers spotted me and pointed to the door. I didn't budge. He obviously had no desire to carry me out "kicking and screaming". Besides, the people around me declared that I was far too young to understand anything, anyway. I saw the show.

The next morning the troupe was served breakfast in the children's canteen, I was there and somehow managed to obtain Marika Rökk's autograph, which I still possess. I remember her elaborate hairdo and expensive-looking, white, long fur coat. I also remember how they all seemed to enjoy our breakfast.

Shortly after arriving in Geislingen

After the school year ended, I spent one more summer in Murnau and then, in the fall of 1946, we moved to Geislingen, early enough to get properly started with the new school session.

In Geislingen life returned almost to "normal", at least. as far, as I was concerned. School; YMCA summer camps in the hills surrounding the town; trips with friends to the movies or the theatre; plus the usual "social life" of one in the early teens.

For mother too Geislingen was a period of respite. All immediate daily worries were over. We had a place to live and food to eat. Mother also had enough friends to pass her time pleasantly. Occasionally we made trips to other camps, to visit friends, relatives or some acquaintances. We even travelled to see interesting sights, that had not been destroyed by the war.

While in Geislingen we also received news, that my father was alive and NOT in Siberia. It took almost another ten years before we learned more. On the whole, he had been very lucky. Thus the first two years in Geislingen passed in relative peace. During the third year, when great numbers began to immigrate to USA, Canada, Australia and even to some South American countries, a new anxiety took root. Where could or should one go? At the beginning not all countries accepted women with children, by 1949 Australia did.

And thus in the month of August, 1949 it was our turn, once again, to journey to - and to face a totally unknown future in a land far, far away: Australia. And therein lies another story.

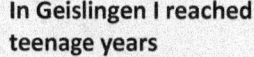

In Geislingen I reached teenage years

> Our life is just out there,
> somewhere
> **Gunnar Neeme "Mist of Time"**

DOCUMENTATION OF OUR IDENTITIES WAS ONE OF OUR TASKS AS DP'S

I am not sure what this document was prepared for. It was prepared about 18 months before we left Geislingen.

It is interesting to note the 'political' designation of Estonia.

I think that the occupation it alludes to is of the order of a wards maid in a hospital, maybe a Geriatric facility. Mother did work in such a facility when I was a baby, doing night watch.

It seems that documentation of one's occupation in Estonia was helpful in obtaining work in Germany

This is an identification we needed before being able to emigrate. I am not quite sure why that extra form was needed. It is essentially a stat dec by two people who had known mother since we lived in Estonia and sworn before a lawyer. We had many documents with our IDs on them but I wonder if this was done because we appear not to have had birth certificates among that collection.

AIRE KOLBRE/SALMRE
AND SO IT HAPPENED

OUR CHILDHOOD IN ESTONIA

Kaare and I were fortunate to be born in the Republic of Estonia in 1930 when the Estonian identity was riding high. We were given names the names Aire and Kaare which abounded in vowels. Father had Estonianised our surname from Kolberg to Kolbre. I have remained loyal to my Estonian first name despite living in America for over fifty years: It was frequently read as "Airy" (airy, according to the dictionary also meaning frivolous, easy going, lively, happy, the antithesis of which I truly am). My foreign name has offered me many opportunities to introduce my place of birth to the Americans who tend to commonly only be familiar with the world's larger countries.

We have many wonderful memories of our childhood: Of Christmas, our christenings, Kadrioru with its swans, Tallinn's Teachers' College Primary School, Tallinn's drama theatre, the zoo, the Central Hospital where our mother worked and where we were both born, Estonia's winters with its abundant snow etc. Our only misery was the war.

A large fir tree was brought into the living room on Christmas Eve: It rapidly dispersed its wonderful scent. I have yet to again see such beautiful fir trees as we had in Estonia. Kaare and I wanted to decorate the Christmas tree. We had to be careful because the glass birds and balls were very fragile: It was inevitable that one of those glass decorations would slip though a child's fingers and break. The decorated Christmas tree stood with great dignity in our living room and at dusk on Christmas Eve the candles were lit: They sure were a temptation for us to play with. Since leaving Estonia I was never again to feel the magic of those sparkling candles.

In USA they don't use real candles, while frequently fir trees which have been ferried in from far off places frequently can be seen for sale: They had already been lopped in the autumn and their dryness renders them flammable unless electric lights are used. Those childhood Christmases are etched into our hearts. To simulate a little Christmas back in Estonia while living in Connecticut we arrange a couple of fresh fir branches into around vase and attach real candles to them.(Scandinavian shops sell magnificent candles and candle sticks) By lighting candles on the bent fir branches with a match we revive the atmosphere of our childhood Estonia.

World War II brought pain and created chaos in our lives. Initially it did not make any sense or we just could not understand it all: After all I was only three years old, and Kaare was only one year old when the Russia set up its bases in Estonia. Father became the adjutant of the Suurup fortress.

The adults were somehow afraid and talked little especially if we were with strangers. We preferred to go for walks in the dense forests around Suurup: Their conversation still remained sombre. We could not understand why they were afraid of Suurup fortress' Russian commandant. That stout commandant would sit us on his lap, and let us play with his many red decorations and gave us candies.

The months passed by and the Soviet Union occupied our country. One day we did not have a father any more: He had been deported together with the Estonian military to Russia. Fate was kind to father and he was one of the few Estonian military to escape from there. Dubiously as a serviceman who had escaped from Russian lines to Germany, he had to bide time as a prisoner in Prussia. I can recall when father walked in through our door in 1942 in Tallinn clad in a strange foreign brown POW uniform.

It had been traditional to christen children during their first year of life. Due to the prevailing circumstances our Christenings were deferred until father returned from Russia. We can remember our christening day. Yes, we can recall the beautiful striped butter balls which were rolled with the butter spatula, also the tasty tortes which were decorated with colorful jellies.

While in Germany as a refugee, at times I fondly remembered these red and green jellies. The red and green jellies (jello's) we could obtain in the school canteen in USA were not nearly as luscious as those back in Estonia which had been made from fresh berries and for our christening. In our memories Estonia's tortes will forever remain the best cakes in the world. Even now many years later when staying in Estonia, Estonian pastry cases too remain the world's best.

On christening day when the adults were chatting we children used that opportunity to slide along the hallway banister. Christening dresses were unsuitable attire for such pursuits as sliding from the second floor to the first.

With the German occupation life was more peaceful than at the blood stained Russian times, but still not quite not normal. I can recall German soldiers frequently visiting us because of father's work commitments. They were friendly, brought us candies and they even made time to play with us. It was fun to play dominos with them. I was taken by uniforms and played on the lower floor with tin soldiers belonging to long standing family friends' sons called Tõnu and Meeme Maasik. I can recall how the older children learned traditional legionnaires' songs for mother's day: "Far, far away is my home…" and "I would like to be at home…"

The years continued to pass and the winds of war were approaching Estonia. Increasingly Russian planes began bombings of Tallinn. I can recall the 9th March 1944 bombing of Tallinn. Our family of four together with some people who lived in another house were sheltering in our cellar. Among us were some German soldiers sitting with worried looks on their faces. During a break in the bombing we went outside. It was night and it was wintery, but outside it was light and warm. Tallinn was burning around us. People came out of their houses and began to douse them with sand and water to prevent the flames spreading. We copied the adults. No one yelled at the children to vamoose and go to sleep! The bombings resumed fast and the Russian planes returned to begin their further destruction.

Even now lightning and thunder outside reignite the vivid flashbacks of the rumblings of the bombings.

After the 9th March Russian bombings of Tallinn mother and my godmother with her family moved to Karksi Nuia in Viljandi region while father had to remain at his work in Tallinn. I can recall at nights seeing the glow Tallinn's bombing in Viljandi. The farm folk feared for the soldiers who were at battle with Russia where the war was raging. My godmother's brother was out there among it all. The family members travelled among the surrounding farms to collect clothes for those young soldiers on the Eastern front. I relished accompanying those journeys across the slow clad fields on sled tracks which were comfortable but perhaps did not quite measure up to the picturesque aplomb of such photos.

The summer in Viljandi was especially beautiful. The large lush red, white and dark blue currant bushes were an ongoing source of yummy sweet currants. The yard had a pond with curious lively leeches and in the middle of the yard was a white garden shed where we could shelter from the sun. It was fun to join the cowherds and shepherds during the day. Each cow, heifer, sheep and ram had its own name. The herdsmen also knew each tree and shrub and were always ready with interesting stories.

They taught us to make willow flutes and shared with us the 'secrets' of the herdsmen's lives. However the war began to come closer and closer: Sometimes the Russian aeroplanes were circling overhead while we played in freshly hewn crop fields. Country children were accustomed to running around these fields but the city children found such activity very painful.

Stories of the Russians misdeeds had left their mark on our young ears: The sight of aeroplanes frightened us. The farm employed Ingerlanders who the Germans had brought to Estonia from near the Russian border. They yearned for Russia's victory. They boasted that soon the Russians would arrive in Karksi Nuia and take away our toys and cut our heads off: Even children were terrified of the Russians.

The war came even closer and the time arrived to leave Karksi Nuia to escape from the approaching Russians.

MEMORIES OF SCHOOL IN ESTONIA

Fate granted me the opportunity to begin my education in Estonia at what was then known as RIK primary school (State English College) though at the prevailing times the school was known as Tallinn Teachers' College primary school. I have wonderful memories of my first school. It was situated on Narva Maantee. Sadly due to the escalation the war I was not to complete my first year there: My schooling there ended that spring.

I can recall meeting the Principal for the entrance exams in the spring of 1943. I wish I could recall the principal's name. I can recall that he had a hefty build and wore a grey waistcoat under his suit coat. Mother later related that family friends whose children had not passed the entrance exams had whined that maybe I got into the school due to father's friendship with the principal and not by my own steam. It is possible that both factors helped as is common in life. I remember being asked to read and do sums. We lived on Laulupea (Song festival) Street. Usually I walked to and from school on my own: I enjoyed that.

Despite our rush to escape from the war front mother had the foresight to take the school reader and religious instruction book with us. They proved to be invaluable. Kaare was to use it after me and thereafter it was handed down among many of our refugee children: Such intensive use reduced both to tatters. Brown tinged by time J. Luuri and A. Arumäe "Religious instruction for primary schools part I, for years I and II", still adorns my bookshelves in my present Connecticut home: There it retains its place of honour.

I have on a couple of occasions visited the Narva Maantee school house which still remains, but it is now called "Peda" school house. In 1985 my younger daughter Tiina and I stayed in the School's old gymnasium. While there I showed her the vaulting horses and gymnastics ladders which I used to climb up gymnasium walls: That brought back memories of games which we played in formed circles. The magnificent Christmas tree stood in that same gymnasium. I was an angel in the Christmas play. Mother made the wings for my angel costume.

I can recall the strict discipline of that school. During class breaks we had to walk back and forwards in pairs up and down the corridor. Some of my most treasured memories are of the school taking us to the children's theatre at Tallinn's Drama Theatre. My captivation with the theatre has not diminished but I still do not like to sit near the front. That is where we had to sit when we went there with the school. When the bats, witches on their broomsticks and other sundry, creatures fluttered in the air suspended by strings and wires, for the children this revelation destroyed the impetus of the theatre.

I also enjoyed the drawing classes: Maybe they were craft classes. There we made coloured paper chains for the Christmas tree. Nevertheless while my time at the school was limited it was a memorable time. In Germany we went to school for a short while: It wasn't the same!

I began my school year in autumn 1943. As I recall soon after Christmas the Germans took over the school building as a military hospital. School was now scattered all over Tallinn: It could never be the same as it had been on Narva Maantee in that prestigious place called Tallinn University Teachers Department.

LEAVING ESTONIA IN 1944

Dad insisted to know what was in store to avoid past problems, so a delegation was organized to check out the facilities. The end result was that no one at Rotenburg knew anything about refugees coming and there wasn't anywhere to accommodate them.

At Fürth there was a camp for Poles and Russians and this was overflowing. No one knew of any camp established for Baltic people. After some reorganization several Estonian families were moved to Fürth and we were amongst them.

We relocated on 12th October 1945 and I called this 'our new home' but reminded dad that 'our real home is far away'.

A week later mum travelled with Harald to Geislingen where a large Estonian camp had been established and secured a room for us. Harald stayed behind, while mum and I joined him a couple of days later. Dad followed on the 4th November. Dad had also secured a teaching position taking the final year classes for commerce, psychology and philosophy.

Mum described the trip by train to Geislingen 'horrendous'. Trains were so packed that part of the trip one was hanging on standing on the steps or the outer porch. At one stop mum managed to get into the carriage but

Harald didn't: He eventually climbed in through a window.

We lived in Rappenäcker Street in one house with just one room and then moved to another in the same street. We were on the third floor in what were actually two attic rooms, and Harald shared one with an ex-soldier, Ludwig Annom. Life took on some normality but food was still rationed and scarce.

Dad worked at teaching and as a legal adviser for Baltic people, was involved in most Estonian organizations, the chess club and Scouts. He attended various courses such as mechanic, English language, farming, and photography.

It is still hard to come to terms and reconcile leaving Estonia and becoming a refugee. I was eight years old in that September 1944. Kaare was six years old. It all happened very fast. It seemed like major confusion in our Tallinn house at the time: I should have been at school.

I can recall how mother packed our suitcases and wanted to include out photo albums: Father said this was needless as the world could not stay in turmoil forever and that we would be able to return in a few weeks. That hurried exit from our homeland stretched out to be a half a century of Soviet occupation of Estonia. Mother had the foresight to include a few family photos among the clothing together with my class 1 reader and Religious Instruction textbook.

In the refugee camp in Germany we awaited for our homeland to become free again. Fear of the Russians carried us a long way away from them to USA. Father, Karl Kolbre, a professional Jürist, had had the honour of Captain in the Estonian army and had fought against the Russians in the War of Independence with the Treffner Kuperjanov Partisans and Tartu's schoolboys'' Battalion. In 1941 he was taken collectively with other officers to Russia. He was fortunate to escape from Russia's hell and return to Estonia via Germany.

Our family in Tallinn 1940. Father E.V. Captain, Jürist Karl Kolbre, Aire, Kaare and Salme

Our mother Salme Kolbre

Our home at Blomberg camp. It was situated at Huxweiderstrasse 20. We lived on the second floor in 1945-9. Our little room is to the right. Mother was the camp's senior midwife. Like Dr A. Norman Meie who lived in the adjoining room they were both valued members of the camp. Our small room also served as an office where people brought their endless problems.

Our parents had no choice. To be captured a second time by the Russians would have been disastrous for father and indeed our entire family. Mother, Salme Kärner Kolbre, a trained nurse midwife was Tallinn's Central Hospitals wounded patients' section senior sister. Mother had completed the Tartu University midwifery course in 1920 and specialised in surgery.

Many high profile state officials hid in Central Hospital to avoid deportation. Had this become known the department head Doctor and mother, as the departments' senior sister would have met an unwished for fate. Mother prized and enjoyed her work in that hospital: She had to leave it behind and together with her husband and family escape from the oncoming Russian onslaught. No one believed that we would remain so far away! The feeling was that we would soon return to Estonia and that life would continue as it had in the years gone by. Even many years later in USA mother would awaken with nightmares that the Russian military were coming to arrest us.

OUR EXODUS BEGINS

From Karksi Nuia we headed towards Saaremaa. Mother packed quickly. Our suitcases contained only needed clothing. Mother piled lots of clothing on Kaare and me, allowing us to carry more clothing with us. As we passed through Tartu my grandmother gave us a small 'Luteri' veneer case filled with tasty food provisions which became necessary quite quickly. Later in Germany that case still retained its wonderful sausage aroma. Our journey led through Hiiumaa to Saaremaa. Those islands were magical despite their 1944 ravages of war.

Their memory left me pining to see them again one day. Many decades later, when Estonia became free again we have repeatedly visited those beautiful islands. My war time memories of Hiiumaa are of junipers and Baltic herrings. It was fun playing 'hide and seek' between the junipers. It seems that our regular diet in Hiiumaa was herrings day after day together with potatoes and butter. The adults were not all that impressed with this recurring menu but for me that hankering for Hiuumaa's herring remains.

I remember Saaremaa for the swish little toy boats built from thick bark and bearing white masts: It fun to sail them in puddles. Life was in survival mode during war time and the adults had neither the time nor inclination to join their children in such activities. The stormy sea ship and Estonia faded into the distant past.

We left Saaremaa on 28 September 1944: The Russians lines were already moving closer from Tallinn. Both Kaare and I were left with unforgettable memories of our parting from there.

We were destined to go to Sweden but this was not to be. It seems that Estonia's traitors had intervened. We can recall being on Saaremaa's shore which was full of endless hopeful people too awaiting that white ship. As the ship became visible the people became livelier. We could hear the words "We will escape". A ship called "Peter Wessel' was seen to be approaching from the distance: it did not berth on our shore.

Only a few small boats lowered from that ship came to our shore. German officers who had been on shore had telephoned the ship and those small boats had been sent to rescue them. Given father's military connections we too were allowed on board. We were lifted onto the boat which ferried us to the deck of the "Peter Wessel'.

Shock and panic broke out on Saaremaa's shore as people realized that the ship would not berth and they were not about to escape. As the small boats distanced from the shore we could hear cries of "They are escaping, what will happen to us, the Russians are coming?" That painful imagery of Saaremaa's shore is etched into my memory. Ilmar Külvet, a journalist writes dramatically in the play "Sild üle mere" (bridge over the sea) of this tragic day.

My name caused consternation on the ship. Kaare was an obedient child but I was restless and wouldn't listen to mother's instructions. As mother called "Aire, Aire "the people on board became nervous and assumed that danger (häire –meaning danger in Estonian) was looming as aeroplanes were circling above. After a while the people aboard the ship twigged that there was a girl call "Aire" aboard who as being chastised and that we were not all at constant risk of an air raid.

On September 29th thankfully we reached the former Polish port Gotenhafen (Gdynia) which was near Danzig (Gdansk): Gotenhafen had been annexed by the Germans at the beginning of World War II. There were to be many more escapes and 'adventures' to follow as the war began to wane and we finally found ourselves free again.

NOW IN GERMANY IN 1944 AND CHRISTMAS IN RATHENOW

On a foggy morning on September 30th we were ushered off the Peter Wessel at Gotenhafen Port. I recall that we were given sandwiches and drinks at the time: They were handed out by German speaking women. Kaare and I learned that the local language was German.

Mother was eager for us to begin learning foreign languages quickly: She engaged a middle aged German lady to look after us.

We were at the nearby Brandenburg transit camp during the week. Gradually together with other Estonians we were loaded onto a train bound towards the Berlin area. Near Frankfurt am Oder the train came to a halt amid a vast empty expanse and the Estonian group of maybe thirty adults were ordered to leave the train. The preceding day allied bombings had destroyed some of the railway tracks and the Estonians were set to repair them quickly.

Our quarters were a vast old barracks in the middle of nowhere: it was our introduction to life in the barracks. We lived in a very large room with countless beds which were called bunks: We shared that room with many families with children and also adults. Privacy was attained by hanging bed sheets between the bunks. I recall that all the adults had to go to repair the tracks: They were given picks to work with. Our mother was not strong enough to lift the pick which had been given to her let alone repair those tracks! The Germans were in a hurry: The wrath of the war had reached Germany and destroyed it. Orders came from above that all adults had to help in repairing the tracks!

The grandmothers were assigned to mind the children while their parents were at their tasks. Mother went to work in her current good clothing, clad in a red fox fur coat and wearing high heels. The Germans in charge told her such clothing was inappropriate for repairing tracks. What was she to do: That is all the warm clothing she had with her.

Accidents occurred at work and the inadequate nutrition and abnormal living conditions brought with them illness both among children and adults. She was transferred to an office job when they discovered that she had been a midwife and nursing sister: From there evolved the barracks ambulance facility.

The autumn was cold and strong winds howled around the barracks. There was a novelty in the life circumstances and all that occurred was different and interesting through a child's eyes.

Very soon Kaare and I were down with chicken pox followed by measles: It was surprising that we survived them: Many children were not so fortunate and many a life was snuffed out on our refugee trek. I can recall my skin remaining itchy and my throat remaining painful for a long time. Mother wrapped large warm scarves around our necks: The scares were so bulky that it was hard to turn our heads. Well maybe it was the sore throats which were the hindrance to turning our heads! However recover we did.

I am sure that mother by working at the ambulance facility allowing her to give us more attention helped. Father's access to better food too helped. The Germans in charge of the track repairs, too needed the ambulance facilities and those grateful for this assistance kept mother in mind when food was available.

While we were being cared for by our grandmothers, our parents at work, the local German children gawked through the windows and scared us. They peered inside, pointed to their heads with their forefingers (a local sign of idiocy), made horrid faces and hideous noises. We couldn't understand too much of their language: We just saw and heard their commotion. Maybe they were Germans acting out St. Martin's day, or maybe they just came to harass us foreigners.

My memories of the German youth are not pleasant. Reflecting back on the negative behavior of the German children towards us it is possible that it arose from their Germanic Arian upbringing.

When we arrived in USA we noticed a vast difference between the behaviour of war time German children and the American children who had not met war. The American children were mostly friendly, helpful and well-meaning.

In the middle of the barracks was a large cauldron: Just like ones which witches owned! Our daily food simmered in them. It was usually soup which was comprised of water and vegetables: Mostly potatoes and kohlrabi roots. The taste was not so bad and it filled our stomachs. Estonian women were known for being creative with limited food. At night the cauldron was used to heat water to wash off the daytime grime. I cannot recall seeing the sun shining.

Blomberg camp Estonian school 1948. The principal Rosalie Rigna is in the middle, to her right the Estonian language teacher Lydia Pold, Back L. Aire, second R. Kaare. The families have now dispersed world wide.

Aire and Kaare at the Blomberg Camp 1945

**Art classes at the Blomberg Estonian school 1948: The teacher was an artist called Albert Uudriste.
Front L: Arvo Podersoo, Ester Ilves, Kaare my sister.
Back row L: Aire, Lilian Klavet Xjeminez, Maie Uga.**

173

The families were occupied by their daily tasks: There was no song, no joy, nor tears and whining. People appeared to be in shock. Once those tracks were fixed we were again loaded onto trains and the journey towards Berlin resumed.

We were heading for Berlin: The Germans had assigned our destination to its nearby Rathenow which housed a factory producing military carriages. In the autumn of 1944 Germany was in a panic, determined to do whatever was humanly possible to avoid losing the war. Our group of Estonians had been assigned to work in that factory.

We had to change trains because we needed to use the U-bahns (underground trains). With Berlin bombed out and in ruins it was hard for my parents to move about with two children and clumsy luggage in tow.

While Berlin was bring bombed its people used the underground train stations as air raid shelters. Mother kept reminding us that "hold onto me" so Kaare and I carefully grasped mothers' hand while we sought out the way to the correct trains and clambered onto them. The stations and platforms were a seething mass of people. At one station mother managed to board an underground train where the doors closed before she could haul her luggage into it. We alighted in a panic at the next station. Fortunately father boarded the next train and our family continued on together.

I recall eating in an eating facility in war torn Berlin. The war ravaged country had little choice of food in those days. We were given a vegetable salad: Mother said "Eat" and Kaare and I ate. That salad contained little oval things: each had two small projections. We were later to learn from the adults' conversation that we had been eating snails. To my recollection the adults did not eat that vegetable salad. The children were given baked minced tripe which we enjoyed eating. We were to learn later that we had been eating horse flesh. The parents ensured that we ate something to avoid us starving.

After many personal and travel induced hardships in a foreign war ravaged Germany (intense cold, illness, weary children and elderly, clumsy luggage, not to mention the helpful fellow countrymen etc) our small group of Estonians finally reached the place the Germans had assigned us to.

The wooden carriage works were amid dense forests and our adequate living quarters were assembled with amazing speed. In the corridor was a kitchen where meals were cooked at the end of the work days. Again the children were cared for by their grandmothers and all able bodied adults were employed in the production of those wooden carriages. Mother was again fortunate to be employed in the factory's ambulance facility. Since there were not that many accidents in that factory mother worked largely in the ambulance office. It sure was less arduous than factory work.

A small group of Estonian children were sent to a German school. I can recall a large stone building. On our first day at that school we stood in threes and fours in front of the class: Suddenly I had to go to the toilet. I suspect that because of the unfriendly atmosphere I had an accident. That set the German children laughing cruelly. The teacher muttered something like "ausländer, ausländer..' (Foreigner, foreigner...) A German boy uttered something which set the class laughing again: The teacher who was a woman clipped him across the ear. Germans had a custom of doing this as I later learned myself when living in Blomberg DP camp. One day while roller-skating on the street in front of our place (the roller skates were my much wished for tenth birthday present) a passing German gave me a clip over the ear.

The war beaten Germans bore the foreigners (ausländer) a huge grudge: The war had taken so much of their past life style with it. Fortunately we only spent one week at that German school. The war was approaching and the school closed down.

The reader and religious instruction book which mother had the foresight to pack among our clothing on that September day when we departed from Tallinn became a boon. Kaare and other children of our age read from those books.

While the adults were absorbed with their future the children were often at a loose end. This was to almost bring me to bad grief. The factory had all manner of machinery and smelt of veneer. One afternoon when work had finished

I sneaked out alone to explore those machines. I pressed a button to set off a loud rumble. I had started the saws and other machinery. People rushed in to see what had happened! I suspect that my parents were relieved that I hadn't been injured and I was spared a bigger punishment. But yes I did receive a haranguing.

The Christmas Eve in Rathenow remains a powerful memory. A willowy fir tree with candles stood at the end of our corridor: Someone read out the Christmas service and "Holy night" echoed quietly. The mood was subdued but the children still were given Christmas presents. Cherry colored covered books of stories printed in large font and written in Estonian were passed around. On the front page was a full page sized picture of the Fuehrer: Mother tore this out fast and disposed of it. The books had come from Berlin. Now we had three Estonian books from which we could learn to read in Estonian.

ON THE RUN AGAIN IN GERMANY: SPRING 1945

Spring had come to Rathenow: With spring came the increasing need to run to air raid shelters. Allied bombers flew over Rathenow which was in Berlin's flight trajectory. There was fear that some bombs could drop on the factory in Rathenow making military wooden carriages: near our current abode. Frequently we had just gone to sleep when the air raid sirens woke us with their screaming. We had to dress quickly, descend two flights of stairs, and cross a town square to the air raid shelter under the house across that square. I have a permanent souvenir of that time: A deep scar sustained when I collided with a sharp stair edge during one such urgent transit. I lost a lot of blood but fortunately the wound healed to only leave its permanent mark of those times.

In the spring of 1944 I developed pneumonia: From my recall I was ill for weeks. Breathing was painful. Mother placed hot compresses on the chest wall to draw out the inflammation and infection: Antibiotics were not available. I cannot recall seeing a doctor on our refugee trek: Mother did her best for us with what she knew.

When the air raid sirens bade us to retreat to the neighbouring house for shelter mother smothered me in heavy clothing: So heavy that it was hard to move, but leaving a sick child in bed was not an option.

One spring day when mother brought me food: Vienna frankfurts, red cabbage my appetite suddenly returned.

Our mother was ninety-five when she left New York and life forever. As an eighty year old she penned down her memoirs. Of our flight in Germany she wrote "in April we could hear the approaching cannon fire . On April 24th before lunch we left Rathenow heading towards the Elbe River where there were English troops. Our group of Estonians now consisted of fifteen adults and eleven children.

We travelled by foot, towing our meagre possessions in a German ‚wägele' (a wooden cart). It was a fine sunny day. We travelled about twenty kilometres on our first day: At 6pm the English cannons began blasting again. We found shelter in an animal stable."

I will add my own memories of that time. Rathenow was almost on the shoulder of Berlin and everyone hoped and waited that the mighty Americans and English would reach Berlin first. We would then be saved. There was disbelief that the Americans and English were so friendly with the Russians: Or were they just naive to allow the Russians into Berlin first? From his military contacts father had obtained train tickets for us but he also had strong nationalistic feelings and said that he would not move sans his national group.

I can recall leaving behind in Rathenow the two grandmothers who minded us and taught us while our parents were at work in the factory. They were sixty and considered too old to become refugees again. As I write these memoirs it seems to me that sixty is still quite young. When one reaches seventy the years begin to take their toll but I feel that I could still tramp twenty kilometers if need arose today. I wonder what became of these elderly folk when the Russian soldiers arrived in Rathenow.

As the Russians approached Rathenow food stores were opened: Frequently no one asked for ration coupons. People bought what they could. The Estonians bought brown sugar, and with hot water turned it into sugar cubes. Mother had a big bag full of brown sugar pieces: They gave us energy when we trudged by foot from Berlin towards the Elbe River. Kaare and I had scooters. At the wagon factory father had made a bicycle for me and Kaare's Godfather made one for her. Both were painted cherry red.

Blomberg Estonian Guides and Brownies 1948.
Front row: I am fifth from the L . Kaare second from the R.

Blomberg Estonian young at the summer camp 1948. Mrs. Leepere is standing at the back. Her daughter Helve has her back turned to the camera and her Helve's brother is to her right. Helve was the choir conductor.

Our family in Blomberg 1949: Father, Aire, Kaare and mother.

When we had to hastily flee Rathenow mother clad us each in two coats. Kaare rode her scooter to the Elbe shore and left it behind there. I felt too hot in that overclothing and it seems that the bicycle was not working as well as it might: I dumped it by the road side and decided to travel by foot.

Mother's recall of the flight from the Russians "The German troops were withdrawing: To avoid the fighting we chose to travel through a dense forest, where the German troops had just abandoned their trenches. After an hours journey we reached the Elbe. We could see English soldiers walking on its western shore and gathered wooden poles onto which we tied white linen and cloths we had brought with us. The kindly English soldiers upon spotting our white flagged posts sailed their boats towards our shore. The panic and uneasiness about the Russians troops was rife.

When the first English rescue boat reached our shore a corpulent Tallinn bank officer from our group ran to the boat and offered the soldiers his gold watch, requesting to be ferried across the Elbe River. The soldier stepped a few paces away from him and gave my husband the boat and its oars: He ferried the women and children first . Two German soldiers and an elderly German lady had joined our group. In gratitude I gave the English soldier a silver soup spoon: He jammed it inside his boot leg.

It had become very dark when we trod along a narrow dewy track towards a nearby manor which housed the English headquarters. The following morning we could see the Russian soldiers celebrating on the Elbe's other shore."

Mother related how one Estonian was so relieved that their family had managed to cross that river that she gave her gold wedding ring to her rescuer. The soldier threw his more basic ring into the river and donned the new gold ring. We were for the second time that year grateful that we had not been sliced by the Russians knife edge. The manor occupants had escaped from there leaving it for the English officialdom. We were advised to take what we wanted. We didn't want such things. The manor had several well adorned young women's bedrooms: From that we deduced that a large family had lived there. We had had to abandon our dolls and toys in Tallinn. Kaare fancied a doll which had a damaged eye. The English gave the doll to her. Later while at the Blomberg camp mother sent the doll to a Nürnberg doll hospital to have the eye repaired.

One night mother dreamed that the Russian soldiers were celebrating in the beautiful manor where we had spent that night. Was that to be an omen! The Estonians had only one dream: To escape as far as possible from the Russians. Some of the group, including Kaare's godfathers' family decided to head towards Celle. Another part of the group decided to head for Detmold. Yes there was a common aim: To be as far from the Russians as fast as possible.

Travel with heavy luggage was difficult. There was discussion about where to access some form of carts. A child had spied a 'wagele' among the carts while passing near a manor. Our accompanying Estonian family found in the manor's surrounds a larger two wheeled cart which needed to be horse drawn. That suited them very well as they were larger in numbers. Their young were older and with their fitter bodies could assume the task of drawing that cart. There were about twenty of us. Those were bewildering times: People were fleeing and roaming: Estonians were to be met wherever one went.

On that same day we left that manor and began to traipse southwards. Soon after the war ended the Americans and English set up a nice community for their Russian allies:

Mother's dream had come true. Our judgement to disappear from the Elbe's shores go further inland had been correct.
Usually father towed our little carriage. Mother, Kaare and I walked beside it unless we were heading up hill when we would push it from behind. At times the road wended downhill: It was fun to stand on the back of the carriage and go for a little ride.

The journey along the highway was pretty. We stopped at villages, where the mayors gave us food coupons and places to sleep. Each day as we reached a new village we were given new food coupons. Thus there was no shortage of food albeit the variety was limited. The sleeping facilities varied. At times we slept in houses warmed by feather doonas. At one large manor the stables were to become our dormitory: We were told that the stables were warm places for children. Of course we did not stay there!

Most Germans we met were friendly and helpful: They too had suffered a lot during that war. I can recall one stopover where we were truly spoiled. In the morning before our departure we noticed that a large knife had vanished. Our family's search for it was in vain. We expressed discomfort at this event but did not have time to ponder on it: It was time to move on again. We had been walking for about half a day when the manor owner's son caught up with us on his bicycle and told us that their knife had been found. Such were the meticulous Germans!

I still love hiking: Maybe this is a legacy of those long treks during and post war in Germany. During inclement weather we just rested.

When the victorious American and English army trucks passed us, the soldiers threw candies, chewing gum, drink powders and cigarettes, etc down to us. They enjoyed watching us run up to them and gather those goodies. Father smoked: That became fateful in America when a smoker requested cigarettes. Kaare and I gathered discarded valuable goods from around those army trucks.

On May 8th, which was also mother's birthday, the landlord announced that "Hitler ist gestorben" (Hitler is dead).

Actually Hitler departed from this world on April 30th but the news took some time to permeate to the villages. People seemed to feel a sense of relief to know that the cause of this major war had gone.

I recall Mother's day. We were resting in a trench by the highway when father announced that it was Mother's day. Kaare and I picked some freshly opened flowers from the trench side and took them to mother. Our parents had huge burdens to carry as refugees.

With the food coupons we obtained plenty of spicy sausages and bread. Mother developed stomach problems. She was often in pain and there was no treatment for this. Fortunately with her knowledge of medicine she slowly recovered as we trekked towards Detmold. We avoided big cities.

On 25th May after travelling for a month with our small cart we reached our destination at Detmold. Detmold was in the Westphalia-Lippe region. The English army gave us a place to live: It was in the former aircraft factory barracks. More and more Estonian and Latvian refugees began to flood in there.

The English ensured that we were fed. The food was basic: There as ample milk, eggs, rice and other kinds of powders to keep us alive. Fruit was in very short supply. Near the aircraft factory was a cherry orchard where the luscious fruit was just ripening.

While the adults worried about what would become of us refugees, we children left to our own resources ran around having fun and at times got into mischief. Having only basic camp food as growing children we needed fresh fruit and the Germans cherries were just yum.

At dusk we set off to pick cherries: The Germans who guarded their trees from the "Verflüchte ausländer" ensured that we could not pick them before they set off home.

When an older businessman from Tallinn found out about our cherry picking he decided to meet us one evening. The bigger boys helped him climb the cherry tree. He shook the branches and as the cherries fell we gathered them up.

On that fateful evening the Germans smelled a rat and armed with (malgad) came with to check on their cherry trees. We children vamoosed fast towards home, but the worthy gentleman up in the tree was caught. The Germans felt sorry for the old man and spared him a beating: That Tallinn businessman and his family felt ashamed of their behaviour.

One day while playing we were just running around because we had no toys, an English army truck arrived with dried foods. As they were leaving a Negro soldier gave Kaare a little black ball which almost matched his own skin colour. We had never seen Negroes before and felt scared of him. Kaare did not dare to accept that black ball from that black man. As the truck drove off the soldier threw the ball to us. Kaare grabbed the ball and looked at her hands: They hadn't changed colour. The small black rubber ball was to provide us with endless fun at the Blomberg refugee camp.

The aircraft factory remained fallow during the spring of 1945. While the adults continued to ponder on our future we children explored the factory and its surroundings. We liked to rummage around the factory and find things. The factory had executive offices with quality furniture. People began to remove the furniture to the barracks.

During the war the Poles and Russian POWs had lived in those barracks. They had been brought in by the Germans to work in the aircraft factory. In a few short days the Estonians and Latvians had transformed those ugly barracks into clean livable accommodation.

At the factory I found a pair of a pair of quality small pliers which father liked and which accompanied us to America. Near the factory there was a deep pool to soak the wooden planks to make them more workable. The big boys began to sail on those wooden planks. I too liked to join in but mother found out from Kaare and put a firm stop to that activity. I couldn't swim: Had the plank tipped over I would have been listed among the drowned swimmers.

Next to the aircraft factory was a secret little stone building. We thought that it would make a wonderful cubby house. The difficulty was that we couldn't open its door. One day a Latvian boy did get inside. He touched something and his right hand turned black: The building had high voltage electricity inside. He had his electrocuted hand amputated. He was his mother's only child. His father was at the eastern front. His grandfather was a Latvian professor. Of course we were all upset by that accident. We were friends with that family in Blomberg. They later moved on to Australia.

In June the English gave the Baltic DPs permission to open a camp at Blomberg. Blomberg town, "Luft kurort"(Air health spa) as the Germans called it was twenty two kilometres from Detmold.

Blomberg, situated near the beautiful Harz Mountains, together with its good and bad, became our home and community for the next four years. Father was one of the Blomberg Estonian camp founders and its first camp director. Asta Randvee, mother's colleague from Tallinn Central Hospital became his assistant. Asta Wachtmeister Randvee's adopted daughter, who is our age and her aged father (a former Tallinn businessman) too moved from Detmold's barrack style camp to Blomberg. In 1941 Asta's husband was deported together other servicemen to Russia. During the Russian occupation he returned to home to Estonia.

Asta Randvee needed her English skills to work with the English administration given that the camp commanders were English Officers. Mrs. Randvee was proficient in English having learned it during Estonia's independence, consolidated it in England, and I believe that she had also travelled to America. The Randvee family were fortunate in being able to leave Estonia with richly luggage and their family were better dressed than the majority of refugees.

Blomberg had a beautiful swimming pool. I recall how we as children used to admire Maie's colourful green toned crocheted swimming costume: She had acquired it during one of her overseas trips, possibly in England maybe even in America. Many years later in America I acquired a similar green swimming costume: However to mind I will always remember hers as being the more beautiful of the two.

I was aged nine when our family; father, mother and Kaare arrived in Blomberg camp on 7th July 1945. We left there for USA when I was fourteen. Our first residence in Blomberg was an old private home at 1 Bruchstrasse. Each family was assigned one room. The largest room was assigned as a classroom for children. This evolved to become Blomberg Estonian School. The landscape around Blomberg appealed to the refugees. Thus Baltic musical artists from Lübeck and other British Zone barrack camps moved to Blomberg: Blomberg was to become the British Zone Baltic Artists Centrum.

During that same autumn came an opportunity to move to a better residence. I can clearly recall the early autumn day in 1945 when the residences were assigned to Baltic refugees. Father took me with him when together with Mrs. Randvee and a Blomberg municipal official sought out suitable accommodation for the Estonians. I can recall father asking me if I would like to live in one of the houses allotted to the Estonians. I answered 'no', because I didn't like living on Blomberg's main road. It was called Neue Tortstrasse. Then we reached Huxweidestr. 20. Father again asked me that question. This time I answered 'yes'. I liked the modern interesting houses in that street. The street had little traffic: I could run around and play ball on it.

Blomberg had allotted ten private residences for the Estonian refugees. They were stylish houses built under the Hitler regime and largely belonged to Blomberg's wealthy.

Initially the British army was responsible for the welfare of residents of the Blomberg camp. Later that responsibility was assumed by UNRRA (United Nations Relief and Rehabilitation Organization) and IRO (International Refugee Organisation).They paid the rent to the owners of the houses we lived in. Initially there was some disharmony with some of the Germans who had lost the war and had too suffered: That included resentment at having to temporarily relinquish their homes to the refugees. As time passed, especially after the currency reform which in 1948 enabled the house owners to be remunerated better, this disharmony about house relinquishment to refugees began to abate.

About 150-170 Estonian refugees lived in Blomberg camp. During the years when the Blomberg Estonian High School operated and while Estonian soldiers lived there the numbers rose to about 300. There were about 700 Latvians and 450 Lithuanians in the camp. Small numbers of Polish and Yugoslav officers who lived peacefully and quietly like the Baltics had found refuge at the camp also. Each Baltic group had their own schools. As I recall only two Yugoslav children went to the German school.

We had become DPs (displaced persons- according to the Silvet dictionary this translates as people who had been dislocated from home, suspended from home. We awaited for Estonia to become free: We hoped that the world's large countries would support our aspirations, albeit post World War II USA and England were friendly with USSR. It is somewhat surprising that we are being cared for at all. It would have been simpler and less costly to return us to our occupied countries. Sweden's government repatriated World War II Latvian war veterans, also a few Estonian ones to Russia. The fear for the future was genuine. We still remembered the journey on the knife's edge and our escape from this.

Our thanks go to our educated and cultured people who were prized by both the Americans and the English: They heard our pleas for Estonia's freedom. The Americans and English particularly enjoyed the Estonia, Latvian and Lithuanian concerts and they liked socializing with our people.

Huxweidestr 20 was to become our home for almost four years. That German two storey red brick house with its high gabled roof and built for one family had seven rooms: Three on each floor. Both floors had a toilet. The bathroom with the heating furnace and also a small room were in the attic. In that house lived five or six families which included children and totalled over twenty Estonians. An elderly lady who lived on the third floor also had a little dog.

Each room housed one family. We were crammed together like sardines. We were one big Estonian family who shared their joys and sorrows. We had to talk quietly because everything could be heard in the adjoining room: Eyes and ears were everywhere.

At times I had a childish wish that the war could continue and that I could see more of the world!

> Time can be the lost and the found,
> the sorrow and the joy,
> the anger and the calm,
> the spent and the gained.
> All is time and waiting
> is the longest part of time.
>
> **Gunnar Neeme:**
> "Mist of time"

ENE MAIDRE/MIKLI
FROM THE SUMMER OF 1944

I was born in August 1936. Thus I had my 8th birthday shortly before leaving Estonia in Sept. 1944. This places me among the youngest people who can remember the events of that time. Actually I have some memories of happenings going further back but for this story I am starting with the summer of 1944.

We were staying with my aunt and uncle on a farm in Valgamaa. My father was working in Valga and mother looked after us: my brother, sister and myself. I am the youngest. I was aware of the troubled looks of adults, heard talk of the battles at Narva and saw the columns of smoke when Tartu and Valga were bombed.

Yet, for a child life went on as normal. This changed suddenly on 13th August. Father sent a word that he had made arrangements for a truck to come and pick us up that night and my mother had to be ready to leave, taking whatever she thought was necessary.

When that truck finally arrived it was overcrowded with people whom the driver had picked up on the way. We were hardly able to climb on. We could see fires on the horizon and hear the noise of the battle. I was truly frightened. I was sitting on top of parcels away from my mother and panicked when the overcrowded truck could not make it up a hill and started to slide back towards a river.

There were some men present and they jumped off and pushed. Eventually we arrived in Tõrva. A few days later we travelled on and stayed with relatives at Tihemetsa. We arrived in the port city of Pärnu on 21st Sept. That night there was an air raid and sheltered in the cellars of Maavalistus. This was my first really close up experience of war. By now my father was with us.

Next day we went to the port. There were 2 small German freighters tied up at the wharf and no more ships were due in. Both were overcrowded with people. Lots more were trying to get on board, but there was just no room. I am told that offers of money and even gold were refused by the captains. Dad was able to produce a case of vodka - and we were allowed on board.

Although I did not understand everything I do remember the wharf, the ships, people, confusion, panic. I knew that we just had to get on a ship. I do remember dad carrying that case of vodka. Dad jumped off the ship to farewell some people and I nearly cried thinking that he could not get back on board. We left that afternoon and the Russian army arrived on the next day.

Why were we so desperate to leave? In June 1941 our family was in the list of people to be deported to Siberia. We only escaped because we were not at home when the truck came to pick us up.

The ship was called "Sonnenfelde". We were sitting on deck on top of stacks of baggage. A storm blew up. Water splashed overboard. The baggage behind us shifted, my brother was nearly buried under it. Mother came to check on us, she was dripping wet having been near the rails and the waves had drenched her. A crane became loose and was swinging over our heads. People were screaming. To me everything was so unreal that I did not know how to react. Scared? Yes, definitely. Yet my parents were there, so things must be OK. At one stage a Russian plane flew overhead. Again I remember the panic around me. Later we heard about the ships that were sunk by Russian planes.

After 3 days at sea we landed at Neufahrwasser.(This was the Port of Danzig, now Gdanzki) . I will skip over the horrors of transit camps. Hunger, crowding, head lice, bedbugs.... Later endless travel in crowded trains. Air raids. Some parts of this time are very clear in my memory others just hazy pictures. Father had severe bronchitis and could not help much, I remember being worried that he could not keep up with us. Mother had to shoulder the difficulties. She was an amazing woman. Finally we stopped in Sudetenland, now part of Czech Republic.

Four months later we were on the way again. The war front was getting close. Father had organized a train to take all the Estonians from the area and move us somewhere south and west. However these passenger carriages were soon taken away from us and eventually we continued in 2 freight carriages. One of these had as small stove, the other one was unheated. We were in the unheated one.

It was end of February I remember being very cold – and hungry. Sometimes warm soup was distributed in stations by a Women's organization. We had very little food with us. The food had been short all the time we were in Sudetenland.

Next place of stay was on a farm in a small village in Würtenberg. We had a small room in one of the outbuildings. It was over the laundry and the windows overlooked the stables. There were flies everywhere. My parents had a lot of problems finding even this accommodation. Now we were really hungry. Food was scarce and of course being foreigners we were the last ones to be supplied even when we had the necessary ration cards for it. I remember standing in long queues outside shops. War was getting closer, there were air raids and cannon fire. Then the French Army arrived and suddenly the locals found that there was food available for us after all.

We moved to Displaced Persons Camp in Kempten. This was the beginning of 5 years of camp life under UNRRA, later IRO. Our camp was moved to Altenstadt, then Geretsried and finally back to Kempten.

The life for the children was quite good. We attended school and lots of activities were arranged to keep us occupied: sport competitions, summer camps, plays were staged, girl guides and boy scouts were very active. There was plenty to do. We all lived close to our friends and as we were all equally poor this was no problem for us. We made our own toys and survived reasonably happily. Food was fair, we were no longer really hungry.

I must mention the school again. We had no text books. Most of our teachers were professional teachers and they worked wonders. We wrote notes by hand, later gradually some typed text books were produced. We were certainly taught work ethics. This was to help me a great deal in Australia. My mother was a teacher and I owe her a lot.

In 1948 IRO began to close the DP Camps and everyone had to emigrate. We chose Australia. But things were not simple. Both my brother and I were under 18, my mother just over the 50 year mark. Not enough workers in the family. My sister had married and she and her husband left for Australia and then undertook to look after us on arrival.

Australia wanted workers, not dependants. Finally in Jan 1950 all the paperwork was ready and we had to wait for transport. My brother turned 18 on the day we left and both dad and he had to sign 2 year work contract.

A train took us to Italy and we left Naples at the end of March on board USNS "General M.L.Hersey." The journey on this US army transport ship was far from pleasant. We were expected to conform to almost navy level discipline. There were lots of rules and regulations of what not to do and warnings that noncompliance would result in severe punishments including refusal of entry to Australia.

Everyone was rostered for duties. My father spent time in the engine room, my mother in the kitchen. My brother was fortunate to get an office job. We slept in huge "rooms" on double bunks. There was a strict segregation of sexes. The sleeping area was hot and airless. Later we read from the papers that the ventilation shafts were packed full of contraband cigarettes! The only good thing was the food! We were on navy rations and US fed its servicemen well.

Sadly Ene passed away last year 2013

HER SONS HAVE SHARED AN ANECDOTE

Ene's memories of the transit camps were that they were cold, cramped and short on food

Ene had happy memories of the displaced camps, as she was kept busy with schooling and activities including brownies and girl guides. She also said that because everyone was poor, everyone was equal, so there was little jealousy over status.

The teachers in the displaced persons camps were fellow refugees who took it upon themselves to teach the children. Since they had no text books or other class materials, they made their own.

Ene first met Heino in one of the camps, not knowing that years later they would meet again on the other side of the world and would fall in love.

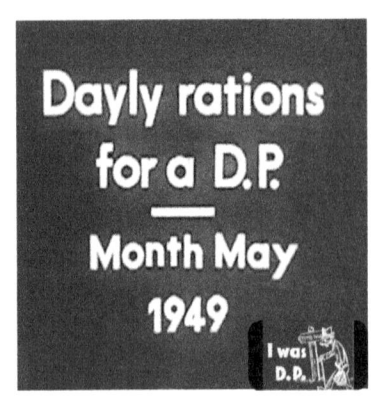

From **ARDO TAREM'S FILM**

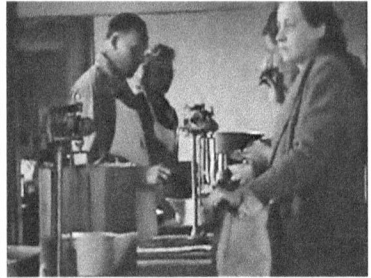

MAIE KAARSOO/HERRICK & ALFRED KAARSOO (THE LATE)

ESCAPE

My parents:
Hilde Kaarsoo (1908 to 2005)
Alfred Kaarsoo (1907 to 1998)

My father was a survivor. Thanks to his courage, decisiveness in crisis, resourcefulness and refusal ever to give up, we, his family also survived. My mother was the glue that held us together. She made a home for us wherever we were, made edible meals even when there was almost nothing to cook, and kept us clean and clothed when there was little to wear. Both parents made us feel loved and instilled in us the belief that we were worthy human beings with a future ahead of us.

The following is a letter, dated Geislingen, November 15, 1948, written by my father asking for help when we were living in a displaced person's camp. It serves as an introduction, and I submit it without corrections, written in English as he was able to do it at that time. All the subsequent segments in italics are a translation of an extensive memoir that he wrote later. I have added information found in a folder of documents which my father fortunately saved, and some of my own memories as I recall. As I assemble and reconstruct our story, I am astounded at the many fortunate coincidences and turns of fate, that guided our lives. Were one to read this story as a work of fiction, one would surely think that the events were too far fetched to be believable.

"My name is Alfred KAARSOO, born in Estonia on March 28th, 1907. My father was a worker and had two children. Both of them wished to acquire higher education, which, however, my father due to his social position, could not afford. **However, I was able to graduate from High-School working with a saw-mill and as carpenter earning money during the summer recesses. After graduation I entered police Training-School. In 1928 I entered police service with the rank of lieutenant.**

My place of employment 1936 was near Tartu, our university town and therefore I took up the study of law at the university.

Meanwhile I had married and become father of two children. Then Estonia was occupied by the armed forces of Soviet Union. The police personnel was fired without any exception. I got a job as an errand boy at a shop in Tartu. In May and June 1941 I was hunted by Communists. I hid together with many other people in the forest until arrival of German troops. So I could save me from falling into the hands of soviets. The German occupation authorities conscripted me into the police service again as a former policeman. By September 1944 Estonia was reoccupied by Red Army.

There was no reason for deciding whether to stay in Estonia or flee to Germany. I could see no chance of escaping persecution by the Soviets, who during their first occupation had made three unsuccessful attempts to arrest me.

In Germany I worked at first in a farm and ulterior I was put into factory as metal worker.

After Germans capitulation I and my family are living in DP camps. All the time I have worked for UNRRA, IRO, and USA Army, as truck-driver, bus-driver, clerk in warehouse, in camp administration office etc. I am able to work as carpenter (have past examination) and worker in metal factory.

My wife Hilde Kaarsoo was born on 04.01.1908 in Estonia. She was graduated from high-school and higher ministerial domestic–school (2 years). She had worked for a long time as a dressmaker and weaver.

My son Enn Kaarsoo was born in 22.04.1932 in Estonia. He is pupil in secondary-school (3rd class).

I hereby ask for job and housing opportunity in USA. I have nor relatives neither friends who could help me

Sincerely yours

(Alfred Kaarsoo)"

My family would not have remained intact, would probably not have survived, had my father not on numerous occasions made crucial decisions and acted quickly.

During the imminent Soviet reoccupation of Estonia as the German forces were retreating, father was ordered by his German police commander to report to an army unit composed of Estonians and being assembled in

Paldiski, near Tallinn, our capital. He arrived there about mid August, 1944, after having moved my mother, brother, and myself to stay with relatives and friends in Tallinn's suburban town Nõmme, since our home in Põltsamaa was in immediate danger of being overrun by the war front advancing from the east.

As the fighting neared, after a sleepless night in the army camp worrying about us, father obtained a permit from the camp doctor, who was a friend, to visit Tallinn on the pretext of consulting a medical specialist. He arrived at Nõmme late at night, and next morning, on September 20, took the train to Tallinn in an effort to take care of us, his family.

"Arriving at the railroad station I met the former Police Academy assistant commissioner, Raig, who was there already waiting for the train. When he saw me in a soldier's uniform, he asked me without long preamble, what my plans were. I explained that I was going to the Police Administration to obtain documents for my family to flee from the country. After these were obtained, and once I had helped my family on its way, I was going to return to my military unit.

Raig's startling answer was: **'Don't be a fool to return to the unit. You know the general situation, hang up your uniform. Begin the refugee path, in order to save yourself and your family.** *I now give you the same good advice that you gave me when I met you on Kalevi street (in Tartu) on the morning of the (Russian) mass deportation. In response to your questioning me where I was hurrying, I said that I was going to work, as usual. I got a sensible response from you, when you said: don't be a fool to go to work today. From you, I received information unknown to me. I did not go to work, and that saved me from possible danger that time'.*

The idea proposed by Raig began to germinate in my brain and developed into the decision to carry it out. **The thought of leaving the army was at first very troublesome for my soul, especially when I thought what my fate might be if discovered in Germany as a deserter. At the same time, remaining with my unit would mean abandoning my family. It would be senseless self destruction, if captured by the Russians."**

That day father was successful in obtaining documents giving permission for us to leave, and by the time he returned to us at Nõmme in mid afternoon, he had made up his mind to take care of us.

"There was no time to be wasted. There was no possibility of obtain any sort of transportation. The only chance was to get to the harbor on foot. *Hurriedly it was necessary to reduce our possessions, which had been prepared for a horse and wagon trip to the harbor that was about 10 kilometers away, to something that could be managed on foot.*

On my last trip to Põltsamaa I had brought my bicycle to Nõmme. On each pedal and on the package carrier I tied a suitcase. I thought that I could roll these, our entire earthly possessions, to the harbor. The others received smaller packages according to their ability to carry.

I heard that somewhere nearby, someone was revving a car engine. It sounded as if the vehicle was mired in a snowdrift in the wintertime and was trying to get going. Looking around, quite a distance away, there was a truck that seemed to be stuck in the sand and was trying to free itself. The side streets in Nõmme, which was a summer resort town, were not paved like the main streets.

At once, the thought arose that perhaps the vehicle stuck in sand might be going to Tallinn. I went to the truck and began to help push it out. At the same time I asked the driver if he was on the way to Tallinn and would he be willing to take me and my family along to the harbor for a fee. The driver agreed immediately.

After some time of shoveling sand, pushing and shoving, we were able to free the vehicle and drove to where we were staying. I cut the ties of the parcels tied to the bicycle. In a short time we were in the truck, even with the packages we thought we had to leave behind, and our friends Maret and Linda Nõmmik who had hosted us, and their suitcases.

Hilde had placed on her head a hat with a low rolled rim. On the way to the harbor, in the speed of travel, the wind soon caught the hat from her head. At first we saw it as hope, that our departure from our country was not final and that soon we would be on the way back home.

Once at the harbor, the truck was not permitted as far as the piers, which were all occupied by ships or scows. The harbor was packed with people. Suitcases and bicycles littered the vicinity of the piers, apparently abandoned by their owners. *We also had more parcels than we could take to the pier at the same time. Hilde remained standing, waiting with some of our suitcases, about a hundred steps from the pier, until I was to return to fetch the parcels left behind. The car that brought us to the harbor had already left. I had offered the driver money for having helped us. He did not take it, saying that we needed it more than he did.*

Arriving at the pier, we headed to the nearest uncovered scow tied there. It was already full of people. Enn and I were still able to find space for our parcels inside.

Before boarding the scow, there was a large white ship visible slightly in the distance. Enn expressed the wish to be able to go on this bigger ship. *Many people were milling about there. I thought that it was more important to get onto the ship nearby, than to go farther, not knowing if even any space was still left there. I did not waste any time and returned to Hilde and the parcels left behind with her. Soon we were all together again, sitting on and between our bundles and taking a breather.*

Dusk was not far away. The scow was filled with people, bundles, boxes and suitcases. The time had been spent rushing and forging ahead.

We had escaped the likely and most dangerous drowning in the waves of the red powers.

Sitting in the scow, I had no idea if this was an independently running boat or if it would be pulled by another ship. Was this the conveyance with which we would arrive at some time at a foreign shore? Someone had directed us to it, and no one had asked for any documents. It seemed that I had been hunting for them needlessly.

We had been sitting in the scow for some time since it was filled. I did not notice when it began to move. It was dusk now. I thought that the flight from homeland had begun. It was getting darker, and a little windy. The scow did not move long. We had arrived at the side of a large ship that had arisen in view.

Probably because of its size, it had not been able to dock at the pier. Now we had to get to the deck of the ship from the narrow end of the scow, along planks and a narrow ladder. The swaying of the scow as well as the ship in the light waves frightened and hampered the inexperienced people carrying baggage.

We had more than one parcel each. As a result I had to make the trip twice. Soon we, and our luggage, were all at the wall of a structure on the deck. The deck was loaded high with people and baggage. The ship was a 10,000 ton carrying capacity German navy "Hilfskreuzer" Hansa according to the information that was known to those sitting next to us. It was already eight thirty and it was getting darker. It appeared that Tallinn was not completely blacked out.

Soon women and children began to be moved into accommodations below deck. Hilde and Maie got a place to sleep. The openings from the deck to below were rather narrow and the descent was along almost vertical metal ladders. I went to see Hilde and Maie in the room below deck. Soon life jackets were handed out to everyone on the deck. When I went again to see mother and Maie, it seemed that only one vest was given for the two of them.

When Hilde had asked for a vest for the child, she had received the answer, that there was no need for that, since the children would be victims of drowning anyway. Then Hilde had tied the vest around Maie.

It seemed terrifyingly impossible for everyone to escape from the spaces below the deck through very small openings for the passageways and ladders. It would only be hoped that the Russian fleet had not yet been able to break through the nets and mine fields near Königsberg. That hope proved to be mistaken as proved by subsequent experiences.

On September 21, at 3 o'clock in the morning, Hansa heaved her anchor and began to move. I had fallen asleep on top of the baggage, and the life vest was crammed around me by someone. The sailors went around ensuring that the life vests were being used. The voyage next day passed without disturbance except for one shot from the ship's cannon. It was not clear if it was directed toward a suspicious enemy target or if it was a test of the cannon. Still, it evidently caused a lot of anxiety.

There was only water on the horizon, no visible shore. There were seagulls circling the ship. Before evening, the wind became stronger, so that those walking on the deck and not used to the sea, were forced to spread their legs in order to remain balanced. On deck rumors circulated, that the ship was not going directly to the German shore, and that the first destination was the nearby Swedish shore and then to a nearest German harbor.

My parents- both photos dated 1946

Many years later 1992

Early in the night of September 22, the anchor chains rattle. The ship has reached Gotenhafen (now Gdynia) about two in the morning. (That day, Tallinn was invaded by the Russian army). *It stopped for a while and about six o'clock it was guided to the dock. Registration and documentation began. No one was interested in permits for leaving Estonia to come to Germany. This activity lasted until midday. Then we were able to carry our luggage to the dock. Now a new worry arose. Where would we go?*

The news of the sinking of Moero quickly reached the place of our overnight stay. Moero was that white ship at the next pier, which Enn had seen and expressed the wish that we would go to as we were boarding the scow. Moero was a German Hospital ship, with appropriate international markings. On board of Moero were soldiers wounded in the war on the way to hospitalization in Germany. In addition to the wounded, refugees were also taken as much as there was space for them. Hansa and Moero left probably about the same time. Moero would have reached Gotenhafen sooner as it took another course and moved faster.

Thus fate had given us one more opportunity to continue our life on this earth."

We spent the first night in a shed, sleeping on hay. Later we were moved to some barracks in Altdam, where we shared large rooms with many people.

"Our leader made daily trips to Berlin. It seemed that he did not like the dispersal of our group. Apparently he had a plan to transport us all to Berlin. Returning from his most recent trip, he summoned the group together in order to give us information. He explained openly that we had not come to Germany to look for an easier life situation. Germany needed help. Help was especially needed in Berlin. Our mission was to offer our assistance there.

Everyone knew that Berlin was a place that suffered the most from bombing by the allied air forces. We had the least need for that. Our move had already been put in motion by the Altdam administration, therefore in order to avoid this fate we decided on our own initiative, and without asking anyone for permission or advice, to disappear quietly and proceed by train in the direction of the residence of Walter's parents. In spite of all possible difficulties on the way and on arrival at our destination, the trip still proceeded fairly smoothly and without great physical difficulties."

Walter Czech was a young German soldier who had been briefly billeted in our living room by our town administration. During his engagement at the Leningrad front, he made several trips to Põltsamaa and always requested to stay with us. Walter did not like Hitler, and a friendship developed between us. He was later captured by the Russians and spent over ten years as a prisoner of war, before being able to return to Germany long after the war had ended. Somehow he then found our address in Canada and actually came to visit us twice. My brother Enn and I also each visited him in Germany while traveling in Europe.

"Now, on his last return trip in the spring of 1944, Walter thought that Hitler was going to lose the war and it was likely that the Russians would again occupy Estonia, *which would lead to great suffering. He had written his parents, that if we should ever arrive at their home as refugees, they should receive us as friends, since we had treated him as a friend. He had received an answer from his parents that they would fulfill his wish if the need arose. Walter gave us his parent's address. Their home was in Silesia in a small town of Noldau, about an hour east of Breslau by train. The town, where they owned a meat products shop, was located near what had been the Polish and German border before the first world war.*

Until now, we had not taken this kind offer seriously. Having become without our country and home, there was a lack of courage in this foreign land to hope to obtain shelter from strangers for the four of us and for our two companions who were still with us. I could not get rid of the troublesome thought that instead of getting farther away west from the red danger, we would now again be moving closer to it in the eastward direction..."

Our family and the two sisters, exited the train in Noldau, in the pitch black darkness of night. While trying to find our way, father stepped off the raised train station platform, and hurt himself, but fortunately, bones were not broken. We found Walter's home and were received with kindness. A few days later, Walter's older sister, Hildegard, began to look for a way for us to find shelter in the nearby county center of Namslau (now Namyslow).

Registration at the employment bureau less than three weeks after arrival in Germany enabled our family and the two sisters to obtain housing in a small, flimsy two room barrack. It had recently been erected on a field at the edge of town as part of a development for refugees.

My brother Enn, twelve years old, and I age nine, were enrolled in school. Enn was older, more outgoing and not shy, but I was terrified every day, especially since I witnessed corporal punishment doled out by the nuns who ran the school. Corporal punishment was not practiced in Estonian schools. The inability to speak German compounded the difficulty, but the total immersion in a foreign language at an early age resulted in our rapidly gaining fluency with very little accent.

"After attending school for a few days, one morning, after having sent Maie off to school, mother and I were looking out the window as she was moving toward town. Before Maie reached the railroad track, the automatic barrier lowered as a train approached. We saw that Maie remained standing by the barrier, but soon turned around and began running

back toward home. She ran, and burst into the room, crying uncontrollably, and said that she was afraid to go to school. We were able to calm her and send her once more on the way.

Near us, on the other side of the railroad tracks lived a girl, one of her classmates, whom she already knew a little. Mother and I discussed, that if Maie would find a close tie between herself and that girl, Maie would be less lonesome and would be relieved of the feelings of fear. After Maie returned from school, she agreed to go with me to the home of the classmate, and invite her to come and play. This is how she found a somewhat closer companion, which helped to lighten her loneliness and fear in a foreign situation for a few months until we once more were hurled into the continuation of our refugee path."

At the employment bureau, father had registered himself as "Jürist" which was correct since he had a law degree, although in Estonia he had been working in the police force as decreed by the German occupation forces. After some time he was notified that an appropriate job for him could not be found. That came as a surprise, since there was plenty to do in the war industry, where the two sisters were already employed.

Father was advised to go to the employment bureau in Strehlen (now Strzelin) to see if something there was available. That proved to be a fortuitous trip. My parents happened to have the address of a friend, Anni Valgmaa, who was a hairdresser and had relocated to Germany a little earlier. Father visited her while in Strehlen, and as a result, she became our contact when in the unforeseen near future, our family was torn apart.

After landing in Germany, father tried to exchange our Ostmark, which was the currency in Estonia at that time, for the German Reichmark, but only small sums were accepted until he was finally able to find a bank who changed all he had, which was not much.

While still in Namslau, father received a notice summoning him to appear at the army induction center in nearby Breslau (now Wroclaw). The following is a description of this event.

"On the designated day I was at the army enlistment commission. So that I would not disappear without any trace, I took along Enn, who had already enough common sense and ability to return to Namslau by train after he had seen and heard what would happen to me.

It turned out, that after passing through the entryway of the commission building, we found ourselves in a large room, where near the door sat a soldier to whom I handed my invitation and who registered my appearance. I was able to take Enn along into this room. There were long wooden benches. On them sat some men without clothes, naked, while others were in the process of undressing. I was ordered to take off all my clothes and wait to be called to see the doctor. I left Enn sitting on the bench, next to my bundle of clothes. That lifted my spirits somewhat, since now I would be assured that I could return to Enn. I did not have to wait long until my name was called.

Going to the doctor it was necessary to pass through a room with several tables, behind some of which sat either an individual in civilian clothes or a soldier, and near the door was an officer in the SD (Sicherheit Dienst) uniform. From there I was directed to the doctor's office. To my unexpected surprise, he turned out to be a youngish German physician who had been part of the enlistment commission for the Estonian legion in my homeland, and through whose sieve I had already passed once in 1942. Later his site of work was in Viljandi. He had been a frequent visitor to the Viljandi security police and seemed to have had a friendly relationship with the Estonian political police reviewer. I had met him there a few times. He was also surprised to see me, knew that I was from Viljandi, and began to ask me about his friend.

I had not heard anything about his friend, but expressed the opinion that certainly he was somewhere in Germany. He asked me about my general health while continuing chatting about Viljandi. I lamented, that my order into the army had come too fast since I had not had time yet to find proper shelter.

To my delighted surprise I heard from him, that my immediate entry into the army was not compulsory, since this was a voluntary recruitment, and my signing up was not mandatory. After a further short conversation and a friendly handshake, I left and was stopped by a soldier sitting behind a desk at the office door. He handed me a printed form to be filled out and signed.

I read that I wished to voluntarily join the army. I said that I was against this idea and would postpone carrying out this plan until I was able to find shelter for my family. The soldier became enraged and jumped from his seat. Holding out toward me the paper I had handed back to him, he ordered me harshly to go to the SD official to explain myself.

I left the application there, and passed the SD desk without a word. I said to Enn, who was waiting by my clothes, that we must get out of there as fast as we can."

Shortly after this event, the westward moving war front caught up with us. We did not have a radio. The news, usually incorrect or outdated, could sometimes be obtained by reading a newspaper nailed to the wall near the town hall.

It was one of the coldest winters in German history. Suddenly we found ourselves in the midst of masses of fleeing people. There was no hope of obtaining transportation from the other refugees. At the roadside, father managed to get mother and myself accepted into one car of a hospital evacuation convoy, and my brother into another.

As my father went to retrieve our meager baggage nearby, he saw that the convoy was moving, and he was left behind.

My despairing mother and I were reunited with my brother when the cars stopped that night. Somehow, mother managed to proceed by train to the home of our Estonian friend in Strehlen, whose address she had previously discussed with father, as a possible destination if they should become separated. Here is what happened to my father:

"As I ran after the convoy I could see a child's hand waving out of the window of a car. Stopping the useless running and remaining standing, there was nothing more I could do as the cars disappeared from my view, taking with it my family. **I did not know if we would ever again meet or see each other, or if we would be lost without trace in the flames of the war.**

It appeared that the convoy of cars which disappeared with mother and children, was one of the last. Most of those that still came, raced by toward the west without stopping. I collected my bundles together and moved them bit by bit closer to the highway, where there was nearby brushwood, so that if I was caught under the feet of the Russians, there was at least the possibility of disappearing into it.

It seemed that they could not be far any more, since traffic had almost completely disappeared. Everyone that had the opportunity had already vanished to the west. I was at the edge of the highway alone with my parcels, still waiting for my savior angel. There were too many packages for one person. If under the worst circumstances, I had to forge on to the west on foot, even through brushwood and forest while trying to avoid the Russians, I would only be able to take along my backpack. In it was butter, a little bit of food, and a partially filled bottle with home brew. I opened the suitcases. From one I took some underwear, from another I took some souvenirs and family photos. **In my pocket I put Maie's doll.**

It was very cold. The ground was covered with snow. I hoped that still someone would come who would take me along. Two or three German trucks came, the first one had a trailer. I begged the sergeant major, who jumped from it, to take me along. The initial response was denial. But bargaining helped. The trunk of the first vehicle was covered. The load was already up to its sides and in it were several soldiers.

After receiving permission to climb into the truck, I began to bring my parcels from the side of the road and started to lift one into the truck. The soldier on top of the load pushed my package out of the vehicle with his foot and said that if I wanted to come along, then the rest of the parcels would be left behind. The truck's tires were poor and they did not wish to be endangered further. He did not let me under the truck's cover and said that I could sit on the hitch connecting the truck and the trailer. I climbed on it and held on to the parcel that was already in my arms. There was a triangular device attached to the truck for connecting with the trailer beam, where sitting was not comfortable or without danger, but it enabled me to move westward. My clothing was skimpy, but the suitcase in my lap helped to sheltered my front from the wind. Two bags and a suitcase were left behind on the highway, containing our goods rescued from our homeland.

The initial unexpected loss of my family had completely thrown me off the tracks and made me unable to think. It seemed as if I had lost everything. A human being can not race with the war machine.

Gradually my thoughts began to function again and to analyze the situation. My wife Hilde, with the children, had at least initially escaped from the grasp of the red wave, despite the fact that she had only a practically empty briefcase with her. There must be some active organizations in the home front that would assist refugees and would help them even a little to keep their heads above the water.

There is only one blacktop highway leading from east to west from Namslau. I knew that the river Oder was not very far and that everyone was forging ahead toward the west, in order to cross it. At the crossing of highways over large rivers there is always a larger settlement or town. I began to hope that my family would be on the same road and that I must begin to look for them there.

The movement of our convoy was not fast, with dimmed lights in partial darkness, yet without obstructions. About eight, we crossed the Oder, where the convoy stopped not far from the bridge, in Ohlau. I thanked my helpers and lifted my packages from the truck and placed them at the side of the road.

It became clear, that I had traveled with the detonation commando. That is the unit that always travels at the end of a military convoy and blows up bridges and buildings in order to obstruct and halt the traffic of the enemy. There was no doubt that large battles would take place here later, which is what did happen.

The remnants of Estonian army units, which had been collected into a nearby large army camp, were also hurled into the defensive battles that took place here. *I would have been there with the unit to which I had belonged before I hung up my uniform at Nõmme when I left to begin the war refugee trail with my family. The battles on the fields of the west shore of the Ohlau river became the end of the journey for quite a few of our countrymen. Here remained lost Põltsamaa attorney Paul Põdra, who was mobilized at the same time as uncle Eugen.*

I was able to leave my packages with kind people in a nearby house and began to look for my family. At the same place where I left my things, I got directions to the railroad station and the location of NSV. NSV is an assistance organization, and I hoped that there could be found an active center for refugee assistance. In the half-dark strange town, it took some time to find these places. The railroad station was packed with people. I went back and forth between the two sites several times. I did not find my family, or any traces of them, either at the station or at NSV. So I tramped around until midnight. I spent the night at the unemployment bureau building and early morning I was again where I had left my baggage, after visiting the station once more.

The hope that I would find my family at this first place after crossing the Oder had vanished. I could not imagine if my family had continued west with the same convoy with which they escaped from Namslau, or if they left somewhere farther from Ohlau a long time before I got there.

Earlier, in Namslau, we had discussed the possibility that if it was necessary to flee again, we would head toward Sindelfingen in southern Germany, where Hilde's high-school classmate, Mrs. Täht lived. Her husband was a physician working in the hospital. Hilde had the address of Mrs. Täht.

There did not seem any possibility of moving from Ohlau into the unknown, in the direction of a town with the droll name of Sindelfingen, except going on foot along with a dense stream of refugees heading in the westward direction. *I decided to join this current with a sled I constructed, and reach eventually the only place known both to me and to my family. From the shore of the Ohlau, pulling my possessions on the sled, I moved with the other refugees to the center of town, where I decided to turn to the railroad station to search for transportation or to find my family.*

Now it was almost impossible to enter the railroad station which was packed with people waiting for an opportunity to ride a train. I did not find my family there. Neither did I hope to get on the trains that were awaited.

I was able to speak to a railroad employee, who advised me to try the Wäldchen railroad which went south from Ohlau and Breslau. It was a little distance from Ohlau, but there might be a better opportunity to get away. The recommended station was located only a short distance from the main station and if I hurried, I could still catch the train which would be leaving soon.

I found that a train was indeed expected at the substation. Only a few people were there. The sled with my bundles tied to it, was lifted into the baggage carriage and soon I arrived in Wäldchen, waiting for a train arriving from the direction of Breslau.

This station was not far from the dome of the Riesengebirge, and was empty of travelers, just like Nõo station during the peace time. In the waiting room, there were a few people apparently waiting for the train. It had become clear to me that trains coming from Breslau and traveling south would pass through Strehlen. That knowledge was in the beginning like a straw for a drowning person. That is where Mrs. Valgmaa from Põltsamaa lived, and whose address was known both to me and mother. Again the hope arose, that perhaps somehow she had managed to go there. I thought that if I could not go by train, I would walk there, pulling my sled.

I sat on a bench near a solitary man, who seemed to be waiting for the train. Starting to chat with him, I asked if he knew about the possibility of a train going in the direction of Strehlen. It turned out that he was a Lithuanian physician, who had become separated from his family and that he had waited unsuccessfully for many hours for a train going to Breslau where he hoped to find them. He knew that a train from Breslau was expected soon and that it would go through Strehlen.

The trains now did not travel according to schedule, but he had questioned the station officials repeatedly about possible trains, and had heard that one was expected to be coming from Breslau. He said that trains coming from Breslau were crammed full of people, and advised me to wait for the train that would hopefully arrive. He promised that he would help me to get my parcels onto the train. I untied my bags from the sled and aligned them at the edge of the platform, waiting for forward progress. I regretted to leave the sled, which I leaned against the wall of the station, for meeting the transportation needs of someone coming to the station later.

After several hours of waiting, a train did arrive. It consisted of commuter-carriages with doors that open completely at each pair of seats. That was lucky for me. The carriages were packed full of people. After I had pressed myself into the carriage, my newly found friend began to push my parcels after me. The people began to yell when I tried to find a place to put down my bags, one even into the lap of someone who was seated. I said that I would relieve them at the next station which was Strehlen, where I was searching for my family. The complaints subsided and soon we were in Strehlen. I myself was not thrown from the carriage but my parcels were gladly hurled out after me. I had been able to salvage our possessions.

Here I found my family again. Incomprehensible luck, as if finding a needle in a haystack. *We were again able to continue our difficult journey of flight.*

Riding in railway carriages without windows or with broken windows was freezing cold. I did not have a coat. When fleeing from Estonia, mother had packed necessary supplies for the children. Fortunately, she had also brought my new suit, with the thought that if I was lost in the war, something could be made of it for Enn. And that now became useful for me after all. I had joined them on the evening before our flight from Tallinn, not having any premonition of the possibility that I would go with them on this journey. The army boots, however remained on my feet. The 'cold remedy' made of sugar beets by myself was still in by backpack, but I had only taken a few sips to treat a cold.

When we reached Nürnberg, it seemed as if it had just recently been bombed. Everything was in ruins, and even the people moved about dazed, like shadows. *There was no water to be found anywhere for drinking. The children were thirsty. A railroad worker directed us to a water faucet that was working, between shattered railroad tracks, quite a distance away. Enn and I went there. I had with me the 'cold remedy' bottle, which was the only container usable for taking along water. I laughed, and poured the cold medicine on the ground. I rinsed* *the bottle clean from its unpleasant smell. Enn and I quenched our thirst and filled the bottle with fresh water for mother and Maie. Who would have thought, that in a few years I would live and work in this city for almost a year.*

In Stuttgart, while waiting for a train on the railroad platform, there was once more an air raid alarm. Everyone disappeared from view. We did not know where one would run. Since the surroundings were already demolished, we thought that it would be unlikely that anyone would come to crush this rubble even finer, and we remained sitting with our bundles. *Soon the signal sounded that the danger had ended.*

In spite of difficulties, losing our way, the cold, heartache and despair, we arrived in Sindelfingen, with our family intact, closer to the western world and fairly far from the danger of barbarians. This trip had started on January 19, and lasted until January 26, 1945."

Until the end of the second world war on May 8, 1945 and for a short while after, we lived in Sindelfingen near Stuttgart, and a neighboring village, Maichingen, where we were lodged by local authorities with a family that had a few extra rooms. My father was conscripted to work making gun parts on a lathe in a converted washing machine factory. He was given brief instructions, and since he had some experience using a lathe in wood shop in high school, he learned quickly.

Meanwhile, we were under siege, and bombing by American airplanes was a frequent occurrence. Sindelfingen was a town of medium size, formerly the site of Daimler car manufacturing. Here the car bodies were molded and the cars were assembled from parts that came from Stuttgart and the surroundings. Now it was the site for manufacturing war vehicles, hence a target for frequent air raids.

Initially we ran to bomb shelters, whether it was day or night, but after a while it became exhausting, especially getting up at night, so that my parents developed an attitude of "what will be will be", and we stopped going.

There was a shortage of all goods, but especially of food. Rationed food coupons were handed out, but there was little to be had in the stores, and even then, only sporadically. No wonder, that much of the time was spent plotting how to have something to eat. During our first bleak Christmas in 1944, while still in Eastern Germany, where we had stayed in the tiny refugee barrack, I had found a sugar beet in an empty field. Mother boiled it and extracted some syrup, and made some tiny cookies on top of our small iron wood burning stove, using a thimble for a cookie cutter.

Later, when living in Sindelfingen, and for a while in the nearby Maichingen village, we were joined by my mother's brother, my uncle Eugen (Eini) Reial. In Estonia, uncle Eini had been drafted into the German army and ended up in Germany, while devastatingly, his family remained in Estonia. Except for a short visit from his son, unusual in 1970, he never had the opportunity to see them again as he died in Canada before Estonia regained its independence.

When the actual war front passed over us in the spring of 1945, we sought shelter in the basement of the house in Maichingen. Artillery bombing was heavy, and when we emerged, we found bomb craters around the houses. The outbuilding of our neighboring farm had been hit and some cattle and the horse had been killed. At least nine people lost their lives at the other side of the village where father and uncle Eini, both past volunteer fire fighters in Estonia, had planned to go help fight a fire. We were occupied by French forces consisting of French officers and black skinned Moroccan soldiers, who were an incredible and frightening sight for our inexperienced eyes. Surprisingly, the Moroccans were generally friendly and kind, unlike their officers. Father writes:

"Our landlady in Maichingen was interested in literature and had left a bookcase with books in our living room. Leafing through them, I found a collection of short stories by a local Württemberg author, Lemmle. One was particularly interesting, and consisted of a tale of a poor man, by the name of Sebulon, who tried to keep his large family from sinking, by honest work as well as by pilfering and stealing.

Our life also was difficult. We did not actually break into a granary, but we were constantly alert, to see if something might be available. Eini and I searched for sites where soldiers had camped. We actually found a few unopened cans of food that had been left behind.

Wandering about, we discovered a large bag full of wheat, barely visible, hidden behind farming tools in a shed surrounded by bushes, hardly a kilometer from the highway. We filled the briefcases we had with wheat. Eini and I had named such activity 'sebuloning', by forming a verb of the name Sebulon. At home we ground the wheat in a coffee grinder. There was enough for several servings of tasty wheat porridge.

The thought developed, that the whole bag of wheat had been sent to us as a blessing from the Lord, and it definitely had to be sebuloned. At this time, that bag of wheat certainly did not belong to anyone. It is unlikely that the rightful owner had placed it there. For sure, it had been stolen from the farmer who owned the shed, by some farm worker who had hidden it there.

Eventually we developed a sebuloning plan. Eini's landlady (in Sindelfingen) had a local friend who was a miller. Eini had explained that he would be able to buy a bag of wheat from the countryside and that he was looking for the opportunity to grind it into flour. Assistance was to come from the miller. The landlady also had a little pull cart (Wägele). Almost every family at that time owned a pull cart as an unavoidably necessary method of transportation. We agreed with Eini that he would come to Maichingen with his cart on the last evening in April. Early on the next morning, even before the nightly curfew was over, we would go with the wagon to the shed, from where he would continue with it to Sindelfingen.

It was an extraordinarily beautiful spring. The gardens, and trees were adorned with blossoms and the ground was green. Only in the evening the air became cooler than usual. We were awake before six in the morning. From the window it appeared that the ground was white. A strong hoarfrost. The thermometer read –7 C. There was no frost on the hardtop of the highway. The grassland between the highway and the shed was white, as if covered with a layer of snow. The tracks of the cart and shoes remained on the frosty surface. The door of the shed was slightly ajar, like on the previous occasion. Eini remained waiting at the door and I went in to fetch the bag of wheat. It was so heavy that I had to strain before I could pick it up from behind the tools.

Both Eini and I had to smile ruefully, thinking of Sebulon. Here we were, one a seasoned lawyer and the other one a former policeman and lawyer as well. The flour made of the sebuloned wheat was divided three ways. One third went to the miller, and each of us got a third."

The frosts of the winter of 1944-45 had destroyed much of the normally abundant fruit crops. The highways were bordered by government owned apple trees. It was permitted to pick up apples that had fallen on the ground and lay in the ditch. Most of the apples were suitable for juice only, but could be taken to a mill in exchange for very tasty juice. Some of the apples were edible as well and were an addition to the diet.

Nature had taken the fruit from people suffering of shortage of food, but blessed them with an unusual abundance of boxwood seeds. There were many boxwood forests and parks. Their seeds were multifaceted, rich in oil, and very tasty. They fell from the trees onto the ground, and it was easy to sweep them together. They could be exchanged directly for oil at a mill where they would be pressed. Since the shortage of fats was especially keen, this oil was particularly welcome. The seeds could also be toasted on top of the stove, and were delicious when eaten. There were other activities that took place.

"Attempting constantly to supplement the shortage of food we kept searching on the highway and along the nearby forest paths. Perhaps something that could be put in the mouth might be found. We saw several horses roaming in the woods, apparently escaped from the army units during the battle activity. Eini, Paul Teder (a friend), and I were willing to catch one and to do something with it. Horse meat is no worse than beef. In our home land horse meat had been sold for food. Yet not one of us three was willing to take the life of a horse.

Since our neighboring farmer had lost his horse during battle, we thought that we would catch a horse and offer it to him in exchange for food. It was not easy to catch a horse. The horse did not have a harness, it was bare like a carrot, and we had nothing that we could use to lead it to the neighbor in case we captured it.

Somehow we caught the horse. Eini helped me to mount it so I could ride it, without a bridle. I grabbed hold of the mane. Paul and Eini helped by walking on each side of the horse. The horse was healthy and lively, but we managed to get it to the neighbor's farmyard. The farmer, who had been in hiding for a few days, had returned home. He liked the horse. **But our hopes for a trade evaporated into the unreachable blue of the sky. The landlord noticed that on the horse's plump, glistening hip there was a prominently branded "F". A certain sign that it belonged to the French army. The horse regained its freedom and we were left without the morsels for which we had hoped."**

On another occasion, uncle Eini and father went on a fishing expedition, which was quite funny, and later was written by mother as a little story. (Appended at the end of this story. MM)

There were numerous other ways to supplement various needs. Father and uncle Eini found a tire from an airplane that had been shot down during an air raid, salvaged the rubber and used it for soles of sandals that they made. Another find was a parachute that provided abundant fabric. Mother made me a white dress, and later a pink one when she was able to obtain some dye. Trips to the woods by father, and my brother Enn, were made to gather firewood. Permits were needed to do that.

There had been no immediate change noted after the peace was declared in Europe on May 8th, 1945. Now another fear arose.

"Rumors circulated, that the occupying French military forces are friendly with the Russians and were sending, by compulsion, refugees and soldiers who had participated in the war on the side of the Germans, back to the territories now occupied by the Soviet Army. There were many refugees of Polish nationality around Stuttgart, who had already formed camps and organized centers. It was rumored, that one such center supplied identification papers on which would be noted the country of origin without proof, based only on the statement of the person requesting the document.

We found such a Polish establishment among the ruins of Stuttgart, where a few streets had not completely been destroyed. Switzerland, which was not far away and was neutral, seemed very attractive to us, and without difficulty we obtained documents with stamps and signatures, stating that we were Swiss citizens. Although we did not have much faith in such a document, it would still serve as an encouraging starting point in an argument if a situation of compulsory return to our home land would present itself."

The need to use these documents never arose, although both my parents received a frightening summons from "Commission de Rapartriement Armee Francaise" to report to Stuttgart for repatriation. I believe that they never responded to it. Later, our French Zone was reconfigured into the American Zone and father found a job as a warehouse worker and truck driver for UNRRA (United Nations Refugee Relief Association) in nearby Böblingen. At some time, he did have a repatriation interview with an American officer, who appeared to be Jewish. **When queried why he did not want to go back to Estonia, father said 'Sir, how would you like to go back to Nazi Germany?' That ended the conversation.**

A small group of Estonian refugees had gathered in Sindelfingen. Mrs. Täht, mother's classmate who had been living in Sindelfingen for some years before the end of the war, and was our reason for going there, had just recently tragically and unexpectedly lost her still young physician husband, and was left with two young teenagers Jüri and Karl, and baby Peeter, born after his father's death. Her mother in law lived with her. Other Estonians were a highly respected and talented surgeon, Dr. Ulrich Karell, his very attractive and energetic young wife Maimu and two young daughters, Anni Valgmaa, who had been our contact in Strehlen and who came with us as we continued our flight to Sindelfingen, Paul Teder with wife, and son Ando, Parfeni Valgemäe with wife and sons Mardi and Tiit, Mr. and Mrs. Rebane with children Tiiu, my best friend, and her younger sister Mari and brother Tõnis, and three young Estonian soldiers who had been badly wounded and were treated by Dr. Karell. Karl Rosin had lost part of his lower face, and through some very advanced and innovative techniques and multiple surgeries, his face was reconstructed by Dr. Karell. Eerik, (his family name), a handsome young man, had lost a leg, and Werner Horn, had a fused knee. There were probably a few others whom I do not remember. Maimu Karell organized the official establishment and recognition of an Estonian camp in Sindelfingen, although the members of the camp lived at various sites.

Eventually this group dispersed, and some of us relocated to Geislingen.

The occupying forces came to the realization that most of the refugees refused to return to their home countries. They had left their homes because of fear of the Russians and would face imprisonment or death if they were forced back.

Camps for refugees of various nationalities were formed, and in the late summer of 1945 our family moved to the picturesque town of Geislingen where Estonians were lodged in three separate districts in homes confiscated from the German owners.

We were housed high on the hillside of Wilhelmshöhe, Karlstrasse #72, looking straight down on the WMF (Württemberg Metall Fabrik) factory. The house was packed with people. It had eight rooms, occupied by eight family units consisting of a total of twenty eight inhabitants. There was a kitchen used by all, and the laundry and bathing took place in the basement.

Our little room was completely filled by four army cots placed around the walls, a table in the middle and a little iron stove in the corner. We lived there for the next four years.

My brother and I attended school that was organized by our fellow refugee teachers. We were busy with our friends and with various activities, especially the boy scouts and girl guides, and the annual summer YMCA camp.

My parents also kept active, and I do not remember ever seeing them idle. Mother was occupied with meals and all the support work needed to sustain our family. Father worked in the camp administration as the second district secretary, and later in 1947, for almost a year, he had a job with the American military Labor Service Company Baltic Unit in Nürnberg, driving a bus during the trials.

This gave him a small amount of earnings that could be exchanged at the PX. Every few weeks he would return with treasures such as some chocolate bars, food items for us, and cigarettes which were a very valuable trading item for food. One time he returned with a pair of nylon stockings for mother, who saved them, and eventually gave them to me to wear when I attended a dance for the first time. On another occasion, the proceeds of his earnings were all stolen on a crowded train.

At the camp, father learned ornamental leather tooling, making various items such as wallets, handbags, belts, book covers and even boxes. I do not know if he ever sold any of these items. He earned an IRO (International Refugee Organization) certificate stating that he had been tested and had been classified as an Ornamental Leather Worker. It appears, that many men in the camp were doing that also. Unexpectedly for father, this skill later became a lifelong occupation.

With the hope of making himself desirable for a job in any country that might open its gates to us as subjects of immigration, father also qualified for a certificate at the Vocational Testing Center Geislingen and was classified as Carpenter 2nd Class. That must have been easy for him, since he had loved his woodwork shop activities in high school many years before in Tartu.

He took an eighteen week course in drafting provided by the IRO AREA 2 Technical Training School and finished with a final evaluation of "very good". From the Testing Committee of Agriculture and Forestry, again under the umbrella of IRO, he received a certificate that he was classified as a Lumberman 2nd class, and as a Farm Labourer 2nd class. I suppose he qualified for these certificates since he had supported himself through high school by working incredibly long and heavy hours in a sawmill in southern Estonia during the summer vacations.

As for farm labor, probably most Estonians of his generation knew how to raise food, whether in a home garden or in the fields, and father was certainly exposed to such rural activities while living with an aunt as a teenager during the summer sawmill job and when working long hours at a farm during one summer, herding cattle as an eleven year old child.

Father also was tested by the Testing Committee of special services and was classified as Cook-master.

Mother was classified by the Testing Committee of Cloth and Textile Workers as Dressmaker 2nd class, and Weaver 1st class.

Numerous letters, such as the example provided at the beginning of this story, were sent out by father to Sweden, to United Sates of America, to Australia and to Canada. We were out of luck, and no one seemed to be willing to receive us. On one occasion, there was a rumor, that Australia was looking for two families as immigrants.

We got up very early in the morning, dressed in our most presentable clothes and took a train to Stuttgart, eighty kilometers away. We found ourselves lined up on a large field with about two thousand other hopeful applicants and waited for hours, until a small cluster of officials walked past where we were standing with smiling faces, hoping that we would be picked. Of course we were not selected, and we returned to our Geislingen camp, disappointed, but not surprised, after we had seen the magnitude of competition.

Finally, in spring of 1949, we discovered the address of mother's cousin, Hans Reil (he had dropped the "a" in Reial) and his wife Hilda, who had emigrated to Canada from Estonia in the nineteen twenties and lived in Winnipeg, the capital of the province of Manitoba. He responded quickly to our letter, and as a result of his sponsorship, we received a visa to enter Canada. By now we also had received permission to go to Sweden, United States and Australia. **My parents picked Canada. None of us ever regretted that choice.**

We embarked from Bremerhaven, a city still totally flattened and in ruins, on the troop transport ship U.S.A.T. General R. L. Howze. After the rough waters of the English Channel, which sickened almost every one, and eight days at sea, we docked in Halifax, Nova Scotia, on June 11, 1949. From there, we journeyed west for three days on a slow train with wooden benches.

We had been given a little money to buy food on the way when the train occasionally stopped. I made my first acquaintance with chocolate covered ice cream on a stick, which still brings back memories of that event.

In Winnipeg, we were met by our rescuing angels, "Uncle Hans and Aunt Hilda", who took us to our new home with which they provided us. It was next to their own home, in a house that they owned and rented to several people. It was furnished, extremely well kept and clean, quite heavenly to our eyes. We had the original dining room and living room, separated by sliding door, and the pantry next to the dining room, which had been converted into a tiny kitchen.

From the small kitchen window I looked at the flashing neon lights saying "SECURITY STORAGE" on the wall of a large building across one of the major thoroughfares. **That first night, I thought it was the most exciting, romantic, sight I could ever see.**

Our trip from Germany to our destination was by no means free. Uncle Hans had provided for us by prepaying the bill sent to him by the IRO officials in Ottawa. They made the point of stating that "The IRO does not provide free rail tickets and subsistence money for the meals from port of disembarkation to destination, but will provide tickets and advance subsistence money. PROVIDED REMITTANCE TO COVER IS RECEIVED FROM YOU IN ADVANCE." The charges were as follows:

(a) Ocean fares   4 at $160.00 $640.00
(b) Inland rail fares   4 at $45.70 $182.80
(c) Subsistence   4x3 Days at $5.00 $60.00
                              TOTAL $882.80

That was quite a large sum of money for someone with zero assets, about $5700 in present terms, my economist husband informs me. Over the ensuing months, my parents repaid the entire bill to uncle Hans in small sums, starting with $12.80 in October of 1949, four months after we arrived.

The beginning was difficult. Father and mother both were 41 years old, my brother Enn was 17 and I was 13.

Although all of us had studied English a little in school, acquiring conversational English was a challenge. Becoming familiar with a foreign culture was not easy for any of us. Father visited immediately the city's unemployment bureau, and was assigned to a highway building project.

Here he was, undernourished, middle aged, and physically not in top shape. It was exhausting work. At some point, he was told to carry a huge pile of railroad ties, one by one to another location. He was alone, and the thought crossed his mind, that if he fell, with one of the huge pieces of lumber on top of him, he would not be able to get up. At another time, he acquired a florid, itchy rash, from sitting in poison ivy, a plant unknown to us, while eating his sandwich for lunch.

After some time, he visited the unemployment bureau again, and told them that he needed to have a job, but that he just could not do the heavy labor required on the highway. He was told that the local Birt Saddlery was looking for help, and he took his small satchel full of leather items that he had made in Geislingen to show them. He was hired on the spot. The salary was low, and while it was increased over the years, it was never munificent.

Winnipeg was a prairie town, among other things, headquarters for the surrounding large farms. The saddlery supplied the needs of the farmers as well as selling leather garments, luggage and handbags, and so on. Father remained with them for the rest of his working life, which continued well past his official retirement age.

He organized and developed a handicraft department in the shop, and single handedly designed and produced a catalogue using many of his own drawings and descriptions, refining it as the years passed. This was the era long before computers, digital cameras and quick printing. Much of the work was done by hand.

There were no such words as "I don't know how" or "I can't do this" in my father's vocabulary. He would and could make anything with his hands. The saddlery became the referral center for luggage damaged by airlines, repair of horse equipment or any other leather items that needed to be fixed, and a resource for any kind of products used in leather crafting.

Father would go to wealthy people's homes to repair leather furniture, found venues for teaching advanced leather crafting, and gave demonstrations at local fairs. Some of these activities were under the umbrella of the saddlery, while others were outside of his working hours.

The saddlery was commissioned to produce the leather covers of the doors of a Torah cabinet, the ARK, which houses the prayer scrolls at a synagogue in Regina, a town in Saskatchewan. This was a giant project, later reported with photographs in the local newspaper. The design was made by an artist and consisted of Moses guiding the children of Israel through the sea, with the giant hand of God, like a cloud, overhead. It included hundreds of faces ranging from large in the front, to small in the distance. Transferring this onto leather, while retaining the expressions on these faces, was truly a work of art which father accomplished beautifully. I never visited that synagogue to see the finished product, and have often wondered if it has survived the times.

Mother, was a graduate of Kehtna "Girls Farmwork and Housekeeping School" (Tütarlaste põllutöö ja – majapidamise kool). That was a well respected school with a two year curriculum for high school graduates.

After finishing school and before marriage, she had been employed by the Estonian government as a teacher who visited rural areas and conducted courses for the local women in nutrition, gardening, and house keeping skills.
Besides being an expert homemaker and cook herself, mother also was a fine seamstress and weaver on the looms. She soon found a job at a sewing factory making blouses, and she stayed there for many years. It was an extremely stressful job for her, as the pay was based on piecework. The more one could produce, the more one earned. Sometimes an entire batch of blouses would be returned to be fixed without compensation. As a result of the constant pressure of speed required to earn even the lowest salary, mother suffered from great anxiety, and often even dreamed of sewing while moving her hands on the edge of the blanket during sleep at night.

My job was to keep clean the common portions (bathroom, hallways and stairs) of the rental house in return of a markedly reduced rental fee. That took very little effort, since the house was extremely well maintained and the other inhabitants were neat. I also cleaned our own rooms and prepared our suppers according the instructions given by mother. It was suggested that Enn should join an army cadet unit, which paid a small salary, but our parents, no doubt as a result of our past experiences, were very much averse to the idea of any connections with the military.

By the following spring, less than a year after our arrival, we had scraped together enough money for a down payment on a run down house, and we moved in. All four of us worked hard, cleaning, painting, and repairing. It was a wonderful, exiting feeling, to have a place of our own. We rented out some of the rooms. Over the ensuing years, my parents bought two more houses, fixed them, rented them, and later sold them. Such rental business can be difficult, with some renters failing to pay, or thrashing the accommodations. It is also a way to increase assets, since we had started our life in Canada with a negative balance.

Enn and I went to school, made friends, and assimilated into the local social life. Enn became an engineer and I finished medical school. We always lived at home, even when attending university.

There were about two hundred Estonians in Winnipeg. Some were old timers, like my uncle Hans and aunt Hilda, but others were newcomers like us. Of course, an Estonian Society was formed. My parents, especially father who served in various leadership positions, were active members. The usual special occasions, such as the February 24th Independence Day were commemorated. A blood sausage making party was a tradition before Christmas, sauerkraut and other Estonian foods were prepared, and birthday parties and other celebrations were held.

My parents' life remained centered around the small Estonian community, and there was very little social interchange with the local Canadians outside of work. Of course they were also aware of, and informed about, the fate of family and happenings in Estonia, and sent parcels whenever that was possible. They kept current with the activities of Estonians in North America and the rest of the western countries and read the Estonian newspapers and books published in the free world.

As time passed, and they had supported their children through a higher education, financial circumstances became easier. Father and mother acquired a summer cottage, fixed it, sold it, and got a second, better one, always near other Estonian friends. Father followed his passion for fishing. Wherever he was, he built something, including a little guest house in our back yard in California. He and mother always had very small, but incredibly productive vegetable and flower gardens, both in the city as well as by the cottage. They even grew potatoes from seed potatoes obtained from Estonia.

Enn moved to Eastern Canada and I went to the United States, first to Ohio and then to California. Spouses and children were added to the family.

Now that mother was no longer working in the sewing factory, there was a continuous stream of hand made clothing that arrived by parcel post. She had a great sense of fashion, and a dress form adjusted to my measurements. Children's clothes were unique and wonderful, even when sometimes they were made of fabric remnants that one would normally not consider suitable for a child.

From mother's fingers also flowed beautiful cloth that she wove on her looms. She made coats and dresses and even drapes from the fabrics, sofa pillows, place mats, and rugs and wall hangings that she designed herself. She wrote stories for children and adults.

Father and mother took at least semiannual, or even more frequent, long car or airplane trips to visit us. They arrived with bags packed with goods, and always a batch of little yeast bread buns with meat filling (pirukad) to be savored. They worked hard for us during the visits, and they deeply loved and spent much time with their grandchildren, even hosting them at their home in Winnipeg when they were a little older, and giving us, the weary parents, a break.

Only after I have become a grandparent myself, do I understand the enormous amount of energy and dedication that it takes to travel across the country, and to care for little active children when one is well past the prime of life.

My parents are deceased, and I regret that I did not ask them all sorts of questions about the past events. In all the years that passed, I never heard them complain about the harshness that life had dealt them. One time, during father's advanced age, I asked him if he ever felt regretful that he had spent his life in a leather shop rather than practicing law. I was surprised, when his quick answer was an unqualified "No".

Yes, hats off to our parents!

This story has been republished from "Elust uuel kodumaal" with the permission of IOR. ISBN:978-9949-9199-6-3

Hilfskreuzer Hansa- image supplied by author

A reflection: The Hansa has an interesting history -see earlier pages of his book- information derived from internet. MM

USS_General_R._L._Howze- image supplied by author

RARE FISH OR FISHING: HILDE KAARSOO

While the trek through the war zone was onerous for all, there were lulls where there was opportunity for timely diversions. I feel that this story by Maie Kaarsoo's mother should be shared. It is indeed part of Maie's journey through that terrain. MM

Characters: "Myself" - Alfred Kaarsoo
"Friend" - Eugen Reial, Hilde's brother

It was April 1945. The Moroccan military units under French leadership had recently conquered a small German town in Swabia. It was promised that all the "Ausländer" (foreigners) who had been badly treated by the Nazis would be assembled in the near future into camps maintained by the new authorities. Thus: free and happy.

Spring in southern Germany entices you to love it, in spite of hating it.

Blossoms. More and more blossoms. Kilometers after kilometers of fruit trees, chestnuts, and ornamental trees and bushes bearing flowers.

And the fragrance.

Even the "verfluchte Ausländer" (damned foreigner) could greedily enjoy this beauty without any restraint.

Even the homeless could fill his lungs with the mixture of rich fragrances.

No one could forbid that.

But it was necessary not to go too close to the farmyard. There was a dominating majestic manure deposit and dung-liquid well. All the pleasant smells paled and retreated from this overwhelming entity.

At a time when our sight and smell celebrated, our stomachs were grumbling.

We were not starving.

We had saved potatoes and a little salt.

Hot potatoes and salt – these taste wonderful. We could eat that endlessly and one more time.

We were skinny, but our stomachs walked ahead of us. As soon as we opened a door to go in, it was always our belly that entered first.

In spite of a filled stomach, our appetite was never satisfied. Our thoughts were still haunted by meat. One never got used to its absence. On the contrary, the longer one has to abstain from it, the more one yearns for it. Yesterday we caught an army horse roaming in the forest. It was strange, but it did not awaken the activity of our salivary glands or remind us of a roast. It was too much alive, beautiful, strong and young. Also, neither of us had ever killed a live being created by God. That means, not if it is large. Only little insects, if they bite. These do not resist and one can always be certain of victory.

Oh yes, but fish. –

That was an idea.

But one that could not be accomplished easily.

    1) Civilians are prohibited from walking around outside.

    2) All bodies of water, without exception, are privately owned.

Everywhere, one was fended off by signs saying "Privat" and "Fishen verboten" (Private, and fishing forbidden). The owners were on guard with pitchforks and sticks. There were reports of fishing expeditions that ended sadly.

Opportunity came to aid: the barber had a need to be friendly with an "Ausländer". While clipping the "locks" hanging over my ears, he talked about his extraordinary, rare fish species which he had "planted" in his pond. He expressed satisfaction that the pond was located in a small forest some distance from town, where it could not be found by "all sorts of elements". No doubt, I also belonged to such "elements". The only exception was that I believed that I knew the forest which he described. We had gathered firewood there.

    3) Now a third deterrent arose: the feeling of guilt. Conscience struggled and called me by some ugly names.

Eventually I found a solution and passed the decision to the "higher court". I said my usual evening prayer for my suffering native land and its people. I added the Lord's Prayer. When I reached the spot "...and give us our daily bread..." I added quickly "and fish tomorrow! Dear Lord, weigh this question and give me your answer. Amen."

With that, I went to sleep.

The morning was still young when I awoke.

The dear Lord had not yet given me an answer.

"Forgive me, but I can not wait longer".

I did not need to go on this trip alone.

I had a friend, a companion in fate. He was sleeping in the adjacent room. I woke him, and in a few moments we were outside in the crisp air.

I explained my plan to him. I must say, that he gave me more opposition than my own conscience. He expressed loudly names and words which my conscience only whispered.

"So you are going to rob the pond? You have sunk so far?"

"Has the Heavenly Father not created fish for food? Did Christ not give fish to the apostles and told them to eat – in the bible, remember? – And now, when we are starving…" I justified my way of thinking.

"We are not starving", he interjected. "That is, not seriously. We have potatoes left for two days. You are even getting fat. Look at your belly. You can't see your toes over it", my friend was sarcastic.

Unobtrusively I corrected my posture: sucked in my stomach and stuck out my chest – as much as it was possible.

"That is not my stomach, it's my chest".

"Since when is your chest located between your belt?" he aimed a short glance toward me. - He stopped and looked me over thoroughly. Something made him angry.

"You are getting really fat! Until now it was only a round belly on top of long bowed legs, now you have a chest, too. Tell me at once what you have been eating lately, that you have not shared with me. I am not talking about the few better morsels that you have fed to the children or have saved, but to make yourself fat while eating when your best friend – I mean, he who was your best friend - is starving…I feel that my fist is itching… and he moved toward me in a seriously threatening manner.

"Don't come! I am bigger. And put your itchy fists in your pockets. – Look!" I opened my jacket buttons for my friend to see.

"Curtains", he wondered.

"Fishing net", I said with pride.

"So you don't have fish hook or any kind of fishing equipment? I have always said that you are an incorrigible optimist and wear rose colored glasses. Going fishing with curtains! Who ever heard of that before! You better think of your blessed soul. You are even dragging me to the path of sin."

"Let that sin fall on my soul. I have already made contact with the dear Lord and have asked his permission for the planned undertaking."

"Did you get permission?"

"Not yet. – But I did not receive an interdiction either. Therefore He does not have a serious objection. And tomorrow is Sunday. I shall go to church and talk to him like a man to man."

We walked in silence. The light tears the cobweb of darkness under the trees.

"Look!'

The remains of a fire. Apparently the camping ground of an army unit.

"We might find something useful here."

"A pair of socks," my friend was delighted.

"Are you going to eat them raw or cooked?" I said with irony.

"There are only small holes at the heels. These can be mended," he ignored my teasing.

"A can of preserved food" it was now my time to be happy. "And here is another one. It's been opened. Half full. We'll eat that one and take the other one home."

"It is said that opened cans are poisoned" reminded me my friend.

"I am willing to make a test."

Ta-ta-ta-ta-ta.

With open mouths we embraced mother earth, our heads pressed to our chests.

From behind the bushes appeared a black man with a machine gun. Black as the night. A memory from my childhood, that black people eat palefaces, flashed through my head. We were certainly pale. I have to explain that black people were a rarity in Europe. He shouted something at us. We understood that we were to stand up. We did that, and also raised our hands. But not without dropping the cans or the socks. The black man searched through our pockets. He found a document, made out a few days ago by a French colonel, who made us free a few days ago. He could not read it.

"No Germans, nix Nazis, no Aleman! – "Ausländer," we tried to explain. Perhaps he understood us. But perhaps we were rescued by the objects that we were holding. The fact that we were collecting leftovers from the army, said to him more clearly than words, that we were not natives. Therefore, not enemies, but rather probably friends.

A wide smile spread over the black face at the same time as his hands lowered the weapon.

He retrieved a package of cigarette from his pocket and extended it toward us. A whole package of cigarettes!! Now our faces also were laughing broadly.

"What a man! Black people are the best in the world," was a thought that flashed through my mind. By the way, that belief has remained with me to this day.

We left the black man after pressing his hand. We continued on our way eating (fortunately we had not spilled the contents of the open can) and smoking. My friend's perpetually glum face had cleared.

There was the pond. Not large. Like a widened creek. Yes, there it was. There was a dam at each end – "Fishing forbidden". But God was up high and the barber was far and perhaps the Heavenly Father was even on our side, since he still had not given me a negative reply and "Silence is agreement." says our old proverb.

We got down to business. We cut pliable willow branches and built a large oval basket-framework, over which we stretched the curtains.

"Let's take off our trousers. No point in getting them wet."

"Both of us?" My friend was doubtful.

"Why not. There is no one nearby. Only the birds. And the sun is also peeking through the dense leafy canopy. I can wager that it has seen more naked men than anyone else."

That is what we did. And into the water we splashed.

The bottom was soft, muddy. The feet sank in, slipped. The water reached to our waists. We waded across and diagonally, sometimes raising the net to look into it. Empty. We splashed from shore to shore. And we did not look into our net any more. We believed we would immediately feel the movement of the fish, if there were to be some.

Nothing like it.

It was cold. Shivering, we climbed to the shore, dragging our net behind us. We turned to inspect its contents carefully.

"Perhaps there is a little one among the reeds", I was hopeful. Our mouths fell open in wonder. There were no reeds or any debris. Nor a net. Only the framework. And the string around it. And only a tiny bit of fabric was flapping from the string. The fingers grab it. It is a tag that says: "Nicht waschen."

"Do not wash" we read in unison.

Our fishing net had dissolved.

We did not speak.

We dressed.

My friend was ready to begin our journey home.

"Let us sit in the sunshine a little while and warm ourselves," I could not leave. I was convinced that there were fish in the pond.

"And let's have a smoke" agreed my friend.

Said and done.

After a short silence, my friend opined: "Then this was not the Lord's will…"

"I am not so sure, I retorted. He just gave me an idea.

"Which would be?"

"If we were to open one dam and drain the water into the creek. We would lower it so that we could catch the fish with our hands."

It was not easy, as it seemed that the dam had not been touched for a long time. We tried the levers. We worked beneath and above the water. Inch by inch, the dam lifted. With power and speed the water fled.

"Now there is nothing to do but wait."

"The devil take it, we were in such full swing, that we forgot to take off our clothes," my friend was startled.

"The sun will dry us. Look, here is the right spot. Let us stretch out on the grass, until the bottom of the pond becomes visible."

The surface of the water sank and our excitement rose. We were not able to tear away our eyes. Here and there we thought we could see fish splashing. The fish were panicking, throwing themselves out of the water.

"They are remarkably nimble", said my friend.

"And slippery." I worried.

"But in some places, the bottom is already visible. Now or never!"

Splashing. Grasping. The mud flew about.

"Caught," exulted my friend.

"I have one also," it was my turn to rejoice.

"And a third one," I straightened my back and held up a struggling fish.

"A goldfish," I mumbled with great surprise. Are we robbing a goldfish bowl? Look, here are more," I was ready to continue with enthusiasm.

"Hold on, you are greedy!" A command seemed to come from somewhere, clear like the crack of a whip.

My back straightened with a start.

"Yes, my Lord," I mumbled in resignation. My conscience was suddenly too vivid. I had to stop my friend.

"Hey, you there! Don't you think we have enough? The barber here is raising something very rare. It would be a sin to empty the pond."

"That sin will rest on your soul, not on mine. And now come over and see what a fish I found."

With a few dragging steps I was by his side. He looked rigidly ahead. I followed his stare.

"A corpse…"

The head and shoulders were clearly visible.

"Let us fill the pond again. It is war time. We have nothing to do with this," was my quick decision.

"There is nothing else we can do," agreed my friend. At the same time he bent down and rinsed the face with water in his palms. It was ash – gray. I looked at it more closely.

"Hitler! Adolf Hitler!" A mistake was not possible here.

My knees were weak. Without thinking what to do with this find, I began to lift him out of the mud.

"Ha-ha-ha," it was such a feeling of relief, that I could do nothing but laugh. "Come and try to lift this 'corpse' yourself. It is stone, copper, bronze or marble – yes, gray marble."

My friend felt it with his hands.

"Here then, the barber has hidden his false idol. The wheel of time pushed him from the pedestal and even the most committed Nazi did not dare to bow to him publicly."

"Let him rest here in the mud, where his disciples have drowned him."

And together we closed the lower dam and opened the upper one.

Silently we watched the water rise until it covered our discovery.

Silently we began our journey home with our three rare fish.

I noticed that my friend was repeatedly glancing at me with amusement.

A wicked suspicion forced me to look at myself. I was not amused by what I found. My only trousers had shrunk, reaching only a little below my knees, leaving bare my hairy bowed legs, which had never been a source of enthusiasm for me.

" I guess you will not be going to church tomorrow," smirked my friend.

"Then you go! Your pants need only pressing."

"But none of this was my doing so it is not I who needs to beg to be forgiven," my friend was obstinate.

"So be it. I will speak with Him tonight in bed and seek appeasement. – But this has still been my lucky day: imagine if only my trousers, both the inner and outer ones, had been made of the same material as the curtains..."

And after a little while I continued quite happily: "And I will go to church tomorrow!"

"You will go? Do not count on my trousers. I'll be in them myself."

BERLIN: A WALL NOW COLLAPSED
SANITY RETURNS FOR MANKIND

And a church reclaimed: The beautiful Kaiser Wilhelm Gedachniskirche which has been rebuilt from the remnants of the shattered church: A reminder of the past and the need for a peaceful present.

MEMMINGEN ANOTHER EARLY CAMP

During our first year in Germany I have hazy memories of a very nomadic life: We seemed to be always on the move. There were so many names of places on my two year old mental Atlas. Thereafter until even today when someone alludes to these places I think : Yes I can remember that name.

Many were set in military barracks as was the Memmingen one. Andres Kurrik was kind enough to act as a guide for those of us who wanted to visit it after Geislingen 2008.

Some Estonians who stayed on in Germany for many reasons continued to live there (as did Andres' family): Germanic versions of Estonian city names still have their place in Memmingen's history: Streets are named after them.

MALL JUSKE/KARP

MY MEMOIRS

I was born in Tallinn, the capital of Estonia on 6th August, 1935, during the prosperous years of Estonia's Independence to Linda and Albert Karp.

My father had inherited a farm, I believe, in Laokula near Paldiski as I had heard my parents often talk about Laokula. During the Soviet's occupation in 1940 Paldiski and the surrounding area was occupied by the Soviets where they established a large military base and a leading training center of Soviet nuclear submarine forces.

We, that is Mum, Dad and little me lived in a flat in Tallinn. Mum worked as a mender (mending weaving faults in textiles by an invisible manner) in her uncle's textile factory and Dad worked as a filing clerk for "Tarmo", a motor car and parts importer in Tallinn.

My first memories from those years are when we visited Loakula and my bed for the first night was made in a large chest. I was not impressed. Also comes to mind when we attended the 18th or 19th Independence Day celebrations held on independence grounds with the armed forces beautifully lined up and a brass band playing. As it was a bitterly cold day we left the grounds earlier for the warmth of our home.

Mum and I watched a soccer match at a stadium. Dad was the goal keeper. My uncle Edmund (known as Etu to the family) was a very good soccer player as he played for the international team.

Christmas was celebrated on Christmas Eve with a family gathering at our place. My uncle Konrad was Santa Claus on every occasion and one year I asked my mother "why does uncle Konrad have the same kind of gloves that Santa did?" The following year he wore the gloves inside-out.

I had a nanny looking after me while mum and dad were at work and at times during the nights when mum and dad were out. I enjoyed being with nanny as she was a good playmate to me. I spent a little time at a kindergarten but for some forgotten reason I preferred nanny's company.

For Christmas it was customary to bake special ginger cookies and sweet bread. Mum and nanny were rolling out the dough for yummy ginger cookies and little me tried to help by removing the strips of dough from around the cutters and saving cooking time for the cooks. I ate the very tasty dough raw with the consequences of a tummy ache and diarrhoea.

I liked walks on snow covered ground and sitting on a sledge being pulled by my parents. As the winters were very cold I had to wear woollen tights which made my legs itch. My pleas to be without the tights were ignored and suffer I did.

I liked going to my grandmother's farm which was known as "Taaramae" meaning a mythological god's place. The living quarters were built from timber with adjoining granary, storeroom and adjoining animal and chicken part of the building both of which were built from local stones. The granary was raised with a wooden floor and separated by timber walls. The granary was for flours ground from farm's produce, seeds for following year's sowing, chicken feed grains and for the animals etc.

In the store room (on dirt floor) was a big boxed area for potatoes and other vegetables, a sauerkraut barrel, a barrel for pickled cucumbers, apples, jams, etc were also stored there. At the other end of the area were farm implements. The attic was stacked with hay and fodder for the animals.

I liked the animals, the fresh air and the meadows to run on, help in the vegetable garden by weeding, pulling up matured vegetables, eating peas, etc. Going to sleep exhausted from the days activities. I remember once being attacked by the rooster when he flew over the gooseberry bush and attacked me on my eye missing the eyeball by a couple of millimetres. I still carried that scar in my fifties.

They say that all good things come to an end and this applied to our secure lifestyle.

CHANGING TIMES: WAR BEGINS

On June 16, 1940 the Soviet government presented an ultimatum demanding Estonia to form a new communist friendly government or the Red Army would forcibly occupy Estonia.

Upon these demands by the USSR government Estonia had to surrender to the USSR government: In a peaceful manner to prevent severe loss of life as the USSR forces and equipment was outnumbered by far to the Estonian armed forces. The USSR forces crossed the border of Estonia June 1940, and the government in Tallinn was overthrown by the communists in June 21, 1940.

On the day of the 'friendly takeover' Mum and another lady were watching the proceedings from the windows of our flat which was facing the street. They were very worried, upset and asked me to stay away from the windows. On the 6th August, 1940 Russia just incorporated Estonia into the Soviet Union.

The mood of the people including my parents and relatives became very sombre as all kinds of terror acts followed- the laughter was gone. Arrests and executions by the NKVD (later known as KGB) became frequent. Radios were collected from all residents. To be found with a radio in one's place was a serious offence.

A mass deportation of Estonians, including whole families with young children, took place on the 13th of June, 1941, when 10,000 people were transported in cattle carriages to Siberia for hard labour.

There were rumours of another deportation coming up. I and nanny were taken to my grandmother's place, dad was in hiding somewhere and mum stayed in our flat. Those rumours proved to be true as another wave of deportations took place on 21st June, 1941. My mother stayed very quietly in the flat. There was persistent loud banging on the door for quite some time certainly from unwanted authorities. This time another 30,000 people were deported but thanks to my parents for the precautions taken we were saved.

Germany declared war on Russia on 22 June, 1941. There was no way of getting true information about the advancement of Germans whose intention it was to conquer Estonia.

Crystal radios were built and listened to in strict secrecy. My father had a crystal radio which I was unaware of until one evening I ventured out of my bed late at night and saw my dad and my uncle listen to it. I was told to keep it an absolute secret as it would be serious consequences for our family.

I enjoyed being in the country where I could help Mamma, play with my own improvised farm with sticks as animals, branches for fences, etc. I also had what I called a small bird cemetery where I buried dead baby birds that had fallen out of their nests in the bush. Nanny was not much of a country person so I tried to be one by helping Mamma with everyday work. Mum would sometimes come and stay for a short time to see how we were but go back soon after.

There was night curfew in the cities and also in the country areas. One late evening 2 Russian soldiers came to the farm and demanded fresh vegetables. We all went to the vegetable garden but I got bored and ventured towards my bird cemetery. That was during the curfew hour. The Russian soldier came at the front of me and put the barrel of his rifle on my chest saying "niet" i.e. no. Mamma turned white from fright and thankfully no harm came to me as I backed back to Mamma and nanny. The soldiers got their vegetables, we were allowed to return to the house, I was put to bed but I doubt about Mamma's and nanny's peaceful sleep?

The German forces advance from the south made it imminent that the front would reach us very soon and therefore we took shelter in a dugout at another farm "Partsa" with their family who I believe were distantly related to Mamma. We stayed in their shelter for a day and night.

A lull came in the fighting and we returned to "Taaramae". On our way to Mamma's place there was more fighting and we took shelter behind an embankment. During another lull we proceeded, as low to the ground as possible to the meadow, and through bush land. On the farm we took shelter in the storeroom between the living area and the animal shed.

After a while some Russian forces set up base at the end of the animal shed and fighting with the German troops followed. I saw a bullet penetrate the storeroom and explode with sparks flying in the timber wall of the living quarter's area. Luckily it did not catch fire. The Russians soon retreated and then became a long lull.

Mamma considered it safe enough and we entered the house through an adjoining door. We cautiously moved about in the kitchen getting something to eat and drink. We saw 4 or 5 soldiers come up to the farm on bicycles. They knocked on the door and when they entered they took their caps off. I could hardly believe them to be soldiers. They were so different from Russian soldiers by being clean, polite and friendly. Mamma gave them something to drink and maybe something to eat. There were smiles- SMILES. They left in a friendly manner.

Fighting around us had stopped and we were able to sleep once again in our beds. Tallinn was occupied by the Germans on the 28th June, 1941. My mother was then able to come to be with us, uncle Konrad turned up and so did my father. We were all safe and well together as a family. A new era had begun under the German occupation.

Life became rather normal. Mum stayed home because her uncle's factory where mum worked had been destroyed as a working factory by the Russians who had removed the machinery to Russia. I am not sure about dad's place of work. With mum staying at home nanny left us.

I developed whooping cough. I was very sick for a long time. They nearly lost me had it not been for my mother's quick reactions. During the recovery I had to receive ray treatment which I hated.

Being an only child I was longing to have a brother. Why a brother I do not know. So while on Mamma's farm I ran after the storks, when they were migrating south, calling out "Bring me a brother".

My father had voluntarily entered the air force auxiliary. He joined the Estonian platoon which was instructed by the Germans. He was stationed at or near Tallinn and therefore was able to be with us during his leave times.

Nightly bombardment with the Russian aircraft became more frequent. With the air raid siren warning we would go down to the cellar with the other residents of the house. At the start of the air raid mother would often go outside to watch the "fireworks" and come down with the progression of the raid.

I started school, 1st class, at the start of the term in Tallinn autumn 1943. Completed 1st half of the year by Christmas and on the 2nd March 1944 Tallinn was bombed and the school I attended was destroyed. A day before the bombardment mum took me to "Taaramae" with me sitting on the push sledge for most of the way. It was about a 10 km journey. Mum wanted to return to Tallinn but Mamma persuaded her to stay for another day.

That night in March Tallinn got a severe bombardment. One of the first bombs fell on the house across the road from our flat and the front of the house was blown in by the force of the blast and the house caught fire. We watched the sky light up red from the fires and the crackling sound of the fires was clearly heard. We lost everything we owned in that fire. Some days later mum dug up from the ashes some silver spoons and a couple of beakers.

From then on we stayed with Mamma at "Taaramaäe". The people, including ourselves, who had lost everything received burnt out certificates from the state for which they received some fabrics and shoes (a pair per person). There were shortages of food in towns but we had sufficient on Mamma's farm. Food was on coupons but not always available.

I learned to ski on my uncle's big skis while the snow was on the ground. I tried spinning very knotty wool on Mamma's spinning wheel. She taught me knitting which I love to this day. Someone had given me the only toy which was a fabric long legged and long armed doll with a porcelain head. For modesty I kept her wrapped in a blanket or sleeping under it. I learned how to make butter which to me was a rather time consuming job. In the spring and summer I picked wild strawberries and what was left over from my 'tastings' were thread on a long straw for Mamma, also picked wild edible mushrooms for cooking.

I occasionally played with the girls at the pastorate but they were real city girls. During the hay making season I tried to cut some hay with a sickle but unfortunately cut my left hand which left me bandaged for a few days. That scar I carried for many years reminding me of the sickle. I saw haystacks made for winter transport. On one occasion while I was being lifted out from the wagon the back wheel of the wagon ran over my pelvis. I was just sore and sorry for the rest of the day. The hay was raked by wooden rakes. The spikes on the rakes would break and I tried to help Konrad to repair the rakes by cutting new spikes from suitable thin branches and securing these into the appropriate holes in the head. Somehow the spikes fitted by me were wobbly but by the next morning they fitted perfectly. Uncle told me that the moist night air did the trick but really he replaced them. I tried!

The Russians were the attackers now with the German forces retreating. With the distant gunfire being heard things looked bleak. Should mum and I have to leave Estonia, for our lives, because Dad was in the Air force, mum and Mamma buried some of our belongings for us to dig up on our return. They were certain it would be only of very short duration as Estonia would again regain its freedom and independence.

The gunfire became rapidly closer and the Germans retreating it became evident there was no option but to leave the country from the advancing Russians. We were able to get a lift on the trench diggers' truck to Tallinn, with me and the packages of our belongings on the floor of the truck, as it was forbidden to pick up other passengers. We went to Viru grandmother's place.

Mum and I went to enquire about getting on a boat to Sweden but it was unsuccessful due to lack of space on the boat. On our way we heard gunfire and therefore kept close to the buildings. The Estonian flag had been hoisted up on Pikk Herman tower by the Estonians. There seemed to be general confusion everywhere. Back at grandma's dad came for a short while with a bandaged hand which mum and grandma redressed. There seemed to be serious discussions. We spent the night at grandma's. During the night there was an air-raid and we all had to spend some time in the cellar of the bigger house with its residents.

In the morning dad came to take us to the port for departure to Germany. After quick farewells with grandma we left in a car. We saw the rubble from the previous night's bombardment in town and at the port. Very quickly we had to get onto the barge for transport to the ship waiting on the harbour with other ships of the convoy. As soon as the barge started to move from the wharf the wharf was blown up. Dad ran off the wharf. He was heading towards the headquarters when he was picked up by the staff car speeding towards the airfield in order to take off by plane. The plane could not be started quickly enough as the Russian tanks were already approaching. The men slashed parts of the plane to make it unworthy to fly and sped away in front of the car in front of the visible Russian tanks.

"Taaramäe"

Mamma, Konrad, Mall, Mum, Koppel grandma, Etu, Viru grandma, Dad

Mall in winter on Konrad's skis

They headed south and were able to board a burning ship at Kuresaare.
Forty five minutes after the departure of the barge on 22 September, 1944 Tallinn was occupied by the Red Army of Russia. The whole continent of Estonia was occupied on 26 September, 1944.

ON BOARD THE SHIP

We boarded the largest ship in the convoy. There were the families of the air force soldiers from the barge, air force servicemen and many other servicemen. The ship, I think was loaded to the maximum because it was the last convoy to leave the harbour. The families were directed to the dining room and we made ourselves as comfortable as possible on the seats around the tables in small cubicles.

Soon after the convoy had sailed out of the harbour there was an air raid by the Russian planes. Two of the bombs fell, one on either side of the ship, making the ship sway a little. During the night the soldiers slept on the floors. In order to get to the toilets we had to step over them. It was quite a task to find space to step on.

We disembarked at Leipaja in Latvia. We were transported by truck to a school house to spend the night sleeping on the floor on mattresses. Good sleep was welcome.

Next morning we were transferred to a small navy vessel which departed Leipaja on 25th September. Mum and I went to check our baggage which was under a tarpaulin. I remember seeing a young air force soldier, who many years later was to become my husband. What a small world! We, the families spent our nights sleeping in the officers' dining room. Otherwise we spent our time on deck.

We arrived at the port of Königsberg, East Prussia which was under German occupation, on 27th September, 1944. It was occupied by the Russians in 1945 and at a conference of the allies East Prussia was given to the USSR and they renamed Königsburg to be known as Kaliningrad.

We were transferred from the boat to a military camp for an overnight's stay. The barracks were clean but to wash ourselves was outside in the middle of the barracks from a tap. Good enough for washing face, hands and feet.

Mum and I went to visit a married Estonian couple living in Town. They put us to a hotel where we were able to wash from a wash bowl in the room. I had developed a fever. It soon went down after mother had given me some 'brontocil'. From there we travelled to a refugees camp in Gotenhafen.

AT GOTENHAFEN IN TRANSIT

We stayed in a large barrack sleeping on hard bunk beds, the toilets and washing facilities were very dirty. We stayed there about 3 days. There was also another Estonian mother with her three sons from Southern Estonia speaking in the southern dialect and we did not find out their origin until they had already left the camp. Mum knew an Estonian lady who lived in town and we visited her.

To get away from the Russian front Mum decided to travel southward to Frankfurt am Main. We stayed in a camp which had a number of Russian prisoners of War who were in a pitiful condition and starving. Although they were Russian soldiers and hated by us Estonians and the Germans, Mum secretly slipped a piece of bread through the fence. They were humans like everybody else. We stayed in a half-built (draughty) barrack with some other Estonian women and children. We were happy, although it was half finished; there were no lice or bed bugs. The toilet! A narrow trench in the ground surrounded by a wire fence with German soldiers on guard on the other side. How humiliating!

We were told by the Germans that there was an Air force base in Frankfurt an den Oder. Hopeful of finding our husbands and fathers or some news of them, we and all or some of the other families travelled to Frankfurt an den Oder. Mum and I met an Estonian lady who worked in a hotel. She was kind enough and put us up for the night. Mum showed her my father's photo and she recognized his face. Dad and her husband had indeed been there but dad had already left. We learned that he was alive.

Mum registered of our arrival on 22.1`0.1944 and was sent to work in Posseil's laundry and also had accommodation in their house up in a little room in the attic. There was a bed, bedding for me on the floor, a very small stove and some room left for privacy to wash from a hand bowl behind a hung-up blanket.

Workday in the laundry was long; the laundry from the Prisoners of War camp was infested with lice. Every evening, after work, in our room Mum would carefully examine her clothing for lice. Through this she kept us free from lice.

The food, though not always available, was on coupons. When I went to the shop to exchange the coupons for a particular item of food I was always told it was sold out. Other people (Germans) were given the particular items but I was a hated foreigner (refugee consuming their short supply of food). Mum as an adult had better luck.

Another Estonian woman worked in the laundry. She had a daughter a little younger than I and we became friends. We would borrow the Posseil's sledge and get branches from a Park for 'starters' in the stove.

We attended a Christmas party for the Estonian Air force wives and their children. Santa gave the children a very small bag of a rarity i.e. lollies (Oz for candies). What a wonderful present!

We had no toys. Mum had acquired some used fuses (electricity), creamy colour about 3cm high with thin 1 cm metal piece poking upwards in the middle. She gave us some rag pieces which we cut up and gathered up on top as dresses for our 'fuse dolls'. We had disagreements. I remember once being very cross with her I locked the door. She put her foot through the wooden panel of the door. What a temper! Mum had a lot of trouble with her boss to get the door repaired.

The Russian front was advancing and again we had to flee again by travelling to southern Germany. It was in February 1945, the fall of Frankfurt on the Oder was imminent. Mr. And Mrs. Posseil had become hospitable towards us. Mum and my friend's mother took our suitcases over the Oder River on Posseil's sledge. The bridge was already guarded by soldiers ready to blow it up. They quickly returned to pick up us and our knapsacks. We safely got over the bridge.

At Posseil's residence Mum packed her knapsack with her clothing and absolutely necessary items. She filled a pillowcase with my clothes. From both bottom corners was a piece of rope tied to the top of the pillow case enabling it to be carried on my back. This was done as a precaution should we become separated in the general confusion. The rest of our belongings including books from home were left behind.

It was very cold at the station filled with people trying to flee from the advancing enemy. Late into the night a train arrived (the last train to leave) packed with people. By really pushing hard we managed to get on board. The compartments were filled to the limit by standing refugees. There were people climbing onto the roof and standing outside on the boards alongside the carriage: Just to get away.

We had travelled for a number of days and nights through heavily bombarded cities, frequently changing trains, packed with people whenever they were running. Often trains had to be stopped before towns due to bombardment and track repairs. On one occasion there was a carriage for women and children only. An elderly lady carrying what looked like a baby boarded the train. During the journey the baby turned out to be a dachshund dog. Poor woman wanted desperately to escape.

In the middle of the cold night on 12th March, 1945 we arrived at Murnau at the foot of the Alps in Bavaria.

There were 4 mothers and their children huddled up on the platform with nowhere to go. One of the mothers was quite vocal and demanded from the stationmaster to have us transferred to accommodation as we were the families of officers serving with the German forces. Incidentally only her husband was an Offi

The stationmaster did organise and a horse drawn wagon was sent for us by the Lord Mayor. Thank you dear lady for making the fuss! That wagon took us to a hotel for an overnight's accommodation. The following day we were transferred to Weindorf, a nearby village where each mother and their children were taken to different farmhouses for accommodation.

We had quite a spacious room with adequate furniture. The farmer was quite hostile towards us but his wife showed kindness. Towards the end of the war food was in very short supply and very hard to buy. Mrs. Petsmeyer, the farmer's wife, would occasionally put a cup of milk without her husband's knowledge into our room for the growing child to drink.

There were 3 girls about my age, including the girl from Frankfurt, and we all became playmates. The 'vocal' lady's child was younger but later on after many years we met again.

We would often play in the sand pit in the churchyard next to where I lived, tell stories etc, and go to one anothers' places etc. Mum would take me to a restaurant in Murnau in search of a meal and visit the Estonians who lived in a hotel. Many Americans flew over Weindorf destined to bombard major cities and military installations.

The American front was advancing and therefore the army stores with supplies for the forces were open to the general public. Mum got some powdered cheese and imitation coffee. She kept the powdered cheese for me. I thought it to be very dry but it tasted delicious. Mum ate the dry imitation coffee ground derived from acorns and some other cereals.

Murnau surrendered to the Americans peacefully without loss of life or damage to the buildings. The first army tanks to arrive carried exclusively black American soldiers followed by tanks with white Americans.

Well at "Taaramaäe" surrounded by icy water and snow

Push-sledge

The American Army set up camp on our neighbour's farm where playmate Aimi lived. They had dug out a deep trench where they disposed of leftover food and food scraps. Aimi came and took me over to see all the beautiful food like bread, oranges, etc thrown into that trench. We were shocked to see it and in disbelief. The soldiers were friendly towards us the refugees and gave us small bars of chocolate which tasted 'heavenly'.

Occasionally they would give us bread and other goodies which were greatly appreciated.

Germany surrendered to the Allies on May 7th, 1945 and after capitulation was divided by the Allies into 4 zones i.e. north-east-Russian Zone: Northwest –English Zone: South-west –French Zone; South-American Zone.

Near Murnau was a Prisoners of War camp with officers from Poland. The camp became under American care and the officers were free to come and go as they pleased. They started visiting the Estonian families. I remember tasting the first American ration, tinned mixed fruit which was given to me by one of the officers- how sweet it tasted.

REUNITED WITH FATHER

Mum was very worried about Dad. Quite some time had passed and no word until one day. On my way to Aimi's Dad suddenly appeared on the road. I happily took his hand and guided him to our room. Because he was extremely thin and in a little baggy clothes Mum at first had difficulty recognizing him. What a happy reunion! He was quite starved and exhausted. He needed bed rest for a number of days.

Because of his very poor condition Mum had to be very careful by feeding him a little at a time and increasing his meals gradually. It took weeks to regain his strength.

He had been besieged by Russians at Gottbus. A farmer had given him some civilian clothes to wear to enable him to discard his uniform. For a week while hiding from the enemy he had nothing to eat but some pig's trotters which he had found in the bush. Suddenly one day he came face to face with two Russian soldiers to whom he had to show the contents of his pockets. Dad had a silver cigarette case with a watch in it. The Russians happily took the watch, gave the cigarette case back and to the relief of my father let him go. He eventually walked through the surrounding Russian front to safety. It took him a long time and many hundreds of kilometres to reach us.

Near Weindorf was a lake and there Mum taught me to swim. We would often go there for a swim and spend the time sun baking and playing with my friends. Every little scratch on me became infected. One day a leech had sucked into it. I started to whack it from side to side and it let go. From this day on the infected cuts healed and no new ones became infected. Nature had cured me.

For my 10th birthday I got a doll's house made from a cardboard box, with the doors and windows cut out, which Dad had made for me. Unfortunately I had no dolls or furniture to put to it- so make believe and improvisation came in handy. I also had a party and my friends decorated a chair for me with greenery and branches. We had something to eat and drink. We played and we were happy.

The Petsmeyers had a teenage son and daughter who worked hard on the farm with their parents. On some Saturday nights the young people of the village would gather on the farm singing Bavarian songs and folk dancing. They were always dressed in their national dress.

Most of the spouses had arrived to their families and the Estonians had become more organized by having church services with an Estonian minister, gatherings of families at the hotel where a lot of Estonian refugees lived and a school in Estonian was started in the hotel.

I started 2nd class at the school on 17.9.45. Subjects covered Estonian, English, mathematics, scripture, nature, drawing, singing, handcrafts and sport. I gained good marks in all except singing.

United Nations Relief and Rehabilitation Administration (UNRRA) had started organising camps for the refugees. In 1947 IRO (International Refugee Organisation) took over the care of the refugees, who had become known as DPs (Displaced persons) and organized the immigration program.

A camp for Estonians was opened during May 1945 in Geislingen. The Germans had to vacate their houses in 3 different areas to accommodate the DPs.

We said goodbye to Murnau at the end of October 1945, and were taken by army trucks with the other
Estonian families to Geislingen, a small town surrounded by wooded hills.

GEISLINGEN

Our family had a furnished room on the ground floor of a joint 2 storey house in the Rappenecker area. The kitchen was shared with all the other residents. There was a cellar and quite a spacious garden around the house. Our room had a large bed for Mum and Dad, a table a sofa for me to sleep on, with a shelf and a mirror above it, a small wardrobe, a cupboard, a small 'tinny' wood stove about 50 x 30 cm for boiling water and for heating.

Food rations were supplied from UNRRA distribution centres. The daily calorie supply to DPs was almost double the calories to the Germans. Our food situation had improved immensely.

I continued 2nd class in a large school building which had been requisitioned from the Germans. Primary classes were held in the mornings and high school classes in the afternoons, alternating six monthly. At the end of the school year on 19.6.46 (summer in the northern hemisphere) my report card was good. That report was written in Estonian. The following years it was written in Estonian and English.

For the first Christmas in Geislingen the American Army gave a Christmas party which I attended. There were sweets and other goodies for the kiddies; I specially remember a fizzy drink. Maybe it was Coca Cola which sent tingles up my nose. At the end of the party the tired children with happy memories were returned to their homes.

With more DPs arriving, the camp became filled to its capacity. A theatre house "Jahnhalle" was requisitioned from the Germans. The Estonians held many drama performances, comedies, three different operettas, concerts, children's plays etc, in the spacious theatre with rooms for ballet classes, choir practices etc.

A sauna was built with 3 rooms: a foyer with a small kiosk, dressing room, washroom and a bathroom platform for whisking oneself in the steam bath.

There was a medical surgery, dental surgery, hospital, baby clinic and ambulances in all 3 areas. A newspaper was published, a bakery to supply bread for the camp, etc.

Geislingen

The refugees were utilized to work in different areas according to their occupation and for other works which required a labour force, eg. firewood was cut by the DPs in the designated timber areas for distribution to the camp on a square metre basis per person. Army trucks were available and used for transport.

Barracks were built to accommodate scouts, girl guides and many different courses were taught to adults.

The American Army employed men from the camp for duties in their warehouses, drivers. etc. Dad joined and was employed in Furth. They had a black uniform, quite handsome in my opinion at the time, and were accommodated by the army on weekdays travelling home for weekends. A couple of times he brought home some bananas and oranges- how delicious they tasted!

After a long summer vacation I advanced to 3rd class. The number of 3rd class students required two classrooms: A and B classes each with about 30 students. I was in 3A. We had a good friendly atmosphere among our classmates. For Christmas each class celebrated Christmas with their class head teacher and the headmaster, then Mr. Mälgi, paid a visit to each class. The Christmas break was very short.

For drawing Miss Hageri and the deputy headmaster was Mr. V. Kaasik. Many years later I met them again as a married couple and we became friends in Australia. We had no school holidays between terms thereby allowing a long summer vacation. At the end of the school year the students gave a concert for their parents and friends with the school choir performing, short plays with dancers, folk dancing, etc.

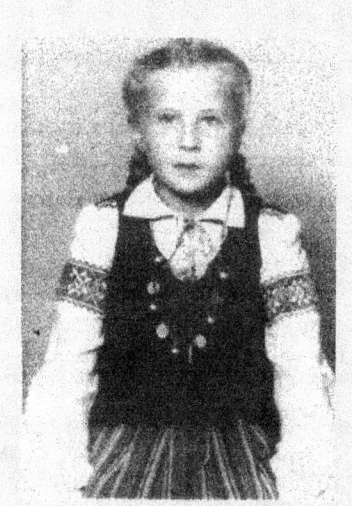

In my original national costume

I joined the Brownies. Each of the three areas in Geislingen had their own Brownies group. I was in the Rappenecker group. Apart from our meetings we helped in the community gardens, on National holiday assemblies and gained knowledge about the Girl Guide movement.

I started ballet lessons in Meta Antje's children's class at "Jahnhalle" and joined children's folk dancing group. The ballet class girls graduated to toe ballet.

I had no proper winter shoes. I was wearing a pair with thick wooden soles and canvas across the front on top. Proper shoes in my size were simply not available. Mum was corresponding with her uncle who had fled to Sweden and he sent me a pair of leather lace up shoes. They were too small but much warmer than the canvas 'clogs'.

Mum sewing my new national costume skirt

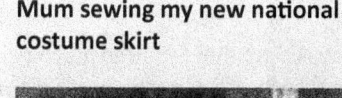

My school bag was a zip up canvas bag with some protective coating on it. The protective coating started to wear off and it became 'unfriendly' towards my books. I must confess it being used under my backside sliding down an iced up embankment was one contributing factor from normal wear and tear.

As dad was working and earning a bit of money my parents were successful in getting me a brief case. Now I was the proud owner of proper shoes though too small, but nice brown lace up shoes and a proper school brief case the future looked bright.

Halloween night: A group of my friends decided to go around singing and begging at people's doors. We wanted to dress up so we had to organise. In the house I lived also lived a lady who was a milliner. She was kind enough to lend me a hat brought to her for repairs. We had been to some places and knocked on another door and to my horror the little girl said "this is Aunt...'s hat". Was I relieved to get out of that place!

The Americans organized screening the refugees of the camp as some people had entered the camp that were not considered as refugees, eg. Estonians who had left the country during earlier years. My friend from Frankfurt stood at the bridge at Rappenecker on the way to school and told mostly her classmates that there was no school during that day due to screening. Her class and also some other classes, especially younger classes had less students attending! What problems this created for my friend! Her Mum was called to the school and the culprit was reprimanded.

During the school days we had 5-6 lessons per day with breaks of about 10 minutes between each lesson which were spent walking along the corridors under teacher supervision. The girls usually spent walking time walking arm in arm with their friends. Occasionally the boys would start pestering us and we would enter the girls' toilets with the boys singing something like "ah-ah-ah the girls' toilet is their holy shelter'. Time did not allow for long meal breaks because the other half of the day the building was used by the High School.

At first I was accepted to sing in the school choir but for the last year my voice was unacceptable. The choir practice was always held during the last lesson and students not in the choir were allowed to go home. One day I picked up my briefcase and it seemed a little too heavy. Upon opening it there was a brick inside it instead of my books which were neatly placed under my desk: Our class' boys playing tricks again. No one owned up. Our class motto was 'one for all, all for one'.

Geislingen had a movie theatre showing American popular and classic movies. For each movie there was a program displaying the actors and actresses from different scenes. Each time we saw a movie we would buy a program. Those programs became a collectors' item. One day at school in the 5th class we the girls were looking at a program with a woman's and man's face very close to one another when one of the favorite teachers, we called him 'vana Valge" suddenly from behind us said with a cheeky tone "wonder if it is taken before or after a kiss?".

We were surprised and speechless but relieved to know that he was a teacher with a sense of humour. "Vana Valge's" son was a member of the folk dancing group where he showed his inherited humour amongst the group. What wonderful harmless fun there was! At school punishment for misbehavior was standing in the corner of a classroom or for serious mischief the student was sent to the headmaster. The cane or ruler was not part of the punishment. The belief to my understanding was that words speak louder than violence- and it worked well.

For Mother's day one year I and my friends went out to take flowers (only a few) from other people's gardens to give to our mothers. We knew that it was not right but did not want to leave our mothers without anything. Just a couple of blooms were all we wanted.

The following year Dad earned some money and I bought Mum a beautiful cup, saucer and plate set which my mother treasured and now it gives me much pleasure looking at it as it is in my possession.

In the camp there was a lot of bartering going on. As dad was a non-smoker the cigarette rations received became a bartering item. To get some fresh fruit Mum travelled to a German farm to exchange cigarettes for fresh apples. She got some tasty fresh apples. How wonderful, but the German's next door farmer had informed the authorities about his neighbor's transaction. Mum received a summons to appear in front of an American court hearing.

Poor Mum she was shocked and terrified. She did appear in front of the court on the specified date with an English speaking interpreter. When mum was asked her age she was under such stress that she could not remember it. The judge did grin I was told. I do not remember if she had to pay a small fine or not but it did show the hostility of some Germans towards dealing with the D.P.s.

The work for Dad in Furth became scarce in the later years and he got work at the bakery in the camp. Sometimes he was able to bring home a little extra bread but most important he was able to obtain some flour bags. These were white bags which had to be thoroughly washed. Mum sewed some bed sheets from the bags and was able to use them for extending my national costume blouse by adding pieces from the bags to the underside of the sleeves and the sides of the bodice.

I had grown out of the skirt. Big problem! Mum used the bags for the skirt by sewing strands of wool, in as close to the original colors as possible onto the fabric and made the width of the stripes on the skirt as close to the width on the original skirt as possible. She fastened the strands of wool by sewing on top of the strands on a sewing machine using ordinary sewing thread.

It was a job that required much patience and time. The completed skirt was exceptional. Then I had a proper beautiful national costume of my own and did not have to borrow from Mum's friends for performances. Mum had borrowed the sewing machine from a German woman. This time she was more fortunate and did not have to appear in court. How stupid the previous appearance was- just for carrying a bag of apples.

During summers we (the school kids) attended a camp on 'Koogimäe' on one of the hills surrounding Geislingen. We slept in army tents on army beds, had our meals served on army utensils, played ball games etc and had a whole lot of fun. Each tent's occupants were responsible for the tidiness of their tents. As this was my first camp it was a great experience and I had no hesitation returning again next year. It was wonderful to be out in the fresh air, in the middle of a beautiful forest with all the school mates and friends.

There were organized sightseeing excursions in which I participated with my parents. I remember the beautiful scenic places along the way to the Alps. We visited Garmisch-Partenkirchen in Bayern, a beautiful Alpine township with its unique alpine houses. I think it was there that we went to the Guesthouse and had a meal in the splendour of the alpine atmosphere.

We went to Zugspitze (2964m) by cable lift car. I was a bit scared hanging up in that 'box' but the magnificent view around helped me to overcome it.

We visited 2 German castles. Neuschwanstein Castle was standing majestically with its towers on top of a mountain. It was very spacious with beautiful artwork painted on the walls, lots of gold in the decor, a grand ballroom and a courtyard at the entrance. It was in my opinion, a fortress. The second castle we visited as Lindenhof Castle which was smaller with beautiful spacious gardens and a theatre built into a hillside. Although it was smaller it was equally lavishly decorated but to me it seemed to have a relaxing and welcoming atmosphere. Both of the castles were furnished in antique furniture with a lot of gold trimmings. What splendour of yesteryear.

Mum and Dad paid another visit to Bayern. This time to visit the Petsmeyers in Weindorf: On whose farm we stayed before capitulation. Mum said all of them were happy to see one another again. The Petsmeyers son had been captured by the Russians and had spent time in a Russian Prisoner of War camp. Mr. And Mrs. Petsmeyer had apologized to Mum for not believing the hostilities of the Russians as told by Mum. With the return of their son and the stories told by him they believed it all. Unfortunately it was their son's sufferings that made them believe it.

I had many friends, mostly from my class at school like Tamara, 2 Heddas and many more. We would visit one another's places; at winter time spend time sliding on icy ground, making snowmen, etc. On rainy days we would play with paper dolls drawn for us by a young mother from next door. We would draw dresses and other items to wear for the dolls, cut them out, fastened onto the dolls by folding extended strips attached to clothing items.

The house I lived in had an attic and a room in the attic leaving sufficient space at the side for us to play with our paper dolls. We had many enjoyable days using our imagination to utilise these dolls as 'people' travelling, keeping house, visiting friends etc.

On warm and fine days we would visit the 12th century Helfenstein Castle ruins on one of the hills surrounding Geislingen. The ruins were very old with a history extending over hundreds of years. We would imagine all sorts of evil and good things having taken placed there. For us it was a spooky place from where we preferred to leave rather quickly but the fact of having been there was important.

We, the girl from Frankfurt, Hedda from upstairs, Tamaara and I decided to put on a variety performance to earn a little for our refreshments. So a blanket was hung up on some twine in our (the Karp's) room, the audience was our parents and on went the performance. With the proceeds of the "show" one or two of us went to the Sauna Kiosk and bought some lemonade and cakes for the performers' for an 'after show 'party.

The Sauna (a communal bathhouse) was used by all the residents in the camp with separate sessions for males and females. Mum and I would attend the Sauna once per week for a good overall wash. Mum would go up on the platform and whisk herself with a 'viht' (hank), made from dried birch twigs, to open up the pores of the skin and sweat profusely. I would sit and whisk on one of the steps going up. Afterwards we washed ourselves in the washroom, got dressed in the dressing room and went home feeling fabulously clean and relaxed.

My father was very strict with me. I was not allowed to go anywhere to be with my friends till all my homework and study had been done. He continually reminded me to straighten my shoulders while doing my homework.

During the war Dad's helmet received the full force of a bullet and it had ricocheted into the back of his neck. It was visible under the skin but had started to move and therefore Dad had it removed by an operation.

**4th class spring 1948
I'm standing 3rd from the left**

Mall hard at the books

Jahnhalle folk dancers. I'm first from the left, Meeta Antje standing behind me

Mall playing patience while awaiting for transport to Australia

On another occasion during the war he was hit by a ricocheting bullet on his chest at the pocket containing a silver cigarette case behind other items in the left side chest pocket. It could not penetrate the metal and fell down on the ground. It must have been more than luck! The cigarette case Dad had inherited from, I believe, his grandfather. Incidentally Dad was a non-smoker and carried it with him as a precious item.

The children were inoculated for small-pox, tested for TB and injections were given for all sorts of infectious diseases. The smells/odours in the clinic, probably ether, caused me to faint after each injection. In years 4 and 5, I was absent from school for quite a number of days through illnesses like mumps and other children's health problems.

The Primary School children were not allowed to be outside by a certain time in the evening unless accompanied by their parents. One evening coming home from the rehearsal in "Jahnhalle", after the 'in time' on the bridge to Rappenecker a teacher came from the opposite direction. We fearfully crossed the road and started talking in German. I'm sure that we did not sound like Germans but the teacher probably had mercy on us as I think that he was aware of us attending rehearsals!

As mentioned earlier I had joined the children's folk dancing group in "Jahnhalle". We had learned a number of dances. The theatre put on a performance of our national folklore including folk songs, folkdances and customs relating to Jaanipaev (Midsummer's day) on "Kiigemae" (Hill with the village swing). On midsummer's night the young and old folk would gather on "Kiigemae" to sing, dance and enjoy themselves by the warmth of the Jaanitulli (fire) to pass the shortest night of the year.

On that night the sun barely sets and almost immediately the dawn breaks. There were 7 pairs dancing in the children's group. My partner was Ain Laats. It was an enjoyable group of dancers with Mart, "Vana Valge's" son always happily joking. With the other artists, folkdance group of older dancers and our children's group there were 3 successful performances during the evenings. The folk dancers were taught by a ballet dancer Meeta Antje who also taught the children's ballet class. Meeta was a schoolmate of my mother from her school days in Estonia.

The children's ballet group in toe ballet shoes participated in a play "Tondioo" (Spooky Night) for children and youth. Some of us had speaking roles and the rest were in dancing roles. The play was about a tailor, his apprentices, mother, children and a teacher (if my memory serves me right). During the dark hours of the night the tailor's scissors, smoothing iron and the tailor's ruler became alive and danced. I danced the part of the smoothing iron with a large body of the iron around me, built by the prop men, allowing me to see straight ahead through the holes in the bottom of the iron.

During the first performance all went well but during the second performance the prop men had not secured the side props securely and soon after my entry the props on that side of the stage collapsed - what horror! The curtains were drawn, props were secured and we started the scene again, this time without mishaps. I also danced as one of the moonbeams who were gentle and left the scenery intact. Due to the beginnings of migration we had only two performances.

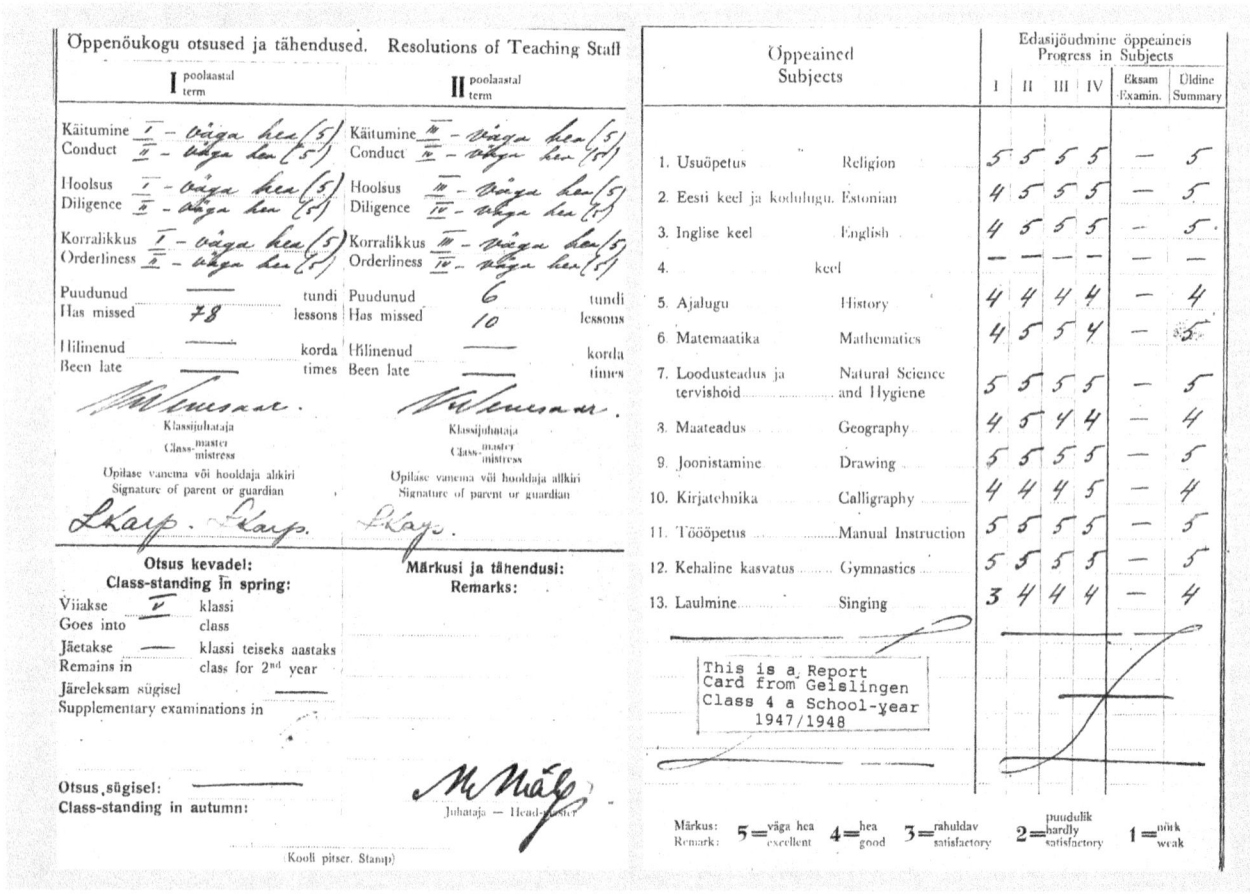

ARDO TAREM
A MAN WITH THE FORESIGHT TO TELL A LOST TALE

As the scrabble to survive among adversity continued, the instinctive behavior would have been to not look beyond one's own needs. Something bade him to look ahead.

For myself it brought many revelations which had become blurred with the decades. Here is a little about this resourceful man.

I am very grateful to Mati Sööts who too lived in Geislingen, with his brothers. He made contact with me to explore access to WNE and the journey of this book. Mati himself was born in Schwabish Hall and left Germany before he was five years old. Thus his memories of the time are limited. His brothers have better recollections of that epoch of time.

Mati told me about *Ardo Tarem's film. His children Anne (Tarem) Saul, together with her sisters Eevi and Astrid, lived in Geislingen. Ardo worked for some of the international relief agencies in Germany and somehow was able to take movies of Geislingen and some of the other camps in Germany." Mati introduced me to Ardo's daughters and they introduced me to Ardo's grandson Erik.   *A photo of Ardo appears in Eric Soovere's photo series earlier in the book.

One of the exciting parts of these book projects is all the peripheral historic material one learns and sets up quandaries in one's own thinking. Mati too shared, that his uncle while in the Czar's army was stationed in Orenburg which is not too far from where my mother and her parents lived in Samara during WW I. That too was an ordeal for those of Estonia's folk who migrated that far away: I will never know the gist of my folks' journey: Too bad we don't have the insight to ask questions when the answers are accessible.

I thank my younger son Adrian for introducing me to the notion of using "Screen grabs" to illustrate writings, and more so for his patience in showing me how to do this effectively. I reminisce to the time when the Geislingen project began in 2005 when I had not the faintest how to create a simple JPG or PDF let alone despatch one! To those USA and Canadian guys who patiently grappled with guiding me while compiling WNE "I dips me lid" as we say down under.

A MYSTERY SOLVED

On page 188 of WNE writing about Maano Milles, one of my playmates I wrote:
....On another occasion he encouraged me to walk up his front steps carrying a large chunk of tree trunk on my head-like a jug! I tripped and fell, and again incurred mother's wrath for defacing my face.

At times I have pondered where this chunk of tree trunk had come from, or was it but a figment of my fantasy. I was a pragmatic child not prone to fantasy so that wasn't the explanation.

That picture is not of Maano, nor is that a large chunk of a tree trunk: But then everything looks large to a small child: There is definite proof that such childlike pranks and challenges were possible in the context: That small children can remember in context of their lives: At times the context differing to that of adults!

IDLE HANDS WERE NOT PERMITTED: THE USA ARMY WORK CORPS

Pastor Karl Raudsepp.
Photo: ER

Post war in the camps many men were engaged in camp management duties. Others were engaged by the USA army bases which were scattered around Germany.

The men were given tasks commensurate with their resources matched with the army's needs. Even the very old were put to work. My grand father, in that photo would have been about 67 years old.,

Many of the children recall army Jeeps driving through Geislingen dropping off their fathers and older siblings. They too recall saying goodbye to them at the train stations when the weekends were over.

The USA troops were generous to little kids and gave them 'goodies'. My only recall of the goodies was chocolate syrup. Despite the food privation chocolate was not my poison and I knocked it back figuring some other child might enjoy it. Needless to say, mother who loved chocolate was not impressed by my actions. The generation gap sure began at a young age.

Many of the children talk of Negro American soldiers: The first time they had seen a dark skinned man. I have no recall of such.

My only recall of skin colour issues than of an American-Estonian half cast child, who from even my little child's ideology seemed to have been outcasted. No one seems to know what became of her.

I hope that where ever she went she found some human warmth.

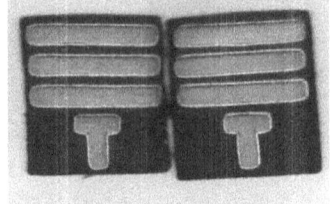

AND IT WAS FROM THE DISABLED THAT WE LEARNED THE ULTIMATE LESSONS

Some were disabled by physical injuries, others by lesser sociological hierarchy or emotional wounds. When need arises something can be made out of proverbially nothing.
Apart from a plenty of nothing , there was plenty of rubble and broken remnants of useful and at times coveted objects.
Time was a plentiful commodity, especially for those who were wounded and needed rehabilitation to find new niches in life or needed distraction from their woes until they had time to reconcile them. MM

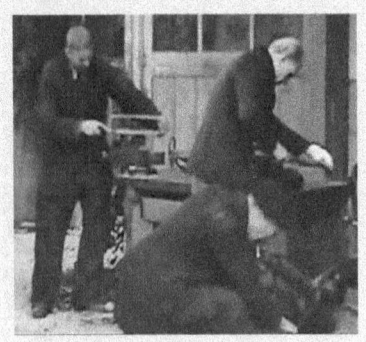

Necessity has always been the mother of invention. Man has always had the urge to move around, at times fast. Who would have believed that these vehicles evolved from nought but rubble.

And on a more pragmatic scale, I recall my youth in Australia.
In my early teens I was using a treadle machine to make clothes for my sister from cut-downs of older worn clothing: And repairing the sewing machine when it went on the blink!
The adults were working hideous hours and if my push bike broke down I was the mechanic who fixed it at even fifteen years of age.
These skills would have been learned from watching the Geislingen folk reincarnating some form of manageable life.
Mind you, after a little high school physics on board mending the iron was not quite so smart: But then we didn't have electric irons in Geislingen: And I did live to tell the tale.

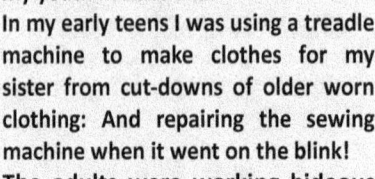 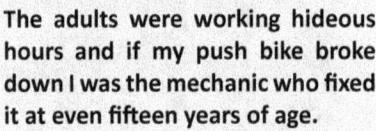 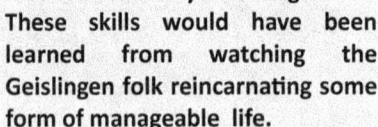 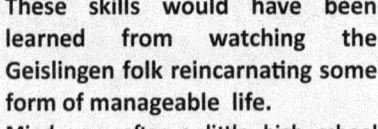 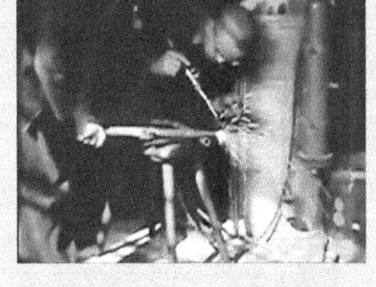 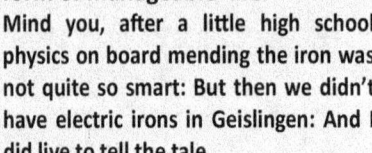  

 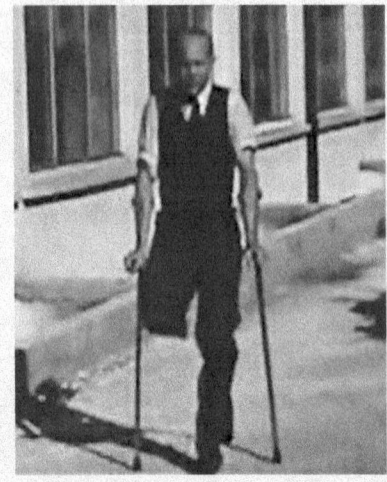 

HANNES JÜRMANN
FROM TARTU TO GENOA

We must have left Tähe tänav when the Soviets were getting too close, or when Tartu was bombed and went to our farm "Maanuse" at Nõo, 14 km SSW of Tartu. I remember a fun evening when mum and a refugee woman who was staying with us dressed up in reversed sheep-skin jackets and played Mardi Sandid. I think that takes place late in the year, perhaps November. It must have also been that Christmas when we went to an evening service in the sled drawn by horses, "kuljused" and all.

The tenants, Pärt and family, occupied the rear half of the house and the upstairs and the front was kept vacant for our use, mostly in the summer.

There was a passageway when you turned right from the door leading to a couple of doors of the toilet (seats with holes to pit – "Dunny" in Australia) There were also hooks for coats and hats before you entered the kitchen through a door behind the one in the picture. Mum got on well with them and we shared the kitchen and dining table when we were there. There was a discarded German helmet hanging from one of the pegs. When we tried to bring it down with a broom handle, it fell and the rim hit Peeter on the forehead, leaving a vertical cut above his nose, the scar of which he still bears.

In the spring of 1944, a German communications unit was stationed with us for a short while. They installed some cables. One of the soldiers, a professional cyclist was Peter Hammerschlag. He was a prisoner of war in Russia for quite a while and when he was released mum somehow established contact with him and his wife, and wrote to them forty years as she did with Hans Aschendorf and family.

We were at Maanuse when the eagerly awaited threshing machine reached our farm, then everyone was flat out assisting in threshing and bagging the grain. Peeter and I had a great time wandering about the farm. Father once took us to one of the old, abandoned peat cutting holes to search for frogs and snail shells.

We also walked down to the cemetery along the road heading south from the farm, having to cross the rail line bordering the back of the farm.

Sometime towards autumn, I remember a night journey in the cabin of a truck carrying our belongings to the narrow gauge railway, where we boarded a train and were met later by mum's parents, who took us to their farm with horse and cart. Grandfather had built a cottage for retirement at the roadside edge of his farm in the 20s. We remained there until autumn. Grandfather taught me to play the harmonica at age 5 and I have had one since then. Father also visited us there from leave at Jõhvi, bringing an old Mauser ("broom handle") pistol and his issue Walther for grandfather to practice. I played with them when unloaded and got into trouble when scoring grandmother's table trying to cock the difficult Walther. Grandfather gave me a tin of old nails to practise hammering them into a wood block.

A pond with log over it as bridge and out-door laundry with tepee like copper support on the other side of the house. There were wild strawberries around the stumps to the left of the garden. The track on the right of the house leads to the main farm house. There was a granite boulder near the pond, and grandfather had sealed the deeds to the farm with pitch in an old artillery shell and buried them under the edge of the boulder. The farm is actually located at a locality of Jalgsema, some kilometres from Järva-Jaani. Peeter and I helped grandfather dig a rectangular pit at the left side of the garden, as a bomb shelter.

It must have been late September when we went to stay some days at the flat of mum's friend Mitsi. I was again in trouble for dropping the wooden toilet seat onto the bowl and breaking a piece out of the inside rim. But Mitsi said not to worry, as we would all be gone soon. While there we also paid a brief visit to Aunt Helga and grandmother Eugenie ('Koosu') who was staying with them. They had a harrowing, last minute escape from the shore to a passing ship on a hastily constructed raft. They were living at Nõmme. I was surprised at how familiar it all seemed when I visited a similar street in 2001. It was just a brief walk, over Mustamäe from cousin Gudrun's flat on Sütiste tee.

Then one evening, we proceeded to the port and amidst great bustle boarded the "Donau" (sunk in '45). Peeter in charge of my teddy bear and I in charge of mum's expensive violin in its case. There was some fuss about a woman who had jumped off the ship onto the dock, or between ship and dock, to commit suicide. Mum had also had 'dog tags' made for Peeter and me out of silver, on chains which hung around our necks. They were engraved with our names and birthdays. Foolishly, mum had them melted down in the '70s to make an Estonian ring for my son Brett.

We were spread out on the first level below the front deck on blankets with our immediate baggage. Mum's notes say it was between 19 – 21 Sept. Other things were stored in the hold. Mum had removed the välves from our valued Phillips radio (which father had rescued from Tiigi tn in '41). This was fortunate, as the radio was stolen as expected. Apparently I would sit in front of the radio at quite an early age, swinging my head from side to side, in time to the music.

One sunny day, there was a siren and the guard with Schmeisser at the head of the steps demanded that no one was to go on deck. Fortunately we suffered no damage. He was a kindly fellow and late offered me and Peeter some of his chocolate. We stopped, probably at Riga to unload some artillery pieces from the level below us. We were all instructed to move to the sides from the removable part of the floor for the crane to gain access. The next I remember was the disembarkation at Gotenhafen. We were met by my mother's friend Felix Urban. He was a medic and later worked at the hospital in Darwin. He had attended Commerce college with my mother in the 30s after mother had to train for a new career as secretary in the Education Department, the positions for cinema orchestra violinists having vanished with 'Talkies'. Felix's family were Baltic Germans and probably responded to Hitler's call to return home.

The Urbans gave us accommodation for a while until we were assigned an unused shop display room with its large window, which we had to cover at the bottom for privacy. Tõnu Kirss, son of our next door neighbours on the third floor in Tartu located us on leave and stayed with us for a couple of days. I played with his rifle. He was in an artillery unit and when mum wrote to him in early '45 the letter was returned, marked,"Für die Heimat gefallen". We were not able to inform his sister Maret until the late '50s. Grandparents were located to a nearby village and visited us on foot. One day on a visit they were chased around a roadside tree by an American fighter which had shot up a milk wagon loaded with aluminium milk cans, like large jugs with hinged lids and carrying handles. We still had one as a peg bucket in Stockwell. Brave chaps, these US aviators!

Later we were assigned rooms at the rear of Frau Willes house by the authorities. It was on a main street and our access was through a large door leading to the back yard. She was a nasty old bat and threateningly told us that her brother was some functionary with the Nazi Party. We were instructed to evacuate the house during the massed bombing raids on Berlin, to avoid being buried in the rubble if hit. After a few occasions, mum in her calm style, said it would not make much difference, and we stayed in bed.

Peeter and I amused ourselves playing at making mud pies and I tried to wipe my hands clean on a shed door at the back. It was weathered and I received two palms full of splinters and was not very brave about their removal. I was a real wimp in those days.

Another spot of trouble arose when, after seeing some film about knife throwing, Peeter and I took turns in lying on the grass outside while the other threw a selection of kitchen knives around the one on the grass. Mum was not happy and we received a good thrashing. I got into trouble again when I exchanged the small model horse to the neighbor's boy, in exchange for a aircraft machine gun shell. We were good friends with the Mayers who owned the next-door shop and I got my horse back, even though I would rather have kept the shiny brass shell. Mum maintained correspondence with them in Australia for many years.

All the Estonians troops were formed into the 20th Estnische Waffen SS Division in early '45 I think. When father came on leave from Neuhammer or Sagan, Frau Wille was quite startled by the tall SS officer looking for his family. No more mention of her powerful Nazi brother. Because of the gross ignorance of the British, and especially the Americans, all families destroyed any photos with evidence of their men having been in the Waffen SS. Consequently I only have a photo of him in his Wehrmacht uniform from December '44, before they were all compulsorily formed into the 20th Estnische Waffen SS Grenadier Division. There is also another photo with a young soldier in Jõhvi in his initial, soldier's uniform.

When home on leave that winter he took us to the small, local lake at Hagenow, taking some photos of Peeter and me. We still had our winter clothes from Tartu, with leather soled, felt boots and fur hats. I was bawling because father made us get down onto the ice and I did not trust the stuff until I had actually been forced to try it. A little later mum went to visit father in Sagan. But we did not see him again until the summer at Schwartzenbeck.

In May the war ended and soon convoys of US Army trucks passed down the street past our house, loaded with German prisoners. During some halt, mum exchanged some of father's cigarettes for tinned meat with some of the prisoners. American soldiers were wandering along the streets. One had a row of watches, robbed from the people, along his arm. Mum knew one of the officials at the Rathaus, who warned her that this region was to be handed over to the Soviets, but there was to be a collection point for (perhaps Baltic) refugees from the nearby German, military airfield by the British Army.

On one of the visits into the city, I pressed the button on stamp vending machine and out popped a stamp bearing the familiar head of Adolf. Having summoned her parents, we all proceeded to the barracks at the airfield. That night we enjoyed horse-lung soup for the evening meal at the dining hall. The next day we boarded the canvas-covered trucks and began the journey. Mum bravely hung a small Estonian flag from a broom handle, out of the back of our truck.

By evening we had arrived at a bomb-damaged, ball bearing factory at Schwartzenbeck. Entry was through a double storey, brick gateway building. Up the main road, and on the corner of a road to the right was a dining hall where we all camped on the bare floor for the night, like sardines in a tin. The next day the men proceeded to gather cabinets and other materials from factory buildings to construct cubicles for each family. We soon had some privacy but were able to climb the bunks to chat with others in the next cubicle. The dining hall was on the first floor and the windows opened to the flat roof of the adjoining factory section. We were soon out there and could climb down onto the street via the fire escape ladder.

Initially there was also a large group of Lithuanians at the factory but they were soon sent somewhere else. We had quite friendly relations with them. The toilets consisted of a long temporary structure with a roof and long board seats lining one wall. There was no door but there was a dividing wall in the middle with one end for women. I remember women and men sitting beside each other in their own section, using the time for chatting. There was some fuss when some Soviet soldiers had been seen skulking in the nearby woods by some of the women. Of course, being Estonians, a sauna was soon constructed near the corner, across from the dining hall. An assembly hall on the left of the road, up from the gate was soon in use for functions. I remember mother laughing about one function, possibly Jaanipäev when father , who was rather fond of speeches, continued for so long that the food was marched in to the accompaniment of music to cut him short.

We kids had a great time exploring all the rooms and offices of the factory and ran freely around the grounds. We got the spirit of improvisation and mounted a hand-basin on the slope opposite the dining hall. We were disappointed to find that the battery operated, factory carts would not work, and they were a bit heavy to push.

Grandfather was soon part of a committee to start a school. They even went to the extent of producing an aabits (alphabet book) with hand water coloured illustrations. Peeter was given a copy by grandfather (who always preferred Peeter to me as he was more out-going and cuter), which is now at the Tallinn educational museum. But I have a photocopy on disc. The only picture I have of Schwartzenbeck is one sent to us in autumn 1945, after we had left.

One sunny day, I met father walking up the main road from the front gate. There was much rejoicing, as we had no idea of what had happened to him. He had quite a harrowing time escaping from Czechoslovakia at the end of the war. It was one full story I got him to put down in detail before his death near Baltimore. He soon managed to get a position with the British Army. Through a couple of their doctors (one was Irish), he got the position of camp doctor at the Polish Camp, located at the nearby, large, brick, ex-German barracks at Wentorf. We were housed on the ground floor of a large barracks near the brick gate. Peeter and I were frequently taken along in the British doctors' cars and an ex-German ambulance truck. Once we went to Scwartzenbeck in a 2-stroke DKW car.

Parents took us for various walks and outings. Mum was rather disgusted when father asked us to keep an eye out for decent, discarded cigarette butts , as he felt the need for a smoke. We also went to the Hamburg Zoo by train. The artificial mountain for goats, had bomb damage but we still saw some animals. There was some excitement when Germans from the other side of the road from the gate, chased some Pole who had been undertaking some sort of robbery in a German house. A military truck was heavily bogged in front of the barracks parallel to ours and it took some effort to extract it from the mud.

After a visit to the US Zone, father located his mother and his sister's family, the Rammos, in Schlosshalde and managed to find a means for us to move there. We also took mum's parents from Schwartzenbeck. That was probably a mistake for father as they were not very fond of him and particularly grandmother could not help inflaming the situation in a marriage which was already stressed.

After briefly crowding in with the Rammos, we were given a couple of rooms in Wihelmshöhe in Turkheimer Str looking towards the mountain and the Germans' vegetable plots on the slope across the road. The Hakk family was in the same half of the house. My parents divorced at the end of '46 and father moved with his mother to a couple of rooms in Schlosshalde. We were at liberty to visit him whenever we wanted as long as we let mum know.

We also moved to Schlosshalde later, probably Weiler Str, the last one up the slope. Grandparents had a room on the first floor and we were on the ground floor below. Peeter and I found an artificial, aluminium leg with a sprung knee in the attic. We were told it had belonged to an Estonian soldier who had hung himself.

A couple of ex-soldiers lived in the lowest level with access from the garden. We were very taken by their little business of manufacturing small sheath knives with colourful handles, made from the plastic handle layers. The garden had at least one apple tree and currant and gooseberry bushes, from which we also got some. Perhaps at that stage the relationship with grandmother became too much of a strain for mum, and we moved to Wihelmshöhe again, to No 86 on the street between the loop in the main road up the mountain. We scrounged some packing cases with grandfather's assistance and attempted to add a wall to the little garden shed to make a cubby house.

Some chap next door was growing tobacco in the garden. In the winter the greatest amusement was the ice making frame, like a wooden, two storey, long house frame which had sprinklers mounted on the top timbers. They were turned on until the structure became quite filled with ice, which was then hacked off by workmen and chuted down to the ice storage shed on Karl Str. However while the ice was forming it formed a magical network of caves between the timbers of the structure and we enjoyed crawling through these. Much of the water not frozen on the framework formed a sheet of ice cover on the slope down to the street. I was terrified once when I had wandered a little too close to the slope and the only way off was a rather jarring slide down to the street level. However, it was not as bad as I feared.

In the summer we would climb up to the plateau above Wilhelmshöhe, up the slope which had been logged, to find wild strawberries among the stumps. I delighted my wife Shirley by finding some strawberries on the plateau. She had never experienced these delights. We drove along a track at the top in the hope of finding the shelter which I remembered.

But we only got to the base of the large cross, which had been erected on the edge of the plateau in remembrance of people who had lost their homes in the East, in Silesia and Prussia. Curiously, the original settlers of the Barossa Valley, came from there and it is sad that the stupid Allies gave this part of Germany to Poland. They had been welcomed to Australia by the original Scottish land owners (Angas and Coulthard) in 1836 when they were being persecuted for their Lutheran religion.

Grandfather would take us for walks and short train journeys all around the Geislingen area. Many of the forest paths had religious icons in shelters, which led to some forest chapel. Father also took us to places like Ödenturm and the museum.

When we visited the museum a number of times, it was crammed with all sorts of antique artefacts like suits of armour, swords and multi-barrelled pistols but when we went there in 2001, there were only a couple of pathetic items on display, including an iron framed school desk which had engraved with 'ESTONIA'. I was quite ashamed when struggling with my broken German, speaking to the older lady who was in charge.

I wonder who got all those fascinating items? In '48 – 49 we often went to the cinema in the shopping area, which is now over-run with Turks and quite run down. One time we bought some glass pens from a stationery shop there. They were shaped like a stylized watercolor brush with the bristles gently curved towards the tip. The twisting glass grooves would hold ink sufficient to write for a short period before you had to dip the pen in ink again, like a normal old fashioned nib. They only had one problem; the tip would wear to a flat with sharp edges, which could then cut into the paper.

By the second half of Grade One, we graduated from pencil printing to writing with fountain pen. This rather surprised the teacher in Australia. We had to revert to nib and ink-well but amazingly, the teacher permitted me to continue using the Copperplate style of script I had learned well. When I misbehaved at Schlosshalde, the punishment was to be sent to grandfather upstairs to do a page of my best writing. Contrary to popular myth, I rather grew to love calligraphy in later life, picking up a few refinements from old documents on my first job at the bank and now have a collection of good quality fountain pens which I use for writing to my ever diminishing number of correspondents.

Grandfather Rehe's main subject at Geislingen was woodwork, but also some basic English. The woodwork room was up in the attic level of the school, next to a room for motor mechanics. I was most humiliated when once stood outside the staff room door for a misdemeanour, to have grandfather come to enter from upstairs.

We were compelled to walk in groups, anticlockwise around the corridor during recess time on the dark red tile floor which was oiled for cleaning purposes. Someone discovered a neat trick, that, if you stood next to an unwary person and slid your foot against theirs, it would bring them down. I tried it successfully on some older, snooty girl who had made some unkind remark. However, in falling, she stained her stocking on the oily floor. Apart from the 'guard duty' at the staff room door, I had the crime written into my bad-deeds book to be counter-signed by mum. I received the appropriate tail-warming.

Another thing we discussed with horror was that the German kids next door could receive corporal punishment at school. I think it was from Grade 2 that we began having some lessons in basic English, in anticipation of our emigration to some English speaking country. I was bemused by one phrase we learned, which was: "I give my dog biscuits to eat". I thought this was rather quaint as biscuits were a rather scarce commodity in those days, and not to be wasted on dogs. I was unaware of the concept of dog biscuits.

From about 1947, mum began to attend the dressmaking school at Rappenäcker and eventually became an instructor there. Those skills enabled her to earn a living as a dressmaker in Australia as her English was not adequate to get a job in secretarial work, for which she had trained in the 30s. We were too far from the city for her to look for other types of work.

From about that time too, father had managed to get work at the big US military hospital in Heidelberg, where he also undertook some study. He came back home a few times on weekends in a Jeep with a Polish driver. I was once given a chance to steer it while sitting on father's lap and had to be assisted when the thing would not straighten out after a turn. I wasn't aware that you had to straighten the steering again after turning a corner. We went to visit Aunt Helga's family in it on one of those occasions and were rather jealous when the cousins also wanted to sit in 'our Jeep'.

On a couple of occasions, Mr. Muru in the next room at 86, took us to evening films at Rappenäcker. They were mostly American films, whereas we saw German films and the Wochenschau at the main, town cinema. I think we saw "The Last of the Mohicans" at Rappenäcker after father had at one time read the German book to us. I was stunned how similar the recent Daniel Day-Lewis version was to my recollections of the book. I think it was early in 1949 that father emigrated to the US with his mother and possibly his future wife Aleksandra. He left me his large glass ear washing syringe to use as a water pistol. Aleksandra Preiman lived about one or two houses farther along father's street. I met her there and again once on a visit to Australia and in '78 when Shirley and I visited father near Baltimore. She was a lovely, gentle lady and they lived happily until his death in '86.

Mum and her parents had agreed to emigrate to Australia and the applications had been submitted but then grandmother had one of her flare-ups and compelled grandfather to change their applications to the US. I think it may have been because of her dislike of mum's friend Paula Altmann who had already settled in Australia. Mum was fed up and continued with our applications to Australia. All my adult life I have been glad that she did. We received Polio vaccinations in a clinic in Rappenäcker, which was a great thing because at that time, Australia was still suffering from this malady to a large extent.

While mum was making final arrangements we went to the summer camp near Geislingen. It was most enjoyable and the young men who conducted activities really knew how to interest us. We learned songs such as "Kusti, Kusti Anna Piitsa" (to the tune of John brown's Body) and the old Australian song "Kookaburra Sits in the Old Gum Tree".

We returned to camp for a second session when in a few days we were called back, as **we were about to depart. After a train trip to Stuttgart and then through Switzerland, we ended up in Genoa for 3 days until the SS Cyrenia departed.**

It was quite a decent passenger ship, but we and other Estonians (among them Mrs. Janov and the Pungars, with children) were assigned to the very bow of the ship. Not the most stable location at sea. I was in the second cabin on the right, with Peeter and some men with the anchor-chain tube running through our cabin.

No. 86 at Wilhelmshöhe

BLACK AND WHITE IS THE LANGUAGE OF YOUTH.

Sometimes everything a child sees seems to involve some degree of good. They have no gut wrenching decision to make. Would it be so easy to chose among degrees of bad?

How would a child struggle to deal with their emotions and actions when the world presents the seemingly less evil option?

How do they cope with what the parents offer perhaps decades down the track?

How does it compare with the seeming Utopia which is but a fight away?

If the parents themselves are struggling to be available to the child, with few resources to offer it, and address their own distress by acting out on the child, who might the child turn to?

How easy is it to coerce a desperate child towards promised warmth, camaraderie and respect? MM

Jahnhalle Christmas 1948

With grandparents in '49

ESTONIA AS THE CHAOS WAS ERUPTING

Hannes, mum (Anna), Peeter, radio on left towards window at Tähe tn. Door to father's surgery on right.

Peeter & Hannes at Järva-Jaani, Aug. '44.

The Pärt family at Back door

Hannes at the front of Maanuse much earlier.

Hannes and Peeter at Maanuse Farm,

Hans Aschendorf

Saun in the background.

Grandfather's cottage in the 30s, no trace of it in 2001. Grandmother's garden

The Donau

LIFE AFTER LEAVING ESTONIA

We still had our winter clothes from Tartu, with leather soled, felt boots and fur hats. I was bawling because father made us get down onto the ice and I did not trust the stuff until I had actually been forced to try it.

Some of the men carrying camp beds.

A performance by Schwartzenbeck pupils

Peeter nailing the wall in cubby, Jüri with saw on left of roof and I on the right beside him.

Peeter on left, under tent corner.

The shelter on the plateau above Wilhelmshöhe with grandparents.

Ödenturm, a lookout tower for the castle

REMINISCING WITH BRUNO LEEPIN

Bruno Leepin's linocut 1962

The plateau beyond the Helfenstein ruins where the market gardens were situated. Photos: MM taken 2003

Melbourne now sprawls for at times fifty km from the CBD with a sector to its south annexed by Port Phillip Bay.

When we as children arrived in Melbourne, the latter was very much smaller and our families bought cheap land clustered around the various refugee camps dotted around Melbourne.

During our student days we clustered together through shared interests and the clusters still keep in touch. Bruno and I both have a love for art which has contributed to our bridging our sprawling metropolis.

One of Bruno's memory clips stays in my mind: perhaps because it matches one of mine and also in some way a snippet of Boris Lees' story. We both still wonder where was that cavernous dark place, where a wall of water gushed amid a hoard of our people in that cavern. We were both only two to three years old at that stage. And it is possible that those images represent three distinct events.

Bruno told of a German man who was popular with the kids both upon the Castle ruins plateau and down town. He had acquired some form of old war machine and turned it into a mechanical farm tool: A very noisy one which could be heard down in the valley and attracted the kids (especially small boys). At times he would allow the boys to ride pillion with him as he worked the fields: What a treat for them.

Food, like everything was scarce: Well except time! Our parents put it to good use. Bruno tells of his mother knitting beautiful ski jumpers which she sold to American troops to go skiing in the nearby lofty mountains. She bought the wool from a Jewish wool merchant in Ulm and knitted well into the night, year after year, to earn those cigarettes and other commodities which were stashed in her wardrobe and which she traded the jumpers for: Those stashes were to buy things which were needed for her twins Bruno and Erika. That is how our folks ensured our day to day survival.

Bruno continued on to talk about Geislingen: High above on the hillside near the Helfenstein ruins the German folks had vegetable gardens which our folks would raid to supplement our food rations. Mothers of course took their children with them. Children were lively and noisy and attracted the Germans who were not pleased with their gardens being raided.

I believe that it is also up there that our folks caught rabbits for the dinner tables: and foxes too. They were good for fur: don't know what happened to their flesh.

Bruno talked yet of another source of vegetables: They were bought with cigarettes, powdered eggs and other commodities from an couple with a sausage dog. They too had a large greenhouse vegetable garden on the Helfenstein plateau. **They were gentle couple who were very kind to children. They had lost all their three sons to the war. Who said Geislingen had been left untouched by the war: How many such stories there were:** My little German friend, Dieter had lost his father, also a soldier in Ulm. Why is it that we still measure loss in terms of real estate..MM

HELGA MERITS
IN THE PARENTS' SHOES: A DIALOGUE WITH ILVI JOE

Helga is one of our cohort: She is currently working on a documentary of our journey. This includes interviews with some of the authors who have shared their stories in "When the Noise had Ended". This is part of one of the interviews.

I have often wondered how it must have been for the mothers in the wartime and post-wartime period. Most of the time they were on their own and had to carry all responsibilities for the children themselves. They could not share their worries and fears with their children and had to keep these emotions inside. But needing to keep these emotions inside, most of the time all emotions were kept inside.

Somehow it seems to me to have been, besides very difficult and traumatic, also a very lonely period for these mothers and I wondered how they kept on going and if later on they have been able to show their emotions to their children.

Although this is not part of your project and not a question, I would make a comment nevertheless. Before the camp in geislingen was opened (Oct.11, 1945) and our arrival there, we who fled in the midst of war and survived it - meaning the bombings, the destruction, the deprivation, the hunger, etc. War is hell wherever it takes place: No question that the experience was most traumatic for the adults, because children are somewhat protected by their innocence, the care and comfort given by parents, etc.

When we consider the Geislingen period, I think it has to be seen in contrast to the hell that preceded it. Also, an important consideration is that our parents were not isolated or alone in geislingen, it was a community of circa 4000 Estonians who immediately went about setting up school, cultural and social life, health care and an administrative structure. All of this activity under the umbrella of UNRRA and the American military (the sight of American military jeeps is indelibly stored in my brain!). The latter was security for the DP camp residents. Quite naturally, the adults wondered about the future, because one could not stay in a DP camp forever.

Reading your part in the book about the flight from Estonia to Geislingen I wondered how long it took for you, as a child, after you arrived in Geislingen, to realize you arrived at a place where you could stay and where it was safe and where was more or less enough food.

We arrived in Geislingen on my 8th birthday, the day on which the camp was opened. I don't recall having any special realization about the place. By that time, we had already been in two refugee centers and it probably felt like another one in a series. However, I do recall starting school (the fleeing had deprived me of starting school in fall 1944), sledding down the hill in Schlosshalde, joining the girl scouts, not being hungry, taking piano and ballet lessons, all of us (mother and four children) living in one room.

Did the fear and anxiety of the flight stay with you for a long time?
No. Perhaps, because I never was in a building that got a direct hit, I did not witness anyone being shot dead, I did not become ill as did my brother (appendicitis) and sister (pneumonia) which must have given much anxiety to my mother.

Did you hope to return soon to Estonia?
Frankly, at that age I did not think about that. Certainly, the adults did have such hopes.

Did you hope your father would arrive one day?
I do not recall missing my father and that's probably because the political situation in Estonia, starting 1939, kept him away from home a lot.

Did Geislingen feel for you as a safe place, perhaps as an Estonian village, but then surrounded by Germany?
Yes, one could describe it that way.

> Wasteland is where a man is not a human being.
> Everybody knows it: everybody denies it,
> and no-one is willing to help,
> Time, only time, is able to help.
> From **Gunnar Neeme: "Mist of Time"**

GUNNAR NEEME

Ants continues: There are also a couple of interesting drawings showing their travels from Danzig and through Germany including Gera where Aarne was born in February 1945 and Ansbach where I was born in May 1946.
Being an artist, the Germans out my father's talents to good use by repainting damaged war trains which is shown in one of the drawings.
There is also a photo of Isa, Ema, Aarne, Vanaema and myself taken at Valga Laager in March 1947.
Valga was our last DP camp before we left for Australia via Naples and the Suez Canal.
I have no memories of camp life in Germany other than becoming violently ill on diesel fumes in the bus on the day we left. I have also vague memories of the harbour in Naples but that is about it.

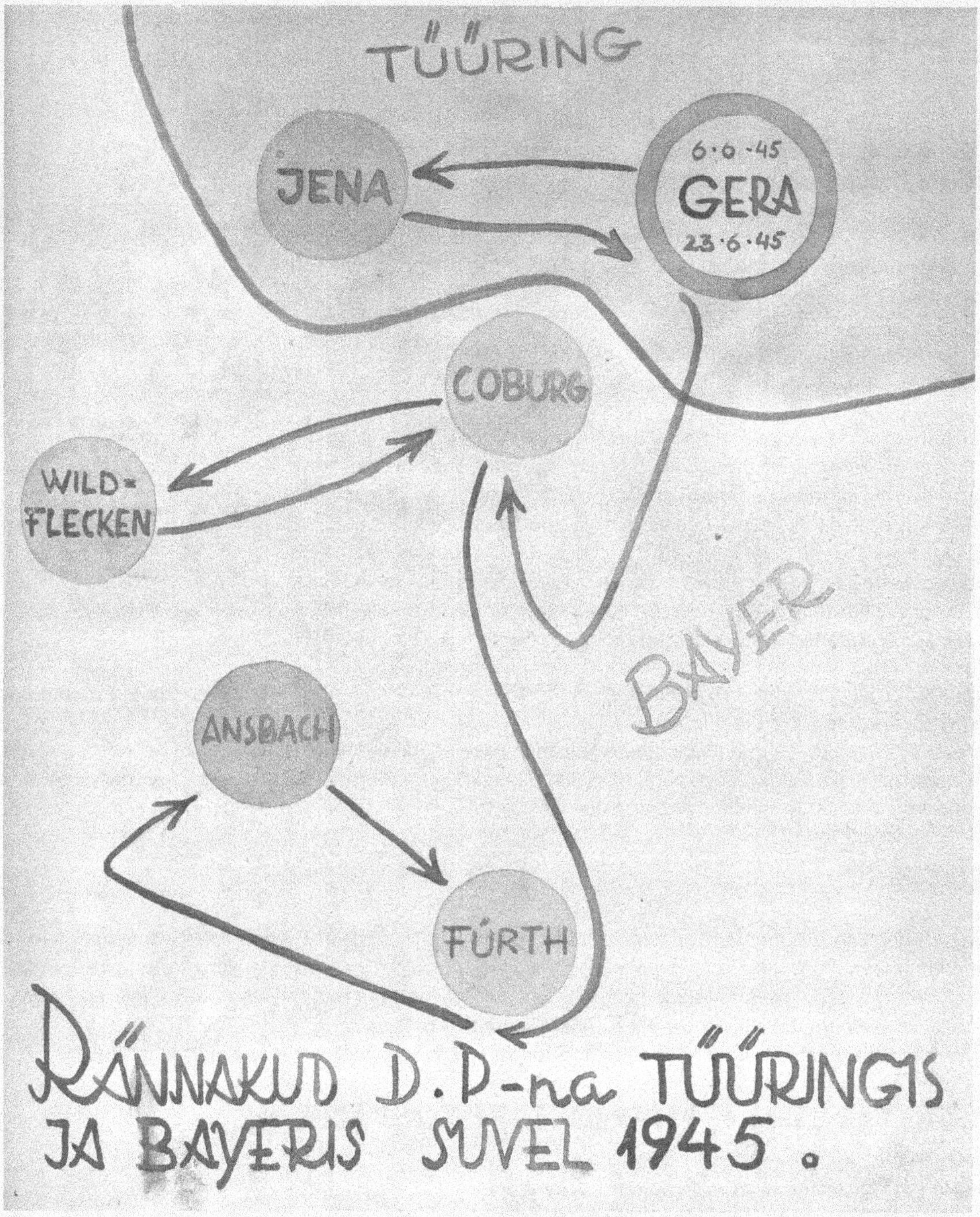
TÜÜRING
JENA
6·6·45
GERA
23·6·45
COBURG
WILD=
FLECKEN
BAYER
ANSBACH
FÜRTH
RÄNNAKUD D.P-na TÜÜRINGIS
JA BAYERIS SUVEL 1945.

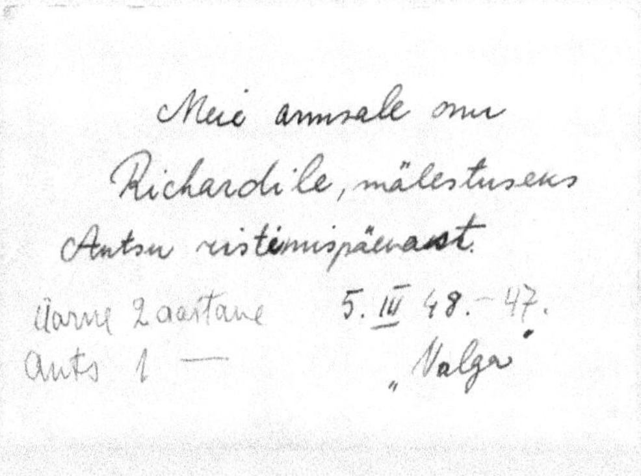
Meie armsale onu
Richardile, mälestuseks
Antsu ristimispäevast.
Aarne 2 aastane
Ants 1 —
5. III 48. – 47.
„Valga"

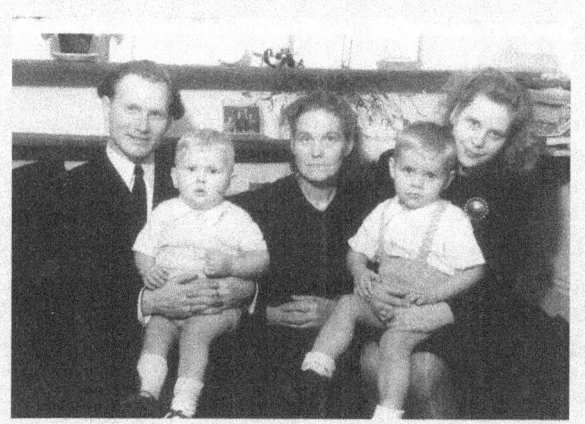

GLIMPSES OF GEISLINGEN CAMP: GGM

RABBITS:

Aino Murk Naeris: Yes, my mother raised rabbits....when we arrived in the U.S. I had to wear my brown rabbit fur coat to Kindergarten and I remember hating it ! I was very happy when I finally outgrew it.

Ulo Kuhi: Apparently raising rabbits was very popular in Geislingen. I recall Aino Murk telling me her mother raised rabbits in their back yard on Rappenacker Strasse.

Merike Tamm; Weren't the rabbits also used for their fur?
My mother came to the US with a rabbit fur jacket, that I believe was acquired in Geislingen.
I think that some parents might have tried to shield their children from the reality of the purpose of the rabbits by claiming, when they disappeared, that they died of old age. That was my thought when I read in our book (WNE) this passage by Peep Aarne Vesilind "Some time during this time we started to raise rabbits. Not sure why this was, since we would not eat them and just waited for them to die of old age". I have had many pet rabbits. Their normal life span is 6 or 7 years. I have had a couple of rabbits live to nearly 10. There was no reason for pet rabbits to die early in Geislingen!!

Photo from Inge Pruks

Mai: I still have a fur collar archived in a box: It came from Geislingen. Maybe its the same one that appears on my collars in some of the photos:
It never occurred to me that it could be rabbit tho I have no idea of what it might have been from, maybe fox given mother talked about such paraphernalia: I should compare it with the photos! I actually cannot recall rabbits in my stay at Geislingen. Strange! Given some folks in our street kept them.

CLOTHING:

Ilvi Joe: I don't recall whether I've commented before in the list, but every time I see photos of us in the DP camp I marvel at how well dressed we are (again, a tribute to our parents). Looking at the photo of the two boys (I presume they are Hannes and Peeter) one would never think that they are war refugees - they are well dressed, down to the tasselled knee-socks (how fashionable!).
In the other photo of a roomful of children, all look very tidy - girls with bows and boys with ties.

PROBABLY STILL IN THE CLOTHING THEY FLED IN

Arriving in Geislingen in people wagons: Why were the people so happy someone asked: Perhaps arriving in purgatory after travelling through hell is a joyous event.

Such mode of travel was pretty typical of those times. There had been countless journeys in whatever wagons were available and where the railroads were intact.

The clothing still looks in moderately good order. Many wore several layers while in transit, and over the years in camps it was to gradually become thread bare. MM

224

MAARE KASK/TAMM

MY ROAD

I was born in Tallinn (Estonia's capital) in 1935, as the oldest child in our family: Our family consisted of my mother, father and grandmother. I had two younger brothers. My parents gave me the name Maare, which means the sea, as in "Mare Balticum" (The Baltic Sea) My parents perceive me to be like the sea: Infinite and tranquil, but also stormy and deep. Perhaps that explains my life long sense of solidarity with the sea.

I was four years old when the Second World War broke out. I do have a memory of that September day in 1939. It was afternoon and I was in the kitchen with my mother. She was about to bake a cake and it smelled sweet. The radio was on, as it used to be. Suddenly the program was stopped and a radio voice announced that the German army had invaded the Polish border and that Great Britain and France were at war with Germany. The war had begun. The peaceful atmosphere in the kitchen changed to nervousness and uncertainly. My mother suddenly became tense and concerned. I was too young to understand her explanation: I could not understood what had happened, but understood that it was something very serious and tedious.

Almost immediately after the outbreak of war, the Russians required to build military bases in Estonia. Ten thousand, upon ten thousand Russian soldiers, along with vast numbers of engineers came into the country. In the middle of June 1940 Tallinn's streets were crowded with Russian soldiers. Estonians, a people that for thousands of years had farmed their fields by the Baltic Sea, were now dragged into the red terror's labyrinth and fear invaded the entire the country.

When the communists took over the country my father lost his employment at the radio, where he had been a journalist. Most intellectual people lost their employment. There was major confusion everywhere. The newspaper Päevaleht (the daily), where father had worked earlier, was taken over by the state and changed its name to Rahva Hääl (the people's voice).

After some weeks, people began to disappear: No one dared to speak openly any longer: One could not distinguish friend from foe.

That summer my parents divorced. Why? The times were very nervous. The arrests continued to increase in numbers; the house investigations likewise. Everyone who had been dismissed from his/her work by the Russians was considered with suspicion, as a "class enemy": That indeed included their families. My parents considered that to optimally protect the family they had to divorce.

In autumn 1940 my father joined the "Metsavennad", i.e. the forest brothers or the green guerilla as it also was called. One of the forest brother's tasks was to collect and to provide information. To obtain the necessary information they needed to have courage, fortitude and strategic skills. It was a dangerous life. To become a forest brother was almost tantamount to signing your own death sentence. For forest brothers, there was no turning back. The red occupation power considered them as bandits, and the penalty for each of them was death. Even if my parents were divorced there still was a persisting threat: My mother and the rest of my family lived in a constant fear.

The war continued. Then one day something terrible happened. On Saturday the thirteenth June 1941 several hundred goods wagons were despatched to Tallinn's station. These were wagons which during normal times transported livestock and goods. In the early hours of Sunday morning before dawn, when people were asleep, Russian soldiers forced their way into the homes, rustled and woke the sleeping people and read their "accusation" documents to them. The children cried. They were pushed aside and the apartments were searched. The soldiers ordered the families to pack together the most necessary: To take with them warm clothing and personal needs. Then the trucks drove them to the railway station. What the solders "forgot" to tell them was that on the station the family members had to go separate roads - men by themselves and women and children together. This was an extensive mass movement of people, determined by NKVD and carried out by Russian soldiers.

After these events, it was impossible for us to stay in Tallinn. I and my brother along with our grandmother moved to a small town - Loksa - seventy kilometers east of Tallinn. Mother stayed in Tallinn since she had a job to deal with. She joined us later. **After the Russian occupation, father came back home** and mother and father **married again.**

THE YEARS AT LOKSA
Loksa is an idyllic place. The small town is a region of great natural beauty at the open sea, seventy kilometers east of Tallinn. It has a kilometer long white beach that is trimmed of pine forest. The pines in the forest belt have stood there since memorial times and transpire a sweet smell of resin and eucalyptus. The seawater at this beach is rather warm in summers.

The summer 1941, when we moved to Loksa, there was an elementary school, a pharmacy and a health care centre. There was also a post office where the post arrived daily. In the middle of the settlement, a very old church was located, surrounded by a beautiful cemetery. The house we leased and lived in during these years, was situated opposite this cemetery.

In the summer of 1941 the Russian occupation came to an end, and was replaced with the German occupation. German soldiers were located in different buildings in central Loksa, where they monitored and checked food production. The food had already been rationed during the Russian times, and this rationing continued.

When the German soldiers were not occupied with their work they patrolled the streets. They wore Nazi uniforms, trimmed with medals and crosses. Several of them had a death skull with crossed bones on their uniform collar. On their head, they usually wore a gray steel helmet. They looked almost like the soldiers in our picture books. The soldiers talked with the local population and also with us children. - Wie get´s ihnen? (How do you do?) they said when we met them on the street. No one of us could understand German: Neither adults nor children, but you could always make yourself understood with the aid of gestures. We children considered the German soldiers to be very polite and kind. They always saluted us, clicked together their shoe heels, and raised their hand to the helmet. They usually gave sweets to us children.

A year passed with relatively calm, at least for us children. We played our games and were rather unconcerned about the future. In the autumn 1942 I began in the elementary school's first class. I had waited eagerly to begin school, partly to become a schoolchild and partly to study and get knowledge. The early childhood with only games and noise was now over for me.

I enjoyed the school from the first day. I had two main teachers, Mr. and Mrs. Aus. Mrs. Aus, who was called Anette, taught the Estonian language which meant reading and writing, and German. Artur Aus taught mathematics, geography and history. What's more, we had a drawing teacher and a singing teacher. There was also a teacher who taught us practical subjects. Religious study was taught by Mrs. Soopere.

Those two school years passed peacefully and quietly. Then 1944 arrived. This year was the fourth year of war in Estonia. The year began with a feeling of unrest and uneasiness. Leningrad which had been under siege for more than two years began its war of liberation. Years of famine, diseases and hostile fire had held the Leningrad's citizens united together as a big family, and now they were ready to liberate their town. Already after a week, on January 22, the newspapers announced that the Germans retreated in a great state of disorder. And on January 27 the 890 day long Leningrad siege was over.

In this chaotic situation the Estonian army, whose purpose was to defend Estonia's boundary at Narva, regrouped. Now, the Estonian civilian population became aware that the war was apparent and becoming precarious. The bigger towns - Tallinn, Tartu and Narva - were exposed to air-raids and the bombs that were dropped created devastation on a large scale. The houses were blown up or were set on fire: Many families became homeless and did not know how they would find a new roof over their head.

In this situation, we children were freed from school and black out paper was placed on the windows. The whole of Estonia was soon in darkness. The aeroplanes flew over the country, both from German and from Russian directions, and the engine noise cut through the air. When the planes flew over Loksa we had to take protection. We hid ourselves in an outhouse in the garden. This little house could protect us against spatter but not against direct bomb hits. It was fairly intimidating to have these sirens alerting people about danger, but there was no real danger for us since no bombs had dropped over Loksa.

In the spring of 1944 I could see that my mother was pregnant. The baby, my youngest brother, was expected to be born in the middle of April. During the entire occupation everything was rationed. It was especially difficult to get clothing. But pregnant women got a special certificate with which they were entitled to buy baby equipment.

Mother got such certificate and had to go to Tallinn in order to buy baby clothes. It was early in the morning Thursday March 9 when she took the bus from Loksa's bus station to Tallinn. She planned to be in Tallinn a couple of days.

Approximately half past six in the evening the first air raid began. Russian aeroplanes dropped their load of flares (a kind of shining bombs) that stayed in the air above Tallinn and lit up the city. Such shining bombs had in popular speech acquired the name "Christmas trees" since they resembled these. The entire sky was covered with "Christmas trees" that helped the enemy to see where to release their bomb loads.

Simultaneously with the sky being lit up by "the Christmas trees" sirens begun howl. German anti-aircraft artillery began to shoot against the bombers and after some minutes the entire Tallinn was in the roars of shooting and falling bombs.

That evening and night it was not a strategic type of bombing, that is customary in many attacks during the war: Instead the bombs fell indiscriminately over the entire city. Over three thousand bombs fell over Tallinn; half of them explosive bombs and the other half fire bombs. The fire bombs were extremely dangerous. An explosive bomb could destroy a building, but a fire bomb could set a big area alight. Approximately five hundred persons were killed that night, another five hundred were injured and over twenty thousand people lost their homes. In the morning of March 10, Tallinn looked like a dead city.

I, my grandmother and my brother Hando, watched the bombing during the entire night. We sat at the kitchen window in Loksa and saw the red fire glow over Tallinn. The sky was a flaming red as the whole of Tallinn was on fire. We heard the aeroplanes passing over Loksa and we knew that they soon would dump their load of bombs over Tallinn. Hour after hour we sat there and listened to the bombs exploding. None of us had any comfort to share. We sat encompassed in our own anxiety and in a confusion of feelings.

After two days, mother came home from Tallinn. She was tired and pale. We ran towards her crying but glad over that she was still alive.

Latter, when we were older, mother told us how she had experienced the bombing night in Tallinn. I will share her story.

"The day after the bombing I saw that all windows in the apartment were broken and there was glass splinters everywhere. The wind whirled around in the rooms and I tried to collect our property into the middle of the room so that they would not bluster away. When I looked out through the window I saw the whole city on fire, houses that had crumbled together, towers that had converted into mounds of ruins.

I and my brother Hando when the war broke out

I could not do anything in our apartment, but started to go towards Loksa. There were no bus connections any longer and one simply had to go. On the road out from Tallinn I saw groups of people from the fire department who gathered together the victims, drew dead bodies from the ruins, and quenched fires. It was smoke everywhere and I had difficultly breathing. I soaked my head scarf and had it in front of my face.

A little bit further along the street I saw five or six dead people lying on that street, and none of them had a head. I became very anxious, fearing that I was going crazy. But I had neither gone crazy nor imagined things that did not exist; rather it was the reality that I saw before me. When I passed some shattered bombed out houses, I saw people digging among the ruins seeking after their relatives.

They were as paralyzed, no loud voices, no panic, not even weeping, but quietly they sat in front of the ruins of their houses that once had been their homes. After some hours, when I had walked five-six kilometers, a car stopped and the driver asked if I wanted a ride. He drove me halfway to Loksa. Another car drove me almost to Loksa, and then I had only five-six kilometers to go in order to come home. Tired and hungry I finally came home and met you, my crying children and also a crying grandmother."

Ten days after Tallinn's bombing, April 20, was Hitler's birthday. That day we were free from school. On the streets in Loksa German soldiers paraded with flags in their hands to celebrate Hitler's birthday.

In our family there was something more important happening than the dictator's birthday. It was the birthday of my younger brother. Mother was very pleased. She was especially pleased that the newborn was a bonny boy. She had been anxious that her traumatic experiences from the bombing night in Tallinn would have damaged the child. But the boy looked normal and seemed to feel well.

In Loksa with Hando

My younger brother was named Raivo. Grandmother, who was a little bit superstitious, was worried that Raivo had been born on Hitler's birthday. - It foreshadowed no good for the boy, she said: That there are always connections between different events and we do not know how these connections could express themselves.

Perhaps it does not matter when the boy is still small but something unexpected can happen further on, she meant: The two, Raivo and Hitler, will always be joined by their common birthday, and if this might lead to success or bad luck for the boy's part only the future can tell.

Time passed and the summer arrived, our last summer in Estonia. One day when I was alone on the beach something terrible happened. Suddenly a bomber plane flew low above my head and dropped a bomb. The bomb detonated with a horrible sound, and there was smoke everywhere. The plane turned and came back to drop another bomb. I ran as fast as I could to a ditch and throw myself down into it.

Everything went black for me, and I was scared to death. I wanted to scream but got no air, and I felt extremely helpless. I do not remember how the bombing ended and how I got back home. This event was one of those aggressive war events when the Russian aeroplanes tried to damage Loksa's harbor.

I turned nine years of age on July 24. Some days earlier, on June 20, there had been an attack against Hitler. The newspapers told us that Hitler survived. His hair and his legs had been burned, his right arm had been injured and his eardrums had burst, but he was alive.

Nevertheless, it was a kind of turning point for the war. About the same time the Russian army had reached Narva and we knew that we could not stay in Estonia forever but had to flee. My father - who had joined the Estonian army (Eesti Leegion) as a foreign correspondent - was on this occasion on leave. Therefore it was decided that he would begin to try to get us tickets to one of the boats that transported refugees from Tallinn to Gotenhafen. He told us that he had to go back to the army himself but that we would meet in Berlin. That was the last time we saw him during the war. It took several years before we could meet again.

I remember my last birthday in Estonia. It was a hot summer day and I was out picking flowers. I picked a bouquet of blue cornflowers and red poppies and mixed them with wheat ears. It was a beautiful bouquet. I knew that we had only some months left in Estonia before we had to leave for Germany. Therefore, I said good-bye to my childhood world, from the idyllic Loksa. My gaze swept over the wheat fields and I remembered how the farmers early in the spring had sown on the land. Now, the grain had matured and ripened. I remembered also the fields covered with snow in wintertime. I also farewelled my loved marine beach with its waves that came from far away from here and told us their secrets. I felt very sad that day because I knew that an epoch in my life was over. I had been happy in Loksa and did not know what the future held for us.

Some weeks thereafter we moved to Tallinn. There, we had to prepare us for the journey to Germany. We had to pack our things, say farewell to my other grandmother and to our friends. We too bade farewell of Tallinn, a changed Tallinn. A lot of the city had been destroyed, the whole blocks where in ruins and the small houses on our street had been obliterated. At last, when our farewell visits were over, the day for our departure from Estonia arrived.

THROUGH GERMANY

It was a sunny afternoon in the middle of September 1944 when we came to Tallinn's harbor and began to start our travel to Gotenhafen. Our family stood there, on an embankment, among many other families and waited to be allowed to board the ship. Mother had a big suit-case and a small bag in one hand and with the other hand she held the baby carriage where Raivo lay. Grandmother carried a big trunk and held Hando by the hand. I had a small suit-case with my clothing, and another suit-case that contained our food. It was supposed to be a temporary leave. We were sure that we would be able to return to Estonia in a couple of months.

The ship, named Watherland, would depart six o'clock in the evening. The time was now half past four. After quite a while, we could board the ship and got our places on lower deck. It was a small cabin with two double sleeping-bunks. I and Hando would lie on one of the bunks, mother and Raivo above us and grandmother on the third bunk. Yet another old woman was in this cabin.

Just when we had taken off our outdoor clothes, and I and Hando were to try out how it would be to sleep with our feet against each other, the sirens sounded. Like a flock of birds, the Russian aeroplanes flew over Tallinn's port and begun to drop their loads of bombs. At the same time we could hear the roaring rumble from the anti-aircraft that shot at the aeroplanes. There was a deafening noise everywhere and the ship shook properly. Put on your safety vests, came across the boat's speakers. Put on your safety vests immediately. Lay down on your bunks. Hando and I crawled to the same bunk; mother crawled with Raivo up in her bunk and grandmother sat at the edge of her bunk. No one of us had time to put on our safety vests.

Then we heard the bombs falling. I felt scared to death. To be trapped in a ship and to have the threat of death above oneself was more than I could tolerate. My feet begun to shake, my teeth begun to chatter, and my heart pounded wildly. Hando panicked. He sobbed loudly, called for mother, and began to cry. "Is this the end?" I asked myself "Does it feel like this when one has to die? "

Don't be afraid, grandmother said when she saw how frightened we were. - Everything has an end, also the bombing, she ascertained. And after a while it really came to an end.

The following day we docked in Gothenhafen. Barely arrived in the harbor we were met by well organized activity. With the precision and effectiveness of Germans the big ship was emptied rapidly, and long columns of trucks were waiting on the dock in order to transport refugees to the railway station or to temporary refugee camps. Already on the boat, the registration had began. Those who had relatives in Germany could continue immediately. The others were transported to the transition camp in Gotenhafen. When we arrived in the camp we were given food. I and Hando got a dish of porridge; mother and grandmother got a cup of ersatz coffee and a sandwich. Even Raivo, who was now four months old, got complementary milk. It was a good thing since mother did not have any milk to give to Raivo, but this milk complement ration at least gave Raivo some food.

Since our goal was Berlin and mother had all the travel documents needed, we went to the camp supervisor to ask how we could leave for Berlin. But there was a obstruction. " You cannot go to Berlin,"the officer said, "no families with children are allowed to go to Berlin. It is too dangerous there. The permanent bombings have turned Berlin into a city of ruins, and it is both difficult and dangerous to go there. Most families with children have already been evacuated from Berlin. I regret," the officer said, "but we must follow our protocol"

What will we do now? We had an appointment with father that we would meet in Berlin and now the road was closed. We were informed that there was a vast number of temporary refugee camps over the whole of Germany. One of them was in Austria near Linz, and it was to Austria that most people who had Berlin as a destination were sent. So, we started our journey towards Austria.

The first stage of the travel was Gotenhafen - Dresden. The train from Gotenhafen was crowded but surprisingly we got sitting places. Our documents were of the kind that German soldiers were obliged to give us their places. In the crowded train the people stood in the corridors and German soldiers stood on the steps. But we were seated. The train did not follow its ordinary route. It took a long time before we came to any place. Sometimes, the train stood still, sometimes it backed. It took almost the entire day before we arrived at the Hauptbahnhof in Dresden.

Almost immediately after our arrival at the station, the air-raid warning went. People ran to the air-raid shelter rooms. We and the other families in this spring group ran also. All our things were left on the platform. Mother carried Raivo, grandmother held Hando by the hand and I had with me the suit-case with our food.

The air-raid shelter on Hauptbanhof contained several thousand people. The shelter lacked ventilation and was almost like a bunker. Since it was crowded with people the air became poor quickly and it was difficult to breathe. Old women sat quietly begging to God. Younger persons looked around in an anxious way. We were anxious too but we still sat quietly, only Raivo started to cry. We heard explosions, but nobody knew what these explosions meant: Our anxiety abounded fast. After a while the sirens sounded announcing that the danger was over for this time. Then it was time to leave the shelter.

We went back to the station. Our luggage was left on the platform. Now, we had to wait for the next train. We asked the railway staff when next train southwards would go. "You do not understand how it is," the man in the ticket box said. "Dresden is filled with military traffic. It means that we have over thirty military trains passing through Dresden every day, therefore we do not know when there is a train for civilian traffic. So continue to wait." And we waited. After some hours a train came and we could proceed with our journey.

Of this long journey which followed I have only fragmented memories. We were on the train but did not know where it actually was or where it was heading. The train went to and fro. Sometimes, we could catch a glimpse of the name on some station, but after some hours we seemed to be back at a previous place again. On some stations, Red Cross sisters stood and divided up food. We got bread and milk. It was cold on the train and we were extremely tired. Mother placed Raivo to sleep up on the net shelf where people usually have their luggage. We others tried to sleep where we sat. Often the train was stopping somewhere because of a traffic-jam further forward. On these occasions we got off the train and moved around to increase our blood circulation. But we had to remain right next to the train all the time, because it started always without a forewarning. Once, grandmother nearly missed the train.

By such means our travel continued several weeks. We were tired, hungry and anxious. The train stopped now and then when there was a bombing attack. Then, we had to leave the train and find protection out somewhere. It was a very frustrating travel situation which lasted day after day, week after week. At last, we arrived in Vienna. When the train stopped in the Hauptbahnhof we picked up our things and got off. Almost immediately the air-raid warning started to sound and people ran to the air raid safety rooms.

Perhaps, it was the fatigue after the long journey; perhaps it was a feeling of helplessness that made us feel quite indifferent. One has to die anyway, we rationalized and that spared us from much anxiety.

THE REFUGEE CAMP IN WAXENBERG
After some weeks in Vienna we had to travel on. It must have been in the beginning of November 1944. Our destination was Waxenberg, a small society approximately 25 kilometers from Linz, high up on a mountain top. In Waxenberg was a big refugee camp. Refugees were housed in a big orange two storey building. The building had originally been a castle, but after the First World War it was rebuilt to one castle - Schloß Waxenberg - and in it was a beautiful chapel in Baroque style. Now the entire building was used as a refugee camp. The camp was a dwelling place for two or three hundred refugees of different nationalities. There were Estonians, Poles, Czechs, Hungarians and even

some Russians. Families without infants were expected to work and were sent to different factories. Those with infants, as was our family, did not have to work.

In the camp there was also a school. The refugee children had to go to school. Since we, the refugees and belonged to many nationalities the education was given in German. I remember that every morning we had to listen to something that Hitler had said and we had to make the Hitler greeting, "Heil Hitler". Both I and Hando went to this school, I in third class and Hando in first class. I do not remember much from the education since I did not understand the German language so well. We were permitted to use an Estonian-German dictionary, but regardless, most of what the teacher said remained unclear. I remember that I often was tired and had difficulty to keep my eyes open.

Daily, we listened on the telecasts from BBC. This British radio station gave once a day news in German. The official German radio was filled with propaganda. To listen to the British radio was forbidden. Our radio was hidden under a blanket under the table. When the telecasts began we laid on the floor with our heads under the table and the blanket over us, so that no other person outside the room could hear the radio voices.

In the beginning of February we heard from the BBC broadcast that the big Russian offensive that had started in the middle of January was a complete disaster for the German army. East - and West-Prussia was isolated from Germany, and by January 27, 1945 the Russian army was approximately three hundred kilometers in on German land. The Russians were now only 150 kilometers from Berlin. We had not heard anything from father and were now nervous about the silence. As a foreign correspondent father had to be near the front and to report from there. Anything could happen in such a situation.

The war came nearer and nearer. Daily the bomber planes passed Waxenberg on their route to Vienna, Linz, Salzburg and Innsbruck. One day in the beginning of April when we, children, were out doors playing, an enormous number of attack planes flew over our heads, so many that the entire sky was colored black. The air planes did not threaten us but were aimed against the cities. We saw how they bombed Linz which was only about twenty kilometers from us, down in the valley. When the airplanes had dropped off their fatal load they fled away and left behind a town in fire. We understood that the war was now very near.

In the camp, there were rumors that the Russian front was already near Vienna. Our family along with another family thought that it was high time to do something, and we realized that we now had to abandon Waxenberg. Our goal was Switzerland since it was a neutral country.

ON THE WAY TOWARDS THE WEST FRONT

It was not easy to leave the refugee camp. Only those people who had a valid reason were allowed to leave the camp. We did not have such a reason. But somehow we managed to get out of the camp. In Linz we intended to take the train towards Switzerland. When we arrived in Linz we had to wait a long time. The trains no longer travelled by timetables. People stood on platforms and waited. The platforms were overcrowded and it was necessary to hold together so that one would not be lost. Many families were separated during these days of escape.

At last, a train came. But it was packed to the breaking-point. I and Hando pushed ourselves in. Mother came just after us. Well into the compartment she opened the window and took Raivo from grandmother who stood on the platform. She gave Raivo to me and tried to help up grandmother through the window. But grandmother was far too heavy. Two German soldiers who stood on the platform saw what was happening, and together they lifted our grandmother in through the window. Then the train started.

We arrived in Saltzburg in the evening. There was no other train leaving before the next day. We had to stay overnight in a church in Saltzburg. It was a big white church, located in a green area. The church had been emptied of benches and was converted to a night camp for refugees. Each family got a blanket that we had to put on the floor as bedding place. This night there were about a hundred refugees in this church.

Next day was the twentieth of April 1945. It was Raivos - and Hitlers birthday. We celebrated Raivos birthday on Hauptbanhof in Salzburg. It was a beautiful day, the sun was shining and there was a smell of early spring in the air. The platform, where we waited for the train to Innsbruck, faced towards the Alps. The mountains were covered with leafy trees to about halfway up, thereafter with snow. In spite of the birthday the day was long and tiresome: It dragged along without any train in sight. We waited and helped time pass through conversation.

However, this double birthday - Raivos and Hitlers – brought for our part a blessing in its wake since no bomber planes were in sight during the whole day. On the evening came at last a train and we could resume our travel.

Our journey took us to Innsbruck. Barely in Innsbruck air-raid warnings started nearly at once. We had to hasten down to the railway tunnel. Standing in the dark underground tunnel we could hear how the bombs landed. People pushed themselves together, feeling extremely anxious. This is the end, I thought. Hando began to cry and Raivo fell into his cry. I pulled myself closer to mother and grandmother. At last the sirens told us that the bombing was over.

We went out of the tunnel. Up on the railway station, there was a chaos. We could see burning fire here and there. The fire fighting brigade tried to put out the fires. The air was filled with black smoke which made it difficult to breathe. We went to the station building to get information about how to get to Switzerland. There, we were told that Switzerland had closed its borders. No one without an entry visa could go to Switzerland. Now, we did not know what to do. After some discussion we understood that what remained was to leave for Germany. For Germany no visa was needed, since Austria was at that time included in Germany. For us it was important to get away from the Russian front.

Therefore, we decided to continue to the west, to try to meet the American frontline.

After a long wait in uncertainty there came a train that we could take. It was cold on the train and we were very hungry. The train's windows had been shattered and a cold wind was blowing in. There was no food available. It was several days since we had eaten. The train staff assured us that we would get both food and drink when the train stopped at the next place. And the train stopped next afternoon, but not to get food, but because the rails were blown up and the train could not continue further. So we had to walk.

Now we were almost in the war zone. There were daily air-raids. The planes flew very low and shot at people on the land. During these attacks, we could not stay in the middle of the road but had to head for the forest and grab onto a tree. In such a way we would not be a target for the air-craft. So every time we heard a plane coming we had to run to the forest. Grandmother was too tired to run to the forest and we had to help her, she herself said that she did not want to run any more.

After many days of travel, hunger and tiredness we arrived in a little village called Marktoberdorf. There we were placed into a closed school house. We knew that the Americans would take over the village probably already during that night: April 27, 1945. We got food, porridge and milk for the children and bread and butter for the adults. When we had eaten we went outdoors. We stood in front of the school house, together with a cluster of refugees who had traveled thousand's of kilometers along fragmented roads, and did not know what the next day would bring with it.

Would the front's transition happen peacefully and free of pain free or would we be shot by the American soldiers? We all knew that this day could be the last in our life.

The next day the Americans were in the village. We could eat our breakfast and after that mother went out to get some information. When she came back she told us that we could stay in the school house until further notice. She had also got food coupons for us. In the evening, some American soldiers came and spoke with us. What they said I really don't know, but the adults laughed and it felt good. The soldiers gave us children chewing gum. Initially we did not know what it was and what to do with it. Hando succeeded in swallowing his chewing gum before he knew how to manage it. The other American novelty for us during that evening was Coca Cola. It was a dark brown and somewhat well thickened sweet drink, considerably sharper in the taste than today's Coca Cola drinks. The soldiers told us that the drink was produced of leaves from coca-bush and had a stimulating effect. During this first evening, we learned also our first word in English, it was "okay".

May 8, 1945, we could hear from the radiocasts that the war was over. Germany had given up and Hitler had already committed suicide. But already after some weeks, we got worrying news. A number of Russian militaries had come to the village, and now they insisted that we should return to our native country - Estonia. It sounded very intimidating. Our entire flight had to do with the escape from the Russians and now they were there again. Mother tried to explain our position for the American soldiers and asked for help. The soldiers listened but had no promises to come up with. It is a political question, they said. So once again we had to flee. We knew that there was a refugee-camp in Kempten, and we started our flight to take us there.

THE REFUGEE CAMP IN KEMPTEN
In Kempten's camp there were refugees of many different nationalities. There were Estonians, Latvians and Lithuanians, Poles, Yugoslavs, Russians and some other nationalities, together four to five hundred people. Our family got a room to stay in; it was a small room with double bunks. The official opening of the camp took place on midsummer evening 1945. The weather was warm and beautiful, not a cloud on the deep blue sky. It was a dignified opening. Estonian refugees stood in semicircle before the school house and our camp manager Arno Raag held a speech.

In the camp, there was a common food catering. Enormous pots with porridge or soup were driven before the houses and from there everyone retrieved their food portion. For breakfast, there was porridge for the children and bread and black coffee for adults, for lunch a vegetable soup and for the evening meal yet another soup. It was a far too low-fat food, but better than the food we had got during our flight.

In the camp, there were a lot of children of different ages. Many of them had during the school year 1944/1945 not gone to school because of the ongoing war escape. Now during the early summer, a school was organized amazingly fast. It started on June 9, 1945. Both I and Hando continued our education in this school. I remember that the school was very crowded and there was a shortage of rooms. Therefore during hot summer days we had our lessons outdoors, sitting under some big trees. We also had to take with us a chair from home. When it rained or was windy and cold we had to sit in a corridor. We did not have any published Estonian textbooks, so our books were written by the people in the camp.

The war was over but we still had no information about our father. We had not heard from him during the whole time, and we did not know if he was alive or not. But now people started to look for their relatives and we started to "wait for father". And one day he came.

Later on father told us his story. He had followed the Estonian battalion when it fought on the eastern front against Russians. When they came to Czechoslovakia everything turned into chaos, and father was imprisoned. The men that were in the prison were innocent, but were accused for different things. When they began to defend themselves they were tortured.

After about six months father succeeded in escaping from the prison and started to search for us. He went from one refugee camp to the next, to get information. The Red Cross had lists of names for the different refugee camps. One of those lists allowed him to find us.

One day in the summer 1945 it was decided that all refugees in the camp would get a kind of identity document. We would no longer be called refugees but DP's (Displaced persons). My registration card stated that I, Maare Kask, was 147 cm's tall and weighed 38 kilos. The card also stated that I had blond hair and blue eyes.

Later that summer repatriation commenced in Kempten. It was a collective deportation of people from their current bases back to the country where they come from. During the entire summer and the autumn 1945 thousands of people were compulsorily transferred back to their homes. After a lot of administrative procedures, we escaped the compulsory transfer, and were moved to Geislingen, an Estonian big camp there. Again, we packed together our belongings and along with other families we were ready for our journey to begin towards a new future.
***

One can ask how I as a child coped with these strains in my life. To be afraid of death, to see the sky on fire when the bombs detonated, to hear the machine-guns roar, and to know that father was somewhere in the war and that mother and grandmother were extremely anxious. As a child I didn't always understand what was happening, but I sensed the atmosphere. Dread and anxiety are feelings that are transmitted from adults to children. But fear never became a part of me. I think that I owe that to my family. My mother and my grandmother could always give both me and my brothers a feeling of calmness and security. **Our family discussed war events very openly, and I could always ask my questions and always get answers. Nothing was silenced down.**

GEISLINGEN

Geislingen, the City of Five Valleys, was located in the southern Germany. It was a town basically untouched by war. We arrived at the DP Camp at Geislingen in August 1945, some month before the official opening of the camp in October the same year. We were assigned to live in Wilhelmshöhe (Villemiküngas). The U.S. Army (UNRRA team 190) had ordered the German families to move out of their homes which were now filled with Estonians. We got two rooms in a house in Wilhelmshöhe. There were two more families in the house. Our house was the first in the row of houses on a slope up to a hill. This slope became one of our playgrounds.

In Geislingen schools were organized very fast. In November the Estonian primary school opened. The ceremonial opening was in November 19 in Jahnhalle, the town's best local theatre with seating for 700. There were 267 students and they were placed in twelve classes. The Estonian teachers we had were all refugees or DPs. The headmaster for the school was Meeme Mälgi.

I was ten and a half years old, and was placed in fourth class. I had not completed the third class in Kempten, but had good grades, so I could "skip" a half class. I enjoyed going to school, as I always had. The school was for me more than homework and grades, it was friendship and unity. When I was twelve I left the elementary school, and continued my education in upper secondary school in Ulm.

On the spring 1946 Hando and I began to take piano lessons. Since the Germans had been forced to submit their apartments to DPs without taking with them any furniture we now had a piano in the room where we lived. Mother and father were of the opinion that if we possess a piano then someone has to play on it. "You children, can learn to play, "they said. Grandmother agreed with mother's and father's feelings. "It is perfect when you can play," she said. "Then, you can play the songs that I like to sing. It is easier to stay in tune when someone plays it."

To learn to play the piano meant exercises and more exercises. We had to exercise scales at least one hour each day. It was fairly boring: Especially during beautiful summer days when all other children were outdoors playing it was a torment to be indoors doing piano practice". To make our practice more pleasant mother had a trick. We got a number of matches that she had counted, and put on the side of the keyboard. Each time we had played one scale we had to move over one of the matches to the other side of the keyboard. When all the matches were moved over we could finish for the day.

Another, more pleasant activity than piano practice, took place on the summers. In nearly every summer both I and Hando were on the summer camp on " Koogimägi " (Cake Hill). "Koogimägi" was more than one hundred meters high hill, and flat as a pancake. Therefore it was called "Koogimägi". UNNRA had decided that children who were undernourished could be in the summer camp for their health. I was one of those undernourished children. The summers on "Koogimägi" will always be in my memory, as a summer paradise. There, we got into touch with other youngsters, learned to know each other, and made friends.

Even today when I hear the word" Koogimägi" I remember the glorious lazy days, removed from homework and other obligations, and filled with games, noise and friendships.

But everything has an end, not only the summers on "Koogimägi", but the whole refugee camp in Geislingen. UNRRA - the help organization that had helped refugees - ended their activity in 1947.

It was taken over of IRO ((International Refugee organization). One of IRO's main tasks was to find a future for DP's. Those millions of DPs that were in different camps scattered over the whole of Europe could not be left in a war ravaged Europe. Together with different volunteer organizations IRO worked intensively to find countries that needed manpower or were willing to take DPs as immigrants.

The years 1949 and 1950 became great emigration years in Geislingen. Great Britain and Belgium had already earlier taken DPs. Now USA, Canada, Australia, New Zealand and Sweden had also opened their doors and wanted to receive immigrants as labor. This meant that screenings and health controls started once again.

Our family tried first to immigrate to USA, but failed the medical screening. The X-ray survey showed that both I and father had a mark on the lung. We continued to apply to other countries. At last we succeeded. It was Sweden that needed manpower.

To immigrate to Sweden was not a first choice for the exile Estonians in Germany. On the one hand, Sweden was situated near Estonia and was both climatically and culturally an attractive country. But on the other hand the country was too near to Soviet Union. The people were also skeptical about Sweden's government: The Swedish government in January 1946 had delivered over hundred people including many youngsters to Stalin's terror. Since the threat of repatriation to the native country rested over Estonians in Germany nobody knew whether one could trust Sweden or not. Despite that approximately thousand Estonians migrated to Sweden. We were one of them.

It was one foggy winter evening, the first of December 1950, when we started our journey. After several nights on a train we boarded the ferry from Helsingör to Helsingborg. I remember that the big ferry floated up and down in low-speed over the dark water. It squeaked and puffed when it worked itself toward Sweden's coast.

On the ferry there was a group Estonians who looked out into the darkness pondering upon a new life in a free country. After five years of war and additional five years in different refugee camps they longed for their own home. The ferry completed its journey and touched against the jagged quay in Helsingborg. We had reached our destination.

A QUESTION

Will life in a future republic be like the one in the familiar frog pond, that some frogs are more like oneself?

Will I and my fellow idealists who by similar means on returning home become strangers?

**from "Not by bread Alone/Mitte ainult leivast"
By Hando Kask, who is Maare's brother**

KÜSIMUS

Kas tulevases vabariigis
on samuti kui tuntud konnatiigis,
et mõni konn on rohkem konna moodi?

Kas mina ja mu aatekaaslased,
kes samasugustena loodi
on koju tulles võõrasmaalased?

Schlosshalde kindergarten children

Bruno with his twin sister Erika and friends

Bruno's house to the L

Bruno's first year at school:
Bruno top L. Erika front 4th L

Our parents did try desperately hard to find less destructive activities for us.
The marionette theatre was one of the fondly remembered ones in Geislingen.
Inge Pruks has shared this photo.

BRUNO LEEPIN
UNKNOWN DANGERS

My childhood home was in Geislingen within viewing distance from where the main railway line ran.

A train line ran through the town, with an old station nearby our home. Next to the railway, there were abandoned burnt out train carriages, ruins and debris that had been dumped after the war.

Warm summer days were spent roaming and exploring places near my home, but for a group of six year or so old boys, the attraction of the unknown and picking things apart to see just how they work was always irresistible.

One day, my playmates and I had made an amazing (or so we thought at the time) discovery at the bottom of the hill next to the road. It was a cylindrical, metal shell that piqued our curiosity and made us wonder how we could best include it in our games.

We decided that it would be fun to roll this along the road. We could always decide later what to do with it, when we got it home to include it in our collections of weird and wonderful things we discovered and played with at that time. I remembered how other older children found and kept pistols they had found amongst ruins, and when we had bon fires some of these children would throw cartridges into the fire – everybody had to take cover! Now we knew that what we found was an unexploded bomb shell. It was fascinating and of course we wanted to keep it!

Absorbed in rolling our new toy down the hill, we didn't at first notice an elderly German man approaching us on his bicycle – only as he got closer and suddenly jumped off his bicycle, waving his hands in the air and screaming in fear, we all looked up in surprise. I realized from the man's reaction that he thought we were up to no good and we stopped rolling my new toy along. The bomb shell had stopped rolling and lay still and innocent near an elder flower bush by the side of the road.

The other boys stopped too and we all stood in stunned silence, with fear and guilt in our eyes. What should we do next? What was the angry man going to do to us? Was this thing his and he thought we stole it? Will our mums find out from him? I'd be in real trouble then, I remember thinking at the time.

The man's screams got louder as he ran towards us. We couldn't understand a word of what he was screaming at us…none of us could understand German that much.

Recovering from the surprise and shock, the first thing that shot through my mind was "run for it!" I didn't hesitate and bolted in fear, not looking back to see if the others are following. The fear pushed me along as I sprinted all the way home…..

We were old enough to understand what danger we just got away from. All of us had heard stories of old bombs being found and it sounded so adventurous. It was just hard to believe we thought of playing with something that was so dangerous!

We could have all been blown up at any moment. Only later I realized that the old man with the bike may have possibly saved us from some horrible injuries and maybe even death……

During the post war period these abandoned bomb shells were just one of the many dangers. It was all just an adventure at the time, but now looking back, and ever since that episode I will never forget, I realized that such dangers were often close at hand.

Aire Salmre writes "Also since I lived in Blomberg DP camp in the British Zone, I'm not one of the 'Geislingen's mudilased' but like you're saying 'we still remain connected' through common experiences. We the 'mudilased of the DP camps share many experiences"

LESS "GLAM" IMAGES RELATING TO THE SAME EPOCH: IS

26 May 1945. In an open rail car from Hermsdorf to Stradoda, have done their job. My my mother Leili Soovere is bending towards me with distressed face.

My Uncle Heino Trees, looks exhausted. Peering over his shoulder is an Estonian soldier Kuusepuu who ditched his German uniform. Kuusepuu was lost to us, likely picked up by Czech partisan units or Russians, and was never heard from again. One sees home woven blanket with Estonian designs, from my father's home farm in Konnu.   IS. Photo Eric Soovere.

Somehow Ilo's narrative connects more closely to my recall: I was maybe one year older. In my one photo from Estonia I certainly did not look undernourished but what I looked like until my fourth birthday will remain a mystery.
  Mother used to relate how she travelled under the German army troop truck seats to farms* to obtain milk for me:
  I still wonder was if I was there too: If not where was I, and if mother ever wondered if I would be alive to drink that milk when she returned: I wonder what was the cost of those rides. Little in life comes free in my life experience.
  Perhaps it there my fascination for bunkers was born, indeed is it there that mother's need to deny that such buildings was born. Try as I might I cannot divorce them from my sense of identity.
  *Possibly in the Parnu region as we had no family elsewhere and even they seemed remote.
  I wonder too, what happened to a brother I may have had. In a photo when mother was younger is a little tot who looks just like me: I was told he was my god-brother. Father's narrative is a little different. In one of father's latter letters is allusion to "Evi (?Evald)" and "oben"- maybe in Heaven!
  Mother certainly talked about what I understood to be "Eva" as a name for me: Maybe she spoke about "Evald"- perhaps it was all too much for me and I did a mental transposition to deal with the undealable. There are just so many engimas.

Maybe the ravages of war had more to them just military might and its attendant fear and deprivation: Perhaps other resources account for the obscure Bell curve distributions!   MM

LIA NOORMETS/NICHOLSON
LEAVING OUR HOMELAND

I was born on September 1st 1929 in Tallinn as Lia Nordmann. The German surname was changed in 1934-1935 to an Estonian surname.

For the last ten years we lived in Saaremaa, in Orissare, a beautiful place. The house was about 2 minutes from the sea, and we could see some farmhouses across the sea in Muhu Island.

I just had my fifteenth birthday when we had to leave our home in a hurry as the Russian forces were getting too close too quickly.

There was a covered truck on the road in front of our house, and we had to get ready within an hour. Everybody had a change of clothes, some photos, mum packed some food and we left the house as it was.

I remember I had a little red case, and my most treasured first ever silk stockings that I got for my birthday were in the case with my change of clothes.

The truck was full of people and we arrived at Kuressaare, the last port from which a ship was leaving. The first day we could not get on the ship: It was a German war ship and had on board some Russian prisoners who started a fire. We saw the smoke billowing out.

The officer told us to come back next morning which we did. The port was full of people trying to get on. We were told that the steel section where the fire was had been closed to stop the fire getting any further. Although the ship was still blowing out smoke that did not stop anyone jostling and pushing to get on board.

The burning ship was a better option than the Russians.

The first night on our journey we had the Russian submarines and planes bombarding the ship. All women and children were sent below the deck and all the men stayed on deck. I remember my mum and I holding onto each other and shaking like leaves. But we were lucky. The Russians were keeping watch for any ship leaving with refugees. There was one ship before us that they got, and most lives were lost. I had a friend who lost his entire family: He was on his own at fifteen years.

Apparently our captain was smart and he knew which way the torpedoes were coming and he turned the ship somewhat and the torpedoes went past both sides of the ship.

We arrived in Germany: Gotenhafen harbour on the 30th September 1944, spending the night on board and disembarked on 1st October 1944.

All the refugees boarded the train. Nobody knew where we were going, except we were travelling north. After two days of travelling and stopping we were told to disembark and then taken to a camp that was a Prisoner of War camp, vacated for the refugees.

The camp was enclosed behind a barbed wire fence, an extremely dirty place. For sleeping there were large wooden shelves. The limited comfort was offered by some straw: There were lots of lice and other vermin.

People were sleepy and tired. For lunch we were given a big metal bucket full of some grey jelly-like soup which no one tasted. Everyone still had some food from home.

Then all the women were allowed to have a shower. It was a big room with a concrete floor and little shower heads on the ceiling. The floor was full of women trying to catch a little water raining down. I remember there were about 4-5 men walking around adjusting some taps on the walls!!!!!

There was also a toilet block: A huge open hole in the middle of the block with handlebars all around, with a horrible stink. Mum and I never used it for the couple of days we spent there.

The second day the German officials came to sort us all out.

My father was a postmaster in Estonia, so my father and mother were sent to Berlin to work in a post office. My brother Ants, who was sixteen was sent to the Luftwaffe. There were about twenty-five young girls, 14-16 years old. We were too old to go with mum and dad as children, and too young to be sent out on our own.

The German officials did the best they could to keep families in touch with each other. Ants and I were given the addresses to write to mum and dad in Berlin and they got the postal addresses of us both. We were always amazed for the thoughtfulness of the German known preciseness even at a time when they were in deep trouble themselves.

So our group of young girls were sent to another camp. It was absolutely horrible. It must have been some Prisoner of War camp for women. We were put into a barrack, a huge room, full of triple level single beds, and women we did know where they all were from.

We were put to sleep with women who had enjoyed single beds. I was on the highest bunk with a little short, fat woman. The beds were so narrow that we had to sleep one's head and other's feet under one blanket.

Lots of the time was spent looking for lice and killing them, and when we had a shower everybody together, one could see lots of lice sliding down the bodies with hot water.

For breakfast we each got a piece of bread and a little cube of margarine and black coffee. That was brought to the barrack by our little German girl soldier.

For lunch everybody had to line up in front of the barrack and we were marched to the dining barrack. For dinner, something was brought to the barrack. Soup was the main meal at lunch time. It was just some potatoes and vegetables boiled together. One day as we were standing in the queue for our soup, there was some loud yelling and a commotion coming from the start of the queue in the front, and we were all told to go back to our barracks and told 'no soup today'.

It came out that one or two women at the soup queue in the front were complaining about the little worms in the soup. They got the yelling and told if they were men they would be shot.

As it was October and the days were getting colder, we still had the same clothes on when we left home, so everybody was given a blue long sleeve outfit (similar to what the plumbers wear).

I so missed mum and dad and our home. I cried so often missing my mum, being on my own among so many strange people. I didn't even know the girls. We were all strangers until we got to the village.

We were in that terrible camp for about a week, then our twenty-five Estonian girls were bundled up and we were taken to an empty Hitler Jungend Camp.

I think that we were taken after the horrid camp we had to endure there for nearly a week. There we had a beautiful holiday, warm beds with feather doonas, three meals a day with second helpings.

That came to an end on a rainy afternoon when we were bundled in a horse drawn carriage that went through the mud and slush and potholes for a couple of hours until we arrived at a village untouched by war.

There was a barrack and we were greeted by two Estonian ladies. They were to chaperone and look after us. They cooked our dinner when we got back for 'work'. We all sat together at the table, the room was warm and the stomach full of warm soup. We were talking and getting to know each other: Then to bed in a hurry because the bedroom was as cold as outside. There was half a barrack for a bedroom with double bunks and feather doonas. The other half was a kitchen-dining -living room.

Next day we were sent out to work in the farms, some had kindly families who just had the girls in the house looking after children and playing with them. I was not that lucky. My farm was 2 km out of the village. I had to walk there in the morning (get up at six) through mud and snow. I was not complaining, when you are young, you just do it.

There was a very small little farmhouse with an elderly couple. The old lady was always very cranky but the little old farmer was nice and he often gave me apples when she wasn't watching. So quite often I sent a little parcel of four frozen apples to Berlin, as their rations were very small and they were always hungry, especially dad. He was a normal size strong man, but after three months there was nothing left of him, just skin and bones. I saw him when he came to see me. Somehow he managed to get on a train. There were no timetables. The platforms at the train stations were packed with people hoping to catch some occasional train going through.

I got such a happy surprise when Dad walked in just as we were sitting down for dinner. So the ladies, who were looking after us and cooked the meal, invited dad to have a meal with us. It was a lovely night, a lot of talking.

My dad was the only person who came to see where we were.

The ladies made up a bed for dad in the dining room, and next morning he walked with me to the farm. It was an unmade road with mud and snow, and every morning I looked at the spot where my father wiped his shoes on the snow, remembering him and missing him.

I don't remember the name of the village, somewhere in Silesia, near the Polish border. On Christmas Eve all of us went to church, and we were singing loud in Estonian, as the music was the same for Christmas songs, and the people of the village were glad and friendly to see us in church.

Every girl got for Christmas a most delicious Christmas cake from the farms. It was the size of a Swiss roll but with poppy seeds and other delicious components. All the girls were nibbling at their cakes, and no one had anything left for after. For years and years I felt so guilty and sad for gobbling it up by myself and not sending it to Berlin for mum and dad who were starving.

We were going to the farms 7 days a week, getting up at 6 am in the morning, getting dressed in our freezing cold bedroom and with no breakfast. We walked to our farms. One of my jobs at the farm was to boil potatoes for the pigs, so I had a few for myself. Warm boiled potatoes have never tasted so good.

As the Russian army was advancing from the East, my father came again and picked me up and took me with him to Berlin. He was not going to leave his little girl where the Russians were sure to come.

We walked to the railway station, about 3 or 4 km. Arriving there, there must have been at least a hundred people on the platform hoping to catch any train. My father somehow got us through the crowd towards the front.

Then a train came towards Berlin and after a lot of jostling and pushing we just made it. The carriage was so full, people were squashed next to one another so tight, if one would faint, there was no room to fall: They would stay unconscious standing up. My father pushed me against a wall, facing the wall. After a while I fell asleep standing tightly against the wall, and I kept knocking my forehead against the wall in front of me due to the movements of the train, so I had a bit of a bruise on my forehead when we reached Berlin at last.

Meeting my mother was the happiest day for both of us after three and a half months of separation in those uncertain times.

Mum and dad were living in a huge five storey building that used to be a school. Mum and I were living, rather just sleeping, in a room full of double bunks and housing about fifty women. Men were in another room.

Dad took me to the Post Office where they both were working and got me a job there too. It was also a huge place. I was in the letters sorting room. I don't remember what I was doing there. Half of the time we spent in the cellar during the air raids.

There was no sleep at night. The sirens were howling in the night more than once. Everybody rushed to the cellar. It was a really big cellar and going along the length of the building.

The school building was an L shaped building, and for some reason our family were transferred from the fourth floor to the ground floor, in the corner of the short side of the L. The air raids were so severe and often. I remember one day, mum and I were washing our hair, and wondering whether this might be the last time ever washing our hair. The next time when the sirens were howling, mum, dad and I were together, so we ran out to the little cellar in the corner where our room was.

Suddenly there was a great bang, the building shook and thick grey dust was blown from the big cellar.

The building got a full blast and all the people in the big cellar were dead or trapped. There were knockings on the water pipes and people screaming for help. Unfortunately there was no one around anymore who could help as the whole city was in ruins and burning.

That was the end of January 1945, and Berlin was a mess. There was no place to get any food. Some water pipes were broken and water was gushing down the streets, so we had nowhere to stay.

Dad went out looking for some food. There was another siren. Mum and I went with other people into a big bomb shelter, way down underground.

That was a horrible experience for us. We felt like we were being buried deep down under the ground. If a bomb hit the entrance of the shelter, it would not kill you: Death would come slowly to all of the trapped. That was the fate of a lot of people, who were found after the end of the war. There was one shelter that was found few years after the war with people still alive: That was a large food storage. The first two years they had candle light, but after that they were in darkness until they were found. Apparently there must have been some air coming through the rubble.

When we got out of the shelter, father was waiting for us. Mum and I would never go to a place like this again. So we went to an underground railway station and stayed there for the night. Dad got some information from a lady about another underground railway station that was bringing some refugees from the East and travelling West.

We were walking in the middle of the road between smoking ruins and there was a lovely lady (similar to our Salvation Army) who was there with a big pot of soup, giving it to everyone who happened to be on the street. Much appreciated.

As it was winter and slippery roads with ice, mum slipped and fell. She wasn't hurt and we started to laugh. Dad was furious with us to be laughing at a time like this, but we could not help it: The desire to laugh was stronger. We managed to stop soon to please dad.

Dad found the right underground station and we settled in sitting against the wall and hoping for a train to get away from Berlin.

After some hours, I think it was night when a train pulled up with refugees, that was also from the best organized humanitarian community helpers.

Dad went to look up the person who was in charge. That train was travelling towards Hamburg and we wanted to go south to a village named Gr'untal, near Freudenstadt in Schwartzwald where our good neighbours from home were living. It was a small village in the middle of the mountains.

Dad had to organise another two train trips to get us down to Schwartzwald and we arrived to our neighbour's doorstep at 6 o'clock in the morning. That was a big surprise to them: They did not know we were coming. There were a lot of hugs and kisses and talking.

Across their room was a big house which belonged to a lovely big, jolly lady. She was a Pastor's wife. He was at war. She was at home with four or five little children. She offered us a room in their attic, window facing our friends.

Now that I was a 'farm-worker' she found me a place in a very friendly family from where I was given a little room with a big soft bed.

I had to help looking after four cows, giving out fresh straw and collecting soiled ones in a wheel barrow. They had three young kids and a French prisoner of war who was helping with the Farmer in the fields. The Farmer was a typical good looking tall German, and a good man. He treated the prisoner of war as family. His wife was a little round woman who had a lot of respect for her husband.

I went to see mum and dad every Sunday. It was about 2 km. When the weather got warmer, on the way through the fields there was a little stream I had to jump over, hopping from stone to stone. I wished I had some time to just lay next to the stream, listening to the gurgle of water and watch the clouds. That time never came.

Near the little village where mum and dad were living, there was a long rail bridge from the top of one mountain to another, about 1 km away. The French war planes came over ever so often to try and demolish it. They did it the day before their army came in. There was no German army to fight them. The village had only two males left: A sixteen year old boy and a seventy year old man.

As my dad was only thirty-eight years old and his friend was the same, they were taken to the prison by the French. They were held there for two weeks, and when they got back, it was decided to try and leave the French Zone and try to go north to the American Zone.

Under the German rule every person had some coupons for meagre rations. Then there was no more coupons but every person got one loaf of bread a week. My dad was so hungry he ate his loaf in one day.

So we got us a little wegel, about the size of a shopping trolley, with four wheels and a handle to pull it. We put all our earthly belongings in it and started to walk.

We were a little apprehensive and scared arriving at the checkpoint between the French and American Zone. I don't know what my dad was telling them, but we got through.

We were walking for days, and relying on food given to us by the occasional farm house we saw on the way. We also had to find somewhere to sleep at night and we were put up for the night. In one farm, the farmer was a little suspicious and took dad to a big bed and handcuffed dad to himself. I don't know where his wife slept. In the morning we were given something to eat and we were on our way again.

I don't know until this day how my father knew where to go: There were no phones or communication of any sort. The German people must have known where is what and apparently dad heard from them about Geislingen.

And there we ended up in front of a big hall, that used to be a cinema, full of double bunks and Estonians. Our bunks were on the stage as the hall was full.

The food was supplied by the Americans. It must have been enough as I can't remember being hungry.

We were worried and wondering about my brother Ants. We didn't know whether he was alive or dead, or caught up by the Russians. Mum was so worried all the time. She had such a good sense of humour but she would not laugh any more.

So dad went looking for Ants in other camps. It was hard to travel at these times as there was no regular transport: Lots of rails and roads had been damaged. Dad got a lift sometimes with an army truck and I don't know really how he got around and how did he know where some other camps might be.

He was gone some days, and when he came back on his own, mum was crying again. As we were safe in the camp, dad kept going out and searching for his son, and coming back on his own, until one day:

It was my sixteenth birthday when dad walked in with Ants. It will be hard to try to explain the happiness of a mother.

Apparently dad went up to the English Zone and to a Prisoner of War camp, as Ants had the German army uniform on so he was taken in with everybody in uniform. They could see he was only a kid, so when dad walked into the office there, he was told which barracks Ants was in and he was free to go.

Neither of them spoke much about that trip except Ants said that they were just so hungry, so dad knocked at a door and woke up the Mayor of the town (at 6am) and explained their situation and the Mayor helped them out with coupons.

We stayed in that camp for some weeks. Then the Americans and UNRRA decided on a solution for us. They emptied a suburb of Germans, who were allowed to take only their personal items with them, but had to leave all their furnishings, beds and doonas for us to use as long as we were staying there.

Once the houses were empty, as people left for other countries, then their houses and furnishings etc. were handed back to them.

The best suburb, Schlosshalde (like Toorak in Melbourne) was emptied first and as we were already in Geislingen, we were settled in first. This suburb was situated on the slope of a mountain. It had a beautiful view over the city. That house belonged to a doctor and family. It was a two storey house with a cellar with a laundry and other shelves and things, and also an attic with a little room also. There were five rooms, kitchen, bathroom, toilet, all in excellent order.

We had the biggest bedroom on the second floor, and another family of three got the next biggest one on the ground floor. Then there was a mother with a young daughter, two single men and two single girls who had the little attic room.

Then everyday life got back to normal. The schools opened: Primary school in the morning and High school in the afternoon.

We had the best qualified teachers: They had to leave Estonia before the Russians got them. The Russians did not like well educated Estonians, so they were sent to Siberia or were shot. The Russians did not want to have intelligent thinking people around.

As there were no books, we had to write down everything on the paper: All that the teachers were teaching us. There was an excellent teacher for every subject. The High School had classes from the first year to the fifth.

Some students from Geislingen went to University in here and became smart professional people: Thanks to the four plus years in Geislingen High School.

Geislingen became the biggest and best Estonian camp in the American Zone. People were coming from all over the free western part of Germany.

Then another two suburbs were made available for us, and at the end there were about 4000 Estonians in the small city.

We had the use of a big beautiful church for Sunday Services. We had religious instructions once a week and a big Confirmation Service once a year. All the girls had long white frocks. I can't remember where my mum got the material from, and all the boys had suits and ties. (Usually thirty to forty kids aged sixteen to seventeen years old)

There was also a theatre for us to use, and there were concerts, plays, shows, operettas, etc. Other rooms were used for rehearsals, also a ballet school, where I was a pupil with eight other girls. We also played a part in operetta "Maritza". The school choir and national dancing was also well attended and enjoyed. (I was singing with the Melbourne's Ladies Choir and dancing in the "Grandmother's group" until I was eighty-two.)

The past school age people also had many activities and clubs: Nobody had time to sit at home and be bored.

The people in the house where we lived, became such good friends, everybody attended the shows and concerts. When we got home from the theatre we all sat around the dining room table and discussed it in depth.

In summer we had to walk about 2km to a little public swimming pool. We were hot when we got there and even hotter when we got back home. It was so full of people and children, how did we want to go in, I'll never know. The water was warm, probably from all the bodies' heat and whatever.

There was also one small cinema opened and they started to show some American really good old happy films. One show went on for weeks and we went to see it so many times that we knew it word by word. They were all in English with German subtitles. For us, school kids, life was good and fun. We went to excursions, had school dances, with the school band. We had school for a week in summer time on a small mountain, sleeping in army tents, five or six girls in a tent. One evening we had a Hawaii night around the fire and dancing around in grass skirts.

Some paper shops opened and we could buy some writing material and pencils. As far as us kids, life was good. The family was together. We had no worries: Parents did all that.

The belief that everybody had on leaving home, that we will be back by Christmas, was only a hopeful dream disappearing fast.

TRAIN STATIONS

Dresden 2003

To me as I travel through Europe, train stations, especially large ones have a 'magic' about them and attract me like a magnet: I have endless photos of them. They have always held that magic.

I can recall my first return to Germany and at Stuttgart station finding a post card of its station in ruins: It felt like returning home.

Perhaps they were a form of home eons before: They sheltered us from the weather when we had no roofs over our heads: Their undergrounds sheltered us from bombing raids and while waiting there, there was a transient optimism that the new destination was safer than our trek had been to date.

How different is that notion to an elderly man I met on my first return to Geislingen in 2002. He had returned to Geislingen after we had departed: He had just been released as a POW from Siberia.

For me there was a powerful connection: I had at last met a man who had walked the journey my father had: On subsequent visits he shared much about that ignoble time in history.

Our partings were always difficult: He told me he hated train stations: It was there that one said goodbye, never to be sure if that person would ever return. The soldiers said good-bye to their families: Their families to them.

There was no "Aufweidersehen" about such occasions. MM

ESTONIAN DP CAMPS IN GERMANY

Most of our folks arrived in East Prussia (now in Polish terrain) their ships landing in Gotenhafen (given Danzig had been demolished by bombing raids). From there they were moved to Berlin and dispersed from there to varying camps and some to private arrangements.

Some folks arrived cross country via the Baltics and Konigsberg.

There was much movement around these camps, some of which were disbanded and others merged into larger camps elsewhere in Germany. The largest of these camps was to become Geislingen into which folk from other camps were moved. The degree of freedom of movement depended on many variables.

The statistics can only ever be approximate because there is no way of being certain how many of our folk fled Estonia. Many perished on their way and others did not reach the camps, and as always statistics have rigid criteria and don't account for all who fled. The estimated number is about 40,000.

USA ZONE I CAMPS
- Almendfeld
- Alenstadt
- Amberg
- Ansbach
- Bad Mengentheim
- Bad Worishofen
- Bayreuth
- Bamberg
- Berechtesgaden
- Dettendorf
- Dieburg
- Dillingen
- Erlangen
- Forcheim
- Furth
- Geislingen
- Gunzenhausen
- Hanau
- Haunstetten
- Heidelberg
- Hochfeld
- Ingolstadt
- Kassel-Bettenhausen
- Kleinheubach (Lowenstein)
- Mannheim
- Marktredwitz
- Memmingen
- Muldorf & Neu-Ottingen
- Neuburg (On Donau)
- Munchen
- Regensburg
- Sindelfingen
- Stuttgart
- Traunstein
- Ulm
- Wielandshag
- Weissenburg
- Weisbaden

USA ZONE II CAMPS
- Aalen (Wasseralfingen)#
- Amsbach I -> Furth
- Amsbach II *
- Amberg KWK *
- Aschafenburg I -> Wurzburg
- Donauworth *
- Esslingen #
- Fohrenwald -> Memmingen
- Fulda*
- Furth*
- Giessen -> Almenfeld
- Goppingen #
- Heidenheim #
- Heilbron #
- Hof -> Marktredwitzi
- Kempten (I,II,III)-> Altenstadt
- Koburg--> Wurzburg
- Landshut *
- Maxhutte ->Weiden
- Mittenwald *
- Necktargartach -> Heilbron
- Neresheim #
- Neubeuren *
- Neumarkt -> Amberg
- Nurnberg -> Ausbach
- Rebdorf*
- Rosenheim*
- Schwabishe-Hall #
- Tirschenreuth*
- Weiden*
- Wurzburg -> Kleinheubach

* Camps which were not dispersed
\# Camps dispersed to Geislingen

Perhaps Geislingen being the largest of the camps gives an approximation of the demographics of the Estonian who did flee.

The camp was declared closed to new DPs when its population approached 4000 but it reached 4400.

Of these 45% were males and 55% females.

In 1948 there were
- 505 grade school children
- 268 highs school students

In early March 1946 there were 214 children attending its 3 kindergartens.
-And of course there were babies and toddlers who stayed with their mothers at home.
Among our cohort we have many who were born into the camps or on the cusp of arrival in their new lands.

CAMPS IN AUSTRIA
- Salzburg
- Linz ->Ried & Salzburg
- Kufstein
- Landeck
- Bregenz
- Lustenau ->Dornbirn
- Insbruck
- Willach

INFORMATION DERIVED FROM: FERDINAND KOOL'S "DP KROONIKA"

For children it was a nomadic time and many of us have little idea of where we actually passed through or lived. As the adults narrated the stories of the trek we would at times feel yes we know that name or it is not familiar. MM.

OTHER USA ZONE CAMPS

Dornstadt
Eggenfelden
Fellbach
Furth in Walde
Geretsreid
Herrieden
Kassel-Mattenberg
Kastel (Weisbaden-Kastel)
Lohengrin
Marburg
Muna- Munster (Dieburg)
Murnau
Marzfeld
Neckargartach
Neubeuren
Obertswehren
Offenbach
Ohringen
Passau
Valga
Vilsiburg
Wildflecken
Windscheim
Wetslar

Many of the smaller camps gradually diminished leaving only a few DPs living in those towns.
Others were relocated to nearby sites and/or merged with other camps.

BRITISH ZONE CAMPS

Alt-Garge
Arnsberg
Bad- Lauterberg
Blocherfelde
Blomberg
Braunschweig
Bremen
Celle
Chile Haus
Detmold
Dorverden
Eckernforde
Fischbeck & Falkenberg
Flensburg
Funkturm (Transmitter)
Goslar
Gottingen
Greven
Hamburg region
Hanover
Hillingsfeld
Holzminden
Hanover
Hanover -Braunschweig
Hanover-Munden
Itzhoe &Horst
Kiel
Lubeck
Luneburg
Meerbeck
Neumunster
Oberkassel
Ochsenzoll
Ohmstede
Oldenburg- Westfahl
Osnabruck
Osterode
Oxford-Rothenburg
Ratzeburg
Rothenhof
Salzgitter group
Sandplatz
Schleswig
Schwartzenbeck
Uchte
Velbert
Wentorf
Zoo-lager

THE FRENCH ZONE CAMPS

Kaiserlautern
Freiburg
Mullheim
Reute Klooster

The camps were small.

Most Estonian refugees in this zone lived in private accommodation and their needs were met via UNRRA or military sources.

THOUGHTS ABOUT REFO FOOD:
A 'MANYLOGUE' WITH ARNE, GUSTEN, HEIKI, SANNU & MM

Arne to Mai,
Re Tony M. Taagen's book: This book, as well as the German Boy make me think that our family had it pretty easy when compared to other refugees escaping from Estonia to Germany at the same time.
 I asked Heiki whether he remembers ever being really hungry during our refugee days. He said that he ate much less than I did and I ate much of his food in addition to mine! I can't refute a word of his claim!

Gusten to Arne:
You raised the question about being hungry during refugee days?
  We had no problems for 1944 fall and 1945 winter and early spring, since we traveled from town to town, in south through Austria, ending north in Flensburg. And my dad had gamed the system to acquire three sets of "Urlauben" ration cards which were good anywhere in Germany. We ate in fine restaurants and lived in good hotels. Until Germany was squeezed to where there was no more room to travel, and no way to renew the triple ration coupons in three different towns, on the same day...
  Over time, I think our memory smooths out what we recall of the really rough times and dangers. But I remember being definitely hungry during the last five-six weeks of the war, and a few weeks after Germany's capitulation. We were now stuck in Flensburg, at the border of Denmark. Missing were the staples that give one the solid feeling in your stomach, grains, bread, potatoes. I think we had some watery "Gemüse" like beets and carrots, but no fat, no butter, no meat. Yet, I am sure, we were still not so bad off that we would have knowingly eaten horse meat.
  At one time a butcher shop had a sign out on the street, that at sometime that afternoon they were going offer beef „Brühe", no ration cards required, bring your own container. I went with a tall water-pitcher. The store had a truly foul smell. A dirty, teen-age kid, probably butcher's apprentice, took my pitcher and disappeared to a back room. Through the door, I saw a huge, walled-in kettle over fire, big enough to boil a whole cow in. The kid dipped a bucket over the kettle rim into the brew, filled my pitcher, and collected some money. I walked home and carried the pitcher to our third floor apartment kitchen. My parents took only a short look and dumped the foul smelling brew down the drain. And washed the sink...
  What Flensburg grocery stores had frequently was fish, mostly flounder, fresh from the sea. But as I said, hardly anything else to cook with it. But the worst: There was NO SALT to be had anywhere! What a shock! Unbelievably hard to fill your stomach with boiled (no fat, or oil to fry it in), unsalted fresh fish... I guess we were never really hungry.
  I have had some people ask me, if in my hunger, I ever scavenged for food scraps in garbage? So I explained that this kind of opportunity did not exist in war-starved Germany. No food scraps ever made it into something to be discarded!

Mai to the group:
Hei,
Something has always perplexed me:
  Over the years I have read about folks whining over the food offered in boats taking DPs to their new lands, and in the reception camps, and I think to myself what are they whining about: What was before them at those places was luxury compared with what they had eaten for at least since the day they were born.
  And yet I have zilch recollection of any food before me in Geislingen to make such an assertion, merely of hanging around the kitchen while something was being prepared on one occasion, and of queuing up for our rations on one day while in Geislingen (alluded to in WNE). It's as it food didn't exist nor tables to eat them off.
  Yet my memory of Geislingen for those years is so intricate that I could, after arrival back there after 53 years, within 2 hours of dumping my suitcase at the hotel locate all the landmarks in the town without a map: including remarking to someone that Kaiser Wilhelm's statue was in the wrong place—to be told it had been moved from the spot I thought it should have been.
  I can recall towards the end of our sojourn there buying one little green fish shaped lolly on a stick, and the probably at the time 'ersatz' torte slices for my seventh birthday a week or two before we left Geislingen and Germany. I still love those tortes tho generally I would forget to eat if nature didn't remind me that I was becoming light-headed.
  Such is childhood memory: we recall the unpleasant by blocking it out (such intense blocking out perhaps the ultimate of validation) and the pleasant by remembering its intricacies. I guess that the streets were my home: That is what I still see Geislingen as. I have no wish to see the room we spent maybe three or more years in.

ARNE ELLERMETS
A FREE ESTONIA, THEN AN OCCUPIED ESTONIA, FOLLOWED BY CAMP LIFE

ICE CREAM AND WHIPPED CREAM!
We were a happy family in the independent country of Estonia. My father was the director of Emlo, a liquor refinery in Tallinn. Mom and Dad took us in the summers to Pärnu for vacations. We spent a lot of time at the beach. One of my favorite memories is of the ice cream shacks, small round buildings with peaked tops, along the beach. Mom and Dad would buy themselves ice cream, served with small metal(DIVIDED "SMALL METAL INTO TWO WORDS) spoons about 2 – 3 inches long. Heiki and I would get tall round cones of whipped cream!

I talked about this story with my cousin Gusten who is a year older than I am. He and his family also visited Pärnu because our aunt Alle lived there and provided us with housing. According to Gusten the beautiful beach at Pärnu was divided into three areas. One area was for men, another was for both sexes and the far end of the beach was for women and children. He says that he was about 7 or 8 years old when his mother took him to the beach into the women's area. The women used that area for sunbathing – naked of course! He said that occasionally he would see men come to the dividing line to get a glimpse of Estonian beauties, sunbathing in the tall grass! At that point I liked the whipped cream better!

GOLD COINS HIDDEN IN THE SOAP.
Those good days disappeared with the occupation of Estonia by Russia in 1940 and the subsequent deportation of many of our friends and family. Our Mom told me, age 10 and Heiki, age 6 what to expect if our family would be chosen for deportation. She told us that families were being separated – men from women and children from parents. Each of us was supposedly allowed to take one suitcase with necessities.

Mom said that since I was the older one I was responsible for the welfare of my brother. She said that she had packed our suitcases. The toiletries included pieces of soap which she had cut in half, carved out the middle and packed some gold coins in the soap before resealing them under hot water. They looked like used pieces of soap. If Heiki would get sick, it would be my responsibility to break open the soap and try to bargain with our guard, to get a doctor to see him. Fortunately it never came to that.

DAD WAS A POOR TEACHER!
It appears that our family was excluded from the mass deportations because of Dad's job of providing liquor to the Russian leaders. There was no one with the technical know how to take over his job. He was given a Russian understudy, but fortunately Dad turned out to be a very poor teacher and the understudy never took over his job!

THREE OF US WENT INTO HIDING!
My grandfather was a meteorologist in Tallinn until he bought a small farm, retired and moved out to the country. When it became apparent that we would be deported Mom, Heiki and I moved to their farm in Lükati.
Grandfather had a large raspberry patch with raspberry plants that were over six feet tall. The patch was fenced in on three sides and the fourth side was an embankment that was even higher than the plants. Grandpa and his neighbors dug a large cave into the embankment and made a camouflaged door out of wood panels that held sod mats with tall grass. We received instructions that in case Russian soldiers came looking for us we should hide on the wooden benches in the cave until the soldiers left. Fortunately the farm was small, located in an isolated area without a road that would carry a truck. If we were on the list to be deported we were not found! Dad visited us on weekends, riding his bike for about ten miles from the city.

DAD'S CRIME- HE HAD BEEN A RESERVE OFFICER IN THE ESTONIAN ARMY.
When the German forces were approaching Tallinn in 1941 Dad was arrested. He was forced to board the ship "Eestirand". It was scheduled to take him and about 4,000 other Estonian men to Leningrad for further shipment to Siberian slave labor camps.

When Dad boarded the ship he found my uncle, Mom's younger brother Endel, on the same ship. The ship had barely departed the harbor of Tallinn when it was attacked by a Finnish dive bomber. Dad and Endel saw the attack developing and decided to split up, one to the front of the ship and the other to the back. They hoped that one of them would survive and get word back to the family.

The bomber was a good shot. He put his bombs right in the middle of the ship and blew out the bottom, causing the ship to sink. Both Dad and Endel survived. They were picked up by fishermen from the island of Prangli who gave them a place of refuge until German troops occupied the area. It was a great day when they returned home.

WE BARELY ESCAPED THE WORST BOMBING OF TALLINN.

After three years of German occupation the Russian forces were once again approaching our home. The nightly bombing of Tallinn was intense. Mom and Dad decided that Mom, and Heiki and I, would go to Kuusiku, about 30 miles from Tallinn, where we would be safe from the bombing.

By pure coincidence our departure was set for March 9, 1944. Dad drove us to our uncle Ott's home. We were welcomed with open arms and cramped quarters.

That night we witnessed the red sky from fires from the horrible bombing attack which destroyed most of Tallinn. The Russian bombers used what we called Christmas Trees to light the city. The flares were hung on a frame that was in turn attached to a parachute.

Today the Christmas Trees remind me of the flares used by US troops in Vietnam to protect military bases from night attack by the Viet Cong. Dad returned to work and we stayed in Kuusiku for five months.

THE BOAT WAS CONFISCATED!

Dad made regular trips to visit us and picked us up during the third week of August 1944. Mom and Dad later told us that a fishing boat they had hired to provide a way for the entire family to escape to Sweden had been discovered by the Germans and confiscated.

There was no other option available to us. We had to split up. Mom and the two of us boys sought transport an empty German transport ship returning to Poland. Dad's work contacts in Germany had promised to take care of us, until he would join us, or we would return to Estonia, depending on the progress of the war.

A PRETTY COOL TRIP

We sailed from Tallinn on August 19, 1944. The weather was beautiful and the ship was empty. Heiki and I had the run of the ship and the sailors were nice to us. We were given a large cabin with some mattresses on the floor. We shared it with one other family! When we arrived in Gotenhafen, now known as Gdynia, Poland, there was a small band playing welcoming music for us on the quay. All of that changed in a hurry!

SOOME PUSS- A FINNISH HUNTING KNIFE - AND LICE!

From the ship we boarded a bus that took us to a barbed wire enclosed camp. We were prisoners!

We shared a large bedroom with 30 or 40 other people from the ship. By this time we were pretty tired and glad to hit the sack! The first sign of trouble was the rustling of the straw throughout the room. The mattresses were straw filled ticks that had seen other occupants who weren't as clean as we were! The lights were turned back on and people asked whether anybody had a knife. My Finnish hunting knife, that I had received as a gift for my 12th birthday, made the rounds. The place was infested and we fought a losing battle until we went to sleep.

The next morning Mom made an appointment with the Camp Commander, delivered a bottle of Dad's finest liquor and bought our way out of camp! We even received transportation to the closest railroad station!

ATTIC APARTMENT AND EITHER A SPANKING OR A SCOLDING

The trip to Auerbach im Vogtland, our predetermined meeting place with Dad, went pretty well. We were guests with a kind German family for a few weeks until they helped Mom find us an attic apartment.

The apartment had a living area with a small kitchen, a sink in one corner and a table with a sofa that wrapped around it in another. The sofa became my bed. Heiki had a small bed against another wall. Mom had a separate bedroom with a steeply slanted ceiling and a window in the roof. The window could be propped open with a metal rod.

Shortly before we had to leave the area because Russian troops were drawing close to Auerbach, Mom had taken Heiki out. I was the only one at home. The air raid sirens sounded. I went to the bedroom and looked out of the window. The sky was full of large US or English bombers, heading in the direction of Dresden or Leipzig. The aircraft were in very good formation. There was no sign of German fighters or anti aircraft fire. I pushed the window wide open against the roof and decided to take a better look. I used some furniture to provide me with steps and climbed on the roof.

Much to my chagrin that was the time when Mom and Heiki arrived at home. Mom grabbed me by the ankles and made it clear that I had to get off the roof and into the basement that served as a bomb shelter! I don't remember whether I got a spanking or a serious scolding! In any case, the allies didn't waste any bombs on our little town.

THE NIGHT MOM CRIED

We had been in the apartment for about three weeks when we got the word. We hadn't had any way of keeping track of the progress of the war. There was no radio in the apartment and the only way was through newspapers, published sporadically. On the 24th or 25th of September Mom came home with a newspaper that said that Tallinn had fallen to the Russian troops. Mom cried!

ALL IS WELL- DAD IS WITH US!

Dad showed up about ten days later. He said he was on the last ship that had left the harbor of Tallinn on September 22nd. The ship followed the same course we had taken about five weeks earlier. There was one big difference. Our trip had been quiet, whereas Dad's ship had been attacked in the Baltic Sea by a Russian torpedo bomber. Dad thought that the bomber took too flat an attack angle as the pilot released the torpedo. The torpedo acted like a flat rock thrown on smooth water. It hit the water, skipped and went through the smoke stack of the ship before disappearing in the water on the other side.

There was no repeat attack and the ship arrived safely in Gotenhafen [Gdynia]. Dad had brought a box of smoked bacon slabs from Estonia. It was almost stolen from the dock. He had left the box in somebody's care and when he returned he couldn't find it. He said that he walked to and fro looking for it. Finally, he saw a woman sitting on something, with her skirt covering the seat. He saw the large letters with his name peeking out from under her long skirt and reclaimed it! We were very thankful since that bacon was a main source of nourishment as we later traveled from Auerbach to Lindau and eventually to the village of Kranzegg in the foothills of the Alps.

HIT THE ROAD ONCE MORE!

The approach of Russian forces forced us to leave Auerbach in February 1945. I turned 13 in November 1944 and Heiki had turned 9 in October of the same year. As I think about it now, we didn't consider our lot to be anything out of the ordinary. Dad and Mom didn't complain. That was a bit unusual since they had locked the doors to our apartment in Tallinn and left everything behind. They did what they thought best for all of us. Dad had enough German money and Heiki and I never even thought about finances.

Somehow Dad, who was 37 years old at the time, escaped being arrested and forced to go to the front to fight the Russians.

Talking about the Russians, they were getting uncomfortably close to us. We packed our suitcases and took a train to Plauen, expecting to travel on through Nürnberg to the Swiss border.

A RUCKSACK WITH A FLAP HELD IN PLACE WITH A LEATHER STRAP

Our goal was to travel to Bodensee, as far from the approaching Russians as possible. We left Auerbach by train. Our first stop was Plauen. As our train pulled into the station that night, there was an air raid warning. We were ordered to leave the RR station and walk to a nearby park that had deep ditches dug for bomb shelters. All the lights were turned off and it was pitch black in the station. I had to hold on - with my teeth - to the long leather strap of the flap on Dad's rucksack as we went through the underground passage in the station.

Dad and I had two suitcases and a backpack each and we didn't want to get separated. We managed to get safely to the park. Some bombs had fallen in the area and some fires were burning, but we were safe.

After a while the all clear was given we headed back to the station and continued south through Nürnberg to Lindau.

The Allied bombing of the city of Nürnberg had taken a terrible toll. The rail yards were totally destroyed with railroad rails bent into every imaginable shape and pointing to the sky. There seemed to be only one track through the mess. Our train moved very slowly and we made it. As I recall the trip to Lindau took two days and we slept on the train.

Pärnu, Estonia ~ 1938-39 Our Family with Heiki on Isa's knee

Arne with Isa kayaking in Pärnu

247

A STARK CONTRAST BETWEEN GERMANY AND SWITZERLAND
We arrived in Lindau in the evening. Dad and Mom sought out a facility in the middle of town set up to handle refugees on a short term basis. We once again faced sleeping on mattresses made of materials like large potato sacks, stuffed tightly with straw. Fortunately they didn't have any bugs from previous occupants like they did in Gotenhafen! Heiki and I got the top bunks of Mom's and Dad's beds. I went to sleep immediately and had a rude awakening in the night. I had rolled over and fallen out of the top bunk. Thankfully nothing was damaged, not even my pride! That's what happens when you are really tired.

Mom and Dad tried to get permission to stay in town with the hope of being able to sneak into Switzerland.

No such luck! We were told that no refugees were permitted to remain in the border area and we had to be out of town in a couple of days. Surprisingly the sight seeing cable cars were still running to the top of a nearby mountain. We took an evening ride up! What a contrast, as seen from the top. The lights on the Swiss side were bright and beautiful while the German side was totally dark. The border was clearly delineated by the lights on one side and lack of lights on the other! We took the last cable car down to town and back to the refugee facility.

RETTENBERG, KRANZEGG AND ELLEG AT THE END OF THE WAR.
A local train took us through the beautiful foothills of the Alps, stopping at every station. We liked the looks of Rettenberg and got off the train. I don't remember whether we stayed there for a night or not. In any case, we heard of a tourist apartment that would be available in Kranzegg, the next station on the railroad track.

When we arrived there we found a very nice small apartment that would be available for us until the tourist season would begin! We held a family meeting and decided that it was unlikely for any tourists to show up very soon and took the apartment on the second floor of a new home. An Estonian mother, a Mrs. Miller lived across the street with two children. The older one was a girl, Silvia. Her younger child, Arvo was my age. We became friends on the spot.

Food became an issue at this point. Potatoes and cheese were the two main foods that were available and we ate a lot of both! There wasn't much variety to the diet!

For some reason, maybe the question why Dad was not in the German Army, caused Mom and Dad to be very cautious and they decided that we ought to move into a smaller village off the beaten path. A very nice German farm family took us in at a small farm in Ellegg, a small Alpine village.

The family accepted me like one of their sons. They gave Mom, Dad and Heiki a large bedroom on the first floor of the farm house and I became roommates with their 22 year old son Hans. He had been injured in the war and lost one eye. We shared a bedroom on the second floor, each of us sleeping in opposite corners of the room.

By this time my earthly possessions had shrunk to one pair of old ski boots, a pair of nice boots with artificial rubber soles, a wrist watch, my Finnish hunting knife and some pants, shirts and socks along with underwear. I kept the boots under my bed and put a nail in the wall next to my bed where to hang my wrist watch. A second, stronger nail held my knife in its leather sheath.

OOPS, NOBODY WARNED ME ABOUT THE FLOOR IN THE BARN!
This farm house, like all the rest in the village, had the family quarters in one end of the house and a barn for about 40 cows in the other end. The hay for the cows was kept in the area above the cow barn.

When warmer weather arrived in late March or early April I was working like a regular farm hand with Hans and some other help. It was time to send the cows to the Alpine meadows for the summer. The cows left and it was our job to clean the barn. The barn floor was level cement where the cows stood and munched their hay. Behind the tails was a cement trough that was designed to catch the manure that could be washed with a hose and collected at the end into a big tank under the floor.

When the jobs were handed out for the day, I was handed a broom and told to sweep the cobwebs off the ceiling of the barn. I was eager to get started. I considered the task and didn't like the idea of the cobwebs and dust falling on me. The best way to handle it was to walk backwards on the boards between the two rows of cow stalls. All went well, but I didn't pay attention to what everybody else was doing. Until... the floor disappeared from behind me and I found myself dropping into about four feet of liquid cow manure!

UGH and double UGH! The other men had removed the planks between the rows of cows to clean the tank. Fortunately I landed on my feet! As quickly as I fell, I came out of all of that good stuff! There was a typical German fountain in front of the house. Cold or not I dove into the icy water! One of the men had seen me and helped me by getting a towel. I removed my boots, shook them out and headed for the house to take a hot bath.

MOROCCAN TROOPS OCCUPIED THE AREA.
We knew that the British and American Forces were north of us, but we had expected French troops to liberate us. However, all of the liberators in our case were troops from Morocco. They took over the area and arrested Dad. He was taken to Kranzegg, about 12 km from Ellegg and locked up in the basement of the house they had established as their Headquarters. This time Mom pleaded his case. She did a good job and Dad was released after two days.

The Moroccans had thought that Dad was a German officer who had put on civilian clothes and hidden on the farm! Meanwhile I discovered that the troops who had searched the farm house had also been in my room and had stolen my watch, my Finnish knife and my only decent pair of boots. We didn't complain since we were now free of Russians and the threat of Siberia!

GATHER THE FOREIGNERS.

The war in this area came to an end in May 1945 and we were gathered and taken to Displaced Persons Camps. In our case the first of these was a school building in Kempten. Twenty eight of us were in one of two large classrooms with two bathrooms on the second floor – the floor designated for Estonians. The Latvians were on the first floor and the Lithuanians were in a different building somewhere in town.

Life in DP camps in Germany!
Kempten – May – October 1945
Altenstadt – November 1945 – June 1946
Geretsried – June 1946 – Spring 1947
Augsburg – Spring 1947 – March 1949

Arne has taken that extra illuminating step and created a correspondence with his brother Heiki and cousins Gusten and Sannu to compare notes of their memories and perceptions. He has marked the sites of those with * followed by a number and they will be appended at the end of Arne's narrative.

GATHER THE REFUGEES IN KEMPTEN!

It was a new experience! The military vehicle that drove around the Alps and collected refugees dropped us off at a school house in Kempten. This building became our home for the next five months! We didn't know what to expect!

Germany was flooded with refugees from the Eastern European countries who had fled ahead of the advancing Russian forces. The Allies had to make some big decisions. The first step was to collect the refugees by nationalities into temporary facilities.

Our school house had three stories and a pretty good playground. The four classrooms on the first floor were assigned primarily to Latvians and the second floor to Estonians.

As we walked into the large classroom we found it set up with bunk beds running the length of both sides of the room and long tables with benches dividing the room. There were 28 of us! Our family was assigned two bunk beds that were pushed together. Mom and Dad got the bottom two and Heiki and I the top bunks. On one side of us, between us and the big window, was a young family from Saaremaa, a nice husband, wife and a baby. We also had a wall locker per family.

WHY THE EXTRA SHEETS?

It became very obvious that privacy was a luxury that was totally lacking. The adults among us worked wonders! The camp was administered by UNRRA (United Nations Relief and Rehabilitation Administration). Our committee talked with the administrators and they issued two extra sheets per family to hang on the sides of the bunk beds to offer privacy in the lower bunks!

Altenstadt :The top level of that large building served as the Exhibit Hall.

A picture from the Estonian exhibit in Altenstadt in 1946. I am the only youngster, at age 15, in the picture with the other older stamp collectors' stamp in the corner. The handwriting on the card is my father's.

Our Ema/Mom, Mari Ellermets, is on the far right of the picture above and the far right of the ladies who are standing on the picture below.

BATH HOUSES IN THE TOWN.

There were two bathrooms on each floor with a few sinks and three stools for both men and women. There were no shower facilities. That problem was solved by families visiting German bath houses where you could rent a bathtub with hot water for a given period of time – it seems to me that the time per family was 30 minutes. We made at least weekly trips to the closest of those businesses that were also used by many German families.

EXPERIENCE WITH THE FIRST SCHOOL IN A DP CAMP!

Within days of our arrival our parents decided to establish a school for the children.

My first year of high school began on the low stone wall at the side of the school building that served us as our home! We had excellent teachers since many of them had also decided that they would not survive under communist rule in Estonia. The best teachers had escaped just like we did!

It was on that stone fence that I learned my first "song", really a ditty, in English. I still remember it -- "Mr. Brown, Mr. Brown are you going down to town, would you stop and take me down, thank you kindly, Mr. Brown!" I don't know what kind of conveyance Mr. Brown was driving, but the song stuck in my mind!

The school building that housed us had three floors. The third floor was a common use area, a fairly good size room, became the first Estonian High School in Kempten. When the weather didn't permit us to sit on the stone fence we assembled in that classroom. Mom was one of the English teachers, even though her diploma from Estonia said that she was a home economics teacher!

ALTENSTADT NEAR SCHONGAU, GERMANY: FROM A SCHOOL TO A MILITARY COMPOUND!

It was time to move to more permanent facilities before the winter of 1945 set in. We took a military bus ride from Kempten to Altenstadt, near Schongau. Our new home was far better than the first camp.

The military base had a central parade ground that was surrounded by four large buildings. The refugee side consisted of one very long two story cement block building with a full basement. I believe that we were the only refugee nationality at that camp.

Our family was assigned a private room on the second floor with two bunk beds, a table and chairs and a military wall locker. There were large central toilet facilities with showers! It seemed quite luxurious after the five and a half months in the old school building in Kempten.

The food was also much better. We ate our meals in a US military mess hall that was in the next building. The allies also provided the materials and allowed our men to build a sauna in the basement of the building!

IT DOESN'T PAY TO PLAY HOOKY, ESPECIALLY IF YOU GET CAUGHT!

I was half way through my freshman year of high school when we arrived in Altenstadt. Our teachers and fellow students moved with us. Therefore, the only thing that changed was the school facility. Our classes met in large rooms across the hall from our bedrooms. We had the same faculty as we had had in Kempten.

Things seemed to go smoothly, but that was before we, boys, were tempted to misbehave! The school hours carried into late afternoon. The American soldiers who manned the mess hall were kind to us. They allowed us to take a 20 – 30 minute break in the afternoon, run to the mess hall and have a nice snack! We had discovered that the American GI's had a movie theater in the same building as the mess hall. There was no charge for the movie and nobody manned the door.

Three or four of us boys decided one afternoon that instead of returning to our last class we ought to skip out and go to the movie. All went well. We had no problem getting into the movie and we enjoyed it. The problem arose when we went back to school. We were told to report to our parents!

My parents were nice, but they were also strict! When I found my Dad he told me that I had to go and stand outside my classroom door at attention for a half an hour. If anybody stopped and asked me what I was doing I had to tell them that I had broken the rules and this was my punishment.

It was bad enough to have to do that with adults, but the really embarrassing part was to have to explain our behavior to the girls, especially in the higher classes!

THE FIRST BALTIC BOY SCOUT CAMP

Our refugee scouting in Germany got a great start in Altenstadt. We didn't have uniforms, but we had plenty of capable leaders and eager teen age followers!

The First Baltic Boy Scout Camp was held in the foothills of the Alps in June 1946 shortly before our DP Camp was relocated to Geretsried near Wolfratshausen. Each of the scouts was given a cloth name tape identifying the place and dates of the camp. Each tape identified the scout with a number. I was scout #27!

The camp was very well organized and set a good example for the camps that followed. I believe that the head of our camp was a Scoutmaster Mihkelson, one of the original scoutmasters who had brought scouting to Estonia.

A large multi purpose building overlooked the military facility at Altenstadt. The refugee family hosted a special exhibit of Estonian culture. The displays ranged from stamp collections to national costumes and art. Our Dad, Arnold Ellermets, was one of the organizers of the festival that was a big success.

GERESTSREID NEAR WOLFRADHAUSEN: FROM A MODERN MILITARY CASERNE TO THE BARRACKS IN THE FOREST!

Pack up your belongings and be ready for the next move! We didn't have much to pack when we received the orders! It was the summer of 1946 and our next home was waiting for us in Geretsried. It was close to the German Autobahn that runs from Munich to the area of famous castles such as Neuschwanstein and the ski areas of Garmisch Partenkirchen and Zugspitze, the highest mountain in Germany.

The caserns in Altenstadt were built around carefully manicured parade grounds. The barracks in Geretsried were hidden under a carpet of tall spruce.

Our living and school accommodations were cramped but adequate. Our family had one good size room off the central hall with a bathroom next to it.

My brother Heiki remembers that our Mom and the other Estonian ladies were surprised when they found a pair of nice socks with a small hole in them thrown in the trash in the bathroom. A Belgian officer had one of the rooms in our hallway. The ladies were utterly amazed that he threw the socks away instead of darning the hole!

THE REAR END OF A BULL!?!

To us he was just Isa (Dad), but he chose to work for UNRRA as a representative for the Estonian part of the camp. He greeted visiting dignitaries, worked in an office and continued as a very active athlete. Ema (Mom) continued teaching and was a girl scout leader.

Heiki began his acting career in the Estonian DP Theater. He was the only child in this play. He played his part barefoot as you can see in the third picture! And what about me ? I was the rear end of the bull! I was active as an Estonian Boy Scout. The following incident happened at a campfire!

Our scout troop had to present a skit.

We decided to treat the other scouts to a bullfight. The matador had a pool cue for a weapon and all we had was a green Army blanket. When the blanket was thrown over us the two of us became the bull. The boy in the front stood up straight and I had to bend over, put my arms around his waist and follow him around and make appropriate sounds.

The problem arose when the matador used the back end of the cue to stab the bull. I couldn't protect myself and he stabbed me behind the jaw, knocking my jaw out of joint. I didn't think much of it since it snapped back in place, or so I thought. Even today my jaw snaps out of place and makes a cracking sound when I open my mouth really wide or eat anything that requires tough chewing! Good memories of our boy scout days!!!

FIELD TRIP TO HITLER'S OFFICE!

The relocation of the camp from Altenstadt to Geretsried did not disrupt our schooling. One of the barracks was converted into a school and we continued with our studies. I think that it was our German language class that took us on a field trip to Berchtesgaden and higher into the Alps to see Hitler's "Eagle's Nest".

During our first trip there the facility was pretty well destroyed. But we could visit the large auditorium type office that had a beautiful view across the valley, even if its windows were blown out and the furniture was in absolute disarray. On a subsequent trip the place was cleaned up and as I recall we had to pay to get in!

My younger brother Heiki sent me a message, saying: Arne, here's one you probably don't remember. It seems that when you came back from the trip to Berchtesgaden, a piece of what you said was Hitler's desktop came with you. I must have envied that piece and eventually

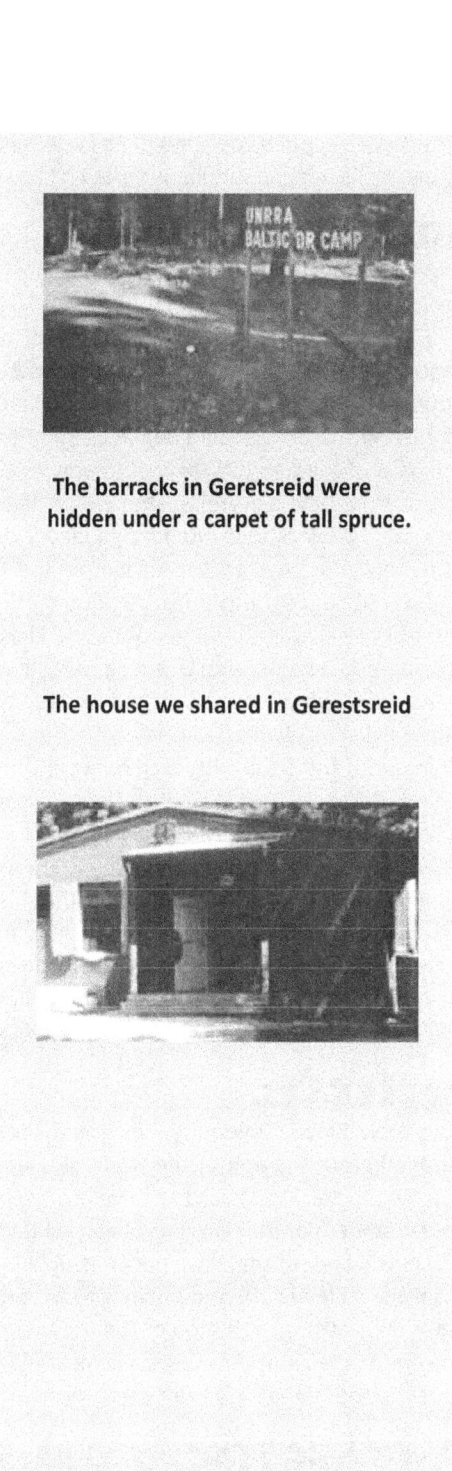

The barracks in Geretsried were hidden under a carpet of tall spruce.

The house we shared in Gerestsreid

Isa on far right with UNRRA officials

251

must have swapped you something for it. Believe it or not but after about 66 years, the piece is sitting on my desktop, next to my desk lamp. I don't know what I had to give up in a trade for it but I would guess that you don't have it any longer!

TOYS FOR DP TEENS!

Play things were at a premium in DP camps. Once we got settled in Geretsried Heiki and I took a good look around and decided to build our own fort!

The basic construction material came from a large roll of German military communications cable covered with a rubber sheath. The camp had a lot of trees. We chose four trees that were about ten feet apart and strung the cable, double strength, from tree to tree at well above our head height, forming a frame for the fort. Then we tied a network of wire so that it formed a bunch of 4 to 6 inch squares. We brought out several of our precious blankets, put them on the base of the net and we were ready for all kinds of adventures.

Books were at a premium, but we managed to borrow some books that gave us many hours of pleasure and ideas for imaginary explorations into foreign lands!

By this time I was a pretty accomplished story teller. When we were still in Tallinn, Estonia we had a small toilet. Mom had a routine. Every evening she would ask me to sit on the toilet and Heiki would sit on a small potty on the floor in front of me. It was a boring routine. Heiki asked me to tell him stories. I recall telling him all kinds of stories about us as crewmen of a submarine traveling to far away seas.

As I think about it now, if I had realized that I would spend 30 years of my adult life as a pilot I would have told him about flying airplanes. However, whether on the toilet in Estonia or the net in Geretsried, we expanded our horizons by sharing our thoughts with each other in stories.

CHESS!

Chess was still one of our favorites. There was a young veteran in our camp who had lost one leg below the knee while fighting on the Russian front. I think that his name was Endel Kool? He was an exceptional wood carver and eventually established a workshop in the community building where he made chess sets, trays, etc.

I don't think that Heiki and I ever got beyond our little folding chess set that we brought from Estonia. We used tweezers for moving the chess pieces in the slots on the board. We must have been careful – I don't remember chasing any lost chess figures under our fort! Endel's hand carved chess sets were beautiful but out of our price range!

CABLE CARS.

Toys took a lot of ingenuity. We talked about the cable cars that had taken us to the mountain top near Bregenz and Lindau before the end of the war. The scenery had been spectacular and we lingered on the top one evening, before catching the last car back to the valley. We had seen Switzerland peacefully sparkling on one side of the border and the total darkness of the blackout of war on the German side.

Thinking about that gave me an idea of building a cable car of our own. I had some fishing line that became the cable from the valley to the mountain top. A matchbox was the cable car and thin thread was the means for moving the car from the bottom to the top of the mountain. Somehow I located a small reversible electric motor that had a pulley on the end of the shaft. Another pulley was placed at the top of our mountain – actually a high window ledge - and we were ready for our imaginary ride to the top of the world!

PATCHING PING PONG BALLS!

Necessity, being the mother of invention, taught us how to perform surgery on ping pong balls! UNRRA had a checkout point where we could borrow a volley ball or a basketball and even baseball bats and a few gloves. They would also issue us ping pong balls as long as the supply lasted. After the end of the war the ping pong balls were of a very poor quality. We hit them hard and pretty soon they would crack.

We were resourceful and figured out how to repair them. We made patches from broken balls by cutting them just bif enough to cover the crack. Then filed the newly made patches as thin as possible with a fingernail file and then glued the patch over the broken part of the cracked ball with Mom's fingernail polish remover. The patched ball would never bounce quite straight, but it taught us a lot how to be ready to handle the ball in a game where the opponent used a lot of English! The process was time consuming, but it allowed us to continue improving our game.

Our stay at Geretsried was comparatively short. By the fall of 1946, I was about to turn 15 and Heiki 11. We packed our few suitcases and were off on the next phase of our refugee travels in Germany.

AUGSBURG - FROM A SCENIC FOREST CAMP TO A BIG CITY.

Our next home and school was in the city of Augsburg that was in utter ruin.

What does the introduction to a move to a big city in the early spring of 1947 have to do with a Spanish jet fighter? Nothing really, except that it triggered memories from another phase in our lives! We were missionaries with Awana Clubs International serving in Europe in the late 1980's. Wilhelmina and I had traveled from Frankfurt, Germany to Coria del Rio in Spain to help American missionaries Ken and Peggy Merriken start Awana clubs in their area. Ken and Peggy had a large bathroom with a sink and a shower. I was shaving and Wilhelmina stepped into the shower. When she turned the water on it sounded like a low flying jet was roaring over the rooftop! When she turned the water off the engine noises from the jet stopped! It turned out that there was a large gas fueled instant hot water heater on the patio outside the bathroom window. The loud noise was generated by that contraption! It reminded me of the UNRRA (United Nations Rehabilitation and Repatriation Administration)

HOUSE IN AUGSBURG!

When we moved from the beauty of nature in Geretsried to Augsburg we had to adjust to quite a few changes. The changes involved our living conditions, proximity to schools, changes in curriculum and many other areas.

LIVING CONDITIONS

Our first home in Augsburg was a very large brick apartment building that was divided between refugee housing and the UNRRA offices. Our family was allocated one of five large bedrooms in an apartment on the second floor. We shared the apartment with four other families. For the first time we had access to a kitchen and we, meaning Mom, cooked our own meals.

Food items were still distributed by the refugee organization. There was no refrigeration or cold storage for food. The families shared the large stove as well as the one toilet and a separate bathroom with a large tub. There was a BIG gas fueled instant hot water heater described above, it was hung on the wall over the tub. Dad worked in an UNRRA office in the same building.

The organization was later renamed the International Refugee Organization (IRO). His position granted him the right to use a US military gym that was a short streetcar ride from, "home". I was delighted since he took me along to the gym and I received some excellent coaching in volleyball and basketball. Coaching was fun for both of us. We made the refugee newspaper when both of us played on the Estonian team at the camp against the teams from Latvia and Lithuania. I have to confess that my part in that games was very limited and took place when one of our older team members fouled out!

The street scene in front of the UNRRA House shows the typical way for moving almost anything in those days, using a wagon even while wearing a business suit on a busy street! Obviously parking was not a problem!

DAD AND HEIKI SURVIVED MY COOKING!

Mom had to go to the hospital for about a week for what was called minor surgery! Since we had to cook our own meals something had to be done. There appears to have been a vote.

I either won or lost, depending on how you want to look at it. There were no cook books and Mom wrote her own cookbook on rainbow colored paper. The menu and detailed cooking instructions were written on different colored paper for each day that she expected to be out of commission. She had been a home economics teacher before I was born. As a result, her instructions were easy to follow and nobody complained about my cooking. On the other hand, I don't remember receiving any compliments either!

SUMMER CAMP.

Our stay at the UNRRA house came to an end while I was at Boy and Girl Scout Summer Camp in Pfronten-Weissbach that lasted from August 25 to September 10, 1947. We lived in tents. I was a part of the Black Anchor Tent Team and competed with the other teams for the Gray Wolf Trophy. We came in second and were proud to show off our trophy!

Since we were in the Alps we also climbed mountains and visited the ruins of castles that had seen their better days! I am the shortest of the boys in these three pictures. I took my growth spurt a year later!

Isa high above the net spiking the volleyball

View from the doorway of our house

Street scene in front of the UNRRA House, Augsburg

Brother Heiki beginning his acting career as a barefoot farm boy!

The camp came to an unusual end. The Girl Scouts had their tents fairly close to those housing the boys. We had many of our activities, such as camp fires, together. One of the girls got very sick and was diagnosed as having polio. She was transported by ambulance from Pfronten to Augsburg. The authorities decided to quarantine everybody at the camp to see whether anybody else was infected.

We went back to Augsburg and were kept in isolation in a US Army hospital for a week, before we were allowed to join our families. Fortunately there were no other cases of polio.

LAST MOVE BEFORE DEPARTURE FOR THE UNITED STATES!

Dad, Mom and Heiki made the move from the city of Augsburg to a more permanent housing complex in Augsburg Haunstetten before we arrived back from the quarantine. While we were at the camp in Pfronten, some of our fellow scouts went on a trip to the International Boy Scout Jamboree in Paris. They had their picture taken under the high gate that they built leading to the Estonian area of the Jamboree grounds.

HAUNSTETTEN AND OUR PRIVATE APARTMENT!

Well sort of! The Allies moved the German residents out of several blocks of identical small apartment houses. We were teamed up with a young married couple, Mr. and Mrs. Enn Eessalu. Our home was on the second floor. It was one of five apartments in the house and consisted of two bedrooms, a kitchen and a small bathroom. The Eessalus lived in the smaller bedroom, Dad, Mom and Heiki had the slightly larger bedroom. I had the corner of the kitchen.

My kingdom had a folding Army cot and a large wooden box, standing on end. The lid to the box had been removed and the box divided into two shelves for my limited supply of laundry and my notebooks for school. The contraption was covered with a cloth cover and it served me well until we departed for the US. There were also two small square kitchen tables with four straight back chairs, one for each family.

All six of us must have behaved pretty well and I don't remember any disagreements. When the Eessalus became the proud parents of twin girls I became the godfather of Anu, one of the twins.

Sanitation and good health rules were always a key for survival. Our apartment had only a small bathroom with a toilet. The sink for doing our daily toiletries was the same one we used for preparing our food and washing our dishes in the kitchen. There was a wash room in the basement with a list of names defining which apartment had the priority to use the facility each day.

When it was our day we heated up the water in the really big kettle, put the hot water in a tin bathtub and took baths. Since we played sports on a regular basis we had to sneak into that room whether it was our day or not and wash up with cold water!

The apartments were heated with a small stove that used ordinary firewood. The same was true of the kettle in the basement. We had to buy logs of wood from the Germans who came by with a hand pulled wagon. I was the family wood chopper and stacker. I still have a large scar on my left hand where I barely missed my index finger and cut a nice slice above the V of my hand. Fortunately it healed well, leaving only a caution sign to be more careful in the future!

ACTIVITIES IN HAUNSTETTEN!

We, the children, were fortunate to have good adult supervision and lots of youth activities. Scouting was big as were sports and games like chess, checkers and ping pong.

Our apartment was in a perfect location for us. The community volleyball court was directly in front of our house and we knew whenever a game was in progress, which was often. View from the doorway of our house that was a copy of those seen on the picture!

A basketball court was only two short blocks away and we practiced a lot. Dad continued working for IRO in the same building where we lived before moving to Haunstetten. He also continued to play both volleyball and basketball.

Mom was a Girl Scout leader and Heiki and I were both in Boy Scouts. We continued with camping, both under the auspices of Scout leaders as well as the guidance of YMCA leaders who had served in that capacity in Estonia. Many of those camps took us to the foothills of the Alps where we learned quite bit about survival out of doors, and the beauty of nature.

NEW SCHOOL- AGAIN!

I really shouldn't say "new school" because the school in Augsburg was well established when we began attending it in the fall of 1947. The school, located in the center of town, became my last high school before arriving in the US.

The other DP's, many of whom arrived in town two years before us, did an excellent job of locating facilities. They also set up the curriculum and identified top notch teachers in the Estonian DP family. The principal of the school was Härra Koljo who had been the principal of the Estonian Real Kool in Tallinn. My homeroom teacher was Härra Ruumet, a superb teacher of mathematics. Our English teacher, Mrs. Williams, was my favorite! All of them prepared us very well for entry into the American school system upon our arrival on this side of the ocean!

The trip to school was a new adventure. Up to this point the school facility had been either a part of the house where we lived or at least on the same compound. Now we had to walk about 1.5 to 2 miles just to get to the streetcar that took us to town. Our stop in Haunstetten was the end of the line!

We were a happy group of youngsters and the walk with friends was a joy. We rode an old fashioned streetcar with monthly student tickets. You can see on the picture a sign that says, "Speaking with the driver of the car while in transit will result in prosecution!" We were happy to be allowed to speak with our friends! The streetcar took us past the Messerschmidt aircraft plant, and runway, as well as a stop where the students from the other camp at Hochfeld met us.

A PROBLEM - LEARN FRENCH REALLY FAST!

The school facility was a real school building, located in the middle of town. It was under the control of the US military government. The curriculum followed the pattern of the one used by the Estonian Real Kool in Tallinn. Upon my arrival in the US I realized that I had been very fortunate to have such good and demanding teachers. The school days were long and diverse. School was in session six days a week.

As good as the curriculum was, I encountered a problem. My previous study of languages included Estonian, English, and German. I am still fluent in all three. The Augsburg school added Latin, and much to my chagrin, French. I was in my third year of high school and the students in classes ahead of me had studied German instead of French as the third major language. But, for some reason, beginning with my class, the German language had been replaced with French. My grades were quite good, except for French. My new classmates who had gone to this high school had two years of French under their belts.

Mother arranged for tutoring with my French teacher. It worked, to an extent. When the report cards came out my progress in French was marginal. Signing up for tutoring raised my grade to satisfactory. When I stopped being tutored they dropped to marginal! Thus, every other semester I had to go to tutoring until I escaped from it by our family moving to the US!

WE WERE THANKFUL TO TRANSIT TO THE NEW WORLD.

Dad and Mom had been very busy, without involving Heiki or me. They had established contact with her brother, our Uncle Karl Vesk, who lived in Long Island, New York. Karl was the first engineer on an Estonian cargo ship. It was hit by a torpedo from a German U-boat before the end of WW II and sank near Cape Hatteras. He was rescued and brought to the US where he accepted employment as a mechanic in a boat yard on Long Island. Mom had written to him and asked him to see whether he could get his boss to sign a document guaranteeing employment to our Dad, providing that Dad could arrange transportation to the US. His boss agreed, signed the papers and after a period of waiting we were provided transportation through the International Refugee Organization.

We arrived in New York harbor on March 21, 1949. Our ship was not allowed to dock that evening. I clearly remember standing on the deck of the USS General Muir anchored close to the Statue of Liberty. I watched the lights of New York City and especially the traffic on the Long Island Parkway that runs along the shore. I remember the thought running through my 17 year old mind, "I wonder what this new country has in store for me?"

I found this page in an old notebook from the Estonian High School in Germany. We had a very full schedule! The page below shows the grade sheet from my first year of schooling in the US as a senior in High School.

The grades marked with an R indicate the results of the NY State Regents Exams that have to be passed before graduation. The results show that

1) the Estonian refugee high school did an excellent job of preparing us for the schools in the US and
2) That I wasn't involved in the social scene since I didn't feel completely at home with the language and spent my time divided between studying and playing Varsity basketball.

Re Mai's questions about **STRESSES ON THAT TREK**

Arne replied.

Your message raises questions that apparently Heiki and I didn't find necessary to resolve! Fortunately we never had to worry where our next meal would come from or what was in the pot. When there wasn't much we didn't seem to care, as long as we survived. We were fortunate to live under the close supervision of our parents through the period where we might have suffered either physical or mental harm.

Thankfully we were flexible enough to establish daily and longer term goals for our lives, received an excellent education and good adult support from the Estonian and later the American community.

Looking back it was all challenging, interesting and rewarding. We both chose military careers that included long periods of family separation in places like Vietnam, Thailand and Africa,

...My immediate thoughts centered on the fact that our escape from Estonia and the requirement for any resultant psychiatric care has never entered my mind! I was almost 13 and brother Heiki almost 9 when we saw our parents lock our doors in Tallinn and begin a new, exciting phase of our lives as refugees! Our parents were both 36 years old and in excellent health. You could say that we rolled with the punches and landed on our feet!

Now that we think about it, we never heard our parents complain about our sometimes miserable circumstances. Life was interesting. As I wrote earlier, Ema, Heiki and I left Tallinn on August 19, 1944 and Isa followed us on what he claimed to be the last German transport ship out of Tallinn on September 22nd. His ship was attacked by a torpedo bomber, but the pilot made too flat an approach and the torpedo went through the smoke stack and fell into the Baltic Sea! We lived in Auerbach im Vogtland in a small attic apartment until February 1945 and then hopped and skipped across southern part of Germany until the end of the war. We traveled through Nürnberg on what appeared to be the only useable railroad track among a bombed out ruin of the railroad station and ended up in Lindau am Bodensee.

We were treated well when we arrived at a building converted for a temporary refugee home where I fell out of the top bunk in a double bed because the bag that served as a mattress was overstuffed with straw! Isa took us on a quick trip on a cable car to a mountain top where we could observe the difference between a well lit Switzerland and totally blacked out Germany.

What really mattered was that we were together as a family and could draw strength from each other.

The end of WW II found us in the villages of Kranzegg and Ellegg in the Alps. Once again, we were well received and supported by German farm families until we were collected into our first refugee camp in Kempten. We learned a lot in process! My lesson was that if you help your host family .... I was single minded in performing my task.

Our education had been interrupted by the war. Once in place at Kempten we were the first class in the Estonian High School. As you can se we didn't have any time or interest in developing any psychiatric problems!

Four years in DP Camps ended with our "cruise" to the US and entry into the US education system. Heiki and I were immediately competitive with our fellow students. We both graduated from College, received Master's Degrees, attended several years of USAF graduate schools and finally retired as Colonels form the US Air Force. I was a pilot and my most memorable assignment was to fly to Hanoi, North Vietnam on March 4, 1973, to participate in the return of US POW's from the hands of the North Vietnamese.

As you can see the escape from Estonia was a challenge, caused a few temporary problems, but didn't have any harmful impact on our lives!

LIFE AT THE AUGSBURG CAMP: COLLAGE

Picture taken under the high gate that they built leading to the Estonian area of the Jamboree grounds

In front of the school house

On the school bus

I am the shortest of the boys in these three pictures. I took my growth spurt a year later!

My high school class led by our homeroom teacher Härra Ruumet.

Venus, laden with refugees, arriving in Örnsköldsvik harbour. Venus, certified to carry 20 passengers, had arrived with 842 souls]. Venus, laden with refugees, arriving in Örnsköldsvik harbour. Venus, certified to carry 20 passengers, had arrived with 842 souls].

The war was still on so the Swedes did not allow pictures to be taken in their harbours. That's why you see soldiers' backs only. It was not that the passengers had come up on deck to witness the docking. That's where they had been for 62 hours. The hold was full of women and children.

Flyktvägen från Estland till Sverige i september 1944.

Flight from Estonia to Sweden in September 1944

SANNU MÕLDER

VENUS

Episode: Venus
Date: 25-26 Sep 1944
Time: Monday night, 25th
Place: Gulf of Finland; From Rauma(Fi) to Örnsköldsvik(Sw)
Square brackets [] contain comments by Sannu Mölder

Background:
Soviet army was re-invading the Baltic States. Many Estonians had fled to Finland to escape another Russian terror. On the 2nd of September 1944 Finland signed an armistice with Russia. Russia was demanding the return of all "USSR citizens", which, in their view, now included all Estonians in Finland. Those who did return were never again seen. The Finnish Government was sympathetic towards the refugees and was covertly aiding them to flee to neutral Sweden.

EXCERPT FROM VABA EESTLANE; 17 Sep 92.

Title: [Page from History; Quest for freedom exceeded fear of death. Tragedy on the Baltic Sea 1944]

Translation:
Finnish authorities helped to organize small motor boats along with the ships "Gustav" and "Venus" to transport refugees from Uusikaupun (Finland) and Rauma (Fi) to Gävle (Sweden). The very last trip of Venus is a drama in itself.

Venus left the Rauma archipelago Monday night 25th September 1944 – destination Gävle. Raging storm made it impossible to maintain a WSW course for Gävle. The Finnish captain of he MV Venus was forced to alter course to WNW. With normal weather the trip to Gävle would take 17 hours.

During the night the wind veered to NW making it difficult to maintain even a northerly course. Seas were washing over the port gunwales, drenching those sitting and standing on deck. When the captain changed course into the starboard seas rumours started, saying that he ship was headed for Vaasa, into the hands of the Russians.

One man lost his nerve and shot himself in the head with his pistol. [(4) continued from the following week's Meie Elu edition – same title]. The captain/helmsman was forced to change course again into the port seas. There was no sign of the Swedish coast all day Tuesday. Faint city lights were seen the next night in the west. No-one knew what town the lights were coming from.

Land was sighted at dawn of the 27th and soon thereafter the ship's motor stopped working and the ship became adrift in the storm. There were seven Estonian salt-water captains on board who suggested that sails be raised. The Finnish crew was not familiar with the sails so the Estonian 'sailors' had to raise the sails. But to no avail – the coast did not come closer.

Around noon, a Swedish coast-guard cutter approached; a tow was attempted; the hawser broke; someone got the engine going; Venus now followed the cutter into the rocky fjord; the engine quit again; a tug was summoned and Venus was finally towed into Örnsköldsvik harbour.

The Coast-guard later informed us that, had we drifted another 20 metres, our bottom would have been punctured by underwater cliffs and we would have sunk. We were 300 km north of our intended Gävle and 27 hours late. **Gävle radio had already announced that Venus had sunk.**

Aside from the suicide, two babies in the hold had succumbed to engine fumes. [I recall being below deck with other chldren as well as all the women. Our place was right below the ladder leading to the deck. This was the route of the communal pee-pot as it was passed hand-to-hand to be emptied overboard. In the stormy seas, it was not easy to keep the rim of the pot and the level of pee parallel. Consequently, seaspray, occasionally washing down the open hatch, was not always seaspray. There was a (very fortunate) lack of drinking water.]

Örnsköldsvik had been warned to expect Finnish refugees. However none had arrived thus far so the people of Örnsköldsvik poured their hospitality on the Estonians. Seven refugee centres were set up [many local public school children got unexpected holidays].

[Refugees soon became dispersed to various places of employment throughout Sweden. My parents and I traveled to Ölsboda Estate near Degerforss where Dad became the caretaker and Mom worked in the kitchen. It was too late for me to start school – my first sabbatical at age 9!].

DIALOGUES WITH ARNE & HIS COUSINS

While Arne was compiling his story he maintained a dialogue with his cousins Gusten and Sannu and his brother Heiki. They have shared this with me.

To Heiki, Gusten and Sannu:

Arne writes: Here's the story of Altenstadt to the best of my recollection. . .
My recollection of our room in Altenstadt and its furniture is very hazy. Do you remember any of it? Sannu, please read it for your info and ask any questions that you might have. Also, I taped a conversation with your mom and dad in Toronto describing your escape from Estonia to Finland and then to Sweden and Canada. May I transcribe that tape and send it to you for editing and then to Mai. Your story was much more dangerous and scary than our escape from Estonia! Thanks for your comments Gusten!

That little commemorative cloth strip with our camp numbers is the most elusive thing that I have had in a long time! I first found it in a Black Magic candy box that is very old. I took it out so that I would know exactly where it would be in case I needed it. Then it disappeared again - I think that it is on my desk, but at the moment its exact location is unknown. Our two numbers, 27 and 29 being so close probably had something to do with both of us being from the same scout unit in Altenstadt. I am also still looking for that little album from the First Baltic Boy Scout Camp in Altenstadt. I am sure that it is somewhere in plain sight, but I just can't find it! **We seem have too many photo albums!**

I have to agree with you that **I also had a very unpleasant feeling toward the German school that I attended for a very short period in Auerbach.** My German was very poor at that time.

Whenever a grouchy man teacher would ask me a question he left no doubt that I was a stupid foreigner. I was very happy that we left Auerbach shortly after I entered that school. The gym teacher was even worse since I could not perform up to his expectation in gymnastics, especially attempting to do the exercises on the bar.

However, the attitude of the German people in the Alps was 100% different. I was accepted as one other family at the farm and except for falling into cow manure in the barn, which was my fault, all went well.

We were also very well received as youth missionaries after retiring from the USAF. Of course the situation was completely different since we came as "Americans" working with German children. My language skills had been polished by that time with the experience of four years of active duty with the USAF after four years of college German. I was even asked to preach in German at many youth camps as well as in German churches.

I was frequently asked whether I came form Sweden. Wilhelmina's situation was a bit different. She had no background in German language and did her best to learn the language as quickly as possible. She attended the Goethe Institute at Rhein Main Air Base when we were still on active duty and continued with her studies once we arrived there in 1985 as missionaries. The German people whom we met at many churches first asked us whether she was an American.

After a few years they asked her whether she came from England. And, before we completed our missionary ministry there they were asking her whether she came from Holland! That showed a definite improvement and brought her "guessed at" home country closer to Germany.

I don't remember anything about the fishing line and the hooks that you mention in your message! The Raag family lived two doors down from us in our hallway on the second floor of the caserne in Altenstadt. Helmo's younger brother Arno came to Union College either one or two years after I started college, but we didn't have any classes together and didn't really see each other except on rare occasions on the campus.

Roman Toi was the Estonian choir director at Geretsried and also an excellent ping pong player. We, the boys, held him in high esteem because he used to come over to play ball with us!

You should write your own "snippets" for Mai and see how she would use them.
Thanks again, ...Arne

Gusten's message to Arne:
Actually, my shocking, ugly and unpleasant memories in Germany are from the treatment of students in the high school I attended briefly -- that was during the last weeks of war; And then after the war, when we, the refugees, came under the apparent protection and care of the western allies, while the German population suffered famine, denazification persecution, prisoner of war camps, west's condemnation for war crimes, persecution of Jews and Communists in KZ atrocities. They could not express their venom against the occupying military, but could take it out against us. And that went on for couple of years, even past the monetary reform and start of economic reconstruction. **We were not wanted in their land.** Verfluchte Ausländer was the frequently heard label, as well as being called "guests of Hitler". (The admission of Baltic refugees to the Third Reich in 1944 was explained in the press as at Hitler's invitation).

Conversely, **for the period of our stay in Germany during the last war year, from when we arrived there until the capitulation and occupation, I must say that we, my family, were treated pretty well by the civilian population and social aid organizations like the NSV.** There was little difference between the treatment of German refugees from the east and foreign nationals like us. At least as long as we were not, and did not behave like the conscripted (semi-slave) laborers of the "lower racial groups" from the eastern lands. My father knew how to "work" the German system and social order, even when we were compelled to escape from possible punishment for disobedience, and had to keep moving for fear of capture as fugitives from the police. Of course, we behaved as if we were all together with "the total warriors" in the same pot of war-time deprivation. Not honest, but a strategy of survival that worked for us.

From: **Sannu Molder**
I guess conditions in Sweden were different. Generally, at the adult level, we were treated with kindness and generosity. At the kids level (9 to 14) a few 'natzist' and 'jävla utlänning' were heard. Especially since the 'utlänningar' stood 1st and 2nd in academics (including Swedish grammar) throughout public school. Had we stayed, we could have easily melted in. Most that did have done so. I visited Sweden last year. The people seem to be less arrogant and more easy-going and intelligent than I remember from my childhood (all this based anecdotal evidence and very small samples). ....Sannu

From: **Gusten Lutter**
To; **Sannu Molder:**
Sannu, **at that time, spring/summer 1946, about a year after German capitulation, I don't think the German police carried any ammunition, at least not in the rural area of our camps. But the guns gave them stature while they could always be scary and threatening even without them.** As with the teasing play of fishing licenses for foreigners, by this time they had learned how to "manage" the local American military authorities. Bowing and scraping in their faces, cursing behind their backs, and often openly brutal and offi cious towards the refugees. They scared me frequently, especially if they were performing some specifi c street duty for the Amis. Because of the behavior of the police, and the animosity of the Germans towards the refuges during the early post-war period, I still have mixed feelings about the Germans in general. I never got to know them during an established peace time after Allied occupation. I am sure that Arne feels differently, having lived there in times of "normal peace and harmony". I guess, my psyche got twisted in my formative years... and the memory lingers.....Gusten

From: **Gusten Lutter to Arne:**
Arne, I have searched through my old diaries for anything that might prompt your memory. But, as I mentioned some time ago, **I am fighting writings on poor, now faded war-time paper,** and my terrible penmanship.
  A (typed) program of "Jüripäeva Lõkkeõhtu" on April 23, 1946 showed that it was conducted by nskm. Edgar Igarik, had a speech by Arno Raag, and two choir songs conducted by Roman Toi, one also accompanied by the camp orchestra.
  At about the time of the end of the school year, I joined a folk dancing training course, along with two other classmates. Helmo Raag convinced me to join because he wanted to, but not alone. Andrus Paap, a steady friend of Helmo over the years had absolutely refused. Then he agreed to come to observe the class and somehow was recruited as well. I danced with a Aino Grassberg, and I have no recollection of her. Helmo was paired with Mall Peelpalu, which was odd, because notably, they did not get along in school. Mall was most independent and opinionated. We thought Paap was very lucky. His partner was Luule Päid, whom many considered a real beauty.
  You probably remember her. I note in my diary that the girl I truly liked was Viive Lind, but she did not join the folk dance group.
  I also found the scout camp commemorative cloth strip. My number was 29.
  I also remarked about fishing. The Germans did not want the Verfl uchte Ausländer to depleted their streams in the Altenstadt area, and convinced the American Military Government to institute licensing. Initially there were to be 60 licenses issued to the camp residents, on a lottery basis. My father got one. But when the applicants were assembled in a hall to be issued licenses, the local Germans had gotten the number reduced to 30. Then the Amis distributed them from the front back, and my father was left out since he was in the back row. Shortly thereafter the area streams open for fi shing were curtailed, so that fi nally one could only fish in a stream from the Altenstadt village bridge, and a few km stretch of the Lech River.
  At about that time I had gotten a fishing line and couple of hooks from you, Arne, and was fishing, sort of secretly, in a mill stream behind the Keller gasthaus where we lived. A German woman spotted me and complained to the German police. A motorcycle cop with rifle slung across his back, rode to where I was fishing and brutally confiscated (ripped up) the line. He demanded my papers and compiled a lengthy report, which he assured me would go to the American authorities. Of course, I heard nothing further, but your very fine, monofilament line and hook were gone forever, and my fishing efforts were ended. .....Gusten.

From: **Sannu** to **Gusten:**
Interesting poaching story :) You are lucky this over-zealous fish warden did not shoot you..................Sannu
Gusten, **of the names you mentioned I know only Roman Toi.** He has lived in Toronto for tens of years. Great guy! At a party a few years ago we got into a discussion on pure mathematics and cryptography. He knew much more than I did about both subjects. I could not get him to talk about aerodynamics :) He must be approaching 100.

DIALOGUES WITH SANNU MÕLDER

There is a magic about e-mail dialogues: There is a certain spontaneity about the stories.

Gusten wrote:
Arne, you wrote, among other thoughts:

"....meanwhile I am enjoying reading "the German boy" by Wolfgang Samuel. Wolfgang escaped from the Russians ahead of the front from Prussia. He is now a retired colonel U.S.A.F. Heiki read it from the library. Our local library was no help so I bought the book directly from Wolfgang. when I finish it I'll be happy to send it to you in case you haven't read it. Reading his story makes me think that we had it pretty easy during our escape. **I still wonder how our isa and yours escaped without having been conscripted into the Wehrmacht**!

While in Estonia, my dad escaped military service because of his job in Kuusiku. He was The Big Boss of an important food producer for Wehrmacht.

As an unusual event in those (1943) times, Wehrmacht brought a legal charge against him in a German (Occupied Ostland) court of some sort, accusing him of producing and shipping to the Wehrmacht a train-car load of sub-standard and defective cheeses! Apparently, the spherical cheeses they made in Kuusiku had failed to maintain their shape in transport. The legal case proceeded slowly and never came up in court before the German defense structure crumbled and Estonia was abandoned.

In Estonia, I am sure your dad also had an important war-work deferment. Vaguely, I remember them being called the UK papers... or something like it.

Sometime in winter of 1945 (February?), Germany declared another conscription of all men up to age 40. That was not into the Volksturm, which, as I recall, was an effort managed individually by each municipality, not across the Reich, but to the regular army.

My dad was born in 1908, and was subject to this call. After our travel through south Germany and Austria, seeking but not getting residency permission there nor being able to escape to Switzerland, we had arrived in Lütjenburg, Schleswig-Holstein, where we had planned to wait out the war. My parents decided to run away again, switching tracks like we had done in leaving Ulm.

Isa told our landlady (a NSDAP member retired school teacher, who still hoped for Hitler's wonder-weapons) that he wanted to follow Hitler's call and join the army. But first, he was going to take Ema and me to stay with the family of his last boss in Estonia (a Herr Thiede, whom you might have met when he visited us in Kuusiku), who had a farm in Pommern.

While we bought tickets to Kiel and Berlin, in Kiel we took the train to Flensburg. We destroyed all our documents, and reported immediately to Flensburg police that we had lost a pack back with all of our papers on the way to Flensburg, and now we needed their help!

Since arriving in Germany we had been able to get all kinds of assistance from all kinds of authorities -- by telling them credible lies (as needed) and seeking their help. This strategy had worked for us everywhere, and it did here again.

While we waited at the Flensburg police headquarters, it took one day to produce complete ID's with photos and required stamps, all on the basis of the info we told them. Isa got older, new birthdate in 1904, no longer subject to draft. I got a year younger (1931 instead of 1930) – just to have an extra measure of safety against possible conscription. Also my name now got to be Lutter, to eliminate the confusion of the family Lutters having a son named Käsper.

Having made this name switch, I had a surprising glitch in recovering the title to my grandmother's farm. The restitution commission denied my request, because my name change implied a legal adoption by Ott Lutter. With Heino's help, I appealed that decision, appeared in a hearing, and told the story of our adventures in wartime Germany. And I got the land back... Gusten

Arne's reply to Gusten:
Hi Gusten, you explained your Dad's method of escape from the German draft. Now I wonder about our Dad's handling of the situation. He was born April 4, 1908. I don't know anything about his successful evasion of the draft except that his Russian understudy never learned how to run the liquor factory. As I have said before, our Isa seemed to be a very poor teacher!!! and the Germans like the Russians needed all of the liquor that Isa's factory could produce under his supervision. Arne

From Gusten to Arne:
Arne, a couple of additional comments: In 1941, after Germany attacked Russia, men were drafted (and grabbed) in

Tallinn. Your dad and Endel got caught in that trap.

In the relatively backwardly Orgita, under the shadow of similarily remote Märjamaa, there was no collection of men under the guise of mobilization. And, as soon as we heard that Germany had attacked -- and therefore there was now hope of liberation from Communists -- our family went into hiding. So if Isa was sought, he was no longer around. And we stayed out of everybody's sight until Wehrmacht arrived in Orgita.

I cannot hazard a guess how your dad managed Hitler's last gasp in 1945. But because your family was moving around and seeking a place to settle, might have provided temporary draft immunity in the eyes of the authorities... And then your area was liberated. In our case, we were anchored to Lütjenburg when Hitler called...you were war refugees in transit from the east. .....Gusten

From Sannu to Mai:
Mai, some stuff from Gusten and Arne concerning the German Army (Wehrmacht) drafting of their dads (Isa) during the German occupation of Estonia (1942 to 1944).

My dad escaped by dying in the Fall of 1942. The Germans had just arrived. We had all been hiding in the woods near Vigala, during the Summer, to escape Russian deportation. The Germans were generally welcomed because they drove out the Russians who had invaded (liberated - they STILL call it that) and oppressed and deported the population since 1940.

Soon, however, the prayers changed to 'Dear God please liberate us from the liberators'. And then we were 're-re-liberated' by the Russians in the Fall of '44. Just ahead of their advance, on 2 Sept. 1944, we set out in an 8 meters open fishing boat from Noarootsi beach towards Sweden.

Two Estonian foot-soldiers who were patrolling the beach threw their rifles in the surf and jumped on board. It was a very stormy night. A few days earlier the flames of Tallinn had been burning on the horizon. We had arrived in a Noarootsi beach-house by open truck. I had a gut-ache because I had eaten unripe pears from a potato sack that the truck-driver had salvaged from his garden. His fare had to be paid in gold coins. All other currencies were close to worthless. German marks had inflated to the point where they were carried in suitcases.

Two fishermen returned with a bucket of eels and we all had eel soup. They reported a very rough Läänemeri. We had waited two days for the storm to abate. Sounds of not-so-distant gunfire was constant. Could not wait any longer - we didn't want to get 'liberated' again. The little diesel, with a red, open fly-wheel was hand-cranked into action and went dunk, dunk, dunk as the boat pitched towards Sweden. .....Sannu

To Susan-Sannu's wife:
This is my cousins' cousin Gusten Lutter writing about his uncle Endel Vesk. Endel was my Mother's brother's wife's brother. (uncle, once removed??). He is buried in the North York Cemetery. I also have a picture of their plane. Met Endel in Sweden shortly after his escape. Most of the latter part of his life he lived in Toronto, working as an aerial photographer..

The airplane was a two-seater open cockpit, single engine, biplane. The pilot sat in the front cockpit and the other three escapees were crammed into the rear cockpit. Had they been caught, they would have been shot on the spot. Sannu

From Gusten to Arne:
Arne, I have just received Hendrik Arro's book "Pommid Öisest Taevast" about the Estonian fliers on the Eastern Front. It tells about the escape from Heiligenbeil, Germany, to Vetlanda, Sweden, on 13 /10/1944, pretty much as I had read it somewhere previously.

The flight group arrived the day before and was told that they would be disbanded. This was a disheartening message, foretelling an uncertain future as a common soldier of the Third Reich. The planes were to be ferried to a nearby field the next day. Since Estonian fliers were no longer trusted, fuel was to be removed from the planes, leaving just enough to reach the next field. The detanking was completed for all, except stopped for two because of darkness.The word of that leaked, and two groups of four decided to take advantage of the last opportunity for escape.

The plane to escape was a FOKKER CVE, piloted by Unteroffizier Helmut Võsari, on board also flier Feldwebel Boris Pärl, flier Gefreiter Endel Vesk, and mechanic (of the same plane) Unteroffizier Harry Liiksaar. They started from the parked position across the field that had enough room for takeoff, and quickly disappeared into low clouds.

The field was patrolled by two new recruits from Estonia who sensed nothing wrong about a plane taking off. They raised no alarm.

The other Fokker started a little later, but on takeoff veered into a parked Arado, damaging both planes. It was piloted by Gefreiter Kalju Vijan, accompanied by Unteroffizier Harri Toi and Gefreiters Kalju Reitel and Valdo Raag. Being uninjured they were able to return to sleeping quarters before discovery. An older mechanic who had arrived on the field told the ignorant guards to raise alarm and create a commotion, or they would be in bad trouble with the German staff. The boys fired in the air after the plane that had disappeared long ago.

The investigation by Germans concluded that two groups of two had attempted escape in two planes, but after the collision had taken off in one. ....Gusten

The picture is from the book "Pommid Öisest Taevast – Öölahingu Lendurid Idarindel" by Hendrik Arro, which I had just purchased. It lists Unteroffizier Helmut Võsari as piloting the commandeered plane, with others on board: Fliers Feldwebel Boris Pärl and Gefreiter Endel Vesk, and mechanic (actually of the same, stolen, plane) Unteroffizier Harry Liiksaar.

From Sannu to Bernt:
Subject: Conquest of Sweden (failed)
Hi Berndt

   Where can I find out how many people lived in Örnskjöldsvik in November of 1944. That is where my parents, I and another 800 Estos docked in arriving from Finland.

   Since we did not come to burn the city, as had happened to Sigtuna sometime earlier, we were most generously received by the local population. It must have been quite a shock to them. The Swedes were advanced in modern entry screening methods - we were all x-rayed. The Swedish doctor had learned two words of Estonian; with great emphasis and some 800 times over he said "hinga sisse" (breathe in). That became the motto of the camp. It was posted at the beginning of the path leading to the outhouses.

   The Finns used different methods. On our previous arrival in Finland we were ushered into a huge sauna. The sauna had two paths through. Clothing went through a very hot side to kill the bugs. Naked bodies through a parallel path that was almost as hot - "hinga sisse" would have been applicable here too.
Cheers,
Sannu
p.s. It takes more heat to kill a louse than an Estonian.
Tuyhis is what those 4 guys flew from Germany to Sweden...Sannu

From Sannu to Mai:
Hi Mai

   This is something I translated into English either from Swedish or Estonian. It concerns the episode from Finland to Sweden. I'll try to find the original. **On retiring (in 2000) I promised my kids that I would not take up golf or the writing of anything that smells like an autobiography.** They have subsequently forced me ('forced' as distinct from 'convinced') to write up some snippets of personal history (non-autobiographical!), -- still refusing to play golf. .....Sannu

Sannu is alluding to the story "Venus" on the following page.

Catharsis-pile of nonsense (or some other substance) There was simply no need for it, especially not among children. Why wash clean hands SM.

Written in context of a book reviewer's comments on "When the Noise had Ended".. MM

FREQUENT MOBILITY WAS THE NORM FOR THE FIRST TWELVE MONTHS

One could not always be where one wanted to be, at a time one wanted to be or have what one wanted. At times regimentation was unavoidable and rules were accepted to facilitate basic survival.

It is perhaps the need to adapt quickly, effectively and without whining that allowed our cohort of children to become resilient in the years which followed. MM

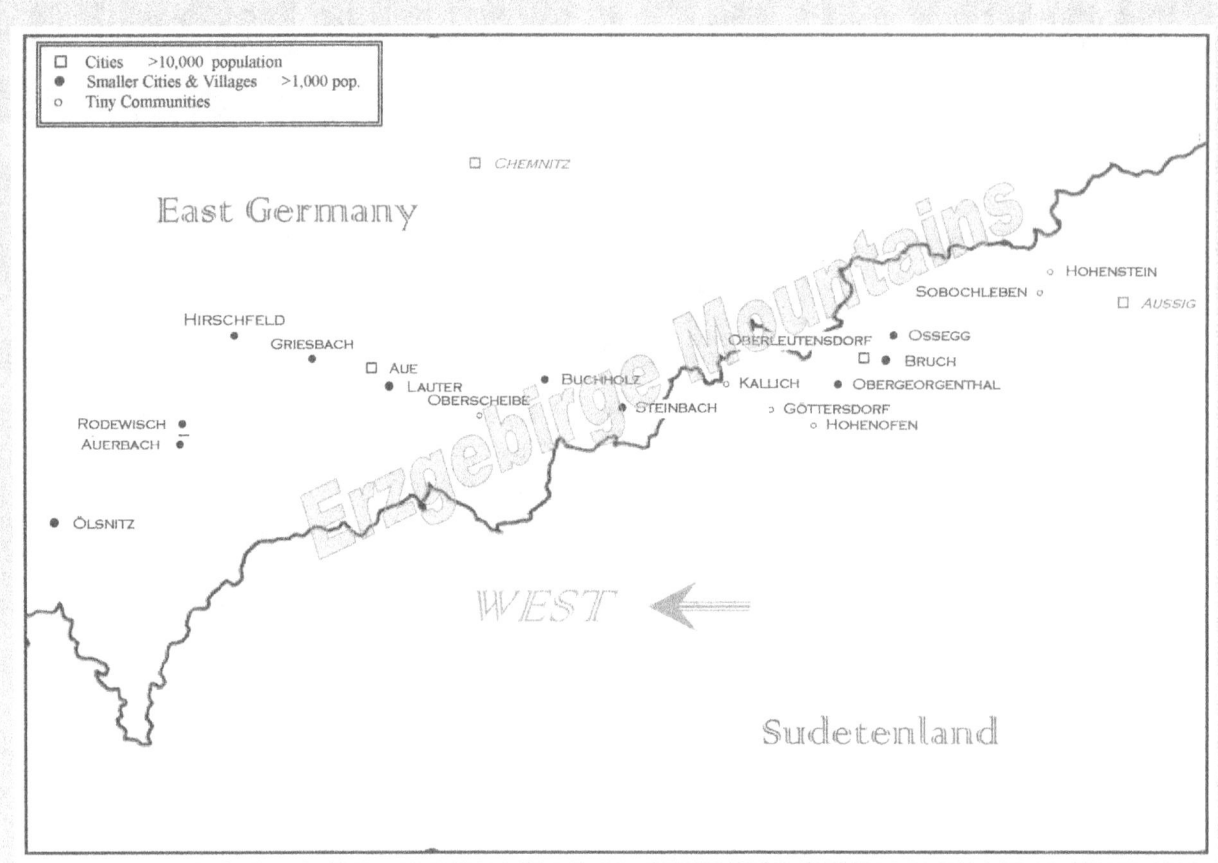

The path from **Sobochleben** to the refugee camp in **Ölsnitz**.

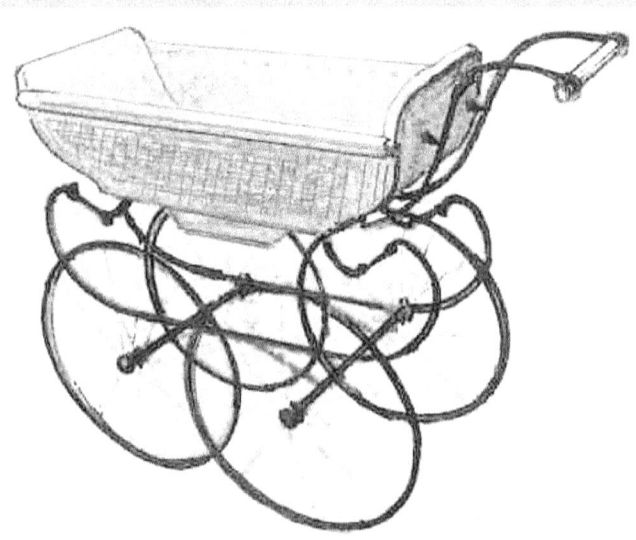

Drawing of our venerable baby carriage.

Indrik has shared considerable effort to ensure that the names for the places he alludes are correct according to present nomenclature.

Given central Europe's writhing serpentine borders in the last century, it is inevitable that there some discrepancies in the nomenclature of places alluded to in the stories in this book will occur. Much as book reviewers are wont to comment on such discrepancies, as a traveller in those time I fell that we will need to accede some discrepancies in such annotations. Indrik wrote to me:

'Please note that I use different Czech names for some communities we visited than Jüri (Indrik's late brother) did in his WNE tale. Both may be correct for their own time periods.'

INDRIK LINASK
ALONE - WITH FOUR CHILDREN

PREFACE
My family was among those tens of thousands of Estonians who planned to flee abroad in 1944, in order to escape a repeat of the terror which they had witnessed during the occupation period three years earlier. However, after mother and the children left home to stay in Tallinn for a while for safekeeping, a sudden change at the warfront caused her to lose contact with father. Mother alone escaped with us, four underage children.

Without a doubt, fear helped mother to make the decision to leave Tallinn on a German ship. But more important was her determination to escape with her sons from the approaching terror regime, as she and father together had decided. That same determination continued on our ensuing journey in wartime Germany, and Sudetenland, East Germany and Germany's American zone after war ended. Mother was determined that our journey succeed regardless of personal hardships along the way.

Much later, mother explained that the main reason for her and father's decision to flee from their homeland was that they wanted their sons to grow up in a free society.

THE BEGINNING
When Estonia was occupied for the first time by Soviet troops in June of 1940, we lived at Palamuse, where father was the Town Administrator (vallasekretär), and our home was an apartment at one end of the town office building. We were then a family of six, including father (Arnold), mother (Elise), three sons (Rein - 4, Indrik - 3, and Jüri - under a year , and grandmother. I don't remember what actually happened when the Red Armies first came in and during the period immediately following, but I do remember that some months later we no longer lived at Palamuse, and, instead, were at a place called "Viru". Rein remembers that our living quarters were not in a house, but in something more like a root cellar or cave ion a mountain side. Neither of us remembers where "Viru" was located, nor do we now know whether we went there to hide or stayed there because no other nearby living space was available. Mother wrote about that time period only briefly*

*throughout, portions in *italics* are an English paraphrase of mother's original Estonian text

In the autumn, Arnold was let go from his administrator's job. Although we initially continued living in the town building, we eventually moved to "Viru"(kolisime „Virule"). Then the mass deportations, sleepless nights, war, German occupation . . . .

Deportations in June and mass killings in July through September 1941 throughout Estonia are well documented for this occupation period. Also documented is that, when driven out by the Germans in October, 1941, the retreating occupiers destroyed almost everything they couldn't take with them. This included burning down the Palamuse town building and our former home.

During the subsequent German occupation, life appeared almost normal again to us children. Father was appointed town administrator at Kaarepere, and the apartment in one end of that town office building became our new home. In August, 1943, our youngest brother Madis was born.

But when the war front spread back onto Estonian soil in the summer of 1944, and the *red army masses continued to forge ahead,* father and mother made an important decision:

Arnold and I decided to escape from the Communist terror to Finland or Sweden, or, lacking a better option, to Germany.

And shortly they started making preparations. Necessities to take along were packed ready to put on a horse cart. Valuables to be left behind were buried in our garden between the apple trees and currant bushes.

But these preparations did not help us. Near the end of August, after Tartu had fallen, the war front was only 30 km from our home, and air attacks by Soviet war planes increased. Then the family decided that mother should take us children to stay with relatives in Tallinn, where it was safer. Also, it would be easier to leave the country from Tallinn, if that became necessary. Mother did not want to go without father and grandmother, but finally agreed, because everyone thought it would be only for a short while. Father, who still had job responsibilities, and grandmother, who stayed to care for the animals, were to follow us with our belongings if the time came.

In Tallinn, we were hosted by mother's aunt and cousin in their apartment on Weizenbergi Street.

War conditions at home in Kaarepere did not change for three weeks. After Rein's birthday, Rein and mine, had passed, mother decided to return home to get more clothes for us. But before she could go, on Sunday, September 17th, the Red Armies broke through at the Tartu front; the trains no longer went to Kaarepere; and, by that evening, the Germans had announced their decision to leave Estonia.

Then, suddenly, life around us became very unsettled. On Wednesday, our Tallinn hosts left for Germany on the Wartheland. They invited us along, but mother found it impossible to leave without father and grandmother. Mother's other cousin and his family, who lived in the adjacent apartment, left for Haapsalu in the evening, presumably with the hope of escaping to Sweden. And his sister-in-law's family, who was staying with them, also for a short while, obtained a travel permit to leave for Germany in the morning. Mother had lost contact with father, we had nowhere to go, and we faced being left alone in an very unfamiliar large city with the Red Army takeover imminent. But somehow we did escape, as mother described:

On Thursday morning, we learned that travel permits were no longer needed, and people were free to go where they pleased. So I decided that our only hope was to join my cousin's sister-in-law and try to escape to Germany with them. I started to pack hastily.

Before I could finish, however, the sister-in-law announced that they were already leaving for the harbor. As an omen of good luck, their departure was delayed by an air raid alarm, which allowed me to finish packing. We had very few belongings of our own, but I packed some blankets, most nonperishable food items that my aunt had left behind, a small aluminum pot, and two quarter liter bottles of vodka, which later might be useful for bartering. I went to the harbor in the baggage car with Madis, Jüri, and the sister-in-law's young daughter, while Rein, Indrik, the sister-in-law, her husband and their son walked.

We, the group with the older children, entered the harbor before the baggage car and immediately started to scout for available ships. We first noticed the stately looking Moero, but it appeared already very crowded and had a long queue still waiting to board. Next was the much smaller RO-2 and then another larger ship, the RO-22, which we decided to board. It took a long while for mother, the younger children, and the baggage to join us. They had been dropped off at the harbor entrance because the car was not allowed into the harbor. It was almost evening when we were reunited onboard. The baggage was carted from the harbor gate to the ship in exchange for one of mother's vodka bottles.

ESCAPE PART I: THE JOURNEY FROM ESTONIA

The RO-22 too was very crowded, and no vacant berths could be found in the main cabin or anywhere else; even sitting room was scarce. But, as in many other times during our escape journey, good fortune and good people came to our aid. As we were looking for a place in which to settle, we met another family in a similar situation who had a sick daughter. Their mother, not nearly as reserved as our mother, noting the number of small children without a place, went to the ship's captain and demanded room for children. A small cabin near the ship's front, normally used by the crew, was then made available for our group of families with small children. That location may well have saved us when a torpedo hit the RO-22 early next morning near Paldiski.

Our voyage at sea took longer than normal due partly to the torpedo damage, but also because the RO-22 reportedly circled farther into the North Sea and close to Sweden, instead of following the usual coastal route to Gottenhafen (current Czech name Gdynia), in order to distance itself from a Russian airbase in Lithuania.

We reached Gottenhafen on Monday, and then, lacking any destination, spent time in several refugee camps until the war ended. Our first night passed in a camp near Danzig (Gdańsk), from where we boarded a train in the morning to the next camp in Wilhelmshagen, – a suburb of Berlin. Mother recalled our arrival at Wilhelmshagen and stays in refugee camps this way:

The long train was crowded with refugees mainly from Estonia. Upon arrival in the evening, everyone was in a hurry to find shelter in the barracks, which were located a half kilometer or more from the station. I too stepped onto the station platform with the children and our few belongings. The children were not yet old enough to help carry these; therefore, we had to be otherwise resourceful. I carried the suitcase some distance ahead and Indrik came along. Rein stayed to watch the younger children and remaining baggage. So I walked back and forth several times until all the bags and children were together again. And then the process repeated with the older boys alternately watching the baggage and younger brothers until we reached the barracks.

The barracks contained many rooms filled with bare wooden bunks. But all near the front had already been claimed by the earlier arrivals or reserved by them for friends who hopefully would join them later. We had to pass through quite a few rooms before finding adjacent bunk spaces for all of us.

After a few days, we were ordered to newer barracks in the same camp. These were cleaner and furnished with double beds instead of bare bunks. But before admittance, everyone was required to wash thoroughly and be decontaminated of head lice (täisaun). Then, after breakfast the next morning, all adults were required to register at the camp employment office, from where recruitment to work started. Of course, no one was interested in me because of the children.

Food in this camp was very poor, watery soup of unpeeled potatoes with occasional turnip pieces. Additionally, smaller children were given a turnip and semolina soup on some days. I used our small aluminum pot to fetch both soups. But eating was difficult at best, because we had only one teaspoon with which to pick out larger potato pieces from the soup. Poor nourishment was beginning to affect the children's health, especially Madis, then only a little over a year old.

Our stay at Wilhelmshagen was often interrupted by air raid alarms and bombings targeted at nearby Berlin – mostly at night. The first night the alarm sounded, I tried to wake the children, but they didn't react at all. Rein and Indrik were in the upper bed with Madis and Jüri sharing the lower bed with me. As the first bomb explosions sounded, I shifted Madis and Jüri closer to the wall and climbed onto the edge of the upper bed, trying to shield all the children this way.

I did manage to wake the children during the alarm the next night and go to the shelter. It was so cold there that the children shivered. But some kind work service young men from Italy – actually boys – placed their own jackets on my children's shoulders, leaving themselves to shiver.

Then one day I heard a rumor that a Mr. Vilms, who had been the Mayor of Viljandi in Estonia in 1939, was organizing a camp for mothers and children. I located him and registered my family immediately. And, on October 11th, we left Wilhelmshagen by train to go to this new camp. On this trip, a good meal was provided by the German public welfare service NSV (National Sozialistische Volkswohlfahrt) between trains in Aussig (Ústi nad Labem). And upon arrival at the Mariaschein (Bohosudov) rail station, our bags were loaded on an ox-cart for transport to the camp located a few kilometers ahead in the village of Sobochleben (Soběchleby) located in "Kreis Aussig, Sudetenland".

It was dark already when we exited the train, and it had been raining. I carried Madis, trusted my handbag to Jüri, while Rein and Indrik also carried something as we followed the oxcart on the unfamiliar muddy road. But a pleasant surprise awaited us when we finally arrived at Gasthaus Mayerhof, which was to be our camp: bread with marmalade and warm coffee made of roasted grain. And we could eat as much as we wanted, courtesy of the NSV.

We were housed in the huge hall of this Gasthaus, tightly filled with double beds, with a stage at the far end. The beds had bags of wood shavings for mattresses and army blankets for cover. In the beginning there were over a hundred people living there, but as time passed, some moved to the surrounding villages where they found both work and better living conditions. Others moved farther away — even to Germany. Although new people came, living conditions became much more spacious for those of us who stayed.

Everyone in the camp received food rationing cards, but these were taken from us on account of our central kitchen meals, except those for the smaller children. I had to cook meals for both Madis and Jüri in our small aluminum pot heated on the large potbellied stove in the corner of the hall. And, through the intercession of our camp director, Mr. Vilms' sister, I started to receive a monthly monetary stipend of 100 DM from the NSV. As our stay in Sobochleben continued and we settled into a more stable life, one enterprising mother organized school classes for the children in a local school house.

Thus arrived Christmas Eve, 1944. The school-children gathered on the stage around a Christmas tree. They sang carols and recited Christmas verses. Smaller ones watched these activities with their mothers from the hall below, and many a tear rolled down their cheeks. After supper, we lit our own candle next to our beds in honor of beloved family members and our home. Then the children repeated their verses, and together we recited evening prayer.

Weeks and months passed. I usually sat up late into the nights mending our clothes, which were falling into disrepair because we didn't have money to buy anything new. All we had was spent for food. We were fortunate to receive a child's bed for Madis from the NSV, where he could again practice walking, and, also, a baby carriage, actually a sturdy old fashioned double carriage with wicker sides and huge one meter wheels, which served us well later.

ESCAPE PART II: FLEEING FROM THE SUDETENLAND

After mid April, the war front was catching up with us, and our stay in Sobochleben became anxious. More people started leaving westward. I too obtained a rail travel permit, but, not wanting to risk losing the children in crowded stations and trains, did not dare to use it going anywhere alone.

Then, on the morning of May 7th, we learned that the Russians were already near. *Some people scurried to the Mariaschein train station, but others decided that the larger Hohenstein (Unčin), station, although a little farther, was a better risk for catching trains and prepared to go there. I too loaded our belongings into our carriage: clothes in the* *bottom, food stuff into the suitcase, Madis in the front end and Indrik, who had contracted a high fever a week earlier, in back. Then we set out for Hohenstein.*

Fifty Sobochleben Estonians, including the Vilms' family, joined the already large crowd in the Hohenstein station. But none of the incoming trains would stop. And the midnight train didn't come at all. We waited until morning when our group bribed the stationmaster with cigarettes, and he stopped a train. It was well after 6 a.m. by the time everyone was aboard, and we started moving very slowly westward.

After we passed the Ossegg (Osek) station several hours later, bombing started to be heard at some distance. Soon after that, the train stopped, and we were ordered into cargo wagons of another train. As Russian war planes started roaring above, strafing something, we took shelter under the wagons. After things quieted down, instead of moving ahead, the train returned to Ossegg station, where we were advised to seek shelter in the adjacent woods. It sounded like a battle was being fought farther in the woods when we moved our baggage. But eventually things quieted and our entire group appeared safe. And here we met the Russians.

Toward evening, the station guard told us that trains will not be running for the time being and our group should seek shelter in town, about a kilometer away. Mr. Vilms' sister, whom we had elected to be our group leader, accompanied by a couple of other women, then went to consult the town's new administration about night accommodations and opportunities for proceeding onward. We were assigned to spend the night in a schoolhouse, which until very recently had been used as a military field hospital, and told to come back in the morning for a travel permit. The permit, which was received, after a long and anxious wait, on the following day, *allowed us to "move freely within the borders of independent Czechoslovakia".*

Since the trains were still not running, it became apparent that we had to leave on foot. Because we needed some vehicles to carry small children and baggage, people returned to town in the hope of bartering for whatever could be found. Mother was fortunate because we already had our carriage.

Meanwhile numerous drunken Russian soldiers were spending time near the station. Rein remembers how one threatened to throw a grenade into our group, but, discouraged by a Czech guard, threw it instead away from us across the railroad tracks at some imaginary Germans, where it exploded with a vicious bang, after which he emptied his handgun in the same direction. Mother remembers another group *amusing themselves by shooting at branches in tree tops.*

By that afternoon our group members had obtained about a dozen small wagons and conventional baby carriages from townspeople and one larger cart from the rail station. Now everyone had to repack what they had and take along only bare necessities due to space limitations. Our suitcase with food was placed on the work cart and everything else into our carriage or the little back packs mother had made in Sobochleben, which Rein, Jüri, and I were supposed to carry, but most of the time left hanging on the carriage.

The group of 50 included 23 children, 22 women, including some elderly, and 5 men. Everyone's goal was to go West and get away from the Russians as fast as possible. We definitely did not have a "yellow brick road" or planned route to follow, but just tried to move in a generally westerly direction toward Germany. A major safety concern on the highways was Russian army convoys, which we encountered especially on the first few days, and occasionally later too. Avoiding the convoys often meant going zigzag on smaller roads, instead of using a direct route. (Refer to map)

Former Russian prisoners of war in Germany were also a nuisance on the first days. They were looking for jewelry, gold, other valuables, and cigarettes and didn't care who the owner was. Our group didn't have much, but they did find a couple of watches and some cigarettes, which they took. However, no one bothered mother with her small children.

During the next 14 days, we crossed many hills and valleys and traveled a total of 200 km on foot with almost every kilometer bringing new challenges, particularly for mother. Most families had one or two children per adult, but mother had four. Our family tended to be the last one to arrive at lunch and evening stops. Mother described this as follows: Mother described this as follows:

My load was difficult to push, because additional to our belongings, two boys were in the carriage – Madis all of the time, Indrik still debilitated from his illness most of the time, and Jüri or Rein occasionally, too. Pushing uphill, I tried to go from one telephone pole to the next, then place a rock under the carriage wheel, rest a bit and recover, and then try to reach the next pole. Down hill would have been easier with our carriage, but the boys couldn't keep up, and I had to brake hard all the way down.

We arrived at the first city Bruch (Lom) in time to witness a Czech takeover and apparent payback to the Germans. Almost immediately after entering the city limits, our travel permit was checked and we were directed from the main road into a dead-end side street, told to sit down on the sidewalk and wait for orders.

While there, and, later on the way back out, we witnessed first hand some gruesome sights of war. We heard volleys of shots from somewhere nearby. We saw dead bodies on the streets, nice houses being sacked, and the unforgettable sight of German soldiers pulling a cart filled with bloody bodies in civilian clothes with hands just dangling downward.

Eventually, after our papers were checked again several times, we were given a rifleman for an escort, ordered to move out of the enclosed street and get out of town. And soon we were on our own heading west on the highway. But there we began encountering large Russian convoys racing in both directions. In between were oncoming speeding single vehicles and occasional foot traffic.

We continued to travel on major highways until we passed Oberleutensdorf (Litvinov) and Obergeorgenthal (Horni Jiřetin), and the highway turned almost northerly toward Chemnitz, Germany. There we took the smaller road westward, very sparsely populated. Since we couldn't reach the next town by evening, we stopped at an abandoned sawmill with an adjacent house for the night. The house had been thoroughly sacked, but the kitchen stove was good, which allowed all the mothers to cook warm meals, usually porridge or boiled potatoes, when potatoes were available. We slept on the second floor of the shed adjacent to the house.

Lodgings on the following nights in Sudetenland and later in Germany, too, were arranged by our group leaders with government officials of the towns that we passed through. Usual places were local schoolhouses or other community buildings. The town officials also tried to arrange food for us. In the smaller villages and outlying areas, lodgings had to be sought from local farmers, and we stayed in farm outbuildings. Both the officials and farmers were accustomed to refugee traffic and responded kindly to our needs, although food tended to be scarce where many refugees had previously passed through. Only once were we refused outright.

The hot afternoon sun was a major difficulty on numerous days. Children wanted to drink constantly, and mothers stopped at houses and brooks to fill water containers. Not only did the sun affect the children, fatigue the adults and make them sweat, but it also softened the asphalt pavement, causing wagon wheels and shoe soles to stick. On those days we traveled much shorter distances.

On one hot day early on our trek, we reached the town of Hohenofen (Vysoká Pec). Here we initially received a cold reception from the townspeople, but were well cared for after they heard our story. The town administrators designated a local sports hall for the night and even organized its cleanup, and then the women and children from town brought us warm food.

Travel until this point had been mostly over gentle hills and valleys, but now we turned onto a tiny unpaved road heading directly into the Erzgebirge Mountains. We needed to cross the mountains somewhere, regardless of which path we chose to reach the American zone in Germany, and this was the shortest path to the German border and hopefully didn't carry any convoys.

Pulling even small carts up this dusty and stone covered road was punishing. The whole group could travel only short distances at a time and then needed to rest. Additionally, the conventional wagons and carriages, which most people had, became immovable when their small wheels hit stones. All carts and carriages had to be pulled up one by one over some steeper segments of this road, with several people helping each other. Our carriage's large wheels rolled over stones more easily, but we still had to climb the hills. That day we traveled much less than a 10 kilometer distance, while ascending high up into the hills.

Towards evening, we reached Göttersdorf ([Boleboř]), where we had planned to spend the night, but we found a large contingent of Russian troops partying in town. Many townspeople had fled, and most of those that stayed were not spending the night in town. This was the only night that we spent in the open air. We "made our beds" on a small side road at a distance from the village center and with a high bank on one side to protect us against a rather chilly wind.

In the morning, everything was quiet, and we found an abandoned house where again meals could be cooked. Also, we were permitted to milk some cows which a Russian soldier was herding, and everyone drank their fill. But this caused a new need for frequent stops during that entire day.

After two more days of traveling up and down the hills, past farm houses and through small villages, we reached Kallich (Kalek) where we crossed the border from Sudetenland into East Germany. Of course, there was no physical border or border crossing here, because both sides were now ruled by the Russians, just as they formerly had been by the Reich.

The road on the German side still continued up and down hills, smaller in the beginning, then getting longer and steeper. Just before evening, we reached the town of Steinbach in one deep valley, where we spent our first night in Germany. Steinbach appeared to be in mint condition because no armies had passed through it. Here German town officials provided us with shelter and arranged food.

As the hills and valleys continued to get bigger on the following day, we met a local man with a huge ox working on the roadside just before one particularly long steep hill. Our group leader negotiated with him to take us up this hill, and, consequently, all children and older women were placed on the oxcart and all of our carts and wagons tied behind, and we climbed that hill without effort. A few days later, some more zealous women in our group hired a farmer with a horse to help bring us up yet another big hill. Everyone was getting physically tired and a little discouraged by our slowing progress, since fewer recent encounters with the Russians had dulled our urgency to push ahead.

When we reached the village of Lauter on Thursday afternoon, May 17th, it was decided to rest for a day. This would allow all of us to recuperate a little and also plan for our caravan's travel onward.

We stayed on a farm and slept in a barn full of straw. Since we had time, Friday also became a wash day – everyone washed themselves and their clothes too, all with cold water, of course. This just happened to be the start of Whitsunday weekend (Pentecost), which is also a customary time for German families to do major cleaning.

On Saturday, we uneventfully passed through Aue, the biggest city thus far, then another town, but then stopped early for the day in Griesbach, because of a threatening thunderstorm. Here we had to spend the night in a crowded schoolhouse, which also housed a multitude of unfriendly German refugees, who initially refused to make any room for us.

Everything was wet and muddy in the morning. Nevertheless, we moved on and by evening were in Wolfersgrün near the American zone. But we were not allowed to spend the night there. The angry Burgermeister scolded our group leader for coming through his village and demanded that we just go away. So we continued on, and, when it was already dark, reached a tiny farm in Hirschfeld where other refugees already were staying, and we too were allowed to spend the night.

On the following afternoon, Monday, May 21st, the 50 in our original group reached a crossroad where we started to separate into smaller groups a, each with different destinations. Mr. Vilms recommended that our family, another mother with two small children, and a third with one child and a grandmother, head toward the border crossing into the American zone in Radewisch and then go to Ölsnitz bei Plauen, where the closest American zone refugee camp was located. The other groups would initially turn towards the Infersgrün zone crossing, and from there continue to their destinations. We had learned from local residents that small groups were more easily allowed to pass through border checkpoints.

Our three families passed the Rodewisch American checkpoint on May 22nd, without a question being asked, and continued to a German refugee camp in Auerbach. The food in this camp was meager, but mother occasionally found ways to supplement it. Once she was able to buy fresh bread from a local bakery and get some potatoes and chives from townspeople, and we had delicious boiled potato and chive sandwiches for supper. Then after we had rested some days, mother met two Estonians from Ölsnitz who had come to Auerbach looking for relatives. They told mother that there was an Estonian refugee camp was in Ölsnitz and recommended that we go there. So we extended our trek 21 kilometers:.

On the morning of June 6th, after we had picked up our daily bread and sugar provisions, we started to move on to Ölsnitz, and with some stops and rest periods, arrived by the evening. This camp, located in the „White Horse" hostel, was full, but we found room somewhere on the floor. Fellow countrymen offered us some very tasty cream soup, but the boys are so tired that they fall asleep without eating.

That evening I met one of Arnold's colleagues from Estonia – we had a lot to talk about. On the next day, this part of the camp is moved to the larger „Deuta Werke" industrial complex, also in Ölsnitz, where 60 other Estonian and a number of other nationalities' refugees already reside.

A fortnight later, rumors abound that the Americans will draw back towards the West so that the Russians can come further into Germany. We are alarmed and terrified. But the camp is moved away to Coburg by military transport on June 22nd, from there to Landsberg on July 1st, and, finally, to Rosenheim on July 5th. We are kept in the American zone while the Russians took larger chunks of Germany.

ESCAPE PART III: THE AMERICAN ZONE

In Rosenheim, we lived in gigantic white tents and were in constant contact with a large number of people of many nationalities. That was an interesting experience for us. But a week after arrival, Rein developed a high fever and was diagnosed to have severe bronchitis. Mother refused to let him be sent alone to a sanatorium and be separated from the rest of the family. Then Jüri, Madis, and I were also found to be sick with bronchitis, some other lung infection, and tuberculosis. Only mother was healthy.

The four of us were then sent to a small-children's sanatorium in Gaissah bei Bad Tölz, located in the foothills of the Bavarian Alps, where we spent the last year of our escape journey. Mother opted to leave the refugee circuit and live on her own during that time, instead of returning to a camp alone, because she wanted the family to stay together. She found a job in Bad Tölz and visited us regularly. Mother recollected:

On July 28th we are taken from Rosenheim to Bad Tölz, where the children are placed into a nearby small-children's sanatorium. I start to look for a job, but spend the first night alone in the loft of a Tavern's barn. On the following day, I was back at the sanatorium to mark the children's clothes and, at the same time, admire nature's beauty in the surrounding area. But I am in despair with worries that perhaps treatment came too late, and the children may never regain their health. And I pray that God give me strength to live through all this.

Two days later, with the aid of an employment agency, I found a job as a housekeeper in the "Haus Frisia" home for the elderly in Bad Tölz. Gradually I become accustomed to being without the children and with my job. Although I am the lowest ranking employee here, I am still treated as part of the family. Then two weeks later, on my visit to the sanatorium, the doctor informed me that the diseases have not progressed to an alarming stage and the prognosis is for the children's complete recovery. And three months later he said that they are recovering quite well.

I visit them every Sunday and on most holidays, which are my free days. I speak Estonian with them and on most visits we spend some time singing familiar children's songs. The older children have not forgotten much, but Madis, who barely spoke Estonian when he arrived here, speaks only German.

We did recover and left Gaissah on June 25th, 1946, and went on to the Estonian refugee camp in Geislingen.

EPILOGUE

The stay in Geislingen started a new chapter in our lives. Most significant was that all four of us attended Estonian schools there. We also got the opportunity to emigrate to America, where we established our new home. Mother made sure that we continued our education as far as possible there, too; and we all completed college with Baccalaureate, Master's, or PhD degrees. And mother, who had already anonymously contacted father from Geislingen, invited him to America.

Father joined us in May, 1965. He was very pleased that we had escaped, how mother brought our escape journey to a succesful ending, and quite proud what all four sons had accomplished under mother's guidance.

Mother with four sons in Geislingen, autumn of 1949.

ART AND HANDICRAFTS TOO THRIVED

Their daily tasks completed, people whiled their time away as they did back in Estonia: Perhaps the only constraint the more primitive materials available to complete the beautiful articles created.

There were art classes, leather work classes and pottery classes to name a few.

I can certainly being taken along to art classes by mother when I was a preschooler: I suspect to abstain me from mischief while out of sight.

My creative skills were to emerge quite independently many years later: Well apart from poetry which I compiled to substitute for the paltry babyish one I was being asked to recite at Estonia's national day. Needless to say the platoon commanders weren't pleased but I was: It was a welcome escape to freedom.

Jahnhalle served as the centrum for all our folks's artistic endeavours: plays, musicals, choral festivals etc. Even we the children were engaged to participate.

Once musical instruments became accessible they too became a feature of the performing arts. I fondly remember the piano accordion for its rhythmic sounds.

And I still wonder where my penchant for listening to military bands derives from: Was it learned in Estonia or whilst we trekked around Germany.

While most of the photos derive from Geislingen, they are but symbolic as Geislingen was the largest of the Estonian camps and thus material became more readily accessible. each ot the camps evolved their own resources and travel among the camps became more common as peace ensued and travel among them became safe.

SIR ARVI PARBO
MY YOUTH IN EUROPE: MY AUTOBIOGRAPHY: PART 1

This autobiography has been compiled for the Tartu University Library collection..
I have translated it from Estonian.

CHILDHOOD

My three brothers and I grew up in the 1930s on my parents' farm near Loodna in Läänemaa. The nearest towns were Kullamaa which was 10 km away and Märjamaa, 20 km away. I was the second oldest. We had no sisters.

Our one hundred hectare farm derived most of its income from meat and milk. We also grew grains, potatoes and flax. Father did most of the farm work with the help of the odd farmhand. All four of us helped father from a young age according to our age and skills.

Life on a farm was very different in those days. Our vicinity had no electricity. Both cooking and heating during the winter were by a wood fired stove with hot plates. The lighting was by kerosene lamps: after dark we had to use these both in the house and in the stables.

Our food was home grown. Mother baked our bread and even made soap from lard and soapstone. The village store was about a kilometer away: we only went there to buy, salt, sugar, salted herrings and so on.

The farm work was done by horse drawn farm tools. We did not own mechanical tools or tractors. We had six horses and we boys quickly learned to work with them, to plough, sow, convey the reaped hay to the barn, and the milk to the dairy. I learned to milk cows and frequently did this, together with the herds woman and mother. The value of the milk was determined by its fat content: At the dairy this was converted to butter and buttermilk. Thus we had to monitor the fat percentage diligently. There was a time when I knew our milking statistics by heart.

We did not have a car and moved around on foot, or by bicycle, horse and cart or sled. During the winter we boys skied. In exceptional circumstances father would take us to school by horse and cart or sled.

At the end of the 1930s we acquired a telephone: Prior to that we used the one at the village store. The newspapers were many days old by the time they reached us. We heard the daily news by battery operated radio: The battery was charged by a windmill at the school. The radio also provided us with entertainment: We listened to music and the then popular radio plays. On special occasions like anniversaries, festivals etc we went to performances at the school hall. These varied from plays to musical presentations. That was about the limit of our entertainment. The nearest pharmacy was at Kullamaa, the nearest doctor and dentist at Märjamaa and the broad gauge train station twenty kilometers away at Risti.

Father used to go to Tallinn occasionally and he usually returned with a case full of books obtained at sales: These gradually amounted to quite a library. We boys read these avidly and I have forever continued to enjoy the companionship of books.

There was still time for play. We could play sport on a large field near the house and the forested farmland was ideal for playing cowboys and Indians. In winter low lying places were iced over and we could ice skate on them. War games were always popular. When my older brother was away at school in Tallinn I was always the general and my younger brothers the officers. Pauka, our dog, was the only foot soldier.

SCHOOLING

We began school aged eight at the local Loodna Primary School four kilometres away. During Estonia's first Independence it was possible to begin high school preparatory classes (or pre-high school) after completing fourth grade. After two years at such a school one could begin high school proper.

In 1939 I began Gustav Adolf pre- high school in Tallinn, living with my uncle at Pelgulinn. I was promoted to the second year in the spring of 1940. Then in June came the winds of political change: Under communism the pre-high schools were closed and in the autumn I returned to Loodna to complete grade six in the following year.

In September 1941 I was successful in passing the entrance exams for Gustav Adolf high school first year. Again I lived with my uncle. I completed the second year and junior high school in the spring of 1943 and decided to transfer to Tallinn Technical School where my older brother had completed his studies for machine construction. I wanted to study to be an electro-technician: But that was a short sojourn which was interrupted by the Red Army breaking through the German front at Leningrad in January 1944 and quickly reaching Narva.

The second Russian Occupation was impending: The last Estonian Prime Minister Jüri Uluots spoke on the radio asking for men to stop that advance and endorsing the German mobilisation.

IN THE ARMY

Two of my friends and I decided to discontinue our studies and answer his call. We were too young to be called up but in February we volunteered for the Estonian Flying Group. It combined the sea plane squadron at Ülemiste (which was involved in reconnaissance and dealing with submarines in the Finnish Gulf), and the two night

275

bombing squadrons which were situated initially at the northern end of the Eastern front in Russia. They were later relocated to Rahkla in Virumaa.

After training at Liepaja Flight School in Latvia (I was in the ground crew) a third night bombing squadron was formed in June and sent to Tammiku air field near Jõhvi. It bombed targets at Narva (later Sinimägede) front and the immediate vicinity until the end of August. Thereafter we flew from temporary airstrips near Türi to the Tartu front. In September we retreated from Estonia. In the confusion I could not make contact with my family and for years did not know of their fate.

After a pause in Lithuania our journey passed through East Prussia and Poland to Germany, where the Flying Group ceased its operations. Until March 1945 we were at first officially in a parachute unit, but in reality in infantry retraining at Esbjerg in Denmark and later in air defence in Dortmund in Germany. In April after various adventures I found myself in the Estonian Reserve Regiment at Odense in Denmark. From there we were despatched at the end of the month to the Estonian Division in Silesia. However, Berlin had already been surrounded by Russian troops and we could not get through. We left the train and marched four hundred kilometers westwards, with the Red Army at our heels, until at the beginning of May we met American troops at Lüblow village in Mecklenburg.

Germany had been divided into American, English, French and Soviet occupation zones. We were in the Soviet zone and the Americans withdrew from there. Before that we were handed over to the English and taken to their zone. For the next few months I became a POW near Lake Uklei in Schleswig Holstein.

DISPLACED PERSONS' CAMP
Camps were opened in Germany for the foreign refugees who were called Displaced Persons (DPs) and at the end of September I was fortunate to enter one of the Lübeck camps. At Lübeck there were many others like me with their high school education incomplete and there were also school teachers. They set up an Estonian high school, from which I graduated in the spring of 1946.

STUDYING MINING
A Baltic University had begun at Hamburg: Its staff and students were from the Baltic States. I spent one semester in the philology faculty. I enjoyed this but my real wish was to study engineering, which I had already begun in Tallinn Technical School. I was also interested in minerals and during my education in Tallinn had often in spare time collected trilobites and other fossils in the quarries at Lasnamäe. Combining these interests, I decided to enter the Clausthal Mining Academy in the Harz Mountains to learn mining engineering.

The Harz had been a lead, zinc and silver mining precinct since the tenth century. A mine at Rammelberg near Goslar had been worked continuously for 1000 years. The Clausthal Mining Academy was founded in 1775 and many American mining engineers, metallurgists and geologists had acquired their qualifications there prior to America establishing such schools.

The mining school which had closed down during the war due to the majority of the professors and students having enlisted in the army opened its doors again in October 1946 and I enrolled. Most of the students were returned servicemen.

The winter of 1946 was very cold, with no fuel available for heating. Both the teachers and students wore heavy coats, fur hats and gloves into classes. Rather than reducing study morale this had the reverse effect: We were not studying to pass exams but to acquire skills. We knew that our futures would be determined by this. Discomforts were irrelevant. **I am often reminded of this when these days I hear complaints about inadequate facilities and conditions.**

While at Clausthal I learned that my family were alive in Estonia: however communication was to be severed for ten years.

During the school vacation in 1948 I worked for the first time as a miner underground near Clausthal: They mined lead and zinc: I was learning and being paid as well. My next vacation was spent working in a coal mine in Gelsenkirchen in the Ruhr Valley.

While working in the mines I came across many German engineers and senior mining people who were employed working below their previous qualifications. They had been exiled from Silesia when it was placed under Polish rule to compensate for the loss of East Poland to the USSR: The Polish eastern border remained unchanged, as agreed between Stalin and Hitler in 1939.

German mining industry was not expanding: There were more mining engineers than were needed, and for someone like me there were no shining prospects in that part of the world. I decided to leave Europe.

I knew that Australia was short of workers and that mining was a major industry there. Coal had been discovered soon after white man arrived there at the end of the eighteenth century. The nineteenth century saw a copper mining boom. Gold mining began to thrive in the mid nineteenth century. Lead, zinc, silver, tin and brown coal followed.

Australian representatives toured the DP camps, recruiting: The immigration formalities were quickly completed. Thus I decided to migrate to Australia.

After a three week uninterrupted sea journey from Naples in Italy, I touched Australian soil for the first time when I landed in Melbourne in November 1949.

PARAMETERS OF DEPRIVATION

I have a very simplistic way of thinking about human demographics and behaviour .
Given a specific demographic within a given epoch and environment, most people's lives would fit into 2-2.5 standard deviations of the Bell curve no matter what the modality.

The narrative in this book has been diverse but perhaps a little hard to conceptualise within the Bell curve notion.

Living conditions and food seem to have been the main parameters alluded to. I have annotated some random quotes. MM

Arne Ellermets recalls:
I can't remember ever being really hungry, although food was scarce in the early days of 1945. When we lived in the village of Kranzegg we had a good supply of potatoes and cheese, but that was pretty much it!

In Ellegg I was accepted as one of the German farm family and worked and ate with them, I don't remember how or what Mom and Dad and Heiki ate.

Once we were gathered into DP camps the food was provided by the US Army. That resource seems to have met our needs until we got into facilities in Augsburg where we had our own kitchen, although initially shared with four other families!

The last two years in Germany we lived in Haunstetten, a suburb of Augsburg, and shared a small two bedroom apartment including a kitchen with another young family who didn't have children. We received food rations from the Camp Commissary with coupons. Our Mom was a home economics teacher in Estonia and an excellent cook who could fix a very good meal from almost anything! She was a blessing!

Sannu Molder Arne's cousin recalls:
In the spring of 1945 we had been in Sweden for half a year or so. We lived in a little village in southern Sweden called Svaneholm. Mom and Dad had jobs at the local rubber factory and I was attending public school. Although Sweden had not participated in the war, it suffered some effects. Coffee, Akvavit, sugar and meat were on 'coupons'. Swedes are addicted to coffee so the Estonians were trading their coffee coupons for Akvavit - their addiction. Occasionally meat was sold without coupons and Mom had bought a tin and made a stew. Dad said he liked the stew and asked what kind of meat it was. I had picked up a smattering of Swedish - enough to know that the label 'häst kjött' meant horse meat!

Dad lost his appetite!

Dad then said that the Germans in Estonia had distributed tins of meat that was labeled as half chicken meat and half horse meat but it turned out to be half a chicken and half a horse.

Arvi working at the coal mine in Germany 1948

Am I granted a choice
or must I wait
For all that is fate?
I do not know.

I need my memories
of all that happened yesterday
To compare the days of tomorrow......

from **Gunnar Neeme**

"Mist of time"

JAAN PAARSON
DONNA PARSON'S (HIS WIDOW) REMINISCES

Jaan Paarson with family and friends in front of his house. Jaan is in front row first left

Jaan Paarson was one of our cohort of children to leave Estonia on that fateful day. He is no longer with us.

Donna his widow, shares some reminiscences shared by Jaan and her her mother-in-law.

When Alma Paarson left Estonia in 1944 with her two young sons, she took with her a cloth bag of flour and during the months they spent in Bachnang and Stuttgart, when there was nothing else to eat she would reach into the bag and fry the floor with a little lard to fill their stomachs. Gradually, the bag of flour became smaller and smaller.

Alma and her youngest son, Jaan, were living in Stuttgart when the war was ending and the French marched in. Jaan was playing in the streets among the debris of war. The soldiers had broken into a chocolate factory and gave the children they came across, including Jaan, a chocolate bar.

Jaan had two strong memories from the time he lived with his mother in Bachnang before the war ended.

One was being attacked by an English Spitfire pilot while playing in an open field. **The plane was so low that he could see the pilot's eyes before he ran into a culvert for protections.**

The second was when he left with his mother to take the train to Stuttgart to wait for the end of the war.

As they were walking up a bank to the station, the allies started bombing the station. He remembered **his mother pulling him down to the ground, wrapping him in her arms, and saying "we are either going to make it or not. There's nothing we can do but wait."** The bombing subsided and they continued up the bank to the station and took the train to Stuttgart.

Jaan is in the back row standing behind the girls

PAUL ÖPIK
A FATHER BEFORE HIS TIME

I visited Paul in Canberra in 2012. He is a quiet unassuming humble man. There is a aura about his quietly spoken voice. It is with such voice that Paul related the story of his adolescence: A sacrifice which most experienced adults would find beyond their comprehension.

I have translated his words into English: Given that, I have used second voice as idiom can vary among people and become inappropriate in first voice.

The Estonians used 'Amis' as a colloquialism for Americans. I have used the Australian equivalent of 'Yanks' given Paul now lives in Australia.

This story is a composite of Paul's narrative, and a translation Juku Pärn's article in Meie Kodu (translated with the permission of all parties concerned)

He fought for Estonia's freedom: He fought for the freedom from war's ravages for a host of boys, some quite young, and who had became separated from their parents during the flight from Estonia.

Among Paul' treasured artefacts are two publications "Eesti Sona" (Estonian word) and "Varemetest tõuseb Kättemaks" (Revenge rises from the ruins), the Estonian divisions weekly newspaper of the times.

Paul's fight for freedom against Communism began as a 13 year old in Tartu in 1941.

Paul's father Prof. A. Öpik with his family including Paul now aged sixteen arrived in Danzig in 1944. Paul already had three years of military experience. They arrived in Swinemunde which included a German naval base. The base endured daily bombings and during one of these Paul's grandfather's portrait was damaged by a bomb fragment which went through the eye. Paul quickly befriended some of the crew of an Estonian tourist ship which was berthed there. They invited Paul to visit the ship many times. It seemed so small compared with the military hardware all around.

A few weeks passed thus: Thereafter the Estonian, Latvian and Lithuanian academics and their families were sent by train to Breslau: Their task to dig anti tank trenches. The women were set to mend German soldiers' uniforms: Some uniforms were still stained with blood.

A few days later Paul was summoned to the headquarters of the barracks where the Estonian Air force boys were staying: He was advised that he was now responsible for those young warriors who had over-stated their age. Yes, they had seen battles in Latvia and Curland from where they had escaped with their units. However they were too young to join the Air force assistants and to stay at their barracks.

A few more days hence when all their ages had been verified they were sent to the Estonian Headquarters in Berlin. Paul was asked to read an article relating to this subject written in "Eesti Sona". The older of these young were to become Air force assistants and work on the land and those aged 8-14 years went to KLV (Kinderlandveschickung) camps. The Estonian ones were managed by Estonian teachers: Their task of the former to bridge their gap in lost education. The children wore black Hitler youth uniforms and the camps had firm rules.

Robert Keres was to become the Principal of the school and Aleksander Puus the teacher. Robert had been Paul's mathematics and gymnastics teacher at Treffner (A high achieving high school on Tartu). He was basketball player who had represented Estonia in the Berlin Olympics. Aleksander later taught at Sydney's Consolidated school.

Another move followed to Bechau in Poland. There they were given a large house to live in: One which had been the home of a Polish 'somebody' or a watch house. It was frequented by high ranking German Officers to go rabbit hunting. On one occasion the boys assisted them by diverting the rabbits and rewarded with two of them.

The Wirtshaftleiterin paid the boys upkeep. "Tiigrinahk" (tiger skin) was her nickname as she wore a leopard skin coat: She was German. The boys slept in a large dormitory on double bunks and refused to wear the Hitler Youth attire: They proudly sported their former Estonian air force uniforms.

Classes in Estonian commenced promptly.

More boys began to arrive; among the earliest a six year old whose mother pleaded that he be accepted given she was penniless and had nowhere to go He was accepted.

Not so, two 13-14 year old girls who arrived with their mother a couple of days later. The boys were excited but the excitement was not to last. In Poland there were similar camps both for boys and girls. The boys' one was run by Paul's desk mate Karl Laantee.

Paul insisted that the boys were kept busy: They did gymnastics, ran and sang. The singing was in unison and comprised of songs from the lost homeland. Paul had learned first aid and with his Red Cross kit attended the cuts, bumps and bruises. While they were at school he had to ride 16-17 km by bike to one of the training venues where he learned skills to pass onto the boys.

Two Polish women prepared their food and washed the younger boys clothing. The boys were now receiving three meals a day.

Paul's and a colleague's task was to travel to Danzig to collect provisions such as bedding, underwear, uniforms, and shoes etc. They sure were young men who had been entrusted with a lot. They made several such trips.

Christmas brought a nice Christmas tree around which the boys sang Christmas songs and each relished a piece of marzipan. Paul received a Christmas Album in German. "The Reichsfuhrer SS Commandostelle –Frauen. Manner des SS und Polizei". Beneath this was written by Himmler himself „Look what great brothers we were". That album contained Christmas songs, beautiful pictures and even Hitler's picture.

They again left for Danzig on 16-1-45 arriving on 18-1-45. They saw trenches being dug and cannons being set up. It was to be their last trip. Carrying the bundles they had just collected they saw that there had been a major air raid and that the train station was alight. Passenger trains had been cancelled and they boarded the only available train: One carrying wounded soldiers. Fortunately it passed through the Bechau vicinity. The nurses were tending the wounded soldiers with food and drink and gave Paul and his colleagues some too.

The train lumbered along slowly and before reaching their destination they threw out their parcels and jumped out into the deep snow. On returning to the camp they shared what they had seen: They could hear the roar of the war outside. It was time to move on. For expedient travel only necessary items could go along: No books, well except the "Nippernaadi" which was the boys' favorite. (The is a book of adventures by a young man with limited insight but very entertaining)

At the train station they were asked "Why have you come here? There are no passenger trains running?" A reply to the question was "What do you think? What should I do with these children? The youngest is six years old."

Finally the stationmaster stopped the next train carrying wounded soldiers. The younger boys were ordered into the carriage and the older ones sat on the steps: Thus they travelled to the west. The train stopped at many stations where the refugees were offered food and drinks. Despite the circumstances things were done in a very orderly way.

Finally on 30th January they reached Berlin. Paul stayed with the boys at the train station: Keres and Puus set off to find them accommodation. It was 3km away in a school house. They had to walk there. They were advised that this was a temporary arrangement until their final destination could be confirmed.

On February 1st General Soodla invited Paul for an evening meal at "Unter den Linden" Hotel: A huge surprise for a lad like Paul. He spruced up his clothing and his shoes as much as possible, and placed a blue-black and white armband on his sleeve.

He arrived at the hotel at 6pm. The porter opened the door, let him in. It was all too much for Paul: red and gold everywhere. All present were high ranking Generals and Admirals. They paraded with their women, drank cognac and chatted.

There was Paul with his paltry blue-black and white armband. He was asked what he needed: He indicated that he had been called by General Soodla. A hello was said but Paul didn't inquire why he had been asked to come. It later transpired that General Soodla needed to know how the boys had escaped from Poland.

Yum! The food was delicious. Paul accepted a couple of glasses of wine which he had been offered. Cognac and cigars followed but he cautioned himself that a boy shouldn't drink cognac. He pined for a cigar but declined it too.

On 2nd February they were given travel documents by the general staff. Their seats were reserved until February 4th to travel to Oberhof in Thüringen.

10.45am on February 3rd brought a major bombing raid upon Berlin: It lasted until 12.30pm. The boys were despatched into a robust cellar.

Paul remained outside to watch for a short time to see what eventuated. He feels that he was one of the few to see the imagery of that day: It was the biggest bombing raid of the second world war. The day when 2600 American designated planes filled the sky. They consisted of 937 bombers and 613 fighter planes. The remainder were English bombers and German destroyer planes. The air battle cannons were lit up. The air was filled with smoke. Planes tumbled down. The city burned and bombs were beginning to ignite near Paul as he headed for the cellar. 2267 tons of bombs were dumped, 2.5 square miles of the city was destroyed and about 25,000 people perished. Hitler's bunker which was submerged under eight metres of steel reinforced concrete while sustaining many hits was unscathed.

Orders came for all who were able to, to evacuate the city pronto. With the trains out of action there was a 15 km walkout of the city to access rail transport. After a couple of hours of travel they had to change trains. That involved a two hour wait. The boys wanted to see the city and promised to return in time for the next train. Two of them didn't keep their promise and the group missed that train and caught one which came four hours later.

When they arrived at the next city it was alight: Both the train station and the train that they had missed were reduced to rubble. Those errant boys had saved their lives.

At Oberhof station we were welcomed by the sounds of the Hitler Youth Orchestra. They had heard of the boys' escape, of Berlin caught in war's fury and the journey to Oberhof The group was relieved of their luggage. It was carried two kilometers to Hohen Luftkurort Hotel, "Der Schweitzerhof". The hotel stood on top of a hill and included a school and hospitals for the children of the hierarchy. During the war they had accommodated wounded soldiers and evacuated school children.

Hell! What a turbulent journey they had just encountered. Yes, they were the closing days of World War II.

On the second day at Oberhof the boys were given classrooms and advised that they had to be seen by a doctor: Even a dentist had been summoned. He fixed the boys' teeth and extracted one of Paul's.

The ground was still covered by a thick blanket of snow. The Germans were skiing and asked if the Estonians too skied. Paul told them yes but that they had no skis. The basement stored many skis and they were allowed to use them: They were off on them fast. Paul sprained his ankle on the second day. By the fourth day they were competing with the Germans: The Estonian boys gained the first three places.

A few days later the mother of the youngest boy arrived and a couple of weeks later further two women whose sons were with Paul. The mothers tidied up the boys' clothes and left with the boys.

Paul Öpik

The Germans gave the group the responsibility for the firewood. Thus each week they traipsed into the forest to collect firewood. Each boy carried on his back as big a load as he could cope with. They were embarrassed by the German boys' lack of enterprise. The latter just brought in small twigs. Paul suspected that they thought that the Estonian boys were stupid to carry such heavy loads. The local Germans noticed the boys' conscientiousness and asked if they would like to work in private houses beating floor rugs etc.

The first job was at the local hotel's 'Wirtschafterleiterin's house. Seven of them went there. That house had huge rugs. Paul had learned to beat rugs at home. They dragged the rugs outside and beat them clean and were paid pocket money and a sandwich. More such work at other houses followed.

The local school principal was interested in the Estonians and often invited Paul to his home. He asked Paul to tell him, his wife and his daughter who was Paul's age of Estonia's fate, of Communism, of Russians. They found this hard to believe and Paul had to repeat many times how evil the Russians were.

Robert Keres
Dec. 29-10-46
Buried at Freudenthal

He taught English. One evening he asked his daughter for the translation of "Pfefferkuchen" into English. Paul automatically replied "Gingerbread": He had remembered this from school. The following day the German boys greeted Paul with "Good morning, good morning". They thought that he spoke English.

One evening the group heard on the radio that the Estonians had escaped from 'Opel's bag': That raised the German's esteem of Estonians further.

Sometime in April before the Americans took over rule from the Germans, American planes flitted above them. Cars in the valley below were burning. Three to four days before the American's arrival the German boys were asked to line up in front of the hotel: Paul's group were asked too. The orchestra arrived and they all marched into a large square with 600-700 young already present. Three helmeted soldiers stood in the middle of the square holding a flag. A German boy marched towards the flag and they were all expected to give a soldier's oath. The salute over, they marched back to the tune of the orchestra.

"Wirtshaftleiterin"
at Berlin camp

Soon after they were asked to go and collect the weapons. Paul told the boys to stay in their rooms and not go. The German young went along and soon returned with "Sturmgweher". One even had a Panzerfaust on his back. The leader of the German boys inquired why the Estonian boys had not gone to collect weapons. Paul felt that they were too young and could not see any use in their possessing weapons.

The next day the group was ordered out. The mayor of the town stood in front of the hotel. He was a big heavy man. He bore a gold colored Nazi oak leaf marking on his uniform front. He insisted that the Estonians collected some weapons and screamed: "Oberhof will remain in German history and then the Americans will be stopped". The Estonians thought he had to be crazy to think that their boys could stop the Americans. Paul said that the boys were not going anywhere.

An American spy plane was circling above them and emitting cannon fire: Some flickering had already reached town. Two tiger tanks stopped in front of the hotel. An SS officer with a Knight's cross around his neck alighted from one of them. According to Paul's friend Hans Einer's recall he was probably a 'sturmbahnfuhrer'.

The tanks drove to the foot of a nearby forest. The officer demanded that Paul and the boys collect some weapons. Paul refused this request. The boys became frightened when he threatened to shoot Paul but then he turned around and vaporized. Einer has a powerful memory of this.

The gun bearing Germans began to order Paul's group about. Keres and Puus took the boys to the classroom and confined them to it.

So began their last day of between rulers. Armed wounded soldiers were ordered to sit by their windows and await the American's arrival. They could see fires flickering in the town. Paul stood in front of the hotel and observed the events unfolding. The mayor arrived with two gunman and ordered "Mitkommen" (Come with us).

Paul thought that it was all over for him. They began to march down the road to the town hall. Suddenly a cannon shot whizzed past them and exploded about 200 metres away.

The Bürgermeister (mayor) screamed "come further, come further!" The next bang was close to them. The two gunmen beside Paul jumped to shelter between two houses. Paul ran downhill looking over his shoulder." Mayor" stopped in the middle of the street and screamed. "Stop! Stop!" Paul said he would give him 'stop' and ran even faster.

Paul had no idea where the mayor had vanished but two days later he saw him captured by the Americans.

All young, old and women were in the cellar. A crazed German boy came in too with his "Sturmgeweher". Paul threw him out. In the rooms peering out of the windows were small boys with guns.

Paul was concerned that if they began to shoot the Americans would burn the building and the boys and Paul with it. Paul ran from room to room and pried the guns from the Hitler youth. He had to slap a couple of them across their faces and then sent them all into the cellar.

Suddenly there was a big bang in the hotel. Paul was on the third floor of the hotel and ran along the corridors towards the direction of the bang to find the walls covered in soot. The building was on fire. The Germans were well prepared: There were large water containers, sandboxes, axes etc everywhere. Two German boys ran up and helped Paul to extinguish the flames. One of the seventeen years olds later gave Paul a present: A photo of himself.

After extinguishing the fire they went into the basement. It was dark in there.

The occasional house was burning. The military hospital across the road began to burn. There was a lot of light weaponry fire to be heard: Then through the window Paul saw the first American. Soon there was much swearing in English: Screaming began to emanate from the cellar. The cellar was emptied: The women and children into one group. Our boys and Keres and Paul joined them.

The POWs stood about ten metres away. Paul was ordered "Hands up" and sent among the POWs as he was in uniform. Someone yelled in Estonian: "Where is Paul?" Paul yelled back that their ways were about to part.

A miracle followed. An American soldier approached Paul. He had Red Cross markings on his helmet. He took Paul's hand and asked "Virolainen?" Paul replied yes. The soldier was a Finn in the American army. He returned Paul to his boys where he stripped off his uniform and was in his underwear. The war noises rumbled on and Paul and the boys were allowed to return to the cellar.

Then things became quiet outside: The laughter and movement was confined to the corridor. Paul peeked out of the door. The Americans were carrying wines boxes which they had found in the hotel cellar. As the laughter and movement abated They all returned to our rooms to give the boys some sleep.

Paul thought wow, if it suits then Americans then it is OK for him to do likewise. He went down to the cellar and filled his backpack with wine bottles and put them under his bed and made a second such trip. He now feels ashamed to talk about this: They used to call this taking booty.

A day later while they were singing Estonian songs in the biggest room there as a knock on the door. Two older wealthy looking women stood there: They were the owners of the hotel. It seems that a couple of days ago there had been a meeting of the town's Germans. It was at the house of the two boys who had helped extinguish the fire. They had spoken of the large flames Paul had extinguished. The hotel owners had come to thank Paul and handed him a large parcel apologizing that they could not reward him better. When Paul opened the parcel it contained five bottles of wine. The space under the bed was full of wine bottles! How would those poor women know that Paul had raided their cellar and stolen their wine? Paul felt ashamed.

The food was very poor. They were rationed a couple of loaves of black bread. They were all starving, and their conversation was focussed on food but the boys did not whine. They all narrated of their past of ample food: Roast pork, sauerkraut, jellied pork etc.

The road leading up from the valley was a typical Thüringen forest road: 3-4 km long and winding. At times trucks would come to grief travelling along it: It would remain there as the other trucks continued on their way. The boys observed this.

Paul had not noticed anything amiss until one day the boys arrived with their legs astride; their trousers tied of at the bottoms and they had something hard in their trousers. He asked what was amiss. They had observed a broken down truck, jumped out of the forest, threw a large carton into the bushes and ran away. Fortunately they weren't spotted or they would have been shot.

Another truck came along soon and resurrected the engine and the truck travelled on.

The boys opened the box which was full of gold coloured chocolate boxes. They had required two trips to bring back all the boxes. They all hoed into the chocolate that evening: All but Paul got diarrhoea. The remaining chocolate was consumed over a few days.

On another occasion they commandeered a box of candles: They were pretty useless and were palmed off to the Germans.

On the third occasion they found a box of ice-cream: They ate it like soup with spoons. Paul forbade any further trips to gather goodies. It was to be their last trip.

Then the Americans arrived and lobbed into the biggest hotel making it their lodgings. The hotel had a golf course. The Yanks asked the boys to be their caddies and rewarded them with chewing gum. Paul was furious. They could have given them some food. The boys informed Paul that there was oodles of food to be had and invited him to come along and see it. They went there to find a rubbish tip: That's where their leftover food went. Thus began daily visits to the rubbish tip. The best pickings came on Independence Day (4th July). There was roast turkey, meat and lots of everything.

Paul still has a souvenir of that tip: Two American army uniform markings. It seems that Paul has specialised in rubbish tips!

Then abruptly that food supply came to an end: The yanks began to pour petrol on the food scraps. Puus could speak English and mustered up courage and paid the Yanks a visit to talk about this. Thereafter they could retrieve whatever was left over from breakfast and lunch. That kept the boys alive and fed. There was coffee by the bucketful. Given they were not coffee drinkers this was passed onto the Germans who relished it.

One fine summer day while the boys were at school, Paul sat outside to watch the world go by. Two former soldiers passed him. One was barefooted; the other's boots were torn to bits. They spoke Estonian. Paul said "Hello, hello!" They introduced themselves. The Officer was Captain Koger. Paul could not recall the junior officer's name.

That is when Paul first heard of the "Czech hell". During the conversation Paul asked Captain Koger if his family were in Germany. He replied yes, his wife and his nine year old son. Paul asked him to wait, rushed upstairs to the classroom, grabbed a blond boy by the hand and brought him down with him. A father and his son were united. That was like a fairy tale come true. Both men were given civilian clothing and shoes. That is the last time Paul heard from them.

Time passed and one day trucks appeared in front of the hotel. They were put on board and moved to Gotha city. There they were taken to a large school house where there were Latvians and one Estonian woman with a daughter.

The Yanks fed them well but one morning raucous swearing broke out. The Latvians had erred badly by breaking into a store room.

Within a couple of hours the trucks were on the ready and everyone was loaded onto them. On each truck were two armed men. The truck drove away towards the east. They were taken into the hands of the Russians at Jena. Red flags were flying and the Yanks were still milling around the city. It was hand over day for the different zones. They were taken to a huge camp which had been a refugee and Prisoner of war camp. Estonians, Latvians, Lithuanians were taken to: Over the preceding two weeks it had been taken by the west from the hands of the Russians. Paul decided it was time to move on again.

They packed the basic necessities, ate their soup at night and slept there for that night. The Estonian woman with her daughter and one Latvian boy went with them. The remainder consisting of a couple of hundred Latvians stayed on.

Hochenluftkurort Oberhof in Thüringen, Hotel "Der Schweitzerhof"

"Hotel Schweitzerhof in winter 8-3-1945

Puus family in Australia in 1950

Next day they pondered on a means to escape.

A couple of Yanks and some Russians stood by a couple of large bivalve iron gates. Suddenly a barrack at the other end of the camp caught alight. Everyone headed that way and Paul and his party walked away unnoticed. No one was there to stop them.

They reached the train station where an American train was stationary. The last three carriages were allotted to people in civilian clothes. They were Hungarian Jews. They climbed into the carriages but the Jews began to protest to have them ejected. Puus and Paul went to the train conductor and asked to be taken along: They informed him that among the group were young boys whose parents were in the west. The group was placed into an empty animal carriage and the train moved on westwards.

On arrival in the American zone they weren't game to stay there and finally jumped out of the train at a station to find a train heading north. They had tragic information from Jena.

At the train stations refugees were given food and drinks, so there was no urgency to move on. They finally reached Cologne and continued west to the Dutch border where the border guards exited them from the train.

They were sent back to Cologne: No food this time! From there they were advised to travel to Bonn which was already better organized. There they became aware of DP camps and on that same day were trucked to Mannheim.

It was a big camp and they were given rooms. They were all scruffy and dirty and doused themselves under warm showers. The children were well fed and for the boys it was back to classes again.

Paul leaned that Augsburg had a large Estonian community and hurried there to rummage among their name records for the names of the boys' parents. He found the mother of two boys was living at Wiesbaden and on the following day returned the boys to her.

Paul returned Ago Kadak to his parents in Augsburg (Ago is now in Australia): They were elated as was Paul. Ago's father was working for the Yanks day and night making donuts. Paul was given a couple of dozen to take back with him.

Paul also met some friends there in including Karl Laantree. Paul had become a sweet tooth. Before departing he exchanged another bag of donuts for bread.

At Mannheim a couple of parents had arrived to collect their children. A Narva Battalion soldier came to collect his brother. Roomets later became an Estonian soldiers' association member in Canada.

The Russian Mission with its red flag full mast was across the road. The Russians intruded the Estonians' camp to brain wash them. They also noticed a few Estonians frequenting the Russian Mission. Paul exploded: Together with the medical students they went a tore the flag down. They felt crazed. The Russians were quick to arrive at the gates asking for them to be identified. Paul packed his backpack and left his friends in God's care ad moved on to seek out this family.

Aleksander Puus had moved onto Geislingen and two years after Paul had left Mannheim he received a letter from Aleksander. Aleksander shared of his travels since leaving Mannheim and about life in Geislingen where he had by then lived for one year.

Keres had been hospitalized in Mannheim, later in Heidelberg and finally in Freudenhal sanatorium where he died from TB. Puus wrote of their friend's death "So departed our great friend". Puus too was not well but worked in Geislingen as a primary teacher.

Puus has recounted the fates of many of the boys: They are here and there and many are real   Yanks. Many were adopted by American Officers and live in America.

Paul is proud of those Estonian boys and their sense of responsibility. Had the Russians not the Americans arrived they would have been sent to battle and Paul is sure that each of them would have taken weapons to retaliate.

ESTONIA PAYS TRIBUTE TO A MAN WHO IN HIS YOUTH MADE HUGE SACRIFICES

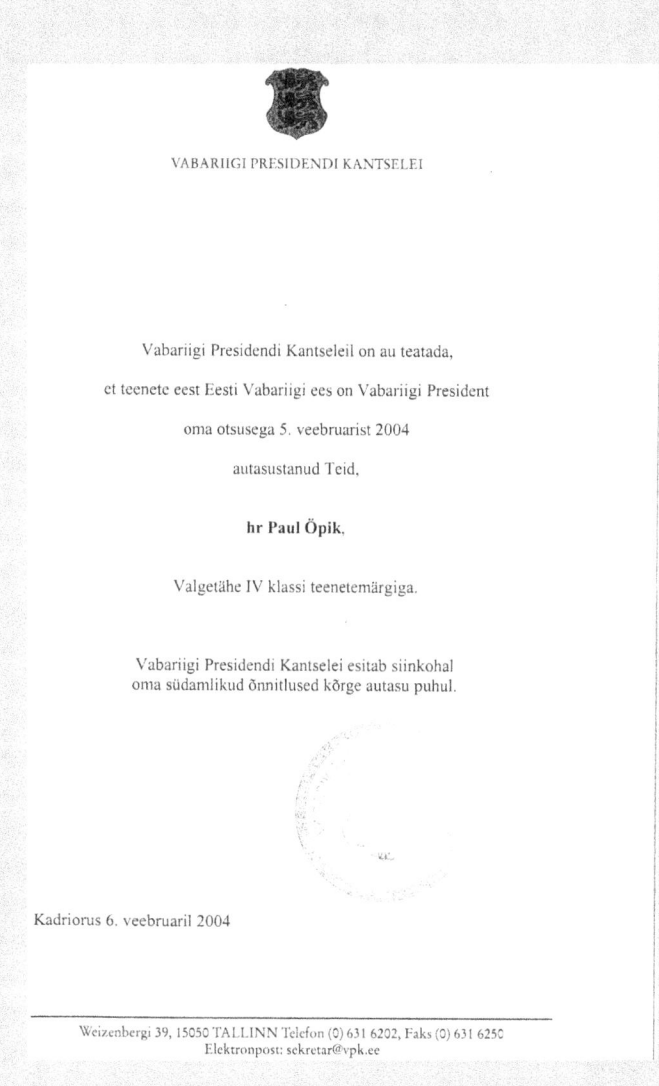

Paul receiving Estonia's "Order of the white star 4th class" from Dr. Malle Tohver (On the right) who was the Honorary Estonian Consul in Australia at the time. To Paul's left is Hilja, his wife

PAUL'S AIRFORCE BOYS

Vello Vilberg

The boys on this page had stated they were 3 years older and had already seen combat in Estonia

Johannes Merila

Kaljo Roomets

Sumeri

Kalju Suitsev

Uno Piil

Kalju was awarded the Purple Heart and the Silver Star by the USA army for his courage in the Korean War.

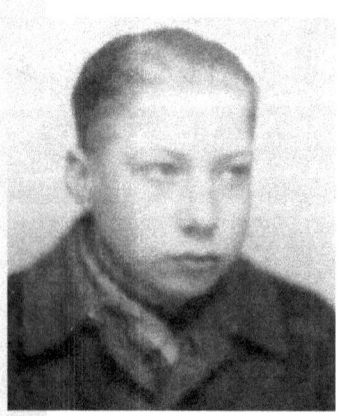

PAUL'S WAR ORPHANS

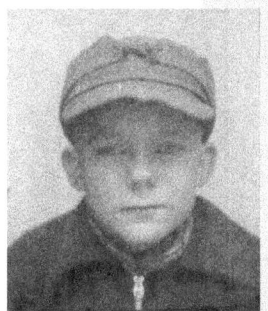
Jüri Raid

Endel Taks

?Ullar Vitsut -2nd photo

Ullar Vitsut

Raul Vitsut

Laul

Boys who were brought to the camp by their parents and ones who were homeless in Germany

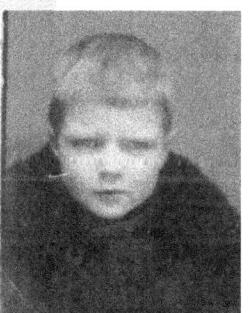

Hans Einer

Koger

Allik

The younger Prima

Vello Prima

Unknown name

SNIPPETS FROM JÜRI RAID'S LETTER TO ME IN FEBRUARY 2012

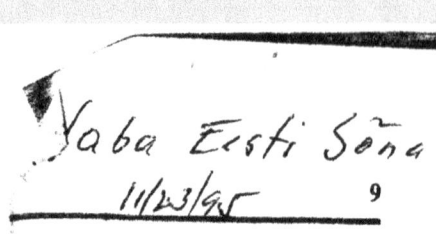

Kas keegi teab, kus on Endel Taks või Jüri Raid?

Andrew H. Deuble, oma endise eesti nimega Ain Tohver otsib teisi orbusid, kes Teise maailmasõja järel paigutati välismaalaste perekonda ja nende kohal toimus nime muudatus.

Orbudegrupp läbis Oberhoffit Aglastehausenisse, kus grupp jaotati. Mõned leidsid kohe sobivad perekonnad või isegi oma vanemad üles, kuid teised mitte. Grupis oli alguses: John Merila, Uno Piil, Jüri Raid, Harry Sakjas, Kalju Suitsev, Walfrid Sumeri, Ain Tohver (Andy Double praegu), Vello Villberg ja Endel Taks.

Oleme leidnud üles kõik väljaarvatud **Jüri Raid ja Endel Taks.** Saime ka teada, et surma läbi on lahkunud John Merila ja Uno Piil. Teame aga niipalju, et Jüri Raid elab Rootsis, kuid ei tea, kuidas temaga kontakti saada. Endel Taksist me ei tea midagi. Võibolla adopteeriti ta ameeriklaste poolt, nagu allakirjutanule juhtus, ja ta nimi muudeti.

Kui teate midagi Endel Taksist või Jüri Raidist, palun võtke kontakti Andrew H. Deublega (Ain Tohver), aadressil: 8379 SW 108 Loop, OCALA, FL 34481-5732; või telefoni teel: 904-873-1361.

Resourcing article to attempt to trace the missing 'brethren'.

My name is Jüri Raid. I was born in 1931 in Võsu. Forgive my writing to you in Estonian but my English, which I learned at school, is no longer adequate for communication. *

One of my friends in USA forwarded your article "Help! Our childhood memories are gradually being shared," to me.

I am one of those children: The young who fled from Estonia to Germany in 1944. Given that our small group's activities were unusual, maybe they would be interesting to share with future generations.

The accompanying articles are copies which have been published in Toronto as "Sauna Antsu Saaga". They were compiled and edited by Hans Einer. To my knowledge about 25-30 books were published. The intent of the publication was initially as a tribute to Hans Einer's father. The book was expanded to include the narrative of these children in Germany. Eerik Purje did the editing.

Paul Öpik (he lives in Australia) has also had his memories published in the Estonian newspaper in Australia. **. To my knowledge these were sent in part to our former homeland to be archived.

My account of those times has tended to remain through a child's eyes: They continue from where Paul's narrative ends. It relates the story of the children and young after capitulation: A time they spent in an orphanage.

There are three other survivors from our group at the Orphanage: Vello Willberg, Ain Tohver (now known as Andy Deuble) and Harry Sakjas.*** They live in USA.

*Jüri has lived in Sweden since he was a boy hence his everyday language is Swedish. He like many of us is trilingual with a varying degree of fluency in those languages according to predominant usage.

**Paul's story is included in this book: It has been translated with the permission of Paul, Juku Pärn and Meie Kodu.

***Communications from Vello, Ain and Harry will appear separately in chapters to follow.

WAR ORPHANS JÜRI RAID

The names in this narrative are ongoing from Paul Öpik's memoirs and thus assumed to have been read. They were written in Sweden in 2003.

PROLOGUE
Endless novels and memoirs have been written about the traumas and sufferings of the Estonians during World War II but a small fraction of our folk's narrative has slipped between the cracks: The story of the war orphans and other children who were to become permanently separated from their families. Why? Yes the readers might well ask this.

A general impression of the story of our young during that war was written in the books "Valgumärgi kasvandused" (The students of the lightning flash) and " Igavesti Noored" (Forever young), both published by Airforce's support workers club.

Whatever happened to those who vanished, who became separated from that group? But then perhaps it is even better that these are now shared with a more distant hindsight: It enables one to share those memoirs with some humour. This avoids such memories again traumatizing with those painful marks visible just post war, those of our injured soldiers and war veteran boys: Those whose lives became ruined by alcohol or a generally detached attitude.

Young have the capacity to forget and the energy to generate new beginnings. It is unlikely that such young felt inclined to maintain diaries of the chaos of wartime. There is lack of accurate data about names and dates: at times they just happened to intercurrently become part of some narrative.

The significance of these memoirs was publicized by a small article in USA's Estonian newspaper while searching for lost friends: Memoirs of those orphans who by their adoption acquired new parents. Some of them, now grey haired gentleman, did eventually find their biological parents when the world predicament improved.

Some of them were never to personally read these pages: The Almighty had already called some of them home. The mother language for many, quite understandably has become a blur and inaccessible for them to read. This collection of pages is a tribute to those determined, conscientious Estonian youth leaders who spared many an Estonian young from the privations of Siberia and gave them another chance at life.

We the surviving orphans bow our head in tribute to their sacrifices: There are no words to convey adequate thanks.

Robert Keres used to wander about with a worried face as he searched for a more permanent home for us. The boys needed adequate clothing. Everyone was given American army shirts: But there were difficulties with trousers and footwear. In the attic there was frantic activity: shorts were being produced for the summer and attempts were being made to alter donated clothing to fit the boys.

One day Robert came into the attic and announced "I have just converted all of you to Jews. I have found an orphanage where Jewish children whose parents can't be located are being cared for. You will be going there soon."

On noticing that the boys still wore belts with a crooked cross on them someone asked "Don't you have any other belts? What sort of Jewish boys are you: You are wearing Hitler youth belts!" The buckles were removed and holes punched in the belts to accommodate the hooks. "Above all don't talk about the Luftwaffe or Hitler youth while at the orphanage" Robert added. "Right now you still look too military like."

AGLASTERHAUSEN
One day Robert and our teacher Puus were left to God's care. An American military truck was standing in front of our house, and a happy go lucky driver hoisted the boys' backpacks onto the truck. The last to descend the stairs was Juss, mumbling somewhat angrily "In old Aadu's time we were still 'somebodies'. It has been said that the Hitler youth and the old monkeys are the last of the Waffen. Now we are sans possessions and just refugees without a homeland."

In those days we could not remotely conceive or relate how much our teachers Robert, Paul and Puus had done for us. We just said God be with you and maybe we will meet again somewhere some day. We climbed into the truck tray and all nine Estonian boys headed for new adventures.

As the truck finally turned off the main road to travel between villages we began to carefully scrutinize the environment. The truck stopped in front of a large gate with a large sign stating "Western District Children's Centre. UNRRA team 507". An American soldier emerged from an adjoining small gateway and opened that large gate to allow the truck to enter.

That group of Aglasterhausen buildings had since its inception been a farm management training center. Subsequently it had become a respite place for German soldiers. There were many buildings and they were surrounded by a high fence. So this was that famous American orphanage!

The boys jumped off the truck dray to explore the surroundings. A sturdy woman in military uniform quickly joined us. She was the camp manager. Her name was Miss Rachel Greene. She greeted the boys with a few English words which we barely understood. Then a Latvian couple joined the boys. In clear German they indicated that they would be the boys mother and father.

We were guided up the steps of a large nearby house and went through an open door and led to a large room. Nine white blanketed beds stood around its walls. There was a white bedside table between each pair of beds. At the end of the room was a large window which brightened the room with the sun's rays. In front of the window was a table surrounded by nine chairs. The Latvian then led us to the bathrooms and a place where "The king walks bare foot". One wall contained large wardrobes: We had little to put into them apart from our back packs and a couple of American army shirts. With little more ado we chose our beds.

On returning from the bathrooms we found nice, soft, white towels at the ends of our beds. We had barely returned to our dormitory when the Latvian came and asked us to accompany him. Juss, the oldest of us was still responsible for our clothing and quietly spoke in our language "If anyone asks tell them that we are Estonian Jews and have just fled via East Prussia."

The Latvian directed us to the lower floor and opened a door where several other young people were chatting. That room had some soft chairs and several sofas for us to sit on. The chatter from those already in the room quietened. The Latvian indicted that we were new students from Estonia. The students already in the room created space for us on the sofas and graciously invited us to sit down.

Initially there was dead silence in the room. One could have heard a pin dropping. Juss put an end to that when he spotted a piano near the wall. "Juku, play a few tunes so that we can somehow break the silence". After Juku had played a few known German pop tunes Juss advised "Don't play these today, maybe they are unsuitable"

A girl with jet black hair pushed her way onto the piano stool near Juku. She began to question him about his knowledge of films. She spoke good German. Juku mumbled that where on earth would he have seen or heard such films. The girl then began to sing "Lily Marleine" in a beautiful mellow voice. Juku found his voice and they sang several songs which were more or less familiar.

Between the songs we had to out of politeness chat with the girl. "Where are you from?" "I came from Oswiecist" she replied "The Germans call it Auschwitz" she added, showing us her forearms onto which were tattooed numbers.

The boys had already heard the KZ camp story at Oberhof. While the city battles were raging he Americans initially threatened that they would allow the KZ residents to come and rob Oberhof. Of course it was only a threat.

Juku eyed the girl and noting her thin body and remarked "I was in the Kapo camp doing the cooking". Kapos* were gaols for criminals, where they maintained internal order. "The majority of those here are survivors of those camps."

Juku thought to himself, now we have really landed in strife! He was trying to conceal his large army boots under the piano stool. Fortunately the gong sounding in the hall resolved that awkward predicament. A young girl poked her head through the doorway and called "Essen" (come and eat).

That meal was our afternoon snack. The Estonian boys were allotted their own table with a white table cloth: We had to watch where we put our hands! Uno spoke with authority "This place has a fine English custom of drinking tea at five o'clock." No tea appeared at the table: Instead fresh rolls from the oven were placed on the table together with large jugs of cocoa.

There was little time to admire such a feast. A stout helpful woman in a nurse's uniform appeared. In clear Estonian she welcomed the boys and said enjoy your food. She explained that across the courtyard is the nursery which she is in charge of. The children there were around one year old. They had been found, their parents having been killed during their flight or been abandoned by them. The boys quickly christened her as the midwife, which she probably had been at home in Estonia. When the boys asked if there were Estonian babies among them she replied "who knows, there could be Estonians."

A married couple accompanied the American camp supervisor into the dining room. They immediately began to converse in Polish. We understood that there was conversation about "Estonskajas". They then welcomed the boys in German and then something else was said. It seemed to be in German. The 'midwife' stated that they were speaking in Yiddish.

The evening meal over, we went to our room and Juss went to inquire from the children, where do the local residents live. On his return he explained that the people here are all Polish Jews, who in the main had escaped Auschwitz. We definitely could not discuss our adventures here. The camp manager knows who we are and what we have been doing. From here we are all eventually to be sent overseas to America, be it by adoption or other means. Juss further explained that explained on Jewish religious occasions there would be special foods, and we will be able to eat whatever we wish. Eventually an Estonian girl joined the kitchen staff.

"I wonder how they let us know of meal times?' Inquired Uno.

"Are you already hungry?' Inquired Juss with surprise.

"You already heard that a gong will sound when the time comes."

"No I'm not hungry yet" replied Uno "But I feel nauseated from the sweet drink."
"Who asked you to guts all those cups of cocoa" the boys tormented.

The evening meal arrived soon and included a very unfamiliar bread. We even had roast potatoes on the table

After the evening meal the girls called the boys to chat but we apologized that we were travel weary and vamoosed into our room. The boys discussed why there were so few boys here: there was a vast disproportion of girls. Some thought that maybe the boys did not manage to tolerate the KZ privations as well.

That night all the boys found it hard to get to sleep. We were sleeping between two white sheets like back home. The mattresses initially too felt strange: they finally adapted to our body shapes. We later discovered that the mattresses had been filled with some kind of grain: That was supposed to be healthy. One could hear a sense of rummaging in the room as the boys tossed and turned in their beds. We had eaten too much and worries about our future loomed before us. Aglasterhausen was to become the boys next phase of life.

*A Nazi concentration camp prisoner who was given privileges in return for supervising work gangs: Often a common criminal and frequently brutal to fellow inmates.

THE ORPHANAGE
The Estonian boys rapidly adapted to their new life. We idled around the surroundings. The camp manager advised us to have a proper rest and eat properly so we could recover. Yes with the ample food our belts soon needed to be let out.

The Jewish children attended school classes during the day. The girls had a small sewing workshop somewhere. There was also a carpentry facility where the future 'Americans' were learning a trade. Endel Taks, one of the Estonian boys (who left for USA in 1946 to be lost contact with) acquired an interesting job in the kitchen. He used to bake bread and thus learned an occupation for his future. Endel was always a little different to us: He had not matured like the rest of us, and the other boys frequently picked at him. But somehow in Aglasterhausen he suddenly came to life and was always happy. He often laughed when he spoke.

One day the Latvian came to advise us that all of us boys were to have a doctor's check-up including a chest x-ray. He asked if any of us were aware of any spots on our lungs. Should we be aware of such he coaxed us that one of our friends have an x-ray on our behalf. We knew that a lung spot meant nix to going to USA. Such action had spared a couple of the girls.

Going to the doctor's added variety to our day! We did not resort to his suggestion about fudging x-rays. A couple of days later we heard from him that all had gone well at the doctors and to not worry about not being eligible to go overseas.

The arrival of two Latvian boys at the camp brought big changes. They had really seen life and had even participated at the Russian front. They were sent here from the refugee camps as orphans. They blended easily with the Estonian boys and became friendly with them.

One day the Jewish students were taken by car to the synagogue at Heidelberg for one of their religious occasions. They pleaded with the boys to join them, just for a change. Juku and Uno accepted the invitation. On the evening before the Heidelberg trip the boys were given a real pork roast, while the Jewish students were given cooked fish.

The girls asked the boys to put some bacon aside for them and that they would collect this later from the boys. Their Jewish faith was strong. The army bus for the Heidelberg trip arrived and the ride in it was quite an adventure.

At the foyer of the Jewish synagogue we were given some form of head gear to cover our heads. The girls were sent to the balcony where they could between covered drapes observe the service. The Estonian boys were

The Air corps building in Oberhof hotel in Thüringen

This is a cutting from a contemporary newspaper. The narrative to it will appear in translated from among the snippets to follow. This document was forwarded to me by Jüri Raid

becoming increasingly drowsy. The Cantor's voice was all that coaxed their eyes to remain open.

After that we could all have a look around the city: That was interesting. Heidelberg was the only city in the vicinity that the airplanes had not demolished. Heritage buildings were being preserved and most of all the American third army head quarters were here.

At the end of the month the camp manager advised us that the Estonian boys had had enough time to lounge around and that a teacher would be arriving: Also a music teacher for the camp. Soon two large boxes arrived into the yard by truck. They were said to contain musical instruments donated by rich Americans. We just had to wait until the music teacher arrived: They would then distribute the instruments according to our desires and skills.

The next day we were delighted to be introduced to Meta and August Pruul (both now deceased in Australia) and their daughter Vaike and son Hendrik. The morale of the boys rose: Estonians were again at the fore front.

The Pruuls quickly set about creating an orchestra. The instruments were distributed and learning in earnest began. Only two Estonian boys weren't in the orchestra. Harry said that he would no longer become a voluntary participant. He stayed in his room hands on his lap and listened to others practising. From that he acquired the name of grandmother. The other to not participate was one of the Summeri boys. He just had no musical inclination and the Pruuls excluded him.

Martin Laab, a young teacher (now living in USA) arrived a couple of days later. Classes began in earnest for the boys. Martin did not find teaching easy but he related well with the boys. A lot of emphasis was placed on learning English. American history and geography too were emphasized. We had to learn about life in our new land. We had to learn the names of the capital cities of all the states and their main industries. The teacher even cut out of cardboard templates of the various states and made us put them together like a jigsaw to form USA. The teacher did a great job and we learned much for our futures. When we sometimes wrote the more important statistics on the ceiling planks no one objected.

Participating in the orchestra too had some fringe benefits. Each of us received dressy new shirts made of parachute silk. Somehow it was inappropriate to entertain the important visitors wearing old Hitler youth shirts.

The orchestra was comprised of whatever musicians were available. Vello and Juku played accordions. Uno played the saxophone and the others played banjos or guitars. August Pruul led with his violin so much that the violin bowstrings broke. We learned a simplified version of Strauss "On the Blue Danube" and the tango "La Paloma", the latter with Meta's beautiful singing.

Five of the girls had made themselves long white dresses and they conscientiously learned some form of ballet. The Jewish girls formed a small choir which Meta conducted.

August Pruul used to frequently play the organ in German churches. He would take Juku with him to change the register at appropriate times. Through this he hoped to teach Juku to try to play the organ. The Pruuls would often be away at other Estonian camps to entertain them:

At times for an entire day and night. Juku was then called to baby-sit and was rewarded with a couple of packets of cigarettes. The boys were not great smokers, but with access to cigarettes they had to share them around.

With the performances we demonstrated to the visitors how the students at the orphanage were studying. Many military uniformed personnel together with film crews and writers came along. The important guests appeared to be pleased with our performances. We had to ensure that our credentials reached the right places.

In the afternoons with the celebrations over, dances were organized for the guests. There were also party foods and drinks. The young were shunted to their rooms when these began. That was not well received and the young demanded to have a dance of their own. An attempt at this was made with Juku and Uno providing the music but their repertoire was somewhat limited. On evening August Pruul showed us his entire collection of sheet music. With Juku they played everything they could access. I doubt that any other music teacher would have been generous enough to sacrifice an entire evening playing tangos and foxtrots.

Thus the time at Aglasterhausen passed enterprisingly. I can't recall how we celebrated Christmas. The Jewish students didn't celebrate this. The Estonian boys went to the local church with the Pruuls and Martin.

LET'S PARADE OUR ESTONIAN IDENTITIES.

The winter passed in the name of learning. The American guards vanished from the camp gates. Their tasks had been simple and they were no longer needed. It seems that they had only been placed there to deter people's curiosity. The boys wandered in and out of those gates, and at times wandered to the nearby villages to explore how German farm folk lived.

The Neckar valley did not endure a typical winter and thus we could not participate in winter sports. The Jewish students had their own classes. They were taught by a Polish married couple.

By early January Martin, our teacher and the Pruuls had begun planning how to celebrate Estonia's

Independence Day to demonstrate to the others that Estonia had once been a free nation. The boys had regular choir practice and with Meta's help they learned some proper choral songs. The Jews were quick to ask why the boys were so busy in the evenings with all kinds of practicing. They had an appropriate word for unusual occurrences: Circus! When the orchestra played something wrongly they yelled "Circus". If our boys got something right they would call out "Mensch" which in Yiddish meant a worthy person.

February 24th, that important day, brought a lot of invited guests and they were acquainted with Estonian culture. Martin gave a short talk in English about current issues. Meta and her daughter dressed up in Estonian national costumes, and they tried to find something more festive for the boys to wear. Together with instrumental accompaniment they sang 'Tuljak" and "Kaerajaan" (Estonian traditional songs) in their varying tones. August accompanied Meta when she sang songs by Estonian composers.

With the festivities over a dance orchestra had been arranged for the evening. There was festive food on the tables and even drinks appear to have been supplied. I find it hard to believe that the camp manager arranged all this. Almost certainly all this was arranged by Martin and the Pruuls. The young were again sent off to amuse ourselves with something appropriate when the dancing began.

Our Latvian friends created some proper mischief. After the performance they joined the Estonian boys, bottles in hand, and boasted that it is the appropriate brew. They wanted to give their friends something special on their festive day.

The Latvians had managed to set up a winery in a forgotten garden cellar which had previously been used to prepare animal feed. In autumn the German farmers made cider from apples and pears which had fallen to the ground: It was just right for quenching the workers thirst. The Latvian boys had bartered cigarettes to obtain this semi-fermented liquid. A couple of packets of yeast and some sugar had been sidelined from the kitchen: The brew frothed in the cellar. The boys had assembled appropriate tubing from old pipes. Since that old cellar was remote from other buildings no one had noticed the Latvian boys' activities. On the appropriate day came the bottling and then proudly the sharing of it with the Estonian boys.

Fortunately the boys did not indulge in too much of that liquid: It was bitter and disgusting. Nevertheless the tasting made the boys happy. Then came the jeering and complaints from the Jewish students that the Estonian boys had made a "Circus": It took quite a bit of effort to restore order in the Estonian boys' room.

The next day the wine making was discovered. The Latvian boys were allowed to stay on at the orphanage and the entire thing was hushed up. It would have been embarrassing for the camp management for others to know that wine had become accessible at the orphanage. The entrance to the cellar was sealed off with large wooden planks to ensure that no one could access the factory. However the event remained a conversation piece among us for yonks.

The orphanage maintained our bed linen meticulously. It was laundered somewhere in the German village. Each weekend we received clean sheets and towels at the ends of our beds. As winter fell we were given warmer clothing: Jumpers and couple of shirts. The footwear was a bigger concern.

In the yard there was a laundry for us to wash out shirts and underwear. We each washed this by hand. The ironing was very primitive. We had irons heating on the stove and with a cloth we alternated these to ensure that they remained hot. Ironing the trousers was cumbersome with this method. At times we decided that it was simpler to just pus the trousers under our mattress to flatten them.

**Confirmation boys 1946; From right
First row:** vello Villberg, Vaike Pruul, Jüri Raid, Pastor Rebane, Hendrik Pruul, Uno Piil, Ain Tohver, Meeta Pruul, Martin's partner Made
Second row: Peeter Elias' wife, Kalju Suitsev, ? Estonian lady from kitchen, Hannes Merila, W. Sumeri, Martin Laas, Harrry Sakljas, the "Midwife", Peeter Elias, August Pruul

1946, all the orphanage students at the confirmation

Just before the departure to USA. From the right first row: 1. Endel Taks, 3. Polish teacher, 4.?, 5. Miss Greene, 7. Vello Villberg. The remainder are Polish-Jewish children

The Jewish girls insisted on helping us with the washing and ironing. We had to downright demand that they went away. It would have been hard to explain where we obtained our brown Hitler youth shirts. In the evenings we sang together. The girls knew a lot of songs from films which we soon learned.

ESTONIAN CONFIRMATION

In the spring of 1946 Martin and the Pruuls decided that we boys needed to be confirmed: We couldn't be sent from here to USA as pagans. The hope was that should the boys when living among the Americans forget their mother tongue their confirmation certificate would remind them of their beginnings.

Pastor Hans Rebane, who ministered to the surrounding Estonian UNRRA refugee camps, conducted our confirmation classes. I cannot recall how long these lasses lasted; maybe only a few days. Eight Estonian boys prepared themselves to become grown ups. Only eight because Endel did not join us: Maybe because he was the youngest of us.

The boys wanted to make the confirmation day a festive one. Many musical items were practised: we needed to show what we Estonians were capable of. To help the Pruuls Peeter Elias a well known cellist was invited to contribute to the music.

Juku had much to learn: There were many performances in the church where Juku was to be part of the quartet. Meta sang as a soprano, August played the violin, Peeter the cello and of course Juku the organ. Sibelius "Our quiet prayer" was one item; "Our mother" had been requested by the Pruuls as an Estonian song and Handel's "Largo" was played on the violin and cello.

Difficulties arouse with the words of the Estonian hymn. It was to be that powerful finale to bless the boys being confirmed. Somehow the words of second verse became scrambled: Martin had to recite them to the boys repeatedly. The words 'dear' and 'beloved' were readily confused.

Our confirmation day brought another big surprise. The boys were given new well fitting new dark suits, new white shirts and white ties, new black shoes and sox. There was chaos with getting dressed into that clothing. The Pruuls had to come to the rescue: The boys had no idea what to do with the ties. We had not seen each other dressed so elegantly. We teased each other with "Who are you?" We introduced each other and shook hands: It was all in good humour.

On the first day of Easter, on April 21st 1946 eight proud boys about to be confirmed headed towards the Aglasterhausen church. At the church door Martin's partner Made, placed a white carnation in our lapels.

"Boys now let's proceed together" our friends called among them.

The church was full of the orphanage children. The Jewish students were unconcerned that this was a Christian celebration. Everyone wanted to be part of our big day. The confirmation blessing too was a festive occasion. Juku had to run from the altar up to the organ repeatedly: That made things even more important.

All went just perfectly: well until difficulties again arose with the Estonian hymn. Juku was forbidden to use the pedals. However during the hymn he felt the need to display his fortes and set the pedals into action. Hell, someone had slipped with the full weight of his body onto to the pedals. The church rumbled with such foreign sounds. Meta grabbed the 'organist' by the armpits and lifted him back where he belonged and stated benignly "Never mind, son, just continue steadily." How great our music teachers were. Instead of lashing out at us they pacified us and even offered praise. There are too few such teachers born into this world.

Celebration of the first anniversary of freedom from the KZ camps and the first relocations. That anniversary was celebrated on the same day as our confirmation blessing.

After the church service we all moved to the large dining room which had been decorated in the fashion of the times. Many visitors had been invited from outside the camp. An American flag hung on the wall. On one side of it hung the Israeli flag on the other the Polish flag: To each side of these hung white and grey striped material drapes with the letters KZ in their centres: They apparently symbolized the prisoners' uniforms.

This was to be a day of intense grieving, but because of the Estonian boys' confirmations all faces looked cheerful. Some official in military uniform gave a speech. Everyone stood up to remember those who had perished in the camps.

I can't recall much about the music. The Jewish girls' choir sang in Polish and Yiddish. Meta had again risen to her form and taught these girls their songs in a foreign language. Meta too sang a few sad songs and Elias played a few prayers on the cello, together with Augusts' piano accompaniment.

After the celebrations came a joint party where all invited guests joined in. The boys who were confirmed were photographed individually and as part of the entire orphanage family.

The following day the first of our students were about to begin their journeys overseas. Those first eight were photographed under their flags together with the camp management. Among them were friends Vello and Endel. That was a big surprise.

It was not conceivable that two friends would be parting not to know if they would ever meet again. It all happened so fast that no one could find a way to stay in contact. That memory of those leaving still looms vividly before my eyes: Vello in his new confirmation outfit and poor Endel in his English army shirt and trousers obtained in Berlin.

The following morning after sending off our mates the mood was low. It worsened when our confirmation outfits were collected: They had been given to us for confirmation day alone. I wonder who really needed them more. We were asked to again don our regular gear: life had to go on.

Finally the Pruuls to left us in the hands of God, They were headed for Hanau refugee camp and thereafter to Australia. The Pruuls calmed the boys assuring them that their successor too would be an Estonian called Adalbert Virkhaus (now deceased in USA). School continued as it had, but somehow one could see that a large exodus was imminent. Everyone was agitated and each of us pondered individually about what lay ahead.

While awaiting the new music teacher music ceased to be part out our lives: Those who wanted to make their own. Most of the instruments had also been removed: They too were needed more elsewhere. We boys whinged among themselves, "Our suits were confiscated, our instruments were confiscated: Let's hope that no one confiscates our food"

Here end the tales those tortuous paths: Their author had to leave Aglasterhausen camp to a UNRRA refugee camp in Germany. Almost forty years later only few of those who began Bechau camp school and then wandered where ever were to ever meet again. Some have been called by the Almighty: They will forever live on in our memories.

EPILOGUE

From later derived documents it evolved that Aglasterhausen orphanage camp closed its doors at the end of 1947. The Red Cross with its worldwide searching found the parents of some of the children and close relatives of others. That search did not extend behind the Iron Curtain. However many years later some parents who were left back in Estonia were able to visit their lost sons.

Sadly many of the adventures of those bewildering times have been lost in the mist of time. Inevitably some of our boys will deny ever having been part of us. We ask their forgiveness that all was remembered according to their perceptions. There is no documented basis for their perceptions. Many of Aglasterhausen activities of that time have been preserved in documents. Some grey haired friends have revived their memories of past friendships. The Almighty has called many young and their leaders to him, but in spirit we remain together.

Sadly some friends have vanished without trace. Perhaps the future may reunite us.

These paltry lines about our courageous youth leaders are but an inadequate tribute to them:
Robert Keres, Aleksander Puus, Paul Öpik, Martin Laas, Meta ja August Pruul. Thanks to the lists compiled by the first three of the above it is possible that Bechau's, Oberhof's Mannheim's and Aglasterhausen's students will be able to read them. Aglasterhausen's teachers ensured that those young stayed alive and treasured their parents.

The young cannot always adhere to their elder's teachings. At times they were even complaining about why they were being picked on that day. Thanks to those committed teachers none of the young in their care has strayed off the straight and narrow. We bow our head in gratitude to those teachers.

Today I can still recall the faces of these young: they remain fixed before my eyes: Those who fled from Bechau's fronts, from the bomb torn Berlin and from Jena which was given to the USSR.

WHAT BLOWS IN THE ILL WINDS?

Perhaps there is a need to review what the children see in their role models, not only their parents but the world in which they are cast to live. Maybe we need to accept children as being more astute than we give them credit for!
Could they be measuring the number of 'goodies' who live in their childhood worlds with the number of 'baddies' who too live there? Might they be capable of reasoning that one or two badly adjusted adults are not representative of any society? How ugly might be the world they leave behind: How ugly might have been the world their captors left behind many years before! Can brutality really evolve from human warmth?

Somehow it seems to me that purgatory is the place where these young run to when they are not comfortable with their nests. Hell becomes the place which they can never leave. At best they will have ugly memories which they will struggle to reconcile, at worst they might become a perpetrator of those memories for others. The world will be left to wonder what can be chang*ed.* **MM**

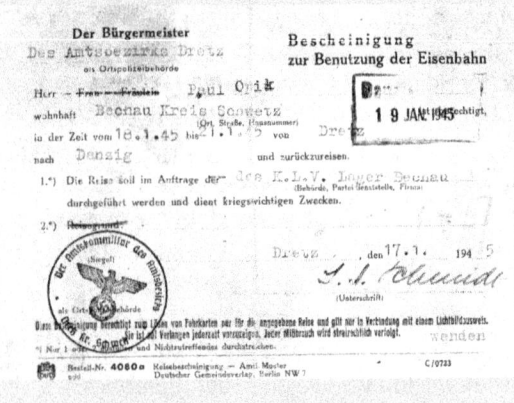
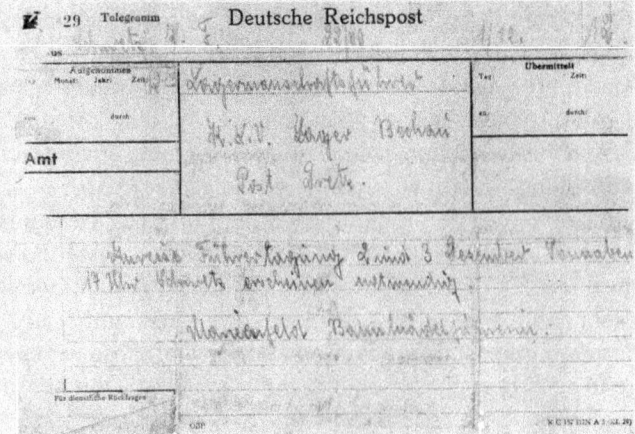

The complex documents required by Paul for safe transit of his' boys' at the closing of World War II

Such documents are but selections of the endless 'permits' on needed to move from A to B in those times.

Hans Einer 1980

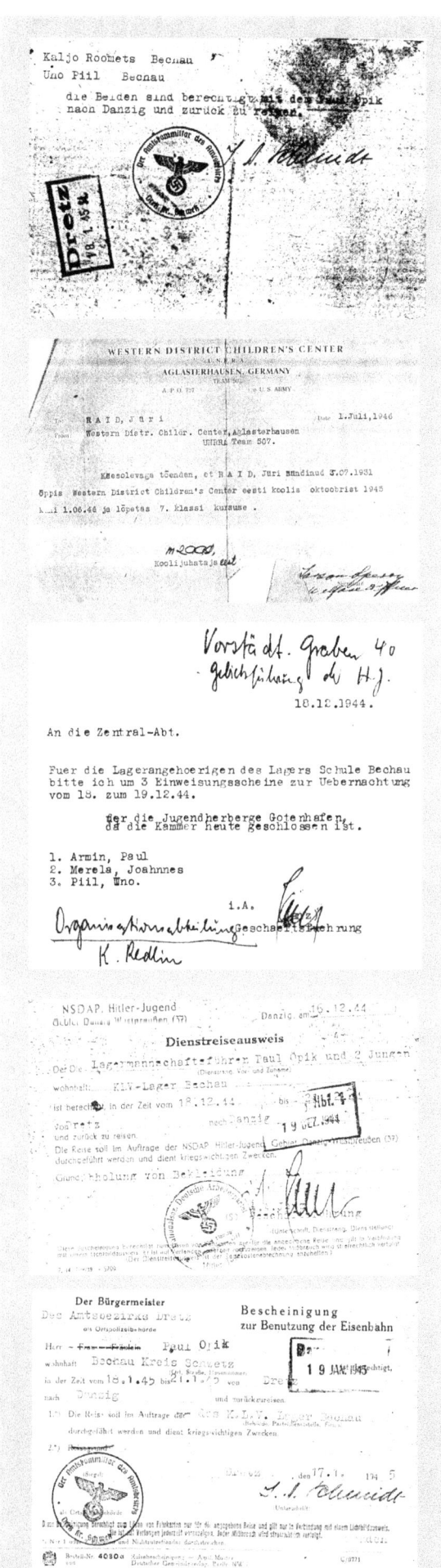

Letter to Paul from Aleksander Puus

WITH GOD'S SPEED AND NEW APPROPRIATE DOCUMENTS ONTO NEW LIVES

```
WESTERN DISTRICT CHILDREN'S CENTER
              U. N. R. R. A.
      AGLASTERHAUSEN, GERMANY
              TEAM 507
  A. P. O. 757           c/o U. S. ARMY

                         1 June 1946.

TO    : Whom it may concern.

FROM  : UNRRA Team 507, Aglsterhausen


     Mr. Wilhelm Raid and his son Mr. Juri Raid
lived at our Center. They are going back to Borkhorst,
near Munster, Germany.

     The food they are carrying has been issued to them
from the regular rations allowed to Displaced Persons
in the UNRRA Assembly Centers. (for two days).

                                   Rachel Greene,
                                   Director
                                   UNRRA Team 507.
```

Yes, there were many necessities on that trek.
Appropriate documents to replace lost ones were high priority.
The religious identity of the young too was considered an integral
part of moving on.

Western District Children's Center. UNRRA team 507
Aglasterhausen, Germany.

Leerilaste õnnistamise Jumalateenistus
Esimesel Ülestõusmise pühal 21. apr. 1946.

Me vaikne palve . . . . J. Sibelius
Kvartett

Kogudus:
Lootuse lastena astume Jssanda ette
Tänu ja kiituse kandle nüüd võtame kätte
Vägeval jõul tõusku me palve ja laul
Üles' kus valguse läte.

Küll on veel raske nii mõneski asjas me algus,
Kui aga koidab Su kullase õiguse valgus.
Jssand, Su nõul ja Sinu vägeval jõul
Võidul saab tõde ja õigus.

Kasvada tahame usus ja edasi jõuda,
Üksmeele-, vendluseaatele ligemal püüda.
Seks meie eel. Wägevam, sammu Sa teel.
Õnnistust alla meil saada.

Leeriõpilased:

Merila, Johannes - Karl †
Piil, Uno - Johannes ?
Raid, Jüri
Sakjas, Harry
Suitsev, Kalju
Sumeri, Walfrid - Hans † 23.1.1996
Tohver, Ain
Willberg, Wello - Peeter.

Kog.:
Elu päew ja elu läige, Kuis särad sa, kui armupäike Mu hauakambri walgustab. Oh mis tunneb õnnis süda, Kui mööda waew ja mure, häda, Meid walgus taewast rõõmustab. Meid wõitja saada sa! Et wõime wõita ka Sinu nimel; Su surma tee Wiib elusse Nii saada maid ka rahule.

EESTPALVED.

Emake . . . . Eesti rahvaviis
Kvartett.

Kog.:
Oh wõta mind, mu Jumal, Käe kõrwale, Et tee mul jõuetumal, Läeks taewasse. Ei suuda üksi astu Ma sammugi, Sest siruta mull, wastu Käed alati.

Su armusülle ase Mull' juhata, Seal rõõmus, waewas lase Mind puhata. End sinna ära peita Las' oma last, Kõik mured su peal' heita Nii ustawast.

Kui ma ei saagi aru Su armust weel, Sa wiid mind läbi maru. Ka surmaööl. Sest wõta mind, mu Jumal, Käe kõrwale, Siis tee mul jõuetumal, Läeb taewasse.

Õp.: Palve.

Kog.:
Minu süda, rõõmustele, Jäta patu kombed jälle, Tõtta ära pimedusest, Mine wälja eksitusest: Sest sind laual' kutsutakse, Õnnistust sull' pakutakse; Jeesus, maa ja taewa Looja, Tahab su sees aset teha.

ARMULAUA TALITUS
ÕNNISTAMINE.

Kog.: Mu isamaa, mu õnn ja rõõm . . .

Õp.: Introitus.

Kog.: Nõnda kui alguses oli, nüüdki on ja jääb igavesest ajast igavesti. Aamen.

Õp.: Kõne.

Kog.:
Sa valgusta, oh Issand, Me rasket eluteed: Ei hävita Su heldust Ka suurte vooge väed. Meil lohutajaks ole, Kui sihid kõiguvad, Ja näita vaenust üle, Kus meie õilsad raad.

Meil, noored, sihte palju, Meil tarvis abimeest: Sa Issand, meie kalju, Meid päästa hädadest. Meil aatetiivad anna, Et sihile läeks lend; Ei tõmba ilm siin alla, Kes Sullo annud ond.

Õp.: Leerilaste õnnistamine.

Hällilaul . . . . B. Godard
Peeter Elias - cello

Õp.: Palve

Kiriku aaria . . . . A. Stradella
Meta Pruul - sopran

Õp.: Pihtitalitus

Largo . . . . G. F. Händel
August Pruul - viiul, Peeter Elias - cello

Kog.:
Halleluuja, koorid kostke, Häält Jeesu ülenduseks tõstke; Ta püham päew on ilmunud! Ta ees lõhkes surma wäli, Ta wõites hauast wälja tuli, Kes meie eest sai maetud. Jah, wõit on tema käes, Ta lõpetas kõik wäes, Halleluuja! Ta lõpetas, Öö peletas Ja surma haua-seletas.

Tõusnud ta meid rõõmustama Ja kõike ära kaotama, Mis rahu riisub meie käest. Tema au on kadumatu, Ta sõna hukkaminematu, Ja õnnis see kes usub tõest. Nii käime armu na'al Ka pisarate maal Üles sinna, Kus elab ta, Kes armuga Meid surmast saadab elama.

JUTLUS.
Õpetaja H. Rebane

SNIPPETS FROM THE OTHER WAR ORPHANS

This is a cutting from an old publication which was clearly written at the time. I cannot trace its origins only that its author had the initials A.S. It was sent to me by Jüri Raid.

It is the article whose photos appear in Jüri Raid's story.

The original is damaged and incomplete: the legacy of a large time warp.

Because of the voids it is impossible to translate this accurately but I feel that I have imbibed its gist: The context is still within my early memory. I feel that it very authentically documents the ethos of those times.

THE YOUNG PREPARE FOR LIFE'S RESOLUTIONS

Stones cannot budge alone: Likewise the new generation cannot assume the interests and characteristics of those born into less turbulence without support. Their exposure to the horrors of war has battered them and some cosseting on feather filled pillows is the first step on that journey. Play and singing have been an integral part of their rehabilitation: To allow them to reconcile the horrendous shadows of their past: To lap up whatever sunshine happens to pass their way while they journey back to the world that most take for granted.

The orphanage carpentry workshop truly shows how those young have taken the bull by its horns: They have become adept at the use of its tools. The girls have learned the secrets of clothing manufacture: Their hours in the sewing room have not been idled away. Beside the master baker stands a boy a metre tall boy paying intense attention: He is eagerly learning how to convert dough into bread. He and his young mates will inevitably become the master bakers of the future: They will know how to bake healthy large loaves of bread.

Some of the young will be fostered by parents who can offer them greater opportunities than the orphanage could: no matter we will all have learned that work is an integral part of life. It is not just about getting it done but about it enriching one's sense of being. Yes even upon arriving in USA, the land of thousands of opportunism they will accept the need to accept what might be hard and tedious: That even in USA people need to be supportive of each other. That each will need to work and love their work.

One can only love their work when as a free citizen they can commit themselves to tasks for which they feel an inner calling. Forced labour has yet to prove as productive or meaningful as chosen work: Just as slavery has never offered a permanent sense of worth. The orphanage has taught us that it is preferable to aim towards vocations where one's skills and passions lay.

Life in the orphanage has reinforced the notion of talent perhaps more visibly than elsewhere. Among us are children from a turbulent time frame and of different nationalities and races. Each race has its characteristic traits and skills which pass on through the generations. Among us are children who know little of who they are or what they inherited from their forefathers whom they have not met or cannot recall. Without such knowledge one cannot even begin to predict what lies ahead for these children: A world famous singer, violist, dancer, writer or artist may well emerge from the ashes.

It makes sense to leave options as widely open as possible to allow those children to follow where their strengths might lead them. Access to music, dance and art during their development may ignite a dormant flame. By allowing the young girls interested in dancing and committed to practice their performances before us their talents will thrive. Likewise it matters not what instruments we cut our teeth on be it a violin, saxophone or another the experience will allow our musical skills to evolve and become stepping stones to other opportunities: Maybe in orchestras in their new lands.

The orphanage is a powerful training ground for our futures. From this humble facility may evolve many life options. Of course should the children access parents who can nourish their talents they will fare batter and maybe become the maestros of the future. Some may find parents who push for academic achievements: maybe doctors, ministers of religion. Some of these children may pine for a different future as a musician, dancer or a baker.

No matter, the ultimate truth will remain that the child who follows their heart and puts their enthusiasm into their quest will reap the greatest riches life can offer.   A.S

From "THE WAVES"

As evening breeze tenderly touches the wings of day, all memories become dreams, filling the breathless hour with a strange quality beyond all longing and hope.

The moment is strangely silent as I await the approach of evening, the golden drops of the melting sun slowly disappear beneath the horizon still tinged with laughter of the passing day. The cliffs rest in their coppery glow and the sand gently clasps, the parting kisses of the sea. A pale mist rises from the water, casting its veil over the sleepy shores, where the heat of sun lingers lazily amongst the half submerged rocks.

As the festival of eventide draws closer, the waves softly begin their song which soon swells into a solemn chorus filling the evening with uncontrollable yearnings and anxieties. The song echoes from down below, climbing along the walls of stone, all the way up from the sea of amber and emeralds. It sounds out of one into another, and then each repetition becomes fainter and fainter, until all this is left is a whisper, a sigh of the soul, a mauve haze of silence that marks the inner awareness of contentment and peace.

Gunnar Neeme

VALE, ENDEL TAKKS & KALJO ROOMETS

PAUL VALENT is one of my most admired and treasured colleagues. He too saw Europe in those treacherous times.

He has spent his life working with troubled people and in his retirement has written much about his observations about life.

Quite correctly he states that there are no shortcuts to intimacy.

The young Estonian boys who became separated from their parents and at times orphaned were to become very closely bonded emotionally. They supported each other in their difficult trek and to this day make every possible attempt to stay in touch.

Much effort was spent locating each other post war.

The clipping from the "Ringkiri" or newsletter is from one of countless such newsletters to circulate among them to enable them to stay in touch and meet where possible.

They are now aging fast and time is taking its toll as one can see from the obituary list.

On this list is Kaljo Roomets who was one of the lads alluded to in Paul Öpik's story.

This edition of the newsletter was forwarded to me by Harry Sakjas.

Aasta 1975

ENDEL E. TAKS

Funeral services will be held Monday, June 30, for Endel E. Taks, 40, 1515 Lake Drive, Town of Wescott, who died Thursday in Shawano following a short illness.

The Kuehl Funeral Home of Gillett is in charge of funeral arrangements. Friends may call from 3 until 9 p.m. Sunday.

Rites will be held at 11 a.m. Monday at the funeral home. Pastors Haresh Sabnani and George Sherman will officiate. Burial will be in Wanderer's Rest Cemetery.

Taks was born Dec. 17, 1934 in Estonia, Europe, the son of the late Edward and Mrs. Vera Taks. He came to the United States at the age of 5 and served with the U.S. Army overseas during the Korean War.

Mr. Taks was married to Caroline Ciesky on March 7, 1970. Survivors include his wife, a daughter Tina Helge, and a brother Henry and his mother who reside in Toledo, Ohio.

Taks was owner and operator of Ed's Body Shop in Pulcifer. He was a member of the Musician's Union and played the accordian at the Alpine Bavarian Inn.

Vaba Eesti Sõ... 11/23/95

Kas keegi teab, kus on Endel Taks või Jüri Raid?

Andrew H. Deuble, oma er... dise eesti nimega Ain Tohver o... sib teisi orbusid, kes Teise maa... ilmasõja järel paigutati väli... maalaste perekonda ja nende k... hal toimus nime muudatus.

Ringkiri (Newsletter)

Head kamraadid ligidal ja kauge...

Aeg teeb oma tööd halastamatu... ajame sõrgu vastu. Vabatahtliku...

Klubi on elus ja tegutseb. Iga ku... kuni tosinani ulatuv toimkond ha...

Pärast läinudkevadist juubelipid... koos kaasade, kallimate ja sõpr... liikmetele kui külalistele. Asuko...

Osavõtust palume teatada korral... post ... Mida nõuame pika tiku tõmbajalt ettek...

Pärast möödunud aasta ringkirja...

Kalju Pada – 20. oktoobril 2009
Jaan Saare – 10. märtsil 2012 – ...
Peeter Sentka – 10. mail 2012 –
Eduard Madissoo – 18. juulil 20...
Erich Priim – 15. septembril 201...
Toivo Kõhelik – 24. septembril ...
Osvald Pajo – 5. novembril 201...
Kaljo Roomets – 26. veebruaril...
Ilmar Värk – 9. märtsil 2013 – T...
Heiki Sillaste – 15. märtsil 2013

That little clipping appeared in Jüri Raid's letter. The news is not always what people wish to hear after being separated for years.

There are no shortcuts to intimacy or friendships. The forging of bonds requires an empathic and altruistic interchange between vulnerable souls.

Paul Valent

HARRY SAKJAS
YOU CAN'T GO HOME

It was 1942 – 43, and the Germans occupied Estonia.

As a youngster of 12 or 13 years old, we were made an offer to go to school in Germany, for one year and learn the German language. After a year in Germany we were supposed to return to Estonia.

The 'school' turned out to be a farm labor camp near Bechau, Poland – occupied by Germany at the time. There we spent the days working on the farm, mostly sugar beets, and the nights at the camp. Working at the farm, you could usually find something to eat, so that was a plus. No schooling of any type in the camp.

After spending some time at the camp, the 'Eastern Front' was getting closer as the Russian army moved into Poland. At that time some older boys were assigned to the German army, and the rest of us were placed on a train headed for Berlin.

We didn't know the destination after Berlin, but based on rumors, we were going to German Air Force Base in Eger, to serve as Air Force Auxiliary troops.

We arrived at Eger, were issued uniforms, and started training with light anti-aircraft guns. We spent a lot of time training in cold weather without the proper clothing, and I got sick with pneumonia.

After coming down with pneumonia, I was sent to a German Army hospital in Karlsbad that was located in a resort area famous for its mineral baths. I met Ain Tohver, (Andy Deuble) at the hospital, we were in the same room.

At age fourteen we were considered as 'babies' of the hospital, and received special treatment. The Christmas that I spent at the hospital was the best time that I spent in Germany during the war. After my release from the hospital, I was told that all boys under the age of fifteen were being released from the German Air Force Auxiliary, therefore I didn't have to report back to Eger in the mountains and a winter sport area.

In Oberhof our group of Estonian boys was placed in large hotel, with nice rooms, but very little food.

Few days after our arrival the American Army arrived, and during the attack on the town, our hotel was hit by an incendiary device on the third floor. Some boys had to leave the cellar, and put out the fire.

The next night the Germans tried to attack the Americans to re-take the town, but they failed.

At that time the food was scarce, and regular meals were gone. Additional food was found in garbage dumps, were the Americans threw their leftovers. Finally our teacher asked the Americans that they no longer throw away the remaining food, but would give it to our group. They agreed, and that helped with the food shortage.

Few weeks after their arrival, we heard that the Americans would be leaving Oberhof, and the Russians were going to take over the area. Later we learned that this was part of the agreement to divide Berlin among the occupying forces.

Hearing this, we left Oberhof that day heading west by walking and riding trains. Eventfully we reached Cologne, and from there traveled to Mannheim and a Displaced Persons camp there. In the camp we were able wash ourselves properly, and eat regular meals. We were warned against eating too much, as the body was not used to all the extra food. Personnel at the camp talked to all of us in an effort to find our parents or relatives.

When none could be found, we were classified as orphans.

The Western District Children's Center, UNRRA, located in Aglasterhausen, near Heidelberg, was discovered by one of our teachers. The center housed Jewish children who had lost their parents during the war. The teacher talked to the orphanage's management that the Estonian boys were in the camp, and had Jewish parents. We were told to remove all remnants of German uniforms before going to the orphanage.

The Children's Center (orphanage) was an excellent facility with provisions for dining, living, and health care areas. The young Jewish people living there accepted us, and no questions were raised about our Judaism. The Jews had their school classes and workshops, and ours started after the new Estonian teaches arrived.

We got along well with the Jewish boys and girls, and they participated in many of our functions and we were invited to attend the synagogue in Heidelberg .

We left the camp, June 1946, and took a train to the port of Bremenhaven.

There we got on board the S/S Marine Perch for our journey to New York, USA.

KALJU SUITSEV: A COURAGEOUS YOUNG LAD BECOMES A HERO IN HIS NEW LAND

Kalju, or "Rocky'/Kal as he was known in USA, is not here to write his story but he remains part of the young Estonian Airforce Boys memories.

Erik Purje/Sail, in "Eesti Elu", a Canadian based Estonian ex-pat newspaper, has written in far more detail about this group of young lads who survived against the odds as the war continued to rage in Germany. The primary writings are in Estonian.

Kalju was amongst a group of Airforce Auxiliary boys, who enlisted with fudged ages in Estonia, and were transferred to Sudetenland. Together with other young Estonian lads who were considered old enough to be separated from their mothers they were placed in work camps. Some spent time at the Bechau camp in Poland: It was a variant of a Hitler Youth Camp. Kalju too found his way to Aglasterhausen Orphanage.

Seven of the boys including Kalju, were through the efforts of the Estonian Lutheran Church, and a Quaker camp leader and USA Major, sent to USA. Kalju became a resident of Seattle in Washington.

It sadly appears that all seven of the boys met difficult lives and tragedy: They were to join the USA army as part of the Korean conflict. Kalju, ranked as a Corporal found himself in a unit which came under heavy fire and casualties. Kalju defiantly stayed on that hilltop when some others withdrew. They destroyed a number of enemy, but finally Kalju was alone with minimal armory and serially used all that was available from his fallen comrades until the last cartridge had been fired. He was taken to hospital in Japan and later USA where he was promoted to the rank of Sargent.

His courage earned him the Purple Heart and Silver Star.

It seems his past had been dissociated from his memory leaving his son oblivious to his past. Vello Villberg was to play a role in reuniting Kalju with his sister.

Kalju's parents were John and Helen Suitsev. Kalju was born in Vera, Estonia.

Kalju has been described as a man who believed that nothing, including freedom came without a price.

He too acknowledged in publications that the price at times was too high.

He spent his remaining years, while grappling with his own physical and emotional wounds fighting for the welfare of USA's younger military casualties. He was quite a man. MM

Kalju died in 2011 and was buried with military honours.

The photos are dreived from articles sent to me by Jüri Raid and Paul Öpik

AIN TOHVER aka ANDY DEUBLE

The last time I saw my mother Sinaida Tohver was in late September or early October of 1944 and I have had no information since then as to whatever has happened to her.

Back to year 1944.... I am not able to recall all those events as vividly as some of my other fellow travelers the "displaced children";

I left Estonia in September 1944 with my mother on a small German ship that was destined to Danzig(Gdansk): To escape the victorious the Soviet army that was closing in on us from the east. After arrival we were shipped to transient camp in Frankfurt am Oder. I may have stayed there about a week and then I was placed on a train, which I believe took us to Bechau, Poland to go to school or assist a farmer in harvesting: Whatever they told my mother On arrival there I met several young Estonian boys who were there for the same purpose as I was, but our primary purpose here was to help out the farmer on picking potatoes, etc/ and I don't remember attending any classes there. After several weeks there we were transported to Eger, Czechoslovakia where we were to support the German war effort.

My mother remained there and that was the last time I ever saw or heard of her. This transfer may have been presented to us as a school, but I can't remember or am not aware of what this transfer was about?

After several weeks at this farm, maybe October 1944, we were shipped to Eger to be Luftwaffe Hilfers or whatever our new title was. Some of us had to participated in the launch of glider planes for training purposes of the German Air force and others had some rudimentary military training with wooden rifles. We were required to listen Nazi propaganda machine on loudspeakers several times a day, which was a useless effort on their part because we did not understand a word of German.

Subsequently I became ill with a high temperature and rash on my body. In November or December, 1944, I was admitted to a German Army field hospital with a possible case of measles. I may have been there for a week or two after which time I began to have difficulty in breathing and they decided to transfer me to a hospital in Karlsbad (Karlo Vary). There I was diagnosed with diphtheria and I was given various herbs or medication to inhale which helped me to get rid of my congestion caused by the inflammation. At that time they did not have any antibiotics and medications were scarce due to on going war so that was all they had available for my illness.

The care this hospital gave me was excellent and enabled me to recover from diphtheria, except for some residual damage to my vocal chords and my heart muscle. I recall another Estonian patient, Harry Sakjas, who was a patient with me and he became my translator to communicate by lip reading my intentions and passing it on to whoever understood us.

The next step of therapy was to give my vocal chords electric shock treatments to restore their original function. I did not speak German language at that time but this treatment helped me to learn German language so well that I was speaking it fluently within nine months. I learned typical "hospital German" or "Hoch Deutsch" without any local dialects affecting my speech.

The problem with my new language was that, the German couple that adopted me in US, spoke a German dialect "Schwabish". Were amazed that an Estonian refugee could speak "Hoch Deutsch" or thought I was an Estonian snob.

Something good always follows something bad, so at the age 80, my vocal chords were somehow regenerated and I am able to entertain several times a month by singing to senior groups. I was discharged from the hospital sometime early of February 1945. Several of us were placed on a train to Oberhof, Thüringen Germany.

I believe that Paul Öpik took over the leadership of our group at that time and lead us through war torn Germany to Oberhof. Our journey took us through Berlin during then worst bombing attack on February 1945 and Paul had the courage and leadership qualities to get us safely though this turmoil. We were welcomed in Oberhof with a parade as heroes of Berlin bombing attack thanks to their propaganda machine.

Our stories will be basically the same from this point until our arrival in America. We don't have many of our "displaced children" remaining: Many of us have completely disappeared or died as of today. I was able to regroup some of us after I retired, thanks to Vaba Eesti Sona, where I read that Vello Villberg's mother had died and was able to trace him to Iowa by having the paper contact him to give him my telephone number in Florida.

He called me in early 1990's and we were able to find most of our group that resided Oberhof. Only one younger member Endel Taks we were not able to locate, who like me, may have had a name change and disappeared. I searched for him via web and found a Getty picture of him and there it ends.

I have lost the ability to speak Estonian fluently, that I regret, but life has many closed doors and sometimes we are unable to open them for whatever reasons.

AGLASTERHAUSEN ORPHANAGE
PHOTOS FROM JÜRI RAID AND HARRY SAKJAS

Our room in Aglasterhausen:
From L. Andy Deuble, Kalju Suitsev, a Polish teacher. Martin Laas (standing). Johannes Merila, Vello Villberg, Harry Sakjas (Standing facing window), Uno Piil (with Saxopone), Endel Taks and Jüri Raid (playing the accordion)

Harry Sakjas

Confirmed: Jüri Raid (L) Uno Piil (R)

Jüri Raid (center) with two Latvian boys

1948: Jüri Raid Leaving Bocholt DP camp to go to Technical School in Bremen

Estonian boys at camp

JÜRI RAUD

MY FAMILY

I mused as I read the word "Juku". That was initially my nick name in Bechau. I think it was coined because initially I was quite and was felt alone. The others were old warriors from war. At the time Estonians used the expression "Pupu Juku" for which perhaps the nearest translation is "Timid/scared Juku". I soon settled in and only "Juku" remained of that nickname. I am not embarrassed by that name.

I left Aglasterhausen because my father was released from being a POW and came to collect me. We went to the English zone: To a camp where our recently freed POWs were living.

My father was a professional soldier. He was one of the youngest of our Freedon Fighters. From late 1940 and early 1941 and the family were living scattered around Estonia. My older brother lived somewhere near Viljandi: My sister in Talllinn. We scarcely saw our father. In 1940 we were with mother somewhere near the Estonian-Latvian border living in a tent on a peat bog. The farmers were worried about the food shortage.

One could only access the spot by a very known agreed path: Any other path would have resulted us sinking into the bog.

In 1949 we learned by the grapevine that we had been sentenced to death by the Russian court. In 1944 my mother and I escaped by ship from Tallinn to Germany. We knew nothing of the family's fate.

We later heard that Father has continued in the final battles co-opted with the Germans on Sörve Island.

My older sister was at Tartu University studying medicine: In 1944 all students were sent to work at the German military hospitals. She was later evacuated to Denmark and later came to Sweden.

My older brother was on with the Legion at the Narva front. Unfortunately his unit became overcome. He acquired documents with a false name, but someone recognized him. I have obtained the records (in Russian) of his trial from Estonia where his identity was revealed and he was sentences to death

My parents managed to escape to Sweden by the help initiated by some Estonians: Then the brought many who were not suitable to for resettlement. There were all manner of screenings at the camps. I travelled to them to help them move to their new home and remained here because their health was not good. My sister was already awaiting us.

NOT BY BREAD ALONE--SLIVERS OF PONDERINGS

One of the highlights for me of returning to Tallinn, is to again meet children who had shared the Geislingen DP camp. Among them is Hando Kask, who in addition to his profession as an architect has written some powerful poetry about our youth.
I felt truly privileged to be invited to the launch of his poetry book. His sister Maare Kask Tamm has written an account of their trek in narrative form.
I have included some of Hando's poetry" It just says so much! Hando and his brother Gunnar Raivo, and sister Maare live in Sweden. MM

RELICS OF ATLANTIC WALL AND BUNKERS NEAR ÅRHUS IN DENMARK

They are similar to the features Boris Lees describes at Hjørring, Denmark

BORIS LEES
VERY MUCH ON THE RUN: TO SOMEWHERE!

The world around us started to change. What happened in 1939 is described in different countries and in different history books in different ways.

Estonia was forced to give the Soviet Union military bases at the Port of Paldiski in north-western Estonia and when Finland refused to give similar bases at the port of Hangö, the Soviet Union attacked Finland. At our home we started listening to Finnish news, not in Finnish, which none of us understood, but in Russian, which was meant for the population of Soviet Russia. The Russians were trying to block the news by broadcasting noise of the same wavelength, but it wasn't always successful. I remember the opening words of the broadcast: "Slushaite, slushaite, govorit Finyandia (Listen, listen, Finland speaking). The broadcast was in very good and clear Russian and it helped me to improve my pronunciation.

In June 1940 the Russian forces occupied Estonia, and we saw it happening just a few metres from our home. Soviet tanks came into Rakvere along Narva St. And turned northward on the corner of Võidu St. (30-40 metres from my father's shop). That street went across the railway and a few kilometers later joined the Tallinn highway. Many years later I heard in a speech at a function in Sydney that the Russian tanks were so poorly made and serviced that dozens of them were left at the roadside, requiring servicing or repairs.

In the autumn when I went back to school a lot had changed. In the assembly room and other parts of the school were pictures of Stalin and Lenin, religious classes had disappeared and teachers, who had been nationalistic, were now very quiet. We were taught new songs which praised the Soviet Union, such as "the International") a communist anthem and a song praising the communist Russian "empire' which started with the words "large and wide is the land which is my home..." But soon the boys had put new words to the same tune: "In the autumn the communist government "nationalization' of private property started and the house at 30 Pikk St., which my father had bought in 1939 was also taken away.

A few months later the tenants were kicked out and the building was converted into army barracks, holding 30-40 red army soldiers.

It was interesting to see the Soviet Russian culture and understanding of how to build a toilet. The confiscated house next door (32 Pikk St.,) had a shed on a backward incline, so that the front was level with the back but at the rear it had a stone foundation nearly 2 metres high. The shed itself had a wooden floor and the Russians cut 8-10 holes, about 40x40cm into the floor for the soldiers to defecate into! (A large number of Soviet soldiers had never used a toilet in tier lives). When I returned to Estonia in 1991, I found that the shed had collapsed because the vertical posts which supported the roof structure had rooted away at the bottom, due to excrement.

The house where the Taliga family lived in 1940 was taken away in sections. First they lost the ground floor where Mrs. Taliga's dental surgery was, as they converted it to a meeting place for a Communist youth organization, but at the beginning of 1941, they were kicked out of the first floor of their residence and found a flat at 47 Pikk St., next to the fire brigade head quarters Behind the headquarters was a park where Ulo and I could play. When the Germans occupied Estonia in 1941, the Taliga family moved back to their old property.

On the 14th June 1941 a mass-deportation of the Estonian population to Siberia started and a number of our friends and acquaintances were deported in cattle wagons to far eastern parts of the Soviet Union.

My classmate Tiiu Lehmets lost both of her parents but she and her brother Tiit escaped because they were on a farm in the country. I met Tiiu again in December 1958 when I came from Christchurch in New Zealand to take part in the Estonian Festival in Adelaide.

On the 21st June 1941 Germany attacked the Soviet Union and I remember that some younger men in our town "disappeared" into forests to escape mobilization into the Soviet army.

Our family went for a walk on the Pagusoo (a swamp near our town), where my parents discussed the possibilities of leaving the town temporarily and stopping living at our usual address on Tallinn St. The nine year old boy remembered lots of details of the discussion, which shows that there are things which should not be discussed in the presence of children. My parents decided that as we had no relatives on a farm somewhere it would be impossible to be away from the town for any length of time.

On the 27th June, almost at midnight, there was a hard knocking on our living room window and when my mother opened the kitchen door two NKVD members (today known as KGB) entered and announced that my father was arrested and was given some time to put together some clothing to take with him. My mother had immediately after their entry taken my father's gold pocket watch, his diamond ring and also her own wrist watch and rings and put them in the pocket of her dressing gown. This was good, because the NKVD men searched the premises and even took pictures off the walls, to see if something had been hidden behind the pictures. When I was in Tallinn in 2005, I visited the Government Archive in Tallinn and they had received materials from Russia relating to arrests of Estonian citizens in 1941. (I had checked this on previous visits but there were no materials then).

It is just as well that I am able to read Russian handwriting, as everything was written by hand in Russian. The authority to arrest and carry out a search was given to comrade (in the communist world "Mister, Mr. is strictly prohibited) Riis and the search carried out by "People's Security Commissariat" member A. Metsik.

The document of arrest was signed by PSC member A. Ellik and had to be signed by both my father rand my mother. Interrogation in the prison in Rakvere took place on 29.06. 1941, after which he was transported to Russia: north of the city of Perm and south of Solikamsk.

The prison camp was in Ussolye on the shore of a lake. Entries into the file stopped suddenly in June 1942. A couple of months before there was an entry saying that my father will not be sent to the forest to cut timber but will be cleaning the dormitories, obviously he was very ill. In 1956, when my mother and I were living in New Zealand, my mother wrote to the International Red Cross in Geneva, Switzerland requesting that they try to find out what happened to my father. Two years later, in 1958, she received a letter from them advising that they had received information from the Soviet Union that my father had died on 15th June 1942.

After my father's arrest my mother visited the prison in Rakvere several times to take a few extra things for my father, but six days later he was no longer there but in the way to Russia. A couple of days after the arrest of my father my mother saw a prison guard in the street, whom she had known before the Soviet occupation. He told her not to walk beside him but behind him so that other people would not guess that they would be talking. He explained a number of things about my father and the prison but my mother did not tell me any details.

A couple of days after my father was arrested, two NKVD men visited us during the day and told my mother that the jewelry business was being nationalized (which means that it became property of the communist government). Although the shop had been locked since my father's arrest, a number of things were stored in the shop which had nothing to do with the business. My mother explained this to the men and they gave permission to take some thongs from the shop to the flat at the back. They then sealed the front door and the door connecting the shop to the flat and access was impossible.

However, immediately after the arrest my mother had been to the shop and removed some items of jewelry and watches and had them taken to my grandmother's home. Some of the watches were taken with us when we left Estonia in 1944 but ended up on the bottom of the Baltic Sea when our ship was torpedoed.

About a week after the first visit half a dozen men came and took jewelry and seven or eight wall clocks, after which they again sealed the door to the shop.

In July 1941 the German army reached the southern border of Estonia, and after the battle of Tartu (the second largest city in Estonia) we started to hear artillery explosions. (Tartu is 100 km south of Rakvere). We also had air raid alarms and my mother thought that it would be safer to spend nights in the basement of a building which used opt belong to the Tivas family, on the corner of Lai and Rohuaia streets.

We heard that the Germans had already broken through to the northern coast and when we went out on the street (early in the morning of the 6th August there were German soldiers riding bikes along Tallinn street in an easterly direction. On the corner was a group of local people who greeted the Germans with great satisfaction. The Soviet occupation had come to an end.

The first thing that the Germans did was the distribution of coupons for purchasing food items, as there was a severe shortage. Distribution of food did not become completely normal during the German occupation and because we had no relatives on a farm, we continued to have shortages.

Now it was again possible to go to church and as I was used to going to the Orthodox Church on Tallinn Street I continued to go there. Because of recent arrests the congregation did not have a person who was able to carry out the selling of candles, taking prayer requests from families and small holy breads to the altar and carrying out the collection. My father did this for a short time and now they asked me, a ten year old boy, to do all these things. I was obviously fully familiar with the running of the services, as certain things had to take place at certain times, in spite of my young age, and I carried on the work for three years until we had to flee from the town before the arrival of the communists.

At the same time as I was helping in the church, the priest of the congregation, Mr. Leets, suggested that the son of the choirmaster Mrs. Kristoffel, who was also my classmate, and I could have Bible studies at his place once or twice a week. Our parents of course were very happy about it and we did the studies until my mother and I fled in September 1944.

At my grandmother's property, at 5 Posti street, the flat in the rear building became vacant and my mother decided that now, without the business, there was no point of living on the main street. We started carrying small things in baskets to the new home and a neighbor's daughter, who was three to four years older than I also, came to help us. Finally there were only the heavy items and my mother found a horse and cart man who transported the rest of our things and furniture to our new address. Another thing worth mentioning is that the Blechmann family, in whose house we had lived for 10 years, had fled to the Soviet Union. Practically all the Jews in Rakvere had fled, as it was known that the Germans would kill them.

We had only lived in our new house for six weeks when two German soldiers arrived and told us that the army needs to place soldiers in private homes and they took one of our rooms for their possession. Compared to many others we were lucky because originally the rear building had two flats, one two room and one, one room unit. The door connecting the two parts had been closed and wallpapered for years and we had recently opened. Now it was possible for the army person to have a separate entrance from the common hallway.

The first 'tenant' was a major, but he stayed only a couple of weeks. The next one was a captain, the next one a lieutenant. Then a sergeant who had nightmares and we could hear him moaning and groaning during the night. He was a nice man, but told us that his family had been killed by an Allied bombing raid in the western part of Germany and it had obviously affected him severely.

Just before Christmas a close to forty year old private, Rudolf Rath, came to live in our house. He explained to us that he was too old to be a front line soldier and he was made a warehouse assistant, from where the soldiers received cigarettes, drinks, shaving gear, soaps, combs, mirrors and other small items which in German was called a "Marketender". Rudolf Rath stayed in our room until the summer of 1943 and we had a very friendly relationship with him. He told us, that should we need to flee to Germany, we could stay at his mother's place. When he left our house he was given a room in the same building as the warehouse.

When the German forces started retreating from Russia and the thought of having to flee from Estonia became more real, he said that we could send some items of clothing in his name to his mother's address in Germany, as armed personnel were permitted to send parcels home about every four to six weeks. My mother packed quite a few items of clothing into a cardboard box and it was sent to his mother's address. That is also the reason why we remembered her address when we arrived in Germany after our ship was torpedoed and sank in the Baltic Sea.

In the winter of 1941 when walking to school I went a couple of hundred metres further to the railway line and discovered that along the line, between the rail line and the street was a timber yard, totally enclosed in barbed wire and steel mesh, where timber was cut into small, 4-5 cm square blocks. This sort of wood was used by German trucks in specially designed burners, because petrol was not available and only used by the air force.

Suddenly I noticed among the prisoners who were doing the work a young boy who was in my class in the previous year. He was a gypsy and came to our school during the Russian occupation.
Now with the German occupation, gypsies were the "wrong race" and the boy had been made a kind of prisoner. I went to Railway Street several times after that but he had disappeared.

I had another classmate, who with his parents fled to Russia just before the Germans came. This boy was Aba (Abraham) Grassman, whose father had a show shop on Tallinn Street. Aba was not particularly clever or noticeable, but his absence was clear to us all.

Another person who went missing from our class was Lia Rogovski, whose father had a medicine and hygiene preparations shop. They too had to flee to Russia. In the 1941/42 school year we went to our usual No.1 primary school, but in the autumn of 1942 our school had been converted to an army hospital and our students had to go to the No.2 primary school a couple of kilometers away.

The hours of both schools were cut by about 20%, so that our afternoon schooling could start at 1pm, but it was already dark when we finished. In 1943 we started in the same basis but a month after Christmas we were told that this school building was also going to be converted into a hospital and in February 1944 education was discontinued and a school report for the year issued. According to this I had finished year five in primary school.

There were no official announcements or information about the war but there were rumors about battles near Narva (100 km east of Rakvere) and the Blue Mountains, which are about 20 km west of the city of Narva and the Narva River.
We also had Soviet aircraft throwing a few bombs on our town in the evenings. My mother decided that it would be safer to spend the nights out of town and we started to walk in the late afternoon to the farm of the Taliga family, which was about 3km west of our town.

On the 9th of March 1944 we were outside listening to the fly over of many bombers. We noticed in the far west, 100 km away, the so called 'Christmas trees' in the sky, strong light sources with parachutes, which were used to light up areas for bombing. We also heard distant explosions of many bombs and we assumed that the object was the city of Tallinn, the capital of Estonia. A couple of hours later all this was repeated and the next day we found out that our guess was correct.

Towards the end of summer my mother started seriously thinking about how to flee from our town when the Soviet forces got closer. She was talking to various friends and acquaintances about fleeing together, as she felt more secure to do it in a group. The Taliga family were not interested and I remember how one day we went to another watchmaker, Mr. Eduard Aavik, who lived and worked at 53 Pikk Street, but Mr. Aavik was not interested in fleeing. That meeting had a strong influence on my mother's being independent and not relying on help from other people. Over many years it became obvious how strong her will and decision making was.

In spite of the war, Government offices in Germany were working very effectively. The refugees affected by the sinking of the ship were helped by NSV (a government help organization "Nazionalsozialistische Volkshilfe") giving them purchase vouchers and money, so that they could buy clothing and other things. My boots survived wet for many hours, but mother's shoes were write-off. Finding shoes in the city of Gotenhafen was almost impossible due to great shortage, but my mother was lucky going to a shop owned by some Baltic Germans who had left Estonia in 1939 and they contacted other shoe shops to find a suitable pair.

The workers at NSV were also helping people contact friend or relatives. We both remembered the address of Mrs. Rath, the mother of the soldier who had been staying in our house, and now my mother wrote a letter to her, which was posted by NSV with an accompanying letter as well. A positive reply came very quickly, so that as soon as I was well enough we could travel. The train tickets were also paid by NSV.

The trip to our destination was quite long. In the evening we boarded a train to Gotenhafen which travelled all night towards the west. Early in the morning we arrived at a station in Rostock and caught another train to Schwerin. The second small station was Kröpelin, where we left the train and started to walk to the village of Lüningshagen.

In the station building in Kröpelin I received some instruction in German words which I have never seen or read until then. When I went to the toilet I discovered that the door was decorated with lots of words and drawings which were completely new to me because I had grown up and learned German in a good mannered society.

We asked the stationmaster how to get to Lüningshagen and he told us it was quite simple, but the distance was about 8-9 km. We started walking and hoped that we might be lucky and get a ride with a farmer's horse and cart but there was no such luck. There was not a single vehicle moving in our direction. The first five kilometres or so we walked on a beautiful road lined with threes and then turned to the left, onto a gravel road, where we had to walk another hour. Towards the end of our walk my right shoulder started aching. The overcoat I was wearing was rather heavy and my shoulder was troubling me for a couple of years. We came to the conclusion that when I was rescued out of the water, they must have pulled me out by my right arm.

Lüningshagen was a typical German village with a road in the middle and farm buildings on both sides.

When entering the village there were three groups of farm buildings on the left belonging to the largest farmers. They had 20-30 cows, 4-6 horses, about a dozen geese and lots ducks and chooks. On the right side were medium size farmers. They had 4-hectares, 2-4 cows, a couple of pigs, a couple of geese and about ten ducks and chooks. They were colloquially called "Budner" and Mrs. Rath was also one of them.

On the left past the major farms, were small houses with a hectare (100 x 100 meter) of garden land, where they grew vegetables. They were called "Hausler", which approximately means "house people". The large farmers were basically a source of income for the smaller ones; without this the smaller ones could not survive.

During our stay in the village the large farmers had Russian prisoners of war working for them, as German men had to serve in the army. Mrs. Rath, who was a widow, also had a helper to do the housework and some of the farm work connected with cows and pigs and feeding the birds. Marusya was a Ukrainian girl, probably on a semi-voluntary basis in Germany. She never complained about anything and it is probable that her life in Ukraine was not the easiest.

Mrs. Rath's house had an attic room under the roof with partly 45 degree angle roof as walls. In the room was a bed, small table and a couple of chairs. There was no stove or heating in the room and sleeping in a cold room was quite normal in Germany.

Mrs. Rath was not a particularly warm and friendly person but was reasonably polite and although food was a bit insufficient, the German coupon system was partly at fault. There was also no shop near the village. Once a week a horse-drawn bread van called on farms with bread and any bakery items. The driver had some sort of disability, so he was not taken into the army. He was obviously good hearted, as having discovered that we were refugees, he gave us three loaves of bread for two coupons, which was a great help to us. Sometimes when we walked out of the village we helped ourselves to a couple of cattle turnips, which when boiled were quite edible.

In the meantime we had become acquainted with Mrs. Schlutow who was living in a small house on less than a hectare of land. She was an approximately 55 year old widow with a golden heart, who had undergone a terrible tragedy. When Germany was about to start the war against France, both of her sons were taken into the army and not long after the start they were killed in a battle.

At her place we spent Christmas Eve. She had her pig slaughtered before Christmas and she had a number of tasty foods, especially a special sausage called "Mettwurst" which she had made herself and which was really fantastic. After the war, when we lived in Denmark, we sent her parcels, because Lüningshagen village had become part of Eastern Germany and there was a shortage of lots of things. Mrs. Rath also lost her son who had lived in our house in Estonia. He had succeeded in reaching the East Prussian city of Königsburg, but when the Russians cut off the city from the rest of the area and he perished there.

The residents of Lüningshagen went to church (and kids to school) a couple of kilometers away in the township of Retschow. The township was small, but the church was very interesting and historical. We met the minister of the congregation, Mr. Frederich Schoop, who showed us very old ornaments and memorial plates, but the most interesting item was a folding altar with six 3 metre tall sections of biblical paintings. It had been given to the church by a local nobleman over two hundred years ago. The nobleman was a ship owner, whose ship had been caught in a huge storm and survived through an absolute miracle. In gratitude he had ordered a special folding altar for the church.

When we needed to buy anything, be it clothing or other items, we had to travel to the township of Satow, which was situated in the opposite direction to Retschow. This township was several times larger and there was even an Estonian family there. Oskar Mänd, his wife and son were living in a flat which belonged to the local pharmacist. Whether they paid rent I can't remember. Mr. Mänd had been a postmaster in the province of Järvamaa in Estonia.

The only connection we had with Satow was the milk cart, which left Lüningshagen early in the morning and returned at lunchtime. This did not leave much time for shopping and a couple of times we stayed at night with the Mänd family. One day was travelled with them to the large city of Rostock, for they too needed some things which you could not buy at Satow.

Soon after arriving in Lüningshagen my mother wrote to several acquaintances. One of these was the younger Mr. Schiller (whom my father and I had met in Tallinn. He and his Estonian wife and son now lived in the city of Pforzheim, west of Stuttgart and only 40 km from the French border. My mother was looking for a place where we could move to, but Mr. Schiller said in his latter that the allies were bombing Pforzheim so frequently that it was unsafe. Much later we learned that his house was hit by an incendiary bomb and they had asphyxiated in the basement which was used as their shelter. In the letter were 200 German marks, which for us was a large sum and helped us a lot.

Another person my mother wrote to was Baron von Stackelberg who at the time lived in East Prussia, in the area which between the two world wars belonged to Poland. The Baron was surprisingly frank about his views about Hitler's Germany. He mentioned among other things that under no circumstances should we move eastward from where we were at the time and he said that he was sorry not to be able to help us.

It is interesting how von Stackelberg was able to come to Germany at all. When Germany started the second re-settlement of Baltic Germans from Estonia, Latvia and Lithuania late in 1040, my father, who knew the Baron from before the first World War, discussed the possibility of moving to Germany although we had no German connections. (The first re-settlement took place in 1939 and a large number of people with German roots left Estonia and the other Baltic states because of the likelihood of occupation by the Soviet Union). But suddenly the NKVD (Soviet secret police) arrested von Stackelberg and transported him to a prison in Moscow, because he was suspected of espionage for Germany. As a result our family lost the chance to leave Estonia for Germany. However in January 1942, a member of Hitler's government, Herman Goring, who was related to the Baron, approached the Soviet Government and von Stackelberg was released Butyrka prison in Moscow and sent to Germany several months before the start of the war between Germany and the Soviet Union in June 1941.

Mr. Schiller suggested that my mother should write to an acquaintance of his. Mr. Konrad Sitz, who was the manger of a canteen at a military aerodrome in Hagenow, in the same state as out village and about 80 km south west from us. Mr, Shiller pointed to two important aspects: Mr. Sitz would be able to get my mother a job and there would be no shortage of food.

My mother wrote to Mr. Sitz and received a friendly and positive reply. He said that the aerodrome was too small for the allies to be interested in and he had already found a job for my mother in a repair shop for military clothing. So we decided to move to Hagenow.

The town had two railway stations: One was in the town and the other 3-4 km to the south, on the Berlin to Hamburg line. As it turned out, the allies were not interested in the small military airfield but bombed the station on the main line a couple of times.

We got ourselves a room with its own separate entrance in a prefab building. In it were two beds, a table, a couple of chairs, a hand basin and a small stove to warm the room. About 50 metres from the prefab was a bomb shelter which could be used if there was an alarm.

It is worth mentioning that Mr. Sitz and most of the ladies in the repair workshop were Baltic Germans from Estonia who had not found better work and living conditions.

All meals, breakfast, lunch and dinner were supplied in the canteen.

There were a few air raid alarms but they were a nuisance because the shelter was a bit far away from both the workshop and the canteen. Even the manager of the workshop suggested it would be easier to walk onto the pasture instead. My mother and I went for walks in the spare time to acquaint ourselves with the surroundings.

On one side was a pine forest with roads sufficiently wide to move aircraft along them. Every 80-100 metres was a parking spot cut out next to the road and Messerschmidt Mw 109 fighter aircraft were placed there. We were told that German was so short of fuel that only aircraft near major cities were still being used. I must say that during our stay, not a single aircraft took off.

In the other direction were large wheat and rye fields and we started walking into the fields when an alarm was given. Visibility was good and should there have been an air raid we could simply let ourselves flat on the ground.

One day we decided to go further along the filed and after a few kilometers discovered an estate. We investigated how far the estate was from the town of Hagenow and found that is was 3-4 kilometers, same as the airfield, thus forming an even sided triangle.

My mother was of the opinion that it was time for us to move out of the military area and she spoke to the owner of the estate. He offered us a room in the building used for the staff and on the first floor all the rooms were unoccupied. This was good, as we did not need to share the kitchen. The rent was also relatively cheap, so we decided that we could manage for a while. We moved with our few possessions at the beginning of April from the military airfield to the Scharbow estate.

Behind the manor and further behind our building was a small building with bars on the windows, where about a dozen French prisoners of war were housed. They were used as farm labourers and my mother noticed that when they had finished their work they were locked up in the small building and were let out again in the morning to go to work.

My mother was concerned that if there as a fire they could not escape from the building and could die from smoke inhalation. When there was an opportunity to talk to a Frenchman in French without anyone noticing it, she mentioned her concern. The Frenchman was interested in what nationality we were and when he found out that we were Estonians, he trusted my mother to say: "Don't worry about this, Madam, we have secretly made a key and if there is a fire we can get out!"

The lord of the manor turned out to be a real Nazi person. One morning I met him walking near the manor and I said "Good morning!", whereupon Mr, von Tiede stared at me and shouted; "You are a German boy and you don't know the German greeting! Heil Hitler!' I was quite startled and said according to his instructions, but in myself I felt like saying "No way!"

While living in Scharbow we had to go to the town of Hagenow a number of times, mainly to buy food. We met an Estonian family here and they told us that there as another Estonian family here and the husband was working as a surgeon in the Hagenow hospital.

Towards the end of April a small army unit with two anti-aircraft guns arrived at the Scharbow estate. It consisted of only a dozen men, led by a lieutenant. Soon after their arrival we started hearing artillery noise, not as strong as we heard in Estonia before fleeing, but it was obvious to us that the war was getting closer. And suddenly in the afternoon of first of May the soldiers got busy.

My mother went to the lieutenant and asked him where they were going. He replied that his first stop was the city of Lübeck and that they were going to leave at about 9pm. My mother asked if we could travel with them and the lieutenant said we could get a couple of seats in a trailer. He asked also whether we knew where we would like to go in Lübeck and my mother said that we would like to go the Swedish church.

In the evening we took our suitcases and went to see the soldiers. We did not need to wait long and it was still light when we started our trip westward. Our unit consisted of three trucks, two with anti-aircraft guns, and the third with a trailer which had about ten seats. It was obvious that the unit was meant to have more soldiers, as there were only four soldiers with us and there were half a dozen empty seats. It was soon dark and we travelled again with a small light on the mudguard just like on the army truck which took us home to Tallinn.

We dozed and even slept sometimes during the trip and early in the morning we arrived in Lübeck. As promised, they brought us to the Swedish Church and the soldiers departed in their trucks. We arrived just at breakfast time and Swedish lady helpers were giving coffee and sandwiches to those present.

My mother started investigating how we could get closer to Sweden and was told that on the next morning a Red Cross bus will arrive to take Swedish nationals from Berlin and Lübeck through Denmark to Sweden. We spent the day at or near the church and in the evening we were allowed to sleep on church benches, as they did not have anything softer or more comfortable.

The next morning was Wednesday 2nd May and about an hour after breakfast the Red Cross bus arrived. It was neither German nor Swedish, but the bus and the driver were Danish. The bus was almost full of Swedes from Berlin: From Lübeck about half a dozen persons were allowed on the bus as well, including ourselves.

We travelled in a north-westerly direction and about midday we arrived in the port city of Kiel. The city had been heavily bombed and most buildings were damaged. We stopped in front of a four storey building which had lost its front wall and you could see into the various rooms from the bus. The driver said that we could stretch our legs and go to the toilet, which we did, but visiting a toilet could be seen from the street.

The bus kept travelling and in the afternoon we arrived in the border city of Flensburg. While driving on a street which had houses on the right side and a park on the left, we were forced to stop by German military policemen. Some policemen came on the bus and started checking passports of travellers. We were sitting almost at the back of the bus and when the policeman came up to us and was shown the identity paper issued in Gotenhafen, he screamed loudly; "Raus!" which in proper German is "heraus" (out!).

We had to get onto the footpath and the driver found our suitcase in the trailer. At the same time another passenger was expelled. He turned out to be also an Estonian, about 40 years old, from western Estonia, and is name was Kirill Nõu. The bus left and we discussed with our new acquaintance what to do.

We decided that my mother and I will stay here with his and our suitcases and he is going to go and find out if there is a place somewhere we could stay. Half an hour later he returned, and said that we were lucky: Only a few hundred metres away was a small transit camp where we could stay.

We took our suitcase and walked together to the camp. It consisted of four prefabs with a square in the middle and each room had four to six two storey bunks. Quite a few had some blankets hanging to separate them and to shield from view. Behind the door were hooks for hanging coats and clothing.

It just started to get darker when there as an alarm and as we noticed, in the middle of the yard were some stairs going underground. Now we hurried out, putting our coats on at the same time, and went down the stairs to the bomb shelter. The shelter was an underground tube, about 3 metres in diameter, with stairs at both ends. Along the sides of the tube were long seats on both sides and we sat down and began waiting.

All of a sudden there was a whistling sound, a noisy explosion occurred, and immediately there was a second explosion with less air pressure. Now a lot more people streamed into the shelter and as the seats were occupied, they walked and stood between the seats. The lights had gone out and only some pocket torches were used here and there. A young woman was slowly moving past me crying and moaning: "My child, my child!" which obviously applied to the small child she was carrying. The woman moved on with the flow and disappeared. We sat in the shelter for a while, then people started moving out of the shelter and we also went out and back into our room. There was no light and we got into our beds and went to sleep.

In the morning we got some coffee from the kitchen at the end of the next prefab, but there was no food. This did not bother us, as we still had some bread with us.

In the yard, close to the kitchen, were two holes in the ground, where the bombs had fallen. Some windows in that prefab were broken and when I was getting dressed in the morning we discovered some blood on my trousers. We heard that a child had been killed, so we assumed that the woman's child who had been hit had been bleeding, dribbled a bit on my pants and then died.

A woman in our room had a different problem. Her overcoat had been hanging on a hook behind the door and when the explosion had created air pressure, the wall in our room had been moved slightly to create a crack for a few seconds and part of the coat was sucked into the crack. One could imagine that the coat could not be removed.

We decided to go into the centre of the city hoping to find a proper shelter for the next night. We discovered that there was a small "mountain" near the centre and from the street where we walked we noticed an opening into a tunnel. We had just walked 10-15 metres and were starting to go back out, when a man came to the entrance and announced in a loud voice: "All those of you who arrived from Berlin this morning please come across the road into the school building, we have an important message for you!"

We thought immediately that this could be interesting and went across the street into the school hall. There were 60-80 persons in the hall and a man in private clothing stood on the stage and announced that for those who had arrived from Berlin as train had been organized to take them to Denmark. They should go to the third platform and the train will leave at 7 pm. This was very interesting and we decided to try to get back on the train although we had no permit of any kind. It was about 2 pm when we started walking back to the refugee camp. We found Mr. Nõu and he was also of the opinion that we should try.

We made some inquiries to find out where the railway station was and found it was a bit over a kilometer away. I can't remember that we would have had anything to eat, we took our suitcase and Mr. Nõu his and started our walk. We were on the station pretty early and found our train. The carriages were such that each had eight doors and each door went into a cabin with seats opposing each other. From memory a cabin could hold about 8-10 persons. We found seats in the third carriage and started writing for departure.

At seven o'clock nothing happened, when it was eight and nine, but the train stood still. My mother went out on the platform to find out what the problem was. She was told that we had no engine, as the one that was on the way to us had been attacked by Allied aircraft and there were bullet holes in the steam engine. A new engine would arrive as soon as practicable.

Our concern was that if there were an air attack on the station we had no idea about possible shelter. We dozed in our seats and it was already getting a bit light when there was a bump and we heard the noise of an engine. The train started moving, gathering speed we were on our way! It was Saturday the 5th of May 1945.

In the brightening light we travelled past farms and we noticed that on every farm there was a flag pole with a Danish flag flying in the breeze. It looked rather festive but we had no idea what was going on. The train stopped at Kolding station and the travellers were offered buns and coffee, then we kept moving northward. About midday we arrived in Arhus (today's spelling is Århus) which is Denmark's second biggest city. Here we were given soup and bread and after an hour or so we continued to move northward.

We had a map of Germany which showed Denmark up to the city of Alborg (Ålborg) but after we passed Ålborg we had no idea about the top end of Denmark. Soon after we crossed the long bridge over the Strait of Langerak we stopped at a small station and some rear carriages were unhooked. The shortened train travelled a few kilometres and stopped at Brønderslev where again some carriages were unhooked.

Finally, in the late afternoon the last four carriages and the steam engine arrived in the town of Hjørring, where all travellers were ordered out. On the platform the refugees were approached by policemen in private clothing but wearing white arm bands. They told the people on the platform that all Germans had to go to the southern end of the platform, while non-Germans were guided to the northerly end. There weren't many non-Germans, maybe twenty persons, among the Mr. Nõu and we. We heard later that the Germans were taken to a refugee camp which was protected by barbed wire.

Non-Germans were taken to the centre of the town, where there was a small square called Torvet (market place), and on one side was a small hotel which had been the head quarters of the local German army unit. The inside didn't look like a hotel, which was natural, considering it had been used by soldiers, but the beds had pillows and blankets and we were given separate rooms.

After we placed out luggage in the rooms, we were taken by bus a kind of social club which was used by the local newly formed police as an eating place. We were treated by the ladies who were serving the meals exactly as politely as the policemen.

Here we heard that we had crossed the border into Denmark at the last moment, because the German forces had capitulated in the early hours of the 5th of May and the train was on its northward journey already under the control of the Danish administration. This was also the reason why they had not had a properly formed police force, although we suspected that most of them had been members of the original police force.

One thing was very noticeable concerning the refugees- they were obviously very hungry and probably been starving for a while, for they all ate a lot more than would have been expected and the Danish ladies serving us were quite surprised. We stayed in the hotel on Torvet a couple of weeks, then we were told that the hotel was going to be repaired and refurbished and they moved us to a wooden prefab building which had been built on the corner of a park. At the same time our eating place was also changed.

We now had to go to an old style building at the edge of town, where about thirty Hungarian refugees were located. The food was also prepared by Hungarians and was typically Hungarian. For the first time in our lives we were given goulash and other similar dishes which contained so much paprika that our mouths were burning when eating.

While living in this prefab, we were given a questionnaire, whether we would like to be repatriated to our own country. All said "No' except for a Russian family, who decided to return to the Soviet Union.

Mr. Zaitsev was a musician and his wife was an artist. They had an 11 year old son Garik who sometimes played with me. The other refugees in the building were quite surprised that the Russian couple were so naive, but they were requite certain that they wanted to return to Russia.

In the middle of June we had to move again. This time all the residents in the prefab were moved about 30 km north of Hjørring*, to an old, run down beach hotel called "Tanishuis".

The building was about 500 metres from the actual beach on the strait of Skagerrak and about 2km from the small township of Tversted. Actually the beach was part of a small bay called Tannis Bugt, so the name of the hotel came from this. Apart from us and the Hungarians from Hjørring*, other refugees were also brought here so the total was somewhere between 150-200.

The administrator of the refugee camp was a Dane whose name was Greve Rasmussen and is first name Greve was unusual, because it meant 'Count', but he was not part of the aristocracy, his parents had simply given him such a name. His assistant was a Hungarian, Mr. Stief, who according to other Hungarians had been a colonel in the Hungarian army, which was fighting against the Soviet Union. The number of Hungarians was again greater than of other nationalities and therefore the food we got to eat was again according to Hungarian taste.

The nationalities represented here were Estonian, Latvians, Lithuanians, Poles, Czechs, Hungarians and Ukrainians, but no Russians, Belorussians, or people from the Balkan area.

The most interesting thing was that a couple of weeks after settling in, a former captain of a ship who was of Czech nationality, but was fluent in English, started giving us English lessons. The unusual bit was that the Czech Republic is completely landlocked and for a person of such nationality to reach the proficiency of a master of a ship on world oceans would be extremely rare. As there were no textbooks, he wrote the words and sentences on the blackboard and we had to write everything down. In the beginning there were about fifty students, but the number was shrinking steadily and after some time we had about a dozen students who were seriously interested in learning.

There were very few children of my age in the camp. I became friends with a Latvian boy, Andrejs Clems, with whom I went to the beach and went wandering in the surrounding area. We had to be very careful not to go onto the areas where the German army had placed explosive land mines.

The so called "Atlantic Wall" was organized by the Germans from the top end of Denmark along the Atlantic coast to the Pyrenees on the border of France and Spain. The strongest and best fortifications were on the coast of the English Channel, but even here in Denmark a lot of work had been done to stop a landing by the Allies.

The old hotel building was about half a kilometer from the beach because between it and the beach were about 30-50 metres high dunes with some dune grasses. These grasses had a very sharp edge so you could easily cut yourself when walking on the dunes.

Not far from our hotel were German mine clearing specialists who had been sent here after the recapitulation of Germany. Everyday there were between a dozen and a couple of dozen explosions and sometimes we could see smoke and dust. The mines were never taken out of the ground but exploded on the spot.

One day when Andrejs and I were returning from the beach that between the dune closest to the shore and the one slightly more inland there seemed to be a walking path. We walked onto the path and walked eastwards. In some places it happened that the path had been dug slightly deeper between the dunes to give it more protection and we walked about 1 ½ kilometers when we came to a concrete shelter. The concrete shelter had a concrete roof, which on top had part of the dune with some grass on it so it could not be distinguished from the surroundings. The camouflage was excellent.

When we went inside, we found that the shelter has a shooting opening, about 60-70 cm high and about 4 metres wide facing the sea and a 70 mm calibre gun mounted on a movable base. The room was about 25 square metres and here were lots of things connected with the weapon, but no shells. On the floor I found a small oil can which I took with me and which I use to this day.

Andrejs' knowledge of German was pretty poor, but it was the communication language in the camp. One day I was near the sheds when Andeys was walking towards me. Suddenly an about forty year old Hungarian came out of the shed, walked past me towards Andrejs and started shouting at him in extremely poor German while gesticulating with his arms. He accused Andrejs for stealing his bike. Andrejs let the man carry on for a bit and then said in just a spoor German: "Ich deine scheise Rad!" (Me your crap bike!) and walked away. As you can imagine, this incident was so comical that I could never forget it.

The beach near us was very nice, lovely sand and great surf but very few resident of the camp went swimming. The reason was the temperature of the water. None of us had a thermometer but many who went for a swim did it only once. The surroundings and the waves were great but the temperature was far too cold.

The summer was slipping away but our living conditions were not changing. My mother felt that I had already lost a lot of learning time and something should be done to get back to school. The township of Tversted was not very far away and it would have been easy to walk to school, so we went to see the camp administrator Greve Rasmussen. He agreed with the idea of going back to school but that it would not be possible to go to Tversted. He promised to do some research on it and let us know.

A few weeks later Mr. Rasmussen called us to his office. His investigation led to the refugee administration offering us to be moved to Copenhagen where I could go to school.

It was already September when we and another family were driven to Frederikshaven on the east coast, from where a train took us southward along Jutland and then eastward on the Island of Fyn to Nyborg. From here a ferry took us to Korsør* on the island of Sjælland and from here a train finally took us to Copenhagen.

Here we were placed in a very unusual refugee camp where most of the residents were Estonians. The camp was situated in a building which contained a tennis hall under an arched roof. On the front of the building on Peter Bangsvej was in huge letters "K.B Hallen". K B was København's* Boldklub, in translation the Hall of the Ball Club of Copenhagen. The large tennis hall was divided into "streets" which contained tiny "rooms" separated by cardboard walls. Each "room" consisted of a double bunk with about 75 cm wide space where one could undress and climb into bed. The cardboard walls had been painted with waterglass (sodium silicate) to make them fireproof.

In the large hall all were Estonians and on the wall on the edge of the platform at the end of the hall Estonian artists had made and painted the image of the mediaeval castle in Tallinn, the capital of Estonia. Adjacent to the hall were a couple of smaller rooms, each holding about 30 persons. Most of them were Latvians and Lithuanians.

Behind the large tennis was a smaller badminton hall which was used for dancing and various meetings. I took part in a simultaneous play of chess, where Ortvin Sarapuu, who later was the chess master of New Zealand, played against 30 participants. He won all but one of the games.

Soon after arrival we travelled by tram to the centre of the city, where the older part was St. Peter's' German church and St. Peter's school. The headmaster was an about 55 year old Mr. Neumann, who was German and spoke Danish with a strong accent. The education took place in two languages. Some subjects were taught in German, others in Danish.

Following some discussion I was admitted to the first class of the middle school. Among other teachers was a married couple with the surname of Christensen, where the husband, who was Danish, taught us maths and geography, whereas his wife, who was German, was teaching her subjects in German. Most of the students were completely Danish, whose parents wanted their children to be bilingual. The main precondition was that the student had to know enough German to understand the details of what was being taught. The refugee students had the opposite problem, their Danish was worse then their German.

In my class were also Aime Aarend, Karin Rosmet and Frieder Treumann. Frieder's father has been a pastor in the town of Vaivara in the eastern part of my home district in Virumaa (about 60 km from Rakvere) and his maternal grandfather, Chistfried Brasche, who also lived in our refugee camp, had been pastor and dean in a northwestern part of Estonia.

A couple of months later we got another foreigner in our class. When the teacher asked what his name was, he spoke so quickly that no one could catch his name. The teacher asked him to speak slowly and then we heard that his name was Leonardo Anagnostakis. He explained that his father was the captain of a Greek ship and his mother was German. It seemed that he was not a refugee, but Leonardo came to our school because of being able to speak German but not much Danish.

The chairman of the Estonians in K B Hallen was Enn Salurand, who later migrated to Canada and was active in leadership there as well. The next leader of Estonians in K B Hallen was Mr. Avasalu. There were also some Estonian boys in K B Hallen, but they were a year or two older than I.

The closest friendship developed between Ivar Wiren and myself which lasted until 2007, when he died. His parents felt that Sweden would be a better country to live in and like many other Estonians moved to Sweden and stayed there. The same of Harri Talve and Aarne Tuuling (he died a few years later). Aime Aarend whom I mentioned before, also died in Sweden a few years later.

Going to school had a fantastic effect on my proficiency in Danish. Although in the refugee camp we spoke Estonian, school work and associating with other students speeded my communication in Danish with incredible speed. However, the German school was soon in financial trouble. It had been supported for many dozens of years by Germany; for it was a private school and whether the Danish government supported it in the past was unknown (the government did finally support the refugees). Now, after the German occupation, the Danes were not pro-German, and Western Germany itself was occupied by the British, French and the U.S., so there was no money to support German schools in other countries.

Soon after my start our class had to vacate the classroom in the main building and go to a basement room in an old adjacent building. When we started in the second class we were told that this was the final year for us, as they could not financially keep the school going.

In the second class we got a new teacher of German and English, Miss Karen Jørgensen. After a few weeks Miss Jørgensen invited refugee students and their parents to take part in a gathering of members of a Pentecostal congregation in the garden of a Danish family. There were three or four students with parents, so we were 8-9 refugees and about 12-15 Danish people.

The gathering brought the refugees closer to the locals, as the Danes were very friendly and the refugees were telling their stories about how they fled and how they got into Denmark. Every story was different from others. There were more get togethers like this but there were fewer families from our camp and after a while my mother and I were the only ones. There were always readings from the Bible and praying, but they were never pushy abut their views.

A year later they invited us to come and listen to a United States Baptist preacher who was preaching in a large hall to several hundred listeners. The preacher was Bran Frary von Blomberg who, in spite of having been born in the United States, still used his title as a Baron. My mother spoke to Blomberg about the possibility of emigrating to the United States and he promised to do some research. There was later correspondence between them and the baron has found that the US had a quota for immigrants from each country and the Estonian quota had already been overstepped.

During the second year our classroom was not in the regular school building but in a very old building on the same block as the St. Peter's church.

When I finished the second class in the spring of 1947, my mother was of the opinion that it was wiser to stop going to school and start learning a trade. My mother was very happy with my father's trade as a watchmaker and she felt that I should also learn that trade. We had newspapers in the refugee camp and my mother found an advertisement where a watchmaker was looking for an apprentice.

We travelled by tram to the fairly distant suburb of Valby, where a section was called "Music Town" because all the streets had been named after composers of all nationalities. The watchmaker's shop of Willy Blytner was at no. 11 Mozartsvej and he was interested in having me as an apprentice. Blytner was not a usual Danish name and it came out later, that his original name Madsen was so common that he decided to change it.

His business was obviously successful as he had an about 40 year old watchmaker and a third year apprentice Gert Andersen. We agreed on various conditions and I started repairing alarm clocks, which I had already tried in my father's shop when I was seven years old.

I am indebted to Gert Andersen for my ability to correctly pronounce the r-sound in Danish. The guttural r in Danish is quite different from German and other guttural r pronunciations. I started at suitable moments saying words like 'rod'* (red) "rart" (rare) etc, sometimes when sitting in the toilet or walking outside. Gert Andersen checked my pronunciation and results were good, because he also checked other sounds. Soon I was an extremely rare foreigner, being able to speak accent free Danish.

I had worked for Mr. Blytner for a few months when an inspector came from the Employment Office to check on apprenticeship conditions. When he discovered that I had started my apprenticeship before Gert Andersen had finished his, he told Mr. Blytner to terminate my employment. Mr. Blytner found through some connections a watchmaker, who was willing to take me for a short time, until a permanent apprenticeship could be found.

Mr. Jensen did not have a shop. His workshop was in the first floor and his flat behind the workshop. Mr. Jensen's workshop was close to our refugee camp, where we had moved fairly recently, only about 1 ½ km from us. He was a very gifted watchmaker and designer of special chronometers for accurate timing. He also had enormous theoretical knowledge and special machinery for making parts and clock wheels. However, although we both tried, there was no luck in finding a new apprenticeship.

I decided to go back to school, but St. Petri school had closed all higher classes and I had to find another school.

The former Estonian Consul in Copenhagen, August Koern, who was the foreign minister of the Government in Exile and who lived close to our refugee camp, had found a new school for the other boys. The problem had been, that high schools refused to admit refugees and Mr. Koern knew the headmaster of Gammel Hellerup Gymnasium, Mr. Jens Knud Eriksen, who was quite willing to take refugee boys into his boys' school.

It was the end of November in early December when I travelled to the suburb of Hellerup and showed my school report from St. Petri School. The head master placed me in year four (jumping one year) but after about a month in the fourth class they decided that it would be better for me to place me in year three.

I started in the third class in January 1948 and at the end of the school year in June I got a good school report and came second in the class. Only a boy, whose name was Hvolby, came first. I should also mention that the suburb of Hellerup is about 20 km from the suburb of Amager where the refugee camp was situated and all the boys that went to that school, where the girls went we never knew.

In the yard behind the school building, where boys spent time during the recess, was a 20 cm diameter bell under a little roof on two posts. Under the edge of the roof was the motto of the school: "Memento vivere" (remember to live), but the boys translated it as "Husk at traekke verjet"*, which in local slang means "don't forget to breathe".

I mentioned earlier that our first camp was the K B Hallen on Peter Bangsvej. Here we stayed about one and a half years, then we were transferred to a camp consisting of wooden prefabs at Artillerivej 63. This was fairly close to the centre of the city, at the northern end of the island of Amager and close to the bridge called Langebro.

A few hundred metres west of our camp, on fairly soggy ground, was a garbage disposal area and Ivar Wiren discovered that among the garbage were some wrecked bikes. He collected various parts and built himself a bike. Observing his success, I followed his method and soon I also had a bike, as buying one was out of the question for such poor refugees.

The most interesting thing when looking at the past, was 60 years later, when I visited Copenhagen in 2007 and discovered that the refugee camp buildings, where we had lived so many years ago, were still the same. Even the "Swedish red" colour of the paint was the same. But now the inhabitants seemed to be some kind of "no hopers' who had rubbish and old furniture in front of their prefabs.

In this camp on Artillrivej we lived about a year and a half, then we moved to a camp on the northern edge of the island of Anager, on a street called Prags Boulevard (Prague is the capital of the Czech Republic).

This camp was much larger and a larger number of nationalities were represented here.

The Boulevard was also a connecting road to the "Oil Island". The bridge to the island was a few hundred metres from our camp and on the island were over a dozen huge fuel tanks and ships came from the Middle East with crude oil, which was here refined.

A couple of kilometres to the south-east were some very nice swimming beaches and during the summer it was great to ride the bike down there and go for a swim. My school mate Ivar Wiren was a good swimmer and taught me how to swim also. One year I decided to harden my body against catching colds and I went for a swim almost every day till the end of October.

In the meantime I went to school in Gammel Hellerup Gymnasium and in year three I came first. Even in Danish as a subject my marks were the best or sometimes second in the class.

During the summer vacation I wanted to earn some money and found a job in the restaurant of the central railway station. The work was divided into two times: From 6am to 2pm or from 2pm to 10 pm. When I was looking for a job I went through the back entrance and asked a man if there would be a possibility of getting a temporary job during school holidays. He suggested that I talk to the trustee of the trade union. Povl Jørgensen* was very friendly and got me job in a couple of days.

With his help I got a job the following year as well. We wrote to each other for many years, until he died during my living in New Zealand. Through his help did my mother get a job in the kitchen, but due to inflammation in the wrist she had to give it up.

In year four I went back to school in October, over two months after the other boys to earn a bit more money. Year 4 was the final year of the middle school. Then came three years of gymnasium studies: Some students left school after year 4 and so did I.

An interesting part of year 4 was the subject Latin. Some subjects in Denmark's universities required that the students had studied Latin for at least one year, but because I started so late I did not think I could do it. My classmate Erling Tiedemann was of the opinion that I should definitely learn Latin as well. He was a Catholic, which is extremely rare in Denmark and he had heard a lot of Latin because of that. I went with Erling to the teacher of Latin, Mr. Jefsen and with his permission started on two levels. I worked through the material for the next lesson and also started with the first chapter in the book. Work went well but I had to memorise a lot. I still remember how I rattled the Latin word to love: amo, amas, amat, amamus, amatis, amant.. and there were lots of similar rattlings off, because of the grammar of Latin verbs in the present tense, past tense and in the subjunctive mood. My mother was holding the book and checking my performance. The interesting thing was, that at the final exam my score was "ug" (udmæket godt), (in English exceptionally good) whereas Erling had to accept "ug- (ug minus). Maybe here is the right moment to explain the Danish marking system. Ug "exceptionally good" was 15, ug- was 14 and two thirds, mg 14 and one third, mg (meget godt) "very good" was 14. Mg -13 and two thirds, g (godt) "good" 12. The lowest was minus twelve (slet) "poor".

The students of Gammel Gellerup did not have to buy text books. Books were lent to students by the local government office. This office was in the suburb of Gentofte, which would have been 6-8 km from Hellerup by car, but by public transport quite complicated. I read most of the books in five to six weeks- they were really interesting to read. Particularly interesting were geography, zoology and botany, they were as interesting as story books. Chemistry and physics were also interesting, particularly the historical aspect, but mathematics I left for normal study. The result was that I knew so many facts before actually studying started that it seemed like repetition.

It was also interesting when in February or March we got an exchange teacher from Norway. Basically such exchange of teachers for a couple of weeks in Scandinavian countries is done to acquaint students with another Scandinavian language, without officially having to learn it.

The teacher was an about 30 year old Norwegian, who came from a township about 200-300 km north of Oslo. We were given Norwegian texts to read, the teacher reading loudly at first and then the student copying the Norwegian pronunciation.

I found it interesting when I was reading about twenty sentences, copying the teacher's pronunciation. I was obviously successful, as the teacher said that I spoke like a Norwegian from southern Norway and I was the only one in our class who was able to pronounce words in their fashion. Although writing in both languages was similar, is a Danish person not able to palatalize r and L so the sounds remain unpalatalised. The Danish r is of course deeply guttural as well.

I can't remember how my mother met an office worker Aage Schmidt, but we also visited him and his wife at their home. Aage Schmidt had lived in Russia prior to the revolution and his wife was Russian. He was empowered to sign documents on behalf of the company where he worked, which was called Skandinavisk Kontrol. The parent company was based in Switzerland and was called Societe General de Surveillance.

The company was interesting in that they had branches in most countries of the world and importers of goods gave them orders to examine cargoes of various products before they went on the way, so that payment was made after analysis and checking was carried out.

I got a job as a junior office worker which also included going to various head offices of importers, delivering to them documents concerning cargoes and very often results of analyses which had been carried out. A frequent type of cargo which came from South America was called "cotton seed cake". Denmark was importing hundreds of tonnes of these, because feeding these to the cows increased their milk production. The address of Skandinavisk Kontrol was Amaliegade 98, which was only three buildings from Amalienborg Palace, where the Danish king lived with his family. Sometimes I saw King Frederick IX driving his car past our office.

The political situation in the world was still unstable, especially in Europe, because the Soviet Union was occupying half of Germany as well as Eastern European countries and there were misunderstandings now and then.

My mother and I were looking for possibilities to emigrate somewhere out of Europe and to be able to earn a living. I went to the Technological Institute of Copenhagen where there were evening courses for radio repairing technicians. I also found a radio repair shop where the owner worked in the evenings as well as during the day, so I could do some practical work.

The final exam at the institute consisted of theoretical electronics, as well as practical repair. I had no problems with theoretical questions, but practical work was at a low level. All the other students (most were apprentices) worked in repair shops every day. There were 23 students in our class and the teachers had made 24 radios 'faulty' by replacing some working parts with faulty ones. The first students had a large choice of radios and they just pointed at one on the shelf, which was given to the student for checking and repair.

At the start all 23 students were given a ticket with a number on it and I got ticker no. 23, so I was the last one to go in for the practical test. There were now only two radios on the shelf and the teachers asked me which one I would like to repair. I had no idea which would suit me better and I pointed at one of them. It was placed on the table and the two examiners sat with me at the table.

The radio was completely 'dead' and I started measuring volts and ohms with the multimeter. Measuring did not yield any results and I suddenly remembered a dream which I had seen five or six days ago. In this dream I saw a radio, which had rarely used valves, which were made in Germany. These valves were called "U series". In our lessons about various valves we were taught that the "U series" were particularly stable, because the internal parts were lying down and were not upright like in all other valves. It was interesting for me, that the radio I was trying to repair had these unusual valves: All "U series' valves were black. In my dream all the valves were also black, except one, which was white and was called UCH 11. My measurements with the multi meter did not give any results and I decided that the best I could do was to replace the UCH 11 with a new one. I explained to the examiners that I suspected that the UGH 11 was unstable (which would have been very uncommon) and requested that I be given a new valve. They brought me a new valve and as soon as I installed it, the radio worked normally. Thus I was totally successful in my practical exam, and my exam results had very high marks.

But the Head master of Gammel Hellerup was very sorry that I decided to stop going to school in the Gymasium part (last three years of total high school). He was of the opinion that I should have kept on studying and got my matriculation. He was sure that with most subjects I would have had no trouble at all and offered that I could come to his flat a couple of times a week and he would teach me mathematics without any charge. That was very generous of him and I studied maths with his help for about twelve months.

In the meantime my mother succeeded in getting a permit to emigrate to Argentina, and aforementioned Karin Rosmet and her parents travelled to Buenos Aires. Another migrant was the former editor of the largest Estonian newspaper "Päevaleht" and also editor of a children's magazine, Voldemar Mettus. He had been studying Spanish in the Berlitz Institute and he gave me his textbook. In the Berlitz teaching system there is no translating and the whole teaching is done in the language which is being studied. I noticed that on the last blank page he had written the dates and the number of pages studied. The usual was 2-3 pages.

When I examined the teaching methods of the institute, I found that the speed of study in classes with several students was far too slow and individual study with a teacher cost 7 Kroner per hour. I decided that if I study hard it will be the best solution. A teacher I was given Mrs. Heltvig, who had also taught Mr. Mettus. She was an Argentinean, who was married to a Dane. We decided on a method of study and instead of learning 2-3 pages per lesson, I did 6-7 pages. My study was going well and I was sure that once we were in a Spanish speaking country I would move forward pretty fast.

But then "the bomb exploded". The president of Argentina Juan Peron* cancelled all visas for entry to his country and every person had to reapply for a legal permit. I did not know the details of how mother obtained those permits, but it was obvious that our trip was cancelled. Some other refugees in our camp, who had made preparations for travel to Argentina, also stayed on. And I stopped my study of Spanish, as there was no need for it anymore.

In June 1950 a so called "Selection Mission" came to our refugee camp in Copenhagen. They were New Zealanders, who had just been to refugee camps in Germany to select suitable migrants for New Zealand. In Germany the refugees had such selectors from other countries, but in Denmark they were the first and only ones.
My mother and I considered New Zealand as a very suitable country where to migrate to, only my mother's wrists, which had disabled her when she worked in the restaurant, were still not well. Her friends suggested that when the medical examination is done, she should not mention the problem at all, but my mother said that she would not lie to the doctors. The selectors were to choose 80 persons from Denmark and we also put in our application for an interview and medical examination. I passed the interview and examination without problems and when my mother was checked she mentioned her wrist problem. That did not bother the selectors at all and they told us that we had been accepted.

Unlike other countries where only 100% healthy persons were accepted New Zealand was very humane. Viktor Vares, who lost a leg during the war and another former soldier whose name was Johannes Merevali*, who had lost his hand and part of the arm below the elbow, was also accepted.

Our trip was to start in August from the port of Bremerhafen in north-western Germany and my former headmaster J. K. Eriksen prepared a School Certificate with an English translation and wrote a reference in English explaining my achievements at school. In 1951, when I wanted to study pharmacy, the Professorial Board at the University of New Zealand made it possible for me to be accepted as a matriculated student.

In the beginning of August we travelled by train from Copenhagen to Bremen where we were taken to a camp in the suburb of Tirpitz. The camp belonged to the army and we were housed in two storey barracks buildings. We were supposed to leave the port of Bremerhafen a few days later, but the just started Korean War put a stop to it. As a consequence we had to stay in Tirpitz for a whole month, until they found a new ship that could carry almost one thousand migrants.

At last we were told that a new ship was to start its journey on the 7th of September 1950. We were taken by buses from Tirpitz to the port of Bremerhafen, where a Greek ship called "Hellenic Prince" was at the quay.

ESTONIA'S WAR CHILDREN: A FRACTURED GENERATION

Inevitably copies of this book will be accessed by those of our generation who were to grow up in Estonia or worse still in Siberia: It is would a rational response on their part shake their heads and wonder what we are whining about.

This book begins at a time when some Estonian parents made a decision whether to leave or stay in Estonia: None of us can ever be privy to their total factoring of their rationale. We were young and only knew the world as we had met it: The world of those who stayed in Estonia but the mythology of our folks. In their youth they lacked the insight to explore further: As maturity heightened their parents began to fail or were too burned out to reminisce. It really required a trip to reality street to begin to question. And indeed the answers may not have come regardless. Having worked in the Australian Veterans' Affairs and with an interest in behavioural medicine I quickly learned that many of the military had their lips sealed for a lifetime, as did those involved in the many underground movements. Even those closest to them were never to even suspect the complete reality.

This book is but the story of the journey of a group of children who were removed from their land of birth for reasons which may remain obscure: It in no way intended to compare their story with those of the others of our fractured generation.

The stories have as many similarities as differences, albeit differently clad. These will emerge in this book's sibling
"Estonia's War Children: A fractured generation: The first five years in their new lands"
be those in Siberia, Communist ruled Estonia or of ex-pat places. They too of course, will contain only that material which is accessible to those who wrote those stories. I hope to have that book published in the near future, and I suspect that we will find much which binds us, no matter what became of us. MM

HOW THE LOCAL GERMANS WERE FARING: KE

Our creature comforts were luxurious compared with that of the local inhabitants around us. Since 55 percent of Hamburg's residential areas had been destroyed by air raids, housing was almost non-existent. On the east and west sides of the camp, people were desperately trying to put roofs over their heads by constructing dwellings one room at a time. As they would get one room finished, they would immediately begin to add another. For construction materials they relied mostly on what they could find in destroyed buildings. Family members would make daily trips to bombed-out sections of the city to collect usable bricks and carry them home in manageable quantities. In three years I watched a new suburb spring up by the camp, built from single bricks salvaged from the rubble of war.

Food was also extremely scarce for the residents of Hamburg and the surrounding area. They had no cigarettes or any other rations to trade with and the old German mark, before its conversion, was almost worthless. I remember occasionally sharing what little I had with some of my German friends after I began to attend elementary school in Billbrook. Meat, even horse meat, was almost non-existent for my local playmates.

I recall one of my father's friends telling us about an illegal meat operation that the Hamburg police had uncovered. The meat in question was human. The officers had found several human corpses hung on meat hooks in the basement of fan unoccupied house. Apparently the body parts were being prepared for the black market. With the large number of refugees, German and other wise roaming the streets of Hamburg after the war, such an undertaking, although gruesome, was not uncommon.

Father warned me again to be extra careful riding the trains or trams back and forth to the city with my friends.

AND ON UNRRA AND THE DP CAMPS

We were not alone of course. After the War, when all the prisoners of war had been exchanged (mostly voluntarily but by some force) and the people who had been uprooted returned to their homelands (some of these folks were also not given a choice whether to return or not), there were still over a million homeless people from different countries left in Western Germany. These were political refugees who knew what terrible fate awaited them if they decided to go back home. Most of these refugees were from Estonia, Latvia, Lithuania, Russia and Ukraine.

These exiles were officially designated as Displaced People or DPs and placed under the Jurisdiction of the United Nations Relief and Rehabilitation Administration or Unrra. The Western Allies (Britain, France and United States) supported UNRRA in their respective zones of occupation, with adequate food,shelter, clothing and medical care. In order to best accomplish that, DP camps sprang up all over western Germany (primarily in the British and American zones). Most of the camps were situated in former German military facilities.

These camps, as much as possible were organized by nationalities. Since the number of Estonian refugees was relatively small, there was only one large camp where they were assembled, although there were several other insignificantly smaller complexes. The main Estonian camp was in Geislingen in the American zone.

In addition to taking care of remaining refugees in Germany, UNRRA also helped the DPs to immigrate to new homelands in the west. That was usually accomplished by finding sponsors for the DPs in countries like the United States, Canada, Great Britain, Australia and Argentina. The sponsors promised employment and housing for the emigres. Some of the DPs, especially those for whom UNRRA couldn't find sponsors, elected to stay in Germany. By 1953 all of the DP camps had been closed.

REPETITION IS NOT SYNONYMOUS WITH AD-HOC PROOF READING

As you read through the stories, reflections and 'clips' you may in exasperation reflect that has already been said by the same person elsewhere in the book. CORRECT!

This book is a composite of material where my primary intent remained not to modify any story should more material derive from the same author: There has been no mutation. However the book also includes many manylogues' where those authors reflected on the themes concerned: At times they used 'copy and pastes', at others they paraphrased to include new content or to revise their thinking.

The book also contains conversations I had with my cohort in Australia and on my visits to Estonia, Germany, USA and Canada over the last decade or so: At times these were with the authors of the stories where we explored the theme with a different polarity.

The 'repetitions' appear where they act as vignettes or reflections on another story/ cluster of stories which precede or follow them. MM

MART KASK
14 JUNE 1941 - AS I REMEMBER IT

The month of June is very special time for Estonians. It is the beginning of summer with long periods of daylight and short nights, accompanied by warm sunshine. It is the time when all that was dormant during the winter is now coming to life. It is the time that every Estonian longs for, having endured a long, dark and cold winter.

June is also the time for many historic celebrations such as Jaanipäev, Võidupüha, and others. **History has added another day in June, not to celebrate but as a day of remembrance. 14 June 1941 is the day that my generation witnessed firsthand the cruel hand of Joseph Stalin when 10,000 Estonians in cattle railcars were shipped to the Gulag in Siberia.**

In June of 1941, my family was living in Tihemetsa, Pärnumaa. Tihemetsa is about 10 kilometers south-east of Kilingi-Nõmme or about 50 kilometers south-east from Pärnu. Tihemetsa was the site of the Estonian Forest Service technical school where about 200 young men were trained annually to administer the Estonian forestlands. My father was the assistant director and teacher at the technical school. Our family consisting of my father Richard, my mother Aino, my older brother Toomas and my younger brother Hans (Ants in Estonia). We lived in an apartment in the Tihemetsa manor-house. Our family had moved to Tihemetsa from Kuusiku in the spring of 1940. In Kuusiku, my father was the Regional Forester overseeing the forest operations of a sizable area, centered on Kuusiku.

In 1939, the Soviet Union established a military airbase at Kuusiku. The airbase bordered our place of residence which also served as the Kuusiku forest service office. During the Winter-War between Finland and the Soviet Union, the Soviets used the Kuusiku airbase to bomb Helsinki. Shortly after a squadron of bombers took off from Kuusiku airbase, the Finnish national radio (Helsinki-Viiburi-Lahti) broadcast in Helsinki that fourteen aircraft have taken off from Kuusiku and are headed towards Helsinki. After the bombers had returned to Kuusiku, the Finnish radio reported that only eleven of the fourteen aircraft had landed in Kuusiku.

The Soviets at the airbase were furious and were determined to find the person who was sending these radio messages to Finland. The Soviets had determined that my father was suspect number one. The Soviet military personnel, in two or three trucks, drove to our house; forty or fifty soldiers surrounded our house and about ten of them thoroughly searched our house looking for the radio transmitter. They found nothing, since my father was not the informant. Then at night, to intimidate us, the Soviets turned aircraft searchlights on our house for the duration of the night. I remember that the Soviets searched our house two to three times, each time finding nothing. The reporting of aircraft takeoffs and landings continued throughout the Finnish-Soviet Union Winter-War. To the day my father died, he did not know who the informant was. I hope that historians will discover the identity of this person and recognize his or her bravery and unselfish service to the Finnish people.

Reporting on aircraft operations at the airbase was not the only conflict that my father had with the Soviets. The other conflict was over the unauthorized and illegal harvesting of timber by the Soviets to heat their offices and the living quarters at the airbase. The Kuusiku (mõis) manor house and the surrounding buildings housed the Soviet military operations. These buildings needed to be heated at winter time. Instead of purchasing firewood or taking out a permit to harvest firewood, the Soviets indiscriminately cut down trees wherever they felt like it. My father, as the Regional Forester (metsaülem) issued the military citations for illegally harvesting of timber. The Soviets told my father to "buzz off" or his dead body would be discovered in a ditch along a lonely forest road.

The relations between my father and the Soviet military became so intense that the National Forest Service in the spring of 1940, out of concern for my father's safety, transferred him out of Kuusiku to Tihemetsa Technical School. At the Tihemetsa Technical School he had no direct contact with the Soviets. I am convinced that by that time the Soviets had labeled my father as an enemy of the State and to be dealt accordingly at some future date.

Back at Tihemetsa, June 1941 was a typical warm summer months. Second World-War had broken out between Germany and the Soviet Union. German military forces were moving north through Poland to Lithuania to Latvia and will eventually occupy Estonia. Rumors began to circulate that Soviets, in the course of retreating, were arresting Estonian dissidents and undesirables and indiscriminately executing them. My father was quite concerned because he considered himself to be on the arrest list.

The Soviets were known to carry out their arrests in darkness, in the middle of the night. So, if you wanted to avoid arrest, you did not sleep in your bed in your house. To avoid capture and arrest by the Soviets, our family took elaborate precautions to escape potential arrests and who knows, possibly execution. Every evening, my father walked about a kilometer to a trusted friend's house and spent the night there.

My mother took the three boys by the hand and each evening we would walk to the nearby orphanage. My mother was a volunteer teacher at the orphanage, having earned a biology teaching degree from Tartu University. At the orphanage the three boys would don orphanage children uniforms and blend in with resident orphan population. At night, we would sleep in the orphanage dormitory dispersed with other orphans. My mother would also don the orphanage staff uniform and at night sleep with the orphanage staff.

The agreement with the orphanage staff was that they had no knowledge of the Kask family. It was further agreed that in the event the Soviets were to come looking for us, they would probably recognize my mother and arrest her. It was very unlikely that the Soviets would recognize the three boys, their identity would not be revealed and the children would be saved.

During the day, we went back to our apartment at the Tihemetsa manor house, knowing that we would be safe there until the nighttime. This was our strategy to avoid arrest until the Soviets were driven out by the German forces and we could come out of hiding. All this changed on 14 June.

In the afternoon of 14 June, the local sheriff (miilits) drove his motorcycle to our yard and had a short conservation with my father. The local sheriff was a trusted friend and hunting partner of my father. The sheriff told my father that he had been ordered to commandeer a truck for the Soviet military enforcement squad to come and arrest our family that night.

My father rounded up the family, packed the food we had, each of us took a blanket and warm clothing and that afternoon we walked about three kilometers to an isolated hay barn that was located in a forest clearing. The first cut of hay had been harvested and stored in the hay-barn. The plan was that we would hide out in the hay barn until the Soviets were driven out by the German army. We had no idea how long it would be.

Life in the hay barn was stressful. We had to stay inside the barn at all times to avoid detection. My father went out at night to his friend's house and brought back food consisting mostly of hard boiled eggs and rye bread. One of my father's friends staked and tethered a cow close to the barn. We had milk to drink. One or two days later another family showed up. Now we had a total of five or six children. It was no longer boring. In the next three to four days, the barn contained about fifteen to twenty people.

One afternoon, someone in the barn notices that a Soviet soldier, carrying a rifle, was walking across the meadow toward the barn. The men in the barn quickly got organized and it was agreed that in the event the soldier finds us in the barn that the soldier must be killed. We were in no position to hold him as a prisoner. Neither could we let him go and have him report on our presence in the barn. I was about to witness a real-life execution. Fortunately, the soldier kept on walking and did not bother to look in the barn.

After about five to six days in hiding, we learned that the German army had occupied Tihemetsa, the Soviets were gone, and we could return to our apartment.

When the Soviets were reoccupying Estonia in September 1944, we had no choice but to get away.
If we elected to stay, we knew what was going to happen to our family.

On 20 September, we boarded a ship to Gottenhafen, Germany. We had no idea what was waiting for us when, two days later, the ship docked at Gottenhafen. We knew the war was ending. Can we survive the backwash of a world-war in a foreign country on the loosing side? Maybe yes, maybe no. But the will to live tops every hardship and obstacle.

Much has been said and debated lately whether the people that left Estonia in the fall of 1944, left to seek a more economically prosperous life in the free world or did the people leave to survive and save their lives? The question is "were these people emigrants or refugees"? Our family left Estonia to stay alive. We were refugees. Our goal was to return to Estonia after the war was over and the sovereignty and the borders of war-occupied nations were restored to their pre-war status.

When the "iron curtain" descended over Western Europe in 1948, we know that returning to Estonia was a far out dream. We had to shift our vision towards the west.

FAMILIES BOTH LARGE AND SMALL HAD TO BEGIN ALL OVER AGAIN

No matter what the size of the family, its unit was very important. Children learned to become independent very fast and also to be supportive of each other and to avoid needless stress on their parents.

The mind boggles how such large families made such a long dangerous trek from Estonia and still stayed integrated: In today's world even a couple of children and relatively ample money seems not to be enough.

Legend has it that such large families did find it harder to find ways to emigrate from the camps.

THEY WERE SARDINED INTO CRAMPED QUARTERS

The smaller children played in the streets and in their back yards, many of which were situated on hillsides.
The toddlers and very young children were kept stimulated at one of three kindergartens and the older children went to school: Be it grade school or high school or trade school. The school yard too provided room for expending pent up energy.
And for the little nomads there was the river with its waterfall and the Helfenstein castle ruins on the hillside. At times I wonder how many of them did not come to grief but then they had seen ample grief of their trek and perhaps had learned some orienteering skills in the process.   MM

BUT DESPITE THAT TOLERANCE PREVAILED

Adolescents of course needed more space to expend their ebullience and increasing energy.
They needed new challenges, apart from learning which was amply provided by highly skilled teachers who too were DPs.
Such camps allowed camaraderie, sport, etc laced with discipline and respect for others to flourish.
They kept alive the hopes of the young who had to reconcile mankind's behaviour which was beyond the insight of the littlies to grapple with: The littlies only knew of 'goodies' and 'baddies'! to quote the late Mati Mesikep. MM

Map of Bruno's trek

BRUNO LAAN
WAR TIME TRAVELS WW II

After initial advances the German war effort against the Soviet Union bogged down in Russia. The German supply routes were long, roads were bad and the Russian winter took its toll. The Germans needed help. So they started to draft men from the occupied countries. Since Harri and I were not yet of draft age we continued going to high school. However older boys from more senior classes were drafted into the German Army starting already in 1942. Most foods became scarce and they became rationed. Clothing and shoes could be bought only with special permits.

In Nõmme many schoolhouses were turned into military hospitals for war casualties. Schools started to work in shifts for lack of space. Supplies were dwindling, schoolbooks were hard to get. History books were nonexistent, because when the Soviet Union occupied Estonia in 1940, they had ordered all history books burnt. History had to be rewritten according to communist Directives. Before new books could be printed, in 1941 the Germans had arrived. Again the history had to be rewritten, now according to German directives.

Thus for the better part of high school we did not have any history books at all. The teachers used to dictate history for students to copy during the classes so the students would have something to take home and study. The effect of this was that I lost all interest in history, since it became clear that teaching history was manipulated and you did not know whom to believe. Later I learned that this was nothing new - already in ancient Egypt a new pharaoh may have had stonemasons chisel out any reference to a previous pharaoh if that part of the history did not please the new pharaoh.

The Russian front at Leningrad was not far from Estonia and Soviet planes flew nightly bombing raids over Tallinn. To hide from the airplanes all windows had to be darkened at night. German patrols on the streets were just as likely to aim a rifle and shoot through a window, which was not sufficiently dark.

When an air raid siren sounded at night we had to get dressed and run to the shelter we had built in the back yard. My brother Harri and I slept in the same room. Sometimes we were just too lazy to get up and go into a cold winter night. Until one night during an air raid one of the bombs fell too close and crushed one of the windows of our room. Broken pieces of glass and parts of the window frame ended up in our beds on top of us. Well, that woke us up!

In October of 1943 Harri's year (1925) was called up for military service. Shortly before this Harri had joined the Omakaitse or Self-defense. This kept him out of the grasp of the draft for a while.

The Russian bombing raids had not caused too much trouble to Tallinn until the night of March, 9th 1944 when all hell broke loose. Russian planes lit up the city with "Roman candles" and then they leveled entire blocks of buildings. Much of the historic medieval old town suffered heavily. Many lives were lost and many people lost all they had. Half of the city lay in ruins. Things were not as bad 10 km away in Nõmme since homes in Nõmme were mostly single family types set relatively far apart from each other. It just did not pay trying to hit them.

THE AIRFORCE

After the March 9th air raid all schools were closed. I was still 17 years old and the mobilization of my year (1926) was imminent. Most of my classmates had already been drafted. Just three or four of the younger ones and the girls were left. What to do? If I wait for the draft I will become a foot soldier at the front. If I volunteer myself I would have a choice between joining the border patrol, the police battalions or the airforce. Why not the airforce! We used to joke that at least then you can still sleep between two bedsheets and not in a ditch.

Thus in April of 1944, not yet 18 years old, together with classmate Villi Kiinros we joined the German Airforce. We were sent to boot camp in Liepaja (Liibavi) in Latvia. This is also where the flight school for the Estonian pilots was at the time.

Two months later, in June the entire flight school with support personnel was moved to Pärnu in Estonia. Fresh out of boot¬camp I was assigned to the clothing warehouse. To learn the warehousing business I was sent for training to Riga, the capital of Latvia. After a couple of weeks in Riga the Russians broke through the German lines in the eastern part of Latvia near Daugavpils, which was called Dünaburg in the German language. To plug the hole at the front all trainees for various specialties in Riga were collected and sent to the front. We were permitted to take only a minimal amount of clothing in addition to our rifles, ammunition and gas masks. All personal belongings were stored in a military warehouse in Riga. As things turned out I never saw that stuff again. Only later I realized that I should have never taken irreplaceable items such as photos of my classmates with me into the service.

We went by train towards the eastern front. The last 20 or 30 km we walked. We arrived just behind the front lines at night in the dark. The first thing we saw was that they were burying two casualties. What an impression. There I was, barely 18 years old, in the airforce uniform and at the front. Disgusting.

We were assigned to units. We were also told that at this spot we were practically surrounded by the Russians and all troops were going to be pulled out that same night. How stupid having made that long march right into the trap. They pointed at two fires at a distance saying that roughly between these two fires the "bag" was still open. We should turn around and start hiking back and find our units afterwards. We were already tired from the long march and still had no hope for a rest in sight. No choice, we started to walk again - backpack, gas mask, rifle, ammunition. Towards the morning, being dead tired and hungry, with another buddy we said to hell with it, found a rail¬road shack and fell sound asleep.

We awoke a few hours later when it was already light outside. It was quiet. We wondered if the Russians had meanwhile closed our escape route and we were in their hands now for good. We heard some shooting. Decided to start walking in the westerly direction paralleling the railroad tracks, but staying out of sight.

After a while we saw some soldiers in German uniforms. What a relief. It turned out they belonged to an Estonian fighting unit. They were also on the move pulling out of the trap. We thought why not join them instead trying to find the German unit to which we had been assigned officially. We thought to look for their command post as soon as we were out of this trap. We kept on walking in the westerly direction. We saw a German freight train heading west. Lucky break. We jumped aboard.

Since both of us were in the airforce and really had no desire to become foot soldiers in the ditches we said why not stay on the freight train and try to get back to our own unit in Pärnu. We were fairly certain that the army's bookkeeping at the front was not sufficiently accurate nor did they really care what happened to some inexperienced young guys, who had been sent to them.

When the train made stops at the stations, it was searched by the German military police to flush out guys like us who had strayed from their units. The stops were brief and somehow they never got to us. We decided to leave the train well before reaching Riga and walk around Riga to the rail line headed north towards Estonia.

Luck was again with us. We left the train and after a long walk we reached the rail line headed north. We picked out another slow moving freight train and jumped aboard. Our spirits were up. We thought that if the military police caught us now we would say that we had been in Riga for training and now we were headed back to our units in Pärnu. Our soldier's passports showed both Pärnu and Riga, but of course we did not have the necessary marching orders. At the same time there was no written indication about us having been sent to the front.

Again, the train was searched at stops, but each time before the police reached our car the train started to move again. At the Estonian border town Valga we had to leave the standard gage rail line and transfer to the narrow gage rail line, which went to Pärnu. All went well and we found an open top freight car with equipment marked for our own unit in Pärnu. Well, no problem here, just climb aboard and lay low. We heard military police walk past our car, but nobody bothered to look inside.

Between Valga and Mõisaküla the thought crossed my mind why not go home to Nõmme for a couple of days and only then go to Pärnu. The other buddy decided not to gamble and rather stay on this train all the way to Pärnu. By the time we reached Mõisaküla my mind was made up and I found another train which would go north to Tallinn. The train engineer was an accommodating fellow and he let me ride in the tender right behind the steam engine. This was a safe place against search, but terribly dusty from the coal on which I had to sit. Of course, as a good soldier I had my rifle, ammunition and backpack with me.

I got off at Liiva, which was the station at the outskirts of Nõmme, and simply walked home. What a surprise to my parents and brothers. I put my air force uniform and my rifle into a closet, washed up, dressed into civilian clothes and went to town.

It was June of 1944 and just then, within a day or two of my arrival, they started to draft young men, who were born in 1926 like me. Thus my holiday at home was short-lived. I put the uniform on again, took my rifle and backpack, went back to Liiva and boarded a train to Pärnu. Went back to my unit and reported to the German master sergeant Oberfeldvebel Müller, "Flieger Laan meldet sich zurück von Ausbildung in Riga" i.e. Private Laan reports back from training in Riga.

Without asking for my marching orders he told me to report to the quartermaster, who was also a German. When this fellow found out that I did not have any papers he wanted to take me back to the master sergeant. I had already briefed his Estonian assistant about my plight and he came to my rescue. Without blinking an eye he convinced the quartermaster that I had already spoken to the master sergeant and he should merely put me on the rolls again. And so he did. I was back in my airforce unit with no one the wiser. I was assigned back to the clothes warehouse and to regular sentry duty as any good soldier.

EVACUATION STARTS

In the summer of 1944 just across the Estonian border on the Leningrad front things went from bad to worse for the German Army. In September the Germans started to pull out of Estonia. The entire flight school, to which I was attached, was loaded on a ship in the Pärnu harbor. Our pilots got orders to fly the flight school planes to Germany. I did not want to leave Estonia thinking that I might be needed here. We had heard rumors that another Estonian Independence War was starting just like in 1918. We would fight the Russians as well as the Germans and free the Estonian soil of all oppressors.

There I was - I had grown up in the independent Republic of Estonia. Since childhood I had known that our freedom had only been possible because of men, who had fought for our independence in 1918. And now, in September of 1944 the country needed us again! We heard that admiral Pitka was organizing an Estonian Army and they needed men. This was my patriotic duty. I was ready.

As the ship was being loaded, at an opportune moment, together with another fellow we left the ship. We went to a friend's house to wait until the ship had sailed, which was supposed to be that same night. Later we heard that our disappearance had soon been noticed.

On the next day we went back to the harbor to see if the ship had sailed. We approached cautiously between some large boxes. To our surprise suddenly my boss's boss, a German lieutenant, was standing in front of us. "Soll ich Sie 'runterknallen?" - Shall I shoot you? and he patted his pistol case. He was really angry and threatening. Apparently some other fellows had also taken off. He felt personally insulted, since he felt that I was his responsibility and I had betrayed him. He took us back to the ship. To our luck, at that moment the ship was being moved along the quay to facilitate additional loading. So he left us at the ship, yelled aboard to watch us and he himself went somewhere else. Well, it did not take us long to disappear again. The ship sailed that same evening without us.

Later I heard, that when the lieutenant could not find me after they had sailed, he had the entire ship searched. He just could not believe that I had taken off again.

That same night together with this other fellow, whose name has escaped me, we walked across the Pärnu Bridge towards Tallinn to find admiral Pitka and his newly formed Estonian Army. There were airplane bombs on the bridge with detonation wires snaking along the bridge. Later the bridge was blown up by the Germans to slow down the advancing Russian troops. It was September 23rd, I believe.

We started to walk towards Tallinn 130 km to the north of us. After a while as it got dark we crawled under some racks of freshly cut rye to catch some sleep. Towards the morning it got too cold so we got up and continued walking towards Tallinn. People with horse drawn wagons, on bicycles, in cars and on foot were all going south to escape the advancing Russians and we were headed north. People kept telling us that we were going in the wrong direction since the Russians had already taken Tallinn. We did not want to believe them. Nobody knew anything about admiral Pitka. We kept on walking north.

We met Olaf Birk a classmate of mine coming from Tallinn. He convinced us that it was true that the Russians were already in Tallinn and nobody knew about admiral Pitka's units. There is no hope. All is lost. It did not seem right to turn back so we decided to head west towards Virtsu on the West Coast of the Estonian mainland. In Virtsu the ferry was still operating which took us to the island of Muhu.

On Muhu we went to a farm to get some food or to get at least a drink of water. At the farm there were a couple of older women, all others had left for Sweden across the Baltic Sea. They asked us to stay with them at the farm, "Children, where are you going? Just stay here, start working, pray to God and nothing will happen to you." We just thanked for the food and water and moved on.

We got a ride on an old fire engine, which someone had commandeered. The driver was drunk and drove like a maniac. The fire engine was full of people, fear was in people's eyes, but nobody said anything. This was still better than trying to escape the Russians on foot. We rode on that fire engine to the southeast coast of Saaremaa, where a large, but damaged sailing vessel was being repaired. A big chunk of the bow was missing. The vessel was already full of people all willing to risk their lives even in a damaged vessel. The main thing was to flee the invading Russians.

We two did not even have a chance to get on board since we were in German Airforce uniforms. The organizers accepted just women and children and men in civilian clothes. They thought they would have a better chance this way to sail to Sweden. Of course officially they were

Bruno aged 18 years

Badge for Right arm

going to sail to Germany. This gave us the idea of trying to find another ship or boat, which would take us to Sweden instead of Germany. So we headed across Saaremaa to the West Coast where we thought to have more opportunity.

We tried to stay out of sight of the Germans, especially the Military Police. We suspected that they would either assign us to some military unit to stem the advance of Russians or just ship us to Germany. All the MP's were German and there was no arguing with them. Their official badge was an oval shaped metal shield about 4 by 7 inches long. It was hung on the chest by a chain around the neck. It had the words "Feldgendarmerie" engraved on it. We called them ketikoerad i.e. chain dogs. Of course never to their faces since they had the power of life and death over you.

After reaching the West Coast of Saaremaa we heard that the going rate for passage to Sweden was 75 gold rubles. We had nothing. Then at one spot we saw a fisherman's boat, about 30 feet long, riding at anchor some distance from the shore. We thought this to be our chance. We found a rowboat, but no oars to prevent stealing by guys like us. This did not deter us. We broke out the wooden seats and used them to paddle to the boat at anchor. Our plan was to threaten them that either they take us along or we will start shooting. Hell, we are in uniform and it does not matter that we are only 18 years old. Well, soon we found out that it is not so easy to start threatening someone with bodily harm let alone start killing in cold blood. You just cannot do it.

As we reached the boat we saw it was only about 1 1/2 feet out of the water. People were sitting side by side next to each other with no space to step or move. It was overloaded. They listened to our demands, or really our pleas by that time, and said that they would be glad to take us along if they only would have the space. The two brave soldiers rowed back to the shore using the seats as paddles.

Thinking about this later the odds were that this overloaded boat never made it to Sweden. The Baltic Sea probably claimed them with or without help from the Russians. The Russians were known to sink boats full of helpless people trying to escape to Sweden. The Germans usually first took the people aboard their vessels and then sunk the empty boat by shooting it full of holes. They needed workers in Germany.

LEAVING ESTONIA
We kept trying to find a way to get to Sweden. We walked up and down the coast staying out of sight of the border patrols but found nothing. After a few days we heard that the Russians had already occupied the entire mainland of Estonia. There really was no hope for us. We decided to come out of hiding and let the German patrols catch us. We told them that we were trying to find our units. We were sent to Kuressaare and in the harbor of Roomasaare we were put on a transport ship to Germany. The ship was full of men, women, children and soldiers like us.

It was an incredibly sad feeling to be crammed into the holds of a ship sailing towards an unknown future. I felt miserably alone. All I had was a toothbrush to call my own. I remember, to fall asleep I curled up into a ball, as tight as possible, which somehow gave me a little sense of increased security.

We still believed, or wanted to believe, that this was only temporary and by Christmas we would be back home in Estonia. Little did we know. As it turned out it was to be 30 long years later when I was again able to set my foot on the soil of Estonia.

We landed at Neufahrwasser near Danzig in East Prussia. After the war this became Poland and Danzig was renamed Gdansk. All military personnel were told to leave the ship ahead of the civilians. By that time we had met a half a dozen other Estonians in German Airforce uniforms. We decided to try to find our own airforce units instead of being assigned to some army units. So we stayed on the ship out of sight mixed in with civilians until all other military people left the ship and were marched off to somewhere.

Later, to the annoyed German officials at the harbor we made it plain that with our expertise at the airforce we were definitely expected to rejoin our airforce units. With German attention to detail they soon found out that our units had been shipped to the airfield at Frankfurt/Oder. We were given official marching orders and sent by train to rejoin our units.

We had been really in luck. Had we gone ashore together with the other military people we would have been sent to a training camp for Waffen-SS and from there to the eastern front into heavy battles with the Russians. By the way, Waffen-SS troops with greenish gray uniforms were really top-notch elite troops like the Marines in the U.S. They had nothing to do with the concentration camps. "Waffen" means "weapons" in English. It was the General-SS with black uniforms, consisting entirely of Germans, who among other duties were also guards at the concentration camps.

All Estonians in the German Airforce had been assembled about 80 km east of Berlin at Frankfurt/Oder. We were not trusted with airplanes any more. Some of our fellows had flown their airplanes to neutral Sweden instead of Germany. Some of them had taken off even after having landed in Germany. Now the Germans would not let us even close to the airplanes.

The shortness of fuel was rather evident. When an airplane landed it just pulled off the runway and the pilot immediately shut off the engines to save fuel. Then a pair of oxen was hitched to the airplane and pulled to the assigned parking space. It is rather odd to see a fast airplane being pulled by lumbering oxen.

I was assigned back to the clothes warehouse. Boy, was the German lieutenant mad when he saw me! The poor fellow could hardly talk he was so angry. He started to say, "If I would be your father, I would, I would ... GET OUT!" At the warehouse I found my backpack, which had not been completely emptied. My buddy in the warehouse, Uno Kuht, had saved some of my personal belongings.

Life in Frankfurt/Oder was interesting since most of us had never been in Germany. Whenever we got passes to the city we walked up and down the streets, went to movies, went to restaurants. We could order hardly any food since we did not have civilian rationing cards. At one cafe the owner either felt pity for youngsters like us or he liked our heavy tipping. The result was that he kept one certain table reserved for us. Somehow he was also able to serve us some cakes and ersatz coffee. The latter was not made of coffee beans, but at least it looked like coffee.

We also met Estonian civilian refugees. One older man, when he heard that I work in a clothes warehouse, cautiously asked if he could buy a pair of underwear from me. I felt pity for him. No problem. I brought him several sets of underwear and socks. The German Reich did not get any poorer because of that.

The Germans decided to train us to be paratroopers, who could be sent behind the Russian lines. The schooling was going to take place in Denmark, which was also under German occupation. Our men started to leave for Denmark in groups. Letters back from Denmark praised the abundance of available food compared to the meager rations in Germany. It sounded like paradise. This was a busy time in the warehouse since the clothing had to be brought up to regulation before men could leave.

The luck of those who were sent to Denmark did not last long. The Danes naturally disliked the Germans for having occupied their homeland. However, towards us, the Estonians, the Danes were very friendly even if our men wore German uniforms. They understood our predicament. The Germans noticed the fraternization between the Danes and the Estonians and did not like it. They may have thought that we may even team up with the Danes and start something.

Then the plans were changed. Instead of sending us to Denmark for paratrooper training they started to send us to Dortmund in western part of Germany for anti aircraft training. All transfers were in groups of around 30 men since the Allied air raids on trains were frequent. Larger groups of men would have attracted too much attention, which would have increased risk.

Since I was working in the warehouse I never made it to Denmark, but went directly to Dortmund. There we were trained to handle 88-mm cannons against aircraft as well as against tanks. The 88-mm cannons were possibly the best versatile cannons the Germans had. I was assigned to be the number two man on a cannon. There were a total of ten men per cannon. Most of them handled the ammunition. The number two man turned the cannon sideways. Number three aimed it vertically. All you did was to rapidly turn a crank to keep a pointer on a dial lined up with another pointer. The latter was controlled from a measuring and computing device nearby. To use the cannon against low flying aircraft or against tanks the number two man became the one who aimed the entire cannon.

As another specialty I was trained to work with a Malsi Gerät. This was an ingenious mechanical computer to calculate the expected location of an enemy airplane for the time when the shot reached the airplane. The device looked like a large table with interacting drums and scales moved by thin cables. It took half a dozen men to run it. My responsibility was to either read off some numbers into a microphone or enter measurements received via an earphone. This was really a backup system when other more modern systems had failed.

The Germans did not trust any soldiers from the occupied countries to be sent to the western front against the Allied forces. They rightfully thought that we probably would have just as gladly volunteered to become Allied prisoners of war.

We spent the winter of 1945 in Dortmund in training and in digging air raid bunkers deep underground. Just like miners. We also practiced some actual shooting at Allied planes as they crossed the skies towards their targets. Either we must have been lousy shots or there were not enough of us for the Allies to get mad at us. They never bothered, just kept on going.

We ate lunch at the mess hall. In the evening we received hot tea and mostly bread and marmalade or margarine. The food for the whole room of 20 men was handed out in one lump amount. Since the food was scarce you had to find ways to divide the rations as precisely as possible. So under twenty pairs of watchful eyes the food was manually divided into twenty portions. Then one man turned his back to the table and another man asked him, pointing to one portion, who will get this portion. And so on until all portions had been handed out. This assured impartiality.

The food had decreased in quantity as well as in quality. Especially an 18-year-old was always hungry.

Near our barracks were potatoes stored in piles of about 3 foot high and 70 foot long. The potatoes were covered first with earth, then straw and again with earth to protect them from freezing. There was always a German sentry standing guard at the potato piles. This did not deter our guys. At night we crawled between the piles, dug with hands through the earth and straw cover, filled a small bag with potatoes and crawled back out before the sentry could see us.

Back in the barracks we boiled the potatoes adding just salt, since we had nothing else. Then we would whip the boiled potatoes as fine as we could. I doubt if I have ever tasted anything as delicious as those whipped potatoes. There is truth to the old saying that hunger is the best cook.

The Germans noticed the little holes in their potato piles and did not like it. They intensified the guarding. They also searched our belongings at times getting awfully close to some of our stolen spuds. They never succeeded in proving that we were the culprits.

TO THE EASTERN FRONT

In the spring of 1945 the situation on the eastern front got worse and they started to send us, again by groups, to the east. We were supposed to join the Estonian units fighting there. A lieutenant headed our group of 30. All were Estonians. Since there were also some Estonians in the quartermaster's office we had two sets of marching orders made out: one for 30 men and another for 100 men. A courageous Estonian Oberleutnant

Kore signed the extra marching order. The risk was great, but the Germans never found out. We used both of these orders to requisition food for our group of 30 men. Finally we had enough food to eat our fill.

After one of such eating orgies one joker came back from the woods, where he had relieved himself, and said, "To avoid suspicion I made two piles instead of one. Only one big pile would be a dead giveaway that this guy could not have been on standard rations."

We were in no hurry to get to the eastern front. Despite of the Allied bombings the railroads were quickly repaired and operated well. Really too fast for us. So we exited the train at a small station. Marched outside the town, found a farmer's barn and slept the night. The next morning there was some explaining to do to the local police. We said that we came from the western front and now we were headed to the eastern front and desperately needed some rest. We moved on quietly, since we did not want them to start checking with the military police.

In April we arrived in the region of Silesia, which is in an eastern part of Germany. It seemed that everybody was headed west to escape the Russians. The Estonian, Hungarian and German units had all gotten mixed up. Roads were full of overloaded civilian and military trucks, horse drawn vehicles and people on foot pulling little wagons called Wägele typical for the region. We were assigned to fighting units, but it did not matter, since the front had practically collapsed. We turned around and joined the endless lines of refugees and soldiers.

Times like this are very unsettling and people do things they normally would not do. Since government warehouses became unguarded people took what they wanted. The worst part was when our soldiers found liquor and started to drink. I did not touch a drop since I knew that I needed all my senses for survival. I would not be surprised if there were soldiers, who woke up from their liquor-induced sleep to find themselves prisoners of the Russians.

Late in April we found that the Russians had gotten around us and cut off our escape route to the west. Now everybody was for himself. I had my backpack, soldier's aluminum eating utensils, my rifle and ammunition. I also had an illegally obtained small pistol in my pocket. Since I did not smoke I had been able to exchange cigarettes for other things like that handgun.

It became clear that Germany could not handle this war much longer. Our main aim was to somehow get to the west so the Americans instead of the Russians could capture us. We were convinced that as soon as the German Army is conquered, the Americans would keep on going to the east to fight the Russians and eliminate communism. We thought that in this campaign the Americans could even make good use of us. There was no doubt in our minds that the Americans were just as anticommunist as we were. We sure were wrong at that.

Little did we know that the Americans and the British were actually friends with the Soviet Union. We did not know about the lend-lease, whereby U.S.A. was shipping military material and food to the Russians through Iran. We did not know about the Theeran or Yalta agreements, where Franklin D. Roosevelt and Winston Churchill had agreed with Josif Stalin that Stalin could do with the Baltic States as he wishes. Later such agreements were well noted. However, at that time, having been first under the Soviet occupation and then under the German occupation, both with censored news reporting, we just did not know about such agreements. Besides, how much interest should a teenager have had to find out about some obscure meetings in Yalta or Theeran?

Since our retreat had been blocked to the west, we turned south, hoping to get through Czechoslovakia to the American side. We felt ready to fight our way through if necessary. All went fairly well for a while. I was able to find some standing room on a truck. We drove through Jung Bunzlau (Mlada Boleslav in the Czech language) towards Melnik. Riding through the town of Melnik on a highway to Prague (Praha) suddenly all traffic stopped. We could hear shooting ahead of us. Melnik is approximately 30 km north of Prague at the confluence of Elbe (Labe) and Moldava (Vltava) rivers.

Why look for trouble if you can go around it? I jumped down from the truck and started to walk back. So did many others. Some truck drivers started to turn their trucks around. I found another road out of Melnik. It was just as full of retreating vehicles, loaded mostly with German soldiers. One truck with a trailer stopped briefly. The truck and the trailer were chock-full of standing soldiers. There was no room for another man. So I climbed on the trailer hitch between the truck and the trailer. I had my backpack on my back, leather ammunition cases and soldier's eating utensil "katelok" on my belt and my rifle hung on my shoulder. How I was still able to stand on the trailer hitch and hang on to the tailgate of the truck and not fall off is truly a wonder.

The soldiers on the truck noticed my rifle. They yelled down to me to get rid of my rifle. Apparently they had already surrendered their weapons. What a shock to me. I had always thought that whatever happens, as a soldier I must keep my weapon. They changed my mind. When the truck stopped again I just took off my rifle and handed it to a Czech standing at the side of the road. You cannot fight a war when you are the only one on your side who has a rifle. Anyway, without the rifle it was easier to ride on the trailer hitch.

We really did not know precisely where we were. On highway crossings the Czechs had torn down the directional signs and placed them loosely next to the signposts pointing ever which way. It was evident that they wanted to confuse us.

PRISONER OF WAR
We came to a wide river. There were no undamaged bridges within sight. The shore was crowded with German soldiers. Rowboats were being used to transport soldiers across. A German officer in a real fine uniform was directing this operation. All insignia had been removed from his uniform.

Only a Ritterkreuz, one of the highest German military decorations, was hanging in its proper place under his chin.

After a while it was my turn to be rowed across. The river was quite wide and you could not see clearly what was happening on the other shore. We soon found out. The Czechs took us prisoners. There was no sensible way to resist. Each boat brought, say six to eight people, all without weapons, since whoever still had weapons had to leave them on the other shore. And there were many armed Czechs with red armbands waiting for us, some wearing a red star on the hat. Now we realized why the Czechs were so willing to row us across. I am sure the German officer with the Ritterkreuz did not know this either.

We were led to a fenced factory yard. We spent the night mostly sitting in a barn type building in that yard. There were so many of us that hardly anybody had enough space to lay down. Hunger started to let itself be known since I had not eaten for a while.

In the morning we were herded into one long row three across in the regular military manner and marched off supposedly in the direction of a gathering place for prisoners of war. We were being guarded by armed Czechs with red armbands. As we started out we had not been searched yet and I still had my small pistol in my pocket. I realized that soon it will be found and it may cause me trouble. I thought it would be safer if nobody else would have it either. So while marching, when the guards were not right next to me, I took the small pistol apart and threw the parts one by one into the bushes. There was practically no chance for someone to find them all and reassemble the pistol.

Soon Russian tanks and foot soldiers met us. Our hearts sank. All is over. With luck we will end up in Siberia. Without luck they will bury us here. The Czechs on the streets greeted the Russians with joy and handed them flowers. Some Czech women climbed on the Russian tanks and rode happily along with flowers in their hands. A terrible letdown for us.

To them, the Russians were liberators who liberated them from the German occupation. This was exactly the opposite what had happened in Estonia four years earlier. We had greeted the Germans with flowers since they had liberated us from the Russian occupation. Ironically, in both cases the liberators turned out to be the next occupiers.

After a while the Czechs guarding us were replaced by Russian soldiers and we kept marching. Or should I say moving along. Going through towns and villages the local people vented their anger on us. We were repeatedly searched by bystanders for whatever suited their desires. We quickly learned to muddy our boots and make us otherwise drab looking to lessen the chance of having to give up our last possessions. In no time at all it becomes disastrous if, as a prisoner, you have to walk barefooted.

We were being spit upon by the Czechs. I remember one well-dressed lady at the side of the road, who swatted each passing prisoner on the back of the neck with a bunch of twigs. In some towns we passed through rows of people who delighted beating passing prisoners with clubs. It is a very demeaning feeling to let somebody beat you and you are well aware that if you would resist there is a good chance of being shot immediately.

There were some dead soldiers laying at the roadside. I especially I remember a dead youngster in a uniform. His face was covered with a pile of earth. This was visible proof not to try anything heroic. Even so in some villages the Czechs shot every unarmed prisoner of war coming through. I do not know how bad the Germans had been towards the Czechs, but I would not be surprised if later on the Russians turned out to be even worse towards the Czechs. What goes around comes around.

I did not know how these damned Czechs looked at Non Germans in German uniforms. They probably thought that these were real bloodthirsty volunteers, worse than even the Germans. I also realized, especially as a prisoner that you do not want to stand out. The Estonian soldiers normally had a patch on the sleeve with the Estonian national colors: blue, black and white, and in the airforce we had also the word Estland on it. We were proud of this distinction, now it had become a dead giveaway. While marching I tore off all insignia from my clothing and tossed away. Except I could not bring myself to discard the blue-black-white sleeve patch. I hid it in a pocket. I still have it.

From there on I was a faceless prisoner of war, just moving along. After a while I recognized Hans Puhk, another Estonian from our unit. He was a couple of years older than I. He had been one of our young pilots. His family was from the "Puhk ja pojad" flower mill dynasty in Estonia. It was quite a relief to have somebody around whom you knew from before. You did not feel completely alone in this wide world.

ESCAPE

I do not remember having gotten any food while a prisoner of war. We did get water although. Some fellows could not put up with the endless marching and collapsed at the side of the road.
They were just left behind since other groups of prisoners followed us who presumably took those fellows along again. Anyway, we noticed that the Russian guards did not shoot them.

Well, in that case... The thought kept coming back that compared to our present situation would it not be much nicer to be a prisoner where the local people were German and not those damned Czechs? One might even get some food and not just harassment and beatings from the civilians.

When the road lead us through a forest I faked staggering and let myself fall down at the side of the road. Other prisoners kept on walking past me. The Russian guards were on bicycles and did not bother to stop either. As soon as I

335

was between two groups of prisoners and no guards were in sight I quickly disappeared into the bushes. Hans had done the same and we met a short time later.

There is truth in the saying that to try, when there is little hope, is to risk failure, not to try is to guarantee it.
We started to walk through forests and along back roads in the general direction of northwest towards Germany. On one freshly planted potato field we dug up seed potatoes and cooked them. We also found that farmers in general were not as unfriendly towards us as had been the people along the streets where we had marched as prisoners of war. We even got some food here and there. The general attitude of the farmers was that the war is over and let everybody go home. Once in a while we met other German soldiers who were trying to get to Germany the same as us.

By that time all I had was my aluminum eating utensil and a small soldier's knapsack, both hanging on my belt. We had not had any luck to obtain any civilian clothing. There was no way for us not to appear anything else than poor suckers who had lost the war and now were trying to go home.

One day walking along a forest path suddenly a Russian soldier with a rifle appeared in front of us. Well, looks like back to the prisoner of war camp, dammit! He motioned us to come closer and asked "Uura yest?" - Do you have a watch? "No, we do not." He did not believe us and decided to search us. He started to search me first and found in my pocket a narrow leather strap. He knew that such a strap was commonly used to fasten a pocket watch to a buttonhole. He held up the strap and asked: "Where is the watch?" - "Your buddies took it already." He did not believe me, since why should somebody take my watch and leave the strap. Smart man. And stupid me for having kept the strap. He searched me more thoroughly. Still finding nothing.

Then he started to search my companion Hans. As I stepped a couple of steps aside I must have smiled, or just on intuition the Russian let go of Hans and started to search me again. By now he was getting threatening: "But what will I do with you if I do find the watch?" - "I don't have it. Your buddies took it." Finally he gave me a kick in the butt with his foot and let us both go. We were still free!

Apparently that Russian soldier was spending his free time on forest paths to rob unfortunates like us. What he did not know, was that I still had the silver pocket watch my father had given me. It was inside a small leather pouch hung from my neck. In such a pouch soldiers carried their identification "dog tags" so that the bare metal would not touch the chest. The pouch was hidden from view under my rough woven gray colored soldier's undershirt. With the jacket open at front the Russian had not thought to pat my chest. Nor had any one of the countless others, who had searched me. To lessen problems later on I did toss the leather strap away. I still have the watch to this day.

To get to Germany we had to cross the Erzgebirge mountain chain. These are beautiful mountains with some peaks rising over 3000 feet (1000 meters). The slopes are covered with tall trees and the highways snake along the deep valleys. We walked along some footpaths halfway up the slopes so we would not be seen from the Russian military convoys on the highways below us. These footpaths had been made for tuberculosis patients from the famous Teplice-Schönau sanatoriums. Walking along these paths would have been fine except, to prevent tanks from using these paths, the Germans had felled groups of large trees across these paths every now and then. We were too weak from hunger to climb across the tree trunks. Next best was to go around them. The slopes were steep and it took real effort to get back to the path again.

Finally we were across the mountains and in Germany. Hunger was gnawing. In the evening we decided to go to a farm near the forest and ask for food. As we approached the gate suddenly we saw a Russian soldier between the large stone gateposts. He was leaning against one of them. The thought flashed through my mind: that's it, back to the POW camp. Oh well, at least we will be in Germany and not in that darned Czechoslovakia.

To our greatest surprise the Russian soldier asked, "Are you hungry?" - "Oh, yes!" Without further ado he lifted a pail full of soup from behind the gatepost, gave it to us, turned around and went back to the farmhouse. Bless his soul! The soup was lukewarm and had one inch size cubes of meat in it.

Like all good soldiers we had never discarded our eating utensils - the katelok and the spoon. It does not matter that for long periods these items may seem to be useless, but what a pity if some food becomes available and you have no place to put it. We sat down right there at the edge of the ditch and gulped the soup. There was so much soup that after eating our fill we still had enough to fill our kateloks to take along. We quickly even tried to rinse the pail in the ditch before putting it back next to the gatepost. Then we just as quickly disappeared into the forest again.

Like with all nationalities and with all armies there are all kinds of people. Some turn out to be mean when given half a chance and others remain good-hearted. So were also the Russian guards in Czechoslovakia. Some were brutal and all you heard from them was profanity and "Davai! Davai!" meaning "Let's go! Let's Go!" to hurry you along. Others smiled and said "Damoi! Damoi!" -"To home! To home!". Why not, the war was over.

There is an interesting thing about hunger that eventually the hunger pangs recede. The body seems to agree that there is no more food to be had in this life. After a while you start weakening, you slow down. You also feel cold as well as heat much more intensely. Somewhere along my travels I made a solemn promise to never complain about food in the future. Any food. I believe I have kept that promise. It does not mean that I do not appreciate an excellent meal, when available.

After meeting this compassionate human being at the gate of a farm our spirits rose again. True, in Czechoslovakia our principal aim was to get to Germany and to be a prisoner of war there. Once on the German soil we felt kind of stupid going to a Russian POW camp on our free will and ask to be admitted. How about trying to get where the Americans are and give ourselves up there? There is not much hope, but what is there to lose?

The Germans we met were friendly so we dared to be seen more freely as long as we kept away from the Russians. After having eaten that excellent soup the body must have realized that there still could be some food somewhere on this earth and demanded more. Some Germans suggested why not request food rationing stamps like everybody else and buy food at a store.

As suggested, in the outskirts of the City of Chemnitz (later, under the communist rule it was renamed Karl Marx Stadt) e went to the municipal office and requested food rationing stamps. We still had kept our soldier's passports Soldbuch just in case we had to prove that we had been in the airforce and not in the SS. These came in handy. An entry was made on the page reserved for the registration of military honors and decorations. Now it said that we had received rationing stamps for one week's duration. Ordnung muss sein! Germans are notoriously precise and bureaucratic.

While in Czechoslovakia we had tossed away most of the German money thinking that money with swastikas on it surely must be useless. Somehow I had still kept some of it. Now it was dearly needed. We went to a nearby store and all they had was bread and sugar. Of course we bought as much as the stamps permitted us. Quickly we left the outskirts of Chemnitz the way we had come. We were still in our, by now battered, airforce uniforms. We asked for directions and we walked around Chemnitz toward the west. The Americans were supposed to be in Thüringen (Thüringia) some 40 or 50 km away.

Going past a railroad station we noticed a passenger train, full of people, all steamed up and ready to go in the westerl direction. We jumped aboard, tickets or no tickets. We did not bother with such little details. After a while the train stopped, everybody got off and the engine moved to the other end of the train preparing to return to the east. This was near the border between the Russians and the Americans.

TO THE AMERICAN ZONE

We started to walk together with a couple of civilians along the tracks to the west. Soon we saw an American soldier doing sentry duty. Compared to the German regulations this was ridiculous. He was sitting on a chair under a large beach umbrella and appeared to be reading a book and listening to music on the radio. He had leaned his rifle against the table. The table was about ten feet from the rail embankment. It did not seem to interest him the least bit that there were people on the embankment walking towards him, two of them in tattered German uniforms.

We felt safer to descend to the other side of the embankment and we walked right past him staying out of his sight. Easy! What a joy! We may even succeed! Just have to get farther away from the border so we would not be sent back to the Russian zone once we give ourselves up to the Americans.

As we started to cross a highway, suddenly an American truck came along full of German POW's standing shoulder to shoulder. We did not get a chance to hide. Still, it did not stop, presumably because they could not have squeezed another two guys onto this truck or they just did not give a damn. Despite our fumbling our lady luck was still smiling and we were still free men! We tried to be more careful to stay out of sight and continued walking to the west farther away from the border towards the city of Gera.

Eventually we were sure that we were in Thüringen. Hans thought that we should now turn to the north. He remembered having an aunt who had settled in Northern Germany after fleeing from Estonia. She could probably help us both. I argued that it is still too risky to start moving to the north since we do not know where the border was and we may end up in Russian hands again. And then it would again be to Siberia. This time for sure.

Neither of us could convince the other. Finally we shook hands and we parted company. Hans went north and I went west. This was a difficult decision to make. It would have been so much easier and pleasanter to stay together. Walking along alone felt like being alone in the wide world, knowing nobody and not having a definite place to go. Still, the fear of falling into Russian hands had firmed my decision to go straight west. Later I have wondered several times how did Hans Puhk succeed? Did he find his aunt and where is he now?

Going through a village I suddenly saw a military truck coming with a large five pointed star on the door. Damn, again the Russians! In panic I turned and thought to duck somewhere. Before I could take a couple of steps the truck had passed. Actually it had been an American truck with a white star. The fear of Russians was so great that only after the truck had passed did I realize that the star was white and not red.

BRUNO BECOMES A FARMER

I got safely past Gera, but then walking became more and more painful. I had developed a huge boil on my buttock. Going through a village I thought to try to stay there and pretend to be a civilian farm laborer. I found a farmer, who was willing to take me on since he needed help in the fields. It was early morning and the farm family was eating breakfast. Without inviting me to the table they asked me to sit there on a bench until they finished eating and then we could all go to the fields. Of course I was hungry, but I did not complain.

Once in the fields they noticed that I could hardly walk. Next morning they put me on a horse wagon and took me to the local clinic. There a man-and-wife team, both physicians, tended to the ills of a number of people all waiting for their turn in the same large treatment room. They took a look at my buttock and asked me to wait until others had left. Then they unceremoniously just cut the boil open, no local anesthesia, no frills and left the dollar size wound open to drain. I was lucky that the farmer had waited, since I could not have made it back on my own.

In a couple of days I felt better and I started to work at the farm. According to German regulations every person has to be registered with the Bürgermeister (the head of a village or the major of a city) certifying that the person lives at a certain address. This was good for me, since this way I received some sort of a paper certifying that I did live in this village. From somewhere I got an old suit. It was really way too large for me. I thought to take the coat apart piece by piece, turn the cloth inside out and sew it together by hand making it smaller to fit me.

ON THE RUN AGAIN

Before I could start on this tailoring project, one evening, it was in June 1945, the local policeman stopped in front of our farm to chat. In our farm there lived also a lady with two small children. They were refugees from Bonn to escape the American bombings. The policeman had come to tell this lady that it had been announced that the Americans would hand Thüringen over to the Russians. The transfer was supposed to take place not sooner than in two days and not later than in seven days.

What a bombshell! The lady was upset complaining that there was no way how she could move 150 km with two small children when the public transportation was not yet functioning. The lady turned to me, "At least you should go." "Yes, but how can I do it on foot that fast over such a long distance?" "Swipe a bicycle." "From where?" "From the farmer." I turned to the policeman and asked him what should I do. He made a sweeping motion with his open hand palm down, clenched the fist and stuck it into his pocket. Turned around and left without saying a word. He had made the well-known gesture for swiping something. Hell of a note. Not being a thief by heart I had asked a policeman and he had agreed, in effect, that stealing a bicycle was the right thing to do in my situation.

I told the farmer that since the Russians are coming I cannot stay any longer and tomorrow morning I would start walking south to Halle. The next morning I asked to borrow a bike for a ride to the Bürgermeister so I could register myself out from his farm. He agreed that this was the proper thing to do.

I bundled up my ill-fitting suit and dropped it out the window so I could pick it up outside on the street. Went to take the bike - the tires were flat. Started quickly to pump them up. The tires were old and had stretched. They did not want to stay on the rims. I worked feverishly. Pump a little, adjust the tire, pump again, adjust again. I started to sweat: unless I get these tires on those rims the Russians may catch me again. I finally succeeded. When wheeling the bike to the gate the farmer saw me, "Have you come back already?" - "Well, no, I am only going now." Little did the farmer know about someone running away from the Russians. I did not give a darn about the records at the Bürgermeister's. To lessen the chance of the farmer sending someone after me, instead of riding south to Halle I started to pedal west towards Jena as had been my plan all along.

Since now I had a document from the Bürgermeister and I did not wear my airforce coat any longer and since I was in a rush I took the highway instead of riding on some footpaths. Soon enough I started to doubt about my wisdom. There was an American checkpoint on the highway.

The guard was looking in the other direction. I thought to just quietly pedal past him. I did not succeed. He stopped me. Showed him the paper from the Bürgermeister. He did not understand German and told me to go back. I kept on gesticulating towards fields and told him in German that I am a farm laborer and I have to go to work. He kept on telling me in English that I do not have the proper documents for travel. I did not let him know that I had learned English in high school and understood him well. There we went back and forth, he in English and I in German, until finally he gave up and let me pass.

Towards the evening I got to Jena and turned south towards Würzburg. Just before getting out of town I was surprised to see a boy on the sidewalk with a blue-black-white armband. He must be an Estonian! "Hey, what are you doing here?" He explained that there is a refugee camp run by Americans in some German military barracks in Jena. There are lots of Estonians and people of other nationalities. Everybody is free to come and go. Since it started to get dark, why not spend the night at that camp? At the camp they did not ask any questions and assigned me to a bed in an attic with lots of bunk beds. Other Estonians there did not seem to be concerned about my news that Thüringen will be handed over to the Russians in a few days.

To continue living as a civilian I needed civilian documentation. So on the next day after my arrival I went to the City Hall of Jena and obtained a Vorläufiger Fremdenpass - Temporary Foreigner's Passport. They did not ask many questions either. Of course this passport did not prove that I had not been in the German Army, since the issue date was 9 June 1945. But it was better than my military Soldbuch, which I still had.

I did not trust to stay in Thüringen. Who knows what the Americans will do? For all I know they may even officially hand us over to the Russians for repatriation to Estonia. Only will it be Estonia? So I stayed in that camp for another day or two and in the morning started to pedal south. In addition to the German Temporary Foreigner's Passport by now I also had an identification card from that camp in Jena, which stated that I was a citizen of the Estonian Democratic Republic. Things were looking up.

As it turned out, those people in Jena were later put on a train by the Americans and the train started to move east where the Russians were and not west. Nerve racking! After a while the train turned south and took the people to the Augsburg Displaced Persons camp near Munich.

After having left Thüringen on my bicycle I asked directions to a refugee camp. I was guided to Bad Kissingen. Getting closer to that camp it appeared to me that I had been directed to a gathering place run by the Russians. That they were trying to repatriate people from Eastern Europe. Sounded again like Siberia to me. Without getting any closer to that camp I turned the bike around and pedaled away towards Würzburg in the American Zone and freedom.

Many years later I learned that my fear of being captured by the Russians had been well founded. My classmate Villi Kiinros did not manage to escape to the west. The Russians sentenced him to ten years into a prison camp in Siberia for having been in the German military. In the eyes of the Russians my sin of having been in a German uniform equaled Villi's. In April of 1944 we had joined the German Airforce together and spent most of the time together for the next thirteen months until the World War Two was over in May of 1945. Easily I could have had the same fate as Villi's.

It sure feels the Almighty had guided every step of my way during the war and finally to freedom. There had been just too many possible pitfalls, which had not been meant for me.

Young Airforcemen training in Libava , May 1944 Bruno is second from the right in the second row

GUSTEN LUTTER PUTS THINGS INTO PERSPECTIVE

I have been working with couple of Estonian travel agents, one in NY (Amest), one in Tallinn (Wris), to lock in hotel bookings and event tickets for the forthcoming Jaanipäev and Laulu/Tantsu Pidu.

The woman agent in NY was going to e-mail me some vouchers, but they did not show up as I expected. So I called her yesterday, and learned that she had had an accident, severely burned her feet by spilling a pot of boiling tea water on her feet, with stockings on yet, and was laid up, immobilized, for over a week.

This reminded me of one of my (and Arne's/Heiki's), cousins, Sven Ellandi, couple of years older than me, who was in the Luftwaffe Auxiliary Service at the end of the war. He was captured in Czechoslovakia, tortured by the Checks (tchehhi põrgus) and sentenced to Siberian prisoner of war labor camps. Prisoners were worked hard and starved and dying.

But, if a prisoner was injured in an accident and apparently judged still capable of work, frequently he was placed into a prison hospital, where they received more food.

Sven told me that one of the symptoms of terminal starvation was the swelling of feet and legs. He reached that stage, and decided to commit a self-inflicted injury that might place him in the hospital.

He burned his feet in boiling water! Luckily, he was hospitalized, regained his health and strength, and was placed into a different prison camp with better conditions for survival.

Eventually, Sven was released from prison, managed his way back to Estonia, was even permitted to enter and finish engineering college. I don't know how Sven's life evolved from Siberia to 1990, when I met him in Tallinn, but in the 1980s and 1990s he was a principal engineering troubleshooter of Kalev (pre-war "Kave") chocolate factory.

(Another cousin of ours, Heino Gustavson, was also in Siberian prisoner of war camps, but after return to Estonia, was denied permission to enroll as a regular, resident medical student in Tartu University . He completed college, though, as a "corresponding student", but in history and German language and eventually was granted the right to be recognized as Ph D in history).

PHOTOGRAPHY WHILE IN TRANSIT: E-MAIL SNIPPETS FROM CONVERSATIONS WITH THE AUTHORS

Mankind has always had the urge to depict, be it accurately, symbolically or using cryptic. It uses many modalities to achieve this. Perhaps word of mouth and body language were the earliest languages but they were limited by their transience. There was no way to accurately convey those notions to the next moment let alone to those centuries or even millenniums away.

Perhaps the earliest form of (semi) permanent depiction was illustration be it on cave walls, rocks, papyrus or whatever. Early writings in various hieroglyphics followed, as did images on portable media such as paper or canvas using tools such as pencil, pen and paintbrush. Yet later man learned to use physics and engineering to immortalize events and thoughts. The camera was born.

Back in 2010 during the HOP project **I, Mai, remarked** among our e-mail dialogues:
The volley of photos has created a new interchange of information which I will add to the photo data base. It has also created an interesting reflection
Peep Vesilind posed the following question:
'Why did our parents take so many photos? It must have been expensive, at a time when they had little money. They must have sensed something about their situation and how the memories of this had to be documented. Interesting.'
Mai continues:
Reflecting on the archive of photos they seem to categorise thus
- official photos eg school, document validation
- recording of personal events i.e. our people as they led their individual lives.....
It would be interesting to explore this topic further......
I have ample photos taken at 'photo sits' in Geislingen, (the more spontaneous ones were taken by Jakob Liholm and Peter Olesk), only two pairs of photos from Estonia and in my first five, even twelve years in Oz only one set of photos (taken as a series in 1961) and two other photos excluding my school photos. Perhaps that is why I remained so attached to the school annuals-- they had photos of me in various activities eg debating.
Among our collection was also a photo of father in his uniform as a German NCO.

It was a real eye opener to me to see all those photos of Geislingen folk going about their lives and to actually see photos of groups of people. I was not really aware that such a richness of social activity existed among our people in Geislingen.

However translations of my father's letters from the Lake Ladoga front relate that mother (who was a good artist) used to send him sketches of me in her letters.

I would be interested to read what your feelings/experiences were with photos in Geislingen."

Ilvi Joe wrote: Pondering the profusion of photographs matter, I have the following thoughts/recollections:
Somewhere in my reading of Estonia's history I recall reference to the fact that photography was quite advanced in Estonia; even some invention occurred here (was it associated with the so-called "spy camera"?). Therefore, it should not be surprising that taking photos was rather common and quite a number of people took cameras with them when they fled (perhaps Eric Soovere is best known among us).

As for Geislingen DP camp, August Sulev was a professional photographer (I think he had been one in Eesti already before fleeing) and lived almost across the street from us. And he wasn't the only one with a camera. All the photos in my family were taken by him and I don't think my mother paid him anything for it - perhaps some cigarettes, or coffee. We have to remember that many DPs worked at American military bases or provided services for Americans (for example, my mother knit tanus, sweaters, etc., and sold to American families) and they obtained goods from Americans and the PX.
Ülo Kuhi was able to offer more detail: My step-father Jakob Liholm had an enlarger in Geislingen. He brought it with him to USA and I still have it in my attic. He took many photos of Geislingen and even made some Christmas cards with some of his photos. He was also into wood burning and made a wooden Estonian coat of arms with two Eesti flags.
Arved Plaks added to the 'spy camera' notion: In 1994 Estonian postal service issued a stamp to honour the invention of the spy camera, which confirms your recollection. The stamp has a picture of the camera.

Tiiu Rodima Gray-Fow shares her reflections: "RE: the profusion of photos taken by our parents in Geislingen.

One of the few items that my father took with him as we fled from Eesti was his camera. I recall him taking pictures throughout our Geislingen sojourn. I believe this camera was manufactured in Germany rather than Estonia. It came with us to the U. S. and was used for many many years.

An insight as to why there were so many attempts to record their life in Geislingen may have to do with what happened to their photos from Estonia. When my parents left, in that frantic three day period between the German withdrawal and the Russian re-entry, they packed their photo albums into a makeshift bundle with sheets and pillowcases. The albums may have been an afterthought. We need to remember that many thought they would be able to return. Anyway, the bundle was stolen and with it all the photos. I remember, as a child, spending hours looking at the photos that my aunts and uncle, on my mother's side, had taken with them. There were a few photos of my parents and myself as well, ones that they had shared with the relatives. My father's family did not escape, and he had no photos of his childhood, or his relatives until the late 1960's when he discovered that they had survived. Even then he only received some current pictures. It wasn't until I went to Estonia for the first time in the late 90's, that I saw photos of my father as a boy and as a young man. He did not live to see them.

Our story may not be all that unique.

I have compensated for the loss of a pictorial history of my family by taking thousands of pictures and having a very hard time getting rid of any."

Peep added: Our father also had a box camera in Geislingen which came with us to the US in 1949. I valued it as a relic of the past, but I did not know what to do with it. I knew that its significance would have little meaning to my children and that it would eventually be thrown away. As a result, I decided to send it, and a small suitcase I used on my trip to the US, to the Museum of the Occupations in Tallinn. They were quite pleased to get these items. I would encourage all of you to consider sending your artefacts to the museum. While their display space is limited, they will at least keep the items safe, and our mementos may someday have value to historians.

Priit Vesilind (Peep's brother) has similar recollections: I remember that Isa had a square black box camera (no flash) that looked like a magician's prop of some sort. He didn't take photos all the time, but had the awareness to record the outlines and happier details of our life. I think he got the film from the US Army PX in Ludwigsburg, where he worked during the week. Sulev's work was professional, and the flattering portraits he made of family groups were of tremendous value to people who needed a rough "P.R. kit" to send to prospective sponsors or employers abroad. One of our family stories is that our sponsors in the US had been planning a laboring job for Isa when we arrived in the US, but then he saw the Sulev portrait of a distinguished, immaculately dressed young professional with his comely wife and children, he rejected that job and went out looking for something more suitable.

Kalju Kubits commented: Why so many photos/cameras? My father too, had a camera and took lots of photos. He also bought several musical instruments. That cameras and musical instruments are costly wouldn't necessarily stop people. When currency could become worthless you don't want money at all - you put it into "stuff," i.e., buy hard assets, things that have a value regardless of what happens to the currency. They are also easier to move across international borders. One reason among many.

Peep introduced some interesting reflections: This is all the more interesting because Vanad Eestlased did not want to have photos taken of them, believing that their "hing" would be transferred to the picture, abandoning their body.

Liivi Joe commented in a diversity of these thoughts. She wrote: Makes perfect sense to me that the spy camera should be invented by the people who don't want their "hing" stolen... we are in the "hingede aeg" (Soul/spirit times) now and I know that they should be sensed but not seen. People still talk about leaving food out for them.
However, with the coming of modernity to Estonia following independence, the move was to become more 'European' whatever that means. I think people from that era spoke of photos needing to capture the very spirit of the person.
I know that August Sulev worked hard at portrait photography, practising (Yep! Practicsing in Oz lingo and I gather USA is not too persnickety about the practise/practice issue so I probably should have typed the former given Liivi grew up in USA. MM) with lights and shadows. Prewar he had a studio in Poltsamaa and had photographed the interior of the huge palace which got bombed July 13, 1941. He took some, but probably not all our pre-war family photos, both formal and informal.

Juri Linask added interest to the reflections: I don't buy Aarne's' s story about the hing. Estonians were not of that mind set. By the time photography came, Estonians were extensively Christianized. Moreover, Estonians, even pre-nineteenth

Jakob Liholm's photo of Ulo Kuhi and his mother with mother and I.

Perhaps this was the photo which was to bridge over 50 years of time.

At Maano Milles' bidding, given Maano too had lived in Hospital weihe in Geislingen, and I had just met him in New York, Ulo contacted me to see if I could add more data to the Geislingen DVD he was compiling at the time.

My reply, that I didn't know who he was looking for but I was looking for someone called Ulo who had lived nearby and whose mother was friends with mine but whose surname I had forgotten.

All searches to date had failed to resolve the quandary.

Across the cyberspace flashed that photo.

It is during those communications that I remarked how remote I felt from all the 'kids' I was separated from.

I was remote no more. Geislingen 2008, WNE and its sibling books were born and then time moved on.

century were quite sophisticated in understanding physical phenomena. My family pictures go back to into that time period, and I never see any fear in anyone's eyes. People were looking to permanentize a record of their existence. Most people who understand the process are! Don't we take picture for the same reason today? It is a natural human instinct to create/have a record. My older brother Rein saved all he could to buy a camera in Geislingen, he was then only about 12, and he clicked away much as we do now. Except, he had to develop and print his own pictures and money was a limiting element for most of us. I believe someone let him use an enlarger. Will have to check on the latter. Anyway there really is no great shortage of historical pictures in Estonia. The limiting element was economics and

vailability of materials and tools for photography. Agfa did not get into mass production as Kodak did in the U.S.

During our exodus Ülo Soovere's father managed to get film for his camera by bartering alcohol for film with Luftwaffe pilots. This was not without great risk to his well being. Even the taking of pictures was in many places prohibited. Unfortunately, some of his art was lost, because he could not develop the film before "the noise had ended."

How imperative it becomes to ensure that people share their various perspectives: It would never have occurred to me that all this rich cultural life was occurring in DP camps in Germany: My more cynical mind perhaps preoccupied by the risks of carrying letters from my father and that photo of him, I believe concealed in my clothing.

One wonders what motivation lay in such actions: was it a situation of blind love or infatuation. or maybe a hope that the German connection would bring us better chances once within German terrain. I guess that is an answer I will never know.

While it didn't plague me while in Geislingen where father was a 'hero' like all Estonian children's soldier fathers,in Oz with learning a little British history about WW I, the Battle of Dunkirk and more latterly the infamous Holocaust leaves me asking, how did we manage to not be shot in transit and perhaps it accounts for the chill I still feel at airports when being asked for my very 'boring' current documents.

As a clinician of course I ask, given most people don't like relating or hearing about ugliness in life what would motivate someone to photograph it. Most of what one sees in our media has a ghoulish flavour to it, but then **there are and have always been honest photographers who put themselves at peril to tell what needed to be said.**

Eric Soovere's photos some of which his son has generously shared for this book are of that ilk: They say so much that words could not depict.

Donald Koppel's book "Ma Hoidsin neid sulle" (I saved them for you) is the ultimate in dignified representation of Estonia's brutally induced fall.

And perhaps another example of soulful representation of such turmoil is Oddmund Joakimsen's "Narvik 1940" which I bought while adventuring along the Norway' arctic region in 2013. While it is about another land's politics it does graphically depict what hideous climatic conditions young men had to endure in addition to the military hardware. It was not too different to the wintery conditions around Narva and towards Leningrad where many of our fathers were deployed.

MYTHOLOGY, SOUL, SPIRIT, SERENDIPITY OR INTUITION

Part of the magic of the Geislingen project which began way back in 2005 were the 'manylogues', which were chatter on all manner of subjects sparked off by someone throwing in a quandary about our youth. We learned a lot with this simple chit-chat and at times came bonuses as the conversation meandered off onto another at times only tangentially related theme. It exasperated some who at times took respite from the e-mails and of course it fascinated others.

I must admit I was always intrigued having been largely separated from Estoniana for years by a twist of fate.

One such manylogue began with an exploration of why our folks had so few photos during wartime and our early days in Geislingen. Many very logical thoughts came forward ranging from access to cameras to the street-wisdom of using or carrying them in dangerous terrain.

Each culture has its mythology which even if considered obsolete at times, continues in our subconscious. We instinctively just do some things.

Peep Vesilind put forward an interesting notion that 'vanad Eestlased' didn't want photos taken of them, believing that their "Hing' would be transferred to the picture, abandoning their body.

How many constructs one could derive from that. It seemed so irrelevant to the theme in hand yet so relevant. We were living in dangerous times: Perhaps we still are in some ways.

I was always adamant not to have my kids in children's 'beauty/cuteness' contests, cute as I thought they were, while others I knew, perhaps more objectively wished them a long way further away. I had always hated contrived photos and the one taken on my first day at school in Australia and published in a local Melbourne paper, I still feel was responsible for bringing me to grief a plenty. I had no wish to expose my kids to such risk: There were other ways of 'earning their stripes'. One could definitely say in a cryptic way that my 'hing' was intermittently transferred from me after that published photo.

Perhaps it all hangs on how we define 'hing'.

Peep had a few thoughts on such a definition. He wrote: '.... "Hing" is difficult to translate. It is not the equivalent of the "soul", which is more like the Estonian "vaim", although "vaim" is also "ghost". Hing seems to be a spirit that occupies a living body (including non-human animals) and is the spiritual essence of a person (or animal). Oskar Loorits has written extensively on this in "Eesti Rahvausundi Maailmavaade" (Estonian Folk World View).[Stockholm, Eesti Raamat, date unknown]. Loorits says that old Estonians believed in two types of "hing". One was the "hing" that was literally one's breath, and this personal "hing" died when a person stopped breathing. The second kind of "hing" was the detached "hing" or "irdhing" which not only survived the death of a person but could wander all around during one's life. After death the "irdhing" might even hang around the house for a while. It did not go to some heaven, but eventually got tired of hanging around and left. The fear during one's life was that the "irdhing" would leave prematurely, and this is why pictures were dangerous. If was believed that the "irdhing" would prefer the picture to the real person and leave.

I am not sure if Jüri (The late Jüri Linask) believes in the two "hing" theory. It seems very reasonable to me. Or at the very least, a lot more reasonable than the beliefs of some of our contemporary religions '

Jüri was very much a philosopher and thinker. His presence in the e-mails always made my day.

Yes many of us looked at religion in a diversity of ways in relation to our own youth. Many of the authors of this book relate to their praying and their prayers for delivery from harm being answered. It was a consolation which gave their folk courage to continue in that treacherous trek: But then one, maybe both of my sons would say what was the meaning of the need for the trek: Why did a deity permit such events to occur. I am no theologian and certainly this is not a theological tome.

Many of us have at times asked ourselves what irrationality prompted us to change our minds and avoid an event which was to produce unexpected carnage. I can certainly recall grandfather, who by life's ravages had been reduced to a pessimist repeatedly alluding to an occurrence where he was walking home from the factory he worked at. The factory was noisy masking surrounding noise, the masking exacerbated to ears which were probably already deafened by chronic exposure to industrial noise. He usually walked that journey and was in no hurry. For some reason he decided to run fast, not something typical of a sixty year old man after a long day's toil. Perhaps out of breath, given his age he slowed down and looked over his shoulder: The spot where he had begun to run had vanished and had been replaced by a bomb crater. It could be that he had not lost his vibration sense which uses different nerve pathways, but who knows: He always believed that something/one spared him.

I suspect that many of us could tell such tales: among them ones who had a change of heart about travelling on the Moero which was a more robust ship, and theoretically protected by humanitarian code being a hospital ship.

I have always been cautious in exploring such notions for fear of opening 'Pandora's box': My attempts have inevitably brought some form of grief with them and always relevant to the reason for trying to open it. I just let Pandora's box be until it begins to flip itself open.

Liivi Joe reflected on this: I think what you have to say about Pandora´s boxes has a lot of merit to it - particularly as I am still mulling over the several paragraphs about the soul and the spirit - which, I think, I have at one point written about to the effect that as far as I know (and here I differ with Peep-Aarne Vesilind who cites Loorits to the effect that there are two different kinds of ´hing´ - one being breath, the other soul) - I recall what I wrote was that Finno-Ugrics scalped their enemies so the ´hing´ could depart forever - when you go to sleep it only departs for the night through your breathing but returns in the morning when you wake, something like that. In any case, your breath and your soul are one and the same in that case. In English ´takes your breath away´ could be construed to corroborate with that as if something moves you to the very bottom of your soul you can associate your breathing with it - or suchlike.

Now, the spirit, or ´vaim´ on the other hand, comes to you from without and can overcome your soul, or ´hing´ As it is abstract I can understand why there can be a lot of argumentation about it. But when you consider the basis of Christianity being ´The Father, the Son, and The Holy Ghost´ then we understand why that abstract presence comes from outside us and we have to account for it in some way - we concur, I think, that all religions are man-made and there has never been a single civilization anywhere in the world at any time that did not create a religion in order to account for this ´spirit´ (ghost, or ´vaim´ or whatever you call it).

For Estonians there is the Kurivaim* (or evil spirit) and the Halastaja vaim (the merciful spirit) and you can conjure either up depending on which your hing (soul) needs at any particular juncture -

*The notion of some form of hex to ward off evil spirits is not culture specific!

Whether this spirit (or ghost) can spook us I am not sure but I think your advice about the Pandora´s box is probably reflected very much in my own family and in Estonia in general terms - burning old letters, memorabilia - things that remind you of horrible events in the past - and there have been a lot here as we know - best not to hold on to them - then as a result we have arguments on the net as we had this winter about why do we need this Diaspora Conference this fall anyway - just let bygones be???"

Maybe Liivi is right, maybe not. There is a lot we don't know about the subconscious mind but then there is something I have learned in my decades as a clinician: During my mental health work I have always had a healthy respect for when it was time to pause exploring some quandary: That the patient's emotional resources had reached their safety threshold. Any time I was by whatever means urged to push past it, both patient and I agreed that my instinct to not explore had been correct: Things went amiss. Again there may be many explanations but do they matter: If something steps in the way, if possible turmoil 'might' follow should we tempt fate? Maybe it is called intuition, maybe a name yet not in our dictionaries.

And perhaps we know when the right time is approaching and we begin to procrastinate: Maybe inadvertently! Since we left Europe I have had a healthy respect for crossing the Czech-Polish border. Many of my colleagues would try to encourage me to visit Prague which is one of the kosher places to visit for Oz folk. My answer was a predictable 'no bl---dy way'. I could never put forward a reason: It certainly seemed not related to the military ugliness which I knew was part of those times.

Early last year there was a flashback: I yielded to the urge to know what lay across the border from Dresden which I had been my closest point to visiting the forbidden apple. I bought a return bus ticket from Dresden to optimize my chances of a safe return.

I had spent the day before touring the terrain around Dresden and Jena: I had carefully mapped out the train routes but missed a well labelled critical major train interchange delaying my return to Dresden till after midnight.

Needless to say I slept in and my trip to Teplice was very curtailed and that to Duchcov (once known as Dux) obviated. Was this subconscious avoidance on my part!!

It was a civilian incident- one where a "hing" definitively ceased to be: I am still procrastinating whether I should follow it up: When I get that typed out letter printed, placed into an envelope and I drag myself to the post office to buy a stamp for it I will know that the time has arrived.** But next time in Europe I will certainly cast an eye on Dux!

** I finally posted it about a month ago (early July 2014) but no doubt the reply will take some time- would I like to know before this book is published: Dunno!!

Liivi's reflection concluded thus: "For myself, ...I don´t like to repeat myself as I did with the Geislingen segment of my life - writing one version in Estonian and then another version completely different in English - that made me feel very untrue to my own memory - I have another segment that I have been itching to write down whose time just never seems to have been ripe, and that is Visiting Occupied Estonia 1969-1991 - that being one of the suggested topics I think it would probably be safer to stick with that." Perhaps Liivi is right: if one doesn't feel true to oneself then one should seriously consider what impedes this and respect that feeling.

Maybe if really doesn't matter what we call the phenomenon: be it mythology, soul, spirit, serendipity or intuition: It is a phenomenon which has a place in all our lives and narratives.

ANTS TAMM SHARES SOME TRADITIONAL ESTONIAN WISDOM

....my father and others told me 50 or 60 years ago: If two Estonians meet, after a while they have created three or four organizations and they immediately start qualrrelling and talk badly of the others, misunderstand each other and so on...

INGE PRUKS PARAPHRASES THIS DIFFERENTLY

I'm sorry this 70th anniversary has brought out so much unexpected correspondence, I guess we are all hurting inside somewhere, and at least you are prepared to speak up. Some pain is too much to put under a microscope, and I guess that's why conferences will be run by academics who deal objectively with secondary sources, rather than ordinary people who only have their painful memories and family stories to tell. I didn't know there was such resentment against us as refugees.

Everyone seems to have a bee in their bonnet, or else some agenda or deeply-held grudge.

...and I didn't know that there was this deep resentment against refugees from Estonia. .....deserting Estonia .... the World War II refugees, whose very lives and children were threatened. I'm sure that no one abandoned their country in 1941 just for a better (economic/material) life.

....her opening sentence has the word 'soovisid', which is a little over-the-top and insensitive to me, as if we (especially we 'mudilased') were presented with a smorgasbord of choice and haughtily pointed to Germany as our choice for the way out to some dreamland. There was no 'soovisid' about it, I was dragged out of Estonia.

....her pointing out the word 'lahkusid', which (like 'soovisid') again hides a multitude of feelings -- envy, condemnation, sarcasm, anger, and a wrong perception of why people left...

My mother suffered all her life for leaving her family behind, even though she grew to love Australia. Those who stayed just think we are all happy millionaires down here, they cannot imagine the ache and deep longing that a person in exile has to live with all their life. And of course these feelings were certainly passed on to me. I have tried to liberate my sons from such feelings, I didn't want it to continue for another generation.

After a life of 'hidden stuff' which has always weighed on me, I am totally against secrecy and double meanings of all kinds. I have tried to be super-honest with my own two boys, no matter how bad that made me look in their eyes.

JUST A REFLECTION.

Over the decades as a clinician, my desk has been deluged with requests for participation in questionnaires within research projects; many on behavioural medicine.

Given my penchant has always been behavioural medicine, I marvel at how glibly trust of another is requested. In a project on refugeeism how many of us would respond (were that our reality) that our father was Estonia's no 1 spy, or the head honcho for a co-opted German unit. Nor would the locals of where ever we now live share such information. Thus any other answers would be based on a contrived answer for the preceding question.

I too marvel at the questions: At times I reflect, had you walked that road you would know that question is not relevant, inappropriate, likely to precipitate needless angst. Etc.

I marvel that the researchers cannot do a data base search among their colleagues for those who do have first hand information about such matters, to at least explore the appropriateness of the question be it related to data or emotional sequelae.

Many a time I have responded: Question not possible to answer.

That has further reinforced my stance that such material needs to be sought in first voice: The author then can find a means of avoiding that which cannot be shared without distortion of further data.

More times, I have been tempted to write "Go where the pepper grows" as the Nordics would say. Discretion is often very thinly spread in those documents. MM

DESPITE THEIR HORRENDOUS TREK THEIR FOLKS KEPT THEIR SERENITY

Boys in Narva did just what little boys do anywhere. They play out the roles of those they admire: Who greater to admire than their fathers and older brothers who were fighting on the Narva front.

Children are resourceful mites: The can adapt and improvise. They don't need toys or the real things.

Among the more powerful lines of Estonia's soldiers' songs are the words "Kiiver peas ja relv on kaes": That the helmet is donned and the weapon is in one's hand.

Who knows whom those helmets belonged to except perhaps who ever owned them no longer needed them. Maybe the insignias were even from another army, maybe legible, maybe not. Small children cannot read and even if they can, they can read improvised meanings into words.

Yes these little fellows of torrid times were in battle with their folks.

WELL, ALMOST ALWAYS! THAT'S LIFE'S REALITY!
PHOTOS BY ERIK SOOVERE : SENT BY ILO SOOVERE

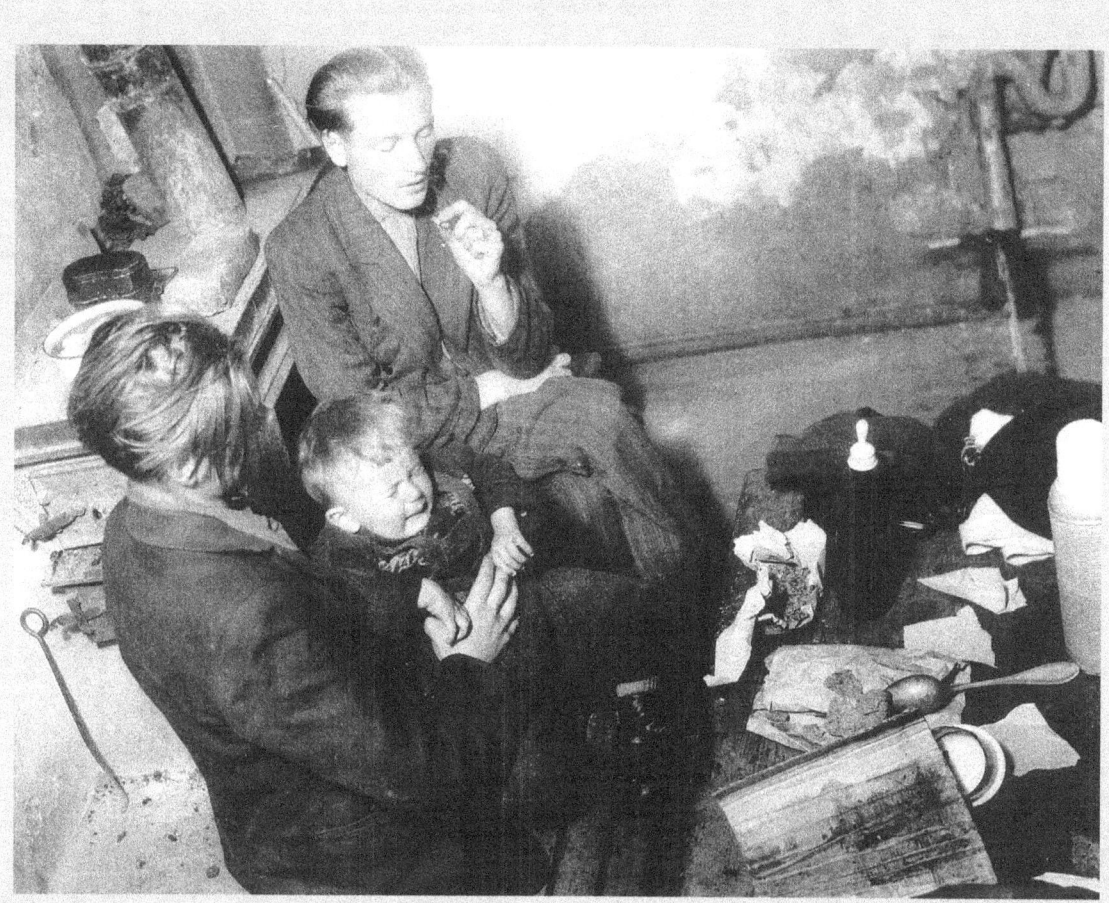

It is human nature to present our journeys in a refined format: That is what society expects of us. But then society has not always walked the streets of hell: Nor does it have such imagery to describe. Perhaps such imagery can only be described in staccato form just as Ilo Soovere has done.

"Heino Trees smokes while Ilo Soovere cries.
Wednesday 23 May 1944. Three days after crossing the Sudetenland –Germany border we awaken at 6.15 am: It is challengingly cold in the barrack at Hof.
In front of the station a crowd, and we sneak our stuff on the train, despite the American commanders' order that no one could ride along.
We next make it to Zeuleroda, and get food stamps for "Swedes", as we were travelling with improvised papers saying we were from there. For each person Eric, Leili and Ilo Soovere, Heino Trees, Leili's brother and Kuusepau, an Estonian who ditched his German uniform, we got 100gm of butter, and over 3 of us managed to get 12 kg of bread. What a treasure!
Leili gets firewood and we move into a small room next to the baggage area of the station. There is a stove, table, 2 benches. We light a fire with torn up picture of H. Hitler..... We eat in warm room and as much as we wanted. Several eggs are boiling. Leili and Eric sleep on the benches, Ilo in the stroller, Heino on the table, and Kuuspuu sets a plank taken from a wall onto one end of the baggage wheelbarrow and the other onto the chair. All night the plank is unstable and creaks."

Such a trek was not the venue for Ph.D. type prose. Nor are memories of such optimally shared via the latter. Ilo has spoken it how it truly felt. It was life as a fugitive: Life on the run.

EPP LÕOKE'S FATHER HAD A CAMERA

Epp writes:
My father also took lots of photos in Geislingen.
I have 2 albums full of photos taken in Geislingen and on the ship to NZ and wonder what will become of them in the future.

The children were christened, some belatedly after the long trek from Estonia to the camps. Pastor Karl Raudsepp was Epp's christening celebrant.

And children played with the children who lived nearby: Given there were four to five families per house and at times more there was no shortage of playmates. The toys of course were improvised.

YES, LIFE WAS KEPT POSITIVE FOR THEM

Geislingen had three kindergartens so routine and learning became a regular feature of their lives, as did grade and secondary schools

And there were celebrations for all manner of occasions be they birthdays or national festivals. While their land appeared to be lost the spirit did not falter.

They treasured the families and friends who too had survived that trek and relished the times they shared together.

ESTONIAN VILLAGES (DP CAMPS) WERE DOTTED ALL OVER GERMANY: SOME LARGE, OTHERS TINY

That trek from war torn Estonia is part of many of their lives: Some of them remember better times in the early 1930s: For others of them their preverbal memory was born amid the chaos of war and for yet others in the camps to where their parents and older siblings had fled.
The latter's identities have partly been formed by a composite of photos taken at those times and their families' and friends mythology.
There appears to be an innate need to touch such a past. While planning the Geislingen grade school and younger reunion in 2008, people who had been born after the camps closed asked to join the e-mail planning dialogues. At the reunion were some who had been born on the cusp.   MM

1949 View from our window in Schlosshalde, Geislingen

Marje Limion/Medri was one of the children born on the cusp. Her parents and her late brother Heikki had fled from Estonia.
I feel that it is important to include those of the cohort born on the cusp in this book because their identities were moulded by the same ignoble events which transpired in Estonian during World War II.

The next ten pages are a picture story shared by Marje, as it was presented to her.

And of course among them are DPs who were truly born on the run. Among them are Kersti Totsas/Linask and Kulla Tõnisson. I am sure that there are endless others- too many to name.   MM

Images of Geislingen, the beginning of Marje's story, The images were largely taken in late 1948, summer 1949

THEY WERE HOME TO THEM UNTIL THEY COULD FIND ADOPTIVE HOMELANDS

That's Dad's car in front (of the barracks)- guess he was home from Nürnberg. He called his car The Titanic. Mom (Maimu Limion, Marje and Heikki Limion

Geislingen 1950? - barakid - Left to right - ??, ??, Marje Limion, Heikki Limion holding the Loorand's dog "Cutie"

1950? - barakid - Mom (Maimu Limion) speaking with an unidentified man who appears in several of our family photos.

Laundry day in Geislingen... mom (Maimu Limion)

Mai, I remembered you were interested in how people arrived in Germany. Mom told me that she and Heikki got on the ship in Tallinn during the day and the ships all sailed at night. They were aboard the middle ship of a three-ship convoy. The ship in front and the ship behind were bombed and sank. She told me she was strangely calm throughout the whole thing thinking that if they were hit and sank, well that's just the way it would be.

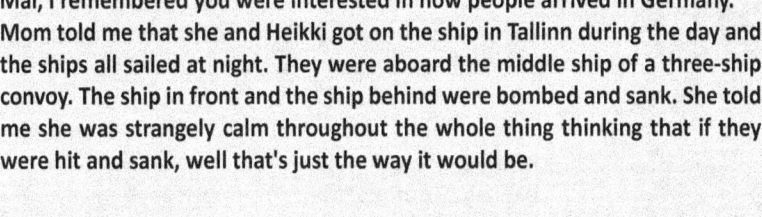

When the DP camps were officially ended by UNNRA (in 1949?), we moved into "the barakid".
These were close to, if not across from the hospital where I was born in 1946.
Many Estonian families lived there. We were there until we emigrated to Canada May of 1952

1949 my brother (Heikki Limion) on the balcony of our room in Schlosshalde

Geislingen 1950? - barakid -Ants Peterson from Sweden, my uncle, holding me, and Heikki

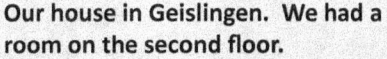

Our house in Geislingen. We had a room on the second floor.

1949 Geislingen- summer. Our house in Schlosshalde

ON THE RUN BUT ALSO ON THE READY

My mother, Maimu Limion, left Eesti at the urging of her parents, in September 1944 with my brother, Heikki, who was born in Tartu in 1942. Of course, she fully expected to return after the war.

Dad, Eduard Limion, was an officer in the military and, after the war, worked with the Estonian Guard Company 4221 in Nuremberg.

In 1952 we emigrated to Canada and I have lived in the Toronto area ever since.

Unfortunately, I remember nothing about Geislingen although mom spoke often about our life there. I have been back to visit four times (day trips), the first time with mom. In spite of the fact that I remember nothing of my early years there, those visits have all been very emotional events for me.

A thought occurred to me - I should scan and send the photos I have in which I do not recognize anyone at all! Maybe someone could identify those people and contact the compiler of the book!

(please do so at the address at the front of the book   MM)

KINDERGARTEN AND SCHOOL BEGAN FAST

Curiously school does not receive much mention in the narrative of the children: It is perhaps more part of the narrative of the adults and the sacrifices they made to ensure that their children were not left behind in their studies.

And it certainly had just that effect: Many of their cohort have found complex vocations and worked to reach significant levels of recognition in such.

One needs to remember that they arrived with scant books, writing materials etc, all of which were initially improvised and later produced by the printing press set up by our folk.

Perhaps kindergarten and the creative activities preoccupied the younger minds, as did the camps and even tours to Sweden: These I am sure were important means of addressing our acquired angst.

It is interesting to note the body language of the children: Some faces are peaceful, even happy while the odd one shows signs of grappling with the journey they had just trodden. MM

WALLOWING WAS NOT ON THE MENU: THEY JUST GOT ON WITH IT: PLAY INCLUDED

1949 June playing in the Geislingen hills- 1Marje Limion, Toomas Normet, ?, ?....

we often went walking the hills. That's toomas Normet on the bottom, Marje (me), unidentified girl though I think it might be one of the 'Palm' sisters?, and Heikki

1949 July -Geislingen hills - Toomas Normet on the bottom. :-) Marje Limion, ?, Heikki Limion

1949 September Geislingen hills- ? (don't know who the child in the foreground is, ? (don't know who the girl is), Marje Limion, Heikki Limion standing, Toomas Normet sitting

1949 September Geislingeni Mägedes - Marje Limion in the middle. Toomas Normet's back.

1949 July Geislingen hills - Maimu Limion and Ed Limion holding up the tower. Front - ?, Heikki Limion, Marje Limion

1949 July Geislingen hills - Left to right - Laine Loorand, Pr. Külmallik, Marje, ?, Maimu Limion. Pointing, behind us, Toomas Normet.

1949 July Geislingeni Mägedes - Back - ?, Maimu Limion, Pr. Külmallik, Laine Loorand. Front - Marje Limion, Toomas Normet, Heikki Limion.

1949 July Geislingen hills - Front - Marje Limion, Laine Loorand. Rear - Pr. Külmallik, Karl Loorand, ?

1949 July Geislingen hills - Rear - Maimu Limion, Karl Loorand, Laine Loorand, Pr. Külmallik. Front - Toomas Normet, Heikki Limion, Marje Limion, ??

Ed Limion July 1949

1949 July Geislingen hills- Left to right - Pr. Külmallik, Toomas Normet, ??, Laine Loorand holding Marje Limion, Dad (Ed Limion), mom (Maimu Limion).

SOME OF THEM WERE BORN ON A CUSP: SOME ON THE TREK, OTHERS IN COSIER PLACES

Marje with Karl Loorand

Heikki and Marje Limion

Marje Limion, Toomas Normet, ?, Heikki Limion

Those littlies have no memories of their parents' horrendous trek. Their narrative but the 'mythology' of their remaining families and friends, and aided by photos of the time: perhaps put into their language by those of their cohort who were a skerrick older.

They played among the smaller of them who had seen war but who too knew nought but not having and thus were not disgruntled by the notion. They were perhaps more bewildered by their parents' angst than their playmates. Their parents mostly ready to console them.

But they too were part of that journey: They were one of Estonian DP kids: They too belonged nowhere.

Many of them were to reunite decades later at reunions of their DP folk. MM.

My late brother Heikki and I.

Summer 1948
Heikki and Marje

Three photos from 1946 in June, year and month I was born! These photos say Tiina Hendrikson on the back and I can only make out the last name of the other little girl... Meybaum? Tiiu Hurt /Høvik who now lives in Norway
Marje in carriagae and Tiiu Hurt HoviK) who grew up in Toronto and now lives in Norway: Photo on the balcony of our room.
PS: I was fortunate to meet Tiiu on my travels in Norway in 2013. MM

IN THOSE ESTONIAN VILLAGES FAR FROM HOME THEY REKINDLED THEIR LIVES

1949 Geislingen Christmas time

1950(?) Geislingen church Christmas tree - Heikki Limion saying his "jõulu salm". (Christmas verse)

1949 Geislingen Christmas- Pr. Külmallik, Marje, Heikki, Maimu Limion (mom)

1949 Geislingen Christmas - Maimu Limion (mom), child (?), Father Christmas, Marje, Heikki

1949 Geislingen Christmas with Santa Claus

Church Christmas celebration - I hid behind that unidentified girl because the flash scared me!

Mom told me that every Christmas, they waited for Jõuluvana (Santa Claus) to show up. I believe he was an Estonian actor living in Geislingen. They waited and waited till mom was often in tears because her children kept asking and she was afraid he wouldn't come. Eventually, he would arrive and.... he would be drunk, of course. He did the rounds of many Estonian homes and at every stop, he was offered drinks. Somehow, he managed to muddle through but mom said he would reek of alcohol. But what did we know? We were just happy to see Jõuluvana. MLM

1949 March Geislingen hills - Heikki Limion, Marje Limion, Ed LImion

Heikki I Limion, Laine Loorand, Marje Limion, Mom (Maimu Limion)

1949 March Geislingen hills

BIRTHDAYS, CHRISTMAS & EASTER AGAIN BECAME THEIR REALITY

Marje's birthday celebration

I do wonder who those three girls are, and that little guy!! -MLM

I have always wondered about all the cakes and pastries. I wonder if mom baked or was able to buy them somewhere. Mai's reply....... Cakes with ersatz cream etc were just becoming available when we were leaving: I had a few slices at my seventh birthday in July 1949 just before we left. I still have a penchant for those German cakes. I'm not a foodie but near a German cake shop my eyes are always bigger than my stomach.

1952 Geislingen- heading for church at Easter time

Their parents very wisely recognized that time out with their friends was an integral part of survival among adversity. MM

Nürmberg Baltic Club -Ed Limion on the left
Nürmbergi Balti Klubis (Club)- 1947 summer Heikki Limion (boy) next to dad (Ed Limion)

The snow was one of the constants which they could remember Estonia by: It was a precious time for parents and children to re enact better times.

WAR HAD NOT ROBBED THEM OF WINTER

1949 March Geislingen hills - Marje Limion, Maimu Limion, Ed Limion, Heikki Limion

Maimu Limion, Heikki Limion, Marje Limion, Laine Loorand

1949 March Geislingen hills

THEY REVISITED THEM, AND MANY WERE FORTUNATE TO STAY IN LETTER CONTACT

Geislingeni jaamas - July 25, 1956 (on the back of the photo)

" Mina Geislingeni jaamas oma saatjatega 25 juulil 1956 asudes teele "tõotatud maale". Vaata ja imesta ku "armastatud" olin."
Could be Linda Piht (lady with dark hair in middle) who is leaving. People who waited a few more years were able to emigrate to the United States... she lived in New York City.
A few more names I can decipher on the back - prl. Milles ja Pr. Prentsel Hilsem tulid veel Mõru ja Teemi ja Vellemaa.

And then one day they each and one of them said farewell to those whom they left behind in the camps: How many such sad but hopeful partings there must have been!   MM

The barakid in 1974 - still standing. that's mom.

(below....) bottom of the stairs where the above photo was taken... in 1974 (that's me)

Back view of the barakid in 1974 (that's mom)

Our house/room (balcony) in Schlosshalde in 1974. That's mom. took her a while to recognize the house from the hill behind it. finally, she saw the linoleum floor which she had been scrubbing the day we left. it was peeking out from under the door!! same floor!!! :-)

Me behind our house in Schlosshalde (see photo above) in 1974

In 1987 when we went to Europe, I had my sons recreate this first photo in the photo below and to the right.
I've also included a couple more photos from that trip taken at the Helfenstein castle "varemed" (ruins).
BTW, I was able to Google some very nice images of that.

358

AND YET PART OF THEM REMAINED BACK AT THOSE CAMPS

This picture was among many photos in my late mother's Geislingen photos box. I guess you gave it to me? The date is 1950. We left in 1952. By 1950, we were living in the "barakid".Before that, we lived in Schlosshalde - mom, my brother and I. Dad worked in Nuremberg at 4221 Kompani. At the time of your photo, I believe the DP camp had ended and we were living the "the barakid", close to the hospital. The "barakid" were still there in 1974 when I visited with mom. Last time, in 2007, (with my husband), they were gone. I was so young at the time that I have no memories at all of Geislingen - just a lot of pictures--Marje.

And some like Marje and Liivi Jõe have already made contact during this project. MM

Hello Marje,
So glad to see all these photos that you have sent around - goes to show that although photos prove we have shared early-life experiences in Geislingen we are at a loss at times to reconstruct real memory - specific people and places - yes, the back of this photo is definitely our mother´s handwriting (Lydia Jõe Laius) - .... For myself I don´t recall a hospital or any barracks around it where your family went to live in 1950. From the photo it does look like the barracks around the Bõlcke tänav complex where all the central administrative affairs took place and which by the time I revisited in 1986 had been fenced off by a private company - can you pinpoint the location - where was that hospital? I know that our family got sent off to Ulm when the Geislingen camp closed officially in 1950 and those not lucky enough to have gotten visas to emigrate somewhere got packed off to those barracks in Ulm - evidently not your family - what was your route out? LJ

ESTONIAN CEMETERY IN GEISLINGEN

And sadly there were some loved ones and close friends whom They had to leave behind forever: Some found their resting place In that cemetery. MM

1948 Oct. Agu Veski lahkumine- my mom is wearing the dark suit and has the clutch bag under her arm. I don't know who any of the rest of the people are. OH, in the second photo, that's my brother, Heikki Limion, in the short pants. Heikki died in 2000 at the age of 58.

A SONG FOR MY LITTLE DARLING

INGE PRUKS/IZZO
A LULLABY LOST

"Sleep, my little one, sleep.
Your worries are still unknown to you,
Your life's journey, windy and stormy, is long and still ahead of you,
Your mother and father are watching over you.
When you grow up, don't forget your people, and your Northern home."

My mother and father were both passionate about music and it was natural that they should meet thanks to their choral activities. My mother, Jenny Henriette Pruks, had a beautiful soprano voice, and her greatest pleasure was to sing in many choirs all her life. My father Albert Eduard Pruks, on the other hand, was a musician, composer and choir conductor, and no doubt he noticed Jenny's voice in the back row and the rest was history.

Family lore has it that my mother did not want to leave Estonia, but my father pressured her, saying he could not leave without her and baby Inge. Although I do not know the exact nature of my father's patriotic activities it seemed certain that he would be killed or sent to Siberia if he stayed.

Some sixty years later, a half-sister I discovered in Estonia would tell me that our father left for other reasons too. She said he complained bitterly at hearing only Russian music on the radio and vowed to return only when Estonia was free again to express its own soul through its own music. Of course that was never to be, because my father died in the Geislingen Displaced Persons Camp in February 1949.

But there was a certain prescience in his attitude, because it was through the Singing Revolution that Estonia did finally achieve its independence. Music and Estonia are inextricably intertwined, and this was certainly true for both my parents, whose very beings were filled with the music of Estonia.

And so it was that our journey into exile began. We escaped to Germany via land, travelling by night in trucks, and it was only by sheer luck that we avoided the bombs which burst all around us as we travelled.

In Germany, we stayed in at least three DP Camps : Augsburg, Kempten and Geislingen. Whenever there is a gathering of Estonians, there will be laughter and singing. Songs such as 'Tuljak' and 'Mulgimaa' and so many others recall the simple peasant life of long ago, and a deep love of the land -- its clear blue sky, its rich black earth, and of course the white bark of the birch trees. These folk songs are known to everyone, and soon my father was involved in conducting choirs again, even though he was far from his native land.

My mother too sang in choirs in Germany, and no doubt music helped to fill the void that had been created by leaving all her family behind. My mother never again saw her parents Pauline and Samuel Joakit, or her sister Ruth. Happily, fifty years later, she would see her sisters Linda and Alma and her brother Jaan, but her childhood home would be destroyed and the familiar landscapes changed beyond recognition.

Perhaps my father was the lucky one, he was spared the sight of so much destruction.

In Geislingen my father worked in a cheese factory where he was forced to lift heavy vats of milk and cream, and this greatly affected his health. He was lean and angular, and in time he lost even more weight, until he was finally diagnosed as suffering from ulcers in the stomach.

At the same time, my mother gave birth to my baby brother, Mart, on 13 September 1948. It must have been a terrible time for her, having to face her husband's illness and caring for a newborn child in post-war Camp conditions, when good food was scarce and there were no family networks to help. Mart and I both suffered from chickenpox, and our mother was particularly anxious when tiny Mart had to spend some time in hospital so early in his life. Mother remembered being shocked at his emaciated condition when he was handed back to her.

It was a black day for me when my father died. I was only five and a half, and my baby brother was 5 months old. I remember the gloomy day of the funeral in February 1949, when everyone gathered at the Geislingen cemetery. I could not believe that my father was gone forever, and when the grown-ups asked me to copy them and throw handfuls of soil into the grave, I was appalled. It was as if they were acquiescing to some terrible ritual which took him away from me, and I wanted no part of it.

I refused to throw any soil into my father's grave, unwilling to bury him and say goodbye.

For me, the time I spent in Germany is filled with sadness, if not horror. I thought Geislingen had been specially created for me, since it had my name 'inge' inside it, a place which took away my father, gave me a brother, and put enormous stress on my mother. It encapsulated my personal wartime story. Of course I now realise that many German towns are named in this way, with the 'ingen' fragment as part of the name. But children see things differently, and that town has marked me for life.

Exile made my father feel even more keenly the power of music and he composed many songs about his longing for Estonia. Fearing perhaps that he would never see me grow up, he composed a lullaby for me in March 1946, in Geislingen, when I was only two and a half years old. It is a song which asks me not to forget Estonia

Yes, the lullaby was indeed prophetic. Four years later, my mother, brother and I would embark on a long 6-week journey on the ship the Anna Salen to sail to the ends of the earth – Australia. I have indeed known stormy and windy weather (who hasn't?), but the love of both my parents has helped me navigate this difficult journey.

This was the last photo of our family.
Mother cradles Mart, whilst I clutch onto my doll.
And father stands behind us all, but a few months
after this family portrait he will sadly leave us forever.

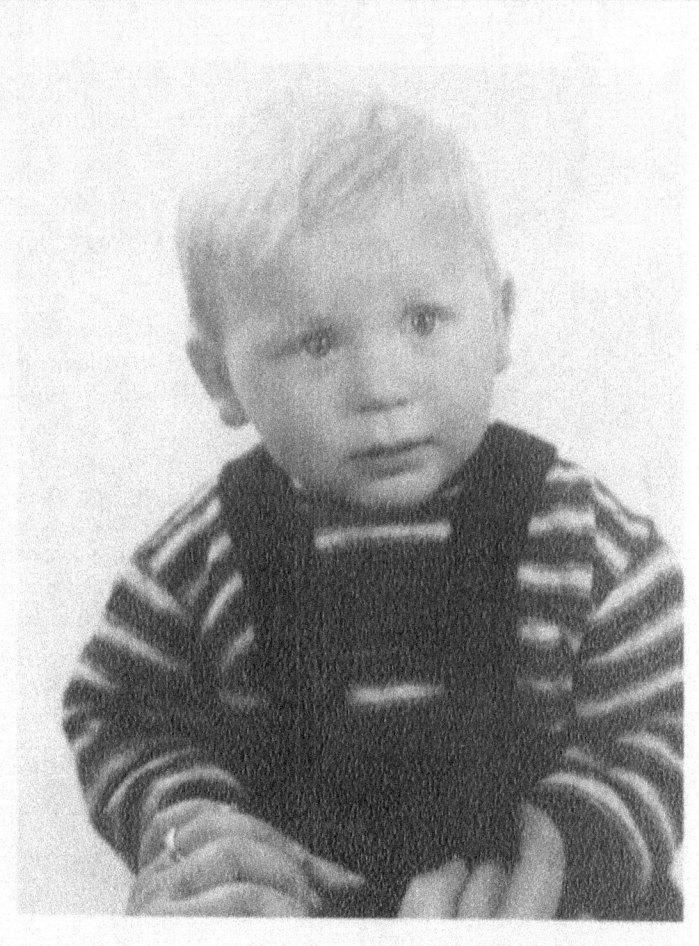

Mart Pruks aged 18 months

Sadly among the many thousands of the young who fled with their parents or were born in the limbo of camp life, are many who could not be represented in this book: They were plagued from early in their lives by badly impaired health and not in the position to share their journeys: Oh! If they had only been in the position to share their pain with us.
Among them are a few priviledged to share but a small window of their journey.
Marty was able to join us at Geislingen 2008: Together there, we were able to celebrate his sixtieth birthday with him: Serendipitously that big "O" fell within the reunion time. MM

FOR MANY CHILDREN MUSIC SOOTHED THEIR SOULS

My father was teaching me the piano, and I was a very willing pupil. I remember that my legs were too short to touch the floor as I sat on the chair, and I certainly couldn't touch the pedals. It was a wonderful beginning to my musical education, and I have managed to pass it on to my two sons Samuel and Miles, who play jazz piano and the trumpet.

AND LEFT INDELIBLE TREASURED MEMORIES: IP

This particular photo documents a historic occasion, as it was the first big song festival organized in the DP Camps. It took place on 10 August 1947, and over 5000 people attended the festival, which took place in Augsburg.

Apart from photographs, I have very few mementos of my father.
However, I do have something that he probably used every day, or at least at every rehearsal: his tuning fork. It is the one tangible and precious link that remains. When I strike it and listen to its vibrations in the key of A, I know that he touched it and heard the same vibrations. It is wonderful that a mere metal object can emit a sound that uncannily imitates the human voice. This is the voice that links me to my father. I can hear him humming the A.

THOSE OF THEM WHO GRACED GRADE SCHOOL AND KINDERGARTEN

Curiously the narrative of their very young does not relate a great deal to school or kindergarten: I have often pondered why. Perhaps in some way their dislocation for such a long window of time made school and kindergarten an irrelevancy in their little lives. Perhaps there was a need for a time to play. Who knows!

Certainly those who wrote about their times at either activity seemed to have focussed more their pleasure in such around musical activities and dance.

Among Inge's treasures is this little song book with its 22 pages of joy for the young. The front page bears an inscription.

MM

WILL FONDLY REMEMBER SONGS FROM THIS BOOK

My mother had asked my auntie Vilma Abel to see if she could find some beginner's piano books. Vilma replied that she did not have any, but that perhaps this little song book would help me learn the songs of my homeland. She apologizes for its rain-affected condition. Vilma ended up living in Germany, but expressed her nostalgia and love for Estonia by making beautiful dolls, each dressed in a different regional costume. Her dolls are now in a museum in Tartu, the Manguasjamuuseum, in 8 Lutsu St, Tartu.

IP

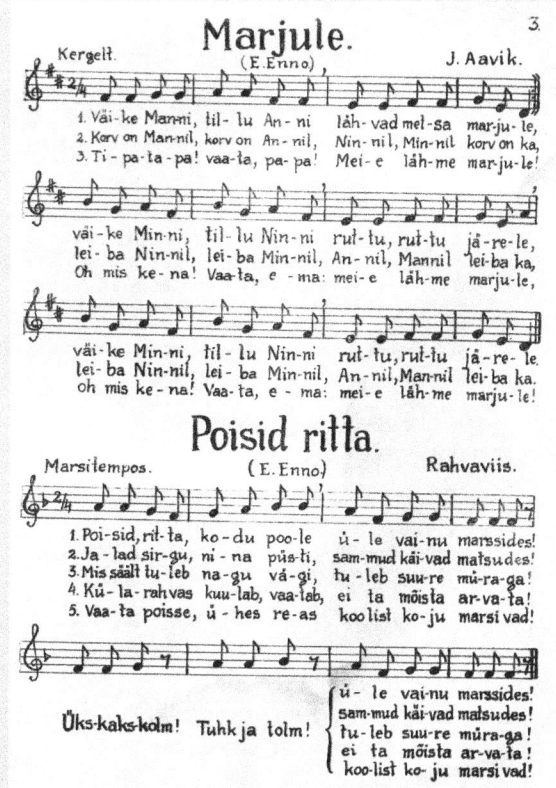

FOR THE OLDER AND MORE MUSICALLY SOPHISTICATED AMONG THEM

Quotes from Inge

As for the 14th June, if you put '14 juuni' into google you'll immediately turn up stuff on the 'Juunikuuditamine Eestis.' It was the beginning of the mass deportations into Siberia (1941), and a black day for Estonia. I started seeing the date in a different light after I saw it mentioned in many places when I visited Estonia. They still commemorate it in different ways. So a date which was once sparkling and happy for me, became dark and dreadful. Like you, I never knew anything about the date, although of course I've heard of the deportations. One of my uncles actually came back from Siberia, although sadly he has passed away now

"thank you for your honesty and willingness to share your experiences"

Inge, I feel privileged to have shared these to allow others to find peace with theirs.
Mai

57. Altenstadt, Eesti Segakoor pidurõivas 1948. Toi vasakul kõrval koorijuht Albert Pruks

I guess I did not want to understand the bigger picture, the sadness of leaving Geislingen where my father lay buried, the sadness of my mother, who never ever saw her parents again, and had to wait some forty years before she could visit Estonia and see some of her family. We stayed 12 months in this camp (In Oz), after which we were moved on to another, in the Eastern State of Victoria.

COMPOSERS SUCH AS INGE'S FATHER WARMED THEIR TIME IN THE CAMPS: IP

, I'm 'only' 69, (2 years ago) hahahaha, I was born in 1943.
I don't want to be 69, it's gloom-gloom-gloom all the way!
I feel and look so old. Aaaaagh!
It's my birthday today! I can't shout it too loudly to Estonians though, because the 14th June is a black day in our history. I had a quiet celebration with the family.

Oh, for the Geislingen days when I was only a cute little girl!

"My mother always said my father died of ulcers ('mao haavad'), because he had had to do hard physical work in a certain cheese factory. I'm not sure where all the various towns fit in, as we lived in Kempten, Augsburg and Geislingen. I have no idea how Altenstadt fits in, and on some photos I see a 'Geriesenstadt', which even my German friends can't tell me where it might be."

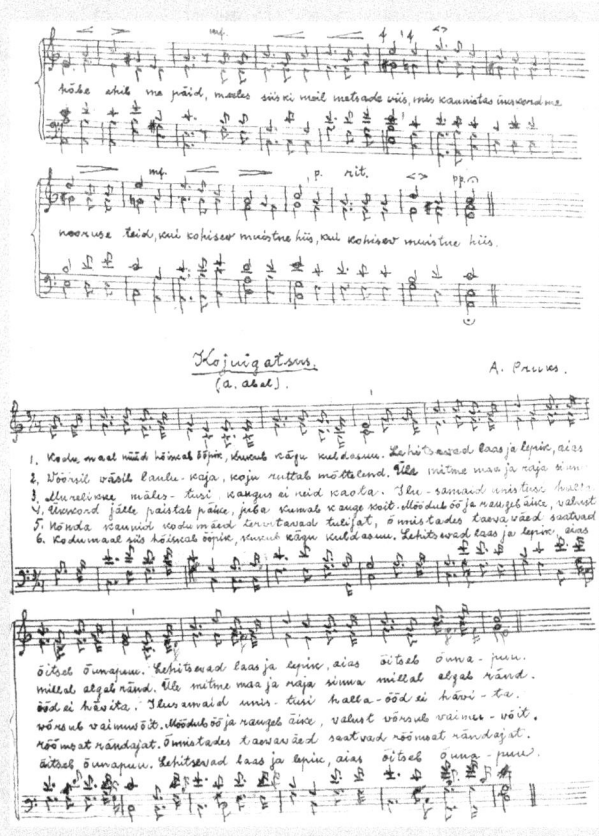

LET US NOT FORGET THEM

The Geislingen project began, dare I say it way back in 2006. From the beginning I had a conviction that the firm modem operandi of the project was spontaneous communication: That I hoped that no one ever felt pressured to share more that they were comfortable with.

The limitation of that strategy of course that much which was uncomfortable was left unshared: My hope that folk would engage at their comfort level, when they felt ready. Not a quick way to produce books but perhaps a more sincere way with less casualties at the end of the journey.

I have learned a lot from my nearly half a century of clinical medicine. That people don't want to talk but they proverbially get a lump in their throats because at a deeper level they do want to do so: That they need a comfortable starting point.

In my consulting room was always a diverse array of paintings- my own: Some patients liked, others they detested. That did not matter because either way the communication was catalyzed by their reason for feeling that way, my empathy to their feelings and of course eventually they shared that which they had dared not to share previously. The outcome was always improvement in the patient's predicament.

Likewise, in the e-mail manylogues to effect WNE some of you may recall my various inter-current allusions to things like as a rookie being assigned to ambulance crews, lest bush fires broke out and the emotions they engendered in me: Of course at the end of that narrative alluding to my sustained apprehensions of being trapped in burning buildings. There were many such illusions and out of such mushroomed many clips which were the seeds for WNE.

The book projects have truly enriched my life: Not because of any kudos but because of some of the wonderful friendships which have evolved.

Among such friends is **Inge Pruks**. Inge lives walking distance from my place (I mean walking distance, not Mai's walking distance which is better defined as a long hike!)

In a recent e-mail Inge wrote
"Everything seemed so easy when I was at your place. Back on my own I don't know what to write...." and **" I feel I can't get started as I don't really know what I want to say, and who would be interested in it. It all seems very remote."**

Of course it was easy doing it at my place . My study is a wonderful clutter among which I feel truly at home: There are paintings of Estonia, bits of printouts of the various books I am working on and shelves loaded with books about the journey of our folk. How much easier it becomes to interleave small painful snippets among other people's painful ones: One no longer feels alone as one does when all one can see are walls, floors, desks, chairs and whatever which don't have such artefacts.

The clutter of my study, also allows body language for the less distressed to create interim knight's moves to create space between the twinges of pain.

One of the limitations of any book is that there is a felt need to restrict the pain one depicts: perhaps Inge says it very adroitly **" the latest e-mail from .... makes the refugee journey sound like a grand adventure. It's not everybody's experience, unfortunately."**

How true are Inge's words: among her other quotations are:

"I now wish I'd had the courage to write something for WNE, because for me it was a traumatic period. A black hole in my consciousness, which represents utter despair. To me it was not a childhood idyll, like it was for the rest of you."

Inge is quite correct. There are so many of my past patients who have presented a stiff upper lip to the world and shared their utter and angst and despair in my consulting room: At times the first time it was recorded in the files: Even then it took until they discovered that I too had been a refugee (given my nondescript name) that they finally spilt their guts. How painful it must have been for them to live in a communicational prison for decades and continue to do so: At times to be bombarded by ignoble DSM labels.

"It seems that the subject of us poor refugees tends to polarize people."

Again how true. That even occurs in the medical world: I have made myself Miss Unpopular by pointing out harsh realities endless times at clinical meetings: It's becoming like a broken record so I am becoming less and less inclined to bother going. Life is becoming too short to waste on the futile.

"I feel there is so much secrecy buried in my Estonian past that I don't even care to unearth it. I was not a part of it, whatever it was, I was an innocent child who got caught in a mass exodus, I lost my relatives, my past, but their stories lived on through my mother's memories. Sure, I'm glad of that. But was my mother's version the 'true' version? Of course not, because we all tell our own versions of the truth.

So, unearthing bits and fragments here and there will only open up a chaotic world which maybe I just want to reject, especially as I played no real part in it. I just got shunted around from place to place."

How poignant are Inge's words: That is the story of all our lives. It is only the details which varied. I can understand Inge's feelings for I too buried such matter until my sixtieth birthday when I for quite the wrong reasons returned to Estonia to escape that reality and left with no wish to return. The enigmas for me lay elsewhere an do not belong to this book.

Despite being Estonia's war children, I am certain that our enigmas at times lay dotted widely around Europe and even further.

"My life is an open book -- with a few pages missing."

Maybe that is true, maybe not. All I can say is that my life is still not an open book: It is hard at times to open it at pages folk want to read. And maybe there is an artefact: Maybe some pages because of nature's wisdom have just become stuck together. Maybe that is nature's/God's caring towards us. I have always had a firm saying "Never open Pandora's box: Wait until it springs open of its own accord." That is why I refuse to interview people, though I have been told by examiners that I make a very good interviewer.

"..you haven't said anything to make me feel uncomfortable, it's probably the whole subject matter that makes me uncomfortable, I don't really like facing the past, it's too sad and I feel I cannot recall as much as I'd like to. My memories all seem to be rather trivial.

Also, I'm not very good at generalizing about experiences, I kind of feel I don't fit in anywhere. You seem to be so good at pulling together all the threads that I am a bit intimidated by you. And I did really mean, Hooray for computers, because it has given so many people (like me) a way of being in touch, despite the fact that everyone's life is rolling on different tracks."

I always desperately hope that I don't do this to people (perhaps the exception being a small number of folk whom I work with who have had difficulties understanding the notion of 'boundaries').

There are no trivial memories: If they were they would be interred among the other trivia in our lives. Each memory remains there for a purpose: At times to offer us encouragement to move on, at others a truncated collection of thoughts to follow up at a more poignant time. Inge talks about extreme sadness which is too hard to face: Which makes her feel uncomfortable. How could anything of such nature be trivial. The trivialisation is a legacy of our life in our new lands where the lack of wish to hear our voices has implied that our voices are not worthy of being heard: What a tragic lack of insight.

None of us quite fit anywhere: each of our experiences by the sheer survival tactics needed to flee has created as many experiences as there are of us.

And of course Inge did not know me ten years ago. She will not remember the stammer which I had should I be speaking with more than two people at a time, no matter what the theme. Perhaps Maano Milles would be the only one who has heard me speak with such a tremulous voice. He may recall that phone message from overseas perhaps a decade ago.

Nor will I forget my tremulousness at the presentations of WNE at its launches. I guess that I read the power points: As I heard some kindly soul remark nearby. I fondly recall Professor Aado Must's compassionate smile indicating "Never mind".

Perhaps the final turning point was at the first War Child Conference I spoke at. Martin Parsons, it's organiser is a very wise man. He asked me if I wanted the lights on or off. He knew that I would feel the angst of folks' body language. When the lights came on, everybody was still there and just as friendly as they had been. For the first time I had known what it felt like to be allowed to own one's soul.

Perhaps Inge is just beginning that journey: Don't despair Inge. Wait for those precious correct moments to arrive. And Inge, just for the record it is the same electronic medium that put me in touch with the world. Ulo Kuhi was working on another Geislingen related project and Maano had suggested that he contact me because I seemed to have a good recall for someone from our cohort. During those project interactions I bemoaned how they all (USA folk who had lived around Lakewood) seemed to be relishing each other's company. How welcome were the words:"Join in". The rest of course is history. That is how the "Micro-Geislingenians" were born.

But there are endless times when I still relish solitude: It will always remain the time when I will have absolute permission to own my soul.

"My Geislingen memories are very sketchy, nothing like yours (Mai)."

Dunno about that. I could readily navigate my way around Geislingen sans map after a sixty three year absence: But I have no 'bl--dy' idea of what the room we lived in for 3 years in Hospital weihe looked like. Perhaps memory is a

Mart Pruks returns to Geislingen 2008

He is but one of thousands of photos I would have liked to include here

Oh, if only all of those unfortunates could come out of the time warp and tell us how it really was for them.   MM

selective thing and we go looking when we are prepared by whatever criterion. I recently visited Geislingen with my Estonian hosts. At their bidding I knocked on the door of No 144 to be declined a visit to the room for a rather paltry reason. I felt no regret: Indeed perhaps a sense of relief.

"I am so glad to welcome Ruth (Inge's sister) home again, because it's very hard looking after Marty on one's own, although he's been pretty good, he's such a sweetheart." How many of us carry such sentiments for a loved one who has been broken by their early life. It is a phenomenon one rarely sees among people who have not seen life plundered at the hands of war.

"that remark by .... sure is rich. .....she tries to exclude you (Mai) as a 'pagulane', trying to focus on the broad brush strokes of 'history', whatever that might be in her mind. She was insulting, too. I don't know what she expects as input from us 'pagulased', nor do I know what the whole 'celebration' (hahahaha) will be about in Estonia, as there is nothing to celebrate about having to escape from your homeland. I could be wrong, maybe they didn't call it a celebration, I forget.
   Sure, some of us made good and became rich and famous, but others did not, drifting into alcoholism and general alienation. Others again, like my family, just tried to survive on a shoestring. These latter stories will not be told, the ones badly affected like Marty cannot speak, and the truly heart-rending stories like yours are often not welcome, because they don't fit into a neat little box, under a neat little sub-heading."

Yes, tragically there are too many "Martys" out there. I recall Jaan Pilli who lived in Melbourne, who died prematurely and I often wonder what happened to Mihkel Tobreluts. Mihkel was a brilliant little guy who too lived in 144 Hospitalweihe and as a small school boy cried when the oldies absentmindedly threw out the newspapers before he could peruse them. He came unstuck in some way in his teens I believe.

HARROWED CHILDREN: THEY TOO BECAME CAPTAINS OF THEIR LIVES: MM

Photos are generally taken at times of elated mood, celebrations, fun times etc. Perhaps the exception being school and kindergarten ones where the child's expression is but a chance occurrence.

But maybe not! I have perused such school photos of my children. There appears to be a consistency. I saw the same hollow looks as they walked into my consulting room which at times was nearby, also when I did the 'mum thing" at tuck-shop and on school committees etc.

I have selected one of my Geislingen Rappenecker kindergarten photos and enlarged some of the faces (accepting the poorer resolution for a greater cause). I have two photos where the same two kids appear: I hope that they were to be transient emotions followed by later peace.

I share a dialogue between Juri Raid and Ain Tohver:
"Sorry for the delayed comment on the psychological effects on us as temporary displaced children, orphans, or whatever is the appropriate term for us.

I passed these comments on to my fellow travelling companion, Jüri Raid, during war years, 1944 and 1945 who made the following comment;

"How many psychiatrist did we have to evaluate us after we survived the worst bombing of Berlin in February 1945 and the warfare later in Oberhof Germany?

Maybe we were already hardened to face these catastrophic events by our previous experience of deportations and partisan warfare in Estonia? As refugees in Germany we were already mature enough to be able to survive on our own and use our "sisu" to help us through these tragic events. In our lives we go through many emotionally shattering events and we cannot be spoiled by our childhood cuddling not to be able to cope with such events which are part of natural life experience. These events should not destroy us emotionally.

Many of us did not have any family support in our new countries and we had to start our lives without any support from any social organizations. The start of Korean War gave us the opportunity to serve this country to be thankful of its generosity to us and we were glad to do it. It also gave us the opportunity to be a part of something and enhanced our acceptance to our adopted country

Many of us have died and the ones remaining have a very short time left but emotionally our life experience has given us to be able to look forward without fear."

Yes, our oldies may have had their squabbles and we too perhaps heaved stones at each other. But as kids we did not have the oldies' hierarchies: Nor did we carry such weight of turmoil lives on our shoulders. I recall that one of the school teachers had lost his son in the Moero sinking: How does one get over something like that!

Given the rooms were cluttered by rationed space we frequently played outside where the oldies' hierarchies became irrelevant: We became Kings of our castles, real or imagined.

And as we matured we became captains of our lives.
I am sure that was equally valid in camps other than Geislingen.

GRIMMER TALES

AIN TOHVER WRITES IN RELATION TO BEING EXILED BY HIS OWN FOLK
(in reply to my allusion to this)

Some ways I had a similar situation in my past. It was not the Estonians who took me in, it was the Germans. That's why I drifted away from the Estonian "close-knit" group and as resulted kind of "americanized" and lost the skill of Estonian language. The Estonians were too busy with their problems.

When we came to America in the 1940's we were a group of children without any parents to accompany us and we drifted in various directions in America and every story is unique. For example Kalju Suitsev and Walfrid Sumeri were about a year older than I and they did not find any permanent placement. I remember that they washed dishes in Bronx for fraternal organization and I met them there.

After several months they found a Estonian couple that had an apple farm in the State of Washington that took them in and gave them food and quarters.

Later on I found out that their experience there was not too pleasant and they were used as cheap farm labor. Subsequently they joined the U.S. Army. This information is unverified but I am sure there is some truth in it.
Apparently all Estonians did not welcome us with open arms and somehow we were sharing their problems. We were group of about dozen children that were loyal to each other as Paul Öpik will tell you. We, or I, still don't know what has happened to Uno Piil as of today.

JOHN SAARMAN ALSO MEETS HIS FATHER ONE DAY
In relation to my allsuion that father died three months before we met.

I'm so sorry that you never met your father.That's such a sad story.
In my case my mother was told that my father had died during the second Russian invasion & it was me in Geislingen who started calling this man who came to see my mother-FATHER.So naturally they fell in love & married & I always called him father to the day he died here in the states.

When I finally met my real father in Estonia he looked just like me except for being older.That weekend all he did was cry as he showed me where he lived & told me what had happened to him in all these years.

He had also remarried & had some children.

Before I left he made me promise to come to his funeral but when that happened I was notified by telegram one day before his funeral-so I never saw him again but I took a lot of video & photos when I was there.One of these days I'm making my own personal film about that weekend.

ILLE LISCINSKI REMINISCES ABOUT HER MEETING WITH VISNAPUU

The poet became very talkative and related a lot about his past in Tallinn, about other Estonian authors, and white nights in summer. The memories brought colour to his face. I did wash his small room's floor......I showed him my first effort at writing. It was a children's play "Ahjukolli Kuusis". He read it and commented favourably on it. When I left Geislingen I never met him again.

A few years later I heard that Visnpuu had died in New York. I cherish his memory because the teachers at BGB were a proud and rather unfriendly with a pair of exceptions: Some had been university lecturers, like Felix Oinas. Pastor Lind was one exception

BUT MERIKE TAMM RECALLS A POSITIVE FROM THAT WAR
(in response to my comment that I was an accident of a troop march)

My conception was also the result of the war and of Estonians fleeing their homeland in 1944. When my father left Estonia in September 1944, he was married to someone else, not my mother (but they had no children). I don't know if my mother and father had even met before September 1944, but their shared refugee path brought their lives together. I was born in Geislingen in June 1946, my sister in February 1948. My parents were married in Geislingen by an Estonian Lutheran minister in 1949, at the same time as my sister and I were baptized. I have photos of the event and a marriage certificate signed by the minister. I don't know what the Estonian law was regarding divorce nor if war situations were considered differently. Maybe five years of separation (or abandonment?) Qualified for divorce. I believe that my father's first wife remained in Estonia and he did, decades later, have a little mail contact with her. **Every one of our stories is so interesting.**

ILLE LISCINSKI/USCINSKI
CHILDREN WITHOUT TOYS

In 1946 I was living in Rappenacker in the DP camp in Geislingen. I shared a room with two total strangers who had ambushed me at the arrival in the camp because they had a room for four persons and they needed me as anchor to secure it, since the fourth person was only a name of the door.

Mrs. M. and Miss B. didn't waste any niceties on me, they only tolerated me. When their lovers: an American Army captain and a Norwegian UNRRA officer came to call, I had to make myself scarce, go sit in the kitchen or the attic.

In the same house lived a charming widow with her three children. When she had to go to town she took the two boys with her, but the little Maia couldn't walk the distance and she had no stroller, therefore I looked after Maia.

It seemed simple enough, but it wasn't easy to pass the time with the lovely Maia because there was no swing, no sand pit, no ball or even a bucket and toy spade to dig soil. The only amusement for us was to watch the little Finns in the next yard. The fence had lost a few palings and we could peep through how five Finns made a racket with a broken garden spade and an old conserve tin of water. There were seven little Finns but the toddler and the baby were indoors while their mother hand washed clothes for nine, bed linen and nappies. She had to wash every single day.

One day when I was looking after Maia and we watched the Finns a jeep pulled up in front of the house. There came the lovers. They went in the house and soon came out again because the ladies were not home. The Norwegian saw me and came to enquire about the ladies. I told them that they were about to arrive home at any time. The Norwegian admired Maia, lifted her up and danced around. The Captain looked bored with a camera hanging from his neck. He stepped closer, told the Norwegian to pose with Maia, pushed me closer to him and snapped a picture. The Captain was an unsavory type I rather disliked.

Once he asked me gruffly "Why did you come to Germany?"

"Because I couldn't buy a passage to America," I snapped back and he understood the irony of it.

I didn't think that he would have this picture developed, but he did.

Soon after I was transferred to Hotel Sonne. Maia's mother was screened out and I never knew what happened to them. It was sad. That's why I cherished this picture of Maia and kept it in a small album.

Two years later I migrated to Australia and worked in a Repatriation Hospital in Brisbane. Again I was sharing an army shack with a total stranger and worked among strangers. I was homesick for Europe and waited anxiously for letters from my friend, Raja, in Stuttgart.

Raja was a beautiful half Russian and half Estonian girl I had shared room at her aunt's unit in Stuttgart. Her father had been executed during the first Russian occupation of Estonia and she was still mourning him when she met John, a Dutch American Army interpreter. Raja fell hopelessly in love with John. When she fell pregnant and told John about it, he promptly disappeared. The Americans refused to give any information about John's new posting.

Raja had a beautiful baby daughter she called Anne. She was lucky that her aunt took care of Anne while she worked in an American Service Club. I visited them quite often and became very fond of Anne. When I received my first wages in Brisbane I bought a big, soft teddy bear and sent it to Anne. Raja had pictures taken of Anne and I had a lot of them in my album. At the time I was eager to make new friends and I showed my little album to strangers. I didn't know that I was a trusting fool.

I had no idea that people gossiped about me and I was horrified when a woman started asking questions about my daughter.

"My daughter? I have no daughter."

"Don't be embarrassed. It can happen to any girl. I know that you sent an expensive teddy bear to Germany for your child."

"I sent it to Anne, my friend's daughter."

"What about the picture where you have a uniformed man and a little girl altogether?"

"What about it? I had nothing to do with that Norwegian or the child I was minding for a neighbor."

"Sorry!" She mumbled.

"Since you are so interested in children, then I must tell you that Anne's mother married a noble German and he adopted her. She had a happy childhood."

WILL MAN EVER LEARN:

Inge Pruks: Oh, the senslessness of war, the waste, the tragedy, the loss.

FORK TONGUED LIZARDS

Back in 2007 I wrote a piece in "Avant" which was the journal of the Diploma of Professional Writing and Editing class. In "Water Shortage" are included the lines:
"Sunshine was an outer-western suburb in Melbourne.......Many of Australia's new post World War II refugees gravitated to Sunshine...because land was cheap...

When I arrived in Sunshine at the age of nine, Sunshine didn't need a drought to create a water shortage. Our house was about eight houses away from the nearest and only tap. The queue was mostly comprised of oldies.

Mostly men carried the water, usually with four gallon buckets. At times women carried it.....That tap site rapidly became a good place to pick up the local gossip..... carrying the water commonly became my job. I was a stubborn and impatient kid. To spare myself the repeated queuing up, I used to insist on carrying full bucket loads. Lugging those buckets, small increments of distance at a time, also spared me the gossip: It seemed so trivial even then...."

Perhaps that is not too different to my WNE remarks about the sauna in Geislingen "... I hated the steam, bare bodies and bitchy women"

While subtly exiled from Estoniana at Estonian House in Melbourne I did not miss the bitching there or indeed among oldies anywhere.

I guess I was always a kid of six, eight, etc going on twenty-six, thirty-six whatever: Today's psych fraternity would have had a field day with my head. I just could see no point in hanging around where oldies had nothing positive to say.

The birds and bees had yet to make sense to me. But yet in a primitive way I had become aware of the 'knitting needle' and drinking stuff and getting rid of babies. I had no idea where from: I guess that was logical as terminations of pregnancy were carried out before what today is fashionably called 'the bump' appeared. The bumps themselves were not part of my cognition yet.

I also understood that mothers could die when having babies: That was a real fear not knowing where those babies were had or their pre-requisites.

In those days I did not ponder too much on such matter: Life was sacred but then it was being taken by the war machine so the incongruity was not that irrational.

Of course from friends who were wiser than I, I learned that illegitimacy was a disgrace but what illegitimacy meant I had no idea for years.

Perhaps the entire gossip scene is becoming a deja vu as this book is nearing completion and increasing focus is directed towards the book about our first five years in our new lands. They too are of reminiscing. None of the stories I have in my possession allude to anything like the above but my mind meanders back to that gossip I pined to escape from all those years ago.

It meanders too, to private communications which have occurred by e-mail and face to face since the WNE project began. Those conversations do not have the sophistication of DNA related matters, just the human pain of children of Estonian parents whom I have befriendewd and who too felt the blight od such exiling remarks. My including this piece perhaps my response to my bewilderment that the full blooded Estonians could not even look after their own folks.

Yes, we were born into times when life was precarious: people were forlorn and at times lived for the day, each knowing that tomorrow might never come. Any transient human warmth at times that little gem that kept the soul alive. Perhaps some serenity began to emerge during the later years of DP status but for many the fear of Siberia continued to loom around the corner.

Husbands and wives were at times never to meet again, and if they did the meetings were often transient and perhaps each time seen as the last time. Emotions swung like fast pendulums as did their outcomes and the fear of the extended outcomes of such. And the little elephant's memory recalls that a person was not declared as deceased until seven years post parting and failing to reappear. Remarriage by the Christian ideology of Estonians 'verboten' until that sentence was over.

How many children born in transit were left to wonder who their father was! That did not even include the DNA consideration. Was celibacy of those who travelled alone a realistic expectation for such an extended period of time: Perhaps even to become more complex should the marriage partner unexpectedly appear.

And how holy were those who peered through slinky eyes at the children thus conceived: The memory of comments about a little half caste negro girl whose mother too graced the sauna still haunts me: She pleaded with the mother to wash her properly so she could blend in (as did many of us for short windows of time and who were invisibly of the same ilk) with other kids.

Yes babies were born, some healthy some not. As a clinician I have become more acutely aware of all that might go wrong, in those precarious nine months and the recurring nine months increments until theirs and my families reached some form of basic nutrition and emotional security. Too, some children became ill earlier or later in their lives. Who is to say how that might or might not have occurred regardless of the circumstances. How does one derive such statistics from among a mobile community with limited constants!

And how on earth did the soothsayers among the gossips derive that a child's ill health could be the legacy of their parent. Where did they derive the right to bleat such painful material among their fellow women. How were they to know that among those were not women in early pregnancy or ones who had had terminations despite the risks they faced in those precarious days.

While I still have issues with termination, and as a clinician struggle with our modern ethical expectations, I ask myself was it so unforgivable for a terrified young woman to have a termination when all that seemed to lie ahead was doom, alienation and 'disgrace' for both mother and child and for that child's siblings. Yes, proper doom, not merely having to resign to living in a twelve square flat with basic food.

How did those bitchy women justify their bleating to dump guilt on their fellow travellers: How did they justify placing the siblings of the aborted fetuses into quandaries of wondering had they themselves just been spared that fate: of might there have been a way to keep their unborn siblings out of Europe's rubbish bins.

I wonder how many of those children succumbed to alcoholism, schizophrenia, and even suicide as a legacy of such sustained bleating. I am sure that I was not the only kid born with the memory of an elephant: Nor was I the only kid born able to dissociate that which would have placed their life into more precarious straits. Perhaps the enemy shrapnel was to prove less damaging to our cohort than the sustained venom from those lizards' tongues.

I am so grateful that I was a stubborn kid who found my way away from such company: Trapped with such company with my dear little mini-philosopher's brain I fear that my chances of it reaching a destination where it could be usefully applied rather than straight-jacketed would have been mighty slim. I feel confident that in today's lingo I would have left the gurus debating if the label was Aspergers, autism, ADHD or complex trauma. Who cares! Well I do care: Not for myself but for all those other kids whom I played among who like I were naive of the adult ideologies. Some of them fared far worse that I did.

Today I stand firm in stating people need to be evaluated in the context of their non-chameleonic lives and not their lives categorised in terms of labels. But that said, solitude is preferable company to living life as a chameleon. MM

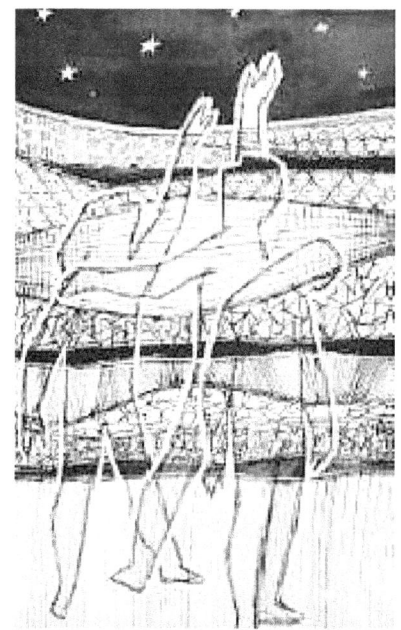

The silent man
was lost in meditation
on Never and Nothing.

His eyes
followed the wind
in the shadows of grey clouds.

There were no memories, hopes, desires,
only colourless dreams
of solitude.

solitude where life
love and time
stood motionless in empty streets.

Gunnar Neeme from "Mist of time"--
illustration accompanies poem in the book.

THE TALE OF THE SALAMANDER

The compilation of WNE created many wonderful dialogues, no manylogues! Ones where the kids who had lived in the Geislingen DP camp shared in addition to what little historical information they knew, also clips from blogs and other writings.
This is one which illustrates children's incredible strategies for survival in a confusing, fast moving world. It truly tells it through a child's eyes.

In the mid 1940s about three thousand Estonian refugees from the Russian onslaught arrived in a south German town called Geislingen. They had travelled through treacherous enemy ridden terrain by foot, horse drawn cart and sea.

The once secret secret fording place. MM

The irresistable waterfall.MM

Finally, they had left the chill winds of war behind them. They older of them were eager to begin their search for a lost normality; one which they had been denied them some years before. With them were small children who faced the perplexing task of learning a new normality. Born during the war, their normality was that of fear, loss and courage. Play was a notion they had to learn to understand.

Geislingen was an idyllic place which had escaped the bombing raids. It nestled in a valley among five hills. In September of 1945 they were ablaze with autumn colour.

On one of those hill-sides among the trees were nestled the old Helfenstein ruins. The town was a fairy tale place, partly consisting of typical German architecture. Some of the houses were similar to the houses that we had left behind in Estonia. These houses were fairly plain with steep roofs and dormers, and were attached side by side in groups of two to five. A river ran through the town. It had several bridges. A railway line connected it with adjoining towns and had a number of loop lines. These enabled the trains to disperse the products from the cutlery factory.

The oldies rapidly began to establish normality. Establishing schools and kindergartens for their children became part of it.

Perhaps for some of the littlies it became an abnormality: Learning seemed to be of little purpose. There was so much to be seen and learnt in that little town. The river, the castle ruins and the endless magic forests surely competed with useless things like learning to read and write.

My place was a short walk from my kindergarten. A railway bridge crossed the river near my place. That was an even shorter walk for me. Beneath the bridge grew blackberry bushes. I don't think that the fruit on them had ripened since war broke out. Indeed I don't think any fruit of the day had a chance to ripen.

The river and the grass under the railway bridge was a wonderful playground for children who were crammed into small spaces together with their war battered parents. Each family, unless large were only allotted a room each.

The chuffing and hooting trains were fun to watch and the bridge itself made a lofty fortress from which to bombard and holler to those who played below it. The splashing of the river water as we dropped stones into it and the whirlpools which those stones created kept us entranced.

The river was a challenge for many of us. It provided bridges which led to other parts of the town including the station, the large cutlery factory and the remainder of the DP camp up on another hill. The children who lived on that hill were truly blessed. They did not have to break bounds to find the old castle ruins. They only needed to climb like gazelles up the hillside through one of those magic forests. They could find Estonia without travelling to it. They could become lords of the town and regally gaze across it.

Breaking bounds was not too hard. The kindergarten was nearby and the children could walk there alone. They could walk anywhere else they wanted to alone too if the kindergarten did not entice them.

I cannot remember anything enticing at that kindergarten except the cocoa and biscuits which were sparingly handed out on special occasions by women who would have been better qualified to run a military platoon.

Had they been more motherly I guess that the Steige River would have remained uncharted and un-navigated by the newcomers to the town. There would have been no need for challenges like trying to get as close to the waterfall as possible without falling down it. The one casualty did not dampen our enthusiasm particularly as he recovered pretty quickly.

Mother had strict rules about me playing near the water. We reached a compromise, reluctant on mother's part naturally. I could sit on the steps into the river a little upstream from the waterfall. Of course there were lots of imaginary widely spaced steps leading well into the river. When I arrived home drenched somehow I doubt that mother believed that I had such long legs as to stretch between those elusive steps.

Coventry became a familiar visiting place.

For some reason the current in the river seemed to vary along it. Upstream it was less rapid than near the waterfall. Behind the hospital, which was upstream there was a fording place. It was the only place where the water was shallow enough to cross it when the bridges were manned by the oldies going about their daily activities. On our side of the river were the vegetable gardens which also grew unripe foodstuffs. They also grew tulips in spring. On the other side was the hospital. It was an imposing structure which concealed the hill and the castle ruins on the other side of it. It also concealed nomadic children.

That fording place was one of my favourite hooky places. I think that it was also one of my friend's favourite ones. I cannot remember the little boy's name. He must have been about my age because he seemed to be able to vanish without his mother being aware of it and he seemed unafraid of fording the river like a toddler would be. I cannot remember what we did when we stayed and played by the river.

I have kept in touch with some of my old playmates and established e-mail friendships with some of the other neighbourhood kids. One day this year I received a letter from a man named 'Klaus'. He is about my age, lived across the street from me in Geislingen and too loathed kindergarten. His mother had given up trying to send him there because he too played hooky. MM

In his letter he told me about playing by the river and trying to catch salamanders which hid under the rocks. He wrote about how if people grabbed the salamander by its tail, the tail would drop off when the salamander retreated. That fording place was one of the few places where the river banks were not too steep to play on.

It seems that Klaus forgot to write that the tail of the salamander regenerates. Perhaps he assumed that I knew.

Below are a couple excepts from Klaus communications when WNE was being compiled

"You're right we probably did all those things together. Actually I was told that I flunked out of kindergarten or I stopped going because I didn't like it. I have a photo of me in school probably the only day I went. If it weren't for Ulo (Kuhi) I wouldn't know any of this.

......I read your story about the salamander. How can you remember all those details? It was very descriptive & brought back one of the few memories that I can remember about Geislingen which is chasing salamanders by the waterfall & having their tails come off. My mother used to call me Klaus in Geislingen. Ulo says we lived near each other so maybe your Klaus is me?? That would be totally amazing!!!!"

But then most little Estonian girls became hooked on dolls rather than playing hooky.

Toy Museum in Tartu: Inge Pruks' aunt's dolls are displayed among the exhibits

RELICS OF THE WORLD THEY LEFT BEHIND

These are photos I took on my first return to Estonia in 2002. It was a place I remained wary of for many years after its independence. Many questions still remain unanswered. I am still perplexed what the urgency to photograph those structures was.

Me thinks that the explanation belongs to a very different book.

These photos were taken around Saaremaa: But such was the shore-scape along much of Europe's western coastline all those years ago.

The now defunct Soviet Submarine Nuclear submarine training center, Paldiski

The 'Pentagon' and surrounds, Paldiski.

WELL, FOR SOME THEIR SHOES STILL CONTAINED PRICKLY BURS

As children of war we were to meet many and varied fates: Some had an outcome which the war touched but didn't visibly buckle, at times perhaps the challenges gave us fortitudes. Others of us fell down many rungs of life's ladder to have to scramble up again at variable rates. For some of us we could see the precipitant of the tumble which may or may not have been declarable.

And inevitably there were many who were to travel through life to not comprehend why burs had been placed in their shoes: Nor could others understand this.

A true compass will always direct one where north is: Our compasses were as scrambled as our lives at times. It was a lottery for each of us how reliable a compass we had acquired in our early years.

Each of us as adults becomes responsible for our own destiny while fate moulds the road. That road can vary- we could not chose the people who programmed our early years. If they were not too smart their influences could haunt us for eons to follow rendering us prey to the indiscretions of others.

Ille Liscinski left Estonia is precarious circumstances at an age where such circumstances have profound effects of the long term outcomes. She is a lady with great dignity but in her poetry she cryptically shares that not all folk prospered as expected. Yes, she talks of

FROZEN MEMORIES

However laced among her writings are memories which left powerful imprints on her. She shares

AN UNFORGETTABLE ENCOUNTER WITH HENDRIK VISNAPUU

In 1947 I lived in Rappenecker and attend the Geislingen Estonian Gumnaasium. I shared a room with two women who talked all the time. It was very hard for me to study.

One day they talked about Hendrik Visnapuu, our foremost poet. They didn't know that I had a lot of my poetry in this room. I was very shy. I didn't dare show my work to anybody and seek an opinion for their worth. On the spur of the moment I decided to go and beg Mr. Visnapuu to tell me the truth about my humble efforts. I managed to grab my long ballads, the ten sonnets and other poems, walk to Mr. Visnapuu's place and knock on the door.

The poet was at home and opened the door. He was a slightly built man somewhat past the middle age and he smiled at me. This gave ne courage to introduce myself and the reason of my visit. I gave my poems to the Poet. He pointed at a rickety chair and I sat down. He sat behind his desk and started to read my work. I felt very frightened. Soon he will say "What a lot of nonsense"

After a long while Mr. Visnapuu started to talk about the poetry of pure rhymes in the Estonian language and how the so called "jrdrhymes' gave more colour and variety to our language. When he noticed my astonishment, to give me free lessons in prosody, I felt as if I was born again and accepted his offer too eagerly.

I would have liked to pay him something, but I had given my Red Cross parcel to the lady who gave me the mathematics lesson. Eventually I figured how I cold pay Mr. Visnapuu for his lessons and asked for a bucket, but there was no bucket, only a big conserve tin. But I managed to make the poet's floor shine.

UNRRA had published his latest poems. He gave me his book and a membership card of "The Estonian Authors Society" with my name on it.

"Stormy roads"
by
Juri Kork , who like
Ille was a student at
Geislingen Gumnaasium.
The image is derived from
the school annual

AND YET OTHERS BECAME ICONS OF THE WORLD THEIR FOLKS LEFT BEHIND

Tiiu Kera

was to become a Major General in the USA Air Force. She like many of her cohort continued to participate in the fight against Communism and towards Estonia's liberation. Mr. Lohmus the museum curator is standing nearby.
She remarks to Arved Plaks who observed her uniform in the Laidoner Museum:
"Arved,
You have a sharp eye!The Laidoner Museum is taking good care of my uniform and I am proud to have my service, as well as that of other Estonians abroad, recognized here. It was a thrill to sit at Kindral Laidoner's desk and sign the guest book"
Arved had remarked to her "I had just come across the photo of Tiiu's uniform in Tallinn, in the War Museums. Who else can come to Tallinn and know that if his or her suit case gets lost on the way,there is a spare outfit already there!

Wow, what an outfit! MM

MAI MADDISSON
ON THE OUTSIDE LOOKING IN

Our world consists of 'be's', 'wanna be's' and 'canna be's'. Perhaps in the context of this book, set when we were young it consisted of much the same: It was a mixture of tenacity, opportunity and the winds of fate which finally delivered us to our nesting places.

Each and every one of us were good people as were our folks: Perhaps the collective variable that war had dealt its vengeance on us variably, and we should not forget that World War I too impacted on our folks and their mythology upon us.

I have in many ways had a privileged life and the last ten or so, as I have been compiling the memories of our youth have brought more blessings upon me than many others: I have been sent letters both private, and ones to be shared with others. Many stories have come my way as have books and DVD's of those who too trod my road.

I have viewed them with immense pride: They have validated my stance with my more despondent patients. To them I have said "When all else fails pretend that you are a refugee and you have absolutely nothing. Let us work together to see what you can rebuild". What a powerful impact it has had on them. I have always been adamant not to disclose specific details but when they again hit a brick wall I remind them "Remember you have nothing. Where to now." Many of them discovered strengths they never believed they had.

Those stories and DVD's of course are the magnificent efforts in resourcing and persistence that only refugee and DP life can teach. My mind boggles at the tenacity of those creators: They like all of us began with nothing as we left Estonia way back in 1944. Those are the stories of the 'be's', some of whom of course at some time were the 'wanna be's'. More power to them.

But what percentage of the 10,000 or so Estonians at the eleventh hour do they constitute or represent. I wish that I could say the figure is 100 percent but my life as a coal face clinician tells me otherwise.

I have worked much of my life in areas where many of our European DPs began their lives in Australia. Their tales are not written anywhere except in medical files and at times misrepresented by colleagues who did not understand the reality of their youth: How many times was I to become the first person to include a past event in those files to improve the patient's self respect. Those patients, keen to become good citizens followed the local more of the stiff upper lip to me too as my name is nondescript: Well only because as an accident of a troop March! I do not carry my father's name on paper, only in my heart.

While examining patients one needs to say something: Perhaps if only to evade the sinister body language which might emerge during that examination: They deserve a gentler introduction to at times grim realities. I would look at their date of birth and their name and remark at what their life might have been in context of the history of those times. Their replies consistently "It was not that bad". Then the cat would spring out of my bag as I announced "That is not how I recall it". The cat from their bag was eager to join in. My new 'news' about their current issues was far from the vague, and seemingly painless once they to then had felt free to narrate of their pasts.

I have always worked among the less affluent patients, remote from those who had fared better. Working as a clinician does introduce as an artefact. One sees more sinister stuff than the average Joe.

One of the DVDs I have relished is one sent to me by Mati Sõõts: It is one he has laboriously edited from a series of silent films made by Ardo Tarem of life in Geislingen. Thank you Mati.

While I was six going on twenty-six during our last year in Geislingen, the birds and bees still lived a long way away and thus they did not invite me to the 'oldies' stuff which I cannot comment on.

The clips of the kids' stuff especially littlies' stuff left me feeling quite forlorn. I was pleased for the kids who appeared to be having so much fun: Albeit there was a sadness, and a look of emptiness in some of their eyes. However in the group represented that forlorn look was not prominent.

I wonder how many other kids stood with forlorn looks beside me, their eyes too, far away, with sadness wishing they were part of the activities: Like a small kid I was absorbed with my own disappointments.

The Sunday Scout, Guide and junior variants' parade to the flagpole which stood just a short ramble under the railway bridge away and near the river stands out clearly in my memory. I wished that I and those who stood with me would have been agile enough to be accepted into the littlies' brigade: My memories of the church service (separate to those events) with its hymn singing by much confusion about how to apply the ideology being preached and rather childishly feeling the pangs of being told to stop singing by the words "ära inise" (I can't quite translate that derogatory expression- it must be idiom, as the dictionaries don't help). How well I knew that expression: They say that repetition reinforces memory: Memory reinforcement of course was the task of the platoon commanders at kindergarten. I still wonder as we boast about the standards of teaching, that the pre-school teachers colleges didn't teach their students that there are more humane ways to communicate with tone deaf and clumsy kids. I don't mean by offering ignoble titles such as Aspergers, ADHD, autism - we wall know that endless list: Could it be that each of those kids just had different strengths: That all they needed was support and morale bolstering.

I recall from the DVD, the streets and kids playing in them but not being part of the games. I recall the folk dancing which the kids were taught and wished I were part of the dancing, as I did in Australia. I rapidly learned that having two left legs was a hindrance as they were for sporting endeavours.

But then more than certainly I was not the only one who felt alone for whatever reason: I did have my little friends and fortunately even then I was a dreamer and mini-philosopher away in a world of my own. I wonder what the modern day psychs would have done with us: I feel confident that it would not have been for children such as I and my friends.

I wonder how many other little kids were left out of the camps and community activities: I wonder how many like I have no recall of fun times: Times such as are alluded to in this book and WNE.

And no I am not whining 'poor me'. I am asking what happened to all those other kids who too walked in those shoes.

My mother wasn't the only person with shattered nerves. Such people figure nowhere in our narrative nor do their kids: Maybe some reach the more ignoble pages of the less noble publications. Can one blame them for their embitterment. Does anyone deserve to be called a 'dreg', which is a term I learned in medical school, and rapidly learned to not disclose that I too was one of those folk who derived from the 'pub culture'.

Nor is much shared about the outcomes of the amputee and disfigured kids. Did the loss of a limb truly eliminate them from activities such as chess, writing etc. Did anyone consider that some of those kids' concentration was suboptimal and pre-occupied by their survival needs. And let us not forget the kids who sustained head injuries in the transit (perhaps unbeknown to their parents given the prevailing chaos): What effect did that have on their futures apart from becoming targets to be maligned:

Neither mental health issues nor head injuries can be tattooed on those children's foreheads to plead for a little more tolerance and compassion from those around.

I wonder how many gave up their will to live: How many learned to self soothe with alcohol and mind altering substances. And it seems that it is unlikely that many would have lived long enough to tell their tale for this or any other book: They tend to perish around fifty five years of age according to current research.

I am one of the lucky ones who has survived to tell the tale. I owe my fortune to a father whose stubbornness I appear to have inherited: My learning from the war trek that people's indifference is nought but water on a duck's back: My learning from mother's shattered nerves that having endlessly belted me to pieces (perhaps by at times by intimidation but almost to pieces which remained attached) was a challenge in life not a handicap. And perhaps most of all I remember that I was one of the lucky ones to win a scholarship to medical school: Had those exams been a day earlier or later I might have performed differently and who knows what I might have been doing.

And reality street lives on: I now work close to the migrant hostel where we began our life in Australia. The streets abound with refugees of new cohorts. I often wonder how they fare. Some time ago at work I was called out onto the footpath because someone had died (well the onlookers' perception): The staff were wary for my safety, but Hippocrates Oath won. Under the passenger side of my car and between shrubbery lay a man. He was still alive. The police were most humane as we reflected on the tragedy of another refugees' life. He was one of the local 'drunks'. Did he not have a warmer and more sheltered place to rest his head. It is a memory which will haunt me for a long time. Given it was dusk and had I not been called out I would have approached the car from the other side. How many others of our folk (including later refugees) shelter in such precarious places.

I close with an anonymous snippet from a private letter: I know its author will not begrudge those words to help another: "It is regrettable that your travels do not take you to......**have very few callers as I have only two friends in ... The third died last year. My life is like a motor with four cylinders, but only one cylinder works...."**
And they do have the correct DNA to be recorded in this book.

THESE WERE SOME OF THE CHILDREN: WHAT HAPPENED TO THE REST?

I lived near that coveted corner for most of my time in Geislingen: At first in a dingy room in Rappenecker Strasse then at 144 Hospital weihe, initially in the attic then in the balcony room below it. I cannot remember inside the room.

Each Sunday morning I would meander either along the river or under the railway bridge to watch the Estonians launch again their mark of loyalty to their homeland and their culture.

I recall the music of the band, the camaraderie of the scouts, guides and their junior variants as they raised the flag and swore their oaths of commitment.

I so wished that I was among those kids: I was just too clumsy to be accepted into their midst. I stood and watched and watched and watched. Almost certainly there were many other kids watching equally longingly. The ceremony over, the parade headed for the Church to join the other Geislingen folks. I don't recall being at the Church.

Of all the sad memories of Geislingen this one still continues to haunt me the most. I was truly on the outside looking in. I wonder how many other such kids there were and for what reasons.

MUSIC AND DANCE WERE BRED INTO THEM FROM TODDLERHOOD

War and the Estonians' exodus from their native land took away their tools and for a variable time shattered many nerves. For some it also took away limbs and caused brain damage depriving their opportunity to optimally engage in what was their birthright. However for most their voices and limbs remained available to most until musical instruments again became available.

Life returned to routine very soon after the camps were set up. In kindergartens and schools singing and dancing their songs kept up their national morale.

Even little children would perform on festive occasions. For occasions where the needed skills were too complex for them they were engaged in other related tasks. Carrying the colourful braids for the song festival parades, acknowledging the performers with flower bouquets gave them an instant sense of participation and goals to aim for.

AN ESTONIA WITHOUT MUSIC AND DANCE WOULD NOT BE ESTONIA

For those of them who by the war's ravages, lost the skills to participate perhaps the greatest loss was not the kudos of performing but the amputation from a culture which kept morale alive and the camaraderie to learn social skills. But then determination bred just that. Many of them found ways to other meanings. For me (amputated from the culture for different reasons) playing hooky from kindergarten was perhaps the beginnings of my interest in psycho-philosophy: I had oodles of time to daydream and reflect on the where's and whys of mankind's inexplicable behaviour.
Perhaps my only regret that the teachers and others, needed to humiliate such kids out of circulation.
But perhaps nature was kind to us and allowed us to blot out of our memories events where we cast to be permanent spectators. The production of these books with their photo exchanges and now Ardo's film, for me and perhaps other children of similar ilk, were to be the first revelations of that such mirth existed for the kids amongst us.

HOWEVER THE STORY OF THEIR COHORT APPEARS TOO GOOD TO BE TRUE:MM

This book has alluded to how adroitly their cohort has moved on: There is little allusion to amputees, or the mentally battered apart from those alluded to in my writings.

Perusing "3 Aastat Geislingenis" (3 years in Geislingen) provides the fleeting allusions on this page. The images are from that publication.
Orthopaedic specialist called E. Laius opened a prosthesis production facility to provide these for invalids. The very need for such a facility indicating that there were invalids among them. We all recall amputees in Geislingen. I wonder what became of them. I know of one who has done well and of another who suicided.

DID THEY FORGET THEM?

The triad of images to the below right is of daily life in the invalids' domicile. They appear to have lived in the Forst Street guesthouse. Pictured is their shared dormitory and kitchen

NMKU clubrooooms: At the apprentice's school there were chess competitions. Let us hope that the less able bodied wer encouraged to participate in such.

Image MLM

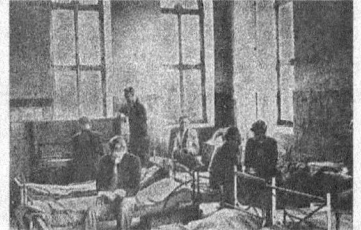

Henrik Visnapuu, with Petro Kusteri hiking-seeking inspiration.

Let us give due credit for the sports people who excelled at such sporting events but let us also reflect on what might have become of the less fortunate: I would like to believe that they were encouraged by Estonia's diversity of talented creative DP folk to pursue paths accessible to them.

In conjunction with the pending emigration, preparations began in September 1946 to perform medicals of the DPs. Each DP needed to have a medical where they were measured, weighed and X-rayed. The latter revealed 274 DPs with lung problems. I wonder how many of these DPs recovered well enough to be allowed to emigrate. What became of the others?

ENDEL TULVING
WE, THE YOUNG

We, the young of the present decade, are children of hard times. Our lives have coincided with a period in the history that is governed by injustice and iniquity, a world in which the ultimate arbiter is brutal power. The harsh reality metamorphosed from our fairy-tale childhood even before we became teens, and at the stage of life when young ones are especially sensitive to their environment we were surrounded by hatred and enmity, destruction and annihilation.

It is clear that these bitter experiences and the environment so remote from normal life, have left deep traces in our souls and have affected our beliefs, our understanding of life, and our behavior. We are often told that we are superficial in thoughts and actions, that we show indifference to the fate of the world, ourselves, and our homeland. We are said to be lacking ideals, we do not have the typical adventurous spirit that characterizes young people, we have no idea what enthusiasm and excitement mean. Our whole being carries a stamp of apathy and lassitude.

It is possible that some older people have indeed gained such an impression of us. After all they see only the outside of us; how we behave, act, and speak. And no one can deny that from our environment over the last few years we have inherited negative traits, habits, and biases.

Perhaps it has been less apparent that besides all this, however, through our own experience we have also learned many valuable lessons; that we have acquired intelligence that augurs well for success in life.

Above all we have learned to be critical of everything that we see and hear; we have firm convictions of what is good and what is evil; we know how to pay attention to what happens in the world around us; we are capable of drawing conclusions from what we see and hear. But all along we have practiced the great art of keeping our opinions to ourselves. We have seen how little words mean if they remain only words.

But for action there also are few opportunities today. We find ourselves in a situation in which we have to tolerate many things that we do not like and that we think are not right. After two difficult occupations of our homeland, when more than ever we experienced lack of justice, we are still astounded when young people are screened out of refugee camps only because of the year they carelessly chose to be born in, a year that less than twenty years later made them subject to forced mobilization by the occupiers. Or when life now is made difficult for those who do not rush to take a menial job overseas and prefer to seek education in high-school or university.

We know that the small group of our compatriots who managed to escape to the West now makes up our fighting force. We know that our trek abroad is not a road of martyrdom, but a journey with a mission. We know we have to fulfil a challenging task that requires the ultimate contribution from everyone, man or woman, young or old.

The young ones are more likely to be successful in this struggle than the members of the older generation, because they are not influenced in their endeavours by political considerations. The young ones are not tethered to any specific political ideology. They are driven by a single dream, by a single objective-- the homeland that is free and independent again.

As said, today we are not in a position to accomplish a great deal. Even so, we must not sit on our hands. Instead we must purposefully make use of every hour. A Chinese proverb says that an army's might depends not as much on the number of fighters as it does on their courage. We cannot enhance our striking group's strength quantitatively, but we can do a lot about it qualitatively. And herein lies our present task.

Above everything we must preserve our national identity and spirit. We must treasure our mother language and the culture of our forefathers. We must use every miniscule opportunity to acquire knowledge and skills that broaden our horizons. We must convert our forced exile to an educational journey that allows us to learn all about the world and its people and that, more than ever, makes us appreciate our worth as children of our people. Lastly, every one of us must use all his talents and wisdom in aspiring to become a "somebody" in the strictest sense of the word. Only when every soldier in our tiny army becomes an officer can we be certain of the final success of our journey with a mission.

We have not abandoned the hope for a brighter future. We have not given up our belief that eventually truth and justice will prevail. In doing so, we are not deceiving ourselves with illusions; we firmly believe that no goal, no hope, no ideal is lost unless we, ourselves, declare it lost.

It has been said that the strength of the young derives greatly from their underestimation of the obstacles to be overcome. It is indeed possible that our plans for the future are based on some questionable assumptions, because we lack experience. We do not possess a huge storehouse of crystallized facts. We are but early matured children of the war, who are more serious than they should be, and who know their obligations by virtue of being a part of a small, brave nation whose huge majority right now is forced to remain silent.

We dare to believe that we are walking the straight path, and fearlessly, full of hope, look forward to the future.

This piece was translated by Endel from the GEG annual where his original Estonian version was written.

GEISLINGEN GÜMNAASIUM STUDENTS

Endel Tulving
Bottom row middle

First graduation year

GEISLINGEN ESTONIAN HIGH SCHOOL STUDENTS

Second graduation year

These pages have been extracted from the GEG yearbook 1945-9

BLOWN BY THE WIND
ILLE LISCINSKI (also from GEG)

(Extract from "Frozen memories" with permission from CopyRight Publishing Company Pty.Ltd)

My kin was scattered
as if blown by the wind:
one dozen lucky ones landed in Sweden
where people had warm hearts
and welcomed them with kindness.
But five of them didn't stay
and sailed in a ricketty boat
away to South America.

Half a dozen poor ones
who had no gold or vodka
to give to the fishermen
to take them across the Baltic Sea
finished up in Germany
including myself.
Three of them went to Canada,
Two stayed in Potsdam
and I alone came
to the faraway Australia.

Two dozen were singled out
by the Red Tsar, Stalin,
and sent to the gulags
and kolkhozes in Siberia
where six of them perished.
Only a few stragglers were left
home in fear and trembling
under the paranoid
rule of the Soviet Union

When the light has gone: Extract from GEG annual

ARVED PLAKS
TEACHERS I HAVE ADMIRED AND SOME OTHERS NOT SO MUCH

This story has been previoulsy published in Eesti Elu/Estonian life.

As I am approaching the age that is expressed by a large round number, I must accept the fact that my productive years are behind me. That is what the statistics show. I also see that my friends are leaving the ranks of the living in increasing number. I call out:"Guys! Are you really leaving? We have not yet finished all our debates and our grand projects!"Reluctantly I have to reconcile myself with the knowledge that I might never see Machu Picchu with my own eyes. So all that remains for me is to look back and think how I got here.

There is enough to be satisfied with: my peasant ancestors became merchants,which led to me having the education that allowed me to work on the team that developed the International Space Station. How cool is that?

Who helped me set my goals and who set me on the path? Of course, my parents deserve most of the credit. But besides them who? It had to be teachers,but teachers in the broader sense of anyone who imparted knowledge to me whether or not she or he had a teaching certificate.

With most teachers the relationship lasted but a short season or a year, and in most cases was very one sided. I doubt if they ever remembered my name after the class and I barely remember theirs. But there are exceptions.

Foremost in my mind is the teacher I had in a Displace Persons' (DP) camp, whose death announcement recently appeared in this newspaper: Mrs. Heleena Koppermann. In 1945 refugees from East Europe in Germany could not return home,but the German economy was in shambles and Germany no longer needed us. The American Military gave us an opportunity to find accommodations in camps in which we were fed. My parents and I moved to a camp named Insula, situated in former army barracks complex near Berchtesgaden, Bavaria. There, among the Poles and Latvians who made up the majority of the camp, were about 60 Estonians,including three grade-school-aged children. I was one of them, a fourth grader.

The Estonians were concentrated on one floor of a barrack. The rooms had double-decker beds, and two families were assigned to a room. In time Mr. Andre fashioned dividers between the families out of Masonite (pressed wood) salvaged from crates. So the Estonian community of the camp became a very close "family" with little privacy and thus few secretes from each other. Of course there were irritations that come with such closeness, but also friendships. We were fed meals from a communal kitchen supplied by the American Army but administrated by the camp inhabitants. Given that the Poles and Latvians did not trust each other, many of the camp administrative posts were given to the smallest minority, the Estonians. But of course each nationality had its own school.

Upon urging from a larger Estonian center three volunteers were found to take on the chore of educating us: Mrs. Heleena Koppermann, Miss Hilda Laas, and Mr. Fritz Andre. They had no children themselves and had no teaching experience. They received mimeographed materials from larger Estonian centers, found an empty room in the barracks' basement and commenced teaching.

The problem with being in such a small school was that there was no chance of getting away with not doing homework assignments. Mrs. Koppermann took on Estonian literature and related topics, Miss Laas Geography and similar, while Mr. Andre taught me woodworking for just half a year, using tools in the camp workshop. In the other half of the year Miss Laas taught us how to knit. An old sweater was unraveled and knitting needles borrowed and so together with the two girls I learned knitting. No problem, I was secure enough in my manhood to endure that. Though I have never used my knitting skill since then,it taught me that I can learn even unexpected tasks!

Mrs. Koppermann was the soul of our school; she was a fiery, energetic young lady with piercing brown eyes. I was drawn to her. As a 12-year old I most likely was in love with her. What I remember most of what I learned from her was what happened on one occasion outside the class room. I had loved to brag of how I hated Russians who were the cause for us having to flee Estonia. I used to repeat, "Give me a Russian and I will wring his or her neck unless it isa very young girl." Mrs. Koppermann heard me during one such tirade. She pulled me aside and asked me, "Arved, did you know that both my parents came from czarist Russia during the First World War, and thus I am an ethnic Russian?" I was devastated. And lesson was learned. I never bragged like that again.

In an earlier incident when we were still in Tallinn,a teacher saved me and my parents from getting into serious trouble. In 1940 I was in my first year of school. The Soviet Union had just claimed Estonia for itself, and the country was in a rapid transition. The flying of the Estonian blue-black-white flag was forbidden. On the front wall of the classroom hung a picture of Stalin in place of our deposed president Päts. My grade school was part of the seminary that allowed teachers in training to practice their skills. One day a student teacher handed out a mandarin to each student. Next the teacher told us that Stalin loved children and understood us because he himself was trained to be a teacher and thus sent us these mandarins. We were now told to write an essay thanking Stalin.

I do not remember what I wrote but I remember that I drew Estonian flags around it. After I handed in my richly illustrated essay,the teacher came to my desk, and whispered in her squeaky voice that the illustrations were not allowed and I should take the essay to my parents. All I remember of her is her weird voice. At home my father subsequently kept his blue-black-white table flag mounted on "Pikk Herman" in a locked desk drawer. Who knows what trouble this teacher kept my parents from by not informing the authorities, as she was required to do?

Some learning experiences were negative. Perhaps the earliest that I remember was when I was six years old and our maid was tasked with making me practice reading in preparation for an entrance exam for grade school. To enter we had to be able to read. It was the word "but" which challenged me. In Estonian it is "aga." The maid told me "read it!" And I would read "a-ge-a." This went on until I was in tears, but I held my ground. Subsequently I mastered reading and passed the exam.

After the escape from Estonia to Southern Germany in September 1944, I ended up in a village grade school. I remember the teacher by name, Miss. Birnbaum and her shrieks when a student had not met her expectations. When shrieks were not enough to make her point she resorted to her bamboo sticks, which were about foot long. The offending student had to hold his or her hand out and she would hit it with a stick. After a while the sticks would splinter, but that was no problem for her, for she kept an ample supply of them.

I too got hit several occasions, with the number of hits measured according to her schedule. This occurred during oral math exercises. She would yell out two four digit numbers, then point to a student who would have to repeat the numbers and then quickly call out the sum. I could speak German fairly well but remembering numbers was confusing for me. For example in German twenty two is spoken as two-and-twenty. So she caught me several times not responding quickly enough.

My worst of memory of Miss. Birnbaum was from the time when she decided to make an example of a kid who was occasionally late. The fact that he had to walk to school a great distance did not matter. In front of the classroom was a life-sized framed picture of der Führer, Adolf Hitler, whom every student entering the classroom would have to salute with a loud "Hail Hitler" while throwing his right hand out straight. This had to be done even when the class work had started. Of course, latecomers were very disruptive. One time when the boy had once again defied the clock, Miss. Birnbaum called in the principal, Mr. Furtmayr, a former army officer who had lost a leg in the war and walked with a crutch. He entered and in front of the class, beat the boy mercilessly with his crutch while yelling. Needless to say, I was never late.

When the war ended Miss. Birnbaum was released because of her Nazi party membership. She was replaced with Mrs. Baumbusch, a kind person. I remember her because of the contrast with her predecessor. I continued to go to the village school until my parents and I moved to the aforementioned DP camp. After I left Mrs. Baumbusch encouraged her students to write me in the camp. I appreciated that and responded with a letter.

I have more complete memories of teachers from my years in gymnasium before emigrating to the US and of high school after emigrating. After leaving our unique small grade school in camp Insula we moved to the city of Geislingen, where over 4000 Estonian refugees were housed. Here I entered the Estonian gymnasium which I attended until emigrating in the middle of my sophomore year.

I have written about my experiences in the gymnasium in the album "Geislingeni Eesti Gümnaasiumi Õpilaste ja Õpetajate Elulugusid,"("Life stories of students and teachers of the Estonian Gymnasium in Geislingen") a compilation of experiences by 260 students and teachers that I edited. Here the contact was less personal between the students and teachers. The teachers were professional and their teaching was targeted. Still there were inspiring moments like when our geography teacher Paul Lannus drew the profiles of Africa and South America on the black-board and showed how the shorelines matched! The land masses must have separated! Only much later was this fact substantiated by of research done on the Atlantic Ocean floor, but I accepted it as fact already in 1948 in Mr. Lannus's class.

The gymnasium had the no-nonsense curriculum of prewar Estonia. Our texts were brought from Estonia by fleeing teachers, retyped and mimeographed. The human side of my experience included watching Mr. Laan, our language teacher, pick on a student called Maise-poiss, whose attendance was spotty and class participation not up to Mr. Laan's standards. Mr. Laan kept picking on him until he quit coming to school. Mr. Laan did something else that I never could quite understand: he took our skull dimensions, one student at a time, and made some kind of judgments based on them.

My best experience was in the Religious education classes with Rev. Johannes Aarik. He allowed freewheeling discussions in class. Rather than conducting the class from the front, he leaned against the window ledge on the side of the class room which I believe was symbolic.

The discussions were frank and engaging. I declared myself an atheist in the process but also formed a lifelong friendship with him. After his return to Estonia upon his retirement I visited him every time I went to Estonia at his home in Nõmme, until his death in 2011. I found it flattering that he would engage me in deep religious topics, but then again he himself was a bit of a rebel. (His articles have appeared in this newspaper.)

In 1949 we immigrated to the United States, and found temporary accommodations in a summer cabin near Bethel, Connecticut. Despite my broken English, I was enrolled in Bethel High school's tenth grade after only a week. This experience was a very new and exciting one.

I recall how kind all the teachers and students were to me. Perhaps they wanted to compensate for the deprivations of the war, but whatever the reason, people bent over backwards to make me feel welcome. I recall names of teachers I never got to thank: Mrs. Carroll (Literature), Mrs. Bishop (Chemistry), Mr. Pointen (Shop) and Mr. Peachy, the principal. Whenever I knew the answer to a question they pointed out how smart I was, and if I did not, they said, "Oh well, he does not know the language".

By my senior year we had moved to Danbury and I attended the school there. My next classroom "wow" moment occurred in the Descriptive Geometry class. I doubt that many people lay wake in bed and contemplate the boundaries of our existence,but for me the breakthrough happened in this class when Mr. Parsons explained the concept of infinity. Most students had such a hard time accepting that you can count numbers 1, 2, 3… and never stop – that there is no final number. I at last accepted at last this concept of time and space without limits and what it says about our importance or unimportance in the universe.

I continued my education at the University of Connecticut , and for this my thanks go the taxpayers who subsidized it. No way could I have afforded to go to any other university on my earnings from my summer jobs.
This being a land-grant school, the only obligation I had was to participate in the Reserve Officers Training Corps (ROTC). We marched once a week in uniforms in an open field for a couple of hours and those who chose the Air Force (AF) option had to take a course in Geopolitics. Of course this was no problem to anyone that came from overseas and I "aced" it. I still feel gratitude being able to afford an education.

Perhaps I should also feel gratitude for the instructors and professors, who did not cut me slack for my less-than-perfect English. **It was a rude awakening that I had to compete for grades on the basis of what I produced on paper.** That D grade that Mr. McGrew gave me in English Composition dashed my hopes of getting onto the honor roll and earning a scholarship, despite the fact that all my other grades that year were A's. But it was also was wake up call for me.

For setting my ultimate goal of making a career in aerospace engineering,credit goes to my AF ROTC instructor Capt. Lang and his staff in my undergraduate years. Whatever they saw in me they took me along on their proficiency flights from Westover A.F. base. I loved to look down from 5000 feet through the twin-engine trainer's glass nose.

At the same time my fellow cadets saw something in me and elected me Commander of the undergraduate AF ROTC

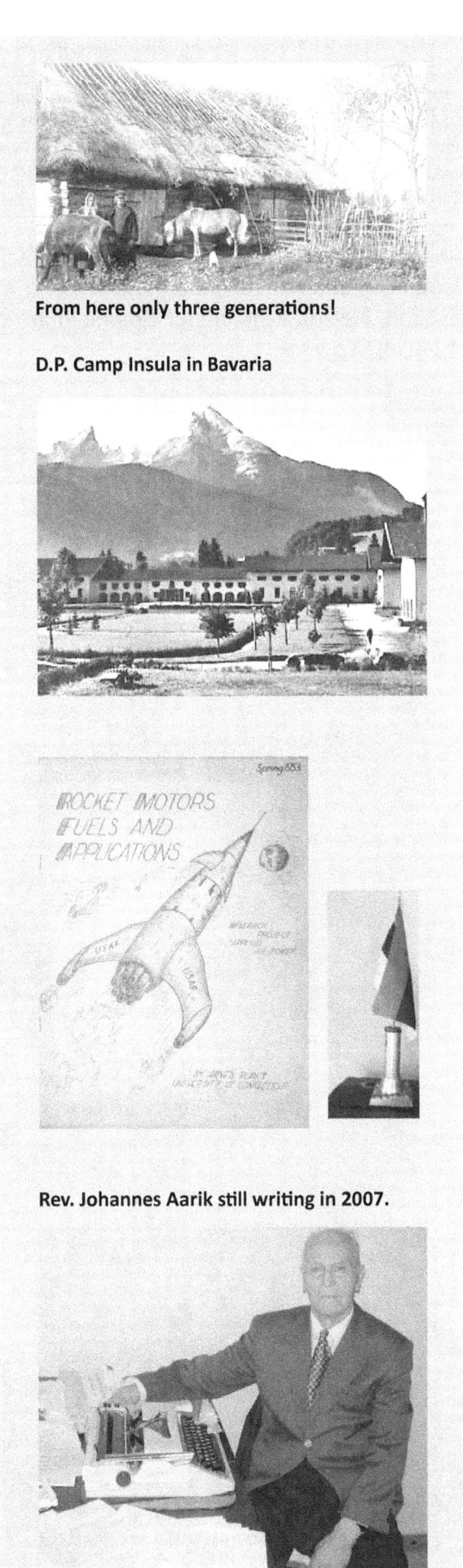

From here only three generations!

D.P. Camp Insula in Bavaria

Rev. Johannes Aarik still writing in 2007.

student organization called Command Squadron. No doubt in part due to this was accepted into the advanced ROTC program in my junior year despite the fact that U.S. citizenship was prerequisite. At that time I had not been in the country for five years and therefore was not yet eligible to become a citizen.

All these experiences caused me to set my sights on a career in aerospace engineering. This I achieved and after 44 years in the industry I retired from the team that developed International Space Station.

Looking back at my learning experience I have been blessed by having been under the wing of Mrs. Koppermann, Rev. Aarik, Captain Lang and many other good teachers,not including Miss. Birnbaum during the last days of Nazi Germany.

What can I conclude from this? **There are no "self-made men."We grow on the shoulders of so many around us and with a "little help from our friends,"parents, teachers, mentors, and our society in general, we can achieve our dreams. I am deeply grateful to so many, and I wish I had thanked them all in person.**

My thoughts grow gentle
and become a whisper of breath
and a velvety flow of silence.
Golden serenity is found
where peace persists
and truth remains undissembled.

In this serenity,
nothing is without,
nothing is within,
everything dissolves
and all boundaries disperse.

Life is sacred,
time is sacred,.
Using them wisely we can make
everything more beautiful
and nobler.

from Gunnar Neeme "Mist of time"

EVE SILLAOTS/NOWACKI
GEISLINGENS DP CHILDREN REMEMBER

This is an e-mail I recieved way back in December 2010: Something about it touched me. Eve was just a few months younger than I and her folks hailed from Parnu as did the folk on my mother's side. I am not sure if the formating was intentional or an artefcat of e-mailing at the time. I have chosen not to modify the format. I sought long and hard to be allowed to publish it. Finally at the eleventh hour I was able to make contact with Dahlia who told me that her mother would be honoured to have that e-mail published. Thank you Dahlia.

Born dec. 4 1942 in Parnu Estonia......mother...Hildegard Sillaots..nee Roose.......father..Elmar Sillaots.......I was ... Eve Mall Sillaots.......father was Estonian Cavallry Officer sent to Siberia......Mother and I end up in Geislingen.........

Mother finds brother in law Oswald Pedajas in hospital, ...the survivor of ship.........torpidoed..... in Baltic Sea....lost wife and daughter....his wife was my fathers sister...after a lenghy....hospital stay....joins mother to search for lost family members........no one found......life resumes.....He is Oswald Pedajas......hired at UNRO.........life resumed to implant similar memories and after reading your book I now at the age of 67 understand my history much better......difficulties lay mostly with immigration.......mother and Oswald who was also my Estonian Godfather, married and I was legally adopted....we ended up in Toronto in 1951.........after 2 weeks spent at our sponsors Oswald decided we were not treated as agreed and we left...........both found jobs, rented rooms ....I went to school for the first time....... time went by gracefully.......

one day we were informed that my father Elmar was alive and back in Estonia........I had assumed he had died.........my stepfather had become my father.......in those days psychology was unheard of for the common man's problems.....my parents decided to ignore the new event though my mother started to develop guilt.....in those days of the communist threats the world was a scary existence.... in 1954 we did not communicate with Estonia...... my life continues in happy childhood..the G bond among Estonians in Toronto prevailed though my parents friends unusually were childless....but slowly now it seemed to me that once the outside threats were eliminated the inside threats emerged....

1957 father O was offered a promotion to work in Montreal.......we moved but it turned into difficult times for Mother.....until then she had worked and had had Estonian friends.......she never integrated into the newy environment and spent a lonely existence at home, resulting in a nervous breakdown. Mental health issues in those years were still unrecognized and we as a little lonely family went underground.

I finished high school and with no input from my parents took time off and went to work in a lab of a pharmaceutial co........the first day of work I passed a young man and didn't take notice.....he left after a short time but on the last day invited me for a date...the year63.....we were married in 1966................

Andre Nowacki is a Polish JEW, born in Warsaw in 1936......he and his mother survived the WWII with Christian IDs........he was hidden for most of the time by a Christian Family of a mother with 3 daughters.......all of his family was lost except one aunt, her husband and daughter....

Andre and his mother imigrated to Israel in 1950............ironically life post war Poland was lived very similarly with heroic Mothers..........

I went to University and finished my BSc...degree....Andre loves to travel and had already been to Europe for a 6 month motor scooter trip.....so we decided to go for a 2 month trip covering everything from Sweden to Italy......this included a visit to Geislingen.......I remembered nothing to my amazement.....but the fondness lingered......

and I continued to recall those beneficial memories and still to muse if I managed my life therefore successfully.....1968 my daughter Daliah was born....we moved to Toronto.....parents stay in Montreal......no link with Estonians in Toronto.....

father O gets cancer and they move to Toronto.....dies shortly after......mother has total breakdown is commited and put on medication...... comes home....

I contact some old friends and am informed that father Elmar is alive and living with my mother's sister in Ootepaa..... letters are exchanged....and in 1973 Mother and I fly to Estonia to meet Father, Aunt and some other family members....

It was bittersweet....communism had done its job.......there was nothing romantic except issues were clarified...Father wanted Mother to come back to Estonia...there was still the old family homestead...the soviets denied her exceptance.......Father died of cancer in 1977.......meanwhile we had all moved back to Montreal in 1973.........in1975 my other daughter, Alexandra was born........we had an opportunity to move to Virginia, USA.......

Mother moves back to Toronto and rents rooms from an old friend from Estonia....... lives there 14 years and finally in a senior apt.for the rest of her years...1997.....87 years....the last 22 years of satisfactory independence and visiting me and my family in our odyssey......Fredericksberg Va........Louisville KY.......Mt.Vernon NY........West Bloomfield MI.......Long Beach NY......

Tel Aviv Israel remains as a haven especially for my husband who has his Mother's old apartment as a healing any time he wants...time passes, the children grow up, get married, have children, have successful careers, ups and downs.........there is always something to be concerned about .....and I keep an eye on the pulse and slowly time becomes just a little planet of amazingly recorded events and memories and one day here I am sitting and musing ....from the beginning

I had to express myself through my hands.........art.....sewing.......knitting.......gardening....cooking.

Memories make us what we are................We want to have our own History...........and as I love to knit........it is the first thing I remember in G------ my mother Knitting and I watching and deciding I will knit and so did and am still doing it.

Knitting has been a common thread that has run through my life.......somehow in the past years yarns become available at bargain prices and I have accumulated a mass of magnificent yarn. The yarn went on to inspire me to leave a legacy in honor of my parents who were denied personal honor of their existence.......I began by knitting basic dresses from all the vibrant yarns and as the saying goes one thing led to another.........

being an artist by nature I have not run out of new ideas and as I advance the collection grows......each has a label designating........HILDEGARD ROOSE.........ELMAR SILLAOTS.................and as a after thought Mother was weaver and Father was from parents who were tailors..............ANDRE [SOLOMON TEBLUM] Father had knitting factory in Warsaw............

life is what you make it.......luck comes and goes.......joy and sorrow will always be there but we have the comfort of religion, great sagas andliterature.Amazingly both my daughters are very stoic and have always met all obstacles head on.

When I comment them about this , they say mother, this is what our home was all about. Now there is Maya 8, Ezra 2 and Zooey 3 months. All are feisty and ready, come what may. Female...........expressed in Art has paralled in my art and Alexandra at a young age was amazing.

Now Daliah's daughter, Maya is showing similar art work but the female is less distressed. Her mother has a no nonesence attitude toward life and deals competently with whatever problem comes her way. Therefore both girls inherited their father's strength and obstinence..so time passes and every once in a while I tell encountered people of our saga.

Then come the computers and I resist for many years. My daughters are offering to me mom get a computer. OK finally. But I approach with caution. Years past and I browse but am not thrilled.

One day Geislingen enters my mind while knitting . Lets see. There it is. Still very active. Wow.........someone wrote a book about. I must get it. It came a week ago.......................................

PS my husbands saga is much more harrowing and has been documented. see google Andre Nowacki... His mother was an amazing mother............Helena Altman....Teblum......Nowacki......Rabinovitz.......survived the Warsaw Ghetto and hid her son for years.

On the top shelf is an autographed milk jug which was presented to me at Geislingen 2008.

It is typical of the jugs we used to collect milk with from the dairy which was at the end of our street. I have no recollection of the dairy or obtaining milk from it. We lived there for three years! MM

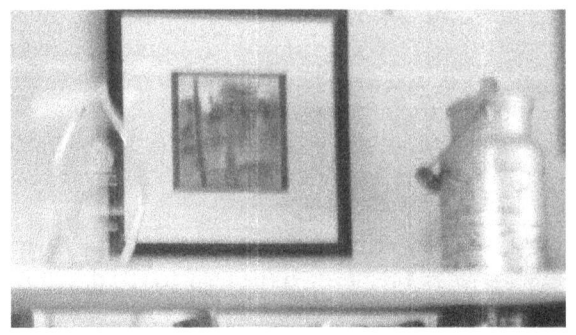

RECYCLED UGLINESS BECOMES A LIMBO FOR SOME

Gustern Lutter writes: "Seems this fits the context of our recent e-mail correspondence and some books of the WWII refugee and DP era we have been discussing. I tend to get hung up on correct reporting of the sequence of events in these tellings, but I guess the nature of events is more important than a correct time-line.

Yes, as we traipsed through those beautiful forests as small tykes we could not imagine anything more sinister within them: And accepted our occasional meetings with them in that context.

In 2011 I visited Dachau, which now of course was no longer the decrepit hole it was when we transited that region. Yet somehow it felt familiar despite it being polished up. It only had photos of the horrifics which we knew little about but according to anecdotal information many of us spent times in defunct concentration camps of similar ilk.

While of course refurbished, these were the fittings and surroundings where many of us spent our early years. Triple/double bunks and all.

The camp at Bagnoli in Italy too had triple bunks. MM

We have all in our past confirmed that "Arbeit macht NICHT frei: And of course "Robote" auch "Niet"! It matters not whether it was enacted in central Europe or the wilds of Siberia. MM

ARTWORK FROM GEISLINGEN GÜMNAASIUM (HIGH SCHOOL) ANNUAL

Unfortunately the names of the artists are not indicated in the journal.

The poetry in the journal is rather beautiful: However it is not a medium which can be translated into another language by anyone but the author: Such nuances are too complex.

ANGST, UNCERTAINTY AND FRUSTRATION WERE RIFE: THEY HAD ROLE MODELS: MLM

Volleyball team? Dad (Eduard Limon) is #11. He was a volleyball player.

Marje is uncertain of the details of these photos. From their format Marje feels that they appear to have a common origin.

The photo above is possibly from the LS Olympics in 1953 in Nürnberg.

The photo below has written on its back "3. Sept. 53. Meie võidurikas 4221 kergejõustiku meeskond L.S. Olympiaadilt Nürnbergis" which translates as "Our triumphant athletics team in the L.S. Olympics in Nürnberg"

Marje's father was very much into sport so her mythology has some sport focus.

As Marje relates her 'mythology' competitive sport was an early priotity while marking time. For the youngies it allowed them to stay fit and vent their feelings in a non-destructive way. Their energy was also diverted to folk dancing which I watched with much envy- If I could only not have had 3 left feet! But perhaps that would not have resolved the sadness. DNA has a habit of carving irreparable wounds. MM

FROM THEIR PARENTS, SPORT WAS ONE MODALITY THEY LEARNED FOR COPING:

Photos from the 1948 Baltic Olympics in Nürnberg

Soccer players (judging from their socks)????

Dad (Eduard Limion) in uniform

These 3 pictures below are probably not from the 1948 Balti mängud (sports) but I've included them in this grouping because they are sports-related.

I think the one below might be from Geislingen judging from the hills in the background but I really don't know.

AS DPs THEIR FOLKS MARKED TIME

Inne Kiipsar/Jonsaar

Sisters Kaare Kolbre (left) wearing Eesti müts and Aire K. Kolbre wearing a knitted cap in Blomberg DP camp in 1945

Tiiu wearing her tanu

Estonia has always had a rich cultural life which has integrated many modalities.

The creative spirit of their folks has allowed their morale to survive where it might have otherwise not done so.

The performing arts in their many modalities travelled with them through the war zones to their new lands. Their literature and creativeness was too: The latter to be their guiding angel and manifest through both art and handicrafts.

For many years art became less accessible as necessity assumed priority of time and resources: Albeit sketches on scarps of paper are to be found!

In the camps there was a need to mark time: What better way than to make use of use intuitive skills passed on through the generations.

Clothing was hard to come by and largely improvised for the children from cut downs of adults' clothing by carefully navigating among the worn out parts, and at times from army blankets and articles from charity parcels .

Warm winter woollies of course were an integral part to survival against the poor living conditions, inclement weather and inadequate food.

Skeins of wool were something their folks left behind in their haste and the needed culling of carried belongings. By corollary worn out woollies became the norm. Their mothers patiently unravelled old woollies preserving sections of wool which was still robust. There were ample colors but of course rarely enough of any single one to make a garment. The knitters among their mothers were quick to improvise: Estonian knitting had always had a colorful identity: They set to work creating jumpers, scarves, gloves, sox and hats.

Those hats live on fondly in many of their memories: They are visible in many of the photographs of the times and many of them still retain them as keepsakes.

IN MANY CREATIVE WAYS

TANUS were definitely 'cool' among our young all those decades ago.

Yes, so 'cool' that one little Geislingen girl cried because she lacked someone to knit her one.

Tanus/Eesti mütsid from Aire's collection

Aire Kolbre wearing Eesti Müts in Connecticut, USA

Doll making, especially of ones in national costume was a popular past time. I cannot recall seeing this but imbibed in me is a fondness for such dolls.

The only doll making I recall is of ones drawn on paper, and garments drawn on separate paper. The latter had tabs to 'clip' onto the dolls - Perhaps the fore-runner of Barbie dolls!! Photos Inge Pruks

While marking time in the camps many of their parents participated in handicrafts of many kinds to a very high standard and often sold the fruits of the hard work to those who were prepared to part with money and other commodities.

The American occupying forces found these arifacts to be wonderful presents to send to the folks back in USA.

Among such wonderful artifacts were items of exquisite leather work, weaving and metal engraving.
I have no idea who made these, presumably in Geislingen but I do know that they are truly the works of master craftsmen.

PORTABLE ASSETS FROM ESTONIA

The performing arts were an integral part of Estonian life: No matter what happened they kept morale high. The flight from Estonia allowed their folks to take little with them: Material possessions were cumbersome. However voices for most who survived were not lost and lost limbs, while tragic, affected a minority only. Musical instruments were not initially accessible but were eagerly grasped as they materialised.

Yes, Geislingen camp was barely afloat when its theater began its productions. Other camps too grasped the opportunities as they evolved.

Clips of theatre performances in Geislingen

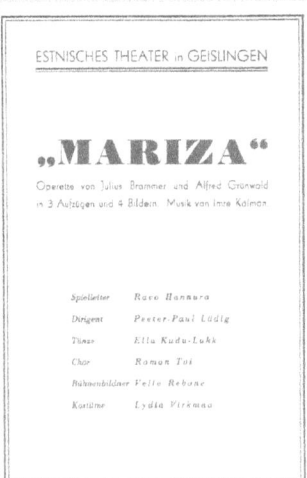

TO THE CAMPS TO THE NEWLANDS: ALAN ADAMS

The greatest assets any child can have are well integrated parents to act as role models for surviving adversity. There were times that all they could do was mark time.
Their parents enthusiasm for the theatre was of course extended to involve the children too. They too performed, sang and danced.
Uncertainty was their constant companion, and continued as they moved onto their new homelands. Again the performing arts were rapidly reborn to keep their bodies and souls together.

These images are part of a collection sent to me by the children of Ravo Hannura who was actively involved in Geislingen's theatre.

"Flags in a storm"

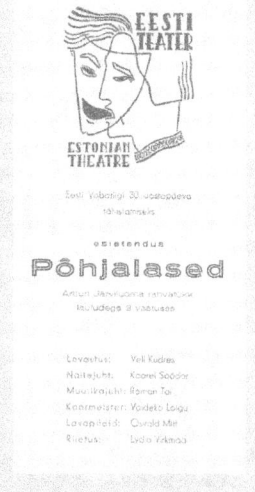

Jahnhalle Geislingen "where it all happened"

Estonian ballet in Germany

MANYLOGUE ABOUT THEIR MUSIC & PERFORMING ARTS: GGM

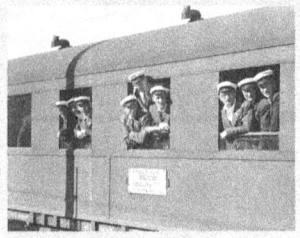

Photos from Ants Toi's collection.
Ants' father, Roman was one of many choir conductors who toured among the camps to help them find them way ourt of hell: Heaven a long way away at the time.

Ilvi Joe: Indeed, Jahnhalle played a central role in our Geislingen lives. Besides those unforgettable operetta productions, ballet was staged and concerts were held there (I heard my first piano concert at Jahnhalle). Also, I recall that school "aktus" was held there and many other activities involving school children. Veronika Lukk taught dance (I was one of her students) and she used to present her students' performances at Jahnhalle.

Regarding our memories of theatre in Geislingen, I'm sure most of us have them, because Jahnhalle was central to our lives at the camp. Not only did we see plays at Jahnhalle, but many of the "kooli aktused" were held there. In addition, concerts and ballet were staged there. I still see Ella Kuddu-Lukk taking a high leap across the stage!

The Geislingen theater question made me look up what I wrote about it in the family chronicle "A Mighty Hand" that I compiled in 1996 before I moved to Eesti. Concerning the Geislingen DP camp period, I visited the archives in Lakewood, New Jersey, where the camp's documents are deposited. In the archives is an UNRRA report containing a wealth information on the establishment of the DP camp. Hence I wrote the following in the chronicle regarding the cultural life: "

An Arts and Theater Section organized almost immediately and in November of 1945, it staged its first performance, a variety show. That show was given four times. In the beginning the artists had for their use some inadequate rooms, but then Jahnhalle was requisitioned, and it became the center for our stage productions as well as school assemblies. A very active theater group developed, owing to a large presence of many professional actors, singers, and production people among the refugees. Jahnhalle housed professional level productions despite material shortages for props and costumes. The theater had its own dance troupe, costume shop and musicians. During its six year existence, 83 full productions were staged, ranging from operettas and dramas to puppet theater for the children. The theater company also toured the other Estonian refugee camps in Germany and the Report boasted that 'the best DP theatre in the U.S. Zone' was in Geislingen'."

Ants Toi: About 2 weeks ago (now 3 years ago**) my dad had an unbelievable 95th birthday organized by the choirs as a combined concert. I sat back aghast in disbelief at what the chorus had organized.** Personal video greetings from Estonian President, Viljandi linnapea, Sakala meeskoor. Letter from Canada's prime minister. Three music faculty representatives came from Estonia to make personal presentations. A breathtaking list of warm greetings from the who's who of Estonian and pagulas Estonian music groups all relating personal experiences where my dad had been a source of encouragement and inspiration to them, and more. The write up in Eesti Elu does not do it credit.

Kalev Ehin writes:
Music as a symbol of Estonia's culture :The Estonian people are noted for their passion for singing. For centuries after they first lost their independence in 1227, singing was their only means of maintaining their identity and self esteem

The two day National Song Festival was undoubtedly most moving and rewarding experiences I have ever had during my entire life they stood with their backs straight and head held high, refusing to be intimidated by their current landlords.

I sensed the strife and emotions of the Estonian people: I had felt their agony and their pride- their willingness to suffer rather than yield to tyranny. I had touched the heart of my ancestral past. I had sensed the vastness and depth of this tiny nation's soul.

MAYBE EVEN SANTAS HAD HIERARCHIES* OR MAYBE THEY DID PRIVATE HOME VISITS ALSO

Viewing Ardo Tarem's film was an absolute revelation to me. I had seen still photos of some of the kindergarten dancing and singing activities when compiling WNE. There was not that much narrative about them. My assumption that they were but part of another festive day where the kindergarten teachers impressed the parents with the agility and song that they had taught their classes. I was quite unmoved by all this as I had no penchant to be where I wasn't wanted.

It seems that at least one Christmas in Geislingen was quite a major event where Santa arrived to hear out the children's confessions of ill doings and then handed out the presents. It is warming to see the gratitude on the children's faces at receiving simple tokens of warmth: How different to the Christmas lists which are in vogue now.

Did the church service precede this event and when was the Christmas Eve dinner eaten? Surely the children would haev been too tired to eat anything after all that excitement!

My recall of Christmases was one of going to church, then coming home to a special meal. I recall that some form of meat and sauerkraut with "Grubbid' (barley) was a delicacy much awaited. I have no recall of sitting at a table eating it or anyone being present.

Santa certainly arrived. By our last Christmas there I had worked out that Santa looked like Maano Milles father: That there had been someone else the previous Christmas and the one before. I can't recall what the response was when I announced this to Santa.

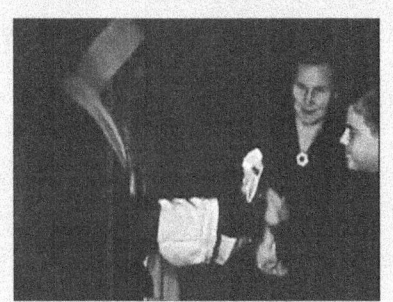

I can certainly recall the notion of the European type of Christmas tree with real candles and glittery decorations and my early disillusionment in Australia when Christmas trees were much less ornate: Though times have changed and of course electricity has made the dry fir trees less flammable in our hot summer Christmases.

I now wonder if we were exiled to the extent that we were not welcome at such functions: There is some suggestion of that as I have researched my past. Or maybe we were there and I have just dissociated the pain of not being allowed to be part of those festive activities. I will never know!

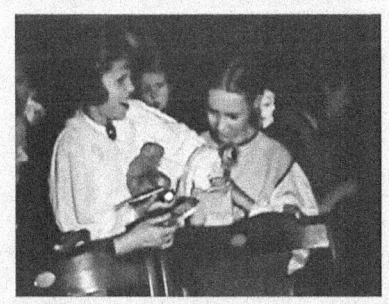

New Year's eve certainly leaves me with more tangible memories. I recall grandfather making up a small metal container and putting something in it which melted and then throwing the hot stuff into a bucket of cold water creating some interesting shapes.

From those shapes we were meant'to fantasise, or see into the crystal ball what the next year held, or maybe wish for what it might bring.

I certainly have no great wishes I recall at those times: Maybe a wish that I were less clumsy, though I suspect I had resigned to that one. Apart from pining to see father out of POW camp I had no real wishes.

In Australia likewise I was a simple child content with the life among adversity and still had no further wishes: And of course then came the time when I realised that more might have been had but wishes don't always come true.

*Marje Limion/Medri's mother shares the secrets of that quandary.

AUTHOR GROUP 'MANYLOGUE' PREPARING FOR THE NEW WORLDS

Inge Pruks:
It is interesting to read about everyone's memories and journeys.
However, the voyage from Bremerhaven to Australia took much longer than the voyage to America, it took us over four weeks.
I wonder how the Americans welcomed their newly-arrived refugees?

Ilvi Joe:
......that the procedure an applicant for immigration had to go through before given a visa was very thorough. Not only medical exams by physicians were conducted, but also political history was scrutinized.

The last medical exam was on the morning of the scheduled departure for the hold in Bremerhaven. In our case (we were in the processing center located at Ludwigsburg), I remember that well, because the physician found scarlet fever spots on my sister Linda's stomach. She was taken forthwith to the hospital and we were quarantined (not only us, but also the folks that were lodged in the same room with us) for couple weeks (needless to say, they were not happy). After Linda was well, we were assigned to the next transport to Bremerhaven and lo and behold! The physician found spots on Liivi's stomach on the morning of the transport. Again, the same routine.

Finally, when we were ready once again for transport, you can imagine our mother's worry lest I have spots on my stomach. The visa would have expired by the time we had gone through that routine a third time. Fortunately, we all received a clean bill of health and were transported to Bremerhaven.

Mai:
It is amazing how one can have a memory like an elephant and not remember one iota of the transit preparations: My only recollection of haggling with the radiographer trying to x-ray may chest and them demanding to raise my right arm higher than it would go. I have accessed a copy of it since: Interesting as was the medical report itself: I would have been flunked if I said that in medical school.

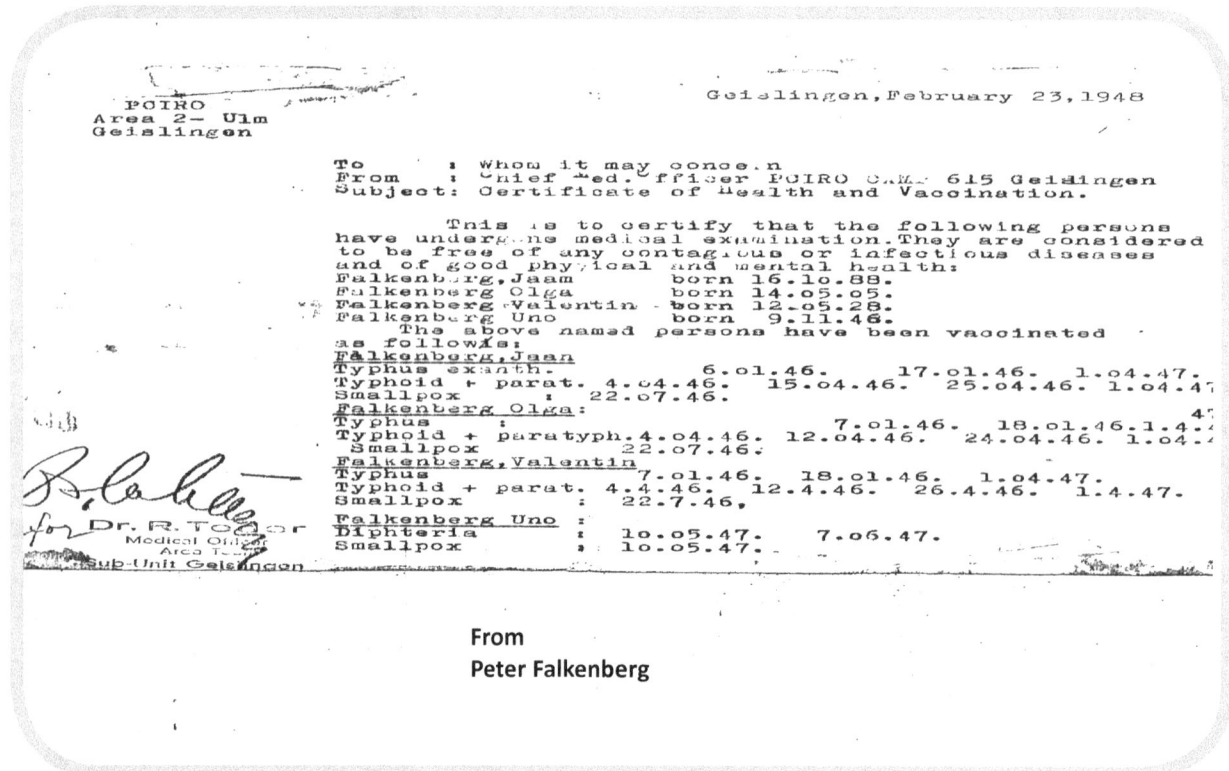

From
Peter Falkenberg

For this book's 'manylogue' I posed a question about the medicals prior to our departure from Europe: I alluded to them as in cold hard reality that which cast the dye for decades that followed, for better or worse.

Ilvi Joe posed a question:
""What do you mean by "medicals which were in cold hard reality"?

My reply "Simple- If you flunked them then you didn't get to USA, Oz, where ever!! Unless somehow a way was found to fudge documents like ours proved to be- I still wonder how!

Ilvi continues: "That helps, Thanks. I don't know of any case where documents were fudged for medical reasons, but in the case of my brother, he fudged a document by making himself half a year older than he was in order to immigrate to Canada. He must have been real anxious to go. He managed to change X to III on his birth certificate and as a consequence, he got to Canada late summer/early fall 1948 (can't remember the exact time) rather than spring 1949!
Imagine that! He was just a 17 year old kid and went on his own to a world he knew nothing about,except that the climate was temperate rather than tropical. He figured out that you can always put more clothes on against the cold, but there is a limit to how much you can take off in the heat.
Ilvi has just been working through her mother's notes which her mother recorded to wards the end of her life- sort of reflecting in a random manner on her experiences, life and people. What she says about immigration explains why, I think, my brother fudged the document.
"1948. aasta kevadel tulid laagrisse Kanada ametnikud oma maa pollumeestele tootkasi varbama. Tiit, kes oli tolleks ajaks tugevaks nooreks sirgunud , haaras voimlausest kinni ja laks Kanadasse. alanud oli ka emigreerimine Ameerikase ja Austraaliasse." (It translates as) Canadian rep came to the camp to recruit farm workers in the spring and voila! My brother decided to go for it!

I chime in again: Well you can definitely say that there was one person you know whose medical documents were fudged: Me! I have a copy of the chest Xray to prove it. Also a copy of the medical which states makes no mention on scars or neurological deficits- albeit there were no questions on the form to place such responses- there was definitely a burn scar on the L chest wall and a partly (recently) paralysed R arm. Visible in the photos in WNE if you know what to look for.
I suspect that mother's too were fudged at least with regard to her eyesight: I don't think that in reality she could see what colour her shoes she was wearing was when she stood up- and she was quite short!
I think that mother's DOB was also fudged somewhere down the track- a 5 was converted to 8: Blind Freddie could have seen it at times I think that we were lucky that we didn't get shot.

Ilvi agreed that it was heavy fudging in my case: she added "and since your mother's was too, probably there must have been some kind person in that committee who had a reason for approving those fudges."

Mai replies:
And it weren't Mai, who feels life would have been simpler in Germany or Sweden. Let us not forget all the families in Oz who lost relatives in Dunkirk when our troops were sent to defend the Commonwealth. The Holocaust issues didn't surface until much later when I was a clinician and my interest in mental health of course entangled me with Mr. Freud and all the psych gurus of the time. (The Holocuast in Oz still remain the ultimate vignette in human trauma).
I have seen father's military documents- some bits missing: He was actually caught up in the Dunkirk battle. That means he was on the front line for 6 years- God knows how he stayed alive that long. Then 2 years in Siberia from where he escaped. Now you know where the stubbornness hails from!!

Linda Dolan writes:
As for the medicals, I personally did not enjoy the nurse nor the doctors attention and cried. That was my only memory. I heard many years later while we were in New Jersey that a friend of my father's did not pass the TB test so he, his wife, and two daughters were not allowed to emigrate. My father urger the Lutheran World ministry to check the man's situation, since the guy was built like a bull moose and was as healthy as a horse, it was not possible he had TB. Further checking his Xray, revealed that his copy was of a much smaller man and could not be HIS. He insisted that another Xray be taken...there was not a hint of tuberculosis at all. The man who had his x-ray was already in New York City and with his Jewish cousins. Imagine that! Amazing what a few shekels will do. (I wonder what currency was used with our documents-MM) Sorry I cannot remember the Estonian man's name. It has been too long.

Hannes Jürmann writes:
The only occasions I can remember about medicals in Aug. '49 was standing in a queue of bare chested women with mother awaiting our x-rays, I think. I found that interesting enough to remember. Somewhere about that time, also towards Rappenecker way, we received Polio shots whereas despite the disease being a scourge in Australia at that time, no one there had heard of such inoculations.

PRE-EMIGRATION MEDICAL DOCUMENTATIONS IN GERMANY

AUSTRALIA
Croupe No. 45/13

I.R.O. Resettlement Medical Examination Form

Part I. Identification form to be completed by Assembly Centre doctor.
I. Teil. Identifikations-Formular, durch den Arzt der Assembly Centre auszufüllen.

1. Name / Name: MADDISSON, Mai
2. Camp / Lager: WG - 229
3. Location / Ortschaft: [DP camp]
4. Age / Alter: 6
5. Sex / Geschlecht: F
6. Colour of hair / Haarfarbe:
7. Colour of Eyes / Farbe d. Augen:
8. Height / Grösse:
9. Weight / Gewicht:
10. Scars or other Means of Identification / Narben oder andere Kennzeichen: none
11. D.P. Number / D.P. Nummer: 616713
12. Claimed nationality / Angebliche Staatsang.: Estonian

I certify that I have seen - Ich erkläre

Mr. - Herrn
Mrs. - Frau   Miss Mai MADDISSON   and
Miss - Fräulein

examined his/her D.P.I. Card, his/her photograph and his/her appearance, and am satisfied the particulars given are correct and that he/she has signed in my presence.

gesehen, seine/ihre D.P.I. Karte, seine/ihre Photographie und sein/ihr Aussehen kontrolliert zu haben. Ich bestätige, dass die Angaben richtig sind, und dass er/sie in meiner Gegenwart unterzeichnet hat.

Date - Datum: 25.05.49

Signature Medical Officer - Unterschrift d. Arztes
Signature of Candidate - Unterschrift d. Kandidaten: L. Maddisson (mother)

Part II. To be completed by Assembly Centre doctor and signed by the Candidate.
II. Teil. Durch den Assembly Centre Arzt auszufüllen, u. durch den Kandidaten zu unterzeichnen.

1. Family medical history / Krankheitsgeschichte der Familie

No. of Children: a) Alive / Am Leben   b) Dead / Gestorben   c) Cause of death / Todesursache

2. Have any of your Family suffered from a) Tuberculosis, b) Mental Illness, c) Epilepsy? If "Yes" give details:
Hat jemand ihrer Familie an folgenden Krankheiten gelitten: a) Tuberkulose, b) Geisteskrankheit, c) Epilepsie (Fallsucht). Wenn "Ja", bitte nähere Angaben:

nein

3. Personal medical history: Have you suffered from any of the following illnesses? a) Tuberculosis, b) Mental illness, c) Epilepsy, d) Venereal disease, e) Kidney disease, f) Nervous breakdown. If "Yes" give details:
Persönliche Krankheitsgeschichte: Haben Sie an folgenden Krankheiten gelitten: a) Tuberkulose, b) Geisteskrankheit, c) Epilepsie (Fallsucht), d) Geschlechtskrankheiten, e) Nierenkrankheit, f) Nervenzusammenbruch. Wenn "Ja", bitte nähere Angaben:

nein

4. Previous illnesses, injuries and operations of candidate, indicating whether he has or requires prosthesis for amputation:
Frühere Krankheiten, Verletzungen u. Operationen des Kandidaten, mit Angabe ob eine Prothese nach Amputation verlangt wurde.

Morbilli, Varicella
Parotite ep.

I certify that the above statements made by me in answer to the foregoing questions are true and complete to the best of my belief.
Ich bestätige die Richtigkeit obiger Angaben und wahrheitstreu, nach meinem besten Wissen auf alle Fragen geantwortet zu haben.

Date / Datum: 25.5.49
Signature of Candidate / Unterschrift d. Kandidaten: L. Maddisson (mother)

PUBLISHED WITH PERMISSION FROM NATIONAL ARCHIVES OF AUSTRALIA: FROM FILE B78, 1957 MADDISSON M

It is interesting to note what was sought out in the medicals of those days. The questions were perhaps occultly searching and I note that in mine a near fatal pneumoia aged about two years old was not considered to be significant of mention, while the childhood infectious diseases were. Nor were injuries considered to be salient to mention. A recently paralysed arm, or an old burn scar on the front chest wall : What might they signify?

In the physical examinations likewise there appears to have been absence of attention to neurological damage, or indeed orthopedic damage. Yet these two would have been the markers of future difficulties for the child. War inevitably produced many such injuries be it, its machinery or the parents' angst. In these photos one can see a clearly paralysed R forearm: Were it in a single photo one might have considered it to be a childhood 'tic'. The normal arm posture appears in the bottom L. hand photo which preceded the others.

FOLLOW UP OF PRE EMIGRATION MEDICALS

MAIE KAARSOO writes:
The pre-emigration medicals I do not remember any of the details of a fairly rigorous medical screening that we underwent, but I know that it took place, and it also must have included a chest x-ray.

I am forever thankful to the radiologist who passed me.

Attached to the Certificate of Identity for the Purpose of Immigration to Canada, which as a dependent I shared with my mother, was the following notice: "The Canadian Medical Card of Kaarsoo, Maie enclosed herewith has been endorsed to enable transportation arrangements to be completed, on the understanding that periodical review of the healed chest condition will be undergone after arrival in Canada. In the interest of the individual, the appropriate Health Authorities in Canada have been notified. This will explain the reason for visits of enquiries by representatives of the Provincial Department of Health from time to time."

This notice fell between the cracks. We were not contacted by health authorities after arrival in Canada, and we were unaware that we had received this significant message.

Before our first year in Canada had ended, at the age of 14, I was diagnosed with pulmonary tuberculosis. A stay of one and a half years in a tuberculosis sanatorium followed, and a few years later a relapse in the middle of my freshman year in college, led to readmission for another year. This brief summary of events does not begin to describe the painful repercussions on me, and as is always the case with illness, also on my parents and brother.

In Germany we had all been in plenty of contact with tuberculosis. In the eight room house, in cramped quarters, where we had stayed in Geislingen, there were at least two coughing adults with openly symptomatic tuberculosis.

One of them, the father of one of my playmates, was rejected for emigration. It was our understanding that after a number of years, he and his wife obtained a divorce so that she could emigrate and help him financially from overseas. I don't know what happened to the single mother with a younger child, whose room was next door to us.

YOUNG CHILDREN'S MEMORIES HAVE NO SENSE OF TIME AND PLACE: THEY LINK BY ASSOCIATION

I had no wish to leave Germany.
Maybe those gentleman in white were the doctors involved in performing the medicals which I too cannot recall apart from the run in with the radiographer: He seemed unable to relate to the simple notion that a child with a paralysed arm couldn't place it where he wanted me to place it.

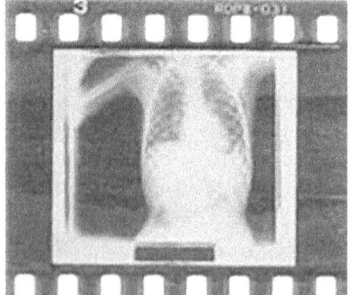

My chest Xray taken back in August 1949: I still recall the tussle with the doctors for not being able to raise my right arm higher: The nerves had been paralysed in the few preceding months leaving a wake of limitations in that arm (now recovered). The fact that the arms were of the same length indicating that no growth had had time to occur. **Published with permission from National Archives of Australia: from file B78, 1957 Maddisson M**

HANNES JÜRMANN
FATHER WAS A MILITARY DOCTOR CARING FOR OUR FATHERS AND BROTHERS
THE ROAD THROUGH CZECHOSLOVAKIA   Dr. Verner Jürmann

Some months before the end of the war, the First Estonian Hospital Company (of the German Army) was located at Neuhammer. Instead of moving to the front we headed towards Torgau and from there on to Nachad. Nearby in Cervey Kosteletz there was still a hospital in the town schoolhouse. There I found two Estonian soldiers recovering from wounds. One was Heino Tuisk, the other's name I cannot remember.(Heino Tuisk is now our neighbour across the street)

The German guards (*presumably attached to the field hospital) ordered that we move towards the west but the Estonian Hospital would not permit this because the Czech 'whites' had guaranteed our safety provided that we handed over our weapons. They then billeted us in some holiday houses in the forest.

After some days however, the Czech Reds seized power and the Whites were embarrassed by us and the protection they had guaranteed. I managed to get out and approached the Czech manager of a clothing factory about our (soldiers and nurses) plight and to get some advice. He was very nervous and rushed me into his office where he told me that his own position was precarious. However he was sympathetic to our predicament.

In reply to the question of our future he said that we had to find our own means of escape because he was hardly better off himself. He managed to find me a used suit and gave me some Czech money. I was now the only one with civilian clothes; the others were all in German military uniforms. Back in the forest we began dyeing the uniforms in a tub from the village. I think the dye came from the village too.

Soon one Czech began visiting us frequently, presumably the owner or caretaker of the cottages. At first he was very friendly but became progressively antagonistic. One day he arrived with a sub-machine gun and took us at gunpoint to Nachad railway station. He intended to ship the men off to Russia and retain the women for his own amusement. However our nurses refused to separate and we remained together. With fear and apprehension I watched the Russian troops on the platform.

The station commandant was a drunken Russian officer who shouted orders in Russian that our Czech captor could not understand. When the train destined for Russia arrived at the station, he could not understand the 'gibberish' which was an order to put us on the train. The Russian shouted, "Papers!" but because the Czech had none he threatened the Czech with a revolver and sent him off. We were all stunned until I realized that we should take off.

When we arrived back at the cottages we held a meeting where we decided that the only route to the west was in the direction of Prague and required trucks. Since I was entirely in civilian clothes I managed to get a lift to Prague. The truck was full of Czechs.

Before reaching Prague we were stopped by some Russian Officers who attempted to strike up a conversation in a casually friendly manner. Understanding their language I suddenly developed acute toothache and was consequently unable to speak, mumbling, "Zub-bolit".

In Prague I located the Doctors' Association Office in the hope of gaining some sort of information. It turned out that the chairman, whom I knew to be friendly towards Estonians, had been removed from office and a new one appointed. I located the residence of the former chairman. He told me that there was an opportunity for me personally but not for the rest of the unit. I was forced to reject the offer and went to the to the railway station where I spent the night dozing at a table. In the morning I awoke sleeping among Russian soldiers.

That morning I began my trip back to Nachad. To escape the Russian threats and propaganda over loudspeakers I went to a Catholic church where I was able to sit and rest in peace. Later that day I chanced to catch the Cerveny train and that night rejoined my remaining companions.

In our trapped situation, considering the predominance of women in our group, I suggested that we should head west towards the American Zone in threes; each man with two women.

With Gunnar Nirg, a medical student I set out as scout with false papers already obtained before Nachad. On the train ride from there to Prague we avoided conversations with Czech fellow passengers. Continuing the journey by train was risky as we did not know where the American Zone began.

Consequently we were forced to hop off before Rockycany. We continued on foot, along the highway. On passing through each village to wish the villagers a good day (denj dobri) without fail, thus appearing to be one of them.

One evening, on passing through a village we heard Russian accordion music and broad Russian conversation. After passing through we came to a copse at nightfall, so we crawled under a pine tree to sleep. Early in the morning Gunnar went to check the lie of the land while I was shaving.

Lieutenant Verner Jürmann

As an ordinary soldier at Jõhvi

I had hardly finished shaving when Gunnar returned with the alarming news that some Russian tanks were camped beyond the trees. We were forced to detour. We decided not to travel together but to take turns in walking ahead with the other following just in sight. Thus if one were caught the other might escape. After a long trek, while Gunnar was leading, we approached another village. Gunnar forgot the mandatory greeting. This appeared to have been noticed as I noticed some excitement at the front of one of the houses he had passed. I caught up to Gunnar quickly and gave him an earful over the omission.

Noticing a copse nearby we ran to it, and then on from there. On the other side of the copse we saw another village and some American tents in its paddock. On reaching the edge of the village

We saw an elderly villager with his grandchild near an American soldier; a sergeant I think. The old man was chastising the child who had his hand in the American's pocket for sweets. We ran to them to escape the two Czech youths following us on bikes, demanding that we be handed over. We produced our false papers and I whispered to Gunnar to muster all his school English.

The American sent the youths packing and they vanished. But our saviour was still the old man who recognised our situation. The American generously suggested that we go to a large house nearby where the

Captain would take care of everything and that we should not worry. When we arrived the Captain was on his rounds and was due to return in an hour. Gunnar was so relieved that he was quite happy to wait for the Captain but my nerves were shot. I didn't trust all this; who knows how much the Captain knows about Estonia. I urgently suggested to Gunnar that we push on.

And so we continued on that dusty road. By nightfall we arrived at a village and found accommodation for the night. But the woman of the house seemed uneasy so we cut short our stay and departed before her husband returned from his night shift.

Eventually we reached Pilsen (Plzen) where we met some Estonians on the city street. They directed us to Camp Carlov where other Estonians had preceded us. After entering the barbed-wire covered gate we were directed to the office. There behind the table sat a committee and interrogator who later turned out to be Latvian. The way the interrogator fired questions at me left the impression that I was in the hands of the Russian G.P.U. Gunnar's interrogation was similar. We decided that we must have landed in the wrong place and headed back to Pilsen.

On the way we passed a Jewish camp and decided that our false papers (*which probably stated that they were Jews according to mother) entitled us to enter. We were welcomed, receiving food and shelter. As we wandered about, we met several Camp Carlov Estonians. They explained that on the day we had been there, the chairman had been a Latvian who adopted G.P.U. tactics, apparently to impress people with his importance. We then returned confidently to Carlov where several hundred Estonians were awaiting us.

*From there father made enquiries and set out to find us locating his mother and sister on the way. He located us in the summer of '45 at Schwarzenbeck, a ball-bearing factory where a Displaced Persons camp had been set up for Baltic refugees by UNRRA.
(* comments by Hannes)

(comments by Anna Jürmann: "Quite strange to read that. To me he said that he escaped from Czechoslovakia together with the nurses, Jewish papers identifying him as Max Jürmann and the help of the Red Cross??? Really quite odd. Of what I have just read here I have no idea. With the exception of NEUHAMMER, where Estonian soldiers were stationed, and I was even there for 2 days. That was during the war. We were then in Hagenow [Mecklenburg State]).

ENN RAUDSEPP
FATHER WAS A COMMUNITY LEADER AS WELL AS A PASTOR

My father Karl Raudsepp (born March 26, 1908 in Puurmani, Estonia; died June 18, 1992 in Toronto) felt the call to the church at an early age. The second son of a Jõgeva mõisa tenant farmer, he was the first in his family to receive a higher education, graduating from Tartu University with a theology degree in 1932. After arriving in Canada in December 1948, he founded eight Estonian Lutheran congregations, including St. John's in Montreal, where he served for 28 years. In 1977 he was consecrated as the Bishop of North America of the Estonian Lutheran Church in exile.

Father writes about his childhood in his memoirs (Ristiga Märgitud, 1982), but provides only a sketchy picture of his parents' families. As a Lutheran cleric, he scarcely mentions his grandparents' Russian Orthodox roots, though he writes that his older brother Aleksander (deported to Norilsk, Siberia in 1945, where he died in a labor camp three years later) was a boarder for a few years at a Russian Orthodox primary school in Laiuse, about 8 kms. from the family farm. Aleksander was expelled for participating in a mock funeral of another schoolboy and never went back to school after that. He stayed on the farm, and eventually took it over from their parents.

Karl began school at age nine in Jõgeva, where he boarded during the week, going home on weekends. Those were Czarist times and school was conducted in Russian. A year later came the Russian Revolution and a brief Baltic German era when the schools dropped Russian and replaced it with German. He recalls hearing the sounds of the battle that took place at the Jõgeva mõisa at that time. By 1918, during the Estonian War of Independence, Estonian became the language of the schools.

Farm boys were expected to help out from an early age, and Karl helped his brother and father by doing chores. He seems to have greatly enjoyed the years when he and other karjapoisid (boys minding herds) got together in the pasture lands to play games, experiment with smoking and play pranks on passing gypsies when the occasion arose. He learned to shoot a rifle at the age of 8 and recalls a time when his brother and he fired their father's hunting rifle during the parents' absence and accidentally made a huge hole in the wall of the log sauna.

But he also had a serious side. He was an avid reader and quickly ran through all the books available on the farm. He talks about first being drawn to the church in Laiuse as a source of additional reading materials and says he received the 'call' at age 12 after hearing an itinerant preacher in Jõgeva. He says he began to pray daily, but didn't yet tell anyone of his intention to become a minister. Encouraged by his mother and supported by an uncle who had a bakery in Tartu, he attended the Treffner Gümnaasium (High School), graduating in 1928 at the age of 20. From his graduation class of 35 boys, seven became pastors.

He was admitted to the faculty of religion at Tartu University, and received his degree in Theology four years later, after taking a year off from studies (after one semester) to fulfil his compulsory military service in a cavalry regiment. He did not enjoy his stint in the military and was glad when it was over. After graduation, he was a pastoral intern for a year, serving in several different congregations, primarily in Pärnumaa, because he liked being near the sea.

He was ordained in 1933 in Tallinn's Toomkirik (Cathedral church).

His first parish was in Häädemeeste in Pärnumaa, where he served from Sept. 3, 1933 to Dec. 31, 1935. While there, he met Ellen Männik, the daughter of the Sindi stationmaster Julius Männik and Anna, his wife. Karl and Ellen were married in Häädemeeste church on July 20, 1935.

He was called to the larger parish of Vändra, also in Pärnumaa, in January 1936. Thirteen pastors vied for that position, but father, a gifted speaker, was selected after the short listed candidates delivered sermons to the congregation. He remained in Vändra until September 28, 1944, when the family fled the Soviet occupation.

Life in Vändra in the 1930s seemed idyllic and in January, 1939, Jaan, the first of four children, was born, then Anne (1941) and Enn (1944). The last child, Karl Johannes, was born in Montreal. Another highlight of that time was father's month-long trip by car with a delegation of Lutheran pastors to a church conference in Hungary in 1937.

THE FIRST RUSSIAN OCCUPATION
In the summer of 1939, Russian forces occupied Estonia and life changed dramatically. Among father's parish duties in Vändra had been to teach religion classes in the 300-student, coeducational local high school.

Suddenly, religion classes were forbidden. Also, everyone had to periodically perform unpaid labor assigned by the local commissar, and no one was allowed to have hired help, so working the farms became extremely difficult. Moreover, farms of more than 30 hectares (including the church farm) were confiscated by the government. Mother had inherited a farm of 29 hectares in nearby Suure-Jaani, which barely avoided that fate and father was able to surreptitiously transfer some church farm tools, crops and livestock to that farm by night.

He himself stayed at the manse in order to carry on church business, but sent his family to Suure-Jaani since the communists were keeping a close eye on all clergy, teachers, politicians, bankers, administrators, and anyone else who was considered a bourgeois enemy of the state.

Father was the victim of several threats and was told that his name was on a list of people to be deported to Siberia, so he started sleeping at different farms every night to avoid arrest.

The Germans arrived in the summer of 1941, and did not interfere as much with local affairs as the communists had done. As long as the Estonians gave them no trouble, the Germans largely left them alone, though they did target the small Jewish population throughout Estonia.

By July of 1944, it was becoming apparent that the Germans were losing the war and that the Russians would be returning. A Swedish-Estonian pastor who had been father's classmate at Tartu University offered to make arrangements for our family to go to Sweden and actually traveled to Vändra to persuade father to go. Father agreed to send his family, but wanted to stay himself, at least for a little while. Mother refused to go without him. Two months later, when the Germans withdrew from the area and the Russian forces were very close, father finally decided to go. Our parents were 36 and 35 years old, mother's aunt Miina Feldmann, known as Tädi, who lived with us, was 63, Jaan was five, Anne was three and Enn was six-months. They could take only what they could carry and had to leave everything else behind, not knowing where they would end up and whether they would ever see their parents or native land again.

By prior arrangement, we were to flee with the families of the Vändra linen factory manager, Reinhold Malm, and its technical director, Martin Tamm. The plan was to use a factory-owned, three-wheeled truck to travel from Vändra to the Baltic coast and then on to Saaremaa, where we hoped to find a boat to cross the Baltic.

The truck had to make two trips. Our family was on the first trip to Hanila church near the coast. The second trip (to get the manager's family) was fraught with many more difficulties since the retreating Germans had blown up many bridges to delay the Russians and they had to drive through a river at one point. Also, the Russians were starting to shut off escape routes, so time was of the essence. They had to avoid at least one Russian patrol, but they eventually made it to the rendezvous point and the combined group drove together to Virtsu, where they caught a ferry to Kuivastu and then traveled south to Roomasaare harbor near Kuresaare.

There were very few boats going anywhere by that time, but we were able to get passage on an R-22 German ship going to Gotenhafen (now known as Gdynia; then a German possession in the Polish corridor.) (Remnants of the German army had retreated to the Baltic Islands and were about to withdraw completely. Estonian conscripts in the German army, who were considered traitors by the Russians and would have been imprisoned or shot, also went to Saaremaa, some hoping to escape, others to get arms from the Germans to make a last stand against the Russians. The Germans didn't think such a manoeuver would be worthwhile and persuaded most of these soldiers to leave with them. If any space remained, they were willing to take civilian refugees as well.)

The voyage almost didn't take place because the German ship, which was anchored in the harbor, burst into flames after an air raid just as the refugees were beginning to board it from the small dinghies they had to use to get to it. Everyone was turned back, but they were allowed to board the next day when the fire had been extinguished. The voyage also just missed ending tragically when a Russian torpedo during another raid passed only a few meters from the ship. Despite those close calls, the ship reached Gdynia safely on Oct. 1, 1944.

WE ARRIVE IN GERMANY

In Gdynia, the family was put on a train full of refugees that went through Pomerania in East Germany to Frankfurt-an-der Oder near the Polish border. We were temporarily put up in some empty barracks where we suffered from a severe infestation of bedbugs. Since no one there knew what to do with a trainload of refugees, we were put back on a train after three days and transported further east to "Maarimaa" in the Sudetenland part of Czechoslovakia, then also in German hands.

Many of the single men or childless couples found jobs or places to stay along the way at various train stops, but no one was willing to take on families like ours, with small children and an elderly dependent.

There was a dearth of food on the train and the children's only food was bread soaked in water or, once in a while, milk, whenever a kindly rail worker took pity on us. As a result the children all became ill. Father was unable to do much to help because his eyes had become severely infected, rendering him temporarily blind -- and in danger of permanent blindness.

When the train stopped for a few hours in Mahrisch Schönberg (now Sumperk in Czechoslovakia), he defied the trainmaster and slipped off the train to look for a doctor. Mother went after him since he could barely see. (One wonders what would have happened to us all if the train had suddenly left?) Father, however, was convinced it was God's guiding hand that directed him to the first house they knocked at, which turned out to be the home of the only doctor in the town, who probably saved his sight.

After three more days, the train reached Jagerndorf in Silesia (now Krnov in Czechoslovakia) with the children's illnesses becoming more and more serious. The refugees all detrained and were housed in a DP camp at the edge of the town. Allied bombing raids, meanwhile, were increasing and everyone frequently had to take cover in the woods.

A short while later, when the children's health had somewhat improved, the refugees were loaded on the train again and told the search for jobs and housing would continue. The train stopped in Bodenbach on the Elbe river in Sudetenland (known today as part of Decin in Czechoslovakia), where the authorities again could not find them any housing or jobs.

Father and another Lutheran pastor went off on their own search and were more successful. As a former cavalry soldier and farm boy, he was able to convince the manager of a stove factory that he was just the man they needed to drive a team of horses, which had been put into service because there was no gasoline to run the factory trucks. His working day was from 5 am to 10 pm since he had to take care of the horses before and after his shift—six days a week. On Sundays he also had to drive the manager's wife into the mountains for a weekly outing.

The family spent Christmas of 1944 in Bodenbach, but left in the early spring when the Russian advance on Germany was only 40 kms. from the Elbe river. An extant letter of recommendation from the factory manager says that father performed his duties well from Nov. 1, 1944 until March 21, 1945, when we left, due to the Russian advance. (The German surrender, which came on May 8, 1945, was imminent and refugees from communist-held lands knew they could be sent back if they fell into Russian hands.)

Father's plan was to travel to Plauen, in Saxony near the Bavarian and Czech borders, to stay with another Estonian pastor, whom father had been able to contact. An Allied bombing raid, however, destroyed Rev. Aleksander Jürgenson's house, killing him, his wife and three children, before we were able to join them.

Since it was necessary to flee before the advancing Russian reached Bodenbach, father decided to simply head west, towards the advancing Allies. We were able to get a train via Karlsbad, Marienbad and Brux to Eger (now Cheb) where the tracks became impassable due to Allied bombing.

By walking two kilometers, all the while pushing and pulling a heavy cart loaded with all their possessions and the children, our parents hoped to catch another train on the far side of the bombed-out area.

Caught up in their exertions and tired, they did not notice a shunting train engine on a track they had to cross, and would have been run down if the belt father was using to pull the

Three wheeled truck leaving Vandra

Sunday school in 1946

Geislingen: Karl in USA military uniform

Raudsepp Family 1948

wagon while mother and Tädi pushed, had not broken. He fell forward and the wagon rolled back, and the engine passed between them, barely missing the wagon.

We did catch another train eventually, but progress was slow because the train had to stop in woods or in tunnels during air raids — of which there were up to six a day. We were dropped off at the small village of Linden near the Thuringian and Bavarian border, where we joined two other Estonian families (Kaljo and Virkus) whom we had known in Vändra.

Jüri Virkus' aunt, Ella Pool, had a job as an English teacher in the German high school in the village and she helped father work up his English skills. We were provided with a ration card and father earned some extra food and money by chopping wood at farms where the men had been drafted into the German army.

After a month, the German army retreated from the area and a day later an American unit marched in. Father found out that from the Americans that the area would become part of the Russian zone and we were advised to leave immediately for Bavaria, which would remain in American hands. So the three Estonian families again packed up everything they owned on small wagons and started walking to the border, four kms. distant, getting through it a short time before the Russians set up check points. We had no plan, just to keep going, among the crowds of refugees heading west and south.

We walked for two weeks, covering about 160 kms., passing through Münnerstadt, Schweinfurt, Estenfeld, and Worzburg before finally getting a lift on a truck going to Lauda. All along the way, we had to buy or beg whatever food was available and to sleep in barns. In Schweinfurt, a Catholic priest helped us find a farm where we were able to wash off the dirt of many days of dusty traveling.

Our journey ended in Bad Mergentheim, where father heard that UNRRA (United Nations Relief and Rehabilitation Administration) had set up a small Displaced Persons camp for Poles and Balts. He was quick to make contact and got us registered for a place in the camp. About 30 Estonians, including our family, were set up in a bombed-out hotel in that resort town. The Americans provided materials and the Estonians were able to make the hotel habitable. Best of all, the refugees began receiving daily rations of food.

LIFE IN THE DP CAMPS

In Bad Mergentheim, father became the group leader of the Estonians and the liaison with the camp authorities. He also helped organize English lessons and cultural events. A major fear of all the DPs was that the Russians would ask the Allies to hand over to them all refugees from Soviet-claimed territories, including the Baltic states. No one, of course, was willing to go back. Father was shaken by one incident when 300 Armenians in the camp, who had been ordered to return, held a church service and then knelt down before the American soldiers who were to escort them back, saying they would have to shoot them, since they refused to go. The embarrassed Americans relented then, but thousands of refugees were sent back at other times. Fortunately, few Estonians were ever handed over by the Allies.

The family, who lived in two rooms in the hotel, spent Christmas of 1945 in Bad Mergentheim, which turned out to be a rather joyous occasion, since everyone for the first time in more than a year felt safe.

Soon thereafter, however, the Estonians in that camp, including our family, were moved further south to the camp in Geislingen, where the Estonian President's brother, Voldemar Päts, had been elected to head the camp's internal administration committee, and father was soon chosen as his assistant.

Since father knew a fair bit of English, his main responsibility was liaising with UNRRA personnel, conducting correspondence and helping to arrange immigration matters. In rotation with the other pastors, he also conducted church services and visited Estonian soldiers who, as draftees in the German army, were being held as prisoners of war. About 200 Estonian soldiers and some German-occupation era functionaries were being held in a prison camp in Darmstadt, and a small handful of others, judged to be war criminals, were held in Dachau, near Munich. At first no one was allowed to visit them, but eventually father requested and, after clearance from the U.S. Army's Denazification Division, received permission to do so, and began paying regular visits to conduct services and to offer the consolations of religion. He also made regular visits to Heidelberg, where several Estonian youths were students sponsored by UNRRA.

In early 1948 Father was made an assistant to Dr. Howard Hong, director of the Lutheran World Federation's Relief Organization, which worked under the umbrella of the American army and UNRRA. He was made an honorary chaplain in the American army, provided with a uniform, a car, a salary and an apartment in Munich, where he worked weekdays while the family continued to live in Geislingen.

Father traveled a lot at this time, but always tried to get back to Geislingen on weekends. Among the places he visited was Hitler's "Eagle's Nest" mountain retreat (picked clean by Allied souvenir hunters by this time) and on another occasion he met Eleanor Roosevelt as part of a reception committee. (He thought she was too friendly towards the Russians.)

By 1948, the possibility of emigration began to open up, as Western countries finally adopted immigration policies to resettle war refugees. In most cases, refugees had to be healthy and find a sponsor who would employ them for a minimum of one year. Most sponsors turned out to be operators of mines, logging camps and large farms, for whom lack of language facility in English was not a drawback. Many of the Estonians in the camps were urban white-collar workers, but ended up working in those rural environments in Canada and elsewhere.

Father's initial fear was that with a family of three children, wife and elderly aunt, he would find it difficult to get a sponsor for emigration. There was also the worry that one or other of us would fail the stringent medical requirements, causing all of us to be refused. Tädi Miina was in particular jeopardy since the regulations required all visa applicants to not only be disease-free, but to have at least 25 healthy teeth. She fell well short of that number, and indeed, in one of the medical examinations the family had to undergo, she was about to be refused.

However, by that time, father was able to produce documents showing that the Lutheran World Federation had guaranteed his sponsorship, so the examining doctor offered no further objections. Passage was booked aboard the Cunard liner Scythia, leaving from Bremerhafen for Halifax and Pier 21, Canada's Ellis Island.

In December, 1948, the family left for Canada, where father's job would be to gather together Estonian and other Baltic and Finnish refugees and establish Lutheran congregations.

Estonian Pastors in Geislingen:
Front row from L: Aleksander Hinno, Bernhard Steinberg, Karl Raudsepp.
Back row from L: Eduard Lind, Aleksander Abel, Johannes Aarik

Dr. Hong with Pastor Raudsepp

Bishop Karl Raudsepp

A QUANDARY:

While in the camps the pastors baptized many newborn in addition to the littlies who had been born as the war continued to rage and during their parents' trek to safety.
The new millennium has brought with it a new phenomenon. Where ever one goes one hears of women suffering with post natal depression.
I ask myself how did their mothers cope: Small babies to care for, older children making demands on them, their homeland in disarray.
There was no money, at times no shelter or food and frequently their husbands were at the battle front: The future was totally uncertain.
What kept up their morale?
Is it possible that despite their fractured lives they felt better supported and less in need than those who have never felt loss.
Is it just possible that a journey of shared hardship confers greater support than all the amenities that people now take for granted.

THE RADIO JAMMER: TALLINN

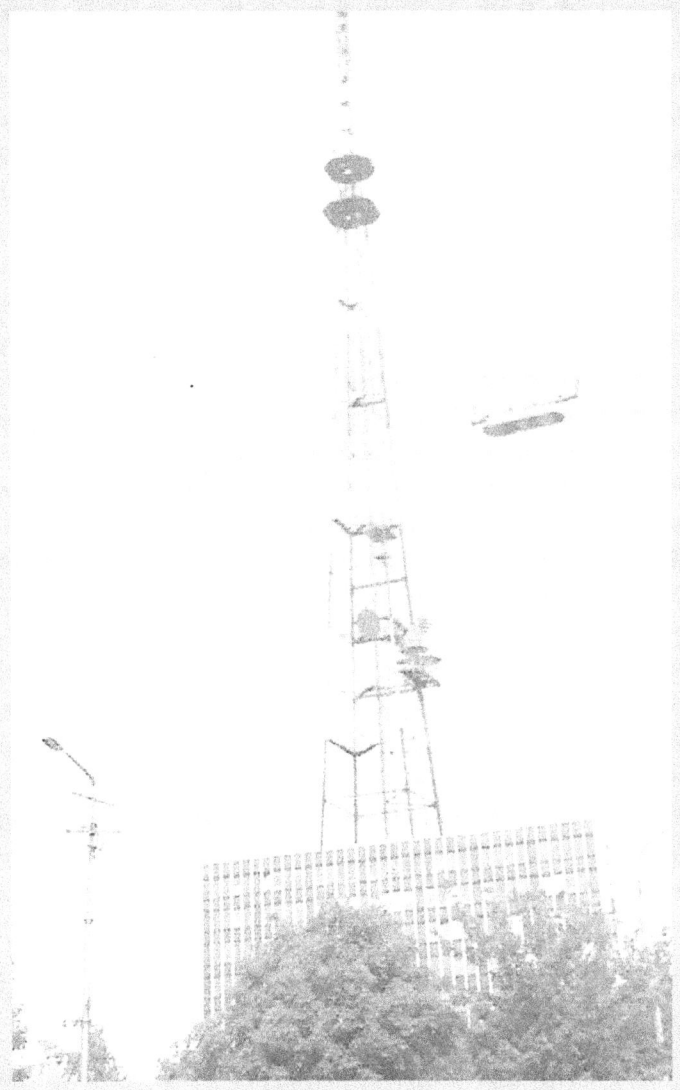

The feared structures which we all knew about and continued to fear until
Estonia again became free.

Photo contributed by Tonu Loorparg

AUTHOR GROUP 'MANYLOGUE' NAME TAGS- THEY HAD MANY TYPES OF SYMBOLISM

Heiki and Arne Elermets' tags

Photo from Helle Puupill/ Girey- en route to Sweden

As a clinician, meetings of various kinds are part of everyday life. At those meetings tags have always been worn to identify each other and of course now security issues dominate their use. I have always preferred another to meet me before the tag: **There is something impersonal about them through my eyes.**

The e-mails dialogues for the compilation expressed a variety of sentiments including thier impersonality. I felt it would be interesting to explore the issue again. Not too many answers came forth: Not as many as I had hoped for.

Linda Dolan writes:
I remember the Tags on lapels very, very well. My mother explained to me that these were necessary so I would not get lost (LOST- Ekks). For myself being labelled with those tags walked towards the positive side of my child's universe. A pick of luggage? My glass of life is always full and do not take umbrage at such perceived offence.

Hannes Jurmann writes:
We were never required to wear name tags. However when we left Estonia, mother put silver banana-shaped tags around my and my brother's necks, which had engraved upon them our names, dates of birth and possibly nationality. It is unfortuante that she used the silver from the tags and chains to have my son, Brett's Estonian ring made as they were a piece of history.

Heiki Ellermets comments:
I noticed some corresoponence on the e-mail recently that some DpP had been upset because they had to wear tags to identify them, like baggage when they were being moved. The attached were my tags on the way to USA. Not totally certain but I think that one may have been for the train to the harbour and the other one for the ship. Consdiering what they got me, Ihave never been upset about having to wear them.

Arne's reply:
Hieki, Amazing that you have them after all these years! I was thinking about them the other day when I read Mai's message. I am in total agreement with you that I am happy to have had the opportunity to wear them.

Heiki's reply:
Arne, I have just verified the tags that I sent you. The number 82 was from Augsburg to Bremen and the 64 was for Bremen to New YOrk. You were 81 and 63.

Arne continues:
Heiki, I notice that your name is written im Ema's handwriting.

Maie Kaarsoo writes:
As for the name tags. I found mine in my father's file. A nameless brown tag with the number 638 that matches my number on my mother's document on which I am listed as a dependent. The tag has a reinforced hole for string, my name on the back, another faded long number, and a rectangular stamp saying "Hospital" and a round stamp saying "International Staging Area" encircled by "International Refugee Organization". We were really happy, and not at all offended by the tags. For us, these were tickets to hope and a new life of opportunities, and not an offensive sign that we were being treated like baggage

HOW DOES A YOUNGSTER'S MEMORY SELECT ITS MENU? DOES IT DISOCCIATE THE PAINFUL AND RECALL THE 'TOUCHABLE'? MM

I have no recollection of leaving Geislingen or any transit points until Naples.

I recall a long tunnel between Germany and Italy while traversing Switzerland: The transit time I believe 45 minutes duration in the dark, did not faze me. but emerging suddenly onto a high up seeminly fragile bridge above a valley far below was scary: What might happen if it collapsed: There were lots of deja vus to base that imagery on. How many demolished bridges did we all pass on that trek!

Naples. was a conglomerate of large white buildings which contained triple bunks (I think) and food was eaten in a mess. Around the area grew strange long red things on bushes (tomatoes).

There we befriended a lovely Estonian family who too had a daughter my age and called Maie. She was a perfect playmate to while away the long sail to Australia.

I was miffed at not being able to visit Pompeii with mother: Would dead bodies really be a novelty to a war child! I suspect that the truth was that I was a handfull to keep track of.

I don't recall boarding the ship, nor its food but I do remember the raised dividers on the tables to avoid the food moving around in synchrony with the waves.

My only other recall in the northern hemisphere was the Suez Canal which I remember in surprising detail, especially for a girl.

DONNA PARSON SHARES SOME RELICS OF HER LATE HUSBAND'S FAMILY'S TRANSIT ACROSS THE ATLANTIC IN 1949

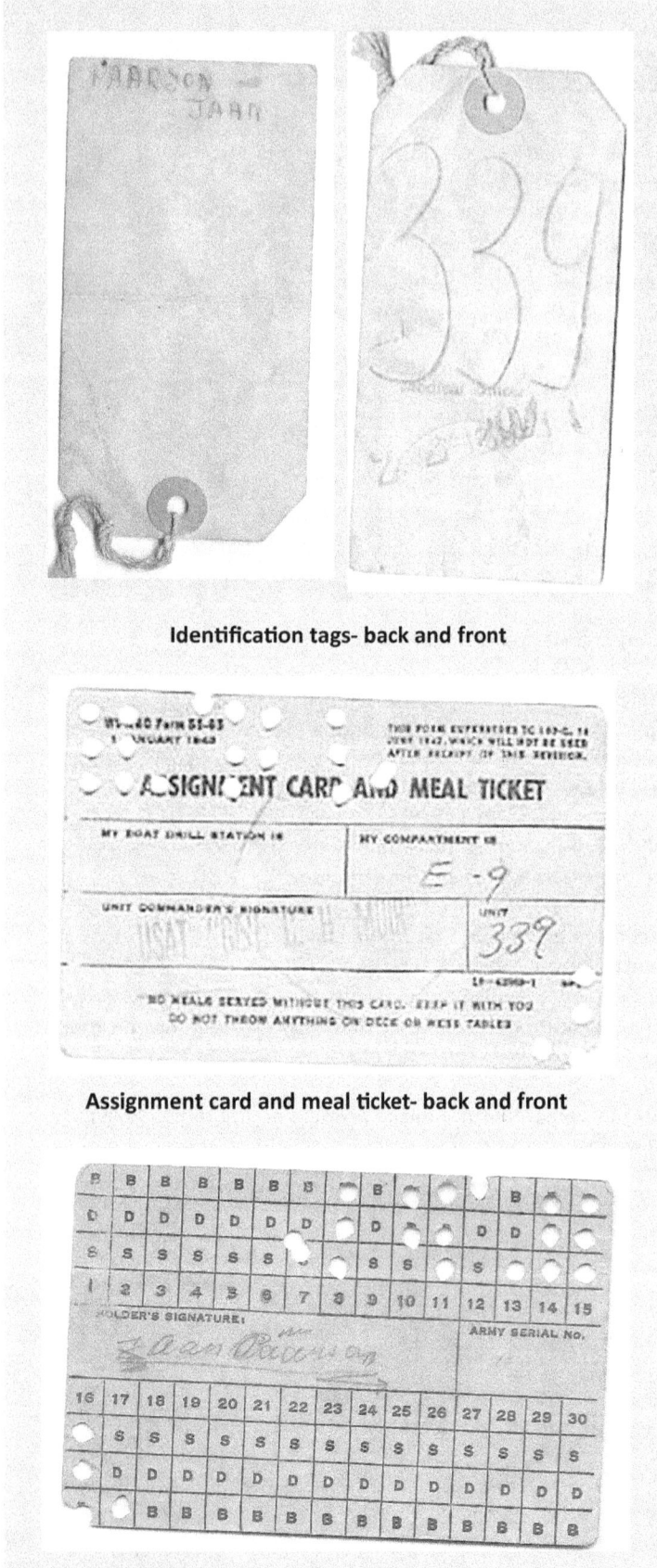

Identification tags- back and front

Assignment card and meal ticket- back and front

DONNA PARSON writes

A few notes about the crossing by Alma Paarson and her son Jaan

1. She was alone with her 11 year old because they were told that the ship was full and her older son, Vaino, could come on the trip, which he did. That meant that at night she and Jaan were separated and he had to go with the grown men to sleep. This was worrying to her.

2. While on the ship a Russian sailor gave Jaan a harmonica. Alma took it away from him- she wasn't going to let her lips touch the instrument the Russian had touched. Who knows what other ill will she harboured at that moment.

My memories of the trans Indian Ocean crossing were not so exciting! The oldies of course thought otherwise.

King Neptune sure was a strange king: An unkind king! Well to a seven year old anyway.

A makeshift pool had been erected on the deck and the oldies and some youngies were excitely milling around it.

Mother, also was there among them. My little friend Maie and I were not so sure of that adventure: Indeed I was terrified (while not terrified of Geislingen's river and its waterfall).

We decided to climb up the funnel's ladder to the first maintenance platform: well away from any threats.

It worked well until King Neptune threw mother in: I screamed as the events of some other more sinister immersion less than five years ago passed through my mind.

Yes, it was back to Coventry for another misdemeanour, as it was when the Fairsea was traversing the Great Australian Bight pitching among monstrous waves.

Kids were forbidden on deck: Maie and I braved it. My doll did not do so well. It had a sea burial. As it careered downward past the portholes it created havoc as people feared a baby had gone overboard.

Many years later at a clinical meeting dinner in Melbourne a colleague related that tale: With an impish grin I advised him that I still had a photo of that doll MM

Transatlantic Pilgrim

No.6   U.S.A.T. "General C.H.Muir"   Thursday, 15.09.1949

Honest Words

Today we say goodbye with this issue, which is our last one. You will, of course, receive a souvenir issue tomorrow morning, but this is the last Transatlantic Pilgrim you will see.

We have provided you with articles and cartoons, some funny and others of a serious nature. I would like to say a few words about the serious articles. We dealt with a variety of subjects, but those dealing with sea sickness and the duty to work produced the greatest response.

There have always been and there always will be people, whose view of the world does not reach beyond the end of their nose, and who will never recognise a communal duty as having priority over their own egoism. It is specifically on this subject that I wanted to speak to you. In a few years time we will obviously see who among us have successfully integrated into this foreign environment, and who was unsuccessful; but don't believe for one minute that in America you can declare yourself simply "seasick" or in other words unfit for work in order to avoid a task which does not necessarily contribute to your dollar income, but should be done for the benefit of the community. Please remember that until very recently you lived in a camp, where you were housed, fed and clothed due to the charity of others and that only due to the compassion of those same people you now have the opportunity to return to a normal lifestyle. It seems clear that you have already forgotten those truths, or what would be worse, simply refuse to accept them. These people, with an indescribable sense of entitlement, lounge in some corner of the ship, feeling like passengers on the "Queen Mary" and criticise everything that comes to their attention. If one wants to encourage them to engage in some task, they are so weak that one gets the impression that they are facing an imminent collapse, if not death. The moment the mealtime signal is sounded, they develop a new energy and appear in the dining room with smiling faces, but are then usually too lazy to return their dirty crockery and cutlery to the service area. The same people are expert at denigrating others behind their back, but face to face, when an honest critique would be appropriate, they are all blandishments and flattering remarks.

These people want to be seen in America, our new home, as representatives of Europe and expect to be treated as equals by the American community!

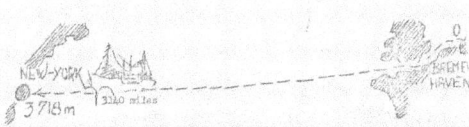

Film Presentation

Tonight, at 17.30 a film "Slightly French", with Don Amiche and Dorthy Lamour, will be shown in the theatre hall.

Ship's Position

12.00, Thursday, 15 September 1949

Latitude: 40 - 12 North   Longitude: 61 - 12 West

Distance from Bremerhaven: 3140 miles   Distance from New York: 578 miles

Speed 16.9 knots

Latest News

Bonn, Germany: Konrad Adenauer, the leader of the Christian Democratic Union was today sworn in as the first Chancellor of the Federal Republic of Germany.

Belgrade: Marshall Tito has been accused of planning to overthrow the Hungarian Government, which had been nominated by Russia, and to occupy the country with his troops. The Hungarian newspaper "Scantela", which published this accusation, claimed that this "act of violence" had the support of the United States, whose intention allegedly is to encourage a state of war between Tito's Yugoslavia and the Russian satellite states. A senior official of the Yugoslav Government rejected this assertion, accusing Russia of using the military manoeuvres being staged near the northern border of Yugoslavia as a means of strengthening the subjugation of the states under Russian control.

Responsible Publisher:	Mr Robert Weil, IRO Escort Officer
Editor in Chief	J Legzdins
Editor	A Szlamowicz
Art	K. Szabo-Czimbalmos
	M Szabo-Czimbalmos
Editorial Advisers	Peter Stross, Asst. Escort Officer
	A Dobrovic

A trans Atlantic crossing newsletter - one of the relics of her mother-in-law's transit to USA.

Its translation from German to English by Harald Korte who lives in Melbourne

THE BEST CHRISTMAS PRESENT EVER: TL

TÕNU LOORPÄRG wrote re 1958:
It was this Christmas I was to receive my greatest present.
Ema called me in one-day and told me to sit down. I sat in front of her as she looked at me and said, "we have received some good news about Isa". She then went on to tell me that through our relative Helga Junkur in USA, we had established through another relative of Helga's in Estonia that my father had survived the war and had then been imprisoned for 10 years in Stalin's slave labour camps in Siberia. He had managed to get home to Estonia in 1957 after Kruschev's reforms when Stalin died. This was fantastic news for me and an answer to my prayers.

Somehow I had retained this belief that one day my father would return. I realized that he was still behind the Iron Curtain and that chances of my meeting with him were minimal. Nevertheless where there is life there is hope as the saying goes. Now at least I could hope. I didn't realize at the time but it was going to be almost 20 years before I would be able to fulfill my wish. At the time I did not give much thought to how this news might have affected Ema, I guess by this time I just accepted the status quo and started to get used to the idea that I now was part of two families one in New Zealand and another in Estonia.

When I arrived home in Waiouru, we had lots to talk about. I started to write to Isa in Estonia but then began to worry about my poor writing ability in Estonian. I also talked to Ema about the complications that may arise from me being in the Army and Isa being in Estonia behind the Iron Curtain.

New Zealand family
Christmas 1958
Waiouru:
L to R: mother
Helene, stepfather
Stan McKeon, sisters
Anne, (Tõnu) Linda

Perhaps among all of our dearest hopes is that there were many such reunions: That they all fared positively.

The latter we of course know is a naive hope for we all know of heart-breaks be they related to meetings or failure to meet after lengthy searches.

Perhaps it behoves on us all to support those who as they reminisce in their aging years are reaquainting themselves with such heartbreak no matter how such unwished for outcome transpired. MM

MAI MADDISSON
"EI OLE VIIMSE HETKE RAVIM" OR "IT'S NOT LAST MOMENT HEALING"

Tiit Pruuli in his review of the Estonian translation of "WNE" wrote "**....... Lugedes veendusin, et see Geislingeni raamat ei ole mitte ainult ajaloodokument, vaid ka viimse hetke psühhoteraapiline ravim põlvkonnale, kes hakkab vaikselt igavikku astuma.**"

Translated into English it reads"**.... From reading the book I felt convinced that this Geislingen book is not only a historical document but also a last moment psychotherapeutic opportunity for a generation which is beginning to fade away." (bite the dust)**

Ilvi Joe was quick to respond " I looked at the last sentence and thought, yes …. why not? I myself don't feel that it's "viimse hetke psühhoteraapiline ravim" for me. **I know that anybody who lives through what we did as children would be scarred, but most of us were not debilitated, which would indicate that we had "psühhoteraapiline ravim" rather early or we were just strong and healthy to start with.**

Maybe there is some truth in both perceptions.

'Traumatology' has in some ways become the flavour of month, or maybe even the decade. Inaccurate bandying of its jargon, at times to cause more angst than the index problem.

Many years ago I wrote an article which contained the lines "Emotional trauma is an inexplicable event that can change the identity of an individual forever. There is no way to avoid this change, just as there is no way to avoid the change effected by a positive experience." Psychotherapy in Australia May 2004: "Is there order in Disorder?"

At one of my ongoing clinical education meetings during 2014, on that theme, the guest presenter asked us each to define 'emotional trauma'. Mine was the shortest definition: An event where that particular person lacks the resources to address/cope with it. That is a fluid definition which depends on a diversity of factors both intra-personal and environmental, and the actual characteristic of the event.

Commonly over my decades of medicine a patient has walked in and shared a distressing event/thought: In my response I at times created a parallel vignette to work from, to allow objectivity. It was presented in third voice and was commonly the story of someone who had shared my road, at times even my own. The relieved patient looked perplexed and responded by asking why no one had done something like that before: My response "That was not taught in medical school. It is something which I learned while living in the western suburbs (of Melbourne)". Our 'western suburbs' is one of the areas where there is major adversity in life. It remains a refugee 'ghetto'. I avoided the refugee bit because it might have introduced a confounding variable: The distressing event rarely matching one of ours, despite the relevant area being set up in another once largely refugee ghetto of the same era. The latter folks brought along problems too, but not of that ilk: They were experts at solving those.

Back on reality street it has repeatedly occurred to me that what I had done was exactly what I (and probably most of my cohort) did walking home from school having lived in a window of adversity, and what's more what I, like any of our refugee cohort, had heard our folks do since the dawn of our memories.

On reflection our journey consisted of endless adverse events: they could have occurred anywhere and at a variable frequency: Perhaps the events' close proximity an opportunity to revise and improve our skills at problem solving. While we had seen more of strife in our then short lives we had also learned to do our "Maths problems" well. Such problems had ceased to daunt us: But maybe there were others which replaced them, depending on our new resources.

Perhaps they will emerge when I explore the story of our first five years in our new lands: Or it may be that history repeated itself because we had become good at 'maths'.

Trauma resolution has many phases: Perhaps the Kubler Ross model is the most adaptable to the diversity of situations which befell us: They could not all be resolved in parallel, nor concurrently.

The war, the need to flee and the misadventures en route were the misfortunes which were out of our control. Our folks had the insight to realize that not anyone of them had the resources to overcome such might: They had to weigh between the risks of staying and those of fleeing, and the complications thereof.

During all those stages: War time Estonia, the flight, life in the camps and our early years in the new lands our folks debriefed with each other sharing their distress and sharing knowledge of options to try to move on. A concurrent ongoing catharsis, an environmental opportunity to debrief with true 'experts' and also to be opportunities to be supportive of each other were occurring. These are all integral stages of addressing adversity/trauma.

Closure is another integral part of coming to terms with the past: It allows us to reassure ourselves that we had not cheated anyone in our problem resolution, or at least allowed us to offer amends.
Among us were significant numbers who couldn't find prompt closure:
- There was wondering of what had happened to our folks whom we had left behind.
- Some who became remote geographically/demographically from other Estonians, lost their debriefing sources.
- There were some who carried enigmas of that journey for many years/decades, perhaps as I did. The Estonia bit was easily reconciled but the German bit including the catharsis did not occur until 2003 when I was finally among a group who had shared that part of the road and could relate to it. To have one foot in the Estonian camp and the other in the German camp created many conflicts in resolution: One foot stood in the camp of the violated, the other of a violator.

However given our environment was one where we shared a predicament we were able to find at least an interim closure until opportunity for more permanent closure presented. Our own folks around us understood that plight and we had all become the experts about that journey and were supportive of each other and helped each other mark time: Marking time perhaps a powerful skill to learn. We needed to learn it to use our lives productively until answers to our quandaries emerged from those darkened caverns, be they the Iron Curtain or the unspeakable ideology of the both of Estonia's invaders. No amount of sitting and pondering would change anything one iota: Well, apart from the reality that we would be left behind on life's ladders where ever we were to grow up.

For many of us new enigmas cropped up unexpectedly, like discovering a loved one was alive and there was a need for a renewed catharsis to address the (at times positive) complexities of existential issues these brought with them. And at times such events occurred repeatedly requiring further catharses and closures.

Mostly we moved on to our new worlds accepting that, our folks had made what was the optimal choice with what remained and that we had not knowingly let anyone down in our actions: We had reconciled our past: And from our past we took away many strengths and moved on. We had all had lots of practice with those 'maths problems' and could readily adapt their resolution strategies to the forthcoming challenges.

While moving on we did more than just live our own lives.
- We continued our fight for people's right to freedom, including many who fought for their new countries in the hope to suppress Communism.
- Some became supportive of a diversity of refugee movements and support organizations.
- Others were active in trying to restore Estonia's independence.
- And I guess I, being one who carried many enigmas for a long time, due to a premature loss of all links for honest relevant information, put that to use helping patients how to clarify their enigmas, and to mark time until the opportunity to resolve these came. I had learned from the past to help find positive outcomes for others.

Thus, the group is quite right in asserting that 'WNE' was not about catharsis which for many had already occurred in a timely way decades ago. Nor is it about closure with a few exceptions. But of course mini-closures occur in our daily lives. This book is built on the same model as will be any other books I compile/d.

Each person we meet on this earth has a different threshold for tolerating another's' 'baggage'. This is dependent on many variables and is not an indication of their individual ability to feel compassion for another: It could at times be perceived as a self protective instinct. 'Baggage' itself can be relative, depending on the setting a person finds themselves and may be emotional/material and indeed both. In many countries where the culture is derived from the British model, and where most of us have lived most of our lives, the 'stiff upper lip' is considered to be a marker of coping. But the absence of sharing doesn't necessarily mean that there is nought to cope with, nor that a person has coped. It is merely a case of respecting a local cultural more.

Each of us fits somewhere under life's prosperity-adversity Bell curve with regard to the amount of baggage we carry and the time required to resolve each episode: For a very few amongst us the number of life fractures has been nebulous, for others an exponential chain where one life's fracture has been the genesis of exponential others, not to mention ones occurring de novo.

In our adoptive countries relatively few locals fit under the thin negative tail of that Bell curve. Most folk fit under the two standard deviations of that Bell curve and life just lulls along. That Bell curve becomes skewed in times of war and its aftermath but when one moves to a war free environment one has to accommodate oneself under a new Bell curve. The emotions are temporarily boxed into an artificial container: At times a long temporary.

Day to day interaction with folk around depends on having sufficient sharable non-chameleonic narrative to keep conversation afloat. A significant percentage of this relates to sharing one's day to day life's journey. Should someone have a paucity of this they may deal with this in a number of ways: These are outside the scope of this book which is one of narrative not of psychotherapy.

However many of us have found the wish to pass on our stories to our descendants and it is in that context that those books began their journey. Parents and grandparents everywhere reminisce about their pasts. One only has to hear the pain some adopted children feel for their lack of narrative of their pasts: Of that which has generated their identities.

Many spend their lives on a painful, fruitless search: Many others prefer to bury such pain to appease others.

"Baggage" is a word we tend to coin for life's events which are not palatable to another's ear. Such baggage has been commonly reconciled long ago and merely becomes a person's life narrative/autobiography: At times the owner richer for having reconciled it. Its sharing is not a request for help, or a release of concealed pain, merely the owner's participation in a conversation about a given window of shared time/ reflection on a given event in mankind's journey. Sadly it is commonly perceived as a request for help with unfortunate consequences,the details not within the scope of this book.

These books are truly about reminiscing how we travelled the journey from meeting a misfortune to where we have moved on and the past has merely become the narrative of our journey. It is possible that some of the stories were written at a time in the past as part of a cathartic exercise but the books themselves have not been compiled in that context.

Perhaps we could say that 'WNE', 'Hats off to our parents' & 'The first five years in our new lands' (to follow) tell of how we readily acquired the resources to move on optimally.

ON A COLD NIGHT I STAND GUARD

I stand guard during the cold night
North Star high in the sky
The wind it dumps flakes on my eyes
But I have a determined task:

Protect you my dear homeland,
that you can sleep in peace my Estonian girl
whom my thoughts are with today
and whose likeness is nowhere else to be found.

Cold are you, my northern blonde,
You seem as remote and as inaccessible as the North Star
I often wondered" Is this coldness otherworldly,
Is it a sham, or really honest?

But I like your crisp complexion,
A frost like look in your eyes,
I guess your love is as clean, clear,
and sister like as ice crystals.

And when I come home again,
I want you to smile at me.
Big words from you I will not need,
but now I have to wait faithfully.

For sure, it was not an easy path,
I have had to travel to win,
Your gaze is calm and clear,
I want to find happiness and refreshment there.

Cold you are too.

G. Helbemäe
This poem was sent to me by **Tõnu Loorpärg**: His father would sing it on request: He received many such requests: Especially for my Elen Arakus whose husband Helmut died in Stalin's Gulag on a cold night in 1944

From: "Freedom is another word for everything to gain" Volume 1

I suspect that it is a song many of us and our folks could relate to: Each in their own unique way!

NOR WAS TÕNU LOORPÄRG THE ONLY ONE TO AGAIN TOUCH THE PAST

Paul Opik's story tells of the journey of a number of war orphans: Children who had lost or lost track of both parents. Harry Sakjas was one of those children who was adopted to families largely in USA.

The tragedy of children who witnessed their families killed, or heard narrative of it is incomprehensible to those who take their families for granted. But they have a form of closure, dismaying as it be.

Many saw their folks deported to Siberia and were left to wonder if they survived and how they survived. That is a story which cannot be written in a few paragraphs or pages: It belongs in another book: Estonia's war children- a fractured generation.

Some were fortunate enough to meet their folks again after they were returned to Estonia. Sadly prolonged separations, no matter how tragic the circumstances, do not always augur warm reunions: Too much has changed in the life experiences of the family members: At times enmeshed in such reunions is a hybrid of emotions: Many ask why, why them, why wasn't evasive action taken earlier. Perhaps there were unreconciled issues which it now seemed inappropriate to reconcile: The battered had endured too much: Was it appropriate to cross that time warp to move on.

FORD GENERAL PARTS NEWS — Page C

Reunion—After 28 Years

At 3 a.m. Easter morning, Harry Sakjas was at Detroit's Metro Airport to welcome his parents arriving from Estonia, a country of the Soviet Union. He had last seen them in 1942 when he was taken from his native land by the German Nazis.

As the travelers streamed through the passenger lounge at Metro, Sakjas wondered if he'd recognize his parents from the photographs in his billfold. Then, the searching eyes of his mother and father met his.

'MOSTLY HAPPY'

"My mother cried a little. And they were tired, happy, a little confused, but mostly just happy," says Sakjas, a Senior Designer at GPD's Product Engineering Office.

Only a few days earlier, August and Amalie Sakjas had left their Estonian home along the Baltic Sea, bound for Moscow and the United States. In Moscow, they had boarded a big jet. It was their first plane trip—a speedy climax to the 28 long years that began in 1942.

Then, Germany's war machine occupied the Baltic Sea countries of Estonia, Latvia, and Lithuania. Those nations had been under Russian control since 1940. The German high command figured to use the area as a strategic launching pad for blitzkrieg thrusts against Leningrad to the north.

Harry Sakjas was 13 at the time. He and thousands of other teenagers of the Baltic countries were to be sent to the German heartland. There, they were to study for one year, then be returned to their native land. Through the window of the train leaving for Germany, Sakjas had waved goodbye to his parents.

He never arrived in Germany as a student, however. Instead, he was sent to Nazi-occupied countries to work as a farm laborer. For the next three years, this would be his life in Poland, Czechoslovakia, and Germany.

"While the war was going in Germany's favor, we were permitted to write home," recalls Sakjas. But that was to change in less than two years, when Russia launched its counter-offensive in the Baltic, repelling the Germans and reclaiming those countries.

When the war finally ground to a halt in 1945, Sakjas was in a war zone held by the Americans near Stuttgart, Germany. He spent the next year in a displaced persons' camp, then a church-sponsored group in the U.S. offered him a chance to come to America. Having no way to communicate with his parents, not even knowing if they had survived the war, Sakjas grabbed at the opportunity.

After reaching the U.S., he was sent to foster parents near Detroit, where he finished high school. After graduation, he joined Ford in 1950 as an assembler at the Rouge. Later, he would complete Ford's Toolmaker Apprenticeship and Design Trainee programs.

In the intervening years since Sakjas' arrival in the U.S., he and his parents have communicated by letter on a regular basis. "But it took me until last summer to persuade them to visit the U.S.," he says.

His mother and father have a six-month-long visa to remain in this country. After their visit, they'll return to their native Estonia where a daughter and two other sons live.

CATCHING UP

In those six months, they'll have 28 years of catching up to do—and an opportunity to become better acquainted with their son and his family. Sakjas' family includes his wife, Helen, whom he married in 1956, and children Mary Alice, 12, and Harry Jr., 10.

"It takes a little time for the children to figure out what Grandmother and Grandfather are saying," says Sakjas. "But with a little sign language and interpretation by me, they always get the job done."

HARRY SAKJAS FOLKS BRAVED THE BUREAUCRACY TO VISIT HIM IN USA

Images from Harry Sakjas

photo album helps reconstruct the past 28 years for Harry Sakjas ght) and his parents, Mr. and Mrs. August Sakjas. They were separated by the ravages of World War II. The PEO Designer's family includes wife Helen and children Harry Jr. and Mary Alice.

The stories of POWs is similar no matter where they were incarcerated. For the children born after their fathers were sent to the front fathers could only be notional characters without any sense of shared identity. I know of POWs from Changi whose children while empathic to their predicament never were able to become close to them. The same applied to German POWs and I am sure it applies to Estonian ones.

The lifestyles in the west perhaps acclimatized many to more comfort than their newly found families could relate to. Such stories are passed on by word of mouth: The true painful emotions never to be shared with mankind: Never to be understood

Others of us found out too late to make contact: At times it was a legacy of an elective decision to protect our loved ones. Many of us instinctively knew that there were perils in making contact: That leaving their folks to wonder about each other's fate was the lesser evil.

As the perils faded so did the courage of the family members.
And perhaps there were quite a number who really did nt want to know of the horrors at the war front: War has its ugliness no matter what flag it travels under. There are black sheep in every mob.

Perhaps the stories that are told are those of positive outcomes.
Where the split families did meet and two families were left to bond with each other knowing of a shared DNA there was that wonder of knowing who they finally were eg,where children met parents, where grandchildren first met their grandparents and where siblings met each other having been separated for many reasons including military commitments. MM

One can only feel joy for those who met such joy.

And wonderful stories like of the IInask boys where their parents were to remain reunited in USA.

A SECOND GENERATION'S DISBELIEF: JR, HS, MM

Grenader *Henry Rüütel.*

My younger son, now aged 35 was addressing some issues with my lap-top while I was scanning these photos, sent to me by Jüri Raid, onto the master computer.

Adrian caught sight of the photos and remarked "They are so young, they are boys".

My mind travelled through the retrospectoscope when he and his brother had been that age. I recall what a struggle it was for them and their peers (all intelligent kids now with honours degrees and Ph. Ds) to remember to pack into their school bags the required books, sporting gear etc.: To leave notes for me to sign on my desk by the required time. I recalled the decades of patients bemoaning the same of their children and my futile attempts to suggest that they demolished their rotor blades. At times I felt I was a very guilty parent.

Yes, I had learned a lot from the bad old days when I decided that I did not own the kids day to day issues.

Perhaps six years later, one of them confirmed my belief: They were grateful that I had not been a 'helicopter parent' and insisted regardless of their grumping that I would only step in if their own attempts had not worked.

Young Air-force service assistants after arriving in Gotenhafen in the autumn of 1944

HOW YOUNG THEY WERE

'I'll Take The Competition'

Harry Sakjas was one of thousands of refugees who came to America at the close of World War II. It was 1946, and he was an 15-year-old boy, alone in New York City and a strange land. He knew only a smattering of the English language. Above all else, he wasn't even sure if his parents and family back home had survived the long devastating war (see story, above).

Sakjas remained in New York for two months, in the care of the Lutheran Charity that helped bring him to the U.S. The organization counselled him to determine what he wanted to do, then found a foster home for the youth in the Detroit area. In 1950, he completed high school in the Motor City.

Immediately after graduation, he landed a job at Ford's Dearborn Assembly Plant. His job was installing brake cylinders on the 1950 Ford. A good high school record in mechanical drawing and shop soon helped him qualify for the Toolmaker Apprenticeship Program.

After completing the program, he worked a year as a journeyman toolmaker, then became a Design Trainee at the Division's Product Engineering Office. More training followed in mechanical drawing, mathematics, and basic physics. As a result of his toolmaker skills, Sakjas completed the normal four-year trainee program in just two years.

In 1958, he enrolled for night courses on his own. Today, 12 years later, he's still continuing his education through the Company's Continuing Education Program. He now has earned more than half his required credits for a mechanical engineering degree.

For a man who came to this country with nothing, Sakjas is thankful for the years since 1946 and optimistic about the future. He has a happy family, a comfortable home, and he likes his job as a Senior Designer at PEO. He was named to this post in 1967.

What's his goal? "Supervision here in the Drafting Department or else an engineering job," he answers.

"But you don't get those jobs unless you're willing to compete hard," he says, looking up from his blue print-covered work table. "Competition—that's the name of this game — and I wouldn't trade it for any other way. I wouldn't like a promotional system that lets you move up only if the fellow in front of you moves first. I'll take the competition."

PEO'S HARRY SAKJAS
... "I'll take the competition."

GP NEWS
Published monthly for employees of Ford Motor Company's
GENERAL PARTS DIVISION
JOE McCAMMON
Editor

Sõrve lahinguis raudristiga väär...
Jaan Tõnts.

Young Jaan Tõnts had already served in the Sõrve battle and earned an Iron Cross

Harry Sakjas, was not daunted by his need to take responsibility early: He thrived on it as one can see by the cutting he sent for the book. At 16 he was despatched alone to begin a new life in a new land.

His bio, at the end of the book confirms that experience is the ultimate teacher.

Harry Sakjas Sr.
9 Guindola Circle
Hot Springs Village, AR 71909-7134   Phone 501-915-8319
E-mail: harrys22@suddenlink.net

To the left, well actually the right on this page one can see that these were but mere children who had been placed into the Air force assitants jobs.

Vasakul on näha, missugused lapsed olid võetud lennuväe abiteenistusse. All samad abiteenistuslased Egeris 1944. aasta sügisel.

433

NO MATTER WHAT WERE THEIR AGES THEIR DREAMS MET BECAME DIFFERENT TO DREAMS TO THOSE OF YORE

MAJOR-CAPTAIN VERNER HANS PUURAND

His descendants too belong to our cohort.

He did not watch the warring world through slits in blacked out windows as we the little tykes did, apart from when we were on the run.

He was out there in the thick of it : At times he saw it at close range at other times through the periscope. No matter he became a legend in Estonian's fight for freedom.

Once away from Russiana he continued to fight for the Estonian troops who had become POWs and working towards their release. Post war he became politically active in expatriate Estonian politics.

That is but a small snitch of information about such a man: The history books will present this awesome man's efforts and his true courage.

He moved to Australia with his family among whom is Hans Puurand his son: While visiting Brisbane I was privileged to meet Hans Jr. who is one of their cohort of Estonian War Children.

Verner Puurand was to become an inspiration to their generation to continue to strive for the firm conviction that no man has the right to own another: And more poignantly, that no government has the right to overthrow another or bring physical or emotional turmoil upon people of any nation.

He like most of us lived out his life perhaps differently to his dreams of yore. He certainly touched more than his share of troubled lives.

Images sent by Prof. Peeter Järvelaid

TÕNU LOORPÄRG
THE REUNION WITH MY FATHER:
FROM "FREEDOM IS ANOTHER WORD FOR EVERYTHING TO GAIN" VOLUME 1

The machinations of Soviet secret police and their possible impact in the near future on me and my father was uppermost in my mind.

In 1974 I started thinking about the possibility of taking my family to Europe, especially to Estonia. I reasoned that being in Singapore made this a much easier and cheaper journey than it would have been from New Zealand. Over the years I had been writing to my father in Estonia but this had only been infrequent since we had discovered he was alive in 1958. Initially we had communicated through my relatives in USA, to avoid having the complication of KGB (Soviet Secret Police) involvement especially in my first five years in the New Zealand Army.

After I had received a negative security classification when I was posted to the Defence Office in Wellington my attitude changed. I no longer worried about how it might hurt my career and I started to have more frequent communication by letter. I knew that my letters to Isa (my father) were most likely being censored or read so I, because of my heritage and existing links in Estonia, kept to a neutral topics or used coded references if I needed to refer to something which could be controversial. I decided in Singapore to take matters in hand and seek Visas for myself and the family from the Soviet embassy there.

I also realized that as an army officer on the staff of ANZUK Force at the height of the Cold War, I would need to seek permission not only from the New Zealand Army but also the ANZUK Force, which meant of course UK and Australian authorities as well. This meant I did not approach the Soviet embassy until I had received clearance from ANZUK Force. No doubt the Soviet Embassy was under observation by our side and it would have raised some questions had I been seen visiting without clearance to do so beforehand.

I drove into the embassy compound which was surrounded by dense tropical bushes and trees. It was quite large compound and I went into a modern building with large airy reception room which would have been the envy of any British colonial administration. I was received by a young man about my own age who identified himself as the consular officer and I explained that I wanted to take my family for a visit to see my father and his family. In the process he asked me about the circumstances of our original separation and I went into some details regarding the war, what happened to my father and my having been a refugee with my mother. I got the impression he was quite empathetic about my situation as we talked, especially after he related that he had lost his father who had been in the Red Air force and had been shot down and killed at Murmansk during the war. He advised me that the approval would take some time and I then departed.

About a month later the approval for a tourist Visa came through much to my delight. At that point I quickly booked seats on Aeroflot the Soviet airline which flew out of Singapore to Moscow. The flight went through New Delhi and was one of the cheapest airfares to Europe. I also made the necessary onward flights to London and back to Singapore via Paris, Moscow, and New Delhi. The flight Moscow/Tallinn /Moscow was considered an internal flight.

I had been communicating with Isa about the possibility of a visit while we were in Singapore but of necessity final arrangements had to be left rather vague until I knew I had Visa approval. Once that came through I had to move fast to finalise arrangements. I recall my hardest task was convincing Avatar about the trip. She was not someone who enjoyed pre-planning and this trip to Europe and Estonia required a great deal of planning ahead. As a consequence I more or less had everything in place and made sure she was able to take leave from school before I announced that we were going. The carrot I used was to organise a European tour for Avatar while I stayed on in Estonia with the children and then met up with Avatar in Paris. *

I had received a letter from my cousin Ariana Crouchinox-Goldmann in 1970 completely out of the blue, introducing herself as my great uncle's daughter's daughter, from the Leesman (my father's mother) side of the family. She related to me how the Soviets had included them in the purge of 1940 when the Estonian Management and intellectual classes were sent to Siberia and where they stayed in Labour camps of the Gulag until 1944. When Hitler double crossed Stalin and attacked the Soviet Union, at that point because Ariana's father was a Polish Jew, under the terms of the agreement with the Allies, all Poles who had been incarcerated and sent to Siberia had to be released and repatriated to their home locations if possible.

Late in 1945 they managed to get back to Estonia and later because Pedro Goldman (her father) was also Jewish they were allowed to immigrate to Poland. They were there for only a short time before they once again left to go to Chile via DP camps in Austria. By this time Ariana had a sister Karin and they both went through the remainder of their schooling in Chile. Ariana had become very proficient in a number of languages and became employed as an interpreter. When she wrote me a letter she was living in Paris and was married to a French "minimalist" painter who was also a movie actor. He had apparently starred in a film which was never released! We were now being invited to spend time with them when we passed through Paris.

Also along our return journey, in New Delhi we had our friends Leki and Wilma Dorji. Leki was my Victoria University classmate from 1972 and they had briefly visited us on their way through Singapore to Leki's first post in the Bhutanese Foreign Service as a Third Secretary in New Delhi. I had made arrangements for us to visit these contacts on the journey.

Under the circumstances Avatar could hardly object and we were off on our adventures as a family with considerable apprehension, especially about the USSR section of our trip. The "adventure" started almost as soon as we stepped on to the Aeroflot aircraft at Singapore airport. The standard of passenger accommodation was very poor in comparison to other international aircraft. It was clearly an airplane designed to cater for minimal standards of comfort in international travel and there was a cabin crew to match. Most of the passengers seemed to be Indians working in Singapore and travelling to New Delhi. The in-flight catering service consisted of boxed lunches and tasteless coffee served in paper cups.

When we arrived in New Delhi in the middle of the night most of the passengers got off and the rest of the journey to Moscow had few passengers. At Shermitmiov International Airport in Moscow, we had to come down the gang plank steps and then march along the tarmac to the air terminal at some half of a kilometer away carrying our cabin bags and Katrina. We then had to go through customs and border control to transfer to another internal airport for our flight to Tallinn. To get there I had to exchange US dollars for rubles and then get a taxi cab. As I could not speak Russian and nobody spoke English it was very difficult to get directions. When I finally found a cab driver to take us to the airport, I later discovered that our hero of the Soviet Union had ripped us off for the taxi fare taking advantage of our confusion over exchange rates. It was not a good introduction to the worker's paradise!

Both Avatar and I were quite apprehensive about our first trip to the Soviet Union. We were constantly on the lookout for undercover agents both on the aircraft and in the airports after arrival. I don't recall much of our trip through central Moscow but we did not stop for sightseeing apart from a brief photo opportunity during our connecting journey by road. I do recall ending up on the Moscow ring road along with mostly dilapidated trucks which spewed out clouds of exhaust. The city itself looked very drab as we passed through despite the relatively warm sunny weather in June. It was a relief to get to the internal airport and find our way to the check in counter. After a considerable wait we were once again marched some distance carrying our bags and children to our waiting aircraft destined for Tallinn, Estonia.

I had sent a telegram to Isa in Tallinn before we left advising him of our arrival time. Now as we approached Estonia and as I gazed down at the changing land mass below I recognized the large expanse of water directly below us as that of Lake Peipus which was part of the border dividing Estonia from Russia. I recall enormous emotion welling up inside me and I shed tears of joy to be at last "coming home" to the land of my birth. I was at a loss to know how I should greet my Estonian family and I guess Avatar would have been even more so.

On arrival at Tallinn airport we were ushered into a rather shabby building which clearly indicated that air travel was not the most popular mode of travel for passengers to Tallinn. We were able to walk straight through to the taxi rank outside and look for the waiting family. There was no one to be seen . We waited for about 30 minutes. I then decided to get a taxi cab from a rank where there was no taxi cabs waiting. Just at that moment, around 1 pm a small Lada sedan arrived, together with another car and out stepped a number of people who I instantly recognized as my family. Isa was ahead of the bunch rushing toward us and I quickly stepped towards him and grabbed him around his shoulders for the first time in 30 years. I think my first words to him were in Estonian as I exclaimed," What language are we going to talk to each other in now?" I forget Isa's reply. Flowers were given to Avatar by Kersti and Anu my sisters and there were hugs and kisses all around. Õie my stepmother introduced her brother Oss (Oswald) who had brought an extra car for us and then we all departed for the family apartment in the central city.

Despite my inadequate Estonian I quickly started to recover long lost Estonian vocabulary and fortunately Kersti my older sister, spoke English quite well so Avatar and the children were able to communicate as well. The apartment was located in a residential area on the top floor of a three-storey building. It must have been over 100 years old. From outside it looked quite shabby but inside it was quite a comfortable two-bedroom flat with kitchen and bathroom and a large living room. Lunch awaited us with the usual array of smorgasbord type delicacies and together with coffee and "schnapps" we toasted our arrival in the "home country!".(kodumaa)

The priority task after lunch for me was to ensure that we adhered to the KGB (Internal Security Department's) tourist regulations and registered our arrival as foreign nationals in the country. To do this we had to go to an office located in the old town where such registrations took place. We left the family home and Isa and I drove through the cobbled streets of mediaeval Tallinn to make an appointment with the KGB agent concerned. The office was located on Vene (Russia) St in a very old building dating back to the 12th century and which had a very Dickensian look about it, as one entered the shabby waiting room through some very solid wooden doors.

Isa spoke to someone at the counter and after what seemed a long wait we were ushered into a large office where a rather matronly woman sat at a desk. She was speaking in Estonian rather rapidly so I had difficulty in keeping up. As I listened to the conversation between Isa and her I started to realize that something was amiss. Apparently she said, we were supposed to have Intourist Visas and not the Visa we had been issued with. Intourist Visas she explained required tourists to also have hotel bookings in "official" hotels, (where foreign tourists were under surveillance) and where they were required to stay. It was not permitted she said for us to stay with my family. We pointed out that it was hardly our fault that the Singapore Soviet Embassy had issued the wrong visas but this did not help. She then telephoned the Estonian SSR internal state authorities (speaking in Russian which Isa could understand), seeking guidance. We were then sent downtown to what was then called the "Viru" Hotel (now Olympia), which was the only Intourist hotel in Tallinn for foreigners and she told us to speak to the head of Intourist there (another KGB senior officer) to see if we could book into the hotel. By this time I was getting quite anxious and Isa was getting visibly angry about all this nonsense. I was anxious to calm Isa down because he could get in trouble with the KGB given his official status as a "rehabilitated enemy of the Soviet people".

Unfortunately, matters got worse when we were ushered in to see the KGB Head of Intourist, an Estonian. He was completely unsympathetic about our dilemma and stated there was no accommodation available at the Viru Hotel and he will "put us on the next flight out!" We had reached the depths of despair at this point. Fortunately Avatar had remained at home or she would have been in a real state of apprehension.

We then travelled back to the registry office to see our previous matronly councilor. This time she had a smile on her face and said that the "head office" had come back and said that "under the latest circumstances regarding relations between the Soviet Union and New Zealand, New Zealand was considered a "friend" and accordingly special permission would be given for my family to stay outside of Intourist accommodation ."At the time I did not quite understand what she was talking about when she called New Zealand a "friend" of the Soviet Union. I was more concerned about whether they were going to put us on a flight back to Moscow that night!

Hearing this, was a great relief for both of us. Isa and I returned home to the apartment where an anxious family awaited the outcome of all these negotiations. The following morning, Isa called us to the window as he looked down on the street below and pointed to a solitary figure lurking on the street corner outside. We were being watched by the KGB! A couple of days later we had a knock on the door and two people were standing there a woman and a man, the woman introduced herself as a "doctor" from the State who had come to check on the "welfare" of the children. We let them come in and as Isa said afterwards "let the KGB count heads to make sure we were all there!"

Later when we returned to Singapore and had access to New Zealand newspapers again, I discovered what they had meant when they described "New Zealand as a friend of the Soviet Union", apparently the Kirk Labour government had decided for reasons of their own to recognise the occupation of the Baltic states of Estonia, Latvia, Lithuania by the USSR in 1940 as "legal". This came as an enormous shock to me as a New Zealand Army officer whose prime understanding was that we were stationed in South-east Asia to hold the line against a further advance of communist dictatorships!

Many years later as the Honorary Consul for Estonia in New Zealand, I was at a reception at the European Union Mission in New Zealand Residence when I renewed my acquaintanceship with Russell Marshall a former Labour Cabinet Minister. He was now retired and was President of the New Zealand Institute of Foreign Affairs. We got talking about Estonia being a member of

Ariana and Karin Goldmann

Katrina's 3rd birthday.

At Toompea

At Muuga.

the European Union now and when I mentioned the Labour Government's decision back in 1974 to no longer recognise the Baltic states he told me that he had "the inside story of how it came about".

According to him, he was part of a New Zealand Parliamentary team who visited Europe and the Soviet Union during the early 1970s. The team had wanted to visit Tallinn in Estonia as part of the itinerary but this had been turned down by the Soviets because of political sensitivities. He said that after the request the treatment they received became very "shoddy" and un-welcoming and they were instead taken direct to Moscow on Aeroflot. He mentioned the ubiquitous Aeroflot box lunches to me also. On their return to New Zealand the party complained about the treatment they had received in the USSR. According to Marshall who was one of the MPs, Frank Corner then head of the Ministry of Foreign Affairs had told them he would "fix" the problem by proposing that New Zealand recognise the illegal occupation of the Baltic states. He proposed that the New Zealand Government could do so and receive very little political flak from those opposed to it in New Zealand and there would be much to be gained by improved relations with the USSR, especially trade relations which were growing at that time. When Marshall realised he was telling the story to the first Estonian Honorary Consul to New Zealand of the reconstituted Republic of Estonia, he became clearly embarrassed, and quickly emphasized to me that it was a policy decision by the Kirk government that in hindsight has looked very bad and that he was sorry about it.

On my part I lowered the level of embarrassment by relating the story of how the Kirk government's decision had saved my family from being immediately sent back to Singapore and laughed it off. I said "it helped us then but in a perverse sort of way". I have to admit that I may not have been so generous if I had discovered this while the Soviet Union was continuing as an ongoing State. Fortunately we saw its demise in 1991.*

We settled into our holiday with Isa's family very quickly. There was much to talk about and to catch up with on my part. We were also getting to know each other as an extended family. Õie my stepmother was a kindergarten supervisor and a lovely person who quickly made us feel at home. Kersti was just about to finish high school and Anu was 13 at the time and we quickly related to them. It was the school holidays and both Isa and Õie had taken leave from their workplace. The family had a summer home at Muuga which was an hour's drive out of the city. Fortunately it was inside the area where foreign tourists were permitted to travel to. In that period, foreign tourists could only visit Tallinn and not move out into the countryside. The reason for this was obvious to me. Even in the city there was much evidence of military personnel and there were Army Bases and Air Force Bases scattered throughout Estonia. The Soviet Navy had the coastline completely closed off and there were highly secret garrisons such as those on the Paldiski Peninsular which were the site of nuclear submarines and where intruders would be shot on sight.

Thus our holiday was restricted to seeing Tallinn and going out to Muuga. Terry at age 7 was full of mischief and very active. Katrina turned three while we were there and was quite the little cheerful miss. We stood out as a family when we went exploring in the city because our dress was so "Western" and of course Avatar with her brown skin and the children with their olive complexion were a contrast to the predominantly fair-haired blue-eyed Estonians. Having said that there was a large number of people living in Tallinn either as military or working there, who came from Russia proper many from the Asian parts of the USSR. They also had darker complexions than the light-skinned Northerners.*

Avatar was booked to go on a two-week tour through Europe and I was staying on with the family during the period and meeting up with her in Paris. We therefore had to condense much of our sightseeing into the first two weeks of our arrival in Tallinn. There was much to see around the city for me, a city with more than 1000 year history. The old town was especially unique and we spent much time wandering around its alleyways and old buildings taking movies and photographs for the record. Isa took me to the place where I was born in central Tallinn.

The old hospital was no longer there but instead they had erected the Communist Party Headquarters building close by and raised Lenin's statue almost on the spot. We both had a good laugh about the irony of the situation and looked forward to a day when they would be removed. Little did we know then that it would happen and that I would become intimately connected with the Communist Party building when it was transformed into the Ministry of Foreign Affairs building for the Republic of Estonia after 1992!

We also visited the old churches, Kaarli Kirik(Church) in particular where I was Christened, also the numerous museums including Kadriorg Mansion which had been built by Empress Katherine the Great as her summer residence. I was to return to the latter in 2008 as a guest when it had once again become the residence of the Head of State, this time for the President of the Republic of Estonia.

I found it quite easy communicating with the family in Estonian particular with my stepmother who used the Estonian language in such a way that I was able to quickly recognise her vocabulary with my limited child level language. It was harder when the discussion turned to politics or economics. Then I quickly lost much of the meaning of the subject being discussed.

What was clear to me from observing the life in the city and in the homes of friends and relatives we visited was the tenacity with which Estonian community was clinging to their culture despite the Soviet (read Russian) domination. For me the annoying part was that I knew that at the time of the incursions in 1940 Estonia was ahead economically from Finland. Now Finland was way ahead and Estonians were being kept under the jackboot of totalitarianism both politically and economically. Surprisingly, my father told me, that even then Estonia was looked upon by the rest of the USSR as the "Soviet West" and as an attractive place for those citizens in the

USSR who were able to visit or work there. By Western standards it was very much in the doldrums however.

I spent much time talking to Isa and learning from him family history about relatives, where we had lived and what happened to him before, during and after the war. I had received very little information in this regard from my mother and so I was receiving much of it from him for the first time. He would later record much of it and wrote a book as a consequence of my urging, but that had to wait until the breakup of the USSR. At the time such a book would have had serious consequences if it were discovered by the KGB. In 1974 Isa was considered a politically suspect person and liable for constant KGB harassment.

On most of our excursions we would be tailed by a KGB spook. I suppose in the context of the Cold War this was understandable considering I was a New Zealand Army Major, even if New Zealand was a "friend" with the USSR now!

We were of course a great curiosity for Isa's and Õie's friends and relatives. Many of them came to visit while we were there from around the country. Even my godfather's wife and daughter called. He had been one of those incarcerated in Siberia and killed during the purge of 1941. When Avatar left to meet up with her travel group in London, Isa took her to Moscow to help her through the bureaucracy. I stayed behind with the children. It was a very sad parting for everyone. They were not going to see Avatar again until 2005 some 30 years later!

After Avatar left there was one important mission I had to accomplish, this was to locate the whereabouts of my Uncle Alexi's grave(my mother's brother) in Tallinn. Isa and I spent a number of days making enquiries. After searching the records of a number of cemeteries we finally were able to find his name on a roll and then locate the spot he had been buried. It was an area of the graveyard where many of those who had perished under Stalin had been placed and those buried here had had their relatives liquidated as well. There had been no one to care for the graves left! Estonians normally take pride in tending their family plots, but this area where Lex was showed unusually great neglect. We cleared the unmarked plot of weeds and shrubs and later placed stone slabs on it and grew flowers. We also were able to get the address where he lived when he died in 1954 and subsequently visited the house with Isa making some enquiries regarding how he met his fate. It seems he was poisoned by a leaking gas pipe in the house where he had been living by himself.*

Our remaining time, we spent mostly out at Muuga at the summer house Isa had built there and the lovely vegetable garden and fruit trees Õie had cultivated around the house. It was very much in the "batch" style, that we know in New Zealand and it was very comfortable for short overnight stays. Most of the family celebrations took place here especially in

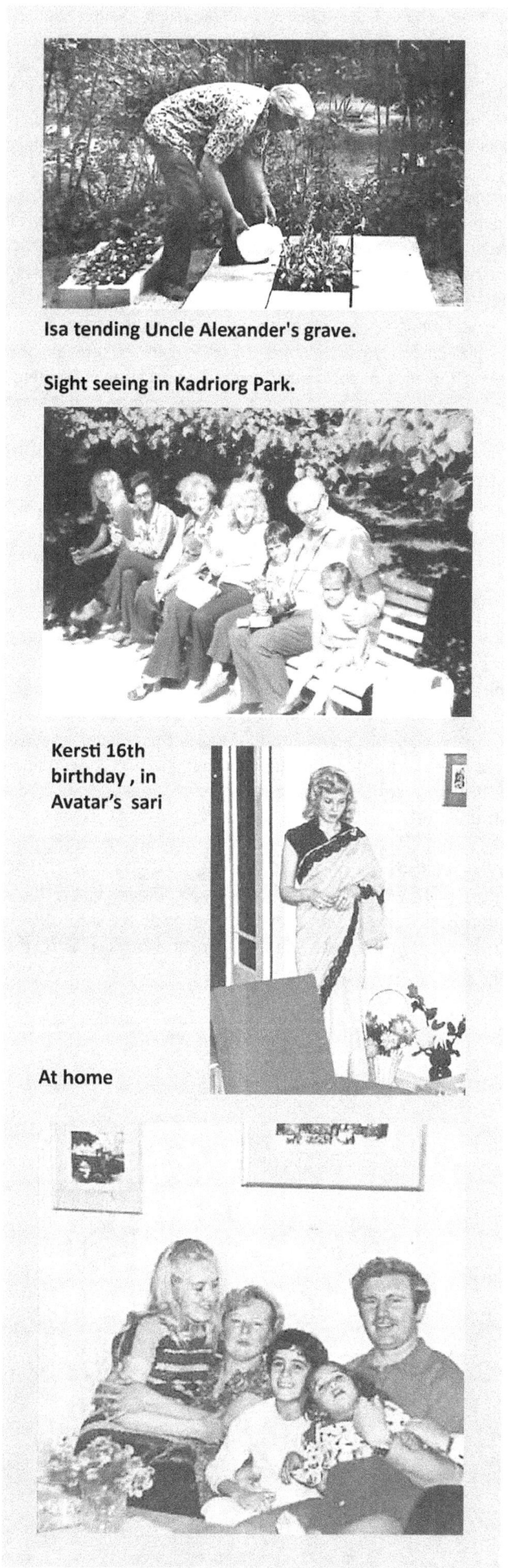

Isa tending Uncle Alexander's grave.

Sight seeing in Kadriorg Park.

Kersti 16th birthday, in Avatar's sari

At home

summer. The one shortage was the lack of a " sauna" and in order to ensure that I was able to partake of a "real Estonian sauna", a scheme was devised to smuggle me out of Tallinn to visit Oss's (Õie's brother) summer house where there was a very efficient one constructed by him. To achieve this we had to create a smokescreen so that the KGB tail watching us would think we were still in the Tallinn house of Oss. I was able to get into another car in a garage and then hidden under the blankets was driven by back roads out of the Tallinn area into the restricted zone where Oss's summer house was located near the beach front west of the city. A similar cat and mouse game occurred on our way back to Tallinn.

Mission was accomplished, I enjoyed the sauna and seeing more of how their family life was able to continue on without the undue interference of "Big Brother". This constant surveillance started to get me down at times. I remember especially the radio jamming masts which were placed around Tallinn area to stop people receiving broadcasts from the West, in particular stations like the Radio Free Europe, BBC and voice of America. These monster like pylons reminded me of the aliens in Orson Well's "War of the worlds."When you tried to listen to one of the banned stations all you could hear was a terrible noise like sunspot interference.

Availability of consumer goods in Tallinn in those days was very limited and to get Western goods one had to have foreign currency which you could only spend in special shops. One had to have "valuta" or foreign currency to purchase items. Clothing of good quality was in short supply. So, before Avatar went she made sure she left most of her garments behind with Kersti and Anu. I in turn was able to buy items in the special shops for Isa and Õie.

Despite this lack of material goods it was very evident to me that the family in Estonia did not lack the essential ingredients for a happy family life, namely, love for each other, enough food, adequate shelter and transport. In some ways it reminded me of the way we lived in 1950s New Zealand as a family except perhaps we had better housing and political freedom without the heavy hand of a totalitarian State. It was obvious to me that there was a strong undercurrent of rebellion amongst the Estonians towards their Soviet Russian overlords. It was a rebellion they were keeping to themselves for the time being and I was heartened by their ability to keep the culture alive and well despite all the handicaps the occupation produced. It was still the Brezhnev era at the height of the Cold War and one had to be very careful or you could still end up in the Gulag as many dissidents did. However, the days of mass deportation had ended for now. Now more subtle forms of reducing the Estonian population was occurring, for example, military conscripts were assigned to the Pacific coast of the USSR for two years and those from Asian areas were posted to Estonia and other Baltic states. Often this meant the recruit would remain in the locality afterwards.

Katrina celebrated her third birthday the day before we left for London.The family made a great fuss over her and she was gifted with a special shaul and hat she had chosen and was presented with a big bunch of flowers when she awoke in the morning to happy birthday song. She was delighted. I think Terry got a little put out by all the fuss being created around her.

When the time came for to me to depart with the children it was not easy to say goodbye. We didn't know when we would be meeting again, if ever, given the nature of the regime in power.
There was many a tear in all of our eyes as we sat in the Tallinn airport waiting to board the aircraft which took us to Moscow and then on to London .Terry and Katrina sat on their grandfather's knee holding him close. They would not see him again for decades.

Terry and Katrina on their Grandfather's knee before departure.

For me it was going to be another 12 years before I returned.*

AGO LOORPÄRG
PARTING THE IRON CURTAIN - A VISIT FROM TÕNU AND HIS FAMILY 1974: EXTRACT FROM "FREEDOM IS ANOTHER WORD FOR EVERYTHING TO GAIN" VOLUME 1

Our correspondence with Tõnu was not as frequent as it had been at first. As it turned out later, there was a reason for this that I had not anticipated. In one of Leeni's letters there was a sentence from which I concluded that my letters may interfere with their life. First, I thought the reason was her family life but it later turned out I was wrong about that.

After Tõnu's graduation from High school, he started his service in the New Zealand Army and spent four years as a cadet in the Military Academy in Australia where he graduated as a First Lieutenant into the New Zealand Army. I think the reason could have been his stepfather who was a New Zealand Army Officer. Also, I had chosen an officer's profession once in the Estonian Republic's Army. Tõnu had probably made his decision following our examples.

Tõnu graduated from the Military Academy after 4 years and stayed in service in New Zealand Army as an officer. When serving in Malaysia in 1965 he met an Indian girl in Kuala Lumpur, called Avatar Kaur and got married. A year later they had a son Terence, my first grandchild. A daughter Katrina-Maria was born in 1971.

Tõnu often wrote about his family, wedding and children. He stayed quiet about the life and service in the Army. It was understandable. In 1974 Tõnu wrote that he was starting to find a way to visit us.

His biggest wish was to finally meet his father. Now he and his unit were stationed in Singapore for two years and he was now a Major in rank. At first this wish remained only a wish.

In 1974 it was difficult for expatriate Estonians to obtain a visa to visit relatives in Estonia. For this a host had to apply for a permit from NKVD. Usually it took months to process the application before a response was received. I could be certain that I would not be given a permit for my son to visit me. The file about my past was at the Tallinn NKVD. They would definitely check that. Even if I had been a „clean" man in their eyes, I would not get a positive response because Tõnu was in the army of a capitalist country, an officer with major's rank. I had no hope to get a positive response.

Thus, all the bigger was our family's surprise in the first days of July when we received a short and clear telegram saying, "We will arrive in Tallinn on 5 July with the whole family. Tõnu!", the Flight arrival time had been added. The telegram had been sent from Singapore.

The impossible had become possible! That was the surprise that I mentioned earlier. How Tõnu obtained a visa, he told us when he was in Tallinn. On the morning of 5 July the whole family, in two cars, went to the airport. We were late. Tõnu's family had arrived on an earlier flight from Moscow to Tallinn. We found Tõnu, Terry and Avatar holding 3 year old Katrina-Maria outside the airport waiting for us.

The first words that my son told me were:" Hello father! How are we going to talk now?". Tõnu thought that his Estonian he had once learnt and still remembered from Estonian kindergarten in Germany was not going to be good enough. He should not have worried, as Tõnu spoke thoroughly decent Estonian and on top of this we had Kersti who spoke English and was a translator for Avatar and the kids. I cannot remember what I replied to Tõnu. The joy of seeing my son again and my daughter-in-law and grandchildren made me speechless. Tõnu was 2 years old when I had last seen him.*

Tõnu's visa lasted until the end of July. They had bought a return ticket from Moscow via London. Our family now had very busy and fun days ahead. Children adjusted with the new environment in no time and Kersti had a lot of interpreting to do because even 3 year old Katrina had lots of questions considering her age. Tõnu and the children were going to stay with us until the end of the month. Avatar was going to fly to London earlier.

On the same afternoon Tõnu and I went to the Department of Ministry of Internal Affairs in Lai Street that registered foreigners arriving in Tallinn. They were not allowed to go further from the town's boundaries. There I was told that they only registered people who had arrived on Intourist visas. Tõnu's visa had been issued by the Soviet Union Embassy in Singapore. They were surprised at how he had managed to reach Tallinn on this visa in the first place. We were sent to „Viru" hotel where tourists with Intourist visas arrived and stayed. Here the situation was even worse. The Deputy Director refused to register them. We were treated very impolitely and he threatened to send the whole family back to Moscow. Now I realized what was wrong. Guests who came to Tallinn were expected to have Intourist visas and they had to stay in Viru hotel, not at the host's home. They were allowed to visit homes but they had to stay overnight in the hotel where it was possible to keep an eye on them.

We returned to Lai Street but there they refused categorically to register Tõnu's visa. We were leaving when a woman wearing a militia uniform in the office next to where we were, waved us over and quietly suggested we go and seek help

441

from Estonian Ministry of Foreign Affairs in Toompea. There they listened to our story politely and told us to come back in an hour. This is what we did. We were sent back to Lai Street and told that the manager of the Department will have received an order to register Tõnu's visa. The same woman who had given me the good advice had already received an order to do so. She registered Tõnu's visa, wished him a happy holiday with the newly found father and winked at me with a smile. I thought that one can find good and helpful people even at places where one does not expect to find them. This is how this story ended for now.

Meeting Tõnu's family had been possible through a bureaucratic error in the Singapore Soviet Embassy. They were now able to stay with us with no worries. Many relatives and friends visited us as they all wanted to see my newly found son and his family. Some days we were sightseeing in town, some days we spent in Muuga where kids could play. Muuga was within Tallinn boundaries where foreigners were permitted to go. Breaking this rule would have meant visa cancellation and deportation. But we had lots to do and talk about in town. We had to make the best out of the time given to Tõnu. We had a lot to talk about and some things to clarify. Because of the censorship we had not been able to write about everything that needed clarifying.

Now we had a chance to do that. Tõnu had subconsciously felt that his father was alive. Receiving my letters he had a plan for secretly coming to to see me. Of course, this was complete nonsense but considering his age understandable. Now I understood the meaning in Leeni's letter that referred to Tõnu's thoughts. Of course, it scared Leeni but it was impossible to write in more detail.

There was another unpleasant fact that Tõnu did not write me about. Me living in the Soviet Union and correspondence with me impacted his military career in the army. As a commissioned officer he could now only go up to the rank of a major. Tõnu and I could not foresee such situation and take it into consideration. When Tõnu first knew about it he was, of course, disappointed. He asked me not to worry about it. When Tõnu had been in service for 20 years, he decided to leave the Army after completing his studies at university.

Initially Tõnu was still serving in Singapore and thanks to a coincidence had found an opportunity to visit us. I felt these days we spent together after such a long time being apart passed too quickly when hosting the guests, walking in town and spending time in Muuga. Thanks to NKVD there was variety during their stay as we were not left alone. It had been only a week since Tõnu's arrival when a doorbell rang. We were visited by a „doctor" and a nurse. They excused themselves and asked whether our guests were all in good health. I thanked them for such good care and said everything was fine. „Doctor" checked whether everyone was still there.

Seemingly the man who was keeping an eye on us had fallen asleep – he was across the street next to the railway bank and was changed every other day - we noticed him already on the first day. Now he was doubting whether we still had guests in the house. It seems that NKVD „tail" was following us also when we were walking in town and driving to Muuga. But on one day we managed to con them. This is how it happened!

Õie's brother Osvald's summer house was in Vääna. We were not allowed to go there. We decided to go there nevertheless by conning our guards. I parked my car outside the house, took the whole family on and drove to Oskar's in Nõmme. There I drove to the courtyard at the back of the house where I left my car as we entered the house. I presumed that they were following my car. We spent a couple of hours at Osvald's. His garage was in the cellar underneath the house with the exit from the side of the house facing the street. Osvald took Tõnu's family with him in his Volga and drove to Vääna. My car stayed in the courtyard. Our guards did not know to check Osvald's car. Half an hour later we drove my car out of the courtyard towards town with Õie and Osvald's wife. We did not care if we were under surveillance or not. The guests were in Vääna long ago. I left the car in the garage and we went inside. The guard at the railway tracks was there. He thought all our guests had stayed in the house. A little later we got into the car in the garage and drove to Vääna. We spent a lovely afternoon there. Tõnu went to their sauna where he very much liked the whisking (with Birch leaves). In the evening we returned to Tallinn in my car. This time through Harku as we were warned off the old route by Oss's guests. In Rannamõisa Road the border guard was checking the cars. We got to Tallinn without problems.

1974 summer was very chilly. It was sunny but with a constant and cool northerly wind which took the warmth away from the summer. We could not think about going to the beach much. It left Tõnu's family, coming from warm Singapore, with the wrong impression of Estonian weather. It was not as cold in the garden in Muuga. Children were able to play on the lawn and if they sat on the terrace that was shielded from wind, it was quite nice. Before Avatar left we celebrated Kersti's birthday on 10 July in Muuga. This time the weather was luckily good and warm. There were quite a few guests.

In mid-July Avatar flew to London via Moscow to go on a European tour. I accompanied her on her way to Moscow. I knew the place better and before she boarded her flight we had time to go on a quick tour by taxi around the central town so that Avatar would see more of Moscow. Tõnu and the kids stayed with us. He was going to fly to London at the end of the month, meet Avatar there and then fly back to Singapore together.

Kersti had a lot to do with the children, who needed help in translating, as they had a lot of questions. It was easier to communicate with seven year old Terry. Katrina was very active and full of energy, curious child. When walking in town she liked to walk separately and independently from us as if she was an adult. Passers-by liked Katrina's exotic look. She turned 3 on 27 July. Waking up in the morning of her birthday Katrina acted like a little adult accepting presents. We gave her a small cherry red poncho fit for a child that Katrina had noticed and liked in the Uku shop in town. Katrina's birthday was also the leaving party because on the following morning we saw Tõnu and the kids to their flight to Moscow.

Saying goodbye was difficult and sad because no one knew when we will see them again. We all hoped that we will meet again. *

We continued our every day activities after Tõnu and children left. We all had a certain empty feeling at first. Something was missing, something was different, but after a couple of days everything was like it had been before. July passed too fast. But the joy from this meeting remained. Now we did not only correspond but we were united by a realistic family bond. Meeting my son his wife and grandchildren meant a lot to me. New meetings with them did take place in the future.

Viewing Old Town from Toompea: Isa, Kersti, Avatar and Terence

1990 outside Tallinn House of Horrors: Father Ago, (nephew Tom) and son Tõnu, indicating (to Stalin) "We beat you, you bastard"

TÕNU LOORPARG

The Soviet Union had lived up to its reputation: It had been a scary place for us to visit. Fortunately our sojourn with our family in Estonia made up for all the totalitarian bureaucracy we experienced in sometimes frightening circumstances.

As the Aircraft lifted off the runway we felt a sense of relief to be on our way back to the "free world".

Visiting Kadriorg: Katrina, Avatar, and Terence, the KGB were everywhere

PURPLE TWILIGHT: MM

It occurred now maybe thirty five years ago: A small boy had made an observation and chastised me for my lack of insight.

Matt, then aged seven had figured out that since I had no brothers the name Maddisson would die out: Why hadn't I given him Maddisson as a second Christian name: Perhaps to one day hyphenate onto his father's surname. The explanation is complex and probably goes along the lines of why he wasn't called Erik, Bjorn or Anders. I explained it away more diplomatically, that his father and I had made a generic decision to not use family names.

Whoops! On my first return to Estonia in 2002 I discovered that Madis is the Estonian equivalent of Matthew. With the explosion of cyber technology I was to recently discover that the Parnu surrounds are loaded with Madis Maddissons for generations back: **None of whom I know anything about.**

He hadn't quite reached understanding the notion of sandman wagons, and that his German grandfather's surname (which I have only documented on my marriage certificate) too would become extinct in Oz.

Matt had clearly already noticed the difference between my side of the family and those of locals where there are family names dating back to perhaps the First Fleet, and extended families were the norm.

Caught up in the treadmill of decades of the second generation effect and the name Madison becoming a popular girl's name that notion has blown away with desert dust.

One's patients grow old with one: Many of them of refugee stock and wearing similar shoes as I was. However Mr. Hippocrates Oath stood firm and my mind remained fixated on finding these folk some comfort as a their few remnants of DNA which had come with them began attrition: The names even faster as in our youth girls assumed their husband's names. Of course for both, their sons and daughters infertility was a statistical factor. I was caught in a whirlwind into which I had been trained: Take care of your flock.

The Geislingen project (perhaps now a larger Estonian ex-pat project) is now nine years old. As the compiler of the narrative of our youth I also receive many personal e-mails: There are patterns about them. Some include photos of their children and grandchildren: There is so much to chat about. I relish that personal touch and it rarely reaches the 'manylogues' unless there is a deep relevance (and then of course with the author's consent).

Others talk about their activities, at times there is a fleeting reference to a distant relative. My mind returns to my working days: Yes that is just how my patients who were becoming

"Lost souls' haven: Paldiski Maantee, Tallinn"
painting by
Mai Maddisson

increasingly sociologically isolated used to talk until the bottom began to fall out of their lives. The muscles in their acquired stiff upper lip were becoming limper.

Maybe it is time to reflect about those among us who too are in such shoes. Maybe it is time to observe the diluting volume of some of the voices. Is it because they too are realising that their DNA, and more often their family names are too becoming extinct. Maybe we need to listen carefully for ruffling feathers during our communications: Maybe we need to embrace our folk in their grief.

Recently I have been working on our photography 'manylogues': One really hit home. I knew of many others who hadn't verbalised their pathos. I chose not to publish their words using their name: But perhaps they do need to be said anonymously. They read

"Thinking of the photos I have taken and what they meant, and they were definitely meant to be a legacy, at least at a subconscious level......I had intended to do some major organizing, sifting and winnowing of the photos. It was to be the initial retirement focus, until it dawned on me that my daughter was unlikely to have children. She had wanted to, had planned it, and it was not to be. Obviously the main issue here is her, and what that means for her, and that is not my story to share, however the photos, as a record of who we are, and whence we came, is.

......was persuaded by.....to do a write up of a close relative. I did so because .....son wanted something that could keep that awkward name (how many of us have such names destined for extinction) propagated for their descendants.......

I think, I'm in a pensive mood, but whining is never attractive, especially when we live in freedom with plenty, and are in reasonably good health."

Yes, we do have plenty, but of what: Our material goods will be dispersed according to our wills when the twilight turns to darkness.

Something returns me to my last visit to Estonia last year. My hosts are a wonderful and generous couple: They work so much harder for what we think we have worked hard for.

During that visit there was a major extended family function (as there had been during my other visits) but this one was less formal and chit-chat was occurring all around. Everyone made me welcome and I felt very much so.

My hostess remarked on my being so quiet: I was quiet but not distressed. I had become mesmerised at the notion of having such an array of family so close at hand, and at their spontaneous communication. She asked me "What's wrong?" I answered "Nothing is wrong. I just haven't the faintest idea how to communicate spontaneously with such a vast number of people one can call one's own."

It occurred to me that one only communicates that spontaneously with those who are part of you: All other communication is measured to some extent. We have all lived variably without a commodity which is not visible: How many of us still feel that we are baring our souls to a relative vacuum: It is at times all that understands us.

Some years ago a patient brought in a painting, their first one, to show me. I could instantly recognise whom they had depicted: It was of a sombre man: Mr. Van Gogh. Pleased with themselves they announced that with a friend's advice they had changed the sky from purple to yellow.

Why is it that we cannot allow those of us who are facing a purple twilight share it without feeling guilty!

> Love is but a wandering friend who sometimes comes your way,
> To share your smiles, your joys, your thoughts, that it might gain,
> A confidence to face the outside storm, that blows onto a gale,
> And leaves again as the storm, invades your home........   MM

THE SINILILLED CONTINUE TO GROW & DESPITE OUR

![Verner Puurand memorial]

VERNER PUURAND
1904-1983
EESTI ALLVEELAEVASTIKU RAJAJA

Estonias Sinimaed have many memorials to men who sacrificed their lives for their nation: Some of the graves are marked others not.

Verner Puurand's memorial has been recently erected.
Professor Peeter Jarvelaid stands behind the memorial.

The photography has been contributed by Prof. Jarvelaid

Visiting Hans Puurand Jr. (second from the left) and his family near Brisbane, Queensland, Australia. In the photo to the right, third from the right is the late Will Tonisson, and his sister Kulla on the left, who were Geislingen kids.

Photos taken in 2007 by MM, WT

CHAGRIN CLOSURE IS AN INTEGRAL PART OF MOVING ON

In a manylogue I recently circulated in preparation for thoughts about a prologue for the sibling book about our fractured generation a reply returned from Kalev Ehin: I think all readers will agree that it should be shared before the sibling book is 'born'

WHAT FEELINGS I WOULD LIKE TO SHARE WITH EACH OTHER —Kalev Ehin.

Feeling the overwhelming emotion that totally engulfs you when you're finally united again, in flesh and blood, with the only persons closest to you other than your dear my wife. In addition, there was this marvellous feeling realizing that you were home again, instead of dreaming, after 38 years of absence. Such long sought after sense of needed closure can best describe it with the help of three pictures.

First, here I'm standing over my mother's grave with tears in my eyes at the Rahumägi Cemetery in Nõmme in 1982. Since I had been very close to my mother made it extremely painful for me to come to the realization that she would never hold me in her arms again. What consoled me a little was that she had whispered to my sister, as she was slowly passed away, "Kalev will return!"

Second, here I'm holding my dearest sister, Maimu, in 1982 in front of the house in Nõmme where we lived during the first Soviet occupation and the German invasion in 1941. This brought about a lot of good and bad childhood memories.

I still vividly remember watching the majestic Tallinn skyline becoming smaller and smaller as the ferry Georg Ots was picking up speed heading out of the Bay of Tallinn towards Helsinki in 1982. Tears swelled in my eyes as I wondered if the Soviet authorities would allow me to return again or permit my sister, Maimu, to visit us in America. I also pondered whether my place of birth would ever be free again. It was an unbelievably emotional moment as Betty instinctively snapped a picture of me at that instant. In 2011 that picture became the front cover of Coming Home. Elagu Vaba Eesti—Long Live Free Estonia!

An enigma of my travels in Germany's cities has been my penchant for visiting church ruins.

It is there I found a curious peace, perhaps even a greater peace than among other ruins: But then perhaps they were taller and more symbolic.

I stayed rather longer than usual inside the ruins of St. Nicholas' Church in Hamburg. I don't know why. It was just so peaceful.

In the back of my mind is a vague memory of some kind of sirens wailing away while I just meandered around the courtyard where a church had once stood: A courtyard which was still presided over by its lofty tower and remains of broken walls.

As I meandered out of the side entrance I found myself staring at two police cars. There had been some commotion outside and it seems I had been quite oblivious to it or its proximity.

On reflection why would any country waste its military personnel or armoury on already shattered buildings:

Yes it was probably one of the safe places to run to when those fireworks struck all those years ago.

History had serendipitously reenacted itself.

MAI MADDISSON
REFLECTION: PEACE AMONG THE RUINS

One could say that there are ruins in everyone's lives: That only the magnitude and extent of them varies. Perhaps one could also say that the extent to which they play a role in their present lives varies, and that perhaps memories of those incompatible with survival are addressed in a diversity of ways.

The pivotal factor to optimizing life after any journey with quandaries is the finding of closure: To understand how an event happened and why the resolution was not as one might have expected as now seen through the eyes of relative predictability and peace: For us once youngsters now looking at the event though much older and mature eyes, through experiences learned by later and mutated verbal acumen.

The first task of an author or compiler is to ask themselves to who is this book directed and what are they are trying to achieve by its production. And how realistic is this expectation given the setting of the compiler and the authors.

The aim of the book is simple as I stated in the prelude. "There were just so many questions to answer. Questions which other babies born at those times might also need answered. I hope that my book answers some of them for you."

The book is clearly directed to those who walked that journey, or a similar one: Each of whom, like I has many quandaries about that trek: The younger we were and the more frequent and precarious the events we crossed the more complex those quandaries: For there were times for us, when this was complicated by the need to translate vague, though at times vivid flashes of imagery into verbal concepts.

How does one disentangle such a jungle of hybrid fractured memories? Perhaps the honest answer is that it cannot be done: Were that possible the management of PTSD (post traumatic stress disorder) would become a cinch: To state that the precipitant and resolution are poles apart at times never to meet, would not be an understatement.

Perhaps as I reflect on the writings, it is the creation of the endless dioramas: It has been the creation of such dioramas, as endless as our differing journeys through the jungle of war, which has been the greatest asset to resolving the quandaries. To be returned verbally or pictorially to the same diorama, is perhaps to recognize in a less troubled state, that there was something present which invalidates current uneasy memories of that time. And at times it was the antonymous imagery which creates the relief: NO my situation was not like that: It as quite different: In my shoes I did OK.

Second voice while of great narrative value and of maintaining an even and cohesive pace in a book, is not conducive to spontaneity of sharing. The interviewer may well through their even subtly different journey omit the very important question which a given author wants to share or present a quandary about: Put differently they would be creating their narrative through a vastly different personal diorama, at times oblivious to what lies entrenched beneath that interviewee's soul. This can precipitate unease, at times dangerously so, in the interviewee or a reply which is not optimally considered and distracting from the more poignant aspects of their sharing. Perhaps one should not ignore the possibility that depending on the interviewer there may be endless variants of the same account.

Something which has been ignored as a powerful influence on shared material is the chemistry between two people: Given many of those stories were not written primarily for my use the chemistry becomes less poignant in the perspective. Thus objectivity is enhanced.

Even in narrative there is an aesthetic consideration: It definitely helps when the reader is not buffeted though what seem to be and indeed are very separate stories which may not relate to each other at all. Uneven narrative concerning a single person presented in diverse variations would make one wonder if the book was produced in fragments or whether in fact the person had become fragmented. This story encompasses many voices: Each remains true to themselves but variably different to the others.

I make no apology for the endless different voices or the heterogeneity they effect on the book: A book which is written with a clinician's cloak with forty-eight years of wear. I emphatically state the most authentic and poignant account of any person's story be it medical or sociological derives when they speak spontaneously: That they don't contrive their language to the language of the clinician, or in this instance the compiler.

Language variants derive from people's place of abode and their demographics: To translate their thoughts into that of another is to question how adequate their linguistic skills are. The translation of "When the Noise had Ended" into Estonian made it abundantly clear that even people sharing the same language speak that language differently with different idioms, have words which don't exist in another variant and at times may need qualification. Likewise people from differing academic, professional, commercial and industrial cultures all speak with a different vernacular: They are neither right nor wrong but that vernacular can more accurately transport them into their shoes and allow us to begin to consider how things looked through their eyes.

Even the choice of photography themes and their background tells us a lot about the environment from where a person may have derived and how to interpret their comments: To put them into proper perspective.

Yes I have made a choice to retain first voice regardless of third person opinion: I make no apology for that either.

It would have been of greater aesthetics to produce a book which looked more even: It is a penchant of many academics that this is so, as it is of our relatively ordered current society. Lets us remember that this book was not compiled for either's readership: For them it can only ever be a fragmented collection of individual narratives and reflections for them to interpret through their eyes, maybe to discover a little about an era of the past.

But such lack of evenness too has a purpose: The book needs to contain vast and varied detail: Much of it emotionally dense. There need to be times to reflect and rest. Those intrusive little vignettes and photo clips serve to allow a more peaceful journey through the book.

Nor can be the book representative of our cohort: That would require many long volumes to represent the many subsets of our then young. There is a vast difference in how the tinies saw the times as compared those who were almost adults (perhaps before their time).

Many who remain alive are not yet ready to share their journeys or even face the quandaries: They cannot be represented. Nor can those who are no longer with us, be it due to age or premature demise. The latter would have added a valuable dimension to the book but what they felt; wondered or endured we can never know. The accounts of their survivors can only be second voice accounts: The more troubled the first voice the greater the chance in the degree of material withheld. Perhaps the same can be said for voices which are in part in denial or dissociation.

Perhaps underestimated is their contribution of what seem to be artifacts of tangential material: For those who at times are silent, or prefer to sequestrate a part of their story, it shares with the intercurrent reader what they treasure, for the person seeking closure that artifact may have been a lost part of their past, of their drama too.

Given my own age, reality has to step in: Each year reduces the chances of a task being completed by death or infirmity. Perhaps it is better to have something acceptable compiled than a set of facts left for another to begin to untangle and place into their style of presentation. And let us remember that the primary readership consists of those who have voids to fill and their children who are relying on the remaining of us to do so: The book needs to be as diverse as possible so that among it they may find those skericks of information which elude them, to facilitate their further research.

Yes this book is a mosaic of diverse material set up in a format of best fit with respect to the time that remains for all parties concerned.

The book has not been written for catharsis or therapeutics: Any such outcome is serendipitous. My quandaries have been solved to the possible stage and given my very different demographics any further answers derive from elsewhere.

Most of us have done the catharsis bit in among our own folks: It is the generation gaps and the diversity of pathways with which we have travelled which have required translation into the age appropriate lingo. This book was not envisaged as a cathartic one nor propagated as such.

No book is totally irrelevant to its world and can offer new tangents to knowledge in many denominations.

For the historian it offers a perspective which perhaps is less politicized as children tend to be more naïve and carried their memories via these. It also keeps reminding the world that children too are part of the war journey: Voiceless once albeit.
For the sociologist it takes them away from academia and data and statistics into a world where an awareness arises that the needs of adults and children, both long and short term cannot always be derived through the eyes of the children's elders: That the latter in their plight may be quite innocently blinkered to what lies ahead for the child who will move in very different circles to their parents.

For the psychologists there is an opportunity to revise their dogma: perhaps not all that they perceive as madness is such: That there is method in madness. Such method the lesser of two evils: The difference between perishing mentally or physically. Does anyone who has not met hell truly have the right to question how hell is most optimally traversed: whether the delayed responses are appropriate? For myself I can say that many of my anxieties learned as a little tyke in the war transit have 'saved my bacon' and maybe my life. Had I had a crystal ball and narrated such apprehensions to someone who had not walked my journey I fear that they would have had many exotic names for those anxieties and had I been naive enough to take their dogma as gospel this book may not have been born.

Maybe also to be learned are the dangers of many decades later sequestrating behavior out of its historical context: Dr. Asperger worked only about 350 km from where I lived my early childhood, and at about the same time. Given that many of the children's folks were involved in the war effort be it honest or perverse, what sane parents would communicate spontaneously with their children, and what children fearing for their family would talk spontaneously to even their dearest friends! Where were such communication skills to be learned? What would be the legacies of a very bright child extrapolating from what they heard had the war rumbled on for another half a century, the child now an adolescent: a bird wanting to urgently fly: To fly with fragmented information to direct their wings. Perhaps we have yet to learn that what is observed in atypical settings may need to be scrutinized for unexpected explanations.

For travelers through the same epoch, in similar terrain the book will certainly help them understand that different age cohorts will view situations differently and one day move on to build a world on the foundations built with their eyes: It may offer cautions in how material is shared with differing age groups but perhaps most of all it may help in reducing the incidence of squabbles of mankind.

For present day refugees apart from showing them that hope is a slowly growing vine with no instant panaceas there may be little to learn or of relevance. The newer refuges derive not from Judaeo- Christian ideologies (or their abuse), not from similar climatic terrains or demographic backgrounds, and indeed not from similar expression of artistic traits which are a common transient panacea to severe distress. Their acting out of distress is done by differencing sociological nuances and to adapt to that of a former group in rarely viable.

Perhaps the one powerful lesson which can be transmitted is that the 'oldies' should never use their children to carry their baggage: That is their load, albeit a tough one in the wilderness of war and terror. Their task in relation to children is to offer them realistic hope no matter how many 'sleeps' away that may be for those children. Children are resilient little folk but also wonderful mimics: They learn not what the 'oldies' tell them but role model on what the 'oldies' show them.

And now for the poignant question:
How many of the unanswered questions has this book, answered for my cohort. From intercurrent e-mail exchanges I will bow to the answer of many, many, many but in the course of this journey many new quandaries have been born. Perhaps true closure never comes: We just move closer to it. We keep on looking and in our reminiscing more answers may come.

AND FOR SOME QUANDARIES THE ANSWERS MAY NEVER COME

Among our documents is an entry referring to Ria Maantee 11, in Pärnu. The street numbering has not changed. No one seems to know much about its history.
In 1939 the Baltic German doctor who had owned it sold out and given the times returned to Germany.
Thereafter according to information I have, it became a Russian military rehabilitation facility.
After our exodus it was to become for decades the local 'Blind Institute'.
Why is it in our documents-?   MM

EPILOGUE: A MEETING OF MINDS AND SOULS: MM

Merike Tamm
Olav Virro

Andres Kurrik
Donna Parson

The success of this venture was due to a collective input: A special thanks goes to **Priit Vesilind** who was supportive of me and ready to step in and continue the festivities should that which we all fear, given our ages, step in and intrude upon me.

In our modern world of hurry scurry it is easy for people to become fleeting interactions in our lives. We forget that they are only there by the grace of God or fate. In the hurry of today, we may never again meet that person who somewhere deep down inside us we felt was an integral part of us: One we one day hoped to know better.

How different was the journey of our war children's youth. But perhaps one has to qualify that those differences may be perceived and prioritized differently by those concerned. Objectivity is a far less tangible commodity because to each of us what we acknowledge as the reality has been tinged by that of our own.

I have been privileged to access some form of objectivity. I planned and coordinated "Geislingen 2008" which was a reunion of those of us grade school and younger who could attend. It was set in the town where we had lived and the town's awareness of the event removed confounding variables of concern about a hoard of strangers roaming around their town.

The planning occurred in tandem with the compilation of WNE and consisted of endless e-mails, both shared and private. It didn't take me long to form some form of diorama of what had taken place all those years ago and the emotions attached to them. Fortunately my ego stopped me from assuming it was a shared perception.

I set several agendas for the reunion:
• To render it an enjoyable and positively memorable event for all concerned.
• To allow the older of us with more memory of the times to fill in the voids for the younger ones.
• And to have a summing up component:
• To allow those of us who felt the need to thank the Germans for tolerating us and allowing us to have a roof above our heads, while they themselves were not out of adversity lane.

There were two dinners.
• The fun one came first to ensure that any vast dissent of opinion could not undo the camaraderie which had blossomed.
• The second dinner was the learning one:

There were four speakers.
• The dinner began with the youngest: Merike Tamm was born in the camp. By speaking first the possibility of bias from material learned from the older of us was minimized.
• Then came Olav Virro who represented those of us born into war and hence pre-verbal for much of the time.
• Andrus Kurrik was the last of that trio of speakers. He had known Estonia before all hell broke loose.
• And the fourth speaker? Donna Parson, the USA born widow of Jaan Paarson spoke about how it had been living a life amid 'Geislingen memories' and Estoniana.

And of course much sharing and deliberation occurred at times when we grouped and regrouped: Symbolically the beer garden adjoining the Jahn Halle where much of the social interaction of our folks had occurred became the watering hole and place for rendez vus.

Imre Lipping and Indrik Linask, born into different age cohorts deliberate while awaiting for others to arrive to continue the day's events.

Yes it was a true meeting of the minds and souls: We were able to walk in each other's shoes and understand that perspectives had many determinants. We all parted understanding each other's shoes much better. We also learned that there were other variables including some quite unrelated to our refugee and DP status, which were to determine our outcomes.

•Some of us were old enough to meet those loved ones before chaos erupted around us: Some of us continued to know them and watched the ravages of life change them from peaceful people to ones who again had to learn to trust mankind. Their children too learned that trust cannot be taken for granted.
oOthers of us were too young to remember our loved ones in better times, only as those who could not trust those around, who feared for their lives. That was our normality and perhaps became our identity too. We could understand just how they felt and at times continue to feel.
oAnd there are others of us who never knew what it was like to lose one parent, at times two. Sometimes we knew how and where they had languished. Others of us could not bear to begin that search for decades, to perhaps become another journey to no avail. Yet others like me lucked in to meet by mail or face to face the other genetic part/s of us late in life. I met father by mail at the age of sixty: But better late than never to know who we who truly are.
oThat the very young could relate to not having, and distressed parents but could not conceive the imagery of how their distress evolved (They only had their folks mythology to base this on).
oThat there were many people of Estonian refugee parentage who were born on the cusp and at times were totally perplexed by their locale and   longed to have it rendered tangible.

And for some of like Inge and Mati Pruks, (pictured below) they were left to forever wonder: Serendipity passed their way when' during the visit to the Estonian cemetery as part of Geislingen 2008 they found their father's name engraved onto that collective gravestone.

Inge and Marty Pruks finally meet their father

It still bewilders me how it is possible to take our loved ones for granted and feel that they have no relevance to our identities.

Our journey will forever be the story of war children, refugee children and DP children. The academic tomes may confound the basic premise by indicating that the local demographics differed. They may have for the 'oldies' but for children wars remain but a series of tussles between the 'goodies and baddies' where the children are cast to bring all their survival resources to the fore: We bid them the courage to do so and trust in that courage to succeed. The names of the countries and the ideologies involved are but confounding variables in their journeys.

'HOP' THROUGH THE RETROSPECTOSCOPE

**Children are sometimes born where the stork drops its bundle to unburden its weary soul,
The more burdened the soul the more precarious its landing place,
That the stork continues to fly perhaps part of nature's plan.**   MM

This book was born way back in 2009 when WNE was completed and a concurrent upsurge of emotion occurred at least in Oz, that the World War II refugees from Europe did not do it as hard as modern refugees were, and statedly still are doing. Through my eyes an injustice had been done to the parents of children who derived from the Central European cauldron.

The only honest way to invalidate such emotion was to provide information to the contrary. Having travelled that trek among Estonian refugee and DP children and their parents it was only natural that such a book would be vignetted by first voice stories from those travellers: An interview format perhaps a contrived version seen through a clinician's eyes: I cannot change what I was trained to do. Such a book would also become perhaps polarized away from the normal demographic distribution of those groups as only the distressed visit doctors.

However that story has two fragments: That before arrival in the new lands and what preceded that arrival. Those stories are inextricably continuous but to make the accounts coherent need to be separated into two sibling books as I have done.

They are books which I wrote, and am continuing to write with my heart in them as I too was part of that trek. I have made some wonderful friendships some of which have evolved slowly and cautiously and hence have developed robust roots which would not become vulnerable in a gale: We could always remain honest with each other whether either was accompanied by good or bad: My demographics but an irrelevancy for the past or future.

For many reasons the book has taken five years to mature: perhaps a sign of how complex such issues are. Sadly a number of events have crossed the path of this book. They have made it clear that I do not wear the same 'school tie' as the British folk would put it. There was initial enthusiasm for my being part of the journey but this has in some poignant quarters now changed to what again British idiom calls 'lip service'. Given the wishes projected by those events the only honest role I could continue to assume was that of a narrator of the stories of Estonian war parents' children.

However it is an ill wind which blows no good: The book about Estonia's war children: A fractured generation, permits greater heterogeneity, but only post arrival in the adoptive lands: That is where that book begins. It is partly finished and promises to be just as interesting as its sibling book. However it does leave a void where some stories proverbially begin midstream.

There is no problem without a solution: One into which I can embed the suggestion for the third book which was suggested to me while I was in Estonia in 2013. Yes, in this world there are many children who are to become

"Nobody's children, nobody's adults". They too deserve the serenity to walk tall among mankind. There have been many children of many stocks, Estonian included, who have perished prematurely on such roads: I am one of the ones who has survived long enough to tell their tale. MM

MEET THE AUTHORS

CHARLES (KALEV) EHIN, Ph.D.

Dr. Ehin is the former Dean and currently an Emeritus Professor of Management at The Gore School of Business at Westminster College in Salt Lake City, USA. He has authored numerous management articles in addition to publishing three groundbreaking books. His work can be viewed at http://www.unmanagement.com/.

Dr. Ehin was born in Tallinn, Estonia but fled his native country during World War II when it was torn apart by Nazi Germany and the Soviet Union. His book, Coming Home, is a graphic personal account of his experiences during and after the war in Europe.Please visit http://www.cominghomethebook.com/ for details.

He joined the U.S. Air Force in 1960 and held several leadership positions, including teaching at the Air Command and Staff College, until 1980. Subsequently, he worked as an internal organization development consultant for E-Systems, Montek Division in Salt Lake City. He began his fulltime teaching career at Westminster College in Utah in 1983.

Dr. Ehin earned his BA degree from Colgate University, an MBA from Syracuse University, and a PhD in Business Administration from the University of Oklahoma.

ARNE ELLERMETS

Arne Ellermets was born in Tallinn, Estonia in 1931. He, his parents Arnold and Mari as well as his younger brother Heiki escaped from Estonia in 1944. Their refugee travels were challenging and interesting. He was active in Estonian Boy Scouts and attended four different Estonian high schools as a DP in Kempten, Altenstadt, Geretsried and Augsburg, Germany before relocating to the United States in 1949.

The Estonian High School education formed a solid foundation for furthering his education. He graduated from Lindenhurst High School on Long Island, received a scholarship to Union College in Schenectady, NY, graduated in 1954 and was commissioned as a second lieutenant in the US Air Force. Wilhelmina Klersy, a pretty young school teacher, became the first member of his family in 1953. It is questionable whether she realized what lay ahead!

Air Force pilot training in North Carolina and Oklahoma was followed by assignments to Morocco, France, Germany, Vietnam and the East Coast of the US. Wilhelmina liked France the best! She speaks French while Arne is proficient in German. Flying was fun, but both of them continued their education. Arne received his MS from The George Washington University while Wilhelmina received an MA from the Ohio State University. Arne was a Distinguished Graduate of both, the USAF Air Command and Staff College, as well as the USAF Air War College.

His key assignments involved flying SA-16 Air Rescue aircraft in Morocco, C-130 transports first all over Europe and Africa, then in Taiwan and back to command a C-130 squadron at Langley AFB in Virginia. He received a below the zone promotion to Lieutenant Colonel and three years later a promotion to Colonel.

Several assignments took him away from his favorite seat, the one in the aircraft! His primary desk jobs included one as the Director of Operations at the Frankfurt International Airport in Germany. This task involved directing the operation of the USAF half of the large German Airport. Another non flying job took him to the Ohio State University where he served as the Chairman of the Air Force ROTC Department for four years. That job led Arne to the position of The Commandant of the Air Force ROTC in the Ohio Valley Area that included 28 major universities. He finished his thirty year military career in that position.

Family life posed some challenges with their busy professional lives. Before getting married Arne and Wilhelmina sat down and discussed their expectations for marriage. They agreed that there would be no alcoholic beverages in their home, that all moneys would be in common and that they would read at least one chapter of the Bible every day. They also discussed children. Wilhelmina thought that four would be a good number while Arne thought that two would be sufficient. As it turned out they had all six happy and healthy kids who traveled with them around the world!

A new career waited for Arne and Wilhelmina after retiring from the USAF. They

became missionaries with Awana Clubs International and served for another 30 years in that capacity. They initially lived near Frankfurt, Germany and served the US military community by starting new Awana Clubs for children and youth across Europe. At the same time they supervised the translation of Awana handbooks into German and helped start many national Awana clubs in many countries. The goal of Awana is to reach boys and girls with the Gospel of Christ and train them to serve Him. It was exciting for them to see hundreds of children and some adults accept Jesus Christ as their personal Savior.

HANNES JÜRMANN

Life in Australia has been interesting but kind to me despite a number of changes in occupation. Brother Peeter and I took to the Australian way of life with enthusiasm and seldom had anything to do with other Estonians until my first visit home in 2001. Despite being encouraged to take up teaching by my primary school teacher, I succumbed to the temptation of earning a wage early, left school after 3 years of high school and started as a bank clerk. After 3 years of this, the greater excitement of Air Force life attracted and I followed my brother and friends into the RAAF, being trained as a Radio (electronics) Technician. Since my wife, Shirley, was a teacher I decided to follow her example and completed my last 2 years of high school while in the RAAF and the following year received a Teachers' College scholarship, having finished my 6 year term in the RAAF. As soon as I completed teacher training I began a part time University Degree, majoring in Geology, as there were great prospects in nickel mining. However that fizzled out and I remained a teacher, concentrating mainly on senior Physics and Chemistry, but teaching all the way down to the lower ability juniors too. Australian high schools are mostly not subdivided; just years 7 to 12 and year 12 is preparation for university.

I developed a desire to experience some kind of farming, and we moved to the western side of NSW where we bought a block which was mostly bush, with some grazing. My dreams of making it a viable grazing property were optimistic and it was hard work having sheep and some cattle to deal with beside teaching duties. After retiring from teaching in 1998, the property used up all my time for not much reward and I had the desire for rural life out of my system. In 2003 we managed to sell the place within 6 months and moved to the coast near Port Macquarie where our twin son and daughter worked.

I was immensely relieved to quit teaching at age 60 as the politicians had completely ruined a profession I once loved. Disposing of the "farm" was not quite as big a relief but a big load off my mind. Retirement on our comfortable pensions has been marvellous and allowed me to indulge in my multitude of hobbies ranging from my favourite of motorcycling, learning to read music and to play the sax, improving my Estonian by reading many books, computers, mechanical workshop and a vast array of other things. I have a handful of really good, longstanding friends but avoid involvement in any kind of clubs and societies.

MALLE JUSKE/KARP

I arrived in Australia aboard the "Cyrenia" on 8th April 1949. I finished secretarial school in Sydney. I met my husband Helmut at folk dancing and we were married in 1955 and decided to take up poultry farming in Thirlmere. We were active in the Estonian community. Our daughters both finished their University degrees and we moved to Thirlmere and I became assistnat manager in 1992. Helmut died in 2002,and I retired to Thirlmere retirement village.

Now as a grandmother of five, I enjoy "Taara Gardens" where we can still celebrate our past national days and also integrate with our new friends in our new homeland.

MAIE KAARSOO/HERRICK

My brother and I lived at home in Winnipeg with our parents who supported us until we both graduated from the University of Manitoba. My brother, Enn, became a civil engineer and I earned a MD. I continued my education in Cleveland, Ohio, specializing in neuropathology. While in Cleveland, I married Tracy Herrick, a financial economist. We live in Palo Alto, California, and in a few months will celebrate our 50th wedding anniversary. We had two children, Alan and Sylvi. Alan lost his life in an automobile accident. Sylvi, her husband Matthias and their two young daughters live in Florida and we go frequently to be with them. We have travelled numerous times to Estonia to visit relatives. The most meaningful and moving trip was the one my husband organized to take my parents back home shortly after Estonia regained its independence. It was an extraordinarily emotional time for the surviving family members to be reunited after almost fifty years, and for my parents to see the land of their birth, and to walk on it, one more time

MAARE KASK/TAMM

We left Geislingen in December 1950, went to Sweden as labor migrants. Our first home was Olofström, a small town in southern Sweden. My father worked as a welder in a factory. I and my mother obtained work in a garment factory. After a few years we moved to the capital of Sweden, Stockholm. where I graduated from high school 1953.

I continued my studies in pharmacy and earned a Bachelor degree in Pharmacy in 1957. A year later I met my future husband Allan, (also an Estonian) in a little town in the south of Sweden, where I was working in the town´s pharmacy and he was working as a medical doctor. We married in 1958 and we have been married since.

As newlyweds we began our lives in Gothenburg where our first child was born in 1960: A boy named Mikael.

In 1963, when I was pregnant with our next child, we moved to northern Sweden, to Härnösand. In this town winter is truly a winter with lots of snow and a cold climate. We stayed there for eight years. Our two younger children were born in Härnösand: A boy, Urban in 1963 and a girl, Katarina in 1967.

When our daughter was one year old I began to study again, this time psychology. and in 1990 I graduated as Ph.D. at Umeå University. However before that we had to move again, this time even further north to a town called Boden.

Boden is a place where the sun never goes down in the summer, and never rises in the winter. The reason we have had to move so often is related to my husband's working conditions. As a doctor in Sweden you can stay at the same place a maximum of eight years, unless you get a more senior position. Thus we have stayed in Boden since 1970.

While living in the far north I have mainly worked as a Senior Lecturer in behavioral sciences both at Umeå University and at Luleå University of technology. During these years I have written many books and I am now the author of fifteen textbooks.

Both my husband and I are now r etired. At present we have three adult children, two boys and a girl, three grandchildren, two girls and a boy, and a great-grandchild, a girl.

MART KASK

Mart Kask was born in Tartu, Estonia, his father being a regional forester, and his mother, a high school biology teacher. The occupation of Estonia by the former Soviet Union at the concluding days of World War II, forced the family to flee their homeland. In 1949, the family immigrated to the United States, settling on a farm near Olympia, Washington. Mart finished his high school studies in Olympia and graduated from St. Martins University (Olympia) with a Bachelor of Science Degree in Civil Engineering (cum laude). He went on to Purdue University (Indiana) and graduated with a Master of Science Degree in Civil Engineering.

Mart fulfilled his U.S. military obligation as a commissioned officer with a rank of Ensign (later promoted to Lieutenant J.G.). He served on board of various ships in the

Pacific, On returning to civilian life, Mart worked as a transportation engineer and planner in various government and private sector organizations in Seattle. In mid 1960s he moved to Dayton, Ohio to become the Executive Director of the Dayton Metropolitan Area Planning Organization. Shortly thereafter, he was appointed CEO of the Miami Valley Regional Transit Authority.

In 1971, Mart returned to Seattle as Executive Director/CEO of the Puget Sound Regional Council. The Regional Council is charged with directing orderly growth and economic development in the Seattle metropolitan region of about 3.3 million people. In 1985 he formed an urban planning and development consulting firm of Kask Consulting, Inc. Today, Mart is a consultant to FEMA (Homeland Security) on catastrophic disaster preparedness planning in the Seattle metropolitan region. He is the Project Manager of the Resource Management and Logistics element of the plan to assure that life saving and life sustaining commodities and services are strategically placed and available to disaster victims.

In his professional life, Mart's achievements have been recognized by his peers and he is a recipient of many awards, including the following: U.S. Secretary of Housing and Urban Development (two), U.S. Secretary of Energy, Governor of the State of Washington, and American Planning Association (two). Mart was also appointed a Marshall Plan Fellow by the West German Government. Mart was one of ten American urban planners invited to tour China as a guest of the Chinese government. In addition, Mart served as a registered lobbyist in the Washington State Legislature and the U.S. Congress. One of his lobbying achievements culminated in the construction of the Washington State History Museum in Tacoma, Washington ($50 million). He was one of two Washington State's delegates to the Whitehouse Conference on Highway Safety.

Mart is the current Chairman and Managing Director of the Rotalia Foundation. Previously, Mart served as the Chairman of the Seattle Estonian Society and was an elder of the Seattle Estonian Evangelical Lutheran Church. Mart also served as the treasurer of the Estonian Heritage Collection dedicated to preserve and display historic treasures and artifacts of Estonian origin. For a number of years, Mart served on the University of Washington Scandinavian Studies Department Advisory Committee. During the fall of the former Soviet Union, Mart was invited to appear as an international political commentator on ABC TV network stations, including Seattle's KOMO.

In 1991, Estonia regained its independence and Mart was nominated Honorary Consul of the Republic of Estonia for the territories of Washington and Oregon. Mart also served as Counselor to the Foreign Minister of Estonia and was the advance man to the Estonian Prime Minister on a commercial visit to Japan. Mart was a delegate (Estonia) to the World Trade Organization (WTO) conference held in Seattle. Later, he was the organizer of the Estonian President's visit to Seattle and the Northwest. Mart is a member of the Seattle Consular Corps and served as Chairman of its International Trade Committee. In 2004, Mart retired from the diplomatic service and now holds the title of Emeritus Honorary Consul.

Mart is married to Linda-Reet Kask, M.D., (internal medicine, University Southern California (USC) summa cum laude, phi beta kappa) retired from University of Washington as an Assistant Professor of Medicine and a member of the U.W. Physicians Group Practice. Mart and Linda have four grown children and eight grand children. Mart and Linda live on Mercer Island, Washington with their dog Bogart.

AIRE KOLBRE/SALMRE

I was born in the independent Estonia in 1936. My recollections of my childhood begin with the Soviets establishing naval bases at Suurupi Naval Base in 1939. I could sense tension, that something was not normal. Memories following the Soviet and German occupations, fleeing Estonia, fleeing from the Russians in the war torn Germany and living in Blomberg DP camp are vivid. Our family: Ema, nurse-midwife; Isa, captain, jurist in the Estonian Army and sister Kaare arrived in USA in December 1949.

Received BS in Nursing from Hunter College, MA in health education from Columbia University and studied Nursing Home Administration at the University of

Connecticut. I have worked in health education in NY and CT. In 1961 I married a fellow Estonian William Salmre, a physical chemist and we moved to Connecticut.

My interests have been Estonian culture, history and literature. I've been actively involved with our weekly Estonian newspaper "Vaba Eesti Sõna", also an editor of the newspaper. I was the US East Coast editor of the global Estonian home and family magazine in exile Triinu from 1985-1995, until the magazine stopped its publication when Estonia regained its independence. Working with Triinu editors in Canada, Sweden, Australia and USA provided most satisfaction. All the work for the magazine was done on voluntary basis. I have contributed essays and articles to various publications. When our three children Pia, Tiina and Ivo attended the New York Estonian Supplementary Elementary and Secondary School I taught Estonian history and literature for twenty years. I have volunteered at the Estonian Boy and Girl Scout Camp at Järvemetsa in Lakewood, NJ and also at the Estonian Summer Camp Jõekääru near Toronto, Ontario. Our three children: Pia Ph.D in communications, Tiina MA in special education and Ivo a computer scientist are married. Pia's husband Gregory Romerosa, CPA is of Philipine extraction. Greg has become a wonderful estophile, has studied Estonian, visited Estonia and likes to attend Estonian functions, Tiina is married to Rauno Jõks, M.D., half Estonian and half Finnish. After twenty years of taking a leave of absence from the NY Estonian School, now when Tiina and Rauno's boys Heikki 9, Markus 7 and Madis 5 are attending the NY Estonian School, I'm back teaching at the NY Estonian School. Ivo is married to a Canadian Estonian Krista Leesment MA in business administration and they have a 2 ½ year old son Mikko Andres, who is also learning Estonian.

In 1990 after returning from a visit to the Soviet occupied Estonia I felt we in the free world had an obligation to help the destitute Estonian families there. With three Estonian friends in Connecticut we established the "Estonian Home Assistance" program. In three and half years, during the first years of regained Estonian independence, much needed help was provided for the needy families in Estonia.

Last year Tiina and Rauno's family visited Estonia and the boys liked Estonia so much that we are planning to visit Estonia this summer. Heikki is wishing we had a summer cottage in Tartu.

My hobbies include reading, walking with Nordic poles and cross-country skiing.

ANDRES KURRIK

Andres Kurrik was born in Tartu, Estonia on April 21, 1937 as the firt of five children of his parents Konstantin and Leonilla Kurrik. His early childhood memories from pre-war Estonia and his wartime and some of his post-war experiences and adventures are highlighted in the accompanying story.

Andres began his formal education during World War II in the fall of 1943 in the Lessingschule in Freiburg, the city in which his youngest brother Thomas was also later born. After the war he attended Estonian schools in refugee camps in Geislingen, where his sister Malle was born, then in Aschaffenburg, and finally graduating from sixth grade in the Kempten Estonian school.

After three years in the Oberrealschule in Memmingen and two years in an Estonian Labor Service unit of the U.S. Army in Germany, Andres at age 18 emigrated to the United States, where he was joined in California by his brother Juhan a couple of years later.

The first 15 years in the U.S. were for Andres again a chaotic period. The two brothers supported each other, alternating college and work. Andres combined work as a draftsman for Westinghouse with college courses, until he enlisted in the U.S. Navy after receiving his draft notice. He then spent six years of active duty in the U.S. Navy, serving on various ships from frigates and destroyers to aircraft carriers, with several tours of duty in the Far East and the Middle East, again taking college courses during several shore duty tours in the United States. After completing his first enlistment, Andres continued his naval service in the active reserve of the U.S. Navy, eventually retiring as a Chief Warrant Officer after 30 years of total service.

After attending college part and full time for a total of 15 years at eight different institutions, Andres graduated from San Francisco State College with a B.A. degree in international relations. After graduation Andres moved to New York City where he worked for American Re-Insurance Company until his retirement from that company as a Vice President. A highlight of this employment was his assignment in 1989 to a small team in the company that was tasked with developing business contacts and exploring future business opportunities in the Baltic region of the Soviet Union during the heydays of the perestroika period. Andres thoroughly enjoyed this unique opportunity for extensive and prolonged to travel to and in Estonia and Russia during this tumultuous era. After his retirement from American Re, Andres continued this work as an independent consultant, expanding it to include advisory work for the newly established Navy of the Republic of Estonia.

Andres Kurrik is married to Katrin-Kaja Roomann. They have two sons: Arne and Kalev, both of them working in the IT field in San Francisco, a city that Andres counts after Tartu as his second home town.

BRUNO LAAN

Born on May 6th in Tallinn. He grew up in Nomme and completed Gumnaasium there. During the German occupation he enlisted in the Air Force: He survived the horrors of war without scars.

Post war he began studies at the Baltic University in Munich and then continued at Karlruhe University.

After migrating to USA he continued his studies at the MIT in Boston, where he completed his masters degree.

Los Angeeles became his adopted home where he worked for Fluor for 33 years as an engineer, his task to manage projects world wide.

In Los Angeles Estonian Society he was in the men's choir, folk dancing troup and a supporter of the striving for Estonian independance. As EOLL's president Bruno particiapted in the organisation of the 1979 Westcoast Estonian Festival in Los Angeles. He was in office for many years at Los Angeles Estonian House and the president for 16 years. Bruno was involved intensively in the despatch of parcels and later books also.

BRUNO LEEPIN

Education:
Diploma of Graphic Design, Caulfield Institute of Technology
Work experience:
Graphic designer -ABC TV Melbourne, ZDF Germany, BBC TV London,
ATV Birmingham
Freelance Illustrator- various agencies and publishers
Lecturer-Illustration and Graphic design at Latrobe University Bendigo,and Moorabbin TAFE
Presently pusuing visual arts full time
Exhibitions:
Robert Jack's Drawing Prize- Bendigo Art Gallery -2005
Castlemaine-State Festival and various local galleries 2005-2008
Ballarat Gallery on Sturt-group exhibition-2009
Castlemaine-Brickworks-group exhibition-2012

BORIS LEES

The connection with my country of birth, Estonia, has been unusual, greatly because of the country's geographical location next to Soviet Russia. I lost my father in 1941, during the Russian occupation, because he was a successful businessman. He was taken to Siberia, where he died in less than a year. 1941 – 1944 we had a German occupation and when the Russians were returning in

1944 we fled to Germany and had our ship's catastrophy on the way. In May 1945 we managed to get into Denmark, just a couple of hours before the Germans in Denmark capitulated, and I spent the next 5½ years in refugee camps in Denmark. I went to middle school in Copenhagen and the Danish language came to me completely automatically without any study. In year 3 I was second in the class and in year 4 I was first, not just in Danish but in all subjects.

In 1951 a "New Zealand Selection Mission" came to Copenhagen to select migrants among refugees to live in New Zealand. They had found about 800 in Germany and took about 150 from Copenhagen. My mother and I travelled on the migrant ship to Wellington and after staying in a migrant camp in the North Island we were sent to Christchurch. I had no means to study chemistry at Canterbury University (at age 13 in Estonia I already had the knowledge of Higher School Certificate) and mentioned my interest in the subject to Gordon Jamieson who used to go to services in the local Lutheran Church. He obviously did not realise that chemistry was not the subject that a chemist (i.e. pharmacist) studied. He introduced me to George Hanafin, a pharmacist, who needed an "apprentice". (In those days the student worked in a pharmacy during the day and went to lectures and laboratory work in the evenings).

He was willing to pay me a better wage than standard pay and I started my "apprenticeship" in August 1951 (not in February, as is usual). In the Christchurch Pharmacy Students Association I became the vice president and of 16 students in my year only 4 passed the final exams in minimum time. I had no problem, as I had "photographic memory".

In 1958 I came to Australia, as in Adelaide there was an Estonian Festival between Christmas and the New Year. I also worked as a relieving pharmacist in Adelaide and Melbourne. In Sydney there was no work, as many students had just received their registration. Estonian activities in Sydney were the best and I decided that we should move from Christchurch to Sydney as soon as the timing was right. By 1963 the financial situation in Australia had improved and we moved from N.Z. to Sydney. In 1968 I bought a small pharmacy and I worked there for 27 years. After that I did relieving until I turned 80 and discontinued my registration.

Now I was able to spend more time in Estonia. I did visit Estonia in 1994 and started procedures for getting back the properties that my father and my grandmother owned before communism. In 1996, after selling my pharmacy, I went to Estonia and stayed there for 6 months to re-organise and repair the soviet-neglected properties. I should mention, that the Russian soldiers who were housed in the two storey building opposite the Lutheran Church, had never seen a toilet and used to defaecate in the back yard!

I made altogether 10 visits to Estonia and stayed there over 1½ years. In 2011 I decided to give the building to the Lutheran Congregation, as it was in excellent condition and most of it was rented by an art school and a music school. (The congregation needed income for restoration of the minister's house, as during communism it had become dilapidated).

In my home city of Sydney I was the Secretary of the Board of Estonian House Co-operative Society for 13 years. I became also the Secretary of the Estonian Lutheran St. John's Congregation and I am working for them to this day.

MARJE LIMION/MEDRI

My mother, Maimu Limion, left Eesti at the urging of her parents, in September 1944 with my brother, Heikki, who was born in Tartu in 1942. Of course, she fully expected to return after the war.

I was born in Geislingen in 1946.

Dad, Eduard Limion, was an officer in the military and, after the war, worked with the Estonian Guard Company 4221 in Nuremberg.

In 1952 we emigrated to Canada and I have lived in the Toronto area ever since.

Growing up, I particpated in most of the Estonian community's functions - Estonian school, summer camp Jõekääru, rhythmic gymnastics, etc., and I was confirmed in the Estonian Lutheran church.

I married an Estonian and I am pleased to say that both of our sons are fluent in Estonian. A lot of their early years revolved around the Estonian House in Toronto, beginning with kindergarten there.

Unfortunately, I remember nothing about Geislingen although mom spoke often about our life there. I have been back to visit four times (day trips), the first time with mom. In spite of the fact that I remember nothing of my early years there, those visits have all been very emotional events for me.

ILLE LISCINSKI/USZINSKI

Ille has had a more complex and turbulent life than many of us, even way back in Estonia. She lived in the Geislingen camp and attanded the Gümnaasium there. Her poetry writing talents began there and and thrived in Australia: She had a manuscript of about 100 poems and two plays when she arrived in Australia in 1948.

She settled in Brisbane aand married an Austrlian citizen of Polish descent and raised a family of four children and then, determined to master the English language in 1975 obtained a BA from the University of Queensland.

She part of the editorial committee of "Ethnic Brisbane"- now defunct and was for some years involved with ethnic media in Queensland. She has avidly contributed to "Meie Kodu" the Oz Estonian paper.

She also has three published books- a novel, poetry and a children's book.

INDRIK LINASK

was born in Tartu, Estonia. He escaped from Tallinn, Estonia, with his mother and brothers on the day before Tallinn was occupied by the Soviet Union in September, 1944. Lived in various refugee camps in Czech Republic and Germany before and after World War II ended, including four years in Geislingen, from where his family emigrated to America in 1950.

He started school in the Estonian Elementary School in Geislingen. And, in America, continued his education in Willimantic, Connecticut schools and The University of Connecticut, from where he graduated with Bachelor- and Master of Science degrees in Mechanical Engineering. For forty years, he worked at Pratt & Whitney Aircraft Corp., where he was responsible for aircraft engine structural design, turbine durability design and development, and then directing development of high temperature turbine durability design technology. He is a life member of the American Society of Mechanical Engineers. Is married to Kersti Luhaäär Linask, and they have a son and a daughter. Although retired from work, his home continues to be in Connecticut.

Indrik's personal life has centered on Estonian activities, including 50 years in folkdancing, about half of which as director of the dance group „Jaanik"; the CES brass band; member of two choirs; and the drama club. He served 14 years as president of The Connecticut Estonian Socity, Inc., where he was succeeded by his son. He is still an enthusiastic supporter of Estonian folkdancing and enjoys playing the Estonian folk instrument Kannel.

TÕNU LOORPÄRG

I was born in Tallinn, Estonia 1942, escaped with mother and grandmother from Second Soviet Occupation in 1944 on a ship leaving Paldiski for Danzig (Gdansk).Father served in Estonian Army and later mobilized in Estonian Legion as Anti Tank Company Commander serving at Sinnimäged. After the war my father was a POW and was sent to Soviet Gulag until 1955 when he returned to Estonia . I became a Displaced Person (DP) housed in Augsburg (Hochfeld) Germany until 1949 when my mother and I sailed for New Zealand (NZ) on Dundalk Bay from Trieste. I attended Estonian Kindergarten at Hochfeld then Primary and Secondary Schools in New Zealand 1949-1959.

I studied and graduated from Royal Military College of Australia Duntroon in 1960-63. I served in NZ Army 1964-1980 as Infantry Officer on Operations in SE Asia, and in Staff appointments in NZ and Singapore.

I obtained a BA, Master of Public Policy from Victoria University New Zealand, served Government in State Services Commission as a Director, and at NZ College of Management as Deputy/Acting Principal. I operated in Private Sector as General Manager Executive Leasing Morgan and Banks Ltd. Wellington, Managing Director of The Management Edge Ltd a Strategic/Total Quality Management Consulting Company, Managing Director of Avatar Estate Vineyard (Rtd), Partner in Taipoi Forestry Investments, Member NZ Institute International Affairs, Member NZ Returned Services Association. Past President NZ Institute of Public Administration, Duke of Edinburgh Conferences Alumnae, Duntroon Society, Convener Estonian Culture Group in Wellington: Appointed Estonian Honorary Consul in New Zealand 2006 to present date 2014

I have been writing research papers and books for publication, also writing/translating books on my families NZ/Estonian Memoirs, and on my cohort of Estonian War Children. Participating in Golf and following sport, especially Rugby Union and tennis.

I have been married since 1966 to my wife Avatar who is a retired University lecturer in English. I have three adult children, three grandchildren and one small dog

GUSTEN LUTTER

EPP LÕOKE/BAUERN
Born in Ronneburg, Germany, November 1944 to Salme and Jaan Lõoke. I spent 4 years in Geislingen D.P. Camp and sailed to New Zealand on the Dundalk Bay in 1949.

My first 3 years were in Mangakino, a small village in central North Island, my sister Anu, was born there but sadly mum died a few months later and we moved to Auckland where I've lived ever since.

There was a small but vibrant Estonian community in Auckland and I remember the gatherings and celebrations.

My working life entailed office administration then later years was involved in a small way with special needs children.

I have three daughters, three grandsons and a great grandson due shortly.

Since 2000 I've had three wonderful trips to Estonia and met lots of relatives. After growing up in such a small family it was amazing to realise I had such a large extended family.

ENE MAIDRE/MIKLI
This is an extract prepared by her sons and extracted from her obituary

Ene Mikli was born in August 20th 1936, in Valga in Southern Estonia. She was the youngest daughter of Villiam and Rosalie Maidre, and sister to Juta and Kasper. She spent her first few years on the family farm before having to flee Estonia with her family from the invading Russian Army when she was only eight years old. She and her family first moved around transit camps, then spent five years in displaced persons camps, mostly in Kempten in Southern Germany. Ene's family migrated to Australia in 1950, first staying at migratory camps in Melbourne in Victoria, Australia.

Ene found the settlement difficult. However she learnt to speak English and excelled in her schooling, earning her a scholarship which led to her earning a dental degree. She also enjoyed sports and made it into Victoria's first state women's volleyball team.

Ene married Heino Mikli married in January 13th 1962 and had 3 children, Arno,

Lauri and Markus. The family moved to Port Hedland, Western Australia and then to Kalgoorlie for over 30 years. Ene was recognised for her long service by the Goldfields Chamber of Commerce. She also became a grandmother to two girls – Caitlin and Anna. Ene was given back ownership to the family farm when Estonia regained its independence in 1991, and together with Heino restored it and grew blueberries.

Ene and Heino moved to an Estonian retirement village in Thirlmere in New South Wales in 2004. Heino passed away in 9th August 2007. Ene passed away in 9th July 2013.

AINO PAAL/MARSHALL

and her family arrived in Perth late in 1951 and built their own house as promptly as possible after their arrival. After completing her high school studies she became a librarian with the Education Department and completed her library studies degree.

By 1973 she was Acting City Librarian: She had charge of five other branches.

Aino, in 1966 married an Australian of Swedish and Scottish descent. Busselton, which is 7 hours drive from Perth was their life's work: They had established a cattle farm in Dunsborough, which is just outside Busselton.

Aino was keen is keen on building design and designed both their first house (in 19740)and subsequently a farm house in the 1980's.

Her interest in dog breeding culminated in her becoming a founding member of the Western Australian Cattle Dos Association, and a founding member of the Western Australia Local Government Women's Association.

Their current abode is not Aino designed: They live in a bungalow built by her husband's parents. They have a daughter and three grandchildren.

SANNU MÕLDER

Sannu Mõlder was born in Tallinn, Estonia, in 1935 and fled, with his parents, to Finland and then to Sweden when the Red Army invaded Europe in 1944. Attended public school in Sweden; emigrated to Canada in 1949; joined the Air Cadets and Boy Scouts; obtained the Flying Scholarship and private pilot's licence and the First Year Aeronautical Engineering Scholarship (UofToronto), from Air Cadet League of Canada; attended high-school in Montreal and Toronto and University of Toronto, obtaining a B.A.Sc. in Aeronautical Engineering, an M.A.Sc. in Aerophysics, an M.Eng. in Industrial Engineering and a Ph.D. from Mcgill University (thesis title: Curved Aerodynamic Shock Waves). Flew fighter-jets in the RCAF, became a commissioned officer, attended advanced flying school and earned pilot's wings. Became a research fellow, and then assoc. prof. at McGill University and, eventually, Chairman of the Mechanical Engineering Department. Was director of the Hypersonic Propulsion Laboratory at McGill (1964 to 1972); Member of NRC Advisory Committee on Aerodynamics in the 60's. Member of McGill Senate (69-71). Project Director of the Gun-Launched Scramjet Program (65-72). Participated as consultant to The Johns Hopkins University's Applied Physics Laboratory in the National Aerospaceplane (NASP) configuration definition (1983-84); Consulted to the Defence Research Board at DRDC ValCartier on chemical lasers. In 1972 moved to Toronto's Ryerson Polytechnic University as the Chairman of the Industrial, Mechanical and Aerospace Departments. Directed joint Ryerson-UofToronto program on Studies of Scramjet Inlets. Lectured and conducted research at universities in Australia, Japan, USA and Europe. Lecturer at Von Karman Institute for Fluid Mechanics (2011). Distinguished Invited Lecturer – AIAA (2012). Graduate lecture series on 'Curved Shock Waves' at University of Queensland, Australia (2012). Reviewer for AIAA Jour., JFM, JPP, JSW. NSERC. Consultant to NASA and the USAF. Molder Is a Fellow of the American Institute of Aeronautics and Astronautics and a Fellow of the Canadian Aeronautics and Space Institute. Listed in the American Men and Women of Science and the Canadian Who's Who. Authored and co-authored 75+ papers on hypersonic airbreathing propulsion and shock waves. Presently Professor Emeritus of Aerospace Engineering at Ryerson University, involved in an international program for solving problems related to scramjet air intakes. Fluent in Estonian, Swedish and English with some knowledge of Norwegian and German.

LIA NOORMETS/NICHOLSON

Lia arrived in Melbourne in early 1949: she has lived here since. On arrival she promptly began work at the Heidelberg Repatriation Hospital (eqivalent to Veterans' Hospital) which at the time was very much a hive of activity. Like many of the adolescents she went to work immediately at relatively menial work but with her resourcefulness and diligence was rapidly promoted to work as an electrocardiography technician, and some years later as an electoencephalography one.

She has been active with ex-pat Estoniana at Estonian House over the years: Both in their choirs and in folk dancing.

KYRA PALANGO/ARONSON

In 1944 fled with my family from Estonia to Germany. Our ship was torpedoed on the way, but managed to reach Germany with a hole on its side. During the war we were moved from one refugee camp to another. After the end of the war, we were placed in a displaced persons camp called Valga in the American zone.

In 1950 we emigrated to the United States and, after several moves, ended up at Seabrook Farms located in Southern New Jersey, joining a large number of Estonians who were working at their plant.

After finishing high school, I went to New York to attend a secretarial-language school where I studied French. Worked at the Swiss Bank Corp. for several years and then moved to Irving Trust Co., where I was promoted to Assistant Vice President. In the meantime I married and began studies at Hunter College, majoring in anthropology and graduating with a BA degree.

My husband passed away in 2011. I am spending my retirement years in attending courses at New York University and a writers' workshop. My black cat, called Diablo, is my good companion.

SIR ARVI PARBO AC

Sir Arvi Parbo was born in Tallinn, Estonia, in 1926, and became a refugee in Germany during World War II. After attending the Clausthal Mining Academy in Germany from 1946 to 1948 he migrated to Australia in 1949.

He is married and has one daughter and two sons.

He graduated from the University of Adelaide with a Bachelor of Engineering Degree with First Class Honours in 1955 and is a Chartered Engineer.

Sir Arvi joined Western Mining Corporation Limited as a mining engineer in 1956 and held a number of positions in mines in Western Australia and Head Office in Melbourne until being appointed General Manager in 1968, Managing Director in 1971 and Chairman and Managing Director in 1974. He relinquished the position of Managing Director and became Executive Chairman in 1986, non-executive Chairman in 1990, and retired in 1999.

Sir Arvi was also Chairman of Alcoa of Australia Limited from 1978 to 1996, a Director of The Broken Hill Proprietary Company Limited from 1987 and Chairman from 1989 until 1992 He was Chairman and Director of a number of other corporations in Australia, USA and Germany, as well as a member of Advisory Boards in Australia, USA, China and Estonia.

He was inaugural President of Business Council of Australia in 1983 – 84, President of the Australasian Institute of Mining and Metallurgy in 1990 and President of the Australian Academy of Technological Sciences and Engineering from 1995 to 1997.

He has Honorary Doctorates in Science, Engineering, Business, and Law from Deakin, Monash, Curtin, Flinders, Central Queensland and Sydney Universities.

He was made a Knight Bachelor in 1978 and a Companion of the Order of Australia 1993. He holds the Queen's Jubilee Medal, the Commander's Cross of the Order of Merit of the Federal Republic of Germany, the Grand Cordon of the Order of the Sacred Treasure of Japan, the Order of the White Star of the Republic of Estonia, and the Centenary Medal.

TOOMAS PILL

I was born on 7th Jan 1938 in Tartu, Estonia, escaped to Germany in 1944 with my father, Johannes Pill and mother Linda Kuiva Pill, and aunt, LeidaKuivaTammemägi and her family, daughterLiina and husband LeinoTammemägi.

After having spent several years in displaced persons camps in Germany, we embarked on the SS Misrfrom Marseilles for Australia in 1948, arriving in Melbourne on the 21 of April 1948, after a three week voyage. We then travelled by train to Sydney, where we rented a room in Strathfield, Sydney.

In 1952 my father bought a house in Lidcombe, Sydney. I attended Homebush Boys High School, and Sydney University, where I got a BA in Latin and History. I continued on to get a Dip. Lib and BA (Hons) in Spanish from UNSW, and subsequently an MA in Latin and PhD in ancient Greek literature from Sydney University.

My working life was spent as a librarian at the University of New South Wales.

Upon retirement, I spend my time reading ancient Greek and Latin, writing the occasional article for the Estonian newspaper in Sydney, 'MeieKodu', playing tennis and keeping in touch with fellow members of the Estonian students' society, EÜS (EestiÜliõpilaste Selts), and giving talks to the Estonian Seniors Group in Sydney.

I am married to TiinaHendrikson, whom I met at the first Eesti Päevad (ESTO) in Toronto in 1972. She was then living in NYC, where she grew up, after arriving from German displaced persons camps in 1951. We were married in 1973 in London, and are now residing in Killara, NSW.

We have two sons, Erik and Jaan. Both have BA degrees from Sydney University, Erik in art history and industrial relations, and Jaan a BA (Hons) in psychology.

ARVED PLAKS

Arved was born in Tallinn in 1933, son of Marie and Harald who had a flower store in the city. The store provided a comfortable living given that flower arranging for special occasion was much in demand. Harald avoided mobilization in 1941 into the Red Army thus the need to escape in 1944 was imperative. The family left by ship for Germany the day before Tallinn fell. After the war the family lived in the Geislingen Displaced Person's camp for Estonians until emigration to the USA. Arved acquired in time engineering and business degrees and was employed in the aerospace industry until retirement in 1995. Job assignments included helicopter-, wind turbine-, missile basing- and the international space station development.

Arved had many uncles, aunts and cousins each with a unique story to tell of escape, survival and restarting their lives. Correspondence and visits provided ample opportunity for recording their life events. To add to that: Arved found time also to collect life stories of his grades school class mates (from Tallinn) and of the Geislingen Estonian Gymnasium students and teachers. Many are in form of booklets and some as albums which are now in Estonian archives, museums and libraries but some also in the US Library of Congress, and USAF Archive at Wright Patterson AF Base.

Hobbies include singing in choirs, folk dancing and writing (though no talent is claimed for that). He is a frequent contributor of articles to the Estonian newspapers in New York and Toronto.

INGE PRUKS/IZZO

Inge studied languages at Monash University, Australia and became an English and French teacher. She pursued further studies in France at both the University of Grenoble and the Sorbonne in Paris, adding cinema studies to her interests.

Inge has two sons, Sam and Miles Izzo, who have kept alive the musical tradition. Both can be heard in gigs around Melbourne, with Sam playing jazz piano and Miles on the trumpet, although both are also computer programmers. Making music has always been an important activity in Inge's family.

HELLE PUUPIL/GIREY

Our family immigrated from Germany to Sweden, where we stayed for one year, the next move was to Montreal, Canada. This became my home for a number of years, finished Bachelor of Science degree in chemistry, married and had two daughters. I worked for 10 years at Royal Victoria Hospital/McGill University research lab on B12 and Folic Acid. Our next move in 1972 was to Los Angeles, California. On our family vacation to Colorado, I visited Mesa Verde archaeological ruins, and realized that my education in the history of native tribes in North America was sadly lacking. To remedy this I took archaeology classes at a nearby college, and finally moved to classes at UCLA. I had the opportunity to do field work as a lab director with a contract firm for seven years. I was asked to organize the public lecture program at the Cotsen Institute of Archaeology at UCLA, where I also was a graduate student advisor. My love for archaeology has allowed me to be part of excavation teams in various countries: Guatemala, Mexico, Peru, Hawaii, Wales, Canada, Germany, and of course United States.

Now I am long past retirement age, but am still actively involved with archaeology at UCLA. I am divorced and spend my time visiting my children and four grandchildren and travelling many parts of the world. Estonia will continue to be a big part of my life.

JÜRI RAID

Juüri was instumental in introducing me to a group of Estonian young whom I had never heard of: A group of orphans whom both he hand Paul Öpik have written about for this book. He made contact with the Estonian house in New York: Without his enterprise many of us would never have learned about this amazing group of young lads. Jüri writes:

Mother rand father escaped to Sweden by the help initiated by some Estonians: Then the brought many who were not suitable to for resettlement. There were all manner of screenings at the camps. I travelled to them to help them move to their new home and remained here because their health was not good. My sister was already awaiting us.

I have been married to a Saaremaa lady. We have no children, nor any other relatives.

I have remained in contact with my homeland by indirect contacts. Interestingly in 1991 we received a communication from Estonia that we could come and visit there., even though we had never sought to do so. The organ remains more of a hobby for me. I help when there is a shortage of funds to pay for an organist. Two days still remain sacred to me. The celebrations of Estonia's freedom and of its restoration of freedom. We celebrate this with four congregations by going away for a day trip to a nice place.

Since 1991 we visit Estonia each year. My wife has many school friends in Kuressaare which we always visit. I have also seen my birthplace, and the house in Võsu, where I was born. I have also explored that region a lot.

It used to be easy to reach Kuressaare by airplane but that ceased a couple of years ago. Travel by ferry, then bus and more ferry travel makes the trip tedious but we will review that sometime when my wife's fractured arm has healed properly.

ENN RAUDSEPP

was born in Vändra on March 20, 1944, and was only six months when his family fled Estonia. He received his higher education at Columbia (MS 1966) and McGill (PhD 1977) Universities. After a 10-year career as a print journalist in Montreal and Toronto, he became a professor of journalism at Concordia University in Montreal. During his 30-year university career, he served as department chair, graduate program director, vice-dean of the faculty of arts and science and president of the faculty association.

At retirement in 2008, he was named a distinguished emeritus professor. He is married to Dr. Dana Hearne and has three children, Karl, Ciara and Rory, and three granddaughters.

HARRY SAKJAS

December of 1951 I was called to military duty, and placed in the U.S. Marine Corps. I received my basic (boot) training at San Diego, CA. and completed the training as the 'Outstanding Member' of our platoon. My next assignment was the Marine Air Wing, and I served as a mechanic and 'crew chief' on the F4U4 Corsair aircraft. I was promoted to Sargent, and left active duty after two years.

I returned to Ford Motor Co., and resumed work on my apprenticeship.

August 1955, I was fortunate to marry Helen Drob, the young lady who I met in high school. That union has lasted to this day – 59 years.

I completed my apprenticeship in 1956, and worked as a 'journeyman' Tool Maker for a few months before transferring to a 'salaried' job. Then I started on a 'Body Designer' apprenticeship, a four year program that I completed in two years because of my previous experience.

Our daughter, Mary Alice, was born 1957, and we purchased our first home in Livonia, MI. Our son, Harry Jr. was born 1960.

I continued to work as a Product Designer, and was promoted to Senior Product Designer 1968.

1970 my parents received travel permits from the Russian government, and visited us for about a month. It was nice seeing them after 28 years. Few years later we traveled to Russia, and visited Moscow and Leningrad.

I completed my work for B.S. degree in Industrial Management at the Lawrence Technological University 1974. This was done in the evening – 'night school'.

Shortly after this I was promoted to management in the design department.

With school completed, we purchased a boat, and joined the Ford Yacht Club, on Grosse Ile, MI. To learn more about boating I joined the United States Power Squadrons (USPS), Sail and Power Boating. Over the years I completed all the classes, including celestial navigation, offered by USPS, and also taught boating safety classes to squadron members and general public. After all this work, I earned thegrade of 'Senior Navigator', (SN). Now I am also a 'Life Member' of USPS.Over the years we had number of different boats, including a 36' Gulfstar trawler.

After 38 years of working at Ford Motor Co., it was time to retire in 1988. My wife, Helen retired a few years earlier from General Motors, after working in their Financial Dept. for 20 years.

We sold our home in Michigan 1988, and moved to North Carolina. We built a new home on the east coast of NC, in Pamlico Plantation, a 'gated community' near Washington, NC. There I served on the Property Owners Committee for five years, including a year as the president.

We continued our boating activities, and the membership in the 'Power Squadron'located in North Carolina.

2003 we traveled to Estonia, and visited Tallinn and Paide. This was the first time back since I left there in 1942. We also made a stop in Stockholm, Sweden, to visit friends.

We sold our home in North Carolina 2005, and moved to Hot Springs Village, Arkansas. We purchased a home in Hot Springs Village, a large 'gated community', with 10 lakes, and 8 golf courses. The 'Village' has its' own police and fire departments, and covers an area of approximately 26,000 acres.

EVA SILLAOTS/NOWACKI

Something in me kept my urge to locate Eve again despite the long lag since her initial e-mail. Finally I was fortunate enough to make contact with her daughter Dahlia. Eva's life has not been one where life has brought too many bright lights but one one which has surely indicated what tough stuff she is made of. During the last two years she was widowed and Hurricane Sandy hit her hard. Dahlia told me that her mother would be honored to have her story in this book:That small events like this will bring her positivity.

Eve! Our hearts are all with you as we read this book. Take care.

ILO SOOVERE

Ilo left Estonia with his parents in September 1944 as past of the exodus from the Communist onslaught. He was only a toddler at the time.

They lived in the. DP camps in Germany until 1949. Among his proud possessions is a collection of photos his father Erik took during that trek: Photos taken at precarious times in at times precarious circumstances.

He lived most of his childhood and youth in the Eastern states of USA.

After graduating from the John Hopkins Medical School he partook of postgraduate study to become a neurologist: Among his interests is an unusual and poorly understood condition called catatonia. His interest has now broadened to neuropsychiatry.

He had been intensively involved with USA Veterans Affairs Neuropsychiatry.

He has retained interest with Estoniana via their Estonian House and other events.

Opera is among his passions.

TOOMAS STEINBERG

Born in Tallinn, I was seven when in September 1944 we left Estonia. We were taken to Oelsnitz, south of Plauen. There my mother worked in the Heinkel aircraft factory. About two weeks before the war's end we received permission to leave the work camp. We tried to get to Baden Baden but the railway was no longer functioning reliably. We made it to the American zone and thereafter very soon travelled to Hamburg. We stayed there in a refugee camp for six months. Our next abode was in the Artillerie Kaserne near Lübeck. We lived there for about three years. I started school. In 1949 we left the camp on our way to New Zealand. I was twelve on the ship.

I went to school and grew up in New Zealand. After working in NZ I started to travel – too complicated to list here. I have worked in Switzerland, Germany, Israel and Australia. Now my wife Judith and I live in Melbourne. We have a son named Zev.

ANTS TAMM

I was born in Pärnu but we lived in Tallinn. I left Tallinn on 22nd September 1944 with my parents, aboard the ship Nordstern. My father became one of the 'police commander' of the Estonian refugee camp in Geislingen. His name was Morits Tamm. My parents divorced and my mother and I went to Sweden in 1948. We stayed in Uppsala with my grandparents in a small flat and soon enough I understood that we where political refugees in a sometimes hostile environment. My father went to New York when the refugee camp closed some years later. He was in Kuperjanovs battalion during the war of liberation

I became a schoolteacher in Sweden, for pupils up to 18 years of age: I taught students with literacy and numeracy problems (ADHD) and I also taught history.

Nowadays I am retired. I live half time in the Stockholm archipelago, sailing and motorboating, and half time in Estonia (in a village near Rakvere). I have a wife, three children and ten grandchildren. All my children and grandchildren often visit us in Estonia.

When I was working I arranged many visits to Estonia with my Swedish colleges. Since 1991 I have travelled around in Estonia many times every year and I am still doing so. I have met ex-soviet teachers, I have lectured for teachers in history, I have met pupils who asked their teachers, "why did you lie to us," and I have heard their answers.

Nowhere in Estonia have I met bitter and envious people. We do not only meet relatives, also neighbours, farmers, politicians, historically interested people and historians, doctors, pharmacists, former members of the communist party, people who studied five years in Leningrad, people who served in the soviet army, people who travelled over the whole Soviet Union. Everybody has behaved well towards us and been friendly and nice. We had relatives in Kaukasus. Now the Estonian village near Sootj has been destroyed.

I have struggled with Tallinn city about houses and renovations: I have argued with renters and learnt the Soviet way of thinking - nothing to recommend: One must remember that, during the Soviet time, everybody tried to cheat "the society" and people they did not know; and then they continued to cheat rich people from the West. I have seen Estonia become transformed from a former Soviet country to a western democracy: Naturally I am very pleased to see Estonia beginning to thrive. The people there are mostly honest, like people everywhere.

I am related to many Estonians who unfortunately were forced to stay in Estonia during the occupation time, and even to people who were sent to Siberia. Some died, some survived. Therefore I have a quite good picture of Estonia, Soviet Russia and Siberia, now and earlier.

One of my relatives is one of the founders of the Vistla memorial: The only memorial for Estonian soldiers in German uniforms. One could write a whole novel about that memorial. They started to create it secretly in 1987 and it had a precarious journey to its survival.

I was involved with Free Europe Radio: Very little was shared with Free Europe Radio, just what everyone already knew, queues, shops for communists which were forbidden for others and...well, we all knew about Estonia during the Soviet time. How incredibly strange it still seems to us.

My stepfather, Harri Kiisk, was not well accepted in Estonia.

And Ants didn't mention that he does some nice watercolour paintings: I just found one in my e-mail box!

ANNE TONDI/ELLIOT

After the end of the war our family was lucky enough to get into the Geislingen DP camp in Germany. We lived there until 1950 when we emigrated to Ontario, Canada. After graduating from McMaster University in 1960, I taught mathematics and English in high school.

I have always been interested in all the arts and am an amateur painter. I have spent many days volunteering in the arts community.

In our retirement my Canadian husband and I now live on the outskirts of Milton where we maintain and enjoy our large flower gardens.

We have a daughter and also a son who has two daughters.

I have no living Estonian relatives in Canada. However there are hundreds of my mother's Tikerpäe relatives in Estonia. Meeting some of them during my two visits back to Estonia familiarized me with my roots.

AIN TOHVER/ANDY DEUBLE

I was just a small part of the whole group and I was maybe very fortunate to emigrate to America in 1946, and there subsequently to be adopted by a childless Germany family in October 1947.

At that time my name was changed to Andrew Howard Deuble from Ain Helmut Tohver and I disappeared from the visible Estonians and became "americanized" in a sense.

I served in US Army from 1952 to 1954 and after discharge became an American citizen. The military service gave me an opportunity to attend City College of New York in the evenings and I graduated with a BBA degree in accounting 1959 and later on became a CPA.

My lifetime as given me an opportunity to be able to serve as an accountant, controller and investigative auditor for several profit and non-profit organizations. I am Certified Public Accountant licensed in New York State, retired in the State of Florida.

I have been retired since July, 1992 and been very fortunate to have the ability to continue with my lifetime hobby of singing (to myself) and then to others who want listen to me and I have great fun doing it. It was something that was a part of me throughout my life which I failed to pursue to a career level due to being pragmatic about its ultimate success. Now as I think back about it, maybe I was I

lucky that I left something desirable to look forward in my remaining years.

I am retired in Florida and have a wife and a married daughter with three grandchildren.

I enjoy singing and entertain at local adult homes several times a month to carry my inherited Estonian tradition of music and vocal ability.

EHA TREUFELD/CARR

Just as I arrived early in Geislingen's 'history' I was also to depart early in August 1948: destination Sydney Australia where Mother's great-uncle awaited. Unlike most I had limited contact with the Estonian Community but enjoyed a wondrous High School career followed by six years of medicine at Sydney University. Having married in my final year I failed to 'quite' graduate due to a family tragedy and instead was to spend the next 21 years in my husband's business family. Two daughters were born from the union which sadly ended in 1980. A brief rebound marriage to a Hungarian aristocrat followed. This had taken me to the beautiful Northern Rivers district of NSW and thence to the Gold Coast region of SE Queensland. Along the path I somehow managed to graduate the Securities Institute and enjoy half an Economics degree study at University of New England. Lack of health and of wealth decided on a tactical move to the then Estonian Village in Thirlmere 100 km S of Sydney. What was to be a temporary journey has become permanent in spite of the sad fact we have now become 'Taara Gardens' and are owned by RSL [Returned Soldiers]. Seem busier than ever with further tertiary studies, working on market surveys and being a panellist and committee member in many organizations. Am a rather well known food blogger worldwide, which has brought many friends, a lot of fun and knowledge. Never a dull moment

JÜRI TULTS

His parents, and sister emigrated from Germany to USA in 1949. He attended Purdue University in Indiana and graduated with a Master of Science degree in Electrical Engineering in 1955. He worked in his chosen field until retirement in 1998. He is a former member of the Estonian American National Council, an office holder in the Estonian Society of Indianapolis, and publisher of the bulletin "Viieoru Viisid" for former students of the Estonian high school in Geislingen, Germany. Jüri Tults was married to Inna Harms, now deceased, and is the father of one son.

JAAN TABUR......

Jaan was a "Mulgimees' - he was born in 1935 in south-central Estonia, at the Tabur farm in the village of Reegoldi.

From Geislingen his family emigrated to USA where he lived in a number of places including Seabrook Farms, New Jersey, Willimantic, Connecticut, Indianapolis, Inglewood, California, St. Charles, Missouri and retired to Cocoa, Florida.

He was married in June 1955, to Joyce Shipp of Indianapolis. They have two children -Jeffrey and Judith.

Jaan was an aeronautics man. He graduated from the Northrup Aeronautical Institute in Inglewood and received a BS in Aeronautical Engineering from St. Louis University Park's College in 1965.

He worked at McDonnell Aircraft Co, later McDonnell Douglas.

Jaan was interested in sound-system technology and installation and he liked to be on the move: Sailing, motorcycling and flying. Both his wife and he had pilot's licences, and explored the eastern United States in their light plane.

Jaan retired in 1990 and has written a book called "The Blessed Refugee and his American Wife- Our Life and Adventures (thus far)"

Jaan and his wife built a house in Port St. John near Cocoa, where they lived until Jaan's death early in 2014

ENDEL TULVING

Endel like most of the authors in this book was born in Estonia and fled during that fateful September in 1944. He graduated from the Geislingen Estonian Gümnaasium (GEG) in 1946. Endel has had an amazing life and one would be very valid in stating that Google , the great simplifier of things, shares his achievements very adroitly.

LINDA VOOSAAR/DOLAN

Born: Tartu Women's Hospital in Tartu, Estonia, on March 22 1944
Father: OsvaldMax Henry (Wiokman) Voosaar
Mother: Eleonora (Mardisoo) Voosaas
Married: John Willam Dolan: July 23, 1972. Two children: Christina Elizabeth Dolan and Brian Kalju Dolan
Education: High school: Arsenal Technical High School, Indianapolis, Indiana (USA) Four years earning Highest Academic Diploma. Top 15 students in class of 1,000.
College: Started with two year diploma for Secretarial Sciences (complete) and added four year degree in Business Administration) (??) Minors in Marketing and Sociology.
Volunteer teaching: Taught grade school Arts and Crafts (combination 15 years) at St. Aloysius, ...Valley, and Immaculate Conceptiob greade schools.
Extra-curricular works and charity: Red Cross, Redway Preganacy Center, RCIA (Rite of Christian Initaition for Adults) and local street committee.
Cultural Interests: Brownie in Estonian Scouts, New Jersey. Folk dance group pre-teen and teenager in Indianapolis. Support for parents in Estonian cultural activities if from pre-teen to adulthood.

AIMI ZECHANOWITSCH

In 1944, to escape the approaching Soviet army, mother and I fled to Germany. Eventually, in 1946, we found our way to the D.P. (Displaced Persons) camp in Geislingen.

After a sojourn of three years we were once more on the move, emigrating to Adelaide, South Australia. There I finished high school , attended Adelaide Teachers' College and began my studies at the university.

In 1960 I came to Canada. The first three years were spent in Montreal; the next thirty seven in Ottawa.

There I married, completed my MA and taught senior high school classes. I also participated in many organizations and associations, forexample: AABS (the Association for the Advancement of Baltic Studies) and CIIA (Canadian Institute of International Affairs).

In 1994 my husband passed away and six years later I moved to Toronto. Here I take part in different Estonian activities and also enjoy travels to various destinations.

My retirement years, on the whole, have been pleasant.

PAUL ÖPIK

Paul is a humble man: He has always been a man amongst men: His guiding light to do that which ought to be done. Thus I (MM) am writing his bio.

Paul was born in Estonia in 1927: His story of the wartime and post war trek already proves his tenacity to address that which needed to be addressed.

On arrival in Australia he was contracted like most of our DP cohort to work for two years in an area of need: At the time they were predominantly the Snowy River Hydro-electric station building scheme, manually digging up chunks of terrain to build airfields in our northern regions (defence priorities) and working the sugar cane fields: Paul drew the last straw. It was hot, dirty and sweaty work. It was also unstimulating and one had to bow to the tenacity of guys like Paul, with their agile minds to be able to endure such droning days: Perhaps they were even too tired to ponder on the subjects.

Australia for many years considered Estonia to be part of Russia and political relationships were enacted in that context. The average person was oblivious to the dramas which had unfolded in those 3 small Baltic lands. Paul was determined to correct this: It took a lot of determination particularly at the times when the left wing of power held the majority vote.

Paul's journey to Australia's recognition of the Baltic States began way back in 1984 in Canberra. He was invited to lead the campaign: It was not an easy task given Paul had family in Estonia and was cognisant of the risks it entailed for many innocents. Paul was also cognisant that trust was a wavering commodity among people who had met betrayal and elected to separate himself from any financial connections. Paul was very much a hands on man.

During this time the group effected the delivery of parcels containing very much needed goods to the EVVA: "Eesti Vangistatud Vabadusvoitlejatte Abi" (Estonian Imprisoned Freedom fighters' Aid). That was not sans complexities.

This was followed by the forwarding to the Australian politicians data about the reality of the Baltic states true predicament.

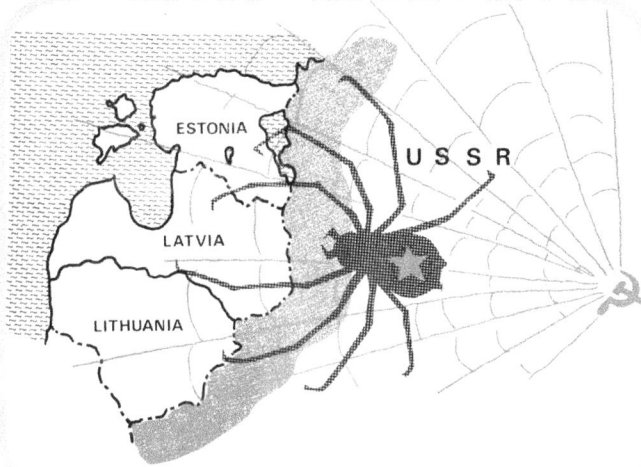

End to Soviet Union's occupation of Baltic States

Among the fundraising activities was the production of a joint envelope illustrating the Baltic predicament: It was a variant on something which Paul had deeply embedded into his memory of the past. Paul, always cautious and pragmatic confirmed that none of Australia's postal decrees had been violated. Those envelopes sold well among our folks! For ESTO 88 the envelopes were reprinted. That was to prove to be a very viable source of funds towards the EVVA cause. It also produced a variable response about the feelings about the sent parcels.

There was a unanimous decision that any further action re status of the Baltic states had to be very disciplined: That emotive protests etc were not conducive to achieving what democracy bade of the group. Among the publications was "A captive nation Estonia" which was suitable for distribution widely. This publication reached some of our schools and other institutions, and also overseas.

A petition from the Estonian Community in Canberra was sent to Canberra for the release of Mart Miklus who was imprisoned in Estonia and for his acceptance as an asylum seeker in Australia: That had endless complications and difficulties.

Likewise Paul was out there for the cause of Estonians sent to mop up the aftermath of Chernobyl.

December 9th 1984 was declared as "Human rights day" in Canberra and EVVA was invited to participate. The pamphlets " A captive nation Estonia" again made their presence, and the envelopes with the spider insignia were again a popular sales item.

Monday 27th August 2001 saw changes in the Commonwealth of Australia, House of Representatives, Hansard. Paul was to pioneer and with his respectful determination bring about the change of heart of Australians in regard to the status of the Baltic states.

No matter what the concern for our folks left behind in Estonia Paul was an action man to improve what could be improved for them. There is no earthly way in which his actions can be summarised into such a small segment of print: Nor can those of his wife Hilja who was with him all the way, 'her sleeves rolled up' ready to do whatever needed to be done.

AND THERE WERE SOME AMONG THEM WHO DID NOT SURVIVE TO TELL THEIR STORIES

Among those were two boys who played among us in Geislingen. They are aluded to in our communications about our memories of life in Geislingen.

Ado Kommendant (photo to left) like **Mark Nigol-Enari** was lost to the Vietnam campaign. I believe there were others also but I have been unable to trace their names.

I believe that Mark was in my kindergarten group in Rappenecker but I cannot be certain.

I believe that there were also losses to the Korean War.

And given the statistical ratio of losses to maimed: How many other of our cohort were to carry the scars of two skirmishes of mankind.

Our hearts go out to their families for needing to grieve the losses from a further war.

A CHAIN IS A STRONG AS ITS WEAKEST LINK

Hell, that was nearly half a century ago!

That is the most important lesson I learned as a rookie intern, from Professor Don Marshall, one of my surgical mentors. If one does not have adequate information to base one's paradigms, one cannot make valid conclusions or participate in effective research. Perhaps his observation is very poignant to the current research on our cohort of expat kids: Is our information sufficiently complete for any ex-pat researchers to even consider researching. Is the locals' own information any more complete!

One has to be sure that one's premises are sufficient: And to have the humility to acknowledge that they may need to outsource for subtle nuances of information: That no one's ego is so important that it has the right to plunder the fate of others.

I hope that this book will become the resource for basing further research on war children and their long term outcomes: Be those children of Estonian or other birth.

Perhaps traumatology is but in its infancy: For the truth about a given setting to be truly evaluated the effects over a lifetime need to be considered: My generation has had the privilege of creating that link: One which only the full hand of life's journey can offer. I hope that we continue to share what we know serenely. MM

www.ingramcontent.com/pod-product-compliance
Lightning Source LLC
Chambersburg PA
CBHW081421300426
44108CB00016BA/2276